High-Performance IT Services

High-Performance IT Services

Terry Critchley

CRC Press
Taylor & Francis Group
Boca Raton London New York

CRC Press is an imprint of the
Taylor & Francis Group, an **informa** business
AN AUERBACH BOOK

CRC Press
Taylor & Francis Group
6000 Broken Sound Parkway NW, Suite 300
Boca Raton, FL 33487-2742

First issued in hardback 2019

First issued in paperback 2022

© 2017 by Taylor & Francis Group, LLC
CRC Press is an imprint of Taylor & Francis Group, an Informa business

No claim to original U.S. Government works

ISBN 13: 978-1-03-247723-7 (pbk)
ISBN 13: 978-1-4987-6919-8 (hbk)

DOI: 10.1201/9781315367217

Library of Congress Cataloging-in-Publication Data

Names: Critchley, Terry, author.
Title: High performance IT services / Terry Critchley.
Description: Boca Raton : CRC Press, Taylor & Francis Group, [2016] |
Includes bibliographical references and index.
Identifiers: LCCN 2016000995 | ISBN 9781498769198
Subjects: LCSH: Network performance (Telecommunication) | High performance computing.
Classification: LCC TK5105.5956 .C753 2016 | DDC 004.1--dc23
LC record available at http://lccn.loc.gov/2016000995

Visit the Taylor & Francis Web site at
http://www.taylorandfrancis.com

and the CRC Press Web site at
http://www.crcpress.com

To my wife, Chris, children, Philip and Helen, and the rest of my now extended family: their spouses, Matt and Louise, and grandchildren, Ava, Lucy, and Ben.

Contents

SECTION II THE PERFORMANCE PLAYING FIELD

SECTION IV   BENCHMARKS AND BENCHMARKING

SECTION V   APPENDICES

List of Figures

List of Tables

Foreword

High-Performance IT Services by Dr. Terry Critchley is an extensive and easy-to-read explanation of IT system performance issues and approaches where his four decades of IT experience are clearly evident. Most books on this topic dwell heavily on the mathematics behind system performance. This is perhaps useful for those specializing in performance enhancements, but they represent a level of detail that is over the head of line-of-business IT managers and their staff.

Instead, Dr. Critchley focuses on explaining these concepts in simple English, supported by numerous figures. As he demonstrates, a clear figure can explain to the layman the meaning of a complex set of equations without needing to be a mathematical genius. This is not to say that he ignores the mathematics of system performance, such as the all-important theory of queues. Rather, he confines the math to a segregated set of chapters and appendices that are arbitrary reading for those that want to dig deeper.

He begins by discussing what is meant by performance. Performance can have many faces depending upon the application, whether it be transaction processing, batch processing, web services, or any one of a number of other uses. He points out that average response time is not a sufficient metric. Rather, the spread of response times is equally important. An average response time of one second is not very good if 90% of all responses complete in 20 seconds.

A major focus of the book is on networks and distributed systems, since systems today do not operate in a private silo. They must interact with other systems, and overall performance is strongly impacted by these systems and the ability to efficiently communicate with them.

He dwells heavily on service-level agreements (SLAs) and on the wide variety of formal benchmarks that are used in the industry. He includes in his discussions cloud computing, virtualization, and high-performance computing.

This book is for everyone in IT. It is especially useful for performance rookies, who can learn a great deal from the book. It should be read by those who know quite a bit about system performance but who can always learn more. The book is for IT managers, IT staff, system operators, and system programmers. Even chief technical officers in an organization can gain important insight into the performance of the systems their people manage and upon which the enterprise depends.

A very detailed Table of Contents (with several headings on each page) makes it easy to scan the book and decide which sections are of interest. Each section typically stands on its own, so that the book serves more as a reference library than as a treatise on performance.

All in all, Dr. Critchley's book is a complete discussion of system performance fundamentals with the added advantage that one can go directly to the issues that concern him or her.

Dr. Bill Highleyman
Managing Editor
Availability Digest

Preface

Preamble

1. This book is not a novel to be read beginning to end. It should be tackled in at least three different ways, tying in with your needs and the learning technique described in it; little and often. Thus, the three methods may appeal to at least three audience types.

Picker	Browser	Studier
• Your interest	• General text	• Specific Material
• Background in other topics	• Skip bullet & reference lists where necessary	• References
		• Use in active IT work

The detailed table of contents and index will help you to follow these modes of learning this quite easily.

2. This book contains many references and links (URLs) for onward learning. Some of these may disappear or be superseded by more modern ones; this is the way with internet material I'm afraid. If this happens, you can chase the information by a search on the words involved, as I and the publisher did in proofing.

3. For hardcopy readers, some links (URLs) are large and complex and difficult to type in to retrieve the desired information but a search on the title and/or the author should yield the material referenced.

The Subject

Systems performance is a subject of great importance, especially in the world of downsizing, right-sizing, legacy migrations and modernizations, distributed systems, virtualization, clouds, and the ubiquitous web. Installations are moving from familiar *classical* territory to the somewhat less familiar *quantum* world of webs, clouds, and virtualization. I had always wanted to write a book on the subject but thought it was too well understood to be of relevance. More than 35 years of dealing with clients and an absolute *howler* by an American IT professor in his book convinced me that I was wrong. The howler, incidentally, was doing a simple calculation on line loadings where he assumed 100% utilization, no network protocol overheads, and no queuing effects. Assumptions like these are the stuff of IT performance disasters, hence this book.

There are many other books covering, for example, queuing theory, but usually from an academic point of view. Often, the erudite authors of such books present a conclusion, after much proof, of the (invented) form

$$\mathrm{T}\eta\upsilon\sigma\,\lambda = \pi(1-\rho^2)+\phi\ldots$$

The question "What does this mean to the IT person or end user?" remains largely unanswered, and I have wrestled manfully with such texts and equations before surrendering and deciding to write my own book. The book deals only with relevant theory, tries to keep a balance between it and what it means to a computer system, and avoids the temptation to indulge in *mathematical gymnastics*, for which the author is eminently unsuited. Often, such equations are the solution to which there is no problem.

The book is about the often misunderstood subject of performance in computer systems, in *measurement*, *interpretation*, *action*, and *prediction*. When a software vendor is asked what computer resources are required to support a certain number of users of his software, the answer is often of the kind "8 Mb plus 8 Mb per user of main storage and 40 Mb of disk per user." The question has then to be asked, "What about CPU power and the number of disk actuators?" This often draws a blank stare from the person questioned.

Another leading question of a vendor is, how many users will your X2000 machine support? One simple answer to this is, as many you can physically attach as long as they are not doing any work. The question presupposes that there is a known transaction rate and that the resources consumed by each transaction are also known. There are applications that can support 100 active users with good response times on a particular machine and others that can render the same machine supine with 10 active users.

A sizing question phrased in the following manner makes sense and is open to a quantitative answer, given sufficient knowledge of the performance aspects of computer systems. "I would like to know what machine you might bid on to support 100 users, each entering an average of 1.2 transactions per minute at peak times, where the transaction uses approximately 250 ms of CPU time on an X2000 and issues 7 disk I/Os for each transaction." To do a precise calculation would require more detailed information than this, but enough information is provided here to undertake a credible sizing exercise.

People sometimes use the results of a benchmark as a sizing exercise, often with disastrous results. There are essentially two species of benchmark. The first kind seeks to represent a particular workload and, subject to margin of error, can be treated as a sizing exercise for the real (or production) application workload. The second kind purports to represent a type of workload at a gross level and should only be used as a tool to compare different systems.

A Definition

An example of the former is covered by A.O. Allen's definition of an objective for a credible benchmark:

> to determine how many active terminals can be supported for a customer with a highly interactive workload, A, on computer model Z with a 90th percentile response time not exceeding two seconds.

This definition does not fall into the "How many users …" trap we discussed above since it is very specific about the workload and required response times. This book was written to clarify many of the perplexing issues surrounding performance. The text is designed to provide technical managers, operations managers, and anyone concerned with systems design and tuning with a technical foundation in performance. It will enable them to tackle questions like the one above with more confidence. It will also be useful to students with IT as a major or minor part of advanced studies.

Systems sizing and performance management are too important, and potentially costly, to rely on guesswork or vendor claims. The book also provides an understanding of some of the factors that affect workstation and multiuser system performance and outlines many of the benchmarks used to measure the performance of a single system or compare the performance of two or more systems.

The subject of performance and benchmarks often assumed religious significance, particularly in the enterprise systems arena, with mainframes competing with UNIX, UNIX competing with Linux and Windows, and so on. Literature warns of the "dangers" of benchmarks and single-measure metrics but offers few solutions. The common theme here is that only the "real" customer workload is representative and benchmarks can be misleading, particularly if the writer has just lost one.

The average person is often left confused about who and what to believe in the minefield of performance measurement and interpretation. It should be self-evident that someone with knowledge of the fundamentals of performance is in a better position to exercise judgment in matters of performance than someone who lacks such knowledge.

The book is about *performance fundamentals*, and though it devotes some space in Section III (Chapter 8) to Linux, UNIX, OpenVMS, and MVS, most of the theory and systems design principles can be applied to other operating systems, as can some of the benchmarks. The performance management aspects, although covering the same environments, can be applied equally to other environments. It is simply a matter of knowing what questions to ask to assess performance characteristics in an environment you are not familiar with.

There are people who know more about the subject of performance than I do—for them I have no message. There are, however, many more people who know less than I do, and less is not enough in the modern world of IT.

I have a simple acronym for assessing IT project requirements: FUMPAS, meaning function, user (aspects), manageability, performance, availability, and security. These should be applied to every aspect of IT developments, from conception through design and down to operation and maintenance. The accent today is almost exclusively on the F and the U since the advent of high-powered systems and "gee whiz" development tools means that we don't need to worry about the M and the P. My experience indicates that neglect of the latter elements causes more problems than minor deficiencies in the former. This is evidenced by the numerous load-related "crashes" of many major websites that occurred during the hectic .com boom and bust (ca. 2000) and is still happening today. Since I thought of FUMP, I have, of necessity, added *availability* and *security*, the buzzwords of the decade, to give FUMPAS.

Finally, don't be put off reading this book by the sight of mathematical formulas. The simple ones are there because they are necessary; the more esoteric ones are there for completeness and for students and purists and will not detract from the IT professional's understanding of the base material. There is a simple math tutorial in Appendix IV anyway.

Audience

The primary intention is to pass on the author's 40+ years of IT experience, which includes a great deal of time spent on systems performance, and more importantly, to classify and categorize that

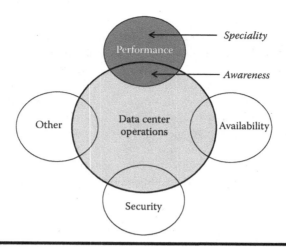

Figure 0.1 Skills: scope of book readership.

experience to reduce the *black art* and *seat-of-the-pants* aspects of the performance management of computer systems to pragmatic terms (Figure 0.1).

Most of the diagrams and graphs in this book are illustrative of the principles and topics under discussion and should not be used to draw any numeric conclusions for use in real life; where graphs are numerically accurate, this is pointed out.

This book should be accessible to most IT personnel, especially those whose responsibilities include performance management, tuning, and capacity planning. IT managers with a technical outlook will benefit from the coverage afforded by the book, as will consultants and people entering the world of computers for the first time in a professional capacity.

Finally, the book was also structured to be of use to students of information technology. One reason is that however brilliant such people are at learning about computing, they cannot learn experience—this book hopes to put wise heads on young shoulders, as well as teaching some of the pragmatic principles of IT systems performance.

> The main point is that this book is not a novel, to be read end to end. Know what you want to learn, consult the table of contents or index and dive in. Afterwards, try browsing and see what you can pick up in far easier fashion than I had to do to write the book.

Navigating This Book

This book is designed to be accessible to most people in the IT spectrum of roles and responsibilities—managers, designers, coders, architects, operators, and others in technical roles. Different people can take different routes through the book by judicious use of the table of contents and the index, which are deliberately detailed and hopefully clear in what each item in them covers.

Even though management may feel they don't need any technical reading, they should gain enough information about different subjects to ask intelligent questions of personnel in technical positions. This book can provide a bird's-eye view of areas to be considered in managing system and network performance.

Book Contents

The book is divided into 5 main sections, 17 chapters, and 7 appendices.

Component Sections

Section I: "Performance Principles and Components"
Section II: "The Performance Playing Field"
Section III: "Performance in Practice," drawing on the knowledge gained in Section I
Section IV: "Benchmarks and Benchmarking"
Section V: "Appendices," which amplify topics referred to in Sections I–IV

Chapter Contents

Chapter 1: Discusses what we mean by performance. Without this, we may be talking at cross-purposes throughout the book. It sets the scene for subsequent chapters, covering performance definitions, expectations, quantification, and an introduction to computer workload patterns that have a bearing on system performance.

Chapter 2: Examines the hardware of which systems are composed and looks at the various architectures and configurations that this hardware evolves into—symmetric multiprocessors (SMPs), massively parallel processors (MPPs), clusters, and others. It also looks at some of the subsystems within this hardware and their effect on performance, finishing with some laws on computer speedup.

Chapter 3: Looks at the components of system and application software that can impact performance. There is a short coverage of data formats and optimization methods to improve performance, but also a discussion of things that can work against good performance. The discussion looks at the overhead imposed by virtualization security and the role of buffers and packet loss in the performance arena.

Chapter 4: This covers the performance of legacy (classical) disks (hard disk drives [HDDs]) and the impact of more modern forms of storage, such as network attached storage (NAS), storage area networks (SANs), redundant arrays of independent disks (RAID), solid-state drive (SSD) storage, and storage connections. There is also coverage of the performance of some of these configurations, along with presentation of some storage benchmarks. The role of processor clusters is touched on briefly.

Chapter 5: The chapter is dedicated to networks and all things connected with them, including Ethernet, Token Ring, and WANs, and goes on to cover performance—things that improve it and things that reduce it. Web performance also finds a home in this chapter.

Chapter 6: Graphics is the theme of this chapter since it is prevalent in some industries and requires performance consideration like any other aspect of IT.

Chapter 7: Presents some of the simpler theory of queuing, which is the basis of most performance work, apart from the obvious speed characteristics and efficiency of the attendant hardware and software. More detailed (but hopefully pragmatic) theory is reserved for Appendix I. It also introduces the ideas of performance management and the life cycle of events to achieve optimum performance.

Chapter 8: This contains the meat of the subject covering the design, sizing, and management of all things performance oriented. The topics of system and web sizing are outlined, and the chapter goes on to look at monitoring what goes on in systems and networks, based on the maxim "if you can't measure it, you can't manage it." The chapter deserves some concentrated study, always with an eye on the requirements of your organization in the management of performance. It is not primarily prescriptive, and you make the decisions about how to implement your management of performance based on what you learn from the chapter.

Chapter 9: This short section of the book is devoted to the thorny topic of benchmarks: understanding, choosing, and running them.

Chapter 10: We come here to the specific types of benchmark in the commercial and scientific fields of business, talking about the topic of benchmarks with fixed decimal point and integer data and with floating-point formats.

Chapter 11: This is dedicated to the Systems Performance Evaluation Corporation (SPEC). There is a website dedicated to SPEC benchmarks that chapter is a short guide to the organization and the benchmarks.

Chapter 12: This chapter is similar in intent to Chapter 11, but for the Transaction Performance Council (TPC). Both chapters have follow-up historical information in Appendix II, better known as *memory lane*.

Chapter 13: This is a short section on network benchmarks.

Chapter 14: This section introduces virtualization and cloud computing, resource management in virtualized environments, and cloud service level agreements (SLAs).

Chapter 15: This covers an outline of high availability and disaster recovery (which inevitably involves backup and restore) and the need for good performance since recovery plans are driven by predefined *time-to-recover* criteria.

Chapter 16: A mixed bunch of topics covering performance and monitoring resource overheads, other important overheads, and a discussion on the meaning and composition of latency. The chapter concludes with a short discussion on performance-related futures of networks, storage, processors, and memory.

Chapter 17: This section of the book eschews gee whiz writing and concentrates on the management disciplines, including service level agreements (SLAs), the *raison d'être* of performance management.

Appendices

Appendix I: "Basic Queuing Theory"
Appendix II: "Historical Benchmarks"
Appendix III: "Terminology" (performance in the main)
Appendix IV: "Some Performance Math"
Appendix V: "Distributed Systems Topics"
Appendix VI: "High-Performance Computing"
Appendix VII: "Summary and Overview of the Book"

Language

The language used in this book is U.S. English, and any humor is predominantly British. In terms of language, I have tried to avoid content-free phrases such as "aligning IT with business strategy or requirements" and "develop a detailed plan" without explaining what they mean or how to do it or even giving an example.

I have regularly examined statements like these from all angles, heated them, cooled them, and bombarded them with protons from the Large Hadron Collider and still cannot make sense of most of them. Maybe you can.

References

In this book, references are given in context instead of at the end of the book, however reprehensible this may seem. In the author's experience, few people actually go to the back of a book to check a reference number or code, but will cast their eyes down to read a footnote or in-line reference. This mode of operation is useful when studying a topic in the book rather than just reading the book as whole.

Many references are to Internet URLs, which are, in general, more accessible than old documents. However, as seasoned web travelers know, URLs have a habit of changing, becoming obsolete, and so on. The ISO 9001 (BS 5750 in the United Kingdom) standard does not seem to apply to the Internet, and so much undated, obsolete, and inaccurate material lurks on its pages.

The author hopes that most of the referenced pages are still accessible and that the perpetrators of random URL changes will feel suitably chastened.

Notes and Graphs

1. Most of the graphs and diagrams in this book are illustrative and are not meant to be accurate representations of data such that they can be used numerically in IT planning.
2. As stated above, many references are links (URLs), which, in the nature of things, often change or disappear altogether. Each link was valid upon producing this book, and random checks were made at the final proofing stage to check that they were still valid. For any that escaped my attention, I apologize. However, a well-structured search on three or four keywords describing the topic in question should produce a new link, assuming the information still exists and is accessible.
3. I have found that learning is best done like someone with a hiatal hernia when eating—little, often, and varied. I have deliberately used repetition at different levels of details so that the same topic can be examined via different perspectives. This, added to references of quoted sources, will give a balanced and more easily digested information menu, which I find conducive to learning.

And Finally

This book is *not* an encyclopedia of topics related to performance, but an introduction and *awareness raiser*.*

It is rather similar to a vacation checklist where I remind you to take your passport, sunglasses, medications, and spare socks. What I don't do is to tell you how to get or renew a passport, whose sunglasses to use, what medications to take with you (apart from some standard ones), or where to buy your spare socks. You don't have time to read that level of detail, and might not need it, and

---

* "When we look at a thing, we must examine its essence and treat its appearance merely as an Usher at the threshold, and once we cross the threshold, we must grasp the essence of the thing; this is the only reliable and scientific method of analysis" (Chairman Mao Tse Tung [Mao Zedong]).

I don't have the skills to deliver it. I do, however, try to provide references to passport and best sock provider websites, to continue the analogy. Everything else is specific to your needs and your responsibility and, in essence, is your responsibility.

One overarching purpose of the book is to make people who read it comfortable with the subject, without fear of discussing it with anyone. The subject of systems performance should fit like a well-tailored suit on the wearer so he or she can face the world without trepidation or fear of being exposed as a fraud. I feel I can do it now, but it took some time and some beatings before I achieved that state. I am trying to pass on the experience to readers and point out the potholes so they don't fall down them as I did.

To emphasize key lessons, you may come across sections or paragraphs titled "WoW," which I define as follows:

WoW: *Words of wisdom*, which may be my own or received wisdom from others. They are the gold nuggets in this book that you should take on board.

Acknowledgments

In writing this book, I have tried to bridge the gap between literature written by experts for experts on the various aspects of reliability and availability, and mundane overviews, so that this knowledge is then accessible to nonexperts in digestible form. I could not have done this without the help of the experts acknowledged below, to whom I am very grateful.

Traditional acknowledgments written as prose bore me, I'm afraid, so I am reverting to a list format. I've named the people who have helped me in a variety of ways and also added minimalist details about them to indicate roughly where the evidence of their help resides in the book.

Here we go, in no particular order:

- Bill Highleyman (Availability Digest): General comments on everything
- Brendan Gregg: Linux performance diagrams and comments (Figure 8.10)
- Roger Parr (ex-IBM colleague): Queuing theory
- Radware: Use of extracts from their paper on users' reactions to slow web access
- Ilya Grigorik (Google engineering): Latency comments
- Bob Wescott: Email discussions and reading his book (cited herein)
- Dr. Muhammad Ali Ismail, Associate Professor, NED University of Engineering and Technology: Cache equation verification and comments

I also acknowledge the work of many others who have written papers and books from which I have either quoted (with permission) or used to hone or advance my knowledge of the subject matter. This book is the result, and I now know 200% more about performance than I did when I conceived the book.

To paraphrase Sir Isaac Newton, "if I have seen farther than others, it is by standing on the shoulders of giants."

Author

I live in northwest England, the fabled land of black puddings and meat pies.

I have been in and out of the IT arena since 1969, with 24 years at IBM, 3 years with Oracle, 6 years working for Sun Microsystems, and 1 year at a major UK bank. I have been involved with more areas of IT than you could shake a stick at: Y2K, Information Management System (IMS), Customer Information Control System (CICS), storage, laser printing, OCR, OMR, UNIX, MVS, MUMPS, Pick, training, platform migrations, benchmarks, data center migration, and customer planning, architecture, and support, among many other things.

In this book, I have made liberal use of diagrams and graphs, as I believe the old adage that a picture is worth a thousand words. In addition, I have tried to lead people to solutions rather than push them with severe action checklists, since I am unaware of readers' company business requirements, but only where the pitfalls might lurk.

I am also a minor authority on the Anglo-Zulu War of 1879, should any queries relating to that topic be raised by the contents of this book.

He that believeth in me and learneth from me, my learned colleagues, erudite correspondents, and other generous information sources shall not perish in the fires of eternal latency but dwell in the Valhalla of optimum performance.

PERFORMANCE PRINCIPLES AND COMPONENTS

Performance work often frightens people because of the apparent complexity of today's environment—virtualization, clouds, redundant array of independent disks (RAID), big data, and so on. If you think about it, these entities are really abstractions on top of physical entities that are understood. Just as all the apparent bewildering substances we see around us are all made up of protons, neutrons, and electrons, similarly, all IT systems are made up of the basic blocks we have always known about—CPUs, disks, tapes, memory, and so on. These are often amenable to calculations and modeling.

In the 1970s, in north England, a customer was experiencing several performance problems with his applications and decided his configuration needed assessment and upgrading. He purchased a bigger CPU as a result of his deliberations, but to his cost, he found it had no effect whatsoever on the system performance since the bottleneck lay in the disk subsystem, which was light in the number of disk actuators, not CPU and not storage capacity. Unfortunately, this book did not exist then. To get back on track....

A simple performance model can be expressed as

$$\text{Performance } P = \frac{\text{Resource Available}}{\text{Resource Needed}}$$

where $P > 1$ is good and $P < 1$ can be bad. The whole area of performance is concerned with resources and their utilization, defined as

$$\text{Utilization } \rho = \frac{\text{Resource Used}}{\text{Resource Available}}$$

where ρ ideally should be less than 1. All will be revealed in due course, but remember these two entities and the items that count as resources—memory, processor, disk, and so on. They also need management.

People may say, "I don't need principles. I, as a geek, need up-to-date technology information." There was an American sage talking about romantic relationships and he said, "Kissing don't last, cooking do." My paraphrased take on the geek premise is that "technology don't last, principles do."

Chapter 1

What Is Performance?

Introduction

In this book, we will look at the often misunderstood, often neglected topic of computer performance—what it is, what is good and bad performance, and what factors affect the performance of a computer system or systems. The subject of queues is central to understanding the subject of performance, so we will spend some time covering this, but only at a high level. We shall also examine the value of relying too heavily on queuing theory in performance matters, especially prediction via models.

We will examine the performance characteristics of computer systems and networks, the "glue" between systems, which can have a marked effect on the performance of online applications, especially those that involve access to other systems (distributed processing).

The main purpose of the book is to help *anyone* in IT feel comfortable with the topic of performance and at whatever level he or she is involved. This covers the spectrum of people from managers through to coal-face operations and systems practitioners (Figure 1.1).

Performance Concept

If you search the Internet for *performance* or even *performance theory*, you will have a large number of hits that, on examination, are concerned with theater, music, or employee business performance. This means that quoting from dictionaries can be misleading in this particular subject; in fact, an Internet search on this will yield some hits that look like IT topics, but are actually about personal performance in work or the arts.

Performance in an IT sense has connotations of speed or *quickness of response* to a query or request for some work to be processed. However, there is more to performance than just this concept, which takes account of the fact that this quickness will vary about some mean value. Thus, a specification of a desired performance criterion might be "the responses must be in the range 1.5–2.5 s when measured at the user workstation."

This might be difficult to guarantee and other forms of words are used, such as "90% of the responses must be 2.5 s or less." This is called a *percentile* definition. In online work, a mean

3

Figure 1.1 Maximum performance example.

response time needs another desirable characteristic—that of *consistency*. At first glance, a mean response time of 2.3 s has to be better than one of 2.5 s, *n'est-ce pas?*

Not so, I'm afraid.

The Paradox: Imagine the 2.3 s response is made up of widely varying responses, say, 0.1, 7.1, 3.4, 0.4, 11, ..., and so on, but averaging out at 2.3. The user will not be pleased with this since (1) it is annoying and (2) it will affect the fluency of his or her work and hence the effectiveness of it. If the 2.5 s response time is composed of 2.0, 2.4, 2.7, 2.5, ..., then the user will be much happier because of the consistency of the response time of a transaction.

The other form of work is the batch job, where the elapsed time to complete it is the main criterion and the batch equivalent of the online response time.

An Approach to a Solution

The precise method of solving the consistency problem may be complex, depending on the underlying cause(s). However, there is one factor that, if not taken into account, can cause this response time inconsistency (or *jitter*). The utilization of each element in the chain of support from the workload is important and should, wherever possible, be monitored or calculated from monitored data.

The service time of a unit of work (UoW)* for a particular device depends on the speed of the device—low speed means low utilization if response times are to be good, and vice versa. If the design or normal operating point of the system has utilizations near the knee of the response versus utilization curve (see Figure 1.2), then it is possible that it can be exceeded with a resulting amplified increase in response time.

If more than one device is near its utilization knee value, then their combined effect may be large inconsistencies or jitter in response times. In Figure 1.2, equal changes in device utilization ρ at points a and b result in large differences (Δ) in response time because of their position on the response time curve:

$$\Delta_b \gg \Delta_a$$

---

* I use this term in place of *customer* in IT discussions throughout this book. It represents a transaction, query, batch job, web inquiry, or any request for work that requires IT service.

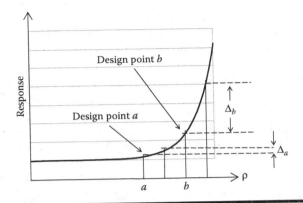

Figure 1.2 Origin of response time jitter (inconsistency).

What this means is that if your operating point is around point *a*, an increase in volumes will have a relatively small effect on the response time. However, if you operate at point *b*, a small increase in volumes will cause an amplified increase in response times.

Hint: There is a relationship between response time and volume of transactions processing for a fixed set of resources. If you measure volumes as well as response times, it is easy to correlate them; if you are on the flattish part of the response versus utilization (volumes) curve, then an increase in volume (utilization) should not cause a significant increase in response time.

Another factor in the response time debate is cost. In general, the lower the desired response time or job time, the higher the cost of achieving it and the cost versus response time curve is not linear. This debate will take place between IT, users, and finance in the service level agreement (SLA) discussions (see Chapter 17).

Note: Performance is thus not a thing that can be discussed in isolation—what the end user is interested (to take a holistic view) in is the quality of service (QoS). This metric will include the response or turnaround time, the consistency of these numbers, and the availability of his or her service. Security will also be a consideration.

I mention this here so that your pursuit of perfect response does not neglect or impinge negatively upon the overall QoS.

Performance: Leveling the Playing Field

The approach to the prediction and measurement of computer systems performance has something to learn from the subject known as operations research (OR). In his book,* Taha discusses the origins of the subject of OR in the British military establishment during World War II. He states,

> Their objective was to determine the most effective utilisation of limited military resources.

---

* ISBN 978-0132555937. My research was carried out in a much earlier edition, but this definition remains the same.

Replace the word *military* with *computer* and you are close to the reason for studying computer performance. In his treatment of modeling, Taha uses a sentence that will explain the treatment of computer performance adopted in this book:

> The model, being an abstraction of the assumed real world, identifies and simplifies the relationships among these variables in a form amenable to analysis.

Incidentally, the book by Taha contains an excellent chapter on queuing theory, covering the various combinations of the situations described by the Kendall-Lee notation (see Chapter 7 and Appendix I of this book).

To construct, and attempt to analyze, computer systems models involving each of the components and subcomponents we discussed above would be an impossible task. It is, therefore, necessary to seek to simplify the analytical treatment of such systems without losing the ability to quantify their behavior with acceptable accuracy.

WoW: Don't try to obtain accurate resource and other information from complex math models or computer systems that in reality are not amenable to accurate analysis using math gymnastics. See "Queuing Theory: Limitations in IT" in Appendix I.

Some of the reasons for this are that systems have

- Mixtures of hardware with different characteristics
- Ditto for the software
- Software architecture and coding
- Varying block and buffer sizes
- Cache hit rates in memory and auxiliary storage
- Load variations*
- Response time jitter
- Other potential *gotchas*

The only true test and measurement of performance characteristics for your application is a pilot trial (benchmark), which will cover functionality as well. So where does this leave standard benchmarks like Systems Performance Evaluation Corporation (SPEC) and Transaction Performance Council (TPC)? The simple answer is they are quantitative indicators of performance or comparative performance and can be used as *rules of thumb* (ROTs) for similar workloads.

It is possible to size your own workload using the standard benchmarks if you

- Understand your workload characteristics, pattern, and volumes
- Can roughly relate standard benchmark transactions to this workload
- Understand the resource consumption of the standard benchmark transactions

---

* For example, a single transaction (UoW) can take various service times, depending on the route it takes with branches for different uses of the transaction, involving more or less CPU time and I/Os than some theoretical average (see Appendix II).

But you should have other ways of verifying your conclusions.

As a simple example, you might try to relate your workload to that of TPC-C in assessing resource requirements.* If your application is already available, then your own benchmark or pilot is the way to proceed.

What *Is* Performance?

There are three kinds of lies: lies, damned lies, and statistics.

Benjamin Disraeli (nineteenth-century UK prime minister)

The performance of a system needs to be considered within a given context. A "good" performance in a play has a different meaning from good performance in a computer system, as we have already seen. In the latter, performance has some connotation of speed; the higher the speed, the better the performance would seem to be fairly obvious. But the speed of what? Certainly not cycle time, as illustrated by the performance comparisons in Figure 1.3, where the importance of processor and other architectures to performance is illustrated.

There are some very *basic* metrics often used to describe the "power" or "throughput" of a single processor, for example,

- Millions of (mixed) instructions per second (MIPS)
- Integer or fixed-point speed
- Floating-point instruction speed
- Clock speed
- Cache size and efficiency (hit rate)
- Elementary benchmarks like the Gibson mix and post office benchmark

Caution: There are several discrepancies between results gained using different measures of power. For example, a processor with higher clock speed and larger memory cache will not always outperform one of lower speed and smaller cache. What this means in essence is that trying to

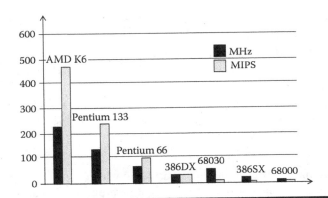

Figure 1.3   Relationship of MIPS to processor speed (MHz).

---

* I did this reasonably successfully many years ago using TPC-A as the basis of the assessment. That, however, does not suggest the technique will always work.

compare how a system will perform in your business environment is not best done by comparing tables of raw characteristics.

There have been a number of benchmarks devised to measure these characteristics, such as post office mix, Gibson mix, Whetstones, and Dhrystones, for commercial and scientific processor evaluations. These are effectively superseded by the SPEC and TPC benchmarks, covered in Section IV of this book, Chapter 12. Older benchmarks are covered for nostalgic and historic recording reasons in Appendix II.

Performance of What?

"So, we have designed and implemented a superb performance system, so that's that." Not so. It depends whether you have delivered great performance for all users and workload types, an unlikely situation. Like a meal, its quality and desirability depends on the viewpoint of the consumer. It's an unfortunate fact that in the performance world, one size does not fit all requirements. Let us look at some of the workload types and their characteristics:

- Transaction-based workloads
- Batch workloads
- Decision support
- Internet applications
- Time-sharing applications
- High-performance computing (HPC)
- Data warehouse and data marts
- Big data applications
- Network bandwidth-hungry applications
- Database-hungry applications
- Program development
- Monitoring applications
- Recovery requirements—standard and disaster (DR)
- Applications needing consistent transmission speeds to endure quality, for example, music or video

This could present a dilemma for designers, but the commonsense cavalry ride to the rescue in this situation. It is normal to bias designs toward the most important business applications for crucial parts of a business. These are often known as strategic business units (SBUs). The main task after that is to ensure the other workloads don't suffer intolerable performance as a result.

Let's look at an analogy. An athlete runs a race 5 s slower than his normal performance. Is that a poor performance? *Yes*, if he is running 100 m, but *no* if he is running a marathon, meaning that performance is relative to the task in hand.

There is also a commonsense factor here in deciding which applications actually need a subsecond response, especially when achieving this might be prohibitively expensive. As an example, consider the use of decision support systems or data analysis applications. If they are for medium- to long-term plans, the work can take 1, 2, or even 20 h and should be planned for accordingly. Similarly, it is often the case that batch work is not very urgent and can be slowed down by some governor method to free up resource for other applications, for example, online payments.

This is sometimes done by reducing the multiprogramming level, say, from four streams of batch to two. Sometimes it may be necessary to use separate machines for different types of workload so they don't hamper each other.

These kinds of considerations should be discussed and agreed at SLA definition time (see the SLA discussion in Chapter 17).

Performance in Numbers

Performance figures are sometimes quoted including clock speeds in megahertz, along with other measures. Some years ago, this other measure was millions of instructions per second (MIPS) and, for scientific work, thousands (KFLOPS) or millions (MFLOPs) of floating-point operations per second.

The MIPS measure fell into disrepute over time, as systems with an apparently superior speed in MIPS proved inferior when measured by a different, more realistic, benchmark.

The original system that was quoted in MIPS was the DEC PDP 11/70 (1 MIPS processor). As the MIPS began to lose credibility, DEC VAX systems were sometimes quoted in VAX units of power (VUPs). The same PDP 11/780, with a particular version of operating system, was used as the base of 1 VUP.

Let IBM try to put this MIPS business into perspective for us:

One of the most misused terms in IT has to be MIPS. It's supposed to stand for "millions of instructions per second," but many alternate meanings have been substituted:

- Misleading indicator of processor speed
- Meaningless indicator of processor speed
- Marketing indicator of processor speed
- Management's impression of processor speed

Unfortunately, no one number describes capacity. Processor speed varies depending on many factors, including (but not restricted to):

- Workload mix
- Memory/cache sizes
- I/O access density
- Software levels (OS and application subsystems)
- Hardware changes
- Partitioning

Workload mix is the largest contributor to the variability of capacity figures.

See *IBM Systems Magazine*, November 2004: "Don't Be Misled by MIPS," http://www.ibmsystemsmag.com/mainframe/tipstechniques/systemsmanagement/Don-t-Be-Misled-By-MIPS/.

Misleading Clock Speed

Look at Figure 1.3 involving some vintage chips and their characteristics. It shows MIPS ratings and corresponding megahertz for a series of systems over a period of years. Years (horizontal) are in decreasing order and values (vertical) may not be exact, but they establish the principle.

It is easy to see that MIPS per megahertz increases as the years go on and processors evolve, and the reason is enhancements in architecture and chip design (Moore's law).

More on Misleading MIPS

What about MIPS? First, it is often difficult to know how many instructions are being executed by the operating system and other subsystems and how many go on useful work. Assuming that MIPS was a valid measure of performance, a 2 MIPS machine is not necessarily capable of twice as much work as a 1 MIPS machine of a different architecture since the efficiency of the instruction use, partly dictated by the compiler, may be different on the two machines.

For example, Table 1.1 shows results for MIPS for some IBM processors.

Question: Which vintage IBM CPUs are represented here by their MIPS ratings?

The answer in all seven cases is the IBM 3081D, announced in 1981.* The reason for the variation in answers for MIPS ratings is the fact that the instruction mixes are different in each case.

The "big MIPS" results could be accounted for by a mix of fast register-to-register instructions, whereas the "low MIPS" results can be accounted for as mixes of complex or *heavy-duty* diagnostic instructions. The metrics of this simple benchmark are so simple that it is easy to deceive people by quoting the performance numbers in isolation.

MIPS and Dhrystones

The origin of MIPS is interesting as it emanated from Digital Equipment Corporation (DEC). An old VAX 11/780, running a certain level of the VAX VMS operating system, was rated at 1757 Dhrystones.

In the past, DEC claimed the same VAX 11/780 was a 1 MIPS machine and hence MIPS for another system, A, could be related to Dhrystones by the following "currency" relationship:

$$\text{MIPs for system A} = \frac{\text{Dhrystones for system A}}{1757} \tag{1.1}$$

Table 1.1 MIPS vs. Which IBM Processor Question

MIPS	IBM Processor
1.4	?
5.0	?
8.0	?
10.2	?
13.1	?
20.0	?
40.0	?

---

* Interestingly, the 3083 was announced in 1983 and the 3084 (four-processor) in 1984.

There are different versions of the Dhrystone benchmark, but the principle of Equation 1.1 for MIPS and Dhrystones holds.

To use an analogy, compare the performance of a sports car versus that of a standard bus. The car is obviously faster (response time), but its throughput (ability to carry many people from A to B) is not as good as that of the bus. The car would have to make many journeys to ferry 40 people from A to B, whereas the appropriate bus will do the job in one journey.

Fixed-Point or Integer Performance

Fixed-point numbers are defined with a number of digits before and after the decimal place fixed throughout the program execution and can be represented as follows:

$$III.DDDD$$

where I and D are integers (0–9) before and after the decimal point. *Integer* numbers are the special case of this format where there is *no* decimal point.

The number representation shown here can accommodate numbers between 0.0001 and 999.9999. Fixed-point numbers are limited to a relatively small range because of the fixed position of the decimal point. This is not always satisfactory for some scientific and other work.

Integer Performance Table

This vintage table shows the nonlinear relationship between power (performance as measured by SPEC) and the cycle speed of the processor (Table 1.2).

Table 1.2 shows that there is no direct correlation between chip speed and measured performance (power). For example, the IBM RS/6000 performs nearly as well as the DEC AXP, but has less than half the rated chip speed of it. An even bigger discrepancy is shown for floating-point performance in Table 1.3.

Floating-Point Performance

Floating-point representation on computers came out of the need to represent a wide range of numbers with a reasonable number of digits. For example, if an astrophysicist is doing a calculation involving Planck's constant ($6.6260957 \times 10^{-34}$ m²/kg/s) and intergalactic distances (say,

Table 1.2 Megahertz vs. SPEC Performance

Processor	MHz	SPECint 92
Digital AXP 3000/400	133	65.3
Hewlett Packard 730	66	47.8
IBM RS/6000 980B	62.5	59.2
Sun Classic Desktop	50	26.4

Table 1.3   Performance: MHz vs. MFLOPS

Processor	MHz	Linpack MFLOPS	Ratio MHz/MFLOPS
Digital AXP 3000/400	133	26.4	5.0
Hewlett Packard 730	66	25.8	2.6
IBM RS/6000 980B	62.5	38.1	1.6
Sun Classic Desktop	50	4.6	10.9

9.4607×10^{21}, 1 million light years), he or she would struggle to have these numbers coexist in a calculation using fixed-point arithmetic.

Floating-point numbers are the solution to this issue and are described by a mantissa and an exponential field. The decimal place is "moved" by changing the value of the exponential field. Examples are

$$1.23456+E06 \text{ is } 1{,}234{,}560$$
$$1.23456-E02 \text{ is } 0.0123456$$

where "$nE0x$" represents $10x$, and n is + ($s = 0$) or ($s = 1$)

The differences in *performance per megahertz* reflect different operating systems, instruction and data cache sizes, and cache handling algorithms, as well as chip and compiler technologies. Similar tables can be drawn up for commercial performance measurements, including online transaction processing (OLTP).

Table 1.3 demonstrates once more the nonlinear relationship between megahertz and power as measured in a floating-point environment.

The numbers are not modern, but they illustrate the point of this argument.

Basically, the frequent discrepancies between supposed power of the same machine measured by two or more benchmarks call into question the validity of one or more of the benchmarks involved.

Note: These comparisons are to illustrate the principle that architecture in machines is an important factor in delivering good performance and that raw clock speeds or MIPS can be misleading. The machines featured in the tables are, in the main, obsolete, and the tables are not meant to be a serious performance evaluation of vendor hardware. This is particularly true for PCs where the number of factors affecting performance, other than pure megahertz, is legion, especially when using remote websites.

Floating-Point Formats
http://www.quadibloc.com/comp/cp0201.htm
IEEE Standard 754 Floating-Point Numbers
http://steve.hollasch.net/cgindex/coding/ieeefloat.html

Single versus Double Precision

There are extended precision, double precision, and single-precision forms of floating-point arithmetic, and the question is often asked in forums, "Which is faster?" A brief look through website articles gives answers that seem to indicate that single precision is faster (though obviously less accurate) than double precision, except for a few special cases.

An interesting point arose when IBM announced the RISC System/6000 in February 1990 and single precision seemed slower than double precision. The answer turned out to be that the system worked in double precision and then converted to single when required, resulting in an overhead that caused the apparent slowdown.

Factors Affecting Performance

There are numerous elements in a computer system that can have an effect on the performance, both good and detrimental. They can be classified under the headings of hardware, system software, supporting software such as middleware, OLTP and database management system (DBMS) or relational database management system (RDBMS), network links, and application design and coding.

The latter can render performance-enhancing efforts in the previous elements totally useless by poor design and coding. This is particularly true in the client/server and RDBMS environments, where performance can be beaten to death by poor design.

The objective of achieving maximum performance is by

- Optimizing the speed of doing things that have to be done. For example, executing program code and transferring data to or from storage across networks are things that have to be done.
- Minimizing inhibitors to this aim—elimination or minimization of any delays (latency) in the execution of the application and the other activities that support the application. These delays are called *waits* or *waiting times* in queuing terms.

Much of the work involved in executing work is serial, and in such cases, the final performance of the work will depend on the performance of the elements in the execution chain.

Some work can, of course, be run in parallel, such as scientific programs or parallel data paths provided to speed up data transmission or storage I/O, but for performance planning and capacity work, it is wise to take the worst case of everything operating serially and not in parallel.

Design

The main factors in achieving adequate performance, apart from the native speed of the system's components, are shown in Figure 1.4.

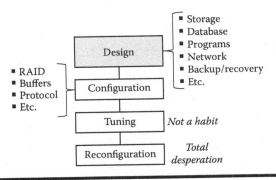

Figure 1.4   Factors influencing performance.

Implementation

Implementation is important inasmuch as the system put into place is the same as the design.

If it isn't, it can have an unquantifiable effect on expected performance and a knock-on effect on the service level agreement (SLA). A failure to meet an SLA on day 1 is not a very good advert for the IT department.

Operation

When the system is operating correctly, there is the usual ongoing task of monitoring performance (as well as other things). The main performance task is then tuning when unexpected workload changes dictate it. If you need to tune on day 1 or 2 of live operation, you've got either the design or the implementation wrong (or both).

Performance Journey

Many of the factors listed in the previous section relate to the speed at which processing is performed by the application and associated software and hardware. Another factor is the response time observed by the end user of the application, that is, the time taken from submission of the request to the receipt of the answer. There are pedantic variations in the definition, time from submission to the receipt of the first character of the reply, or sometimes receipt of the last character.

Another way of looking at the response time is to examine the journey of the work unit or transaction through the system—user to system to user. Each leg in this journey costs time in the form of delay (or latency) and needs to be understood to maintain control of the system performance. An analogy is a real journey where the voyager estimates his or her outgoings at each leg of the journey so that he or she can provide the correct resources (money), perhaps with spare capacity.

In planning this performance journey, the use of numbers is often valuable, but to my mind a visual representation of the numbers and where they lie in the topology of computer systems is more valuable since it allows the visualization of what end-to-end performance means. This is what the end user sees and not the individual elements of performance—they are the province of the operations and performance people.

Figure 1.5 shows the end-to-end picture of a single system (there may be others connected) and a summary equation of what the final performance numbers are and what they mean.

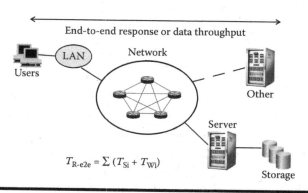

End-to-end response or data throughput

$$T_{\text{R-e2e}} = \Sigma\,(T_{\text{Si}} + T_{\text{Wi}})$$

Figure 1.5   End-to-end system performance.

It also tells us that *visibility* of the elements in a performance chain is important, as we will see time and again. Visibility usually implies tools to measure our resource and time expenditure at each measurable point in the journey. However, remember that interpretation is a key factor, and *a fool with a tool is still a fool.*

The equation in Figure 1.5 shows the basic idea of performance quantification. The time taken to do almost anything is the time taken to actually do it plus any wait time where nothing can actually be done.

For example, buying a loaf from a supermarket should take about 1 min, but if you have to queue behind a person checking out a month's shopping, the whole exercise will take a lot longer. For an IT system with many components involved in the performance of work, the time in each component (assuming they are sequential) will be the sum of all service times and all wait times combined. If it can be arranged that certain activities can operate in parallel, so much the better.

For a system of *n* components where work flows sequentially through them, the total time taken is as shown in the following equation for system total response time:

$$T_{\text{end-to-end}} = \sum_{1}^{n} \left(T_{\text{service}-i} + T_{\text{wait}-i} \right)$$

$$\text{for } i = 1 \text{ to } n \, (\text{components}) \tag{1.2}$$

Performance Terminology

This is sometimes variable, depending on the writer, so I will spell out here what we mean by certain terms. The main entities that allow us to quantify a service are

- Response time as seen by the user
- Response time within the systems (which excludes network times)
- Throughput (of transactions, queries, jobs, or units of work [UoWs])

Response time is the elapsed time between a work request being submitted and the receipt of a response by the same submitter, normally measured as the last character sent by the user to the first character returned. Some people define the latter condition as the time from submission to receiving the first byte of the response, a point we raised above. Examples of response time are

- Time for a database or other data query
- Time an OLTP transaction to complete successfully
- Time for a web page request, access, transmission, and display

Throughput is the measure of work completed over a fixed time, for example,

- OLTP transactions per minute or second
- Bytes or megabytes of a file transferred per unit time over a network
- Bytes or megabytes of data read or written per unit time
- Web server pages accessed per unit time
- Time to dump a file of a certain size to tape (e.g., for backup planning)
- Time to restore a file from tape

These entities are not related in any fixed way so that, for example, it may be possible to increase the throughput at the expense of response time, or vice versa. The setup of the system will in theory be done to satisfy the performance criteria in a service level agreement (SLA).

These numbers, when used in an SLA, are essentially those that are reproducible, unlike, say, analytical queries, which may takes seconds to hours to complete, depending on the parameters involved in a particular query. Numbers regarding and helping to quantify performance in systems are normally referred to by the generic term *performance metrics*. Management consultants J. Magretta and N. Stone (2002) coined the following phrase in a business context, but it is eminently applicable to IT performance:

Given our mission, how is our performance going to be defined?

Performance measurement and resulting metrics are key elements in an organization's business plans for various reasons, some of which are outlined in the next topic. Some metrics related to physical elements of systems, such as hardware and software, but they are not usually an end in themselves. They should allow us to translate them into business value, which is part of the mission of SLAs.

Thus, the key numbers requested by an SLA normally are generated from lower-level metrics, such as resource utilization and data throughput, and other metrics, such as response time, which are measured. This is a theme we will return to several times in this book under headings such as "XXXX Management," where XXXX is some system resource, such as network router, server, or storage.

Does Performance Have a Value?

It is always useful to promote a subject if you can put a value, preferably monetary, on it. There are ways of showing that adequate, consistent performance of transactions and other workloads has a positive effect on the service offered by a business and hence has a value. However, there is a limit where the extra cost of reducing response times or increasing throughput does not have a corresponding business benefit.

I well remember dealing with a UK electricity board and trying to sell IBM's Information Management System (IMS) for their customer records. Our argument was that the records would be updated far faster than the current evening batch update method. The IT manager pointed out (politely) that this offered no real business benefit that would offset the extra cost of using IMS, giving sound reasons why. The IBM team then retired crushed.

There are two papers I have come across that try to put a value on good performance, one a general view, and the other related to the website environment:

Web Performance Monitoring 101
http://www2.smartbear.com/rs/smartbear/images/SmartBear-AlertSite-Monitoring-101-eBook.pdf

The Economic Value of Rapid Response Time
http://jlelliotton.blogspot.ca/p/the-economic-value-of-rapid-response.html

Interaction of Resources

At first glance, it seems that changes in the magnitude of one resource should not affect another resource in the same system, but this is not exactly true, as Figure 1.6 and the following description will show. This I call the *knock-on effect*.

Increased supply of ↓	Affects → CPU	Memory	Disk I/O	W/station	Communications
CPU		★	★		★
Memory	★		★		★
Disk I/O	★	★			
W/station	★	★	★		★
Comms.	★	★	★		

Figure 1.6 Interaction of changes in system resources.

CPU: An increase of CPU power can increase throughput, which places extra demands on memory and disk I/O and possibly communications, depending on workload type.

Memory: An increase in memory size can increase throughput, which places extra demands on CPU and disk I/O and possibly communications, depending on workload type. This will depend on whether memory is a constraint.

Disk I/O: If disk I/O capability is a constraining factor, then an increase in available I/O capacity will put a bigger load on CPU, probably memory, and maybe communications, depending on the workload type.

Workstation: An increase in the number of workstations or terminals, or some change that makes interaction with them faster, will obviously increase the demands on CPU, disk, and I/O capacity. This happened at a chemical company where extra terminals were added for new users and the IT department wasn't told about this. They found out when they noticed the jump in utilizations of the other resources.

Communications: Again, if the network has been the slowest link in the work chain, then increasing its capacity will *suck* more work from CPU, memory, and disk.

Moral: Simply increasing the supply of one resource to solve an apparent response time or throughput problem may not have the desired effect since it may alter the demands on other resources in the system.

Conversely, I have seen a customer upgrade a CPU to solve a performance issue and it having no effect whatsoever. The problem was with the disk I/O. The essence of this is to keep the system in balance.

Resource Management

We mentioned resource management in the section above "Performance Terminology," and it will be useful to define here what we mean by the term *management* in the IT context:

$$\text{Management} = \text{Design} + \text{Measurement} + \text{Analysis} + \text{Action} \qquad (1.3)$$

Others may define it differently, but as long as everyone understands the meaning in context, it should not matter.

The definition I present above will hold for this book. It is like playing a game of cards when someone states that the rules are "according to Hoyle."

Correct management of resources, for example, those affecting performance, includes good design, accurate measurement, intelligent interpretation of those measurements, corrective actions where necessary, and planning for the future.

If you get the design badly wrong, you can all go play golf, because tuning will be like tuning a tractor for an F1 race; if you throw the correct hardware at the wrong problem, your golf will also improve; if you measure the wrong things or get the analysis wrong, your handicap will plummet because of excess golf practice.

> ***Moral***: One major aspect of quality, which in the end means quality of service (QoS), is *getting it right the first time* since changes due to *getting it wrong* may exacerbate the issue or cost megabucks ($$$$M).

Table 1.4 lists some of the characteristics of commercial and scientific applications and illustrates the fact that for different types of work, one size does not fit all. IBM, for example, used to have different systems for these types of work, culminating in S/360, which was meant to cover the 360° spectrum of work.

IBM did not follow up its successful 1130 scientific system, but concentrated instead on development for the commercial environment. It was easily overtaken in the scientific arena by Cray, DEC (with coprocessors), and others.

The world has now polarized into commercial and HPC, and it is rare to see commercial work sharing resources with serious scientific work. Some people go as far as to say that there should be separate networks for scientific and commercial traffic. This is covered in Chapter 5 under the heading "Enterprise and Science Networks."

Table 1.4   Characteristics of Commercial and Technical Workloads

Characteristic	Commercial	Technical/Scientific
Performance metrics	• No. of users • Transactions/second • Jobs/hour • Etc.	• Elapsed time • Instructions/second • Parallelism
Floating-point code	Low	High
Amount of code	Medium	High
Amount of supervisor code executable	Medium to high	Low
Disk I/O and capacity	High to medium	Low to high, depending on the work involved
Terminal/workstation I/O	High	Low
Memory requirements	Medium to high	Medium to very high
Cache memory requirements	Medium to high	Variable

Similarly, floating-point measurements expressing millions of floating-point instructions per second (MFLOPS) can be misleading since there are a range of floating-point calculations and some CPUs have hardwired multiply or divide instructions.

Benchmarks concentrating on these fast calculations can show artificially high results for MFLOPS that might not be achieved when running realistic numerically intensive programs with a wide range of scientific computational operations.

Another case of misleading results occurred when *UnixWorld* published a variant of the Neal Nelson (among others) benchmarks in December 1990. The results showed a larger model of the IBM RS/6000 to be approximately equivalent to a 486-based PC in floating-point performance, using the UNIX **awk** utility.

The Neal Nelson benchmark uses **awk** to test floating-point performance. Tests show that **awk** is more than 100 times slower than an equivalent C program on the RS/6000, compared to factors of 20–30 on other workstations. The fact that almost no commercial applications use **awk** seemed to have escaped the reviewers.

To put the hardware aspects of performance in context, we will now discuss some aspects of hardware performance factors in more detail.

What Can We Do about Performance?

This depends on whether we are talking about preoperational or postoperational periods and activities. There are things that can be done (or not) in both phases of a project to ensure its success. It is well known that the cost of correcting errors in operations phases is more expensive than in the planning and design stages.

Preoperational Options

- Ignore performance altogether (not recommended).
- Establish the need for it and quantify the requirement for the workload in question. One size does not fit all. Design for it in relevant areas (servers, storage, and network) to meet requirements, normally specified in a service level agreement (SLA) and organized by business priority.
- Predict it analytically, by simulation or by rule of thumb (ROT). ROTs are usually based on received wisdom or an organization's own experience.
- Benchmark it or relate it to standard benchmarks.
- Document it (recommended) and amend in the light of experience.

Note: If the preoperational aspects of performance planning are skipped or relegated to *couldn't care less* priority, it is almost certain that there will be problems and any solution will almost certainly be in the *sticking plaster* class, which is an implementation of the *make do and mend* architecture.

We shall see very shortly that cutting corners at the design stage for *financial* or *easy life* reasons may cost more to correct later than to get it right the first time.

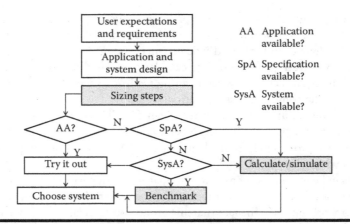

Figure 1.7   Preinstallation performance activity.

Note: Figure 1.7 is not all encompassing, but it shows a high-level view of activities, and within these there will be subactivities. For example, the "Application & System Design" panel might include a series of activities for program development: feasibility, design, code, walk-through, test, and so on.

Postoperational Options

- Ignore performance altogether (not recommended).
- Measure (*monitor*) it and plot it (makes a pretty picture but useless unless you can interpret it sensibly).
- Measure it, plot it, and make a record for posterity (noble, but useless).
- Manage it (measure, record, analyze, act, and plan). *This is the recommended route.*

A key performance concept in this phase is performance management, which we touch on in several areas throughout the book. It has several parts to it, as expressed by the pseudo-equation for performance management components:

$$\text{Management} = \text{Design} + \text{Measurement} + \text{Analysis} + \text{Action} \qquad (1.4)$$

For measurement, we can use the frequently employed term *monitoring*, which itself is made up of several parts, as shown in Figure 1.8.

The legend and explanation of this figure follow:

1. T_R is the total response time (user to system to user) for a *unit of work*, which in most cases will be a transaction, a query, or a batch job.
2. T_N is the network transit time both ways, in and out.
3. T_S is the CPU time in the server (processor).*
4. T_D is the storage access time.

---

* This is a tricky area and depends on what is measured by a monitor and called *server time*. See Appendix VII under "Response Time Interpretation."

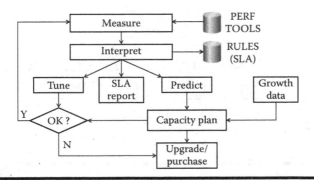

Figure 1.8 Post-installation performance activity.

5. So, in the simple case where the server, disk, and network represent our system, the following relationship holds:

$$\text{Total Response Time } T_R = T_S + T_N + T_D$$

6. However, the three times that make up T_R are themselves composed of other times, some of which are shown schematically in the figure as t_X, where X represents the various subsystems that make up the server, network, and storage resources.* Thus, as an example,

$$T_N = t_L + t_R + t_F + \text{similar terms for other network elements}$$

where L stands for the link (wires, cable, or fiber), R for router, and F for firewall in our simple example.

There will be similar relationships for T_S and T_D involving the service times, t, of their subcomponents. If there are other resources in the overall system that contribute to the service (and hence response) times, they would be included. Very interesting, I hear you say, but so what? In this book, other books, and numerous papers you will see the term *visibility*, which in essence means how well you know the route between the user and the system and back. Such intimate knowledge of the landscape means using monitors to see what is going on at various points, which might be bottleneck points for access to various IT resources.

These operational activities should tie in with *change management* since uncontrolled changes are often a cause of extra demands on resources that must be visible. Unauthorized, but nominally valid, user access can usually be detected via consistently higher resource consumption. I know; I've seen it happen.

Why? The more proactive of these activities are necessary to balance the demands of service level agreements (SLAs) against feasibility and costs. For a discussion of SLAs, see Chapter 17. To take an early look at SLA requirements, we might note that three key elements in modern SLAs should be *performance, availability*, and *security*, and each will have a diagram like those shown in Figures 1.8 and 1.9, but for availability and security aspects in the areas of design, monitoring, and corrective actions.

Figure 1.10 illustrates schematically the costs involved in making changes to aid performance at various stages of choice and development. For example, finding the architectures chosen are

---

* The ones shown are illustrative and not meant to be an exhaustive list of subcomponents.

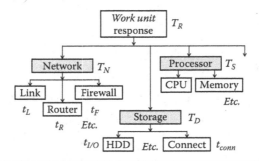

Figure 1.9 Hierarchy of total response time contributions.

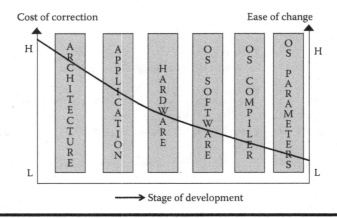

Figure 1.10 Elements of system performance: cost and change as project progresses.

incapable of delivering the required performance involves a great expense, followed by a large expense involved in changing an application by either rewrite or a new commercial off-the-shelf (COTS) application. Later changes, such as operating system or compiler and other system parameters, present less effort and cost.

The moral of this story is *get it right the first time* or incur large expenses in later corrective actions—the later, the more cost involved. Remember, a stitch in time saves nine. Figure 1.10 means that if, as a result of poor design or planning, you have to retrace your steps through OS software, hardware, application, and finally architecture, you are faced with ever-increasing costs of repair, possibly exponential.

Monitoring Performance

The techniques and tools of monitoring performance in different environments are dealt with in Chapter 8, where normal (traditional, classical), web, and virtualized environments are covered. The virtualized environment is the foundation of cloud computing, although it has been around much longer than the cloud.

The value of monitoring is not in the accumulation of performance data and the production of pretty graphs, but the generation of *metrics* that quantify how the system is performing and whether it is meeting the terms of the SLA.

Performance Metrics

Metrics: These are the standards of measurement by which the efficiency, performance, progress, or quality of the components of IT systems can be assessed.

It is a fact of life that to manage something that involves numbers, you need to measure it and present those measurements in a form meaningful to the appropriate people at different levels.

On the Internet, you will find papers on metrics specifically aimed at different environments: classical, Internet, virtualized systems, cloud environments, HPC, and others. Some of these metrics are supplementary to the usual, familiar ones.

There will in general be scores or hundreds of numbers that can be measured, but the art of managing performance is to consolidate these few numbers into what are sometimes called key performance indicators (KPIs). This highlights the difference between data and information, illustrated in Table 1.5.

Role of Testing in Performance

Testing usually has connotations of *function test* (does it do what it should do?) and *stress test* (what maximum load will the system handle before collapsing in a heap?). There are, however, other aspects to this that can offer an insight into expected performance at normal loads. This performance will be dictated by a service level agreement (SLA), and if it cannot be met, it is back to the drawing board for either the configuration or renegotiation of the SLA.

Testing Steps: These can be found in various places, usually under the heading "best practices," but I'll summarize the consensus here by outlining the typical steps in the process.

1. Involve someone who knows enough about the generic practice of testing.
2. Make sure you have the correct workload mix specified with volumes, peaks, averages, and times of day for application usage.
3. Define the service level performance acceptance rules:
   a. Response time of individual transactions—mean or a percentile value (see Appendix I for percentiles).
   b. Throughput (transactions per second [tps]) at which these response times must hold—"a maximum response time of T seconds at N tps".

Table 1.5   Performance Data: Conversion to Key Metrics

Raw Data	Operational Metrics	User/SLA Metrics
01110100110	Average Disk A utilization	Average response time
00111000110	Average wait time Disk A	90th percentile response time
00110000110	Average response time Disk A	Throughput (transactions/second)
00111100110	CPU utilization %	Throughput (queries/minute)
10110110110	CPU wait time %, etc.	Etc.

    c. Any other riders and conditions specified or expected in the SLA, such as availability or recovery.

4. Define and construct the test environment. This need not be the final production environment, which may not prove adequate for the job. It can be performed on a pilot system as long as you can measure the resource usage of the transactions and then prorate them to the correct sized system configuration to handle the production load. See Appendix II under "CPU Loading" for a discussion of transaction resource estimation.

5. Define and design the test scenarios and, importantly, the scripts that simulate the transactions and the delivery mechanism for them. The tests should ideally be constructed with input from end users or web shareholders who know the scenarios better than IT. The scenarios should then approximate to a real production environment.

6. Run the tests and document the results; this is vital since any reruns will want to avoid repeating the mistakes already made.

7. Analyze the results against the objectives and the proposed SLA. If the objectives are met, then do the final documentation and present the results to the SLA "shareholders."

8. If they are not met,

    a. The tests could perhaps be rerun with some tuning.

    b. The tests could be rerun against a renegotiated SLA.

    c. A more suitably configured system could be envisaged, costed, and approved, based on the extrapolated pilot system or a system previously envisaged as being suitable for the task enhanced in the configuration.

References: The first link outlines testing principles that, although ostensibly aimed at web services, is general enough to apply to other testing as well. The others offer some testing best practices advice:

Fundamentals of Web Application Performance Testing (Chapter 1 of eBook)
https://msdn.microsoft.com/en-us/library/bb924356.aspx

Performance Testing Guidance for Web Applications (eBook)
http://perftestingguide.codeplex.com/releases/view/6690

Modern Load Testing: NeoTys eBook
http://www.neotys.com/references/whitepapers.html (register and retrieve eBook)

Chapter 2

Processor Hardware

Computer hardware has progressed rapidly in the past 30 years or so in terms of raw processor speed, architecture, and instruction sets. History has something to teach us, as Table 2.1 shows the state-of-the-art performance figures for a number of machines between 1976 and 1996.

> We are talking about performance increases of factors of between approximately 30 and 300 in 20 years, depending on the system, and the same again in the last 20 years.

Moore's Law

Moore's Law Giveth and ...Taketh Away

The number of users supported, however, has not increased by the same factors in general because of the use of middleware, fourth-generation languages (4GLs), and more complex databases, such as relational structures in native mode and sometimes emulating hierarchical structures. This represents more resources being used to achieve the same business function, perhaps originally developed in Assembler code, through COBOL to 4GLs and other code generators.

In 1974, at the 11th hour, I increased the system memory on a mainframe, destined for a large UK local government account, from 512K to 768K after having second thoughts about its ability to support large numbers of users on the VM, MVS, or Customer Information Control System (CICS) system being proposed. My current PC will not operate properly on less than 64 MB today with a single user. How times and resource requirements have changed. I can also remember a time when operating system gurus at IBM attempted to shoehorn the flagship operating system MVS into 64K. The moral today seems to be if you have storage, flaunt it.

However, hardware vendors today are happy to provide ever-increasing power to developers and users alike. Figure 2.1 shows how Moore's law fared against the real delivery of power and chip density over 40 or so years. In essence, most of the points on the graph are close to the line, showing that Moore's law has held up quite well over a considerable period in "chip" timescales. History has indeed repeated itself.

For a more detailed look at processor development and people involved, see the paper below the table.

Table 2.1   Processor Power Increases over Time (20 Years)

Vendor	Machine/Date	Power (unit)	Machine/Date	Power (unit)
IBM	3033 (1977)	5 RPP	ES9000-820 (1993)	170 RPP[3]
IBM	6150 (1986)	0.36 MFLOPS	RS/6000-59H (1995)	132 MFLOPS
DEC	VAX 8600 (1980s)	33 tps[a]	Alpha 8400 (1995)	More than 3000[a]
Sun	SPARC IPC (1988)	13.8 SPECint92	SS20 HS21 (1995)	131.2 SPECint92

Source: Digital estimates from *System Enhancement Guide*, April 1995.

[a] tps, transactions per second. MFLOPs are from Linpack runs on these systems.

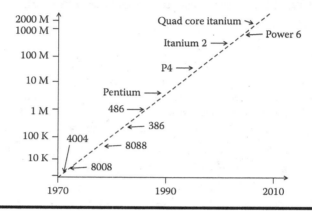

Figure 2.1   Forty years of Moore's law: the test of time.

History of Processor Performance
http://www.cs.columbia.edu/~sedwards/classes/2012/3827-spring/advanced-arch-2011.pdf

Central Processors

Some of the factors contributing to the spectacular increases in CPU performance are

- Processor architecture (uniprocessor, superscalar, vector, symmetric multiprocessor [SMP], clustering, parallel systems, massive server farms)
- Processor speed (megahertz, SMP power ratios)
- Message Passing Interface (MPI) speed and architecture (parallel systems)
- Instruction pipelining
- Instruction cache size
- Data cache size (large ones used in *benchmarks in cache* tricks)
- Levels of cache (L1, L2, L3) and cache handling algorithms
- Memory size
- Memory bandwidth
- Optimizing compilers
- Built-in graphics hardware functions

Processor Usage

The utilization of a processor (or any other item) is the percentage of time it is actually doing work. Thus, we may hear the statement "the processor is on average 45% utilized." This sounds fairly sensible and simple, but when you think about it, the processor (or CPU) is either working or not working; that is, it is either 100% utilized or 0% utilized. How can this be?

The reason is that the *average* is a figure derived from some periods of 0% utilization and those of 100% utilization, as shown in Figure 2.2. A CPU cannot run at, say, 40%; it is either 100% or 0% busy; it can only average 45% over some period.

Processor Utilization Breakdown

Figure 2.3 illustrates the states of activity that can exist in a CPU's *life*.

A processor is either busy or not busy, but this doesn't help us solve performance problems since we want to know what share of the processor is taken up by the application, which is key to its performance. The breakdown of the processor's day is as follows:

- *Idle*: No work to do at all.
- *Wait(ing)*: Is trying to do work, but is held up by lack of a certain resource.

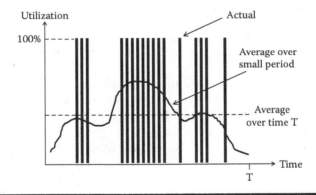

Figure 2.2   CPU utilization in detail.

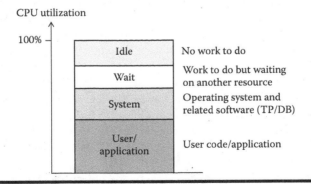

Figure 2.3   Components of CPU (processor) usage.

- *System (state)*: The processor is doing work for the operating system and its supporting software, for example, middleware or a database instance.
- *User/application (state)*: It is doing work on behalf of an application or, in the case of program development, a user.

The key to efficiency is to minimize or eliminate *idle* and *wait*, to minimize *system* so that *application* is maximized. The minimization of idle and wait is achieved by balancing the system resources to match the workload wherever possible. If the system is forever waiting for a disk, it means you need more actuators or capacity.

Operating System

Operating systems (OS), or system control programs (SCPs), have developed rapidly, sometimes from a performance point of view, sometimes from the functional aspect. Whether they enhance performance or not is a moot point, but they certainly have an impact on the flow of work through the system, batch or online (online transaction processing [OLTP]).

Some features of the modern operating system are

- Multitasking, multithreading—some applications and operating systems
- Clustering of CPU nodes
- Memory management
- Network bandwidth management
- Alternate I/O path selection—storage and sometimes network
- Dynamic I/O buffering
- Data caching (memory buffers)—on-chip, off-chip, peripheral devices
- Terminal handling (character, block mode, graphics, graphical user interfaces [GUIs])
- Virtual storage (paging, swapping)
- Compiler technology, especially optimizing
- Handling coexistence and control of transactional work with batch work
- System utilities and commands, some related to performance
- Maintaining logs of system activity for current and future analysis

Supporting Software

The software lying between the application and the operating system ("green" layers in IBM parlance, middleware in others) has progressed rapidly in the last few years. Witness the functionality of the many manifestations of UNIX, Linux, and Windows today compared to that offered by the creators of UNIX, who aimed to produce a developer's operating system for technically minded people ("techies").

These layers have almost certainly not increased performance over traditional supporting software over and above that provided by the hardware, but the functionality has increased dramatically, taking advantage of the extra power available from the hardware.

Some middleware is listed under the heading "Middleware" in Chapter 3, but a few are mentioned below:

- Database (flat file, relational, hierarchical, network, object oriented, etc.)
- Online transaction processing (OLTP), for example, CICS and Tuxedo

- Security layers—proprietary, open, packages, web-specific, and so on
- Other middleware, such as Websphere, Weblogic, and so on

Practically all these items and others listed later can impact performance and possibly need optimization.

Peripherals

Peripherals have shown steady improvements in raw performance for many years now. From the 7 and 11 MB IBM 2311 disks of 1970 to the multicached, high-speed, high-capacity disks and disk controllers of today is a remarkable improvement. The supporting performance tools and diagnostics are also a revelation since in the old days the only way to tell that an IBM 2311 was working hard was to measure the speed with which it *walked* across the floor when the actuator was flying to and fro.*

Careful design of data set placement was crucial in preventing the disk from walking out of the door of the machine room. Some storage enhancements are

- Disks and disk cache (performance and capacity)
- I/O architecture (I/O bus, SCSI, fiber channel, Serial Storage Architecture [SSA], High-Performance Parallel Interface [HIPPI])
- I/O bandwidth (number of paths, parallel vs. serial bit transfer, etc.)
- Optical disk (capacity)
- Tape characteristics (performance, capacity, backup striping)
- Tapes (performance and capacity)
- Printers (performance and function—3D)
- Terminal adapters (performance and function)
- Graphics adapters (performance and function)

> ***Note***: It is often the case today that many functions in peripherals are handled in software or microcode and not fixed in hardware. This allows upgrades in function and often in performance that were not possible with pure hardwired components.

Processor Performance

By processor performance we mean program execution time where lower times mean better performance. The factors involved can be shown as follows in the processor performance equation:

$$E = P \times C \times T \qquad (2.1)$$

where:

    E is the execution time of a program on the machine
    P is the path length or instructions executed in the program

---

* This was usually due to poor data set and index placement.

C is the *average* number of machine cycles needed to process an instruction

T is the cycle time (time for a single cycle) of the machine

T, the cycle time, is a function of the machine hardware clock.

For the mathematically inclined, the general formula for C is derived as follows:

Imagine a reduced instruction set computing (RISC) processor with N instructions in its instruction set, $I_1, I_2, I_3, \ldots$, and so on, to N terms. If n_1 is the number of cycles taken to execute instruction I_1, n_2 to execute instruction I_2, and so on, then the *average* number of cycles per instruction is

$$C = \frac{\sum_1^N n_i}{N} \tag{2.2}$$

Equation 2.2, however, assumes that all the instructions are used equally in any program, which is never the case. To allow for this, it is necessary to introduce a *weighting factor* to bias the summation toward the most frequently used instructions. If N_i is the weighting factor for instruction I_i, then C, the average weighted cycles per instruction, can be expressed as

$$C = \frac{\sum_i^N \left(N_i \times n_i\right)}{\sum N_i} \tag{2.3}$$

P, the path length, depends initially on the programmer, but when the program is written, the onus is on the compiler. The compiler can shorten the path length, or perhaps use faster instructions in combination to achieve the desired result. To illustrate this principle, consider a hypothetical machine that had incredibly fast *add* instructions but average speed *multiply* instructions in its armory.

A compiler that understood the machine architecture might replace the program instruction $(4 \times A_1)$ with $(A_1 + A_1 + A_1 + A_1)$, and some compilers do have a hardware selection option for compilations of executable code. This, however, will reduce the portability of the code since it relies on the underlying instruction set of that processor.

C, the number of cycles needed to execute an instruction, is basically a function of the hardware architecture.

For example, a machine clocked at 50 MHz has a cycle time of 20 ns or 0.02 μs. Obviously, the smaller we make all the factors on the right-hand side of the equation, the smaller the value of E and the better the performance.

Central Processor (CPU) Architectures

In the heady days of proprietary systems, there were a number of computer architectures offered by vendors, each developed for competitive advantage and necessitating a unique operating system—provided by the vendor, of course. Some of these architectures still exist, for example,

IBM 370/390, but in the main, Intel and reduced instruction set computing (RISC) architectures have taken over. Even IBM bowed to progress and introduced IBM RISC architectures into its mainframe and AS/400 (now iSeries) offerings.

IBM does, though, involve other parties in it power architecture via the OpenPower Consortium. Conduct a search on "OpenPower Consortium" to find the paper referenced below since keying in the URL will shorten your life considerably.

What Is OpenPower?
https://www.ibm.com/developerworks/community/wikis/form/anonymous/api/wiki/61ad9cf2-c6a3-4d2c-b779-61ff0266d32a/page/1cb956e8-4160-4bea-a956-e51490c2b920/attachment/4edf7757-2e36-41d3-9869-b62d534be05b/media/VUG%20What%20is%20OpenPOWER%20v%201.7.pdf

RISC and CISC Architectures

Until comparatively recently, most commercial systems, especially proprietary ones, used complex instruction set computing. In 1976, Dr. John Cocke, an IBM research fellow, produced a prototype system, the 801 project—named after building 801, in which he worked—using reduced instruction set computing hardware, which eventually became known as RISC.* As a consequence, the complex instruction sets became known as CISC, although it was the architecture with no name before RISC arrived.

Origins: The first RISC projects came from IBM, Stanford, and University of California–Berkeley about 40 years ago. The IBM 801 project, Stanford MIPS, and Berkeley RISC 1 and 2 were all designed with a similar philosophy, which spawned the name RISC. The generic characteristics of most RISC processors are

- *One cycle execution time*: RISC processors have a clock per instruction (CPI) of one cycle. This is due to the optimization of each instruction on the processor.
- *Pipelining*: A technique that allows for simultaneous execution of parts of instructions to more efficiently process instructions.
- *Large number of registers*: The RISC design philosophy generally incorporates a larger number of registers to prevent large numbers of memory interactions.
- More complex operations that could not be done via a single instruction would be performed by combinations of simple instructions in the instruction set. Table 2.2 shows some of the RISC and CISC architectures from various manufacturers. The main point to remember is that all RISC implementations are not the same and, like CISC instruction sets, vary across architectures (Figure 2.4).

> RISC has now found a home in some supercomputer implementations (high-performance computing [HPC]).

---

* The acronym RISC was not coined by Cocke, but apparently by students and teachers at the University of California–Los Angeles. CISC did not exist as a popular acronym until RISC arrived.

Table 2.2 RISC and CISC Architecture Implementations

RISC	*CISC*
IBM RS/6000 Power/PowerPC	IBM 360/370/390/zSeries[a]
Digital Alpha	Digital VAX
Hewlett Packard PA	Intel x86, Pentium
Sun Sparc/SuperSparc/UltraSparc	Motorola 88000
SGI MIPS processors	IBM AS/400[a]

[a] There are now versions of these machines using IBM's CMOS (S/390 and follow-ons) and PowerPC (AS/400) architectures.

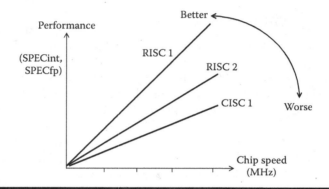

Figure 2.4 Chip performance vs. chip speed.

One of the great advantages of RISC over CISC is the cost of developing and producing hardware instruction sets. The cost of developing and creating RISC machines is cheaper than doing the same thing with CISC because of the hardware implications of complex instructions, like MOVE LEFT LONG (Assembler) and other leviathans.

An article outlining the relative merits of RISC and CISC can be found at

RISC vs. CISC
http://cs.stanford.edu/people/eroberts/courses/soco/projects/risc/risccisc/

A general review of the RISC world is covered in

Reduced Instruction Set Computing
https://en.wikipedia.org/wiki/Reduced_instruction_set_ computing

Traditional System Design

Up to the 1980s, RISC and CISC workstations and machines used a *linear architectu*re for both commercial and scientific work. A typical basic system, shown in Figure 2.5, would have a floating-point card added to it to cater to scientific work.

The problem with this design is that the integer instruction unit often had to *fetch and carry* instructions and data for the floating-point card, rendering parallel instruction execution difficult. Such designs usually needed 1.5–2.5 cycles on average to execute an instruction, sometimes more.

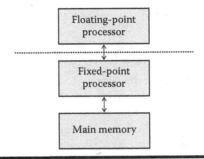

Figure 2.5   Traditional workstation architecture.

The addition of a faster floating-point processor, instead of increasing the overall performance, could have the opposite effect by overloading the intermediate fixed-point processor that does all the *fetching* and *carrying* for the floating-point unit (FPU).

The resolution of this problem demanded a new architecture.

Superscalar Architectures

The research objectives in RISC (and CISC) architectures included the parallel execution of instructions, initially aiming at one instruction per machine cycle. Subsequently, designs sought to execute more than one instruction in a single cycle of the chip.

Recent RISC designs implement the latter architecture, which is called a *superscalar* architecture. Sun, HP, IBM, Digital, and other vendors have implemented superscalar architectures on their UNIX hardware systems, and we will the superscalar *principle* by reference to the original IBM RISC System/6000, shown schematically in Figure 2.6. This does not imply any superiority of the RS/6000; it merely illustrates the basic principles of superscalar computing.

In Figure 2.6, three instruction execution units and two caches are shown, along with the system memory. Superscalar performance requires that the processing units in the architecture are given enough work to keep them all busy. This requirement puts a great deal of responsibility on

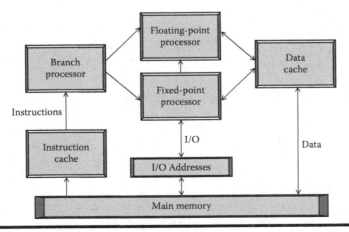

Figure 2.6   Superscalar workstation architecture.

the compilers, which need to populate the instruction cache in such a way as to achieve maximum processing overlap.

In the case of the original seven-chip power architecture, it was possible to have the branch processor performing two instructions, while the floating point and integer units performed one instruction each. This gave the maximum throughput of four instructions per cycle of the machine clock. However, in certain cases, the floating-point operation would be a combined floating-point multiply-add, giving five operations in a single cycle.

Anyone who had the opportunity to look at code produced by the AIX compilers would notice that there were thousands of floating-point multiply-add instructions even if the multiplier was only 1.0000.

Uniprocessor (UP) Architecture

Traditional computer architectures employed a CPU accessing *core storage* for data and instructions, for example, IBM System/360 systems. Later systems, for example, IBM System/370 systems, added an extra layer of memory between the main memory and the voracious CPU. This layer, known as *cache*, was typically much smaller than main memory, but much more expensive per byte. Its purpose was to act as a *buffer* between the CPU and main storage, where data and instructions could be accessed as quickly as the CPU demanded them. It later expanded to more levels, as we shall see later.

Cache Memory: This is random access memory (RAM) that a processor can access more quickly than it can access regular main storage RAM. As the processor processes data, it looks first in the cache memory, and if it finds the data there (from a previous access to the data), it does not have to do the more time-consuming reading of data from larger memory because of the higher speed of cache when compared to main memory. Higher speed of cache memory, however, does not produce faster performance since it all depends on how the cache handling algorithms work.

Cache memory usually comes in levels in some sequence, each supporting the level above in finding data that that level doesn't have in its memory. Most cache implementations can make use of the following sequence of memory:

- Cache level 1 (L1)
- Cache level 2 (L2)
- Cache level 3 (L3)
- Main memory

To take an analogy, consider a craftsman doing work on a house that is 5 km from his own base. He takes a subset of his tools in his van to do the job in hand. If he is really smart, he will have anticipated what tools he needs for the job and loaded his van accordingly. He parks the van outside the house he is working on. When he needs a tool, he simply retrieves it from the van, but if he doesn't have it, it means a longer journey back to base for the tool. The smart tradesman will be faster finishing the job than the one who has to travel back to base one or more times (assuming they work at the same rate). Tool bag, van, and so forth, are the cache levels in this analogy.

Supplementing L1 cache with L2 cache can have a significant effect on system performance, as illustrated by the (old) example of IBM systems shown in Table 2.3. The addition of 1 MB of L2

Table 2.3 Performance Effects of Cache Memory

IBM RS/6000 C10 with L1 cache	IBM RS/6000 C10 with L1 + 1 MB L2
404 tpmC	485 tpmC

cache to the IBM RS/6000 C10 system improved performance by more than 20%, as Table 2.3 shows.

The performance contribution of level 2 cache depends on the hardware architecture, and the same performance enhancements suggested by the example in Table 2.3 should not be assumed to be universal. Neither should it be assumed that a big cache is faster than a small cache. It all depends on the efficiency of the cache handling.

Symmetric Multiprocessor Architecture

In the 1970s, the increase in single-processor power did not match Moore's law, and to cope with increasing demand for power required innovation on the part of vendors. Digital developed clustering techniques and IBM (and others) developed multiprocessor architectures. Indeed, in those days, processor power was increasing by about 18% per annum, whereas demand was increasing at 40%. An answer to this dilemma was to have more than one processor tackling the user workload. This solution became known as symmetric multiprocessing (SMP).

An early attempt at this was made by IBM using two System 360/65 processors, but this only yielded a 10% increase in throughput over a single-processor system—not a bargain in view of the price of the 360/65. The problem was worked on, and eventually SMPs matured and yielded a throughput increase for two processors of 1.7–1.9 over a single-processor system. The actual increase depended on the software being used on the SMP, for example, CICS, Information Management System (IMS), batch, FORTRAN, and so on, and numbers are usually separated to reflect this in the IBM Large Systems Performance Reference (LSPR), a publication dealing with these numbers.

It was thought at the time that the maximum number of processors that could be used in an SMP system before throughput actually fell rather than increase was about 10 or 12. This restricted the number of processors used in IBM SMPs for many years. However, later systems, such as the Cray CS6400, displayed nearly linear performance increases up to 64 processors. The Cray eventually became the Sun E10000, after Sun acquired Cray Research in about 1994, which showed similar linearity.

The SMP does not normally scale linearly, that is, an n processor SMP delivers n times the throughput or transaction rate of a single processor of the same type. In fact, after a certain value of n, the performance degrades. Figure 2.7 shows a schematic view of an n processor SMP.

Clustered Systems

Digital Equipment was the first vendor of any note to produce clustered systems, although for some time the performance enhancements per processor added were far from linear.

Later, IBM introduced the mainframe MVS Sysplex and the AIX HACMP (High-Availability Clustered Multiprocessor) cluster, to be followed by other vendors such as Sun Microsystems and HP.

Today, any self-respecting piece of processor hardware is expected to be able to take part in a cluster. Commercial clusters can accommodate many nodes, each of which can be a uniprocessor system or an SMP system. The fact is that the theoretical number of nodes supported in a cluster

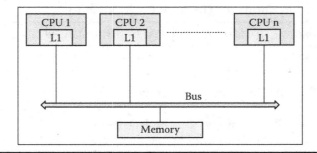

Figure 2.7 Symmetric multiprocessor.

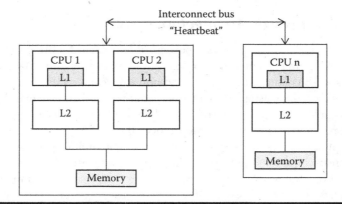

Figure 2.8 Cluster system.

is probably far more than the number of nodes that have been tested for performance and stability. Always remember this when evaluating cluster technology (Figure 2.8).

Massively Parallel Processor Architecture

Massively parallel processing (MPP) is a form of collaborative processing of the same program by two or more processors. Each processor handles different threads of the program, and each processor itself has its own operating system and dedicated memory. A special interface is required to allow the different processors involved in the MPP to arrange thread handling. The MPP processors normally communicate using a messaging interface so that their programming work is coordinated. This is often called a Message Passing Interface (MPI).

MPP is the simultaneous processing of a program by multiple processors that work on different parts of the program in parallel. Each processor commands its own operating system and memory. In some MPP implementations, a hundred or more processors can work on the same application and an *interconnect* arrangement of data paths (MPIs) allows messages to be sent between processors to maintain data and execution synchronization.

An MPP system is often used in preference to a symmetric processor system (SMP) for applications that allow a number of databases to be searched in parallel. These applications include decision support systems and data warehouse applications, but a specialized configuration used for these may not suit other applications.

An MPP system is also known as a *loosely coupled* or *shared-nothing* system.

Parallel Processing

Traditional computing involves the sequential execution of instructions as dictated by the programmer, except where instruction branches are taken or other modules of code are called for execution. It would be nice to be able to do things in parallel to speed things up, rather like a number of people in a kitchen preparing different parts of a meal.

Rather like the meal, parallel computer processing needs multiple *chefs* or, in reality, processors. If a problem can be broken into smaller subproblems, then it should be possible to execute the code representing these problems at the same time, that is, in parallel. A parallel computer then is one comprising multiple processors working in tandem and connected by an interconnection mechanism (MPI) and some control software acting as umpire or referee.

Parallelism has been employed for many years, mainly in high-performance computing, but interest in it has grown lately due to the physical constraints preventing frequency scaling. As power consumption (and the attendant heat generation) by computers has become a concern in recent years, parallel computing has become the dominant paradigm in computer architecture, mainly in the form of multicore processors. Vector processing and processors (Cray) were early examples of parallel processing.

Of course, if one module of code needs information from another module of code before it can execute, then the two cannot run in parallel. For example, a tax program might calculate gross earnings for a person and then assess the tax and other deduction liabilities. The liability code cannot calculate the tax due until it has the output of the gross calculation code.

Figure 2.9 shows schematically code that is partly able to be run in parallel and part not, and shows the overall speedup in performance as a result.

In Figure 2.9, P is the fraction of code that is capable of being parallelized and, obviously, (1 – P) is the fraction that cannot and remains sequential. A is the time taken to execute the code sequentially, including the code that is amenable to parallelization, and B is the time taken when the parallelizable code is run in that way.

The speedup ratio observed in such scenarios is described in some equations or laws; Amdahl's, Gustafson's, and Gunther's are examples, which are dealt with below.

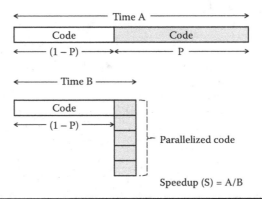

Figure 2.9   Code in sequential and parallel form.

Implementations of Parallel Computing

There are three main ways of implementing parallel execution of code:

1. Multiprogramming, the capability of executing more than one process at a time
2. Multiprocessors, using a computer composed of many processors (>2), each executing a process but all sharing a common memory
3. Multicomputer, where the processes are executed across more than one set of processors or computer system, for example, in a cluster

Of course, there is a cost involved in implementing reliable, parallel processing, and it is not a *given* for all types of workload, particularly commercial workloads. Sophisticated parallel processing systems are usually reserved for use in solving large technical and other problems, a few examples of which are listed below and shown in Figure 2.10.

■ Oil exploration
■ Pharmaceutical drug design
■ Medical imaging and diagnosis
■ Human genome studies
■ Other scientific, financial, and commercial work, mainly in analysis and prediction rather than pure processing
■ Studies of the atmosphere and weather

Such work often goes under the name high-performance computing (HPC). Some of the work undertaken can last days or weeks, so high-availability systems are desirable since a failure of 95% through a 2-week calculation is not a nice thing to happen.

Aside: An amusing incident occurred when a meteorologist was explaining to an IT audience how an IBM 370/195 (a behemoth system in its day) was employed in their work. One attendee asked how they managed to forecast the weather if the computer failed. The reply was "We have a piece of seaweed hanging from the wall and we use that."

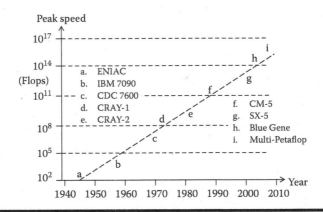

Figure 2.10   Evolution of supercomputer processing, 1940–2010.

Evolution of Parallel Processing

There were a number of entrants in the MPP race in the 1980s and 1990s, but most of them couldn't stay the course mainly, according to Cray, because of lack of knowledge of how to program them effectively. The URL reference in the following section is a link to a paper by Cray about its Cray XE6, but it has much to recommend it as a guide showing what MPPs need to operate properly.

Introduction to Cray MPP Systems with Multicore Processors
http://user.cscs.ch/fileadmin/user_upload/customers/CSCS_Application_Data/Files/
Presentations/Courses_Ws_2011/Multi-Threaded_Course_Feb11/Day_2_Session_2_all.pdf
It shows the basic processors required in MPPs, compute nodes, I/O nodes and service (control) nodes to coordinate the activity of the system (Figure 2.11).

MPI is a Message Passing Interface, the communication vehicle between the nodes in the system that needs to be extremely fast to deliver the power offered by the multiple processors. Realistic parallel processing in this environment cannot take place without it.

Processor Summary

We have done a whistle-stop tour of the processor developments aimed at increasing the performance and throughput of computer systems and involved various stages:

- Increasing the clock rate of single processors and enhancing the I/O attached to balance the system
- Symmetric multiprocessors (SMPs) where processors operate together in close coupling (tightly coupled SMPs)
- Clusters of processors (nodes)
- Non-uniform memory access (NUMA) architecture systems
- Massively parallel systems

There may well be hybrid combinations of some of these systems used for special purposes. One such hybrid is grid computing, which harnesses the power of disparate distributed systems (and workstations) to yield greater power for work from distributed power. Another hybrid is a

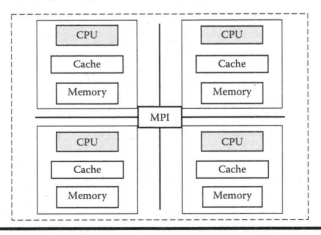

Figure 2.11   Massively parallel architecture.

small processor or workstation preparing work for a back-end HPC processor to do the number crunching and pass the results back to the workstation for analysis and resubmission if necessary. This is often how molecular modeling and similar types of graphics HPC work are performed.

Which architecture is best depends on your workload, although some choices are often obvious, plus cost of ownership and ease-of-use considerations.

References: For a fascinating look at this processor evolution, see the following articles:

From Kilobytes to Petabytes in 50 Years
www.eurekalert.org/features/doe/2002-03/dlnl-fkt062102.php

Difference between Parallel Processing and Vector Processing
http://www.answers.com/Q/What_is_difference_between_parallel_processing_and_vector_processing

Also see "IBM Massively Parallel Blue Gene: Application Development," which is a large presentation on supercomputing developed jointly by IBM and Biomedical Informatics and Computational Biology (BICB):

https://www.msi.umn.edu/~cpsosa/MoscowStateUniv-JUL-2010_lecture.pdf

NUMA Systems

We have seen above some architectures involving different configurations of memory—shared (SMPs) and unshared (MPPs). There are two others, one of which we will cover here: non-uniform memory access (NUMA). The other, *uniform memory architecture* (sometimes *access*) (UMA), is a subset of NUMA.

The NUMA architecture was thought of in an attempt to get around the issue of processor speeds outstripping the ability of memory to deliver data as they were developed. In an SMP, processors can compete for memory, and operation of such architectures over about eight processors can lead to unacceptable contention and performance degradation. This is where NUMA fits in, between SMPs and MPPs.

NUMA is an alternative approach to memory access by multiple processors. It links several small, inexpensive nodes using a high-performance interconnection and seeks to alleviate SMP access bottlenecks by limiting the numbers of processors supported on any one memory bus.

Each node contains processors and memory, much like a small SMP system. Looking at Figure 2.12, all the processors (CPUs) in the configuration can access memory in both nodes in a coherent fashion (one portion of memory is not out of step with another); thus,

- A CPU in node 1 can access its own memory (local or *near* memory in NUMA terms).
- The same CPU can access memory in node 2 through its own memory controller and via the system interconnect shown in Figure 2.12.
- Similar access can occur in reverse, node 2 to node 1.

The access to memory in another node is obviously somewhat slower than memory access within the node, hence the name non-uniform memory access (NUMA). The *cc* prefix denotes the coherency of the access to both sets of memory. Numerically, the ratio of the time taken to access local memory to that taken for remote (far) memory access is called the *NUMA ratio*, with 3:1 being an optimal ratio. Higher ratios will obviously have an effect on the performance of any software requiring this kind of access.

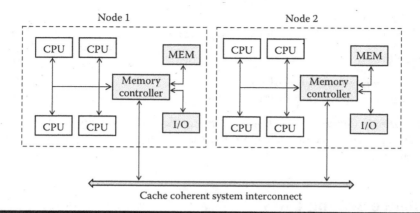

Figure 2.12   Cache coherent NUMA architecture.

In addition, a memory controller allows a node to use memory on all other nodes, creating a *single system image*. When a processor accesses memory that does not lie within its own node (remote memory), the data must be transferred over the NUMA connection; this type of access is slower than accessing local memory.

Memory-access times are not uniform and depend on the location of the memory and the node from which it is accessed, as the name NUMA implies.

NUMA Performance

NUMA performance is not guaranteed unless the configuration is used to best effect. This implies knowledge of the memory requirements of the workload components and optimum programming techniques for NUMA architecture operation. See the following reference:

Optimizing Applications for NUMA
https://software.intel.com/en-us/articles/optimizing-applications-for-numa

Other NUMA References: The references below are useful introductions to NUMA and other memory architectures.

Non-Uniform Memory Access (NUMA)
http://cs.nyu.edu/~lerner/spring10/projects/NUMA.pdf

Understanding Non-Uniform Memory Access
https://technet.microsoft.com/en-us/library/ms178144 (v=sql.105).aspx

> **Note**: The above reference differentiates between hard NUMA and soft NUMA, the latter being a *software split* of memory instead of a *physical split* of separate memory modules as there is in standard *vanilla* NUMA.

Understanding Non-Uniform Memory Access/Architectures (NUMA) [SQL skills]
https://www.sqlskills.com/blogs/jonathan/understanding-non-uniform-memory-accessarchitectures-numa/

Cache Coherence [definition]
http://whatis.techtarget.com/definition/cache-coherence

For Black Belts:

NUMA: An Overview [quite detailed]
http://queue.acm.org/detail.cfm?id=2513149

A Primer on Memory Consistency and Cache Coherence [detailed discussion]
https://class.stanford.edu/c4x/Engineering/CS316/asset/ A_Primer_on_Memory_Consistency_
and_Coherence.pdf

Performance Scaling Laws

Introduction

It has long been a problem achieving better performance through a single, faster processor, as IBM
and others found in the 1970s. This relatively slow performance growth (ca. 20% per annum) was
not up to the 40%, and more, growth in demand for power to run businesses that were increasingly dependent on IT. This led to the linking of processors to combine their power in meeting
this demand, which continues unabated.

Unfortunately, in terms of combining processor power, 1 + 1 did not equal 2. It could be cost-
effective for batch work where the sequence of activity was shared across two or more processors,
but this combination was not effective for transaction processing or other real-time work. The
outcome was the development of clusters of processors or, more accurately, of systems or nodes,
and variations on this theme.

> *Scalability*: Scalability is the ability of a system, network, or process to handle a growing
> amount of work in a capable manner or its ability to be enlarged to accommodate that
> growth (Wikipedia).

Linear scalability means that if we, for example, double the number of units in the system
(processor), it will support double the workload with the same performance (throughput, response
time). This is rarely achieved, and what should be a linear 45° line of a graph of processors versus
workload tails off after a few processors are added. Some of these are shown in the following sections covering three *scalability laws*.

In the symmetric multiprocessing (SMP) arena, IBM used to quote the power or throughput
of a combination of two processors in an SMP configuration at 1.7–1.9 times that of a single processor, and usually gave actual numbers for different types of IBM software, Time Sharing Option
(TSO), Customer Information Control System (CICS) (an OLTP), and so on, yielding these averages. However, with SMPs, the law of diminishing returns applied when adding more processors
(CPUs) to an SMP configuration, hence the development of the new configurations discussed in
the previous sections of this book.

These developments helped to alleviate the problem, but the solutions were not immediately
accessible to the numerical analysis of performance increases as a result of adding processors.
Gene Amdahl, an IBM System/360 pioneer and founder of Amdahl Corporation, made an early
attempt to quantify what became known as a *scale-up* or *speedup* factor, a number to represent

the performance increase per added processor in a configuration, as an aid to planning for capacity.

This became known as *Amdahl's law*, which was a precursor to subsequent modifications and restatements based on experience gained in multiprocessor systems—*Gustafson's* and *Gunther's* laws.

Amdahl's Law

Amdahl's law was mentioned earlier when discussing the advent of clusters. It was aimed at quantifying the increase in power or throughput of two or more systems in tandem, often called scalability. Amdahl's speedup law is expressed algebraically as follows:

$$S(N) = \frac{1}{(1-P) + \dfrac{P}{N}} \qquad (2.4)$$

where:

- S is the speedup factor
- P is the fraction of the program that can be parallelized
- N is the number of computers/nodes involved

$(1 - P)$ is the part of the program that cannot be parallelized; that is, it remains a serially executing piece of code.

As an example, if P is 90%, then $(1 - P)$ is 10% or 0.1 in Amdahl's equation, and the execution of code can be speeded up by an asymptotic maximum of a factor of 10, no matter how large the value of N used. For this reason, parallel computing is only useful for either small numbers of processors or problems with very high values of P, which is sometimes the case with scientific work. In Figure 2.13, no matter how parallel the code elements are, there will always be a portion (shaded) that make the achievement of a speedup of 10 impossible.

Plotting speedup against number of processors for a variety of parallelizable percentages shows a tailing off of speedup at high N, what is called the *law of diminishing returns*. Writing parallel

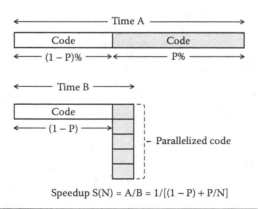

Speedup S(N) = A/B = 1/[(1 − P) + P/N]

Figure 2.13   Amdahl's law: parallelization speedup schematic.

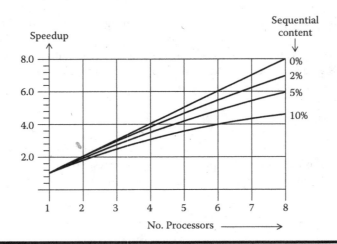

Figure 2.14   Amdahl's law: speedup curves.

code for commercial applications is more difficult than for scientific ones because of the essentially sequential nature of commercial processing.

Figure 2.13 shows the schematic of parallel and serial code that yields the Amdahl equation.

The plots in Figure 2.14 show the speedup (S) of programs containing 0%, 2%, 5%, and 10% sequential content with no overheads involved. You can see that the speedup only tails off slightly as the number of processors (N) increases.

Obviously, the percent content that can be made parallel is a major factor in speedup.

The extent of predictions made by Amdahl's law can be seen in Figure 2.15, which shows the speedup factor extended to very large numbers of processors and for higher parallelization factors.

Since Amdahl's law was proposed, there have been iterations of its principles, two of which are presented in the next sections.

Gunther's Law

Gunther's law is a modification to Amdahl's law to take account of overheads when combining processors to produce an increase in speed (speedup).

The multiprocessor effect is a generic term for the fraction of processing cycles *stolen* by the system (both software and hardware) in order to execute a given workload. Typical sources of multiprocessor overhead include

1. Operating system code paths (system calls in UNIX, supervisor calls in MVS and other operating systems)
2. Exchange of shared writable data between processor caches across the system bus
3. Data exchange between processors across the system bus to main memory
4. Lock synchronization of accesses to shared writable data
5. Waiting for an I/O to complete

Even single processors apparently having no work to do have a percentage CPU loading called the *zero utilization effect* where the processor is busy checking queues and other system blocks to

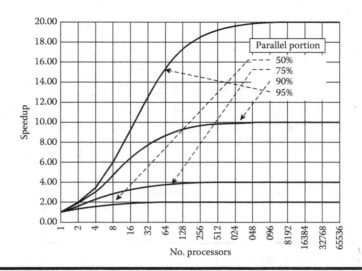

Figure 2.15   Amdahl's law: large N, high parallelization percentage.

see if any work has arrived. When several processors are working in tandem, their interaction also consumes cycles that the program in question might otherwise use.

When these factors are taken into account, Amdahl's law needs something to recognize this. Figure 2.16 shows the effect of Gunther's law, where the graph illustrates the speedup factor against the number of participating processors.

The multiprocessing (MP) factor causes the *diminishing returns* curve predicted by the Amdahl equation to tail off earlier and flatten off sooner.

The definitions needed to understand this law are as follows:

- *Linear scalability*: Without contention and coherence, linear (perfect) scalability will be achieved, that is, $C(N) = N$.
- *Contention*: The factor α represents the degree of contention because of shared data.
- *Coherence*: The factor β represents the *penalty* incurred for maintaining consistency of shared data, a major departure from Amdahl's law.

The modified Amdahl equation now reads as follows, which is Gunther's speedup law:

$$C\left(\alpha, \beta, p\right) = \frac{p}{\left(1 + \alpha\left[(p-1) + \beta p(p-1)\right]\right)} \tag{2.5}$$

where p is as before, α is a parameter that is identified with queuing delays, and β is a parameter for additional delays due to pairwise coherency mismatches (see next section)

In the absence of shared memory, multiple processors (or cores) need to ensure data cache consistency, hence an overhead. The resulting graph is shown in Figure 2.16.

Scalability/Coherence Effect: In 1993, Gunther defined this universal scalability law (USL), which bears his name. His equation quantified scalability quite closely to realistic systems.

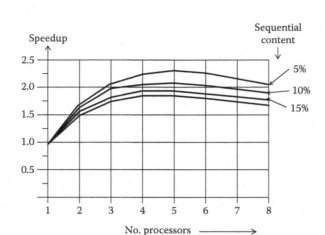

Figure 2.16 Gunther's law: speedup curves.

In addition to *contention* α (e.g., queuing for shared resources) addressed by Amdahl's law, USL included a term for the *coherence* factor β (latency for shared data to become consistent) to account for this nonlinearity trend described by Gunther's law.

When β is 0 (zero), the equation reduces to the Amdahl version of the speedup formula, an analogy to the difference between classical and relativistic physics that depends on the speed of light. The two papers referenced below are very useful in understanding Gunther's law and its extra parameter β over those in Amdahl's law.

How to Quantify Scalability: The Universal Scalability Law (USL)
http://www.perfdynamics.com/Manifesto/USLscalability.html

Parallel Scalability Isn't Child's Play, Part 2: Amdahl's Law vs. Gunther's Law
http://blogs.msdn.com/b/ddperf/archive/2009/04/29/parallel-scalability-isn-t-child-s-play-part-2-amdahl-s-law-vs-gunther-s-law.aspx

> Gunther's law adds another parameter to the well-known Amdahl's law. Gunther calls this parameter *coherence*. Parallel programs have additional costs associated with maintaining the "coherence" of shared data structures, memory locations that are accessed and updated by threads executing in parallel. (From the reference above)

Gustafson's Law

This law, often known as the *Gustafson–Barsis* law, proposes that large data program access to large data sets can be parallelized; that is, computations on it are done in tandem, as opposed to sequentially. This should result in a speedup of the operation and a reduction in elapsed time. It is a modification (some say refutation) of Amdahl's law, which, it is said, puts a limit on the speedup that parallelization can give.

Gustafson–Barsis says Amdahl's law does not fully exploit the computing power of an increasing number of processors. The Gustafson–Barsis law is often written as

$$S(P) = P - \alpha(P-1) \tag{2.6}$$

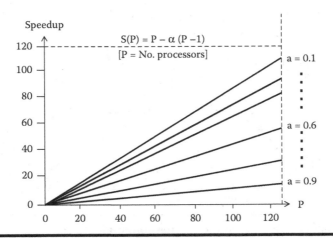

Figure 2.17   Gustafson's law: speedup vs. number of processors.

where S is the speedup factor, P is the number of processors and, α is the fraction of processing that is not parallelizable.

It is easily seen that if all the processing can be parallelized, that is $\alpha = 0$, then the speedup factor is P, the number of processors. If nothing can be parallelized (unlikely) then $\alpha = 1$. This type of speedup is known as *linear* speedup (Figure 2.17).

Note: It was in 1988 that Dr. Gustafson wrote the paper "Re-evaluating Amdahl's Law"; he summarizes the work as follows:

> The model is not a contradiction of Amdahl's law as some have stated, but an observation that Amdahl's assumptions don't match the way people use parallel processors. People scale their problems to match the power available, in contrast to Amdahl's assumption that the problem is always the same no matter how capable the computer. (http://johngustafson.net/glaw.html)

Amdahl versus Gunther

A paper by Schwartz and Fortune titled "Forecasting MySQL Scalability with the Universal Scalability Law" observes that this USL has a point of maximum throughput after which performance actually degrades, which matches the observed behavior of real IT systems.

Although this paper discusses scalability in terms of a MySQL environment, much of it is applicable to other software environments. The authors support their arguments with benchmarks applicable to scalability studies, although some relate to Percona's own version of MySQL, plotting throughput against processor concurrency. They conclude,

> The USL is a model which can help predict a system's scalability. It has all of the necessary and sufficient parameters for predicting the effects of concurrency, contention, and coherency delay. It applies equally well to hardware and software scalability modeling. (http://www.percona.com/files/white-papers/forecasting-mysql-scalability.pdf)

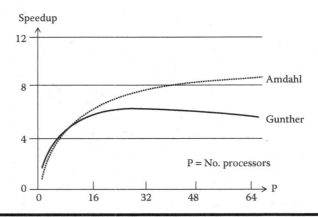

Figure 2.18   Amdahl and Gunther formulas: speedup results.

It is difficult to compare the Amdahl results with the Gunther results without a graph. Figure 2.18 does that, with Gunther predicting a fall in speedup more dramatic than that forecast by Amdahl's law.

Also, see Gunther at

http://arxiv.org/pdf/cs/0210017v1.pdf

and

http://blogs.msdn.com/b/ddperf/archive/2009/04/29/parallel-scalability-isn-t-child-s-play-part-2-amdahl-s-law-vs-gunther-s-law.aspx#9576239

Speedup: Sun–Ni Law

The laws of Amdahl, Gunther, and Gustafson have been tinkered with and discussed widely since they were proposed. A law that usually accompanies these discussions is the Sun–Ni law, outlined in the definition below, and is a generalization of Amdahl's and Gustafson's laws (Wikipedia).

> The Sun-Ni law is an approach used in parallel processing that attempts to improve performance. It is also called memory bounded speedup and was proposed by Professors Xian-He Sun and Lionel M. Ni. This law scales up the problem size and tries to find a solution limited only by the amount of memory available. It is a generalization of two other approaches used in parallel computing called Amdahl's law and Gustafson's law.
>
> One of the challenges in parallel computing is to figure out how the performance of the system improves when it is scaled up. As this can be hard to measure, one of the most well-known scalability metrics studied is speedup. Speedup relates the execution of parallel programs running on a certain number of processors and the execution time it takes for the fastest sequential program to solve that problem. One type of speedup approach is to keep the problem size constant, allowing the number of processors that work on the problem to be increased. This is called Amdahl's law and is known as fixed-size speedup. (http://www.wisegeek.com/what-is-the-sun-ni-law.htm)

NASA Contractor Report 189726
http://www.dtic.mil/dtic/tr/fulltext/u2/a259227.pdf

Memory Hierarchy

Cache

Cache memories are fast buffers between the CPU and traditional main memory to speed up the effective memory cycle time. It is analogous to real and virtual memory (disk), but one level removed. Cache is essentially a technique for accessing data and instructions recently accessed and kept in a fast holding area (cache) for faster subsequent access.

The obvious design of a front-end cache is a large, fast RAM fronting the relatively slower main memory. However, this would present latency problems and cache implementations have developed as multilevel hierarchies as a *lead-in* to main memory.

Cache Hierarchy

As a result, here are levels and varieties of cache memory supporting main memory:

■ No cache, single CPU, physical addressing, and main memory only as storage, with or without the use of virtual storage.
■ Single cache, single CPU, physical addressing. This was the first cache implementation.
■ Cache hierarchy: L1, L2, L3, and so forth.
■ Cache replacement policies: Associativity, random replacement, least recently used (LRU), and so on. This can have a more significant effect on overall performance due to cache than just chip speed and cache memory size.
■ Split cache: I-cache (instruction) and D-cache (data), on top of a unified cache hierarchy.

Early examples of level 3 cache usage were

■ DEC Alpha 21164 (1995): 1–64 MB off-chip L3 cache
■ IBM POWER4 (2001): Off-chip L3 caches of 32 MB per processor, shared
■ Itanium 2 (2003): 6 MB unified L3 cache
■ Itanium 2 (2003) MX 2: Two Itanium 2 processors along with a shared 64 MB L4 cache

Level 4 cache is used in fairly special cases and is not a regular member of common cache hierarchies and finds use in graphics processors. If you think about it, main memory is the L4 "cache" in most hierarchies.

The hierarchy of memory is shown in Figure 2.19. It is a generic diagram, and it must not be assumed that all systems have all the elements shown.

The objectives of cache memory are to reduce the average time to access data or instructions in memory and to reduce the traffic between main memory and the CPU.

Two important *metrics* in cache performance are

■ Hit rate, which is the probability that the processor will find the data it requires in a particular cache. If it cannot be found there, it must move down the cache chain L_x to $L_{(x+1)}$, for example, L1 to L2, and so on, down to main memory until the data is found. If it isn't there, an external storage access is required.
■ Miss rate, which is the probability of not finding the data it requires in that particular cache.

Hit rate = (1 − Miss rate), Miss rate = (1 − Hit rate), and (Hit rate + Miss rate) = 1.

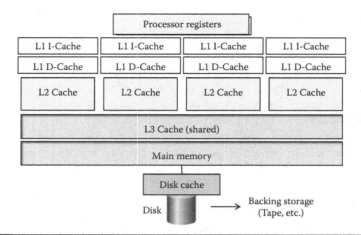

Figure 2.19 Memory cache and storage hierarchy.

The access times and typical sizes of the various levels in the hierarchy are roughly as follows:

Registers	Very fast	Small
Level 1 cache	Units of nanoseconds	10s of kilobytes
Level 2 cache	10s of nanoseconds	100s of kilobytes
Level 3 cache	10s of nanoseconds	1000s of kilobytes
Main memory	100s of nanoseconds	1000s of megabytes
Disk/SSD	Units of milliseconds	100s of gigabytes or terabytes for *big data*

However, there is much more to performance enhancement using the principle *bigger is always faster*. This is not always the case, and I have seen benchmarks for systems with roughly the same processor power where the one with the smaller cache (single level) outperforms the one with the larger cache. In one case, the larger cache was twice the size of the smaller one. The trick in performance enhancement using cache is in the *design* and *operation*. There are more tricks and techniques in cache design for performance than most people would think possible, and size is only one of them.

There are various types and levels of hierarchical cache memory to complement main memory—level one (L1), level two (L2), and level three (L3), the first two normally residing on-chip. This configuration is known as *multilevel cache*. A variation of cache is called *split cache*, where instructions and data are housed in separate caches. Another problem is where an I/O addresses main memory directly retrieving stale data, which has been updated elsewhere in the memory hierarchy.

One way round this dilemma is *write through*, where all writes go to main memory as well as to cache. Another technique is *write back*, where updates are made initially to cache, but an update bit is set to indicate this (*dirty bit*). If the block is to be replaced, main memory is updated if this bit is set. Consistency between data across multiple caches is maintained by a technique called *cache coherency*, too detailed for discussion here (and beyond the abilities of the author).

A Definition:

> In a shared-memory multiprocessor with a separate cache memory for each processor, it is possible to have many copies of any one instruction operand; one copy in the main memory and one in each cache memory. When one copy of an operand is changed, the other copies of the operand must be changed also. Cache coherence is the discipline that ensures that changes in the values of shared operands are propagated throughout the system in a timely fashion. (Whatis.com)

A (Good) Reference:
A Primer on Memory Consistency and Cache Coherence
https://class.stanford.edu/c4x/Engineering/CS316/asset/A_Primer_on_Memory_Consistency_and_Coherence.pdf

Cache Consistency

A problem may have struck the reader about the consistency of data blocks moving between these cache levels, main memory, and anywhere else. This is often known as *dirty memory* or *stale data*, which are older versions of data already changed in another tier of the hierarchy but not reflected elsewhere.

There is a presentation, URL below, which discusses the elements of cache design in some detail. Even if you don't understand the whole presentation, you will be made aware of just how much the design of cache matters in implementation for optimum performance.

Cache Design
http://cseweb.ucsd.edu/classes/fa10/cse240a/pdf/08/CSE240A-MBT-L15-Cache.ppt.pdf

Cache Structure

The structure of a typical cache memory is illustrated in Figure 2.20. Cache is typically 20 times faster than main memory but 100–1000 times smaller, mainly because of the costs of cache.

Costs aside, there are technical reasons why the optimum size of cache is much less than the size of the main memory it supports.

As a consequence, cache only holds a small part of the data and instructions of a program, the rest being in main memory.

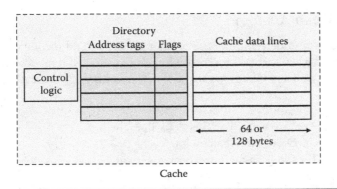

Figure 2.20   Cache design principles.

When the CPU requests data that is not already in the cache, it must be fetched from main memory. The number of cycles that the CPU waits while main memory is referenced is called the *cache miss penalty.*

The number of times that data is found in the cache, divided by the total number of requests for data, is called the *cache hit rate*, usually expressed as a percentage.

The effective memory cycle time (T) is the weighted mean of the access times of the cache and main memory; thus, the following equation shows the effect of the cache "hit" rate on performance:

$$T = h \times T_{cache} + T_{main}(1 - h) \tag{2.7}$$

where H is the cache hit rate expressed as a fraction, and T_{cache} and T_{main} are the access times of the cache and main memory, respectively. Obviously, $(1 - h)$ is the cache "miss rate."

The case of more than one cache level, together with detailed references, can be found in Appendix IV under "Cache Memory Performance." In such studies, the h for the first cache level is taken as 1. In simple terms, the access time for data is the access time for a hit plus the time penalty for a miss and subsequent searches down the cache chain.

There are a number of cache types in existence, including

■ Direct mapped cache, typically used in level 1 (on-chip) cache
■ Fully associative cache, giving the best cache hit rate
■ Set associative cache, best in general for medium to large cache

Most systems today employ both level 1 and level 2 caches in their hardware storage implementations, yielding excellent performance enhancements. Discussion of the cache types listed is beyond both the scope of this book and, more importantly, the knowledge of the author. The second reference below is a series of lecture notes, many of them concerning cache memory, and will prove very useful.

A detailed exposition of cache memory can be found at the following links:

Functional Principles of Cache Memory
http://alasir.com/articles/cache_principles/

Lecture 14: Cache and Virtual Memory
http://flint.cs.yale.edu/cs422/lectureNotes/L14.pdf

A Cache–Workman Analogy

It is sometimes easier to understand the use of multiple caches and memory hierarchies plus the service times obtained when there are successful hits and unsuccessful misses when accessing data. The basic principle in understanding this is as follows, assuming a three-level cache hierarchy:

1. I want some data please.
2. Is it in cache n? Yes. carry on. No. Then look in cache ($n + 1$).
3. Is it there? Yes. Carry on. No. Then look in cache ($n + 2$).
4. Is it there? No. Then look in main memory. Carry on.

Obviously, there is a penalty in not finding the desired data in the first cache and having to travel down, perhaps a far as main memory, to get the data.

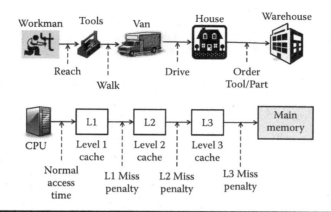

Figure 2.21   Three-level workman analogy of cache data retrieval.

Figure 2.21 illustrates this dilemma with the analogy of a workman doing a job in a house after making the choice of what tools to carry in his toolbox, what to bring in the van, and what to leave at home.

This is exactly the dilemma faced in using cache to speed up the work in hand. The efficiency of the work carried out by the workman will depend on his knowledge of the task in hand and how well he stocks his toolbox and van with parts and tools. If he leaves most of the tools that he needs in the van, he is going to lose time going back and forth to the van. If his tool and equipment selection in the van is poor, he will need to go home or to wherever he stores the bulk of his material.

If he completely misjudges his work, he will have to suspend the task and wait until his order for a part or tool arrives. This is not a perfect analogy, but it helps to visualize the way cache operates and how it is possible to have a larger cache yielding inferior performance to that of a smaller cache.

The cache analogy is to decide on size, organization, and other factors to achieve maximum throughput for the workload in hand, although the rest of the configuration is important. Systems rely on teamwork to achieve success.

> For some math associated with cache performance at three levels, L1, L2, and L3, see Appendix IV under "Cache Memory Performance."

Cache Coherence in Multicore Chips

There is a problem with the shared cache in multicore chips with large numbers of cores, since it is important to keep a record of who has what data, and it requires different thinking than small numbers of cores. If one core tries to update data in the shared cache, other cores working on the same data need to know. So the shared cache keeps a directory of which cores have copies of which data. That directory takes up a significant chunk of memory, and frequent access to it can impact performance. See the reference below for more information on this topic.

Cache-Coherence Mechanism Could Enable Chips with Thousands of Cores
http://www.scientificcomputing.com/news/2015/09/cache-coherence-mechanism-could-enable-chips-thousands-cores?et_cid=4808216&et_rid=784345100&location=top

Chapter 3

Software and Performance

There are a number of ways that system performance might be enhanced with software tools and techniques, although their success is not always guaranteed. Badly written applications are probably not amenable to tuning any more than a tractor is for competing in a Formula 1 race. Some of these techniques are outlined in the following sections, and they cover network aspects as well as system concepts.

Performance Role of Software

The spectrum of software types and variations in today's IT environment is wider and functionally richer than it was 30 and more years ago. The *good thing* about this is that much more can be achieved; the *bad thing* is there can be performance impacts on IT systems work, particularly if the software is poorly designed and written and does not dovetail with the rest of the software and the encompassing hardware scenario.*

In this chapter, we will look at some of the techniques used to enhance software performance and mitigate poor performance that arises due to poor design or the intrinsic nature and circumstances of the systems environment.

Data Tiering

Data tiering is the arrangement of data media in a hierarchy of storage media that might be done for three very different reasons:

1. Studies suggest that the breakdown in storage usage shown in Table 3.1 dictates the sense of data tiering in many instances.

---

* I have seen the performance of a Digital Equipment Corporation (DEC) system emulating IBM's Systems Network Architecture (SNA) with dire consequences. It should have been measured with a calendar and not a stopwatch. I am not sure whose software it was, probably not DEC's. Other forms of emulation can also be performance *showstoppers* and need careful pilots and speed tests before committing to them.

Table 3.1 Organizations' Data Access Patterns

Access and Usage	% of Data
I/O intensive (indexes, tables, etc.)	3–5
Business critical (sales, online web, etc.)	10–20
Support (test, reference data, etc.)	20–25
Archive/backup	45–60

2. Data storage *savings* by using slower, less expensive media for data that is not frequently accessed or whose speed of retrieval is not a major concern. It is not a major concern in this book either.
3. Speed of access or *performance* where the tiering is done with storage media of differing access characteristics balanced against costs. Typically, this might be a hybrid configuration of flash, solid-state, and normal disk storage media, rather along the lines of a cache hierarchy, arranged in that order outward from the processing system from fastest to medium to slowest.

Data Compression

Data compression possibly originated in reducing the traffic flowing across networks to optimize the use of the bandwidth available. Another reason for the technique was the saving of disk space some years ago when the price per megabyte was factors of 10 or even hundreds greater than it is today (or will be tomorrow). In fact, any resource housing data is a candidate for compression routines, particularly if that resource is expensive.

However, the act of compression itself has need for a resource to accomplish it (CPU), and if that resource is costly, the exercise becomes one of balancing costs on both sides of the equation. Thus, if the cost of a bigger processor needed to compress data is more than the costs of extra disk space to accommodate uncompressed data, then perhaps all bets are off in the compression stakes. Today, however, the cost of both these resources is such that it is an installation's choice which route it takes.

There are means of using *hardware data compression* that reduces the CPU load and has been an option on IBM large systems for some time. Tape compression can also be achieved in hardware via the control unit that drives the tape subsystem. In the *software compression* arena, there also exist a number of commercial packages to achieve this.

One use of compression is in the replication of data across the network in, for example, disaster recovery or remote backup and archiving. When compression is enabled in such circumstances, data is compressed on the source computer, replicated across the network to the destination computer, and uncompressed on the destination computer, thereby reducing the network load. As well as reducing the network load, the performance of the activity is improved.

Key metrics in data compression are

- Compression/decompression time. For batch workloads, this may not be an issue, but for online work it will be.
- Compression ratio (CR), defined for normal data as shown in Equation 3.1:

$$CR = \frac{Uncompressed\ Size}{Compressed\ Size} \tag{3.1}$$

For items like video and audio, the time taken to decompress so that one can see or hear the start of the video or sound quickly is a key factor in which case CR is defined

$$CR = \frac{Uncompressed\ Data\ Rate}{Compressed\ Data\ Rate}$$

Compression is supported in some relational database management system (RDBMS) products, as the example of the SQL Server below indicates:

- *SQL Server 2000*: No compression/decompression.
- *SQL Server 2005*: Compression on one data type.
- *SQL Server 2008*: Compression on all data types. Data and backup can also be compressed.
- *SQL Server 2012*: SQL Server provides two methods, page and row compression, to reduce data storage on disk and speed I/O performance by reducing the amount of I/O required for transaction processing. Page and row compression work in different, yet complementary, ways and are worth further discussion. Page compression uses a deduplication algorithm.
- Data compression is also available on RDBMS products DB2, Oracle, Sybase, Informix, and MySQL. The level and functionality of compression and decompression depends on which product you choose.

In the era of *big data*, the transmission of audio and video information takes on new importance, especially as some pundits say that the Internet is running out of capacity (November 2014). There are numerous algorithms for compression and decompression that are designed for different scenarios. Names like Huffman and Lempel-Ziv will feature prominently in any detailed study of compression and decompression of various forms of data (but not in this book).

Data Compression Benchmarks

A data compression benchmark measures compression ratio over a data set, and sometimes memory usage and speed on a particular computer. A description of the compression metrics and some of the benchmarks are outlined in reference 1 below.

In general, data compression benchmarks, techniques, and products are operating system dependent—Windows, Linux, UNIX, z/OS, and so forth—as are the formats supported.

See the following links:

1. *Data Compression Explained*
   http://mattmahoney.net/dc/dce.html
2. *Data Compression Tutorial: Part 1*
   http://www.eetimes.com/document.asp?doc_id= 1275417
3. *Data-Compression.com*
   http://www.data-compression.com/index.shtml

The latter reference contains a lot of detailed sections covering many aspects of compression and decompression, should this level of detail be required for planning purposes.

> ***Moral***: If the costs of extra CPU (processor) power outweigh the savings made by reducing the disk space required by employing compression, then the exercise is not worthwhile unless there are extenuating circumstances.

HTTP Compression

HTTP compression is a capability that can be built into web servers, such as IBM HTTP Server and Apache HTTP Server 2.x and above, and web browsers to make better use of available bandwidth and provide faster transmission speeds. Compression-compliant browsers announce, to the server, what compression methods the browser supports, so the server can provide the compressed data in the correct format. Browsers that do not support compression simply download uncompressed data.

A useful document on the uses of compression on Windows systems can be found at the link below. It is general enough, though, to be useful information for other environments.

Transparent Compression for Windows Operating Systems
http://www.realtimepublishers.com/book?id=260

Software Formats

The format of numeric data in programs is important when doing calculations of any sort since if the formats are not compatible, the results will unlikely be correct. There are, therefore, standards for formats of numeric data to reduce the likelihood of random incorrect answers to math involving such data.

IEEE 754-2008 Floating-Point Standard

Reference:
http://grouper.ieee.org/groups/754/
   http://docs.oracle.com/cd/E19957-01/806-3568/ncg_goldberg.html
In floating-point calculations, errors of precision can occur, for example, subtracting numbers where the difference between them is close to the accuracy of the floating-point system (hardware or compiler). Depending on the floating-point implementations, machines from different vendors would get different answers for the same calculation.

The Institute of Electrical and Electronic Engineers (IEEE) now specifies exactly how floating-point numbers should be represented and the results of floating-point operations (add, subtract, etc.). The standard, IEEE 754, is for binary arithmetic, and there is a separate standard, IEEE 854, for decimal arithmetic. Today, most vendors offer IEEE 754 floating point and portability of code, and accuracy of calculations are not the problems they were. The IEEE 754 standard specifies four floating-point formats:

- Single precision
- Single extended precision

- Double precision
- Double extended precision

Remember, such standards are important in the areas of compatibility and consistency of results produced by software calculations (Figure 3.1).

Table 3.2 shows the characteristics of n and X for the normal single-, double-, and extended precision cases offered by most vendors.

The range of numbers that can be represented by these precisions are

Single: Smallest 1.2×10^{-38} Largest 3.4×10^{38}
Double: Smallest 5.0×10^{-324} Largest 1.8×10^{308}
Extended: Smallest 3.65×10^{-4951} Largest 1.18×10^{4932}

which should be an adequate range for most purposes (except Bill Gates's wealth).

The floating-point operations specified by IEEE 754 are addition, subtraction, multiplication, division, square roots, and remainders. There are also rules for error handling, rounding, and so on.

It does not necessarily follow that single precision is faster than double precision, nor do they give the same numbers for certain calculations. The original IBM RS/6000 showed that single-precision calculations were slower than double-precision ones simply because the RS/6000 was designed for double precision and had to convert a double-precision answer to single precision.

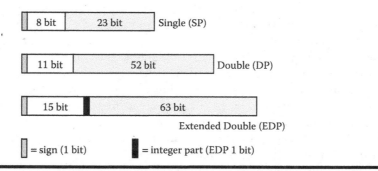

Figure 3.1   Single-, double-, and extended precision formats. Diagram is not to scale.

Table 3.2   Summary of Single-, Double-, and Extended Precision Floating Point

Format	Total Bytes	Bits in n	Bits in Exponent X
Single (32 bit)	4 (32 bits)	24 (1 sign)	8
Double (64 bit)	8 (64 bits)	53 (1 sign)	11
Extended (80 bit)	10 (80 bits)	63 (1 sign)	15 (+1)

Software Optimization

Software can obviously have an effect on the performance of a system, but performance-associated optimization depends on the type of software and whether it is bought in or in-house developed. For *bought-in* software, optimization will depend on

- The software developer's skills; test it before purchase
- The purchaser's choice of execution parameters for the software
- The purchaser's in-house tuning skills
- The resources provided to support the software
- The number of interfaces with other software and systems
- The performance of those interfacing systems
- The choice of database, database design, access methods, and associated parameters
- The type of software—commercial or scientific
- Other factors, some may be specific to the organization

However, in general, one is at the mercy of the application software vendor for application performance, and user modifications often invalidate any warranty given on the software by the vendor.

Compiler and Other Options

For *in-house* software, there are some routes to optimize the performance of the application software:

- Application design. This is a subject in its own right, and a detailed discussion of it is beyond the scope of this book.
- Code rearrangement. This is a simple technique where invariant code is taken out of loops so that it is only executed once or when it changes in value.
- Reduction in data I/Os by the use of in-store *parking areas* in memory for transient data (often called *scratch pad areas*). This kind of facility is useful in passing data between multistage or multiple transactions comprising a business transaction. The scratch pad area is cleared when the transaction is complete. In the days of unreliable hardware, this was a risky business, but nowadays it is feasible.
- Matrix manipulation. Much scientific and some commercial work involves the manipulation of matrices, some of which may be sparsely populated with numbers or data. There are methods of handling such matrices to reduce the time spent trudging through blank or zero elements in matrices. There are a number of books on handling sparse matrices that can be found easily with a simple search.
- Compiler options. When compiling programs, there are often option parameters for the compilation depending on the reason for the action. If the purpose is debugging and checking out basic functions, a speedy compilation without too much attention to execution speed may be used to save time. When the program is ready for use, it is often possible to specify an *optimization* parameter to compile the code in such a way that the performance of the resulting code is optimized. It may be that the compilation itself takes longer in the interests of execution performance. Such performance compiler options will depend on the compiler employed, the language, and the vendor.

■ Use and optimization of data and other buffers. This can have a remarkable enhancing effect on some programs and is worth experimenting with before a piece of software goes live in an organization. The actual detail of what to do where depends of course on operating system, database, and other factors, but typical enhancers might be the number and size of the *in* and *out* buffers in IBM's Virtual Storage Access Method (VSAM) or the flushing of Domain Name System (DNS) buffers in a Windows environment (ipconfig/*parameter*). There are also various tricks of the trade for RDBMS systems, often vendor or product specific.

■ External software routines, mainly applying to scientific work. When subcomponent software* from other sources is used, it is important to verify that the function it provides is what is needed (a type of service level agreement [SLA]) and performs in line with expectations. In addition, the calling and results delivery interfaces and formats (application programming interface [APIs]) need to be properly understood.

■ Other *enhancing* factors in the field of software engineering and testing.

Pipelining

Software pipelining is a loop optimization technique to make statements within an iteration independent of each other. The goal is to remove dependencies so that seemingly sequential instructions may be executed in parallel. However, not all instructions can be executed in parallel simply because of dependencies. The technique is often used in high-performance computing (HPC), which facilitates the use of vector parallel processing. See
http://en.wikipedia.org/wiki/Instruction_pipeline.

Lecture on Pipelining and Cache (Professor David A. Patterson)
http://www.cs.berkeley.edu/~pattrsn/252F96/Lecture02.pdf
(If you alter the "02" in "Lecture02" to different numbers in this link, you will get some other interesting lecture notes from Professor Patterson, though not all "0x" references work.)

Cache Misses

Cache Miss: The CPU requests data that is not in cache. The aim is to minimize this. The miss time is how long it takes to get data, which can be variable and is highly architecture dependent.

Cache Hit: The CPU requests data and it is already in the cache. The aim is to maximize this. The hit rate is the percentage of cache hits.

There are various levels of cache memory that complement main memory with a view to enhancing the performance of applications using the system. The cache hierarchy design has a great influence on performance, but sometimes compiler or programming options can assist too. Consistent *cache misses*, where expected data is not present in a cache and has to be retrieved from elsewhere, have a detrimental effect on performance.

Some cache configurations split data and instructions across separate caches, and there are some compiler optimizations that can reduce these misses, thereby enhancing performance.

■ *Instructions*
  - Reorder procedures in memory to reduce misses.

---

* Scientific functions (sin, cos, arctan, etc.) plus FORTRAN matrix subroutines like *saxpy* (used in Linpack and elsewhere).

- Profile to check for memory conflicts.
  This can apparently reduce misses by 30% in an 8K I(nstruction)-cache.
- ■ *Data*
  - Reordering can result in a 40% reduction in misses for an 8K D(ata)-cache.
  - Merge arrays to improve locality using a single array instead of, for example, two arrays.
  - Change the nesting of loops to access data in the order stored in memory (loop interchange).
  - Combine independent loops that have the same looping and some overlapping variables (loop fusion).

Since the *miss rate* is directly related to the *hit rate* and both appear in performance equations, these reductions can be significant:

■ Hit rate = (1 − Miss rate). Performance follows almost exponential decreases as the hit rate decreases.

Software Performance "Gotchas"

There are numerous areas affecting performance that might trap the unwary, and a few of them are outlined in this section. Some don't just slow down the work but, in some cases, stop it completely. Some *drop-dead* issues that prevent the application working leave the realm of performance issues and become ones of availability or, rather, absence of it.

Some of these are sacrifices made for additional functionality, high availability, and fault tolerance. Their impact on performance depends on too many factors to list here, but it is wise to be aware of them in circumstances where response time constraints are tight.

Security or Fault Tolerance

In the world of remote access (particularly bring your own device [BYOD]), increasing security and reducing exposure may come at the cost of performance or, at the very minimum, a perceived loss of performance in the user's view.

The paper below from SanDisk outlines a case for *self-encrypting storage* to get round some security-induced performance issues.

> Hardware and software encryption can result in a wide range of performance slow-down, from hardly noticeable to outright task halting, resulting high levels of frustration among users. The standard line is that encryption imposes a single-digit percentage impact on performance, while others cite a 25–33% drag on laptop operations.

You Don't Have to Sacrifice Performance for Security
http://www.sandisk.com/assets/docs/you-dont-have-to-sacrifice-performance-for-security.pdf
The NASA publication link below contains some information about some of the potential performance hits in developing and executing fault-tolerant software.

> Note that the fault tolerance redundancy is not intended to contribute to system functionality but rather to the quality of the product. Similarly, detection mechanisms

detract from system performance. Actual usage of fault tolerance in a design is based on trade-offs of functionality, performance, complexity, and safety.

Software Fault Tolerance: A Tutorial (NASA/TM-2000-210616)
http://www.iet.unipi.it/c.bernardeschi/didattica/ANNO 2014-15/DEP/SoftwFT.pdf

Encryption

Encryption can be an overhead but will often depend on the encryption algorithm as the detailed reference below indicates, covering experimental and simulation exercises to determine overheads of the technique.

Performance Analysis of Data Encryption Algorithms
http://www.cse.wustl.edu/~jain/cse567-06/ftp/encryption_perf/
Another paper, referenced below, has the following to say about performance overheads:

Encryption must be planned carefully to make sure it does not slow your system's performance. Encryption can be done at three levels, but only one level is required. Performance is ranked from best to worst—

- Hardware such as chips or hard drives.
- Operating systems such as Microsoft Windows or Linux.
- Encryption applications from NIST-certified vendors.

Details about Data Encryption
http://www.cdc.gov/cancer/npcr/tools/security/encryption2.htm

Deadlocks

A deadlock is a situation in which two computer programs sharing the same resource are effectively preventing each other from accessing that resource, resulting in both programs ceasing to function (stalling).

1. Task A requests resource X and receives it. It issues a hold.
2. Task B requests resource Y and receives it. It issues a hold.
3. Task A requests resource Y and is queued up, pending the release of X.
4. Task B requests resource X and is queued up, pending the release of Y.

Now neither task can proceed until the other task releases the held resource. The operating system traditionally did not know what action to take, and the only alternative was to abort one of the tasks. This is the *deadlock*, similar to a Mexican standoff.

Learning to deal with deadlocks had a major impact on the development of operating systems and the structure of databases. Data was structured and the order of access and hold requests was constrained in order to avoid creating deadlocks (Figure 3.2).

An undetected and unresolved deadlock is, to say the least, a performance inhibitor. Deadlocks can occur in a number of ways depending on the environment—online transaction processing (OLTP), batch, and so forth. In the case of RDBMS, a discussion can be found at

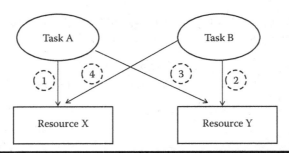

Figure 3.2 Software deadlock overview.

SQL Server Deadlocks by Example
https://www.simple-talk.com/sql/performance/sql-server- deadlocks-by-example/

There are numerous articles on the web on the topic of resolving deadlocks, but a good start might be the following Wikipedia article:

Deadlock Prevention Algorithms
http://en.wikipedia.org/wiki/Deadlock_prevention_ algorithms

It also contains further references.

Runaway Tasks

I have experience of systems running at high utilizations, but my job seemingly stalled, as it is taking 10 times its normal elapsed time. This was sometimes due to *runaway tasks*, which are sections of code that have fallen into a loop or eternally iterative process within a program and consume much of the system's CPU resource. This obviously has a serious effect on the performance of other, well-behaved tasks that are sharing the system.

There is no generic method I know of for spotting these rogue tasks, but they can be highlighted with suitable monitoring tools to see which processes are consuming what resource and deciding if those processes should actually be running. The reasons for such behavior are many and varied, but loops are often the cause, especially in code not executed on a regular basis, for example, that relating to year-end processing, which has not been as rigorously tested as other code.

Bad and Overdesign

I have experienced IT shops that have taken on a new software product and used many of its features without consideration of their possible effect on performance. They may read that it can handle up to 1000 users and 100 different other things and use it to these limits in their application implementations.

I saw one IT department that had taken on IBM's Information Management System Database (IMS DB) and saw it could support structures down to *n* levels in a hierarchy, which they promptly implemented in a relatively simple application. I think they are still waiting for the response to the first transaction, which started in about 1975.

Moral: The moral of this little true story is that overdesign can be the enemy of good performance, and the solution is to either be practical in design or run a pilot scheme before going into production. A short pilot scheme might have saved them a lot of trouble, if it ever finished.

Indexing RDBMSs

Indexing a database, particularly relational, requires a good understanding of the data, the user functions, and how databases use indexes. Indexes use key parts of data from a table in a binary structure to enhance searching capability. Each record of data in the table must have associated data in the index.

Efficient indexing can greatly increase search speeds, but a drawback of indexes is that for each insert, update, or delete, the index must also be updated. Database administrators often apply many indexes to a table to enhance searching, and then sometimes find that other activities have slowed. Review the indexes to ensure that you have the right balance for searching and for updating tables.

Indexing: A Cute Trick

I came across this many years ago when talking to an estate agent IT person about this and that. They had had a large database of properties (not sure what database it was) that took quite a time to search, which was a problem if you had a customer on the telephone or in front of you asking about specific types of property.

They got around this by creating a supplementary database that was coded with binary codes and numbers to represent different types of property so that it could be accessed very quickly. Although it did not contain full details on each property, it enabled the takers of the call to say, "Yes, we have three of that type of property." While he was talking, the system would be searching the large database for the full details of the properties, ready to tell the caller about them and show them on the screen. If the caller wasn't happy, the quick search followed by the longer search would be repeated.

The system, incidentally called Orion (the hunter), was essentially a metadatabase that gave access to the main database. I thought then that it was quite a clever idea.

Poor Software Mixtures

If there are a variety of application types running on a single system, there might easily be contention for resources that slow the system down. For instance, applications that are CPU hoggers make poor bedfellows, as do I/O-hungry applications. The effect of this is similar to a temporary deadlock situation where there are great swathes of wait time for CPU, I/O, and possibly other resources.

The solution to this might be separate systems or a sensible running schedule for the jobs, but this is organization and requirement specific. An extreme and obvious case for a system split is the need to run high-performance scientific work (HPC) alongside the OLTP and database applications.

WoW: Be aware of jobs that are interdependent and need to stick to a timetable. For example, if the online day begins at 9:00 and the overnight batch that feeds it does not finish until 9:20, you have a severe performance problem for 20 min. You also have for your pains a 20 min outage of the OLTP application, which will blow your promised SLA 99.99% availability clause out of the window.

Java Performance

Java environments are somewhat different from classical environments in the range of options available for implementation of software. There is a document from AppDynamics that addresses the top 10 performance issues one might meet on the Java road, and it makes useful reading.

Top 10 Most Common Java Performance Problems
http://info.appdynamics.com/Top10JavaPerformanceProblems_eBook.html?utm_source=
dzone&utm_medium=email&utm_campaign=Dzone_sponsorship&utm_content=top-10-
java-problems&utm_term=ebook

Transaction Processing (OLTP)

Transaction processing, often called online transaction processing (OLTP), is not really an overhead, but it is a resource over and above that used by the actual application code. It is analogous in
a way to virtualization, using resource but delivering huge benefit. As you might expect, there are
tools and techniques to monitor the performance of OLTP and related software and to optimize
them, just like we might do for any other software employed in delivering *IT services*.

> An overview of OLTP and implementations of it can be found in Appendix V under "Online
> Transaction Processing."

15 Performance Factors

The article at the link below is paraphrased here, with permission, from APMdigest (apmdigest.
com),* and the full article was written by a plethora of IT luminaries, covering factors what can
adversely impact application performance.

1. Application complexity: More equals more chance of something going wrong, especially in
   multisourced environments.
2. Application design: A potential performance *gotcha*, especially if the application has multiple
   development *stables*.
3. Application testing: Its quality is the "last chance saloon" for an application's performance.
4. Butterfly effect: Small anomalies in development can have a disproportionate effect on subsequent performance.
5. Infrastructure and components of the application service: Consistency and ability of third-
   party products to cooperate effectively.
6. Network: Quality and latency (jitter, packet loss, poor design, and implementation).
7. Dynamic IT environment: Virtualization and the cloud—complexity and control.
8. Mobility: Adds requirements to performance planning and design.
9. Web browser: Blind spot for end-to-end visibility.
10. Configuration changes: Control, velocity can impact performance.
11. Peak usage: Knowledge of this is vital.
12. People: Communication: Dropping the baton between participants.
13. People: Skills: Suitability and currency.
14. Unknown unknowns: Not knowing the application environment; users, peaks, variations,
    and other factors.
15. Lack of proactive monitoring: "What's going on?" is a recipe for failure.

---

* I have found this a useful site for objective and pragmatic articles and information.

15 Top Factors That Impact Application Performance
http://apmdigest.com/15-top-factors-that-impact-application-performance

Virtualization Overheads*

Virtualization involves a hypervisor that runs with the operating system that normally functions in native mode. It is therefore no surprise that it will involve an overhead, stealing cycles from the CPU and often I/O cycles to do its job, which is at the expense of the systems below it: operating system, database, applications, and so forth.

Hypervisors are now an integral part of the cloud scenario, and it is to be expected that the virtual environment will add an overhead to the previously native work running alone. There has been some work done on assessing these overheads for various applications using different hypervisors.

VM Overhead Reasons

Virtualization has an overhead because a hypervisor is interposed and it needs resource to run and do its job. Much of the overhead is in how the virtualized environment is set up, and much is made of overheads associated with

- Under- and overallocation of memory and storage
- Idle and redundant virtual machines (VMs), which are, in essence, being looked after but not earning their keep
- Other items, many covered in the Red Hat and Jack Li et al. papers listed below.

Cloud Resource Management the Right Way
https://dsimg.ubm-us.net/envelope/146663/297682/1385505154_Cloud_Resource_Management_the_Right_Way_WP.pdf

Jack Li et al. carried out benchmarks on several applications using three hypervisors:

Performance Overhead among Three Hypervisors: An Experimental Study Using Hadoop Benchmarks
http://www.cc.gatech.edu/~qywang/papers/JackLiBigdata13.pdf

VMTurbo Operations Manager (www.vmturbo.com) seeks to improve the performance of VMs by assessing each VM's use of resources and recommending the reallocation of relevant resources to optimize performance. The reference below illustrates the results of a two-phase resource reallocation resulting in a reduction in response time of nearly 50%. The *acceleration* functions in VMTurbo are aimed at cloud and virtualized environments.

Get More Production from Your VMs with VMTurbo [Principled Technologies Report 2015]
http://www.slideshare.net/PrincipledTechnologies/using- vm-turbotoboostperformace0315

Other Reports: Detailed reports on VM overheads are to be found at

---

* In the early days of IBM's VM/370 (ca. 1973), a colleague and I tested an application running native and then again under the same operating system with VM/370 as the hypervisor. The application lost 40% of its "power" when run under VM, a lot, but VM has changed markedly for the better over the years. The test was, to be fair, a fairly hasty affair.

Virtualizing Latency-Sensitive Applications: Where Does the Overhead Come From?
https://labs.vmware.com/vmtj/virtualizing-latency-sensitive-applications-where-does-the-over-head-come-from

An Updated Performance Comparison of Virtual Machines and Linux Containers [IBM research report]
http://domino.research.ibm.com/library/cyberdig.nsf/papers/0929052195DD819C85257D2300
681E7B/$File/rc25482.pdf

Also, see Chapter 14 for a discussion of virtualization and paravirtualization environments where the overheads of them are compared to those of nonvirtualized environments running the same work.

Buffers and Performance

Is Bigger Better?

There is a myth that the bigger the buffer anywhere that data is retrieved and written, the better the response time, throughput, and file transfer times. This, apparently, is not true, although in some cases it may be. Here we cast an eye over just one area where buffering can be manipulated for optimum performance of the network. Buffers are also key to the performance of individual components in a network, such as routers and databases.

Networks: As the glue between systems and users, networks can be sources of slowdown due to suboptimal buffering. The most common network protocol used on the Internet is the Transmission Control Protocol (TCP). For maximum throughput, it is critical to use optimal TCP socket buffer sizes for the link employed. If the buffers are *too small*, the TCP congestion window will never open up fully, so the sender will be throttled. If the buffers are *too large*, the sender can overrun the receiver, which will cause the receiver to drop packets and the TCP congestion window to shut down.

Network File System (NFS) and DNS buffers will probably benefit from some scrutiny and optimization.

For more information and *computing the buffer size*, see the following papers:

How TCP Works
http://www.onlamp.com/2005/11/17/tcp_tuning.html

Buffer Sizing in the Internet
http://yuba.stanford.edu/buffersizing/

Routers: Routers make use of buffers in their store and forward activity on network links, and their size matters in terms of performance.

The first paper listed below implies that widely used rules of thumb (ROTs) that advocate very large buffers in routers are possible out of line, and that equal or better performance might be obtained by using much smaller buffers. They state that a backbone router buffer could be reduced from 1 million packets to 10,000 packets *without loss in performance*.

Part I: Buffer Sizes for Core Routers
http://klamath.stanford.edu/~nickm/papers/BufferSizing.pdf.pdf

Router/Switch Buffer Size Issues [points to other useful papers]
http://fasterdata.es.net/network-tuning/router-switch-buffer-size-issues/

Characterizing Network Processing Delay
http://www.ecs.umass.edu/ece/wolf/pubs/globecom2004.pdf

Delay Performance in IP Routers [Internet delay processes]
http://www.academia.edu/14912203/Delay_Performance_in_IP_Routers

Database: This sort of buffering depends on the access method used (relational, hierarchical, indexed, chained file management system [CFMS]) and often requires decisions on numbers of buffers as well as size of buffers.

For example, in my IBM days, I was struggling with the performance of a program that I couldn't alter, but altering the Virtual Storage Access Method (VSAM) data buffers—input buffers and output buffers—yielded significant performance gains. There were no equations or rules to help, but a few trials showed which direction to take when altering the buffer sizes.

Configuring I/O Buffer Space
http://docs.oracle.com/cd/E18283_01/network.112/e10836/performance.htm#i1007572

Disks: Disks have buffering that should be optimized to balance what the disk can deliver with what the processor can send and receive. Disk buffers are also called *disk cache*. The excerpt below is quite illuminating on the subject of *bigger is better*.

> As memory prices have fallen into the "dirt cheap" range, drive manufacturers have realized that they can increase the size of their buffers at very little cost. Certainly nothing is lost in doing this; extra cache won't hurt performance; but neither does it greatly improve it. As a result, if interface transfer rate is the "reigning champion" of overrated performance specifications, then cache size is probably the "prime contender". Some people seem to think a 2 MB buffer makes a drive four times as fast as one with a 512 KB buffer! In fact, you'd be hard pressed to find even a 4% difference between them in most cases, all else being equal. (From reference below)

Does *Hard Drive Buffer Size Matter*?
http://superuser.com/questions/107486/does-hard-drive-buffer-size-matter

Summary: There are buffers in various parts of a system and network, but bigger is not always better. Another useful tip is not to always accept default values for buffers and caches and check if they can be optimized. After all, the person who set them doesn't know your organization and its requirements.

WoW: This, however, may have a knock-on effect in user satisfaction. Consider the scenario where a new application goes live, but initially only supporting 50 of the planned 250 users within a year. Those 50 will experience far better performance than everyone will when all 250 users are on board. I have heard it suggested in such scenarios that the system be deliberately slowed by some amount, then speeded up gradually as the users come aboard.

Perhaps holding on to your piece of performance enhancement to deliver in stages might do this trick. I am not suggesting or recommending it—just making you aware of it.

Middleware

In IT, *middleware* is a general term for any programming that serves to perform a function not carried out by the operating system or the application software. There are many examples of this, and because of their often major role in system performance, they are worthy of some study. Examples of middleware are

- Online transaction processing (OLTP), such as IBM CICS or Tuxedo.
- Relational database software (RDBMS), such as Oracle or DB2.
- RDBMS connection software to allow different RDBMSs to interact with each other and share data.
- Monitoring software as a general category. This can impact the very performance metrics it is supposed to be measuring if it is too intrusive.
- Security software and the way it operates.
- Queuing software, such as IBM MQSeries.
- Message passing software, often used in scientific work, especially in parallel processing.
- Other software, such as object request brokers (ORBs), application programming interfaces (APIs), and emulation software.
- Internet software, such as browsers and Domain Name Services.
- Other software plus niche software designed for very specific purposes.

Security Overheads

There are performance overheads to many aspects of security, and their magnitude depends mainly on what products and protocols are employed and how they are configured. For instance, checking *all* security aspects for *every* transaction that passes through the system would introduce a relatively high overhead. Traditional systems can suffer this degradation, but web-based activity can be worse if the wrong options are chosen. A detailed presentation outlines some of the performance considerations when using WebSphere Application Server (WAS):

WebSphere Application Server Security Performance and Tuning
http://www-01.ibm.com/support/docview.wss?uid= swg27011084&aid=1

Conclusions

It is often the case that the user of middleware cannot do much to measure, assess, and enhance the performance of such software, but should consider the overall performance of a combination of middleware. This is the normal state of affairs in many IT installations, and a pilot scheme may be the wise thing to start with. I consider middleware performance prediction practically impossible.

Certain elements of middleware may be *star performers* individually, but in tandem with others may be a disaster, particularly emulation products.* Monitoring and tuning middleware is a job specific to the product and cannot be generalized here except to say that tuning

---

* *Don't Overlook the Importance of Middleware to Database Application Performance* https://www.progress.com/blogs/don-t-overlook-the-importance-of-middleware-to-database-application-performance.
Middleware Monitoring http://sl.com/solutions/middleware-monitoring/.

individual elements of middleware does not necessarily mean you have tuned the middleware combination.

A sample of the detailed analysis of a Common Object Request Broker Architecture (CORBA) middleware environment can be seen at the link and may serve as a model for examining other middleware products:

Middleware Performance: A Quantitative Modeling Approach
http://www.cs.vu.nl/~mei/articles/2004/spects2/art.pdf

Note: Other items that can adversely affect performance are covered in Chapter 17.

Network Losses

Losses of data in networks depend on the quality of the transmission medium and the intervening modules, such as routers. The performance impact is due to retransmissions of data considered by the receiver to have been erroneously transmitted, and a retransmission is requested. Incidentally, Universal Datagram Protocol (UDP) is less caring about transmissions and thus manages greater throughput than TCP for the same network links.

Causes of Packet Loss

Packet loss is the failure of one or more transmitted packets to arrive at their destination, and the outcome of the loss depends on what is being transmitted over the network links.

The effects of packet loss are

- For pure data, uncorrected packet loss produces unpredictable errors.
- For videoconference environments, it can create jitter of the picture.
- For audio communications, it can cause jitter and frequent gaps in received speech.
- In the severe losses, dropped packets can cause severe distortion of received data, broken-up images, unintelligible speech, or even the complete absence of a received signal.

The causes of packet loss include system noise, router software errors, weak signal strength at the destination, natural or human-made interference, hardware failure (along the link), software corruption, and overburdened network nodes. There may be more than one of these elements involved in any losses experienced.

Today's media are reliable, but packet losses are a reality. Transmission Control Protocol (TCP) is a widespread transmission agent, but the requirement for acknowledgments can often cause a bottleneck (congestion) if the packet rate is high. Another fact to remember is that bandwidth may be limited by the speed of the slowest link in the path of a transmitted packet, although it might not always partake in the transmission.

Often, TCP will throttle this down by discarding less important transmissions based on some sort of priority scheme decided by the business. The analysis of TCP throughput and congestion limits was examined by Matthew Mathis and others using link or network parameters to describe the situation. The parameters are as follows:

Rate: TCP transfer rate or throughput
MSS: Maximum segment size (fixed for each Internet path, typically 1460 bytes)

RTT: Round-trip time (as measured by TCP)

p_{loss}: Packet loss rate, expressed as a probability ($0 < p < 1$)

The value of p depends on a number of factors, including protocol, but figures suggest a loss percentage of between 0.1% and 1.0%, that is, $p = 0.001–0.01$.

When packet loss occurs in a transmission, an additional load is imposed on the connection. In the case of light or moderate loss, when the TCP rate is limited by the congestion avoidance algorithm mentioned above, the limit is calculated with the Mathis et al. formula for TCP throughput (1997):

$$Throughput = \frac{MSS}{RTT\sqrt{p_{loss}}} \tag{3.2}$$

> ***Aside***: Another parameter is *RWIN* (TCP Receive Window), the amount of data that a receiving node can accept without acknowledging the sender.

TCP Loss Graph

The graph in Figure 3.3 shows schematically (but reasonably accurately) the degradation in throughput achieved at various percent loss levels. It obviously varies with the type of data transmission method. Two useful references on this topic are given below.

Myths of Bandwidth Optimization [white paper by www.f5. com]
https://www.f5.com/pdf/white-papers/bandwidth-myth-wp.pdf
The graph in Figure 3.3 was taken from f5 documentation.

Throughput versus Loss
http://www.slac.stanford.edu/comp/net/wan-mon/thru-vs-loss.html
The paper above was written by Les Cottrell, an old friend of mine who worked alongside me at the Manchester University Van de Graaff machine in the 1960s and is now at Stanford Linear Accelerator Center (SLAC).

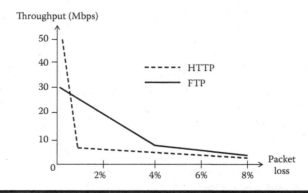

Figure 3.3 TCP performance with packet loss. (Reproduced courtesy of f5 and can be found at www.f5.com.)

The paper has some very detailed but digestible and useful information about various tests carried out on packet loss in networks. The paper also has some valuable links to tutorials and other papers of similar genre.

Note: Data loss prevention (DLP) is concerned with the impact and prevention of loss of sensitive and confidential data either by physical loss (as above) or by network intrusion of some kind.

Chapter 4

Performance: Magnetic Storage and Clusters

This title is a catchall for direct access magnetic media, which now includes solid-state drives (SSDs) and flash storage, in addition to just a bunch of disks (JBODs). In the old days, I/O performance was often increased by using faster disks or spreading the data across more disk actuators for concurrent access. For the record, the media used in online and other time-critical work are*

- Traditional hard disks (hard disk drives [HDDs]), introduced to the world via IBM's RAMAC
- Solid-state drives (SSDs)
- Solid-state flash storage
- Magnetic tapes, normally now used for backup and restore
- Mass storage systems, such as the old IBM 3850 MSS†
- CDs, optical, floppy, stick, and other devices, used mainly for backup or transportability

Today, we have the task of mixing and matching standard disks, SSDs, and flash storage. The common term nowadays for mixing and matching these storage components is *hybrid*. Using them in a hierarchy, fastest to slowest outward from the server access, for economic reasons is called *tiering*. This used to be known as hierarchical storage (management). Use of tiering will be dictated by the workload involved.

---

* The days of storing information on punch cards expired with the demise of Thomas J. Watson Sr. of IBM fame. He was adamant that cards were the way to go, but others, including his son, favored a move to magnetic media.
† This device had a honeycomb structure of storage cartridges accessed via a moving arm. An IBM customer was being shown the system in operation and he put his head inside the open panel. A shout from the salesman caused the customer to retreat, just before the time he would have lost his head, which the MSS would probably have filed away.

Disks and Disk Architecture

Traditional Disks (HDD)

Most people know what a disk is without seeing a diagram—it consists of magnetic platters or disks, connected together on a spindle and accessed by read and write arms that traverse these platters from their outer to inner extremities and back, looking for requested data. The characteristics that dictate the performance, read and write accesses per second, and data transfer rate are as follows:*

- Disk diameter: From about 14 in. in the *old days* to 3.5 in. now.
- Formatted disk capacity (gigabyte, terabyte, etc.): Not equal to stated capacity due to data organization.
- I/O rate at ca. 40% average utilization (for performance reasons).
- Interface: Small Computer System Interface (SCSI), fiber, and so forth.
- Number of access heads (disk surfaces): Typically eight.
- Rotation speed: 7,200 or 15,000 rpm.
- Internal disk cache size: Variable number of megabytes.
- External interface bandwidth (megabytes per second): Varies.
- Sustained transfer rate: Not equal to the bandwidth maximum because of protocol overheads and other latency factors.
- Minimum seek read and write time (milliseconds): Varies.
- Average seek read and write time: Varies.
- Mean time to failure (MTTF) (hours): >1 m typically.
- Unrecoverable read errors and bits read: <1 per 10^{15} I/Os is typical.
- Buffering and cache on the system involved. If the system can't handle the data, the disk will look relatively slow.

Disk Operation Timing

The time for a record or block access on an HDD can be expressed as shown in the equation for disk data access time breakdown:

$$T_{CPU} + T_{CTL} + T_{SEEK} + T_{WAIT} + T_{SEARCH} + T_{ACC} + T_{XFR} + T_{COMP} \tag{4.1}$$

where:

T_{CPU} is time to parse and generate the I/O request in the processor.

T_{CTL} is the time for the controller to format and issue the request to the HDD, plus the time for the request to reach the HDD.

T_{SEEK} is the time to move to the correct track on the HDD (called a SEEK).

---

* I have refrained from putting too many numbers in this list since progress in disk technology will render them obsolete fairly quickly.

T_{WAIT} is the time waiting to reach the required record.*

T_{ACC} is the time to access the record (SEARCH), which will have an overhead, depending on the format of the data (RDBMS, flat file, redundant array of independent disks [RAID] x, etc.).

T_{XFR} is the transfer time of the accessed data to the processor via the controller/channel.

T_{COMP} is the time to complete or post the end of the I/O. This, too, is CPU time.

The CPU initiation and completion and post times may be small and probably overlapped with other operations, but they do exist. Incidentally, the average seek time (as they vary obviously) is approximately one-third of the maximum seek time.[†]

Data Format: The format of data and associated control information varies, but in essence, it consists of a header, the data, and error detection and recovery data (error correction code [ECC]).

Other Factors: Another factor might add latency (wait time) to a disk's performance or channel contention. If other drives share the same I/O channel as the one we have been talking about, there will be channel contention (competition) for bandwidth on it from the other disks attached to the server. This, like any other delay, will depend on the utilization of that particular resource.

I have refrained from putting representative times in the equation above since, by the time you have your eager hands on this book, these will have changed.

An example would be writing 10,000 4K blocks to a disk and reading them back twice to simulate the observed pattern of commercial work where there are more reads than writes to typical files and databases. However, the results obtained from such tests will depend on whether the disk I/Os are random or sequential accesses to files. This in turn will be a function of the workload type.

It is also possible to get results that are in excess of those that would be observed in real life if the test or benchmark file is much smaller than the production file. Much of the test file could reside in main storage during the benchmark run.

Possible Tests: Disk I/O performance is often tested using programs that read and write records at various block sizes to and from disks. Measurements can take the form of elapsed time for doing a fixed number of reads and writes or the access times for various retrieval and update activities.

An example would be writing 10,000 4K blocks to a disk and reading them back twice to simulate the observed pattern of commercial work where there are more reads than writes to typical files and databases. However, the results obtained from such tests will depend on whether the disk I/Os are random or sequential accesses to files.

It is also possible to get results that are in excess of those that would be observed in real life if the test or benchmark file is much smaller than the production file. Much of the test file could reside in main storage during the benchmark run.

---

* In case of disk subsystems with *set sector* capability, the channel disconnects from the particular I/O until the record position is about to be reached on the track, and then reconnects to complete the I/O. In the meantime, it can do something else with its time. Prior to this feature, the channel would wait until the head reached the right position and then release it after the I/O was complete.

† See "Hard Disk Drives," http://pages.cs.wisc.edu/~remzi/OSTEP/file-disks.pdf, for a proof of this. The associated document, "Redundant Arrays of Inexpensive Disks (RAIDs)," http://pages.cs.wisc.edu/~remzi/OSTEP/file-raid.pdf, covers similar ground for RAID devices.

IOPS Myths

The performance of an application depends on the availability of adequate IT resources, such as CPU, memory, storage, and so on. Storage metrics of interest are

- Data capacity
- Input/output capacity (I/O performance)
- Durability, space, cooling, cost, return on investment (ROI), and other mainly commercial factors

We are concerned in this section with the second item, I/O capability, which is not as simple as "my system does *X* input/output operations per second [IOPS]." First, let us look at some background to input/output.

Records: A record to an application usually means a *logical* record, for example, the name and address of a client. This can be made up of more than one *physical* record, which is normally retrieved as a block of a certain size, for example, 2048 bytes. Sometimes, though, a physical record may contain more than one logical record.

Disk Access: An I/O operation consists of several activities, and the list of these depends how far you go back in the chain from data *need* to *fulfillment*. This is shown in Equation 4.1.

Myth 1: This myth is propagated widely in Internet articles and is totally erroneous, so beware. The misconception is a follows:

- If an I/O operation (seek, search, read) takes *x* milliseconds, then that disk arm is capable of supporting 1000/*x* I/Os per second (IOPS). Yes, it is, if you don't mind a response time of approximately infinity, give or take a few milliseconds, as the arm would be running at 100% utilization.

A sensible approach would be to do this calculation and settle for, say, 40% of the IOPS rate as an average that might be sustained.

Myth 2: If we make the allowance above, then a storage subsystem supporting *x* IOPS will perform better than one supporting 0.8*x* IOPS. In its raw form, this statement is not true, I'm afraid, since the I/Os needed to satisfy an application's request for data depends on other factors, many within the designer's control:

1. The positioning of the physical data and its fragmentation, the former no longer in the control of the programmer, and the latter a fact of life, except for the ability to defragment when necessary.
2. The type of application (email, query, OLTP, etc.) and access mode (random, sequential, read or write intensive).
3. Block sizes and other physical characteristics, such as rotational speed (up to 15,000 rpm).
4. The use of memory caching or disk caching, which can eliminate some I/Os.
5. The design of the database layout, which is crucial, and trees have been sacrificed writing articles about this topic.
6. What RAID level, or other access method, is employed.
7. The program's mode of accessing logical records (see below) might be suboptimal (to be mild about it). Does the chain read, save records, or retrieve them again, and so on?

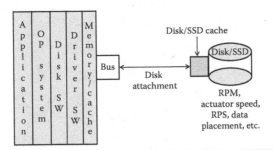

Figure 4.1 Elements affecting in disk or SSD performance.

8. The key and indexing should be optimized to avoid long synonym chains to compose a single record. This can result in diabolically long response times, as I found in a real-life situation involving a customer.
9. Other factors, including storage subsystem operational parameters.

The upshot of this is that very fast physical I/O performance can be negated by poor design and often is.

Tiering is another level of disk access that is mapped (Figure 4.1) (see "Hybrid SSD/HDD Tiering" later in this chapter and "Data Tiering" in Chapter 3).

If the items above are properly thought through, then, and only then, will the system supporting 1.0x IOPS outperform the system supporting 0.8 x IOPS. These design features assume that any *metadata*, such as logs, indexes, copies, and so forth, are not written to the disks containing the application data.

See the following paper and other Fujitsu papers on the topic of IOPS:

Fujitsu Primergy Server Single Disk Performance [white paper]
http://globalsp.ts.fujitsu.com/dmsp/Publications/public/wp-single-disk-performance-ww-en.pdf
A very good, detailed paper by Dell on this subject is

The Ins and Outs of IOPS
https://software.dell.com/whitepaper/the-ins-and-outs-of-iops-as-a-measure-of-storage-performance823117/

Measurement of Disk Characteristics

Do It Yourself Method

The results of a simple I/O benchmark are illustrated schematically in Figure 4.2, where a *good performance* disk displays low utilization for each I/O per second achieved. Thus, disk 3 shows that at 40% utilization, it is sustaining about 17.5 I/Os per second, whereas disk 1 is saturated at close to 100% utilization at the same I/O rate and would be showing a horrendous I/O response time, like *infinity* of seconds.

Such a benchmark is relatively simple to construct by coding random accesses to a database (which does not have to have any real data) with the access code in a code loop that is "tightened" every so often to increase the rate at which I/Os are thrown at the data. The I/O rates and utilizations should be easy to ascertain from standard monitors for the operating system in use.

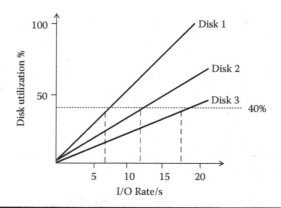

Figure 4.2   Benchmark: disk utilization vs. I/O rate.

Measuring the characteristics of a disk subsystem can be achieved by some simple C (or other) coding. What follows is a description that outlines the way disk performance characteristics might be measured since just studying seek times and data transfer rates is not necessarily foolproof. I know it works because many years ago I specified it and a colleague coded it:

1. Create a file, which need not contain any data, say 50 MB in size.
2. Code an access subroutine to retrieve a block of data from a random position within the file. A random number generator might provide this number.
3. Embed the code in a loop that has a delay at the start to dictate the access rate of the retrieval.
4. Perform some arbitrary processing, or perhaps a loop round a single instruction, on the data to simulate an application.
5. Run the program, measuring utilization and other factors with suitable I/O measurement tools.
6. Tighten the loop (faster access rate) and repeat, tighten again. and so on. If you are clever enough, you might do this "on the fly" and run the program only once.

After say six or seven runs, you will have enough data to plot a graph of disk utilization versus I/O rate, as shown in Table 4.1 and Figure 4.2.

The diagram above shows the results for three disks, but you can imagine one of the lines as the output of your exercise described above. If you are evaluating more than one type of drive, you may get a graph very similar to this one showing characteristics of three disks (but not real ones). The graph can be used to measure the I/O rate of the different disks when they cross the line at what is considered the maximum average utilization that can be tolerated.

Table 4.1   Disk Performance Assessment Characteristics

Characteristic	Disk 1	Disk 2	Disk 3
Access time	19 ms	14 ms	10 ms
I/O per second at 40%	7	12	17
Capacity (MB)	350	700	2000
Cost per disk	500	1100	1500

An Example

Assume that a sizing estimate has been done for an application planned for a system to be purchased. The calculations indicate that the system must support up to 60 disk I/Os per second without significant deterioration of response times. An examination of Table 4.1 shows that this requirement can be met by one of three nonmixed disk configurations available.

1. Nine volumes of disk 1
2. Five volumes of disk 2
3. Four volumes of disk 3

Assuming each disk type has a single actuator, then the required numbers of actuators are nine, five, and four, respectively. A simple costing exercise might enable the right choice to be made quite quickly. Or will it? There is obviously a need for storage capacity as well as storage access ability, so the choice is not quite so simple.

Look at the table of disk characteristics (Table 4.1) and the graph in Figure 4.2 from which these numbers were derived.

On the I/O rate requirement, the choice of nine volumes of disk 1 makes the best economic sense. However, another requirement says that the database will occupy 5000 MB, and these nine volumes would only supply 3150 MB, whereas five volumes of disk 2 fulfill the I/O rate but not capacity requirements. Disk 3 is the obvious candidate despite being more expensive than the other options. This exercise might have been approached from the capacity viewpoint where three volumes of disk 2 would have sufficed but fallen short on the I/O rate requirement.

Using Bonnie++

Bonnie++ is a free file system benchmarking tool for UNIX-like operating systems, developed by Russell Coker. Bonnie++ is a benchmark suite that is aimed at performing a number of simple tests of hard drive and file system performance. There are a number of articles on the Internet about the use of Bonnie++ for file system performance trials such as the ones listed below.

Performance Monitoring for SQL Server [Bonnie++ home page]
http://www.coker.com.au/bonnie++/

Using Bonnie++ for Filesystem Performance Benchmarking
http://archive09.linux.com/feature/139742

RAID Types/Levels and Benefits Explained
http://searchstorage.techtarget.com/answer/RAID-types- and-benefits-explained

Quite a few of these articles cover RAID performance at various levels, often separating read and write performance in results.

Storage Configurations

Configurations of disks (HDDs) and solid-state storage devices (SSDs) can take several forms, depending on what they are required to do:

■ Directly attached storage (DAS), where disks are assigned to a server on a one-to-one basis.

- Shared DAS, where HDDs and SSDs are shared between servers, for example, in a cluster of processor nodes.
- File area networks (FANs), where a set of technologies facilitate file sharing and data management over a network. See http://www.snia.org/education/storage_networking_primer/fan.
- Network attached storage (NAS), as the name implies. This is dealt with a little later.
- Storage area networks (SANs). This is a network of storage devices attached to a network of servers, not all necessarily homogeneous. This is dealt with a little later, along with NAS.

Within these configurations there may be different data organizations, for example, redundant arrays of independent disks (RAID) for performance or availability reasons. There may also be storage (not memory) caching to enable reuse of frequently accessed data by storing it in the front-end fast storage cache of disks and SSDs.

WoW: Storage architectures, connections, and configuration mixes are changing regularly, and it pays to keep abreast of the latest information by subscribing to the relevant newsletters and white papers on the various storage websites.

I feel it is important, in general, to base your technical decisions on a consensus of thought rather than believe any single source implicitly.

Network Attached Storage

NAS Overview

Disk storage used for application data access normally resides on hard disk drives (HDDs), which are attached to the server running the application. NAS is simply storage attached to a server via a network, very often a local area network (LAN). It is often used as a repository for local workgroups and might cover a variety of purposes—email, file storage and so on. One difference is the protocol used to access the data since the NAS drives have an IP address and not a channel, sequence number, and so on, on a data connection medium.

Access to a NAS configuration is thus via TCP/IP, and the two application protocols most commonly associated with it are the Sun Network File System (NFS) and Common Internet File System (CIFS). These were in operation in client/server mode before NAS was developed. NAS is flexible and simple enough to be used in home computing and small and medium businesses and can cater for large enterprises as a shared medium and as a data backup medium. NAS also has a minimal operating system that allows it to perform functions without imposing load on the server.

Introduction to NAS: Network Attached Storage [a]
http://compnetworking.about.com/od/itinformation technology/l/aa070101a.htm

The next reference outlines the differences between traditional disk storage and NAS and between NAS storage and SAN storage.

Introduction to NAS: Network Attached Storage [b]
http://compnetworking.about.com/od/itinformation technology/l/aa070101b.htm

There is a very clear and objective presentation of the differences and similarities between NAS and SANs in the following references:

NAS/SAN Technology Overview
http://www.nas-san.com/differ.html

Section 3: Network Storage Introduction
http://www.slideshare.net/sagaroceanic11/understanding- nas-network-attached-storage

Storage Area Networks

A storage area network (SAN) is any high-performance network whose primary purpose is to enable storage devices to communicate with computer systems and with each other. (Storage Networking Industry Association [SNIA])

What Is a SAN?

A storage area network (SAN) is a connection methodology so that magnetic storage can be shared across multiple servers instead of being dedicated to one server or set of clustered servers. SANs differ from normal switched disk or solid-state drives (SSDs) in several areas, which gives them their advantages.

Refer to Figure 4.3 when reading this text:

- It can connect disparate storage devices to disparate servers.
- It is controlled and driven by an internal *storage processor* (SP).
- Within security confines, any sever can access any device. In the standard case, if server 1 (S1) wanted data from disk 2 or 3 (D2, D3), server 2 or 3 would need to access that data and pass it to server 1.
- The SAN can be configured for high availability.
- The SAN can scale upwards and, moreover, separate data traffic to give each type optimal transfer service.

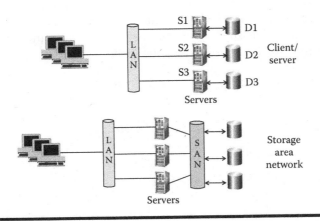

Figure 4.3   Storage area network and standard storage.

There is a raft of information, from elementary to detailed, on the Storage Networking Industry Association (SNIA) site, and a good starting point is at the link below, from where links to other avenues of information are offered.

What Is a Storage Area Network?
http://www.snia.org/education/storage_networking_primer/san/what_san

SAN Conceptual and Design Basics
http://www.vmware.com/pdf/esx_san_cfg_technote.pdf

RAID Storage

In 1987, Patterson, Gibson, and Katz published a paper, "A Case for Redundant Arrays of Inexpensive Disks," now known as RAID, to distinguish them from single large expensive disks (SLEDs). The acronym nowadays is taken to mean redundant arrays of *independent* disks. The principle of RAID is to introduce some level of data redundancy into a disk subsystem to allow the continued access to data in the event of media or other failure and, in certain cases, enhance performance. There are a number of techniques for implementing this redundancy, which are known as RAID levels.

Some of these levels are rare or even obsolete, but we will cover them here for completeness.

RAID level 0: In this implementation, the data is "striped" across the disks in the array, effectively giving the impression of a multiple actuator disk and thus enhancing performance. There is no redundancy and thus no recovery in the event of disk failure in this level of RAID. It is only named RAID for consistency across the various configurations.
RAID level 1: RAID 1 is essentially a mirroring feature with sometimes an option to make an extra copy (Figure 4.4).
RAID level 2: See Figure 4.5.
RAID level 3: See Figure 4.6.
RAID level 4: Raid level 4 is rather an unusual and rare implementation and is covered here only for completeness (Figure 4.7).
RAID level 5: See Figure 4.8.
RAID level 6: RAID level 6 is similar to RAID 5 but has a *second parity disk* as a belt and braces configuration for added recovery options. The performance of each RAID configuration (level) depends on the application, and the recovery times after failure depend in general on the security provided in that configuration.

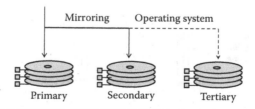

Figure 4.4 RAID level 1 with tertiary copy.

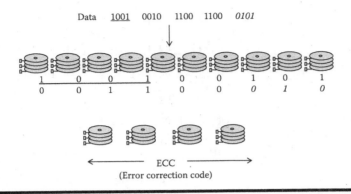

Figure 4.5   RAID level 2 showing bit distribution.

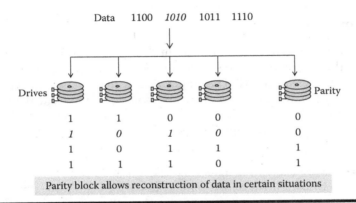

Figure 4.6   RAID level 3 showing bit distribution.

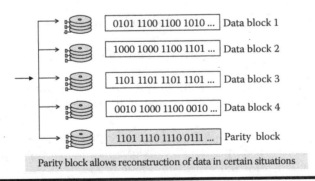

Figure 4.7   RAID level 4 showing bit distribution.

More redundancy, hence greater reliability, usually means longer recovery times. This is a performance issue, but not in day-to-day operations. It will, however, have an impact of service level agreements (SLAs) and in particular *time to recover*—recovery time objective (RTO). The rebuild time for a corrupted RAID configuration depends on that configuration with the *penalty clause* that higher availability is generally longer rebuild time after failure.

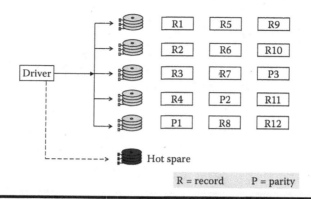

Figure 4.8 RAID level 5 with hot spare.

RAID Performance

RAID levels (configurations) will obviously vary in their performance characteristics because of the different ways they implement their particular levels of availability and their recovery modes. The performance characteristics of RAID configurations will depend on the type of access to the arrays. A paper by Intel on RAID suggests that workload type will dictate the access required to RAID data, and this should therefore be a key factor in deciding which RAID level to employ with which workload (assuming the choice exists).

Intel RAID Performance
www.intelraid.com/files/6Gb_RAID_Performance_1_1_Final.pdf

The workloads and access characteristics are summarized below. The structure of the list is essentially access type and typical applications fitting that bill:

- Streaming read workloads: Sequential I/O seen in media servers or virtual tape libraries (VTLs).
- Streaming write workloads: Sequential I/O seen in media capture, VTLs, and backups and archives.
- Workstation workloads: Random reads and a mix of sequential reads and writes.
- Web server workloads: Typically random read requests.
- Operating system workloads: Random I/O with a read–write ratio of 70:30.
- File server workloads: A large number of random read and write requests with a read–write ratio of 80:20.
- Email server workloads: 50:50 mix of random reads and writes.
- Online transaction processing (OLTP) workloads: Transaction processing and database I/O; typically random reads and writes with a ratio of 2 reads for every write. (This of course will depend on what logging mechanisms are employed and what other work may be done at the same time, for example, updating other databases.)

So What? Having established the fact that different workloads have different I/O patterns, it is instructive to look at the performance characteristics of popular RAID configurations so that the RAID level can be chosen to match the workload to be supported.

Hardware versus Software RAID

Hardware implementations provide guaranteed performance, add no computational overhead to the host computer, and can support many operating systems; the controller simply presents the RAID as another logical drive. Hardware RAID costs more than software RAID, and opinions differ on which offers the better performance.

Recent papers I have consulted say

- Software RAID is faster.
- Hardware RAID is faster.
- They are both about the same speed.

Conclusion: I am inclined to call it a draw.

There are several RAID configurations that one can choose, but only a subset satisfies most commercial requirements. These requirements vary from pure availability to performance, and some need a combination of both. Cost is often a consideration, plus performance in recovering data in outage and disaster recovery scenarios. This is a classic case of "one size does not fit all." For a detailed comparison table of *hardware* versus *software* RAID, see

www.cyberciti.biz/tips/raid-hardware-vs-raid-software.html

RAID Access Characteristics: 1

Figure 4.9 shows a rough indication of the performance of different RAID levels (configurations) for various types of I/O accesses. The performance is indicated by the length of the black line; longer is better, indicating that the configuration is suitable for that type of access.

The lines replace what might have been numbers, but that would lend the numbers credibility far in excess of the accuracy of the measurements. Some people who have benchmarked RAID levels use even broader categories of performance, like *average*, *medium*, and *high*, in their results.

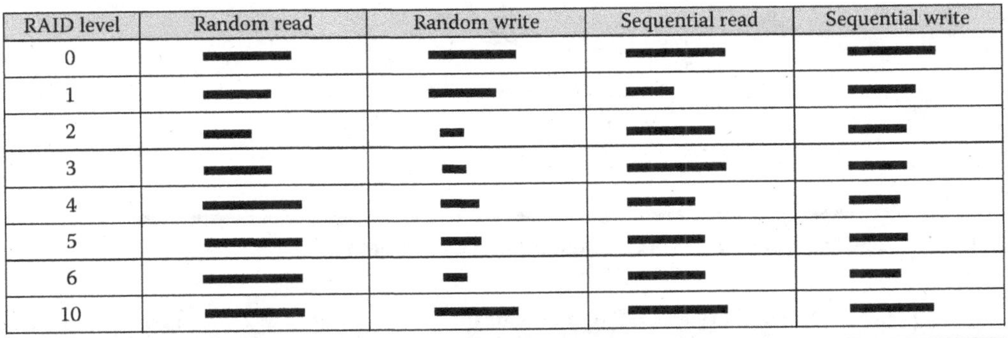

RAID level	Random read	Random write	Sequential read	Sequential write
0	▬▬▬	▬▬▬	▬▬▬▬	▬▬▬
1	▬▬▬	▬▬▬	▬▬	▬▬
2	▬▬	▬	▬▬▬	▬▬
3	▬▬	▬	▬▬▬▬	▬▬
4	▬▬▬▬	▬▬	▬▬▬	▬▬
5	▬▬▬	▬▬	▬▬▬	▬▬
6	▬▬▬	▬	▬▬▬	▬▬
10	▬▬▬	▬▬▬	▬▬▬	▬▬▬

Figure 4.9   RAID read and write performance characteristics.

The numbers depend so much on all the characteristics involved at measurement time that simple line representations of performance, rather than numbers to three places of decimals, seem more appropriate.

RAID Access Characteristics: 2

There are many RAID benchmarks to be found, but the ones with detailed numeric performance figures are nearly always for specific storage systems doing specific jobs. There are, however, some generic estimates to be found (one is shown above), and they work on a rating basis of some four or five categories—slow, average, fast, and so on. You could, if you wish, use a numeric scheme of 1, 2, 3, 4, and 5 to categorize them.

If precise performance information is necessary, you perhaps ought to perform your own benchmarks on the storage subsystem. For the record, there are two more generic RAID performance papers referenced below.

RAID Level Summary
http://www-01.ibm.com/support/knowledgecenter/P8DEA/p8ebj/raidlevelsummary.htm

Summary Comparison of RAID Levels
http://www.pcguide.com/ref/hdd/perf/raid/levels/comp-c.html

RAID Access Characteristics: 3

The graph shown in Figure 4.10 is a comparison of RAID 5 versus RAID 6 performance using the IBM CPW* benchmark on 5737 disk configurations, both with 90 MB of write cache.

The graph is shown as being typical of the difference between the two RAID configurations where performance is sacrificed for higher availability using the RAID 6 option. This does not mean that all RAID 5 or 6 configurations behave exactly the same way, but it is indicative of the difference in performance. This is compensated for by RAID 6 having higher reliability than RAID 5. See

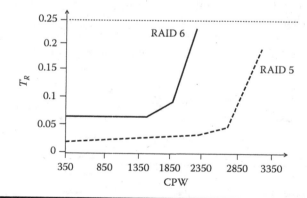

Figure 4.10 RAID 5 vs. RAID 6 performance: CPW benchmark.

---

* CPW is an internal iSeries (previously AS/400) benchmark used as a relative measure of performance among iSeries processors. Compute intensive workload (CIW) is another internal iSeries benchmark that is significantly more CPU intensive than the CPW benchmark.

IBM System i: V5R4 Performance Update GOP02 (2006)
http://citeseerx.ist.psu.edu/viewdoc/download;jsessionid= 0ADBCF29678DF69F25618A4996D
416CD?doi=10.1.1.127.1741&rep=rep1&type=pdf

RAID Performance References

Some performance tests have been carried out by individuals as opposed to standards bodies. Most admit that sometimes their conclusions are personal preferences and that sometimes results depend on the vendor and hardware configuration. Nevertheless, their conclusions do seem to put the various RAID levels in order of performance.

Note: One should also remember that the choice of performance RAID will normally be influenced by the attendant high-availability needs and a compromise is frequently needed.

Summary Comparison of RAID Levels
http://www.pcguide.com/ref/hdd/perf/raid/levels/comp-c.html

Comprehensive RAID Performance Report
http://www.zdnet.com/article/comprehensive-raid-performance- report/

RAID Level Comparison Table
http://www.datarecovery.net/articles/raid-level-comparison.html

RAID Applicability

RAID subsystems are often used for availability purposes, but they can offer performance enhancements over SLEDs in certain configurations and degradation in others.

Figure 4.11 shows the *availability versus performance* characteristics of the main RAID configurations (RAIDs 0, 1, 3, 5, and 6).

Avoiding SAN Performance Problems Whitepaper [Virtual Instruments]
http://www.hds.com/assets/pdf/avoiding-san-performance-problems-whitepaper.pdf

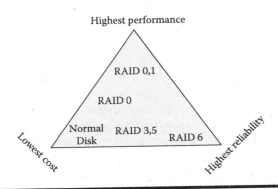

Figure 4.11   RAID positioning factors. (From UNIX News 3/95.)

Which Is Faster: SAN or Directly-Attached Storage?
http://www.sqlteam.com/article/which-is-faster-san-or- directly-attached-storage

I/O Perf Tool (SAN/NAS)
http://sourceforge.net/projects/io-performance/

Is There Life after RAID?

There are a number of reasons why RAID, though technologically sound, is becoming an issue, a major one being performance with large data aggregations, for example, very large databases and *big data*. The reading and writing speeds of RAID devices depend on the level of RAID chosen, and it is usually a balance of reliability and performance. You can't have the best of both worlds.

Recovery times after failure in RAID systems can also be an issue, which can affect recovery in normal failure situations and especially in disaster recovery scenarios. The latter normally have a recovery time objective (RTO) for complete recovery of systems after a catastrophic failure at a primary site. This, more often than not, forms part of the service level agreement (SLA) between users and IT.

Although the bit error rate (BER) may be small, the larger disks being touted today will mean that there is more likely to be an error on every disk, and with RAID, it means a large reconstruction of some sort.

When reconstructions are necessary and are very lengthy, there could well be an error occur during recovery. This is known in common parlance as a *double data whammy*. The paper cited below covers this topic in more detail:

RAID's Days May Be Numbered
http://www.enterprisestorageforum.com/technology/features/article.php/3839636/RAIDs-Days-May-Be-Numbered.htm

> As an aside, the possible follow-on to RAID are structures based on *erasure codes* (ECs). See "RAID and Erasure Codes" in this chapter.

RAID vs. Erasure Coding
http://www.networkcomputing.com/storage/raid-vs-erasure- coding/a/d-id/1297229

Solid-State Drives (SSD)

These devices are often called, erroneously, solid-state disks, and disks they are not since they have no moving parts. They have been with us for many years, and I can remember a vendor chasing IBM business with these devices, particularly for operating system paging where a very large disk dedicated to a few tens of megabytes of page space seemed a waste (and it was). They were, however, not very reliable and not capable of being produced with large enough capacities at that time.

SSDs, as we have just seen, are not new—they have simply come of age in an IT world where more needs to be done and done faster than your competitors, and their current speed, reliability, capacity, and costs now make them viable as a major storage vehicle.

Flash Storage

Flash storage technology is the main *ingredient* of the SSD *meal* and gains several advantages over magnetic hard disk from the fact there are no moving parts to go wrong or suffer from wear. You might find flash memory in the following:

- SSDs
- Nonvolatile dynamic random access memory (NVDRAM) in an existing memory slot on a motherboard
- BIOS chip
- CompactFlash (often employed in digital cameras)
- SmartMedia (most often found in digital cameras)
- Memory Stick (most often found in digital cameras)
- Personal Computer Memory Card International Association (PCMCIA) Type I and Type II memory cards (used as solid-state drives [SSDs] in laptops)
- Memory cards for video game consoles

There are essentially two types of flash storage, SLC and MLC, and these are the differentiators when it comes to the choice of flash or SSD types used in tiering of storage media outlined below. This is because of their different characteristics.

Single-level cell (SLC): Stores data in individual memory cells with two possible states so that one bit of data is stored in each single-level cell. It can therefore have two states within each cell. It has the advantages of faster write speeds, higher cell longevity, and lower power consumption than MLC.

Multilevel cell (MLC): A flash memory technology using multiple levels per cell to allow 2 bits per cell to be stored using the same number of transistors, giving four states per memory cell. It yields a better profile because of higher density. However, because of its higher potential error rate, it uses error correction code (ECC) to counter this tendency.

These individual characteristics of SLC and MLC cells give them a natural place in the tiered hierarchy often used in hybrid SDD/HDD configurations. Their position in the hierarchy depends on the requirements demanded by the workloads in question.

Table 4.2 shows these differing characteristics (and hence applicability) in the use of SSDs in tiering.

Table 4.2   SLC/MLC Performance Details

Entity	Write-Intensive (WI) SLC SSDs	Read-Intensive (RI) MLC SSDs
Workload	Mainstream applications	Mostly read 90/10 R/W mix
Capacity	Ca. 400 GB	Ca. 1.6 GB
Write endurance	Very good	Moderate
Full drive writes/day	30	3
Random read performance	Very good	Very good
Write performance	Very good	Moderate to poor
Relative costs	4×	1×

Source: Dell.

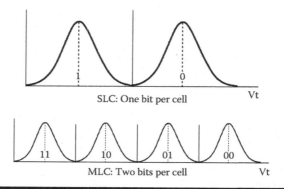

Figure 4.12   SLC and MLC cell and bit structure. (From http://www.samsung.com/global/business/semiconductor/minisite/SSD/uk/html/ssd850pro/overview.html?gclid=CKW2j72ZvMcCF UnlwgodnUcAuA.)

Figure 4.12, taken from the referenced Samsung document, shows a schematic view of the SLC and MLC configurations, which accounts for their different performance and other characteristics.

Source: Samsung 850
http://www.samsung.com/global/business/semiconductor/minisite/SSD/uk/html/ssd850pro/overview.html?gclid=CKW2j72ZvMcCFUnlwgodnUcAuA

This reference takes you to an introduction page that links to several PDF files on various aspects of the technology. If the URL is too big to type, do as I did with the search "Samsung 840" (yes, "840") to find the paper again.

All-Flash Data Centers?

In June 2015, HP announced enhancements to its flash storage, and the media interpreted this as a move toward promoting the *all-flash storage* data center. HP launched the 3PAR StoreServ Storage 20000 enterprise flash family of Tier I all-flash arrays for data center storage with increased speed and decreased footprint requirements and with a new benchmark price of $1.50 per gigabyte. HP claims this price per gigabyte is just a starting point in the promotion of flash in the data center.

These new 3.84 TB SSDs are further enhanced with flash optimization software and hardware-accelerated data compaction, and the use of new cMLC* SSDs are responsible for the drop in price. The new arrays boast 3.2 million IOPS at submillisecond latency, and more than 75 Gbps of sustained throughput. However, HP is not alone.

Coho Data (cohodata.com) is a start-up specializing in enterprise flash storage, and around the same time it announced its all-flash DataStream 2000f. No doubt there will be others going down the same road. There is some disquiet among shared storage vendors about this shift, as the article in the link below suggests, saying that some are like a deer caught in the headlights of a car.

---

* Consumer MLC. See http://www.slideshare.net/IvanIannaccone/hp-3par-enterprise-grade-cmlc-ssds for an up-to-date outline by HP.

The Innovator's Dilemma: Disk Drive Vendors Getting into the Array Business
https://www.langtonblue.com/2015/03/innovators-dilemma-disk-drive-vendors-getting-array-business/

> The only possible issue I see is reliability of these devices over time, which may entail organizations, in a review of backup or recovery strategy, to cater for any shortfall.

Flash Information: Useful flash references include

How Flash Memory Works: Technology and Market Overview
http://computer.howstuffworks.com/flash-memory.htm

Flash in the Enterprise
http://cdn.architecting.it/tech-brief/LB_AI1401_01S_Flash_In_The_Enterprise.pdf

It would also be wise to subscribe to data center and storage publications to keep abreast of these developments, remembering that consensus of opinion is a wise way of assessing the validity of claims for these devices.

Solid-State Drives Overview

Solid-state drives (or devices) differ from traditional hard disk drives (HDDs) in that they have no moving parts and are mainly based on NAND flash storage; that is, they are electronic devices. They house flash storage modules and add electronic interfaces compatible with traditional block input/output (I/O) hard disk drives, thus permitting simple replacement in common applications.

In essence, SSDs = flash + connections to systems via channels. SSDs are nowadays often used in conjunction with HDDs in a hierarchy. Also, hybrid drives or solid-state hybrid drives (SSHDs) combine the features of SSDs and HDDs in the *same unit*, containing a large HDD and an SSD cache to improve read and write performance of frequently accessed data.

A Guide to SSD Storage
www.notebookreview.com/news/an-introduction-guide-to-ssd-storage

Tutorial on Solid-State Disk (SSD) Devices
http://searchsolidstatestorage.techtarget.com/tip/Tutorial- on-solid-state-disk-SSD-devices

History and Trends in SSD [I have assumed this title, as the document doesn't start with one]
http://www.jedec.org/sites/default/files/Ed%20Dawson%20[Compatibility%20Mode](3).pdf

Hybrid SSD/HDD Tiering

In the 1970s, IBM carried out a short survey of its own data volatility on the time-sharing system TSO (Time Sharing Option) user data. It was found that only about 3% of the data was changed in any one day, yet all data was being backed up each evening across a large number of systems and workstations. This prompted the idea of only backing up *changed* data and led to the introduction of the hierarchical storage manager (HSM), both as a concept and eventually a product of the same name.*

---

* As a matter of interest, Bert Latamore discusses a five-tier data model in the link http://wikibon.org/wiki/v/Five_Tier_Storage_Model.

Hierarchical storage management became known as data tiering, but has different connotations depending on what storage type is in question:

- Cache storage or memory is basically hierarchical with levels 1, 2, and 3 in the main. Each has its own its own role to play in the cache hierarchy, based on its size and speed at each level.
- Static hierarchical storage management is where data movement between tiers is done on a time basis, perhaps each night or week. IBM's Hierarchical Storage Manager (HSM) was such a product.
- Real-time or *hot* tiering is where data is moved to more quickly accessed parts of a storage hierarchy dynamically, depending on its access requirements at the time. The following extract perhaps explains the hot or real-time scenario well:

  Once a tiered LUN is created, Windows Server 2012 R2 analyzes disk IO requests on the fly and keeps the most frequently accessed data blocks located on speedy SSDs while moving less frequently accessed data blocks to HDDs—all transparently to applications and users. (Microsoft on Windows 2012 R2)

Note that sometimes tiers are numbered 0, 1, 2, and so forth, or 1, 2, 3, and so forth, but as long as you remember which scheme you are involved with, you should not get in trouble. In the first scheme, tier 0 is the top level of the hierarchy; in the second scheme, tier 1 is the top level. In the discussion following, we use 1, 2, 3, and so forth.

The following references outline some factors about SSD/HDD data tiering, and one includes a pricing element as well. The Dell reference also contains a table suggesting what storage type might be recommended for different workload types—web, OLTP/DB, email, and so on. The recommendation is based on the I/O characteristics of these workloads (Figure 4.13).

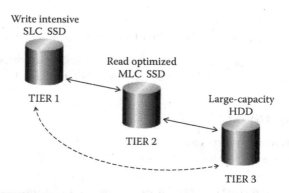

Figure 4.13 Storage tiering schematic: SLC/MLC SSD and HDD. (Based on Garrett, B. Dell Compellent: Breakthrough savings with Flash optimized SSD tiering. October 2013. Dell. http://i. dell.com/sites/doccontent/corporate/secure/en/Documents/ESG-report-Dell-Compellent-Fluid-Flash.pdf.)

Solid State Drive vs. Hard Disk Drive Price and Performance Study
http://www.dell.com/downloads/global/products/pvaul/en/ssd_vs_hdd_price_and_performance_study.pdf
This Dell paper outlines manual and automatic data tiering. The latter involves moving *hot* data from HDD to SSD and returning to HDD is when it is no longer *hot*. Hot data refers to active data being read and written frequently.

Maximizing the Benefits from Flash in Your SAN Storage Systems
http://www.dothill.com/wp-content/uploads/2014/07/Maximizing-the-Benefits-of-Flash-WP- 6.26.pdf

Real-Time Storage Tiering for Real-World Workloads
http://www.dothill.com/wp-content/uploads/2012/08/RealStorWhitePaper8.14.12.pdf
This final reference discusses (and touts) the following subjects:

- Autonomic (automatic) real-time tiering, the migration of data in real time to cater for changing access patterns
- Thin provisioning, a storage alert to avoid initial storage overconfiguration
- Rapid rebuild after errors, spreading LUNs across data sets to minimize the amount of data to be recovered
- Simple user interface
- SSD flash cache option, a variable-sized cache option to speed up performance

They aim to overcome the static positioning of data regardless of access patterns.

SSD versus HDD RAID

Solid-state drive RAID (SSD RAID) is a strategy for improving performance that involves dividing and storing the same data on multiple solid-state drives instead of normal disk drives (HDDs), which are the normal mainstay of RAID arrays. SSDs can be used in RAID configurations, offering the same benefits, and has some advantages over HDDs:

- A sustainable I/O rate (IOPS) can be up to 100 times, but in practice about 10, that of an HDD (benchmarks on this vary significantly). Samsung has measured a factor of 100-fold improvement in IOPS, others 10.
- Its power consumption can be much less. A typical SSD consumes 2 W, whereas an HDD might require 10 W of power.
- The environmental costs of using SSDs can be much less than those of HDDs.
- RAID is seen as one large disk, but because read and write operations are being spread out over multiple disks, I/Os, which are faster, can be carried out simultaneously, thereby speeding up overall performance.
- SSDs in general require less cooling and associated power than HDDs.
- SSDs are lighter and quieter than HDDs.
- SSDs with error correction codes (ECCs) can be extremely reliable.

However, there are some disadvantages to SSD RAID:

- Their longevity is not as good as that of HDDs. An SSD can execute a certain number of writes before it needs to be replaced. In SSD RAID, writes are often distributed equally to all drives with the result that multiple drives may wear out at the same time.

■ The cost per megabyte is higher than HDDs, and although decreasing, HDD price performance is not waiting around to be caught.

■ Many RAID controllers are aimed at HDDs and do not optimize SDD facilities. Ideal SSD RAID performance requires the optimum combination of microprocessor, cache, software, and hardware resources. Failure to properly synergize the underlying technologies can result in performance that does not exceed, and may actually fall behind, mechanical HDDs.

There are numerous papers on the web with arguments for and against SSD RAID as a competitor to HDD RAID, and two are listed below—one completely for and the other more circumspect about the situation.

Accelerating Performance with SSD RAID Arrays
http://www.kingston.com/us/community/articledetail/articleid/8?Article-Title=Accelerating-System-Performance-with-SSD-RAID-Arrays

The Pitfalls of Deploying Solid-State Drive RAID
http://www.research.ibm.com/haifa/conferences/systor2011/present/session5_talk2_systor2011.pdf

A useful article on SSDs versus HDDs can be found at

SSD vs. HDD: What's the Difference?
http://uk.pcmag.com/storage-devices-reviews/8061/feature/ssd-vs-hdd-whats-the-difference

SSD Benchmarks

It is now recognized that benchmarks designed with HDDs in mind do not necessarily show SSDs in the best light, and that SSDs need time to reach their normal operating state.

Benchmarking Enterprise SSDs
http://www.cio.co.uk/cmsdata/whitepapers/3516899/White_Paper_Benchmarking_Enterprise_SSDs__WP006-EN-A4-0313-04_1.pdf

This article is very readable and makes the point above forcefully. The extract below illustrates this.

> Traditional benchmark tests used to evaluate HDD performance cannot accurately measure SSD performance and endurance. This is the case because an HDD is characterized by rotational latency and seek times. Existing benchmark scripts are designed to measure performance over a short time interval. By comparison, SSDs have no spin or seek functions, so the access results obtained using HDD benchmark scripts typically show very high IO rates and low latency. SSDs that are tested with these benchmarking scripts will deliver wildly optimistic performance scores that do not accurately reflect how the drive will perform under enterprise conditions.

A number of parameters can affect the performance of SSDs, among them current and previous workload, block size, fragmentation, read and write mix, queue depth, and a variety of other factors. The first SNIA publication below shows SSDs going through the phases of life from initiation of activity to what can be best described as a *steady-state* condition where meaningful benchmarks can be carried out.

The graphs in the documentation indicate that this occurs after about 3–4 h of SSD activity. Refer to the SNIA publication links below for further information on this topic.

The Why and How of SSD Performance Benchmarking
http://www.snia.org/sites/default/education/tutorials/2011/fall/SolidState/EstherSpanjer_The_
Why_How_SSD_Performance_Benchmarking.pdf

SSD Performance: A Primer
http://www.snia.org/sites/default/files/SNIASSSI.SSDPerformance-APrimer2013.pdf
    The reference below is a useful pictorial look at the characteristics of SSD and HDD storage
(it needs sign-in or registration):

SSD vs. HDD Infographic [information graphic: a concise visual representation of facts]
http://www.informationweek.com/whitepaper/Business-Intelligence/Business-Process-Management/
infographic-ssd-vs-hdd-wp1426289414?_mc=NL_IWK_EDT_IWK_daily_20150410&cid=NL_
IWK_EDT_IWK_daily_ 20150410&elq=d85f69aa9891485bacf58547103d06df&elqCampaignId
=13776&elqaid=59784&elqat=1&elqTrackId=774f86a418d14c77bd76adedc13b8a40
    The last reference, below, is a detailed look at the write performance of SSDs and gives an
insight as to how the I/O operation works. It is quite advanced.

Analytic Modeling of SSD Write Performance [for Black Belts only]
http://ycassuto.eew.technion.ac.il/files/2012/11/write_amp_systor12.pdf

Future of SSD

There are factions who believe that hard disks (HDDs) will be replaced eventually by solid-state
drives (SSDs) and possibly *all-flash* (technology) storage arrays (AFAs), but then the cinema was
going to be replaced by televisions and DVDs at home, wasn't it?
    The link below offers you the opportunity to download a paper that poses the question asked
in its title. The author, Kenneth Hess, counters some fears about SSDs and flash and tries to alleviate them. One is the reliability of SSD, where he points out that EMC offers the same 5- to 7-year
warranty for flash as for SATA (Serial ATA*) drives. His outline of SSD and flash pros and cons,
covered in detail in the paper, follows:
    SSD and flash pros

- Energy efficient
- Low latency
- Durable
- Control of unstructured files (big data)
- Compatibility with operating systems
- Commoditized components

    SSD and flash cons

- Questionable life expectancy
- SSD technology is nascent (emerging)
- Not ideal for all (purposes)
- More expensive

---

* Advanced Technology Attachment.

Hess also states that comparing flash with HDD is not quite the way to go; rather, compare flash with RAM, the former being 50 times less expensive. To me, this approach might suggest that high-performance *databases in memory*, using a single address space instead of disk extents, are quite feasible.

Solid State Drives: The Future of Data Storage?
http://www.infostor.com/index/NAS.html

Flash Storage:

> Flash storage's memory is actually a form of EEPROM (electrically-erasable program-mable read-only memory). Unlike standard EEPROM, however, flash is a non-volatile memory type. This means that it does not require power to maintain stored data integrity, so a system can be turned off—or lose power—without losing data. Flash also erases whole blocks of data at a time rather than on a bit-by-bit level as conventional EEPROM does and so does not require complete erasure for a rewrite.
>
> Flash is solid-state storage, storing data using electricity in surface-mounted chips on a printed circuit board (PCB). There are no moving mechanical parts involved, which reduces power consumption. A typical SATA flash drive consumes 50 percent or less the power required by mechanical drives and may be capable of sequential read speeds more than 500MB/s in consumer drives, faster than even the fastest enterprise-class mechanical hard drives. That is only a part of the picture, because access times are where flash really shines. (TechTarget Glossary)

Other authors' views of flash are that there are trade-offs to be made:

■ Disks are limited by I/Os per second (IOPS).
■ Flash is limited by capacity.
■ A compromise is to have a hybrid flash–HDD system.
■ Striping as in RAID is IOPS inexpensive, so one doesn't have to agonize over which *x* to use in choosing RAID *x* for performance and availability requirements.
■ It may be just a flash in the pan.

Moral: Only the future (not me) will decide the outcome, and that will be based on user experience gained over time and not a sudden decision based on some *gee whiz* technological factor; the organizations who depend on IT don't like revolution, preferring evolution and less depreciation and amortization of existing investments.

Take a look at the links below to get a picture of the issues involved in using flash storage.

How Flash Changes the Storage Equation
http://www.infoworld.com/article/2912373/flash-storage/how-flash-changes-the-storage   equation.html#more

Everything You Need to Know about Flash Storage Performance
http://www.infoworld.com/article/2914841/flash-storage/everything-you-need-to-know-about-flash-storage-performance.html?phint=newt%3Dinfoworld_tech_storage&phint=idg_eid%3D36d5d934825c41283fc0e9c68846524d#tk.IFWNLE_nlt_storage_2015-04-29

Stop Press: Intel Optane

In the last stages of reviewing the text for this book, Intel announced what they call the biggest revolution in storage technology since 1966, planning shipment of devices based on it by June 2016. A brief overview of this technology (*3D XPoint [Cross Point] nonvolatile memory*) follows:

- The Optane SSD is able to achieve 7.2× times more IOPS at low queue depth and up to 5.21 times the IOPS of conventional SSDs at high queue depths.
- An Optane Technology–based SSD has 10× times the density of conventional SSD drives.
- The marketing material also claims it is 1000× faster than the competition available on the market, but it isn't clear what exactly they are referring to—a good guess would be latency, as opposed to bandwidth.
- Optane SSDs will have 1000× the endurance, which, if true, should mean the device has virtually unlimited life span for practical purposes.
- All Optane-based devices will feature a cross-point array structure, which consists of perpendicular connectors connecting around 128 billion memory cells (16 GB per chip).

References to this technology are below and will obviously be more detailed closer to shipment. Hopefully benchmark information will verify these claims, or otherwise.
http://wccftech.com/intel-optane-technology-3d-xpoint-ssd-2016/#ixzz3nK6EOiVs
http://wccftech.com/intel-optane-technology-3d-xpoint-ssd-2016/#ixzz3nK5ylddr
http://wccftech.com/intel-optane-technology -3d-xpoint-ssd- 2016/

SSD Myths and Legends

There are a number of articles promoting SSDs as a replacement for hard disks (HDDs) either in the short term or immediately. Two of these articles look at what they call myths about SSDs in trying to position them against HDDs. They make interesting reading in what they call *debunking SSD myths*. Many of the arguments are about SSD cost, security, reliability, and durability. Performance is an issue beyond dispute, as SSDs win hands-down in this contest.

Even though the writers claim a solid case for SSDs, they recognize that such a change or migration is subject to a learning curve, matching requirements to what SSDs offer and, importantly, the investment in HDDs, which is unlikely to be written off overnight to accommodate SSDs.

Debunking SSD Myths
http://www.networkworld.com/article/2873551/data-center/debunking-ssd-myths.html

6 SSD Myths Debunked
http://www.networkcomputing.com/storage/6-ssd-myths-debunked/d/d-id/1321102?_mc=NL_NWC_EDT_NWC_converations_20150702&cid=NL_NWC_EDT_NWC_converations_20150702&elq=c2abdf11e575449ebceb5dfb8d3ad9b8&elqCampaignId=15315&elqaid=61739&elqat=1&elqTrackId=8a532534ebc145cd9cbf5f96d76fc358

SSD Performance

SSD performance is without a doubt superior to that of HDDs, but it hasn't overwhelmed the latter yet. However, the arguments in the previous section make a good case for migrating, or thinking of migrating, to SSDs over time. The approximate status of SSDs in mid-2015 might be represented by a July announcement from Samsung of a range of SSDs with a 10-year guarantee.*

The top of the five-model range boasts the following characteristics:

- Capacity: 2 TB
- 2.5 in. form factor
- 550 MB/s sequential read, 520 MB/s sequential write performance
- Up to 100,000 random I/Os per second
- Full-disk Advanced Encryption Standard (AES) 256-bit encryption
- $1000 price tag

SSD References: RAID, SSD, HDD, and flash memory, coupled with post-RAID technologies, are evolving subjects that are far too volatile to commit to paper here. They can be found in the usual places in the Internet, many involving the name of Professor Jim Plank. However, there is what looks like a "living" set of SSD documents to be found at http://www.storagesearch.com/enterprise-ssd-ha.html.

I think the only advice I can give on this topic is "watch this space."

Storage Performance

Introduction

Storage performance 30 years ago was a matter of either calculating performance from simple disk characteristics or devising a benchmark or two. Now we have RAID, NAS, SANs, and a variety of cache (memory and head of string [HoS]) and connection configurations. I maintain that this makes calculation virtually impossible and simulation only in carefully defined situations and configurations.

The way forward seems to be rules of thumb (ROTs) and benchmarks, either standards or organization defined ones. One of the main things about storage is that it needs to be managed, as it is not (yet) self-managing.

Storage Performance Management

Definition:

Processes to ensure that applications receive the required service levels from storage systems, while storage systems are efficiently used. This means ensuring that the storage hardware resources are used efficiently with neither unnecessary hardware components nor (other?) components reaching critical utilization levels! It is not the same

---

* I am not sure whether they replace any data lost through malfunction, as well as replacing the SSD. That, as usual, is the responsibility of the user.

as Storage Resource Management (SRM) as SRM is about space management.* (Brett Allison, first reference below this section)

Storage performance management, like the management of any IT resource, requires monitoring and visibility of all elements that affect that resource's capacity and performance. Remember that for a resource X,

$$\text{Management of X} = [\text{Design} + \text{Measuring} + \text{Review} + \text{Actions}]\text{of X}$$

Storage monitoring software should therefore give a unified view into the health and availability of online storage devices. Deploying storage performance monitoring software should also help identify how storage resources are currently being used and form the basis of storage capacity planning (which includes performance capacity). The rules in this arena usually apply to the various configurations of storage–RAID, SSD, SAN, NAS, and JBODs.

Tape performance, unless tapes are used in applications,† would apply to backup, recovery, and disaster recovery (meeting RPOs ‡ and RTOs), and adding extra storage to existing configurations needs management too.

There are a number of tools and techniques in this area of management, from simple monitors to all-embracing tools looking at storage and the associated applications. The references below should give you enough information to put together a credible plan for your organization.

Storage Performance Management Overview [Brett Allison, SNIA publication]
http://www.snia.org/sites/default/education/tutorials/2012/spring/storman/BrettAllison_Storage_Performance_Management.pdf

Storage Performance Management: 10 Storage System Performance Tips [Techtarget]
http://searchstorage.techtarget.com/tip/Storage-performance-management-10-storage-system-performance-tips

The paper below, also from TechTarget, covers benchmarks other than the Storage Performance Council (SPC) ones, for example, Systems Performance Evaluation Corporation (SPEC) SFS:

Performance Benchmarks [TechTarget]
http://www.techtarget.com/search/query?q=performance+benchmarks

Storage Benchmarks
http://www.techopsguys.com/2010/06/15/storage-benchmarks/

Isolate Problems and Optimize Performance Anywhere in the Stack [EMC/Precise; covers database as well as storage]
http://www.emc.com/collateral/software/solution-overview/h7108-emc-precise-so.pdf

---

* I won't bother splitting hairs over the definitions, as they are all about managing storage.
† Older IT people may remember tape *sorting*, which used Fibonacci series math (apparently) in this task. The tapes would oscillate back and forth like the ball in a tennis match, with the operator's head moving in similar fashion to tennis spectators.
‡ Recovery point objective, where we wish to recover data after system failure.

NAS and SAN Management

SAN:

SAN Management [Solarwinds storage management]
http://www.solarwinds.com/solutions/san-management.aspx
   NAS: The link below contains other links to NAS storage management topics and not just performance. It is a good starting point for managing NAS and, in addition, links to a NAS storage introduction.

Storage Network Attached Storage Management
http://searchstorage.techtarget.com/guide/Network- attached-storage-management
   This next link is specifically aimed at NAS management in its many aspects.

Network-Attached Storage Management Overview
http://searchstorage.techtarget.com/news/1158592/Network-attached-storage-management-overview

SAN Performance

The SAN performance metrics reference below lists and gives details of the important metrics that are needed to assess the performance health of a SAN. These are listed below and described in detail in the publications, including suggested numeric values that might serve as baselines for acceptable performance.
   Storage processor (SP) metrics

- SP utilization (%)
- SP cache dirty pages
- SP response time (ms)
- SP port queue full count

   LUNs* metrics

- Utilization (%)
- Queue length
- Average busy queue length
- Response time (ms)
- Service time (ms)
- Total throughput (I/O per second)
- Write throughput (I/O per second)
- Read throughput (I/O per second)
- Total bandwidth (MB/s)
- Read bandwidth (MB/s)
- Write bandwidth (MB/s)
- Read size (KB)
- Write size (KB)

---

* A SAN can have its physical disks partitioned into logically addressed portions that allow host servers to access these partitions as *storage units*. The partition is called a logical unit (LUN).

There are another 15 metrics outlined in the paper that are "recorded for completeness." The products mentioned as providing these statistics are

Navisphere Analyzer
http://www.hecomputing.org/files/clariion/Navisphere_Analyzer_Admin_Guide.pdf

SAN Performance Metrics
http://thesanguy.com/2012/09/25/san-performance-metrics/
Solarwinds offers a free SAN monitor that caters for SANs from several vendors.

Gain Visibility into Storage Performance & Stay Ahead of SAN Slowdowns
http://www.solarwinds.com/products/freetools/san_ monitor/

*EMC CLARiiON Best Practices for Performance and Availability**
http://www.emc.com/collateral/hardware/white-papers/h5773-clariion-best-practices-performance-availability-wp.pdf (older version for Clariion)

Best Practices for Benchmarking SAN Performance
http://www.networkworld.com/article/2239465/tech-primers/best-practices-for-benchmarking-san-performance.html
The link below contains other links to SAN performance, including testing best practices, and is very thorough.

NAS and SAN Storage Performance Testing Product Suite
http://www.loaddynamix.com/blog/nas-and-san-storage- performance-testing-product-suite/
The EMC website is a good place for information on general storage topics, as well as EMC products.

For details of standard storage benchmarks, see "Storage Benchmarks" in Chapter 12, where two Storage Performance Council (SPC) benchmarks, SPC-1 and SPC-2, are discussed, along with a SPEC storage benchmark.

NAS Benchmarks and Test Tools

Some of the references below contain a comprehensive list of characteristics of the disks under test, as well as the usual megabytes or megabits per second ratings normally given as key metrics for NAS configurations. NAS configurations will also have their own response time, measured as time of *request from network* to time of *answer given to network*, which will then be rolled into the overall response time as seen by the end user or requestor. This, of course, is not the total response time as seen by the user.

NAS and SAN Storage Performance Testing Product Suite
http://www.loaddynamix.com/blog/nas-and-san-storage-performance-testing-product-suite/

Intel NAS Performance Toolkit [used in Tom's Hardware benchmarks below, but no longer supported by Intel]
https://software.intel.com/en-us/articles/intel-nas-performance-toolkit

---

* Rest of the title: *Release 30.0 Firmware Update Applied Best Practices.*

All Network Attached Storage (NAS) Charts [Tom's Hardware]
http://www.tomshardware.com/charts/network-attached-storage-nas-charts/benchmarks,87.html

HGST 4TB Deskstar NAS HDD Review [Storage Review, April 2014]
http://www.storagereview.com/hgst_4tb_deskstar_nas_hdd_review

Other Storage References: The following reference is an IBM Redbook on the IBM DS8800 but contains useful information about storage on other platforms, such as Linux, Windows, and VMware. It also covers some SAN topics.

DS8800 Performance Monitoring and Tuning
http://www.redbooks.ibm.com/redbooks/pdfs/sg248013.pdf

Measuring Storage Performance [detailed but readable]
https://wiki.terena.org/display/Storage/Measuring+ storage+performance

Storage Performance Council
http://www.storageperformance.org/home/

Storage Futures

This is a tricky one since in my experience, most futures come from what the user organization needs for its IT and the costs. It is not concerned with international standards, but pragmatic solutions; witness the garbage dump with *de jure* ISO standards ousted by *de facto* standards like TCP/IP and OpenGL. Also, it is not over concerned with blue skies predictions, as its problems are here and now.

Having said that, there are some storage predictions that have to come to fruition because of performance issues. We have alluded to the SSD/HDD battle, which will follow the customer-led course unless, of course, everyone succumbs to the storage hype peddled by some vendors and gurus.

The other looming change in storage techniques is the follow-on to redundant array of independent disks (RAID) in view of its shortcomings in performance in the era of massive data stores. One contender is erasure code (EC) techniques, which masquerade under a variety of names but are in essence variations on the EC theme.

RAID and Erasure Codes

The basic issue with RAID in large data environments is the time to write the high-availability RAID configurations, RAIDs 5 and 6. An even bigger problem is the time taken to recover large volumes of data configured in this way for normal recovery and disaster recovery (DR) purposes. Another issue is the time to failures (MTTF), each of which requires some kind of data recovery. Studies show that EC has a much greater MTTF than RAIDs 5 and 6.

Figure 4.14 is the briefest possible introduction to EC, and I cite references to follow up the topic. The *nomenclature* in the EC literature varies in specifying numbers of disks for data and those used for recovery coding. We use the Jim Plank conventions here, where **n** is the total number of disks in an EC situation, **k** is for data, and **m** is for coding (the EC equivalent of pure parity in RAID 5 or 6).

Briefly, the nomenclature used in erasure coding and retrofitted to RAID is as follows (refer to Figure 4.14):

■ **m** is the number of coding disks (sometimes referred to as fragments), which in essence are the recovery vehicles.

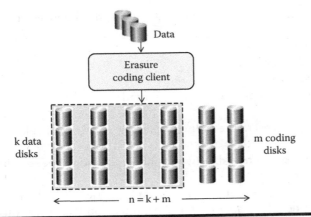

Figure 4.14   Erasure coding data flow and disk configuration.

- **n** is the total number of disks.
- **k** is the number of disks dedicated to data.
- **n = m + k**.
- **r** is called the encoding rate and is equal to **m/n**.

The way the data and recovery code information is stored can take at least two forms:

1. A *horizontal* code separates the data and codes onto separate sets of disks, as illustrated in Figure 4.14.
2. A *vertical* code mixes data and codes on the same disks.

The RAID 5 and 6 equivalents of this configuration have one and two sets of parity data for recovery, which would logically sit where the "**m** coding disks" are in Figure 4.14. EC uses a mathematical function to describe a set of numbers or codes so they can be recovered if one is lost. For the record, these mathematical functions are referred to as *polynomial interpolation* or *oversampling*.

Applying this nomenclature to RAID configurations, the following are true:

- For RAID 1, **m** = 1, **n** = 2
- For RAID 5, **m** = 4, **n** = 5
- For RAID 6, **m** = (**n**:2)
- Replication with two copies, **m** = 1, **n** = 3, **r** = 1/3

EC Recovery Scope

In the diagrams labeled **n**, **k**, and **m** as above (Figure 4.14), it is possible to recover (tolerate) up to **m** failures with **m** disks encoded supporting **k** disks of data.

The maximum distance separable is written as MDS (**k,m**), which means that when **m** devices are added for redundancy, up **m** failures anywhere across **k** and **m** can be tolerated. Another way of saying this is that (**n – k**) failures can be handled since **n = k + m**. A typical set of numbers might be 16 devices, 10 for data and 6 for coding, that is, MDS (10,6).

Applying this nomenclature to RAID configurations, the following are true:

- For RAID 1, **m** = 1, **n** = 2
- For RAID 5, **m** = 4, **n** = 5
- For RAID 6, **m** = **(n/2)**
- Replication with two copies, **m** = 1, **n** = 3, **r** = 1/3

The next reference covers erasure coding *technology* (the *theory* is older than RAID, believe it or not):

http://www.intel.com/content/dam/www/public/us/en/documents/white-papers/big-data-amplidata-storage-paper.pdf

The next link is a presentation by James Plank entitled "All about Erasure Codes." The link following it is a detailed paper on the same topic and represents a useful adjunct to the presentation.

http://web.eecs.utk.edu/~mbeck/classes/cs560/560/notes/Erasure/2004-ICL.pdf
http://static.usenix.org/event/fast09/tech/full_papers/plank/plank_html/

At the next link is a paper covering RAID, its problems, the possible use of SSDs. and erasure codes and object storage.

It also contains an appendix with short notes on the various RAID levels, standard and proprietary.

http://www.amplidata.com/pdf/The-RAID-Catastrophe.pdf

A large, mathematically detailed paper, submitted in partial fulfillment of a PhD and entitled "Reliability and Power-Efficiency in Erasure Coded Storage Systems," covers many aspects of EC.

http://citeseerx.ist.psu.edu/viewdoc/download?doi=10.1.1.160.1517&rep=rep1&type=pdf

Storage Connections

Like the old saying, a chain is as strong as its weakest link. A modified version of this applies to storage performance in that having a superfast server with hyperfast disks is pointless unless the connection between them can keep pace. For a slow connection trying to handle traffic from a fast storage device to a fast server, it will feel as if it is trying to drink from a fire hose at full power. In the development of storage, it has always been the intention to make performance enhancements across the board and not just to specific elements of the subsystem.

One key area is the channel between the server and storage device, often called a bus, a channel, a connection, a LAN, a WAN, and so on. Some of the more common connections between server and device are discussed in the following sections.

Data Bus

A memory data bus is a device to transfer data from disk connectors and other devices to memory. There are synchronous and asynchronous busses that use clocking or a handshaking protocol as the arbitration for transfers.

SCSI Architecture

SCSI is shorthand for Small Computer System Interface (typically pronounced *scuzzy*). SCSI is a standard mechanism for connecting peripherals (disks, tape drives, other magnetic media, CD-ROMs, scanners, etc.) to a computer via an SCSI controller. (Remember, normal attachment of peripheral devices is via a controller for that device.)

SCSI was designed as an alternative to expensive mainframe connections via control units and channels and was designed for small systems initially. It has developed over the years (SCSI-1, SCSI-2, SCSI-3) and been complemented by other peripheral attachment architectures, like fiber channel. SCSI provides a method for allowing access to multiple devices on the same "chain" or interface *at the same time*.

SCSI has evolved into several forms, wide SCSI, parallel SCSI, iSCSI, and so on, and a fairly recent addition is Serial Attached SCSI (SAS), which is capable of mixing with other connection architectures such as SATA.

SCSI Evolution and Future (2011)
http://wikibon.org/wiki/v/SAS:_The_Next_Evolution_of_SCSI

The Storage Networking Industry Association (SNIA) has published a presentation (referenced below) that shows the projected speeds of Serial SCSI as 3 Gbps today, through 6 Gbps, 12 Gbps, and 24 Gbps by about 2018.

SAS Roadmap (2013)
http://www.snia.org/sites/default/files2/SDC2013/presentations/BlockStorage/MartyCzekalski_-SCSI_Standards_and_Technolgy_Update.pdf

Organizations: The T10 technical committee of the International Committee for Information Technology Standards (INCITS) develops and maintains the SAS protocol; the SCSI Trade Association (SCSITA) promotes the technology.

SATA and ATA

ATA stands for Advanced Technology Attachment and is a type of disk drive that integrates the drive controller directly on the drive itself. Computers can use ATA hard drives without a specific controller to support the drive. The processor must still support an ATA connection, but a separate card (such as an SCSI card for an SCSI hard drive) is not needed. Some different types of ATA standards include ATA-1, ATA-2 (or Fast ATA), ATA-3, Ultra ATA (33 Mbps maximum transfer rate), ATA/66 (66 Mbps), and ATA/100 (100 Mbps).

SATA is essentially Serial ATA. SATA transfer rates start at 150 Mbps, which is significantly faster than even the fastest ATA/100 drives (100 Mbps). The SATA interface has several advantages over the ATA interface. One is that SATA drives each have their own independent bus, so there is no competition for bandwidth like there is with parallel ATA.

SATA Discussion
http://msdn.microsoft.com/en-us/library/windows/hardware/dn653577(v=vs.85).aspx

SATA Website
http://www.sata-io.org/

Fiber Channel Architecture

Fiber channel (FC) is a high-speed network connection, running at speeds up to 16 Gbps, and is also used as a connection in storage area networks (SANs). It normally runs optical fiber (UK fiber), but can run on copper with the same protocol—Fiber Channel Protocol (FCP).

FC can be implemented in a number of topologies, the main ones being

1. Point to point, directly connecting two devices
2. Fiber channel arbitrated loop (FC-AL), where devices are on a loop or ring, similar to those on a Token Ring
3. Switched fabric

There are five FC layers: F0–F4. Layers 0–3 are specific to FC and layer 4 (FC-4) is what is called upper layer protocols, which are transport mechanisms for data in

■ Data channels
  - IPI (Intelligent Peripheral Interface)
  - SCSI (Small Computer System Interface)
  - HIPPI (High-Performance Parallel Interface)
  - SBC CS (Session Border Control)
■ Network
  - IEEE 802.2 (logical link control [LLC])
  - IP (Internet Protocol with its partner TCP)
  - ATM (asynchronous transfer mode)

Some advantages of using FC are

■ Sustained transmission bandwidth over long distances (to 10 km at time of writing).
■ Support for a larger number of addressable devices over a network. FC can support more than 15 million device address on a network.
■ Support speeds up to 16 Gbps (16 gigabit fiber channel [GFC]).
■ Hardly worth stealing. Copper transmission media are very attractive to thieves, as my days without a home telephone connection after such a theft demonstrated.

Fibre Channel Overview
http://hsi.web.cern.ch/HSI/fcs/spec/overview.htm

Networked Storage Concepts and Protocols (EMC² TECHBOOK)
http://www.emc.com/collateral/hardware/technical-documentation/h4331-networked-storage-cncpts-prtcls-sol-gde.pdf

Fibre Channel SAN Topologies (EMC² TECHBOOK)
http://www.emc.com/collateral/hardware/technical-documentation/h8074-fibre-channel-san-tb.pdf

Note: The first EMC reference above is 370 pages long and the second 279 pages. The first reference gives basic details about FC and then its use in SANs. The second reference follows on from this one.

IBM Serial Storage Architecture (SSA)

Serial Storage Architecture (SSA) was introduced by IBM in 1995 as a high-performance disk subsystem for UNIX and other platforms. SSA is a high-performance, serial interconnection technology used to connect disk devices and host adapters and is an open standard. The specifications have been approved by the SSA Industry Association and are approved as an American National Standards Institute (ANSI) standard through the ANSI X3T10.1 subcommittee.

It was designed to bypass some of the limitations of Small Computer System Interface (SCSI) connections. Before SSA, the method of transmitting data to storage devices used a parallel architecture, such as SCSI. It was recognized that although this is a fast and low-cost method of transmission, there are a number of factors that prevent speed increases and connectivity. These are

- Address limitation—only up to 16 addresses available.
- Data skew—as the bits are transmitted in parallel, the faster they are accessed, the more likely it is that received packets will have a bit missing.

Total bus length—this is due to the above issue. To prevent skew, the bus length is reduced. Typically, even with differential SCSI, it can be no longer than 30 m, which must include internal SCSI cabling in the devices.

Cross talk and electromagnetic interference—to keep cable costs low, the data lines are rarely shielded, which means the more the bandwidth, the greater the possibility of unwanted signals being induced on the lines.

SSA eliminates this by serializing the SCSI data set and using loop architecture that only requires two wires—transmit and receive (SCSI, with data and control lines, requires up to 68). The SSA interface also supports full duplex. This means that it can transmit and receive data simultaneously at full speed.

Understanding SSA Subsystems in Your Environment [IBM Redbook]
http://www.redbooks.ibm.com/redbooks/pdfs/sg245750.pdf

IBM Channels

IBM has different channel types depending on what device is on the end of them. These were developed for, and mainly used on, mainframes (DOS and MVS). IBM adopted SCSI and other I/O technologies on its UNIX and other operating systems.

Byte Multiplexors: These connect slower devices, such as card readers and printers, to the system and multiplex the data to and from them byte by byte. To use an analogy, this is like orderly queues of cars joining a road one at a time, interleaving cars from each queue alternatively. In this way, every device receives a service essentially simultaneously.

Selector Channels: These were fast channels that often serviced tapes successfully at high speeds. However, their use in disk I/O was hindered by the fact that a stream of data from one disk would hold up a potential I/O from another one. This was alleviated by the introduction of another channel type.

Block Multiplexor Channel: This type of channel allowed interleaving of disk I/O (rather like the byte multiplexor) but at a block level. Disks could receive concurrent service then, instead of having to wait for each other to complete a large I/O transfer.

Initially, disk I/Os had to complete on the same subchannel that the I/O started, which could be an issue if that subchannel was busy with another I/O. This was solved by allowing I/Os to start or complete on different subchannels (paths), which added more flexibility to I/O operations and lessened wait times for completion of I/O.

Storage Performance Gotchas

The first thing to say about this is that *no man is an island*, a well-worn phrase. The performance of a system overall depends on teamwork and balanced components. Just because we solve our storage performance issues doesn't mean we have solved a slow system issue because these components work in a chain. Look at an analogy.

Let's imagine we want to speed up the car journey from San Francisco to Los Angeles by road improvements. We just build a faster freeway. That doesn't help the crawl in and out of both cities, and all the fast stretch will achieve is a bigger queue at the slow stretch at the end of it. This is what I've called the *knock-on effect* in the section "Interaction of Resources" in Chapter 1 and Table 1.4.

It is pointless speeding up your storage if the processor cannot supply it any faster or the network dispose of the data at the appropriate speed. The overall effect on, for example, the resulting increase in a transaction's response time can be small or even negative.

> *Moral*: Balanced systems and teamwork, and remember that the final arbiter of the improvement in any resource in the system is the end user's perspective.

The references cited below basically echo this theme.

Six Things That Can Wreck Storage System Performance
http://searchstorage.techtarget.com/feature/6-things-that-can-wreck-storage-system-performance?utm_medium=EM&asrc=EM_NLN_38128528&utm_campaign=20141229_Word%20of%20the%20Day:%20secondary%20storage_mrouse&utm_source=NLN&track=NL-1823&ad=897915 [best found via a search of the article's name]

I/O Bottlenecks: Biggest Threat to Data Storage
http://www.enterprisestorageforum.com/technology/features/article.php/3856121/IO-Bottlenecks-Biggest-Threat-to-Data-Storage.htm

Clusters of Compute Nodes

A (computer) cluster refers to a group of servers and other resources that are connected through hardware, networks, and software to behave as if they were a single system.

Processors in clusters are more usually referred to as *nodes*, and there are always two or more nodes in a cluster. Clusters can be implemented in a variety of ways to cater for different requirements:

- Load balancing (LB)
- Performance

- High availability (HA)
- Parallel processing, mainly scientific high-performance computing (HPC)
- Systems management, easier on a cluster than on several separate systems

It is in the implementation that the desired functionality resides, and we are mainly interested in performance and load balancing in that such control over applications may be necessary to separate *warring factions*. For example, we might want to separate I/O-intensive applications from each other and similarly CPU-intensive ones.

Clusters allow different types of work—web, core business processes, and other processes, such as network functions—to share data that is normally a requisite for them all. A cluster setup allows this, as well as offering work separation as outlined above.

Cluster Architectures

Clusters are connected systems or nodes with software to make processing cooperative (Figure 4.15). There are four types (plus hybrids, of course):

- High availability, a cluster to eliminate single points of failure and give the ability of failover from one system to another in case of failure.
- Load balancing, clusters that route network service requests to multiple cluster nodes to balance the workload among the cluster nodes. Load balancing provides scalability in an incremental fashion.
- Storage, where a shared storage system exists for clusterwide access by the nodes.
- High performance, which allows parallel execution of work, usually with many low-cost nodes in the case of scientific computing. In the case of commercial work, it provides the opportunity to *borrow* power from other nodes when needed.

A similar lend–lease arrangement occurs in virtualized environments like the cloud.

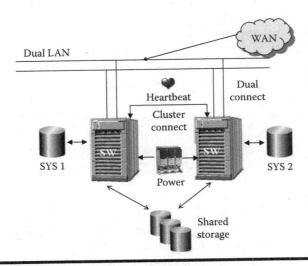

Figure 4.15 Basic commercial cluster configuration (two-node).

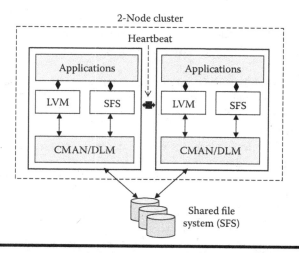

Figure 4.16   Cluster management software components. LVM, logical volume manager; CMAN, cluster manager; DLM, distributed lock manager.

Cluster Components

As we have said, the functionality of a cluster of nodes depends on its purpose, and that in turn depends on the *hardware configuration* and the *type of software* employed. There are obviously network connections also involved.

Hardware Components

- A network, here (Figure 4.16) shown as a wide area network (WAN), connecting users to the system
- A duplicated local area network (LAN) connecting the two processing systems (switches are not shown explicitly in the diagram)
- Dual-connection LAN to processors
- Two processors, each with its own *system* disks, but sharing *data disks*, which themselves may be RAID configured
- Power switch connecting power to both systems (processor and disk), which can be used to isolate a failing processor ("fencing")
- Dual connections (fiber channel [FC] or SCSI) to shared disks or storage area network (SAN)

Software Components

Cluster software includes a "heartbeat" for processors to monitor each other's "health," namely, "Are you still there, Charlie?" Cluster software can be given *life and death* decisions over which applications survive when, for example, two working systems are reduced to one by the failure of one or the other. There are also pieces of software to handle any contention issues that will arise when two or more system nodes try to access the same resources. A cluster manager keeps track of cluster quorum by monitoring the count of cluster nodes.

The software normally involved in a commercial database-based cluster is shown in Figure 4.16:

■ If more than half the nodes are active, the cluster has what is known as *quorum*. If half the nodes (or fewer) are active, the cluster does not have quorum, and all cluster activity is stopped. Cluster quorum prevents the occurrence of a "split-brain" condition, a situation where two instances of the same cluster are running. A split-brain condition would permit each cluster instance to access cluster resources, for example, data, without knowledge of the other cluster instance, resulting in corrupted cluster integrity.

■ Quorum is determined by communication of messages among cluster nodes via Ethernet. Optionally, quorum can be determined by a combination of communicating messages via Ethernet *and* through a quorum disk. For quorum via Ethernet, quorum consists of 50% of the node votes plus 1.

■ Lock management is a common cluster infrastructure service that provides a mechanism for other cluster infrastructure components to synchronize their access to shared resources. A distributed lock manager does what it says on the tin and runs in each cluster node; lock management is distributed across all the nodes in the cluster.

■ The usual operating system, middleware, and applications software.

A number of vendors offer clustering software for various operating systems, and you should consult their websites for individual details of clusters and their implementation:

■ HP ServiceGuard Solutions for HP-UX
■ IBM Power HA System Mirror for AIX
■ Oracle Solaris Cluster 4.1, Oracle Real Application Cluster (RAC)
■ Symantec Cluster Server (Veritas Cluster Server [VCS])
■ VMware High Availability 5.x
■ Sun Cluster
■ Microsoft Luster Server
■ Fujitsu Prime Cluster

Computer Cluster
http://en.wikipedia.org/wiki/Computer_cluster

Chapter 5

Networks

Networks are the glue that connects processors and users to each other in various configurations and, as such, form part of the performance chain of computer systems. A system is usually as slow as the slowest link in the chains that comprise it. In addition, increased workloads affect different links in the system to different extents.

For example, if an increase in transaction workload only has a marginal effect on processor response time, it does not mean it only has the same impact on the network. The effects of such increases depend on the characteristics on the link and its position on the queuing curve of response time or throughput versus utilization (Figure 1.2).

Factors Affecting Network Performance

Some network elements affecting performance, both beneficially and adversely, and which you should be aware of, are

- Network hardware (WANs, lines, LANs, Fiber Distributed Data Interface [FDDI], hubs, switches, etc.)
- *Lossy* transmission media where retries or retransmissions become frequent and affect overall latency
- Network design
- Network protocols (TCP/IP, Open System Interconnection [OSI], frame relay, asynchronous transfer mode [ATM], X.25, remote procedure call [RPC], messaging, program-to-program communication), security overheads, error rates, retries, and so on
- Acceleration tools and techniques
- Network software and architectures (OSI, Systems Network Architecture [SNA], DECnet, IPA, Novell)
- Emulated network protocols*
- Access architectures

---

* A file transfer via Digital Equipment Corporation (DEC) emulation of the IBM Systems Network Architecture (SNA) protocol I came across in the 1980s was so slow it is probably still running (May 2016).

- Classical "dumb" terminal-central server architectures
- Client/server architectures
- Internet or web application architectures
■ Distributed database (Relational Distributed Architecture [RDA], Distributed Relational Database Architecture [DRDA], two-phase commit)
■ Distributed online transaction processing (OLTP) (OSI distributed transaction processing [DTP], X/Open DTP)
■ Network traffic volumes and traffic prioritizing (shaping)
■ Any other additions to the network in the form of hardware or software

Network Performance Measures

These are the metrics that give an indication of how well the network and the links within it are performing.

■ Bandwidth—speed of transmission, usually in bits per second (bps)
■ Line or link utilization at various speeds
■ Throughput—frames, files, packets, blocks per second (or other unit, if time) achieved
■ Latency—delays at various points in the transmission
■ Jitter—variation in the time of receipt of a message, packet, and so forth, at its destination
■ Error rate—number of corrupted bits in the transmission, usually necessitating a retransmission if the sender is alerted of the error by a checksum or other redundancy bits
■ If using wire data (see the terminology in Appendix III) monitors, other metrics relevant to your installation and service level agreement (SLA)

For these measurements, you can use either tools native to the operating system or commercially available tools, but don't overbuy for unneeded functionality.

Some of these metrics depend to a great extent on the network protocols used and algorithms for facilitating transfer in times of stressed networks (congestion control). A detailed discussion of all these elements is beyond the scope of this book and, more importantly, beyond the knowledge of the author (once again), but suffice it to say they will have an impact on the performance of systems using them. The selection, design, and tuning of operating systems, OLTP, and database systems are subjects in themselves and have their own literature. However, measuring the physical resources they consume in a system is covered in this book, in a simplified, but rigorous way.

Documentation: There is an online course that looks very good and readable:

Network Performance and Evaluation
https://sites.google.com/site/netperfeval/

It consists of 48 parts plus slides and videos that complement these parts, but be selective; otherwise, you will suffer from network trauma.

Communications Architectures

Communications performance can be measured in three basic ways:

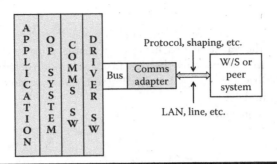

Figure 5.1   Elements affecting network performance.

- Overall end-to-end times for file transfer, transaction shipping, file access, and so on. This can include remote data access, for example, via Network File System (NFS), and remote process access, for example, using Network Computing System (NCS). This is the normal metric of interest to end users and service level agreements (SLAs).
- Speeds of individual elements of the system, for example, the number of frames per second that an X.25 adapter can support or raw line speeds.
- Latency of total time in transmission. I have something to say on this topic, so see Chapter 16 under the heading "Latency: An Examination." In that section I differentiate between the intrinsic speed of work in a network and additional time due to queuing and other delaying factors.

There are network benchmarks and network simulation to aid in sizing networks, but the old hand calculation with rough workload figures will not be amiss in assessing the rough accuracy of any esoteric output from such tools. These tools are covered in Chapter 8, not as recommendations, but setting out the available goods for you to choose from, based on organization needs (Figure 5.1).

Network Protocols

There are a number of ways of transmitting data across networks, both local and wide area, and some are better than others at transporting specific forms of data with specific delivery metrics in mind. Some of these protocols are in software, some in microcode, while others live in firmware units across networks.

Several of these protocols are outlined in Appendix V and, where possible, assigned optimum usage areas for them.

Network Performance

In this section, we examine the performance characteristics of networks, both wide area (WAN) and local area (LAN).

Network Performance Factors

In review, network performance depends on

- WAN or LAN speed (Mbps)
- Bandwidth, the maximum transmission rate, known as *throughput*
- Latency or time for the transit of a packet of data, that is, *response time*
- Other delays, including software overhead, transmission node delay, and so forth
- Transmission reliability, lossy or lossless, leading to retransmission overhead
- Jitter, the variation in delay times
- Data volumes and frequencies
- Frame or block sizes of data parcels
- Network protocol
- Intermediate nodes (systems)
- Other nodes—routers, boosters, switches, and so forth, and their protocol exchanges
- Buffer sizes throughout
- Design of the client/server applications and their *personal* interface protocol
- Security software and resulting performance overheads
- Ancillary services
- The use of "speedup" techniques, such as compression and WAN acceleration

> **WoW**: *Throughput* and *response time* are the key metrics around which all network design, tuning, and measurements revolve. Latency, wait times, queue lengths, and the rest mean nothing to end users; they need comprehensible numbers that are specified in their SLA.

It is impossible to develop a single, general formula for the transmission of data across any type of network. This is because LANs and WANs have different characteristics and may contain bridges, protocol converters, and so on. To treat networks to any sort of analysis, it is necessary to break them into components.

Latency

This is a fascinating name that always gets me on my pulpit. *Latency* in the English language means a hidden potential delay and not a fact of life. Latency applied to networks (and other resources) is often taken to be the mean time taken to do a transmission across a network, and not an overhead to be avoided. A definition in Wikipedia says the following about the word:

Latency (engineering), a measure of the time delay experienced by a system.

> **Note**: I am not saying that others are misleading us when they simplify latency; it is just that to understand exactly what latency comprises gives you a chance of solving network slowdowns. I will cover this topic in some detail in Chapter 16 under the heading "Latency: An Examination," where I break down what is traditionally called latency into more manageable pieces.

Networks to Be Examined

We will look at four main components:

- Lines and links
- Ethernet LANs
- Token Ring LANs
- Internet-based traffic

We will look at them in three basic architectures:

- Classical dumb terminal mode
- Client/server mode
- Internet or web mode

Classical Online System

Systems Network Architecture (SNA) was conceived by IBM in the 1970s and announced in September 1974. It basically defined a distributed architecture with intelligence outboard from the computer in the form of a programmable communications controller. The early communications controllers (370x) were hardwired systems, later replaced by the 3725 and 3745 programmable controllers running the Network Control Program (NCP).

There were other network architectures defined in the 1970s and 1980s, but in terms of configuration characteristics and having a functional layer composition, they are similar. An example is DEC's Distributed Network Architecture (DNA), which linked into the VMS/VAX architectures.

Classical Network: Parameters

Ts represents the service time for the messages traveling up and down the line. There is, however, an overhead on top of the raw data for transmission protocols and error correction code. This is estimated normally to be between 10% and 15% of the raw data. We will take 15% as the overhead, again for safety reasons. This means increasing the transmission time calculated for raw data by 1.15 (115%) (see Figure 5.2).

Using this 15% overhead factor, the service time for a single message pair becomes

$$Ts = (\text{transmission time}) \times 1.15$$

$$\text{Transmission time} = \frac{(\text{input msg size}) + (\text{output msg size})}{(\text{line speed})}$$

Arrival rate = A transactions per second

inmsg

outmsg

Service time Ts = (Transmission time) × 1.15
(This allows 15% data overhead for transmission protocols)

Then line utilization $\rho = A \times Ts$

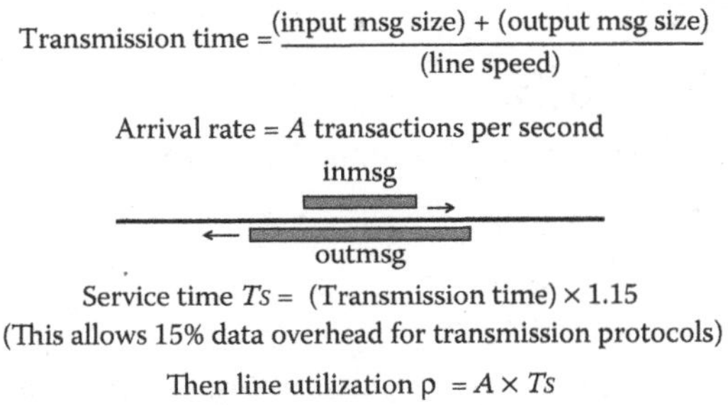

Figure 5.2   Classical SNA network transmission.

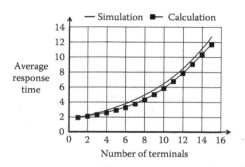

Figure 5.3   SNA network: response times vs. finite number of terminals.

If *A* is the arrival rate of transactions (customers), each taking time *Ts* to be processed, then the utilization of the link is given by

$$\rho = A \times Ts$$

The average line response time is

$$Ts_{line}/(1-\rho)$$

The average total response time is therefore shown by the line or connection response time equation:

$$Ts_{line} / (1-\rho) + \text{average time on host} \left(\text{CPU plus disk}\right) \tag{5.1}$$

Twenty-five years ago, this discussion would have ended here and moved on to the next topic. However, things have changed with the advent of client/server, big data, multiform data, the Internet, and cloud/virtualization.

The resulting response time versus number of terminals in the classical environment (some of which still exist) is shown in Figure 5.3, the results of which are courtesy of Mike Tanner, author of the book quoted below it.

The curve is for a finite number of terminals; that is, the population entering transactions into the system is finite (see Kendall–Lee notation in Appendix I).

It shows the classical rapid degradation of response time as more work is absorbed and the utilization of the system rises, following the traditional ever-upward path as the load increases (as given by the number of terminals).

Practical Queuing Analysis
Mike Tanner (McGraw Hill, ISBN 0-07-709078-0, 1995)

This book is a useful adjunct to the queuing theory in Appendix I, and it will take the reader much further into the topic.

Client/Server Operation

The arrival of intelligent workstations, the antithesis of dumb terminals, heralded a change in the way IT work was carried out and presented various options as to where sections of the application and communications hierarchies resided. Typically, a PC or workstation sitting on a person's desk would communicate with a server (local or remote) and work cooperatively with it. The split of work between client and server depended on what model was adopted, from minimum work on the client (thin client) and most work on the server through to a fat client and a slimmer server.

Client/server (CS) computing is now a dated term that has largely been replaced by *distributed* or *network* computing. The term might be outdated, but CS architectures are still important today. In the 1980s, it was made possible by new networking architectures and implementations, computer hardware developments, and support software. Client/server middleware was developed to make the architectural models of this mode of operation practical.

The cornerstones of the development of client/server computing were

- Remote procedure calls
- Remote database access
- Distributed transaction processing
- Message queuing for asynchronous work

This model gradually evolved into the more flexible distributed processing we see today and eventually into the world of the cloud, where the end user does not have a mental picture of the systems he or she is using.

Ethernet LAN Operation

Ethernet, or carrier sense multiple access/collision detect (CSMA/CD), is a type of local area network (LAN) devised by Robert Metcalf when at Xerox Research Park.* It employs a contention protocol to regulate message access to the physical medium, which can be coaxial cable or fiber-optic cable. Each station on the Ethernet is allowed to send a message to another station or computer at any time.

As with people in a conversation where two of them speak at the same time, two or more stations may send a message and cause a collision on the LAN medium. As in the case of the conversation, the stations wait for a random time before resending the message.

It is these collisions that limit the effective data rate of an Ethernet. In Figure 5.4, station A is seen sending a message to Z, which tries to send a message while the message from A is propagated down the medium. These collisions are handled via a *collision detect* mechanism.

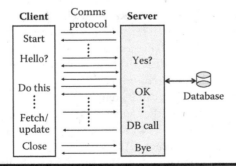

Figure 5.4   Client/server interaction example: Oracle.

---

* Where, incidentally, most of the graphical user interface (GUI) stuff used on Windows and elsewhere was pioneered.

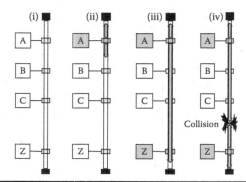

Figure 5.5 Ethernet network operation.

When stations detect a collision, they cease transmission, wait a random period of time, and attempt to transmit when they again detect silence on the medium.

Hopefully, this time the transmission will succeed.

Practical Queuing Analysis
Mike Tanner (McGraw Hill, ISBN 0-07-709078-0, 1995)

Collision Detect
http://computer.howstuffworks.com/Ethernet8.htm

The shaded stations in Figure 5.5 are the ones attempting to transmit a message or other communication, cases ii–iv.

The random pause time and transmission retry is an important part of the Ethernet protocol. If two stations (A and Z in the figure) collide when simultaneously transmitting, then both will need to transmit again using the same protocol, but hopefully at different (random) times so that a collision is avoided.

Token Ring LAN Operation

Token Ring (TR) is another form of local area network (LAN), but unlike Ethernet, it uses an orderly, collision-averse protocol based on a *token* that circulates around the LAN. Token Ring was initially defined by IBM at its research facility in Zurich, Switzerland, in the early 1980s, and they pursued standardization of Token Ring under the 802.5 Working Group of the Institute of Electrical and Electronic Engineers (IEEE). The first implementation of TR was at 4 MB/s, eventually reaching 16 MB/s, 100 MB/s, and counting.

As the token passes round the ring, it can be removed from circulation by a station that wishes to send data to another. The sending station appends the destination address to the message and sends it out on the ring. No other station can send data until it has possession of the token. This avoids the collisions that occur on Ethernet LANs.

The TR therefore apparently had an edge over Ethernet since its orderly operation allowed it to run at about 70% utilization (or higher) without significant degradation due to queuing effects, whereas Ethernet saturated at much lower utilizations, typically 40% in the early days. This defect becomes less serious as transmission speeds increase and maximum sensible utilization goes with it.

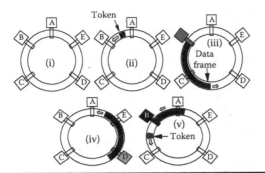

Figure 5.6   Token Ring network operation.

This has not prevented Ethernet from becoming a *de facto* standard for local area networks.

With the development of switched Ethernet and faster variants of Ethernet, Token Ring architectures lagged behind Ethernet, and the higher sales of Ethernet allowed economies of scale that drove down prices further, and added a compelling price advantage. The hardware around the Token Ring LANs was also more complicated than that involved in Ethernet operation (Figure 5.6).

See Tanner (pp. 339–341) for a more detailed description of the process, as well as

Lesson4: Token Ring
http://pluto.ksi.edu/~cyh/cis370/ebook/ch03e.htm

For a comprehensive look at *high-performance networks*, see one of the detailed papers from the University of Wisconsin, several of which are cited in the link below.

Leaky and Token Buckets
http://www.slideshare.net/UmeshGupta3/leaky-bucket-algorithm

Network Transmission Management

Data Compression

Data compression, which we have seen earlier, is simply a means of condensing data to be transmitted over a network link and uncompressing it at the destination. The reason is to minimize the bandwidth taken by the data, and thus allowing greater numbers of packets to be transmitted without causing high utilizations, which cause queuing and hence delays. It also arrives faster.

Compression and decompression can be achieved by either hardware or software, with the former method offloading work from the processors involved. The latter method of compression, software, can be of two types: CPU intensive or memory intensive.

The measure of compression success is the compression ratio, which is the size of the uncompressed data stream divided by the size of the compressed one. There are algorithms for compression, among them stacker (CPU-intensive) and predictor (memory-intensive) compression, and also vendor algorithms such as Cisco's IOS data compression. These are covered in the first reference below. Compression ratios vary, but 3 or 4:1 is an achievable goal, according to the literature.

Understanding Data Compression [Cisco]

http://www.cisco.com/c/en/us/support/docs/wan/data-compression/14156-compress-overview.html

The next reference outlines the difference between *packet* and *session* compression and then goes on to discuss the details of Heap's law and Zipf's law* used in these algorithms. The article contains good illustrative diagrams where appropriate and offers a PDF download of the material for clear printing.

Understanding Advanced Data Compression [white paper]

https://f5.com/resources/white-papers/understanding- advanced-data-compression

There are other terms you may come across in considering the compression option for data transmission, such as *lossy* and *lossless* transmission, *spatial* and *wavelet* compression, and quite a few others to be studied by you on a *need-to-know* basis.

Data Compression

http://www.webopedia.com/TERM/D/data_compression.html

Network Traffic Control

Much of the control of data flow in networks is based on *algorithms* that employ real-time data on an active network. These are some of them:

- Error detection and correction, for example, checksum, cyclic redundancy check (CRC)
- Medium access control, for example, carrier sense multiple access/collision detect (CSMA/CD), Token Ring, and carrier sense multiple access/collision avoidance (CSMA/CA)
- Routing, for example, shortest-path algorithms of Dijkstra, and Bellman and Ford[†]
- Scheduling, for example, first in, first out (FIFO), round-robin, and priority queues
- Congestion control, for example, Transmission Control Protocol (TCP) window control and multimedia rate control
- Traffic shaping, another form of transmission priority for network traffic
- Packet filtering, for example, firewalls
- Overlay network, for example, virtual private networks (VPNs)[‡]

Error Detection and Correction

There are various reasons why data in transmission may be subject to errors, for example, cross talk or noise on a line. Errors vary from single-bit errors through to double-bit errors and then to burst errors, where a series of bits is altered. Sometimes this may not be a big issue for some data, like video and music, although the quality may suffer. Business data is a different matter and steps needed to be taken to remedy any such errors. The steps needed are obviously

---

* You will need to refer to the white paper for a discussion of these intricacies, hence the white paper name "Advanced."

† See http://www.quora.com/How-do-Bellman-Ford-Algorithm-and-Dijkstras-algorithm-work-differently-in-routing-protocols.

‡ "How VPNs Work," http://computer.howstuffworks.com/vpn.htm.

- Error detection, the minimum requirement even if correction is not possible, so that retransmission can be invoked
- Error correction where possible

Detection of errors in transmitted frames (the unit of transmission, sometimes called a *packet*) is achieved by means of *parity checks* and *cyclic redundancy checks* (CRCs). This involves sending extra bits along with the base data (payload) to check that the data received is the same as the data sent, and if the check fails, a retransmission is requested, as something has been dropped along the way.

Parity Check: The sending agent adds a single bit to each byte or frame to indicate the number of 1s even. This is a 0 for even parity. If this is not found to be the case at the other end, then an error has occurred. The error might be a flipped bit in the data or the parity bit has flipped. In either case, the error is detected by the bit count.

Cyclic Redundancy Check (CRC): This involves some math involving an algorithm similar to that used for check digits with a sum being done and a remainder appended to the data. If this exercise is repeated at the receiving end and does not tally with the sent data, an error is detected.

Correction of errors is normally done in one of two ways:

- Backward error correction, where the receiver requests a retransmission of the frame (or other data unit) by the sender. The overhead of backward error correction depends on how frequently it is needed, and that depends to a large extent on the reliability of the transmitting medium.

    This overhead is added to any latency already being felt and will decrease the data transmission rate for such work or increase the response time for OLTP-like activity.
- Forward error correction (FEC), where error correction code is employed when an error is detected. Redundant bits are added to the frames in such a fashion that the receiver can reconstruct the erroneous frame without a retransmission, essentially an *in-flight* correction.

For information on FEC see

Definition: What Does Forward Error Correction (FEC) *Mean?*
http://www.techopedia.com/definition/824/forward-error-correction-fec

Routing Control

A router is a store and forward unit that can connect to multiple networks and other routers, and its job is to get the data frames to their destination based on certain criteria. For example, a router might sit on the edge of an Ethernet network to forward the traffic from users on that network to the appropriate destination.

There are various types of routing:

- *Unicast routing*, where the destination is specified already.
- *Broadcast routing* is a unicast routing, but sent to all possible connected destinations.
- *Multicast routing* is similar to broadcast routing, but only routes work to destinations that want it. The router must be aware of these destination nodes.
- *Anycast routing*, where multiple nodes have the same logical address and the routing is done using a Domain Name System (DNS) server, which provides the IP address.

Within each of the routing types described here, there are a number of routing protocols, and these can affect transmission performance. See the references below for a deeper introduction and a more detailed exposition of routing.

Routing and IP Gateways
http://www.linux-tutorial.info/modules.php?name= MContent&pageid=146
  A lot of useful and digestible detail on the topic of routing can be found at this tutorial site.

DCN: Network Layer Routing
http://www.tutorialspoint.com/data_communication_computer_network/network_layer_routing.htm
  Guru and Black Belt References: There also exist algorithms used for aiding routing:

- *Dijkstra's Algorithm*
  http://math.mit.edu/~rothvoss/18.304.3PM/Presentations/ 1-Melissa.pdf
- *Bellman–Ford Algorithm*
  http://en.wikipedia.org/wiki/Bellman%E2%80% 93Ford_algorithm
- *Floyd–Warshall Algorithm*
  http://en.wikipedia.org/wiki/Floyd%E2%80% 93Warshall_algorithm

  Routers use *routing algorithms* to find the best route to a destination. The *best route* involves parameters like the number of *hops* (the trip a packet or frame takes from one router or intermediate point to another in the network), time delay, and communication cost of packet transmission. They clearly can impact performance.

How Routing Algorithms Work
http://computer.howstuffworks.com/routing-algorithm.htm

More on Routing

Routing algorithms can be classified according to the following different metrics:*

- *Adaptive routing*: The state of the network is incorporated in making the routing decision to adapt to network state, such as network congestion.
- *Oblivious routing*: No network information is used in making the routing decision.
- *Minimal routing*: Minimal number of hop count between source and destination is traversed. Depending on the network topology, there might be multiple minimal paths.
- *Nonminimal routing*: The number of hop counts traversed en route to the destination node exceeds the minimal hop count. *Nonminimal routing* increases path diversity and can improve network throughput.
- *Source routing*: The routing path is determined at the source and the *path computation* only needs to be done once for each packet, like Multiprotocol Label Switching (MPLS).
- *Per-hop routing*: At each hop en route to the destination, the packet goes through routing computation to determine the next productive hop.

---

* See Dennis Abts and John Kim, *High Performance Datacenter Networks: Architectures, Algorithms, and Opportunities* (cited elsewhere), http://bnrg.cs.berkeley.edu/~randy/Courses/CS294.S13/ 2.2.pdf.

Congestion Control

Network congestion is similar to traffic congestion and occurs when a link or node is carrying so much data that its quality of service (QoS) deteriorates. The service baseline is that derived from the service level agreement (SLA) translated into network terms that can be related to the carrier protocol, usually TCP/IP.

Typical effects include queuing delay, packet loss, or the blocking of new connections. A consequence of the latter two effects is that an incremental increase in offered load leads either only to a small increase in network throughput or to an actual reduction in network throughput. This will show in the typical "cliff edge" curve for transaction response and the drop-off in data throughput for data transfer. This becomes a performance issue.

Control of congestion involves regulating the data flow into the network to prevent what is known as *congestive collapse* by preventing the overload of network media and nodes between sender and receivers. Methods of avoiding this collapse include

- Network scheduler—a program in routers to do active queue management (i.e., the arbitrary reorder or drop of network packets under overload)
- Explicit congestion notification—an extension to the IP and TCP communications protocol, which adds a flow control mechanism upon which both ends react appropriately
- TCP congestion avoidance algorithm—several implementations of efforts to deal with network congestion
- *Avoiding* work that requires network transfer from entering the sender node until the congestion eases due to these other methods

The basic message here is that *congestion = overutilization of resources = delays*, which is bad news, particularly for online transaction processing (OLTP). This type of issue occurs on a huge scale with distributed denial-of-service (DDoS) attacks, which is their main purpose in life.

Congestion Control Mechanisms
http://www.linktionary.com/c/congestion.html

Bulk Data Transfers

This is a separate topic but of interest to many organizations. There is a large presentation on this topic, covering TCP issues (including performance), TCP parallel streams, bulk data transfer tools (including GridFTP and bbftp), network management tools, and new TCP stacks.

The network management tools covered we would call *native* tools since there are no commercial tools covered.

Bulk Data Transfer Techniques for High-Speed Wide-Area Networks
https://fasterdata.es.net/assets/fasterdata/Tierney-bulk-data-transfer-tutorial-Sept09.pdf

Traffic Shaping

Sometimes in cases of high volumes of traffic, it is necessary to apportion available network resources according to some control or regulatory mechanisms. This is rather like vehicle traffic where the traffic policeman controls traffic flow in such a way that traffic to and from different directions flows equitably. In some cases, it is necessary to assign priorities of one form of traffic, for instance, emergency vehicles—ambulance, fire, and police. In such controlled circumstances, the usual calculations of throughput or response time will be modified in the light of the controls in force.

> Traffic shaping (also known as "packet shaping") is the control of computer network traffic in order to optimize or guarantee performance, lower latency, and/or increase usable bandwidth by delaying packets that meet certain criteria. More specifically, traffic shaping is any action on a set of packets (often called a stream or a flow) which imposes additional delay on those packets such that they conform to some predetermined constraint (a contract or traffic profile). (Wikipedia)

Since one can't control the speed of the transmitting medium, it is necessary to control or buffer the traffic trying to enter the transmitting mechanism. The paragraphs below are a good introduction to the topic before diving headfirst into the other references, most of which are for networking *black belts* only.

Traffic shaping works by measuring and queuing IP packets, in transit, with respect to a number of configurable parameters. Differentiated rate limits and traffic guarantees based on source, destination, and protocol parameters can be created, much the same way firewall rules are implemented. Traffic shaping works by

- Applying bandwidth limits by queuing packets that would exceed configured limits, and sending them later when the momentary demand for bandwidth is lower.
- Dropping packets if the packet buffers are full. The packet to be dropped should be chosen from those that are responsible for the "jam."
- Prioritizing traffic according to the administrator's choice; if the traffic in a higher-priority increases while a communications line is full, traffic in lower priorities should be temporarily limited to make room for the high-priority traffic.
- Providing bandwidth guarantees. This is typically accomplished by treating a certain amount of traffic (the guaranteed amount) as a higher priority, and traffic exceeding the guarantee as the same priority as "any other traffic," which then gets to compete with the rest of the nonprioritized traffic.

Well-built traffic shapers do not normally work by queuing up immense amounts of data and then sorting out prioritized traffic to send before sending nonprioritized traffic. Rather, they attempt to measure the amount of prioritized traffic and then limit the nonprioritized traffic dynamically so that it won't interfere with the throughput of prioritized traffic.

Traffic Shaping Guide (and references within the document)
https://doc.pfsense.org/index.php/Traffic_Shaping_Guide

Network Monitoring

See Chapter 8 for a discussion of this element of network management.

Network Performance Article Series

There is a series of nine (I–IX) articles on network performance in an application performance context that are quite amazing in their coverage. They are quite advanced, but for the nonguru picking his or her way through them will be very instructive. You may also learn a lot from the *comments* on these articles by erudite readers.

Understanding Application Performance on the Network—Part I: A Foundation for Network Triage
http://apmblog.dynatrace.com/2014/06/10/understanding-application-performance-on-the-network-part-i-a-foundation-for-network-triage/

Understanding Application Performance on the Network—Part II: Bandwidth and Congestion
http://apmblog.dynatrace.com/2014/06/19/understanding-application-performance-on-the-network-bandwidth-and-congestion/

Understanding Application Performance on the Network—Part III: TCP Slow-Start
http://apmblog.dynatrace.com/2014/06/26/understanding-application-performance-on-the-network-tcp-slow-start/

Understanding Application Performance on the Network—Part IV: Packet Loss
http://apmblog.dynatrace.com/2014/07/03/understanding-application-performance-on-the-network-packet-loss/

Understanding Application Performance on the Network—Part V: Processing Delays
http://apmblog.dynatrace.com/2014/07/10/understanding-application-performance-on-the-network-processing-delays/

Understanding Application Performance on the Network—Part VI: The Nagle Algorithm
http://apmblog.dynatrace.com/2014/07/24/understanding-application-performance-on-the-network-the-nagle-algorithm/

Understanding Application Performance on the Network—Part VII: TCP Window Size
http://apmblog.dynatrace.com/2014/08/12/understanding-application-performance-network-part-tcp-window-size/

Understanding Application Performance on the Network—Part VIII: Chattiness and Application Windowing
http://apmblog.dynatrace.com/2014/08/21/understanding-application-performance-on-the-network-chattiness-application-windowing/

Understanding Application Performance on the Network—Part IX: Conclusion
http://apmblog.dynatrace.com/2014/09/05/understanding-application-performance-on-the-network-conclusion/

You may now stand at ease.

Web-Based Applications

Why should we be worried about the details of website performance since it's really about function and *gee whiz* impressions? There are a number of reasons, but one comes to the fore when a business relies totally or significantly on business coming though a website. Studies of people accessing websites have demonstrated that clients have a very limited patience when accessing one and will either abandon their mission or switch to another, possibly competing, website. This equates to not only loss of business, but a possible boost in a competitor's sales.

I am a recognized authority on unusable and irritating websites that are, for all intents and purposes, "down" because they are not delivering the response times they were designed for and possibly divert me to other sites to transact my business.

> See the section headed "Poor Web Performance: Consequences" later on in this chapter.

Monitoring performance and user experience at the sharp end of things should be mandatory for *designers* and *operators* of websites. Marketing people too have a major part to play in this as well, although you may have to advise them of the facts above since they are unlikely to have read this book.

Wide Area Networks

Wide area networks (WANs) are the links between IT systems that are too far apart to be serviced by the faster local area networks (LANs). They come in several shapes and sizes and were developed over time as the requirements placed on such networks grew in size and variety. Today, networks are expected to carry data, video, and voice, which was never in the plan when networks were originally designed.

Early networks concentrated on delivering data accurately, hence the development of error correction codes* and retransmission protocols to bypass the error-prone nature of earlier transmission media. Incidentally, some of these techniques have been applied to error detection and correction in storage, for example, in redundant array of independent disks (RAID).

A more detailed discussion of some of the WAN protocols used today and some of their performance characteristics can be found in Appendix V.

WAN Introduction

The ability to link one computer network with another is often desirable, especially for businesses that operate a number of facilities. A WAN is a communications network that makes use of existing technology to connect local computer networks into a larger operating network that may cover both national and international locations. This is in contrast to both the LAN and the metropolitan area network (MAN), which provides communication within a restricted geographic area because of issues with data transmission over large distances. The concept of a WAN was developed prior to the birth of the Internet and was employed for normal business work.

Linking one computer network with another is often desirable for businesses that operate a number of facilities. Beginning with the local area network and going up to the wide area network, this is most easily accomplished by using existing telephony technology. It is also vital to disaster

---

* Cyclic redundancy checks (CRCs) and longitudinal redundancy checks (LRCs).

recovery (DR) activity—sending backup material to a remote secondary server and the recovery of the primary by retrieving data from this secondary (DR) site fast enough to meet recovery time and other criteria set up by the business in an SLA.

WAN Design

WAN design is a specialist job, but some basic points need to be addressed and understood by others involved in performance and availability of the system:

- Involvement of business people: their requirements dictate all
- Business volumes and the resulting transmission traffic
- Peaks and peak-to-average ratios
- Growth patterns and possible exceptional workloads
- Possible use of design and simulation tools
- Switching technologies to use—circuit, packet, cell
- Routers to optimize the technologies chosen
- Which protocols to use and where
- Evaluation of monitoring tools for the final design
- Bandwidth optimization and acceleration
- An eye to growth, especially Internet and intranet, voice, video, and *big data* transmission
- Availability and reliability considerations
- Security considerations and their possible effect on performance
- Remote working considerations (bring your own device [BYOD])
- Costs incurred and support skills needed
- Consideration of outsourcing

See the Cisco WAN design paper:
http://www.ciscopress.com/articles/article.asp?p=25259& seqNum=3
Also see

WAN Design: What to Consider
http://searchenterprisewan.techtarget.com/tip/WAN- design-What-to-consider

WAN Acceleration

It is often thought that the limiting factor in speed of network transmission is the bandwidth of the medium involved, but this is not strictly true. There are techniques for getting better performance from WANs, often by biasing data transmission priorities toward more important business processes. Having designed the WAN network and its components, is that it? Not really, since there are tricks you can employ to enhance performance, but that is a bonus, not a panacea for poor design.

WAN Speedup

These techniques usually go under the title "WAN Acceleration" or "WAN Optimization." The normal definition is the optimization of available bandwidth through the following techniques:

Table 5.1 WAN Optimization (Speedup) Techniques

Layer	Optimization Areas	Comment
Application	Application optimization	Careful control of how and when data is transmitted elsewhere
Layers 7 and 6	Deduplication, data compression, caching	Deduplication is often used in backup/disaster recovery (see tricks of the optimization trade listed in the "WAN Speedup" section)
Transport	TCP and appropriate protocol optimization	Adjusting the network congestion avoidance parameters of TCP connections over high-bandwidth, high-latency networks
Network layer	Route optimization, forward error correction (FEC)	See tricks of the optimization trade listed in the "WAN Speedup" section
Data link layer	Header compression	See tricks of the optimization trade listed in the "WAN Speedup" section

- Don't send what you don't need to send, especially large files.
- If it must be sent, try to schedule it appropriately so as not to interfere with critical workloads. Use business prioritization as the decision yardstick.
- Use techniques to optimize use of the available bandwidth (discussed below).

Some of the tricks of the optimization trade are (see reference 6 in the "WAN Optimization References" section below) as follows and shown in Table 5.1:

1. *Caching*: This is the storage of data transmitted from a source to a destination at that destination. If the same data is requested at the destination, the optimization software recognizes this and stops any request to the original source for a retransmission.
2. *Deduplication*: "Data deduplication is the replacement of multiple copies of data (at various levels of granularity) with references to a shared copy in order to save storage space and/or bandwidth" (Storage Networking Industry Association [SNIA] definition). Data deduplication can operate at the *file*, *block*, or *bit* level.
3. *Compression*: This is fairly obvious and the data transmission is reduced by an amount dictated by the efficiency of the data compression or decompression algorithms used.
4. *Forward error correction*: A "receiver makes it right" transmission technique where extra bits are added to a packet or message for analysis at the receiving end. In general, it means that the receiving end of the transmission is able to detect, and in most cases correct, any erroneous transmissions.
   Packets warranting retransmission may be
   a. Corrupted due to errors, for example, noise
   b. Lost in link or host failures
   c. Dropped due to buffer overflow

    d.   Dropped due to aging or *sell-by date* exceeded, for example, the time-to-live (TTL) field in the Internet Protocol (IP)

5. *Traffic shaping*: Traffic shaping is the practice of regulating network data transfer to ensure a certain level of performance or quality of service (QoS). The practice involves favoring transmission of data from higher-priority applications over lesser ones, as designated by the business organization. It is sometimes called *packet shaping*.

6. *Congestion control*: This TCP function is designed to stop the sender from shipping more data than the network can handle, as if trying to drink from a fire hose. TCP uses a number of mechanisms based on a parameter called the *congestion window*.

7. *Protocol acceleration*: A class of techniques for improving application performance by avoiding or circumventing shortcomings of various protocols. There are several forms of protocol acceleration:

    a.   TCP acceleration

    b.   Common Internet File System (CIFS) and Network File System (NFS) acceleration

    c.   Hypertext Transfer Protocol (HTTP) acceleration

    d.   Microsoft Exchange acceleration

    See references 5 and 9 in the "WAN Optimization References" section below, which present good coverage of some of the factors listed above.

8. *Choose* your transmission protocol according to what you are transmitting—some protocols are better than others at transmitting certain types of data. This will also dictate the expected loss (and hence retransmission) rate.

9. Take advice from outside if you aren't sure what you are doing.

WAN Optimization References

There are a number of useful references on this topic. I found all the following ones useful in various areas as well as being quite easy to follow. I have therefore decided to list them all and let the network experts among you choose your favorite.*

1. *WAN Optimization Part 1: TCP Limitations*
   http://www.networkcomputing.com/wan-optimization-part-1-tcp-limitations/d/d-id/1234136?

2. *WAN Optimization Part 2: Put Performance Second*
   http://www.networkcomputing.com/applications/wan-optimization-part-2-put-performance-second/d/d-id/1234216?

3. *WAN Optimization Part 3: Overcoming Bandwidth Limitations*
   http://www.networkcomputing.com/applications/wan-optimization-part-3-overcoming-bandwidth-limitations/d/d-id/1234240?

4. *Technology Primer: Protocol Optimization*
   https://www.bluecoat.com/sites/default/files/documents/files/Protocol_Optimization.0.pdf

5. Part of *2012 Application & Service Delivery Handbook* [Webtorials]
   https://www.bluecoat.com/sites/default/files/analyst-reports/documents/2012%20Handbook%20-%20Bluecoat.pdf

---

* You may want to employ here Hilaire Belloc's philosophy about the Ten Commandments: "Candidates should not attempt more than six of these."

6. *The 2014 Application & Service Delivery Handbook Part 1: Introduction and Challenges*
   http://www.ashtonmetzler.com/2014_Handbook-Part_1.pdf
   [Search "Application and Service Delivery Handbook" to find versions from 2011, 2012, and 2013. Add the search term *webtorials* if the hit list is too large.]
7. *The Definitive Guide to Cloud Acceleration*
   http://www.realtimepublishers.com/book?id=219
8. *WAN Optimization as a Service*
   http://www.aryaka.com/products/wan-solutions/
9. *WAN Optimization as-a-Service: The New WAN, Simplified: Optimization for On-Premise and Cloud Applications*
   http://info.aryaka.com/rs/aryaka/images/Aryaka-The-New-WAN-Simplified-WP.pdf?mkt_tok=3RkMMJWWfF9wsRoivqjNZKXonjHpfsX57ukvUae11MI%2F0ER3fOvrPUfGjI4DScFmI%2BSLDwEYGJlv6SgFTrfCMbdu1rgFWBc%3D
   http://info.aryaka.com/rs/aryaka/images/Aryaka_WAN-Optimization-as-a-Service-DS.pdf?mkt_tok=3RkMMJWWfF9wsRojs63KZKXonjHpfsXw6OovUKeg38431UFwdcjKPmjr1YAESsF0aPyQAgobGp5I5FEMTbfYS65st60OXQ%3D%3D [July 5, 2015]

[The Aryaka reference dated July 5, 2015, contains a useful consolidated list of features assisting WAN transmissions.]

10. *An Introduction to IP Header Compression*
    http://www.effnet.com/pdf/uk/Whitepaper_Header_Compression.pdf
    [Effnet specialize in header compression and not general WAN Optimization].
11. *Bandwidth Management Techniques—Tips and Actions*
    https://www.techsoupforlibraries.org/planning-for-success/networking-and-security/tools/bandwidth-management-techniques-tips-and-actions
    Reference 11 discusses in *layman's terms* many of the speedup techniques we have covered above.

WAN Optimization Vendors*

Aryaka: http://www.aryaka.com/. Aryaka's WAN optimization as a service (WOaaS) with a core network platform built using redundant private links across a series of globally distributed 25 points of presence (POPs). These aim to cover 90% of the world's enterprise users.

Silver Peak: http://www.silver-peak.com/. Users can deploy Silver Peak as a virtual machine or physical appliance. The company offers the only multigigabit virtual WAN optimization solution, and runs on every major hypervisor.

Ipanema Technologies: http://www.ipanematech.com/en/. Ipanema is a global, automated system that employs various features to achieve the best application performance over the WAN. This encompasses application visibility, application control, WAN optimization, dynamic WAN selection, and network rightsizing.

---

* Source: http://www.enterprisestorageforum.com/san-nas-storage/wan-optimization-buying-guide.html (December 2014). This is a selection of vendors and does not constitute approval of, or recommendation for, the products listed.

Riverbed:* http://www.riverbed.com/. Riverbed Technology offers Riverbed SteelHead and Riverbed SteelCentral AppResponse products. The basic concept is to provide optimization for any app, visibility from the data center to the cloud, and simplified control across hybrid networks with network path selection capabilities that make it easy to group applications via policy.

Fortinet: http://www.fortinet.com/. Fortinet is a major player in the security marketplace but is also becoming a growing presence in WAN optimization. Its tool allows you to improve WAN performance and more intelligently manage bandwidth. It does this in such a way that data center storage and client devices use far less bandwidth by applying compression algorithm, data caching, and other techniques to reduce the transmission of data.

WAN Optimization: Aberdeen Magic Quadrant

An Aberdeen Magic Quadrant report for WAN optimization vendors, dated March 2015, lists the following vendors in it (and four others):

- Riverbed
- Cisco
- Silver Peak
- Citrix
- Blue Coat Systems
- Ipanema Technologies
- NTT Communications
- Exinda
- Aryaka

Enterprise and Science Networks

The link below is a detailed presentation, looking at the WAN (and LAN) requirements of networks carrying science traffic and those used for enterprise (business) computing. The conclusion, with reasons given, is *don't mix them*. Connect them yes, but don't have the different traffic types sharing network resource. There are several explanatory diagrams to illustrate the possible configurations to achieve this aim.

Network Architecture for High Performance
http://www.internet2.edu/presentations/jt2009jul/ 20090721-metzger03.pdf

Web Performance

The performance offered by a website is partly dictated by WAN speed and latency, but to a great extent by the design of the site, its constituent pages, and other factors unknown in the classical mainframe (legacy) era. The reference below gives some figures (and source) for the typical composition of a web page as retrieved by a user and shown here.

---

* Acquired by Thoma Bravo, December 2014.

- Images + Javascript 77%
- Other, flash, HTML, and cascading style sheet (CSS)   23%

You can see immediately the impact of images, and this is made clear in subsequent information and links to Radware and others in discussing web access optimization.

Measuring Web Performance [Dave Olsen on SlideShare]
http://www.slideshare.net/dmolsenwvu/measuring-web- performance-18921979
   Another paper discusses the use of queuing models in the analysis of web server performance. In particular, they use an equation for queue response time involving the following key parameters, which they expand upon in some detail:

- Network arrival rate
- Average file size
- Buffer size
- Initialization time
- Static server time
- Dynamic server rate
- Server network bandwidth
- Client network bandwidth

The authors draw some conclusions about the "upper bound on the server capacity of web servers." The paper is quite detailed and probably for black belts and gurus in the main.

Using a Queuing Model to Analyze the Performance of Web Servers
http://iomelt.com/capacitricks/file/2011/11/7923431-10.1.1.19.3667.pdf
   Another web server performance paper, which lists the same parameters as above, is:

A Model of Web Server Performance
http://www.lchr.org/a/18/pv/webmodel.pdf

On careful consideration, these last two papers seem identical. Over to you.

Web Performance Working Group

The World Wide Web Consortium (W3C) is an international community where member organizations, a full-time staff, and the public work together to develop web standards. Led by web inventor Tim Berners-Lee and CEO Jeffrey Jaffe, W3C's mission is to lead the web to its full potential. A list of current (December 2014) activities follows:

   W3C Standards: "W3C develops these technical specifications and guidelines through a process designed to maximize consensus about the content of a technical report, to ensure high technical and editorial quality, and to earn endorsement by W3C and the broader community."

- Web design and applications: Web design and applications involve the standards for building and rendering web pages, including HTML, CSS, SVG, AJAX, and other technologies for web applications.

■ Web architecture: Web architecture focuses on the foundation technologies and principles that sustain the web, including URIs and HTTP.

■ Semantic web: W3C is helping to build a technology stack to support a *web of data*, the sort of data found in databases.

■ XML technology: XML technologies including Extensible Markup Language (XML), XML namespaces, XML schema, XSLT, Efficient XML Interchange (EXI), and other related standards.

■ Web of Services: Web of Services refers to message-based design frequently found on the web and in enterprise software. The Web of Services is based on technologies such as HTTP, XML, SOAP, WSDL, and SPARQL.

■ Web of Devices: W3C is focusing on technologies to enable web access anywhere, anytime, using any device. This includes web access from mobile phones and other mobile devices, as well as use of web technology in consumer electronics, printers, interactive television, and even automobiles.

■ Browsers and authoring tools: The web's usefulness and growth depends on its universality. W3C facilitates this listening and blending via international web standards. These standards ensure that all the crazy brilliance continues to improve a web that is open to us all.

W3C Standards
http://www.w3.org/standards/
W3C and Performance: The Web Performance Group is a subgroup of W3C. The areas and standards they work on are sketched out below.

Web Performance Group Publications
http://www.w3.org/wiki/Web_Performance/Publications

Website Access Flow and Bottlenecks

There is an estimate that one-third of the planet's population has online access to IT systems with the estimated growth patterns (Cisco) shown in Table 5.2.

This was not the case in the old days when the organization had essentially complete control over the network and the parameters relating to it. Let us take a brief look at the reasons for delays, using Figure 5.7 as a guide.

The delay (latency) areas in a web service are often classified thus:

■ The *last-mile* problem, a phrase used in telecommunications to describe the technologies and processes used to connect the end customer to a communications network. The last mile is thus called because the end link between consumers and connectivity has proved to

Table 5.2 IP Traffic Growth: 2010–2015

IP Traffic[a]	2010	2011	2012	2013	2014	2015	Growth Rate
Internet	14,995	20,650	27,434	35,879	46,290	59,354	32%
Managed IP	4,989	6,839	9,014	11,352	13,189	14,848	24%
Mobile data	237	546	1,163	2,198	3,806	62,654	92%

[a] Petabytes per month. In the world of websites and Internet, some factors are within an organization's control, and others are not.

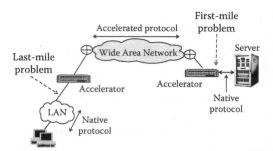

Figure 5.7 Internet problem and acceleration points.

be disproportionately expensive to solve. Anyone using the Internet with normal telephone lines will often fail to see why his upload or download is slower than his neighbor's (as mine is). The neighbor has probably installed high-speed fiber via his or her Internet service provider (ISP).

■ The *first-mile* problem arises on the website's connection to the Internet and is usually due to bandwidth limitation (see Figure 5.7).

Another type of Internet bottleneck can occur at the interconnection points between independent networks, usually where the network provider has no interest in expenditure outside its network space due to cost and no return on investment (ROI). There are probably thousands of networks making up the Internet, so trying to get a consensus would be like trying to plait sawdust.

Bandwidth Explosion: As Internet Use Soars, Can Bottlenecks Be Averted?
http://arstechnica.com/business/2012/05/bandwidth-explosion-as-internet-use-soars-can-bottle-necks-be-averted/1/

Web Performance by Design

There are several aspects to web systems design—for visibility, attractiveness to clients, and performance, among other things. We are only interested in the latter aspect of design, having said elsewhere in this book that trying to tune your way around poor design and configuration of hardware, software, and applications is probably a waste of time. First, let's examine what we are trying to design around to achieve optimum performance for our website.

Web Access: Where Does the Time Go?

If you want to know how long it takes to access and retrieve a page from a website, use the link somewhere in a web article to test it. The results comprise a detailed, timed journey through the web query, which can easily be repeated and results compared after any web tuning activity. In any website access—and a typical website session consists of many of these—there are numerous discrete activities not found in normal online transaction (OLTP) or query processing.

The common elements are network transmission time, image handling, and database access, but even these differ in structure and frequency so normal query analysis or simulation is not applicable to the web accesses. Web access response factors, aside from these, are server response time and load, content size and composition (images, etc.), DNS activity, and client-side delays (AJAX, etc.), plus other web-related activity.

Listed below is an itinerary of a web access's journey through the system:*

- navigation start
- redirect start
  - *redirect*
- redirect end
- fetch start
  - *app cache*
- domainLookupStart
  - *DNS lookup*
- domainLookupEnd
- connectStart
  - *TCP secureConnect*
- connectEnd
- requestStart
  - *request*
- responseStart
  - *response*
- responseEnd [time to first byte]
  - *processing*
    - *domContentLoadedEventStart* [document loaded and parsed only]
    - *domContentLoadedEventEnd* [as above, plus style sheets, images, and subframes loaded]. *This denotes a fully loaded page.*
- loadEventStart
  - *load*
- loadEventEnd

Good Web Performance References

For a discussion of many of the components of web testing and website response time, see some of the following links:

1. Website Testing Tool
   http://www.webpagetest.org/
   Reference 2 uses the Waterfall notation in reference 1 in its discussion of web performance and concludes, "Studies have shown that time to first byte† can dominate web page latency."
2. *Diagnosing Slow Web Servers with Time to First Byte*
   http://www.websiteoptimization.com/speed/tweak/time-to-first-byte/
   Reference 3 offers a lot of advice on its subject title.
3. *Best Practices for Speeding Up Your Website*
   https://developer.yahoo.com/performance/rules.html

---

* Reference 4 in "Good Web Performance References" section.
† The time to first byte is the amount of time it takes after the client sends an HTTP GET request to receive the first byte of the requested resource from the server.

A detailed look at the journey of a web access can be found at the World Wide Web Consortium's (W3C) document:

4. *Navigation Timing*
   https://dvcs.w3.org/hg/webperf/raw-file/tip/specs/NavigationTiming/Overview.html
5. In addition to these references, see the information in the next section ("Poor Web Performance: Consequences"), which outlines a discussion from a Radware (www.radware.com) document, which they have kindly given permission to publish in this book.
6. The guide referenced below covers some of the material presented above but also spells out and expands upon monitoring *strategies* and *viewpoints*:
   a. Help desk, tech support, and social media—Responsive monitoring
   b. Real-user measurement (RUM)—Passive monitoring for end-user experience
   c. Application monitoring—Passive monitoring for applications and infrastructure
   d. Synthetic web performance monitoring—Active monitoring
   The Ultimate Guide to Improving Web Performance with Monitoring [Catchpoint]
   http://resources.idgenterprise.com/original/AST-0145802_Improving_Web_Performance_with_Monitoring_Ebook.pdf
7. On the *dynatrace* website (www.apmblog.dynatrace.com) there are a number of articles in three categories that may be of interest regarding web best practices, performance, and the users' experience in this area.
   Performance Best Practices
   http://apmblog.dynatrace.com/category/best-practices/
   User Experience Management
   http://apmblog.dynatrace.com/category/user-experience-management/
   Mobile and Web Performance
   http://apmblog.dynatrace.com/category/web/
   There are a few other categories on the referenced website that may be of interest, such as dev/ops.
8. A white paper from SITESPECT has some interesting observations about web performance, including links to several sources for *web users' patience limits* (see the next section):
   Optimizing for Speed: Five Key Techniques for Faster Web & Mobile Sites
   http://info.sitespect.com/e/37032/1pnUtBH/dx3r/315438572

Poor Web Performance: Consequences

This poor-design thesis is supported by the 2012 report "How to Stop Webpage Speed from Killing Your Marketing" by Limelight Networks, Inc., which indicates that when website page loading is slow, 62% of mobile device users abandon their session and nearly one-third of those never return. Not good for business. What does that suggest to us?

Other research shows that the 7 s *patience limit* quoted may be too optimistic. In 2009, a study by Forrester Research found that online shoppers expected pages to load in 2 s or fewer—and at 3 s, a large share abandon the site. Only 3 years earlier, a similar Forrester study found the average expectations for page load times were 4 s or fewer. See the *New York Times* article below, where it talks about 250 ms being the patience limit.

For Impatient Web Users, an Eye Blink Is Just Too Long to Wait
http://www.nytimes.com/2012/03/01/technology/impatient-web-users-flee-slow-loading-sites.html?pagewanted=all&_r=1&

There are numerous other studies all pointing the same way.

The overall outcome of them all is the website bad business equation:

$$\text{Slow and/or inconsistent web response times} = \text{Bad business} \qquad (5.2)$$

A Radware (www.radware.com) document takes up the theme *slow web = bad business* in a 2015 document that puts forward solutions as well as defining problems.*
The paper begins:

> When it comes to website load times, user expectations are in a constant state of escalation. In 1999, the optimal load time for an ecommerce site was 8 seconds. In 2006, that wait time had been slashed in half, to 4 seconds. By 2010, 57% of online shoppers stated that they would abandon a web page after waiting 3 seconds for it to load.
>
> Three seconds. In case study after case study, this is the point at which most visitors will bounce if a page is not loading quickly enough. Not coincidentally, case study after case study shows that this is when business metrics—from page views to revenue—are affected by slow page rendering.

For this study, Radware tested the load times of 100 leading retail sites and collected metrics such as page size, composition (contents), and the adoption of performance best practices. Their key findings are discussed in detail in the report, but I have summarized them below.

Key Findings:

1. The median time to interact (TTI), that is, get your information back, was 5.2 s, which is slower than the median users' reported patience limit of 3 s.
2. Only 14% of the top retail sites render feature content in less than 3 s.
3. Nine percent of the top 100 pages took 10 s or more to become interactive.
4. The slowest page had a TTI of 25.1 s.
5. The median page is 1354 KB and contains 108 resource requests (1007 KB and 86 resources in spring 2013). Page size and complexity (= resources needed) typically correlate to slower load times.
6. Images comprise 50%–60% of the average page's total weight, and 43% of the top 100 sites failed to implement image compression, a core optimization technique.

These are simply design faults and errors of omission, and the paper points out some of the best practices to optimize performance of website retrievals and general interaction.

---

* The times quoted in these various papers vary because the studies are partly subjective, but the main theme is that web users' patience with tardy sites is limited, and this causes them to leave the site. This is the main point I am pursuing and not the precise patience time limit.

Best Performance Practices

The following are edited headlines in the Radware publication that should be consulted for detail and authenticity (nonwebbers may jump to the next section).

1. Consolidate JavaScript (code) and cascading style sheets (CSSs) to be shared across pages.
2. Minify code, eliminating nonessential characters such as spaces, newline, and comments.
3. Enable keep-alives of TCP connections, as multiple connections slow down a site.
4. Compress text, with technologies such gzip.
5. Sprite images: Spriting is an image combining technique.
6. Compress images without degrading quality.
7. Reformat images, as some formats take up more space than others by factors rather than percentages.
8. Ensure that feature images are optimized to load early and quickly.
9. Rethink the design and location of call-to-action links in feature graphics, repositioning so that the viewer sees them earlier than waiting for the whole images to unfold (meaning *appear*).
10. Defer rendering "below the fold" content, delaying the rendering of content below the initially visible area.
11. Defer loading and executing nonessential scripts, for parsing and rendering from libraries not needed until the main page has finished rendering.
12. Use AJAX for progressive enhancement; it is asynchronous JavaScript and XML that is a technique for fetching data from a web server without refreshing the page where the code is running—a sort of background activity.
13. Preload page resources in the browser, where all the user paths through the website are recorded and an auto-preloading engine uses this to predict where a user is likely to go based on observed user viewing movements.
14. Implement an automated performance optimization solution, where manual implementation of performance techniques, which can be time-consuming and chasing a moving target, are replaced by automated performance optimization tools and solutions.

The list and its details are concluded with the remark that faster networks and devices are not a performance cure-all. In this area, Radware offers FastView:

FastView: Web Performance Optimization and Acceleration
http://www.radware.com/Products/FastView/
Some of the information and quotations in this section are summaries of information in a paper from Radware, cited below, and who kindly granted permission to use it.

Page Speed and Web Performance (State of the Union: Spring 2015)
http://www.radware.com/spring-sotu2015/

Other Optimization Papers

1. There is also a detailed SlideShare presentation on web optimization that takes a cynical swipe at poor web design and access techniques but offers solutions as well. It illustrates an example of a poor design where there are multiple accesses and transfers to retrieve a limited amount of information and suggests a simple way round it.

*Web Performance Optimization **for Everyone***
http://www.slideshare.net/itnig/web-performance- optimization-for-everyone

2. Another, lavishly illustrated and informative presentation can be found at the following link:
Mobile Web Performance Optimization [Blaze]
http://www.slideshare.net/blazeio/mobile-web-performance-optimization-tips-and-tricks?related=1

3. The following reference contains detailed subsections dealing with various aspects of website optimization. These include
   a. Critical rendering path
   b. Optimizing content efficiency
   c. Rendering performance
   Optimizing Performance [Google Developers]
   https://developers.google.com/web/fundamentals/performance/index?hl=en

4. This Infosys reference is also very detailed and useful:
   Presentation Tier Performance Optimization
   http://www.infosys.com/manufacturing/resource-center/Documents/web-performance-optimization.pdf

5. A detailed web and database performance was carried out at the end of 2014 to the start of 2015, and the results can be found in the link below.

Performance Analysis: Benchmarking Public Clouds
http://cloudspectator.com/wp-content/uploads/report/internap_performance.pdf?

My Take: These papers support my view that throwing hardware and software at a performance issue without knowing the cause is probably totally wasteful. The physical resources of a system are not necessarily the source of a performance problem; they are physical, whereas poor design is a logical performance issue that is not easily spotted by simple monitoring of physical resources. I feel the *gotchas* in this and other papers will enable people to relate physical resource anomalies to problems outlined above and treated with the solutions laid out in the papers.

Web Scalability

Web scalability is the ability to expand to meet growing workload without excessive expenditure on extra hardware or software. The complex nature of web environments makes this scalability doubly important, as it is difficult to predict with theory and customers are unforgiving of slow websites.

Load testing is probably the optimum solution to verifying this.

The paper below reviews four models of scalability and shows how they relate to web and other distributed applications. The applicability of these models is demonstrated with a case study.

Web Application Scalability: A Model-Based Approach
http://www.perfeng.com/papers/scale04.pdf

Web Bottlenecks

Like any IT system, things get in the way of unconstrained performance and cause wait, which add to response times and throughputs. The SlideShare presentation below outlines some show delayers in the web computing arena. It identifies common website performance bottlenecks and deals with them under the following categories:

- Application server
- Database server
- Network

Each of the above categories is dealt with in the following areas:

- *Source*: On what component do they occur?
- *Symptom*: How do you know there is a problem?
- *Causes*: What (or who) created the problem?
- *Measurements*: How to tackle it.
- *Cures*: How to get rid of it.

The whole topic is illustrated with examples of B2B, E2B, and B2E cases (E=end user, B=business).

Web Server Bottlenecks and Performance Tuning
http://www.slideshare.net/GrahamDumpleton/pycon-us-2012-web-server-bottlenecks-and-performance-tuning

A Small Experiment

I used a web testing site to measure the effect of using the command ipconfig/flushdns on response times for simple access to a website on my PC. I accessed the BBC site in the UK from New York *before* using this command. The response time was 5.57 s. *After* using the ipconfig command, I repeated the call and obtained a response time of 0.53 s.

I repeated the test for another website an hour later and got a factor of about eightfold decrease in the response time after running the command again.

I am not sure exactly what this proves, but it is indicative of small hidden performance enhancing gems in systems. Look for them.

WebSitePulse
http://www.websitepulse.com/help/tools.php

Nielsen's Internet Law

Nielsen's law is concerned with Internet speed growth over time and has a parallel in Moore's law for processor speed. The law is in essence that *Internet bandwidth grows 50% in capacity every*

Table 5.3 Moore's Law and Nielsen's Growth Laws

Law	Growth Rate	10-Year Growth
Nielsen's law: Internet bandwidth	50%	×57
Moore's law: Computer power	60%	×100

12 months. However, this does not necessarily mean that performance of applications will increase since there is creeping use of image and video transmission entering the Internet equation.

There are also doubters who think Nielsen's law may break at some time, unlike Moore's law, which seems to have stood the test of time. This remains to be seen, and in the absence of better predictions, it might be wise to rely on it. The factor that makes predictions of requirements for extra bandwidth is the variety of information now passing through networks: bulk data, interactive (OLTP) data, audio and voice, video and image, email and data collection from sensors, application-specific integrated circuits (ASICs), and so forth.

Decisions have to be made, on a business basis, as to which data takes precedence over which data when congestion occurs; for example, online orders outbid company circulars for bandwidth when it is in short supply.

Table 5.3 compares the two laws: Moore's and Nielsen's.

What this is saying in effect is that processor speed, and by implication workload, can grow faster than the network supporting it, which might be a problem. The problem, if it exists, will be exacerbated by the nature of the transmitted data; for example, an image is much larger than a normal OLTP transaction but may only be considered a simple transaction in existing network capacity planning, perhaps devised 10 or 20 years before.

Lesson: This really hammers home the need to understand your workload—volumes, variability, and characteristics—in planning and design.

See

Nielsen's Law of Internet Bandwidth
http://www.nngroup.com/articles/law-of-bandwidth/

Financial and Productivity Aspects of Performance

I have come across two papers that tackle the issue of the value of good, consistent performance; there may well be others. They are summarized below and the links to them given. It should be noted that not all links within these referenced documents work today, but the document contents still have value. I have referenced these papers before in this book, but they bear repeating here in context.

1. IBM Paper. This discusses the effect of reduced response times on user productivity and knock-on effects for the organization, including shortened project schedules, improved quality, improved individual productivity, and attendant cost savings:

   Arvind J. Thadhani, of IBM's San Jose Laboratory, suggests that the number of transactions a programmer completes in an hour increases noticeably as system response time falls, and rises dramatically once system response time falls below one second. To illustrate (Figure 2), with system response of three seconds, Thadhani found that a programmer executes about 180 transactions per hour. But, bring system response time down to 0.3 seconds and the number of transactions the programmer can execute in an hour jumps to 371, an increase of 106 percent. Put another way, a reduction of 2.7 seconds in system response saves 10.3 seconds of the user's time (Figure 3). This seemingly insignificant time saving is the springboard for sizable increases in productivity. (Paper referenced below)

The Economic Value of Rapid Response Time
http://jlelliotton.blogspot.ca/p/the-economic-value-of-rapid-response.html
2. An Alertsite/Smartbear paper. This is mainly about web performance monitoring, but praising the benefits of this achieving good response times, of which monitoring is a key ingredient:

> In a widely quoted study of e-commerce sites, the Aberdeen Group found that a one-second delay in page response time results in a 7% reduction in online customer conversion, 11% fewer page views and a 16% decrease in customer satisfaction. In monetary terms, that means if your site earns somewhere around $100,000 each day, you could be losing nearly $7 million annually due to a seemingly modest lag in performance. (Paper referenced below)

Web Performance Monitoring 101
http://www2.smartbear.com/inbound-alertsite-web-monitoring-eBook-apm-digest.html
The main theme of both these papers is that improving response times can yield productivity gains and the accompanying cost–benefits for internal staff. For clients or customers using a website, response time improvement and maintenance of response time consistency (QoS) pay dividends in sales and customer satisfaction.

WoW: Studies elsewhere have shown that poor response times experienced by customers and potential customers alike result in a significant proportion of those users abandoning their use of the website. They often go to another website, usually a competitor.

Useful Reference: Lectures: *CSE123 Lecture Foils: Computer Networks—Alex C. Snoeren (University of California, San Diego [UCSD])*
http://cseweb.ucsd.edu/classes/fa10/cse123/lectures/123-fa10-l**xx**.pdf
where **xx** is 1–17, representing the 17 lectures on networking. Much of the material is quite detailed but gives pointers for searches and deeper insight into the material.

Summary

This has been a hard slog through network topics and an even harder slog researching it and putting it together in a chapter. The reason should be clear: there are 100 ways to mess up your network performance, but there are methods of monitoring networks and employing speedup techniques. Getting these speedups, however, demands knowledge of

1. Your organization's data transmission needs and any SLAs in force
2. The network and network theory in order to select the correct methods to beef up your network

In addition, your network design should be optimized from the start and then add the enhancement techniques to round it off. If you intend to add them retrospectively, make sure in advance whether you can bolt them onto an existing network without extended service interruption.

Do not just throw a network together and use the performance enhancers to get you out of jail. In these areas, a little knowledge is dangerous and you need to know what you are dealing with, taking specialist advice where necessary. If necessary, reread this chapter when starting any network design. As well as knowledge, there are several tools that will help in getting it right the first time and ensuring top-class quality of service.

Chapter 6

Graphics and Architecture

Graphics Overview

Graphics *functionality* in its simplest definition is the visual display of information, new or previously obtained and displayed in the form of tables or lists, in a meaningful form to the observer. This form can vary from a simple two-dimensional line graph of sales against calendar months to a complex three-dimensional graphics representation of an object with multiple colors, shading, shadows, animation, and other esoteric ways of observing data and information. It depends on the business or aesthetic purpose of the display.

The speed of manipulation and display of such data will depend on the complexity of its representation and the speed of the hardware and software delivering it. It will also depend on how efficient the software is. There are standards for graphics software and, like other standards, such as Open System Interconnection (OSI) and TCP/IP, there are *de jure* and *de facto* forms.

Graphics *performance* is often taken to mean the speed at which the workstation graphics hardware can create visual images on the screen once the data is handed to the adapter to be drawn on the screen. Sometimes it is interpreted as the speed at which the CPU can handle the user requests to generate graphics output and present it to the screen for viewing. The combination I suppose is what we would call the *graphics response time* (Figure 6.1).

The performance of the graphics subsystem will depend on

- How fast the individual elements of the system, both hardware and software, perform
- The function contained in the graphics adapter—coordinate transforms, clipping, scaling, shading, texture, and so on.
- Which software standards are employed (OpenGL, Programmer's Hierarchical Interactive Graphics System [PHIGS], Graphical Kernel System [GKS], native modes)
- How the program was written
- What you are trying to achieve with it, being extremely clever or developing pragmatic solutions (Figure 6.1)

On the last point, it is useful to try to categorize graphics requirements into a few areas depending on user needs:

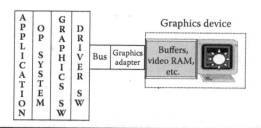

Figure 6.1   Elements of graphic display performance.

■ Simple two-dimensional (2D) mono representations. An example of this might be a power systems analysis program, plotting circuits with numeric information added.

■ Color 2D diagrams with alphanumeric information added, possibly the power systems program again, with warnings and other information denoted by color and maybe flashing.

■ 3D diagrams with color but no animation, offering detailed and possibly cutaway representations of various objects.

■ 3D pictures with animation, such as a representation of an engine or a human heart, using color to illustrate various features and parts and their operation.

■ Video games with high-resolution graphics and advanced animation and sound.

Figure 6.2 illustrates the development of graphics programming from total programming effort to programming assisted by intermediate graphics software and graphics hardware adapters. The two main ways of writing to graphics screens are

■ Low-level code, sometimes at device command level, requiring some knowledge of the hardware.

■ Higher-level code, such as PHIGS, GKS, or GL. These may be used in conjunction with a "windowing" system, for example, PEX (PHIGS with X).

Several manufacturers now develop special chip sets to accelerate graphics rendition, such as shading and luminosity. Modern chips implement many functions, previously in software, in the hardware, making them faster while lifting the load off the CPU and the programmer.

The number of hardware-supported functions plays a decisive role, especially in the 3D world, and most of the development work is currently being conducted in this field.

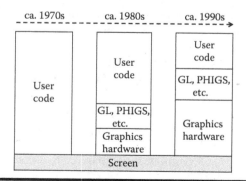

Figure 6.2   Development of graphics coding.

It can be seen from Figure 6.2 that the thrust in graphics hardware development is to put more manipulation function in the adapter cards and do less with the program software in the CPU.

The fact still remains that having a nominally faster graphics adapter or card does not necessarily mean the best overall graphics performance, as we saw previously. Some types of graphics performance metrics are covered later in Section III dealing with actual benchmarks.

Graphics Performance

Look at Figure 6.3 representing a graphics application generating "pictures" and displaying them on a device.

Q: Which workstation is the best graphics performer?
A: Depends on your viewpoint—render and write or overall speed?

Normally, performance for graphics is quoted in raw *drawing speed*, but it must be remembered that for any real application, running the job is the only real test of graphics end-to-end performance. If the answer is overall speed (response time), then B beats A, even though B loses the *write* lap of the race.

Incidentally, this principle applies to most speed *trials* where there are multiple elements or steps in the race. Saying "we have the fastest disks" means little if the rest of the journey through the system is at a snail's pace.

Graphics Speed

Graphics benchmarks measure the speed of particular graphics operation rather than an idealized instruction mix. The actual application performance is difficult to estimate from such figures, however. Some of the component benchmarks used are covered in the following sections.

Characters per Second

This is the speed at which bitmapped characters were moved from the character read-only memory (ROM) to the screen random access memory (RAM). On systems with many fonts, this figure is not meaningful since the fonts have to be retrieved as well as displayed.

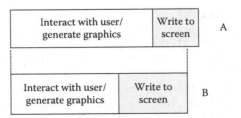

Figure 6.3 Graphics performance factors.

BitBLT

BitBLT is bit block transfer in millions of pixels per second. A common operation in graphical user interfaces (GUIs) or 2D graphics is to move a block of (picture) bits from one part of the screen to another, for example, in a cut-and-paste operation. This speed can depend on a number of factors, and there are no defined standards (metrics) for measuring the BitBLT rate unambiguously.

2D Vectors per Second

This is how quickly 2D lines can be drawn. When comparing quoted figures, it is important to remember that the rates can vary significantly depending on

- The length of the line drawn
- The orientation of the line
- Whether the line is drawn as part of a polyline or a simple line

In an application, lines pass through a number of stages before they are actually drawn. They are *transformed* from an idealized (world) coordinate system to the device coordinate system, *scaled* and *clipped* to an area on the screen. Other things to note therefore are

- Whether the line is transformed
- Whether the line is scaled
- Whether the line is clipped

The apparent performance of some adapters can be increased by up to 50% if none of these operations are carried out prior to drawing.

Moral: Take care in quoting or refuting such figures, more so if you don't understand them.

3D Vectors per Second

The factors affecting 2D draw rates also apply to 3D. Additional factors are

- Whether the line is drawn with perspective
- Whether hidden line removal is carried out

Again, the moral is as before.

Shaded Polygons per Second

Solid models are usually composed of many small 3D segments. This benchmark measures how many segments are drawn and shaded per second. A typical solid model comprises 10K to 30K polygons. A special case of this type of shading is Gouraud triangles, which are triangles drawn where the three primary colors start at the vertices and merge at the center. This is often called *intensity interpolated shading*, which aims to eliminate intensity discontinuities. The next topic follows on nicely from this.

Gouraud Shading

This is an interpolation method used in computer graphics to produce continuous shading of surfaces represented by polygon meshes. In practice, Gouraud shading is most often used to achieve continuous lighting on triangle surfaces by computing the lighting at the corners of each triangle and linearly interpolating the resulting colors for each pixel covered by the triangle.

It is a very simple and effective method of adding a curved feel to a polygon that would otherwise appear flat. Henri Gouraud first published the technique in 1971, and sometimes the operation is performed to assess aspects of graphics speeds.

See the URL below for examples of this shading:

http://search.aol.com/aol/image?q=gouraud+shading &v_t=client96_inbox

X Windows Performance

An X-terminal is typically a diskless computer especially designed to provide a low-cost user interface for applications that run in a network X-server as part of a distributed X Window System. Typically, X-terminals are connected to a server running a UNIX-based operating system on a mainframe, minicomputer, or workstation. This was typical of the client/server model of computing in the 1980s and 1990s.

The performance of an X Window System or an X-terminal is even more difficult to define than graphics performance. The performance parameters involved in assessing X Windows performance are

- The CPU or adapter speed and buffer size of the X-terminal
- The efficiency of the windowing software (Motif, OpenLook, etc.)
- The speed of the "host" processor
- The speed of the network "feeding" the X-terminal
- The utilization of the network

Despite these issues, attempts were being made to develop objective X Windows benchmarks.

Use of Graphics Power

Depending on your use of your spare time, you may think that graphics performance is all about the speed of graphics cards (rendering, shading, etc.) for gaming, and this is partly true. There are, however, other uses for graphics where other components need to deliver high performance too, often in a balanced arrangement. Some of the application areas that take advantage of graphics power and quality are

- Computer-aided design (CAD), the use of computer systems to assist in the creation, modification, analysis, or optimization of a design. CAD software is used to increase the productivity of the designer, improve the quality of design, improve communications through documentation, and create a database for manufacturing. Designs can be 3D for shapes or simple 2D for electrical power systems design.

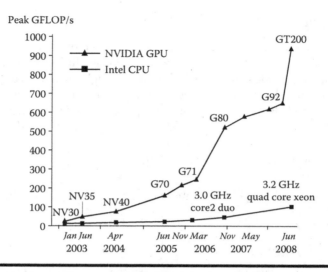

Figure 6.4 GPU power growth vs. commercial power (Intel).

■ Complex representations of various types of contour data from ground, sea, and space data collections.

■ Molecular modeling (or quantum chemistry), the design and study of representations of molecules, often used in pharmaceuticals in the drive for new drugs. This is very often a client/server application where the setup work is done on a workstation and the resulting study sent to a high-performance computing (HPC) system for number crunching. The results from the latter are then sent back to the originating workstation for analysis.

The phrases "Hartree–Fock SCF" (self-consistent field) and "docking substrates" echo down the years from my brief sojourn in this area (not that I know what they mean).

■ Games, now feasible on PCs because of the advances in graphics chip development. In fact, much of the development today is focused on games and their displays.

■ Myriad other areas where sophisticated graphics output adds value to the tasks at hand and is not just a pretty *gee whiz* exercise.

Growth in Graphics Power

Figure 6.4 shows the relative speed of growth of graphics hardware processors (GPUs) when compared to commercial processor growth.

It illustrates the fact that graphics power is increasing very quickly, but as I have said, a major driver is the games and entertainment industries.

Implementing the Lattice Boltzmann Model on Commodity Graphics Hardware
http://iopscience.iop.org/1742-5468/2009/06/P06016/fulltext/

Graphics Performance Factors
http://www.mindcontrol.org/~hplus/graphics/ogl-perf.html

THE PERFORMANCE PLAYING FIELD

Performance is not a quantity to be just measured, but managed. This means knowing what the numeric characteristics of a workload are, why they are what they are, and what control we have over them if they deviate from what is required by the users and their service level agreements.

This necessitates measurement tools, but also a methodology for interpreting and acting upon these measurements, which differentiates *monitoring* from *managing* as an activity. Monitoring is not just undertaken for recording purposes, pretty graphs, and impressing managers, but for the subsequent management and control of the performance of important business functions entrusted to the IT department. The business end of things is what pays the IT salaries; neglect it at your peril.

Chapter 7

Performance: Simple Theory and Concepts

Queuing Theory Concepts

Note: To understand discussions on performance aspects of IT, it is necessary to have the rudiments of queuing theory under your belt before proceeding, hence the interposing here of a section on simple queuing theory, prior to a more detailed discussion, should you need it, in Appendix I.

Word of Advice

Many years ago, it was almost possible to calculate or estimate the performance of a system of a simple server, simple storage, and a single link to end users where performance characteristics were known. Today, the hardware and worlds are far more complex and the workloads more varied with different requirements for performance, and trying to estimate performance numbers to two decimal places is silly.

Fortunately, the cost of resources (at least hardware) is very cheap compared to that which was the norm 40 or so years ago. IT departments would spend days estimating memory and disk requirements, as well as CPU power, needed to service their business workload. Many years were spent shoehorning programs into requiring smaller and smaller memory whose costs were prohibitive. Similar obstacles arose in CPU power and disk requirements.

There were no small CPU increments available—just the next model up, which was usually a quantum leap in price over the one you had or thought you might need. Today, those costs are more granular and hence containable. In fact, to upgrade the PC I am working on at present will set me back about $40 to $50 for an 8 GB memory upgrade. When I started out at IBM in 1969, that size of memory increment was not available for any system on this planet, and if it had been available, it would have cost a king's ransom (plus taxes).

This means that today it is possible to make educated guesses at resource requirements for optimally performing business applications and not bankrupt your company if you are a little out on estimates. The days of needing a very accurate estimate, and a sizing guru to make it, are long gone.

Making Performance Estimates

There are a number of ways of making estimates of resources needed for applications given that they need acceptable response times and throughput rates:*

- *Rules of thumb* (ROTs), which are guidelines based on experience and found to be of use in similar circumstances. Examples I came across were of the following nature:
  - 3 GB of disk storage per relative processor power (RPP) for IBM systems, covering both capacity and I/O rate requirements
  - 1.5% of a certain processor type or size for each transaction per second to be processed
  - x MB per customer record in a relational database management system (RDBMS)
- *Calculations*, using queuing theory and other similar math. These can work fine for a single server (generic), but following through a system with the same math may not be wise, as the initial input distribution will almost certainly not apply to the next (generic) server in the service chain. This limitation is one reason I have not *gone to town* on esoteric queuing theory in this book. The other reason is that I don't know enough theory to do this.
- *Simulation* methods and software that mimic the situation being modeled, for example, by generating transactions and measuring response times or incrementing use of some resource and repeating a simulation each time.
- From *standard benchmarks*, assuming the workload in question can be related to these benchmarks. I have done this, relating the TPC-C benchmark transactions to the customer's estimate of the resource requirements of his transactions.
- *Personal benchmarks* on the real application, for example, in a pilot scheme. The application might be a commercial off-the-shelf (COTS) one, in which case the vendor can assist. If it is an as yet unwritten in-house application, it can be simulated by coding the basic I/O and simulating the transaction code by timed coding loops.

Probably the best method is to take a consensus of more than one of these methods, if possible, which gives one a warm feeling if they nearly agree. Some network sizing tools are discussed in Chapter 8.

Queues and Resources

A measure of how well a system or part thereof is performing is best understood via the generic relationship

$$\text{Performance Indicator} = \frac{\text{Max Resource Required}}{\text{Resource Available}}$$

---

* Please do not apply these ROTs today: they are quite old (1980s) and only illustrative of the principle.

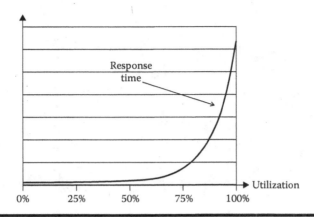

Figure 7.1 Queuing effect of utilization on response time.

If this is less than 1, the performance can be said to be good since there is no shortage of the required resources. This means no queuing with its attendant delays, as we shall see in this chapter.

Another important performance measure is the utilization of a resource, which is a measure of how much of it is being used:

$$\text{Utilization}\left(\rho\left(t\right)\right) = \frac{\text{Resource in Use at Time } t}{\text{Resource Available}}$$

Common sense tells us that this number should be as high as possible, approaching 1, if possible, to make *resource available* small with attendant smaller costs. Queuing theory and practice tells us otherwise, although some writers don't seem to grasp this. I read statements of the kind "Disk X takes 10 ms for an I/O access, so it can support 100 I/Os (1000/10) per second (IOPs)." Yes, it does, if you want a response time of infinity, give or take a few microseconds, because that's what you will get at 100% utilization of that poor disk. This is illustrated in Figure 7.1, which is repeated *ad nauseam* in most queuing theory texts. It shows the rapid deterioration in response time (or throughput) of a generic server as its utilization approaches 100%. This resource might be a server processor, a disk unit, or a network link.

The main lesson is that it is not a linear process but has a response time *knee* followed by a rapid rise. You should design so that you operate in normal circumstances well away from the rising knee point.

Queuing: Two Railway Scenarios

1. A train arrives at a station and a number of people alight from it and head for a telephone to arrange onward transport. There is only one telephone booth available and a queue of people forms outside it. The average time taken to telephone for a taxi or contact a friend is 2 min, and a queue builds up as people are arriving every few seconds to make their calls. Eventually, the queue shortens and, after a time, everyone has made their calls. This scenario is, of course, before mobile or cell phones, iPads, and the like were around.*

---

* Even in these cases, there can be queuing for bandwidth from the telecommunications supplier. This is nearly always the case when there is some form of public disaster.

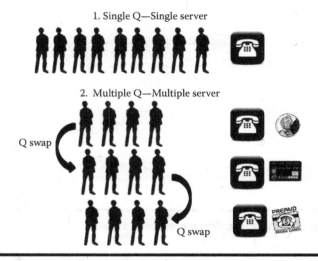

Figure 7.2   Queuing concepts: railway scenario.

This illustrates a simple queuing scenario where the service pattern is "first come, first served" or, in queuing terms, first in, first out (FIFO). There are more complicated serving methods than this, as we shall see in scenario 2.

Note: This scenario will be more complicated if a second train arrives while the people from the first one are still queuing to make their telephone calls, a double queuing whammy.

2. Let us envisage a slightly different scenario at a larger train station where there are multiple phone booths available. Let us imagine there are three phone booths available, one accepting coins only, one accepting credit cards only, and the third one accepting prepaid phone cards. They are all clearly marked, so the rush of people split into queues, one queue for each booth, according to their payment preference. After a short time, people in a slower queue leave their queue and move into another one, assuming they have the means to use the booth being queued for (cash, credit card, and phone card). These scenarios are illustrated in Figure 7.2, and some of the queuing terms involved are shown.

Scenario 1 illustrates the queue of people waiting for the single phone booth, and this is called a single queue with a single-server configuration.

Scenario 2 represents a more usual situation where there are multiple queues waiting for service from a number of servers; here they are telephones. This is a *multiple queue, multiple server configuration*, the multiplicity of queues caused by the need for different service mechanisms.

These mechanisms are called *dispatching algorithms* in queuing theory terminology. The departure from a queue by a disgruntled customer is called *reneging*. The departing person may go into another queue or abandon the request for service and disappear from the system. Leaving one queue to join another in the hope of faster service is known as *jockeying*. A customer refusing to join the queue in the first place is said to be *balking*.

Note: In IT, a unit of work (UoW) doesn't have the intelligence to *renege* or *balk*, but it may be persuaded to do so by operational parameters or actions. An example of this is changing priorities of print jobs in a queue or deleting some of them.

In a scenario where the service mechanisms were all the same, the most efficient operating configuration would be a *single queue, multiple server* one. This is particularly true in banks and post offices and is seen at airport check-ins.

However, in real life the multiqueue situation can be fraught; often one always seems to be joining the queue where someone has a vast number of transactions to complete with the teller.

Basis of Theory

Why Does It Matter?

There are many concepts in queuing theory, but not all are relevant in all situations. Certain metrics and parameters may be important in one area and not in others. It is therefore important to understand the basics of queuing theory and its application to the IT world and, in particular, your organization. In IT, key areas are resource utilizations, response times, wait times (latencies), capacity, and trends in them for capacity planning purposes.

Nobody ever got fired for spending a little time understanding base queuing theory (as far as I am aware), but you may get fired if you use it as the only way to assess or predict performance and get it wrong. More on the place of such theory as we progress.

Workload Queues

Information technology workloads are often mathematically simulated using simplified queuing theory, with the transaction requesting some service from a server or servers. In the analogy above, it is difficult to plan for it, as there are too many unknowns involved.

Another analogy can be drawn by considering the problem of deciding how many counters and how many clerks are needed to adequately serve customers in a shop. It should be noted that there is no single answer to the problem; it all depends on what *level of service* is to be offered to the customers. Having many counters and many clerks will give good service even when many customers arrive at the peak periods. However, this would be very expensive and would need to be viewed against turnover.

The information required to build the correct number of counters and hire the right number of clerks is

- How long, on average, does it take to serve each customer? This is the *service time*.
- How many customers arrive each minute or hour? Call this the *arrival rate*. The time between arrivals is called the *interarrival time* (see the "Arrival Process" section below).

Based on the answers to questions 1 and 2, how long will the queue of customers be, and how long must they wait to be served, and is that time acceptable, given the level of service the shop wishes to offer? These numbers are the *queue length* and *queue time*, respectively, the latter being the most important in IT.

In this simple model, the total time taken for the customer to be served, total response time (the customer "experience"),* is given by the pseudo-equation

---

* In our IT queuing discussions, we will call this time the *response time*, mainly written in this book as T_R. It may, however, be called *total service time* in some contexts.

$$\text{Time spent waiting to be served} + \text{time spent being served} \quad (7.1)$$
$$\text{(Wait Time)} \qquad\qquad \text{(Service Time)}$$

If the customers arrive faster than they can be served, there will be an ever-increasing queue of people. Conversely, if the time between customer arrivals is greater than the time it takes for a customer to be served, then there will never be anyone in the queue. Assumptions in this simple model are

■ The time to be served (service time) is constant.
■ The time between arrivals (interarrival time) is constant.
■ When actually serving, the clerk is 100% busy.

In real applications, whether we consider customers arriving at a bank for some sort of service, or transactions arriving at a CPU for processing, the service and interarrival times are normally variable. This variability introduces another important factor called the server utilization. This affects the total service time, defined as wait time plus service time, depending on the nature of the variability.

In IT terms, the customers equate to transactions and the counter and clerks to the computer system. The analogy can be comfortably extended by considering the journeys to and from the shop as the equivalent of communications line or LAN time taken traveling to and returning from the system.

If the shopping exercise is timed from the moment the shopper left home to the time he returned, it would vary depending on the time of day. The time of day might dictate how busy the roads and shop are which, will add to the total time because of queuing in traffic and in the shop itself. The times are normally called *latencies*.

Arrival Process

As a reminder, we should note that the progress of a unit of work (UoW) through a system consists of arrival, waiting, service, and departure for servers new to the arrival and service processes, often described mathematically by distributions.

Imagine that UoWs arrive for service at times t_1, t_2, ..., t_n. The time between their arrival is called the interarrival time (*IAT*) and is given by

$$\text{IAT}(\tau) = (t_j - t_{j-1})$$

where $j = n$ to 1. The IAT is the parameter that follows a mathematical distribution such as Poisson, exponential, and so on (see Appendix I). The IAT is important in queuing theory, and it should be self-evident that if the mean (average) IAT is less than the time it takes for the server to service a request, then a queue will build up, but may shrink as well as a result of the distribution pattern. If the IAT is fixed and always less than the service time, then the queue will build up indefinitely and response times will go stratospheric, if not interstellar.

The IAT for an exponential arrival distribution is illustrated in Figure 7.3.

Response Time Factors

In our analogies, as in IT systems, the total time to be served is the sum of

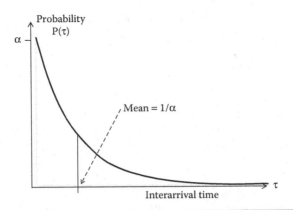

Figure 7.3   Exponential arrivals: interarrival time distribution.

- The total time spent waiting to be served
- The time to be actually served

Obviously in IT systems, there are several server types that a transaction or unit of work will use, for example, CPU, disk, and LAN or line. For each server,* the total service time, or response time, T_R, is

$$T_R = T_S + T_W$$

where T_S is the actual server time and T_W is the wait time. The total response time will be the sum of all T_R factors from each server in the chain, assuming it is linear (in series).

$$\text{Arrival} \rightarrow \begin{array}{ccccc} \text{Server 1} & & \text{Server 2} & & \text{Server 3} \rightarrow \ldots \\ T_{R1} & + & T_{R2} & + & T_{R3} \quad + \ldots.. \end{array}$$

It should be noted that each server in the chain need not necessarily have the same server characteristics, although we would expect the arrival pattern not to change as the work passes along the servers, unless work items are lost. Also note that what is illustrated above are servers in series and not in parallel; that is, each element is a *single server* in queuing terms.

What Determines Wait and Service Times?

The service time may be constant or variable. We consider several cases, depending on whether the resource in question is a LAN, WAN, disk, CPU, and so forth.

The waiting time depends on the factors that we will expand on shortly. Dispatching priority is a factor that can determine wait time when *first in the queue, first out* (FIFO) does not apply. Some online transaction processing (OLTP) and other software may not work in FIFO mode either. To take a homely example, think of the queue at a bar in a public house or bar. If you

---

* In this discussion, I use the word *server* generically, not just in the sense of a computer. The server here can mean any resource that does something with the UoW, that is, gives a service.

are new to the place, it is often the case that the regular customers get served before you even though they are behind you in the queue. This illustrates the importance of logical versus physical considerations.

The list below illustrates most of the service disciplines or algorithms met in queuing theory:

■ Algorithms specific to the server software, for example, IBM's Information Management System (IMS), where the software selects work on a type of work basis
■ First in, first out (FIFO), irrespective of any other properties of the work or server
■ First come, first served (FCFS), the same as FIFO
■ Last in, first out (LIFO)
■ Last come, first served (LCFS), the same as LIFO
■ Round-robin (RR), cyclic selection of work from a queue or queues
■ Infinite server (IS), a fixed delay
■ Shortest processing time first (SPT), deal with *tiddlers* (small fries) first
■ Shortest expected processing time first (SEPT), ditto
■ Biggest in, first served (BIFS)*

You can find more detailed discussions of the service scheduling algorithms at

Comparison and Analysis of FIFO, PQ, and WFQ Disciplines in OPNET
http://www2.ensc.sfu.ca/~ljilja/ENSC427/Spring11/Projects/team2/ENSC427_Team2_Presentation.pdf

Session 1813 Traffic Behavior and Queuing in a QoS Environment
http://web.mit.edu/dimitrib/www/OPNET_Full_Presentation.ppt

General Service Theory

The detailed theory of modeling IT systems and communications is well covered in several books and online presentations, to which the mathematically literate reader should refer. However, please note that some of the terminology used in them differs from that used in this book, in particular, the ideas of queuing time and waiting time. In this book, we use *queuing time* and *waiting time* interchangeably to denote the time spent waiting to be served, that is, the delay between arrival at a service and being served.

A notation used to describe this general case of work arriving at queues and requesting service is the Kendall–Lee notation (see Appendix I). In brief, this notation specifies many of the variables one might encounter in the general case of queuing.

The Kendall–Lee queuing notation normally used is

$$A/B/c/K/m/Z \tag{7.2}$$

■ A—*Arrival process (distribution)*
 – M—Poisson distribution; random arrival process
 – D—Degenerate distribution; deterministic or fixed arrival rate

---

* Some of these and others are listed in a presentation by Raj Jain, a queuing guru. For his lecture notes, search the term *CSE567M*, which should pull up a series of them.

- – G—General distribution
- – E—Erlang distribution
- ■ B—*Service time distribution*
  - – M—Exponential service time
  - – D—Degenerate distribution; deterministic or fixed service time
  - – E—Erlang distribution
- ■ c—*Number of servers*
  - – Can range from 1 to many
- ■ K—*Capacity of the whole system, that is, maximum number of customers allowed in queue plus those being serviced*
  - – Size of the waiting area
  - – By default taken as infinity
- ■ m—*Size of the population from where customers are coming*
  - – Denotes the population of potential arrivals to the queue and server. If the arrival population is small compared to the number in the waiting area, then this will have an effect on the arrival rate and hence the way the problem is treated mathematically. If the arrival population is very large in relation to the waiting area population, then the former can be considered infinite.
  - – By default taken as infinity.
- ■ Z—*Queue discipline, that is, the order in which the customers in queue are being served*
  - – FCFS—First come, first served; default; sometimes known as FIFO
  - – LCFS—Last come, first served
  - – SIRO—Service in random order
  - – PS—Processor sharing
  - – PNPN—Priority service

Note: These letters can vary depending on the source of the writing, although their positions have the same meanings. They are often numbered 1–6 instead of using alpha characters, which makes life a bit simpler, as we have in Appendix I.

In the case of OLTP, the population of transactions is very often of the order of many thousands per day, whereas a queue of more than a few transactions is unusual, except in a badly sized or designed system (see Appendix I for more details on Kendall–Lee). That is all we need to say here about the general theory, except to say that we deal with some examples of subsets of this notation when dealing with systems and networks.

Statement of the Problem

In applying queuing theory to IT workloads, the following concepts are important in throughput and response times; why they are will become clear later:

- ■ The workload population. In OLTP terms, this means the number of transactions that might arrive at the system over a period of time, for example, 1 day. It does not mean the number of users entering UoWs.
- ■ The length of the queue of work waiting for service.
- ■ The size of the "waiting area" for the queues.
- ■ The number of queues.

- The number of servers.
- The relationship between queues and servers.
- The service time and its variability.
- The dispatching algorithm (the order in which requests are serviced).
- The waiting (or queuing) time.
- The arrival pattern and its variability.

The last item, arrival pattern, is normally called a distribution, and there are several that are used in detailed queuing theory, listed here for completeness and dealt with in more detail in Appendix I:

- Poisson
- Exponential
- Erlang with parameter k
- Hyperexponential with parameter k
- Deterministic
- General

It is easy to get into a mathematical maze with these distributions, and they are only pragmatic approximations to what happens in real systems. If we do not have a mathematical representation of the arrivals, then theoretical treatment is not possible.

Terminology and Notations

In this book, we will use the following notation in the discussions of queuing and performance:

- ρ: The utilization of a server and equals λ/μ (see below for λ and μ)
- τ: The interarrival time (IAT) of work units
- λ: The arrival rate of work units
- μ: The service rate of work units
- E_k: For an Erlang distribution, parameter k
- M: For an exponential distribution and so on
- T_S: The service time of a single server
- T_W: The wait or queuing time before receiving service
- T_R: The total time to be served (response time or latency), which is service time plus waiting time, $T_S + T_W$

These metrics are repeated and expanded upon in Appendix I (part of the immersion process), and their applicability to different functions within an organization outlined. They are not all things to all people. Also note that some articles and papers use slightly different characters for the same metric, but as long as you are *on the ball*, this should not trouble you.

Figure 7.4 shows the arrival and flow of work (e.g., batch and transactions) through a system.

A very readable introduction to queuing theory can be found at the link below:

Queuing Analysis [William Stallings]
http://cse.csusb.edu/ykarant/courses/f2006/csci530/QueuingAnalysis.pdf

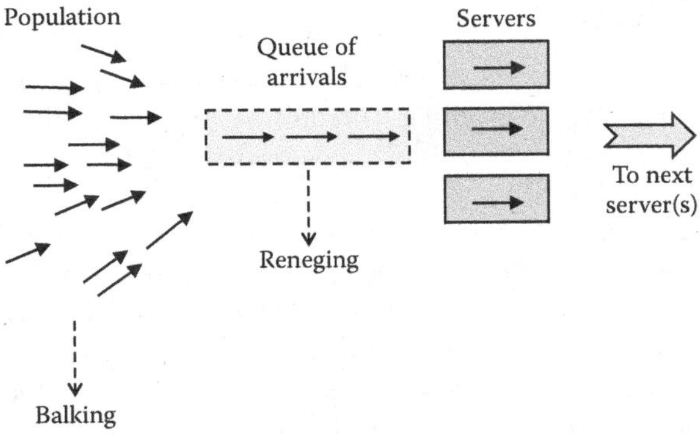

Figure 7.4 Arrivals, queuing, and service.

Utilization: What Is It?

In IT systems, a key measure to monitor across the various resource types is *utilization*. Utilization can have a considerable impact on performance, as we will see. Resource utilization (ρ) can be defined as

$$\rho = \frac{\text{Time a resource is being used}}{\text{Time it is available for work}} \tag{7.3}$$

Why Is Utilization Important?

The utilizations of the various physical resources are important because if they exceed certain limits, they will cause performance degradation. This degradation is manifest in two main areas:

1. The response times for transactions will increase.
2. The throughput drops as a result. This may not apply to batch work since there is no response time to worry about—the higher the utilization of resources, the more work you get through the system.

In the classical IT dark ages, a transaction meant a unit of work (UoW) that read data from a screen, traveled down a link, accessed a data record from a file or database, processed that record, and replaced it with an updated version. It was clean, clear, and capable of being visualized. Today, however, these transaction types still exist, but now live alongside emails, audio, video, and web pages on systems, and particularly over the links user-to-system and system-to-system.

This means that theoretical treatment of such workloads is much more difficult, particularly in the areas of sizing, monitoring, and understanding just what is going on.

> *WoW*: For a more detailed look at pragmatic queuing theory, including Kendall notation, see Appendix I, but we will find that more and more, we are using rules of thumb (ROTs) and simulations to make assessments in the field of sizing, performance prediction, and performance management.

Management of Performance

Performance management (PM) is one of several management disciplines, collectively known as systems management, that cater to running, monitoring, and controlling complex IT systems. These disciplines have been used in mainframe environments for many years, but were virtually unknown in the UNIX world until some 20 years ago.

One reason for the awareness of their importance is that UNIX, Linux, and Windows are now the vehicles for important commercial applications and not just scientific work and program development. These applications help to run businesses, and so integrity, security, availability, recovery, and good performance, among other things, assume a greater importance. Of course, the resilient mainframe continues on its merry way despite premature predictions of its demise. It is still the mentor for nonmainframe systems management, I feel.

Importance of *Systems* Management

The preceding statements are often disputed by IT people, particularly those without exposure to mainframe culture. To counter this, consider the following statistics about the *availability to users* of IBM mainframe applications. Although these figures cannot be applied directly to UNIX and other environments, they will certainly give food for thought when planning for system resilience. The moral is that however much you spend on hardware redundancy, there are other factors that will cause nonavailability or poor performance of online software.

The online workloads represented are a mix of Time Sharing Option (TSO) and the IBM mainframe OLTPs, Customer Information Control System (CICS), and IMS. Nonavailability of an application to end users should not be considered synonymous with system failure, since an application that is not available because the databases are still in the process of backup or reorganization will be considered by the users to be a "system crash."

The statistics presented here relate to commercial mainframes, but it is unlikely that UNIX-based systems will show a markedly different pattern in terms of factors preventing application access by users.

What is this to computer performance, you may ask? The simple answer is that if an application is not available to an end user for x hours, the response time for any transaction using that application will be (x hours + normal response time). It is unlikely that this level of performance will be acceptable to the average user.

The figures in Table 7.1 were collected from various sources by an IBM systems engineer of such professional and technical stature that he or she is to be believed.

The moral is that high availability goes hand in hand with performance SLAs.

Importance of *Performance* Management

WoW: Why worry about performance? If it gets worse, we can tune it, can't we? Not so. However clever you might be, you can't tune a tractor to take part in a Formula 1 race, especially if the system design is *suboptimal* (a polite term I use for *rubbish*). The term is less likely to upset management of your organization or that of a customer.

Table 7.1 Causes of System Outage: 1990s

Outage Cause	Percent Time	Notes
CPU failure	2	Includes all elements of CPU complex
Disk failure	9	Includes errors in recovering
Environment	8	Power, air conditioning, cooling
Tape	0	Near-zero failure rates
Other hardware	0	Switches, consoles, local screens, and cables
Operating system	9	System control program (SCP) plus supporting software
Database/OLTP	1	IMS, CICS, TSO
Application	15	Applications running under the above
Network: Host	9	Includes Virtual Telecommunications Access Method (VTAM), NetView, etc.
Network: Processor	0	Outboard of the main CPU, e.g., IBM 3745
Operators	2	Includes operator error, e.g., causing reruns
Support	22	Nonhardware setup, e.g., buffers
Late start	14	Late availability of online service
Other reasons	9	Anything else, e.g., engineer error

Performance management (PM) is the collection, storage, and analysis of relevant system performance data through the development life cycle for the purposes of

- Checking that the performance is within predefined limits (baseline), probably dictated by a service level agreement (SLA). More often than not, *performance* means the response time of a query (transaction) alongside the throughput (number of UoWs per unit time) of these queries. If there are no predefined limits, or at least expectations, then PM is a rather futile exercise. A formally defined set of performance requirements agreed upon between users and the IT department is known as an SLA.

    The SLA may contain items other than performance, for example, availability and recovery times. It is crucial that such measurements are carried out during software development or acquisition, so there are no surprises when the application goes into production, which means *stable, predictable response times.*
- Monitoring the system for performance *bottlenecks* or potential bottlenecks. For example, if the average CPU utilization of a system is creeping steadily up, there will come a point where the performance will become unacceptably degraded. The speed of degradation will increase as the knee of the throughput versus utilization curve is approached (see Figure 1.2).
- *Tuning* the application or system if an imbalance is detected. A properly sized and installed system should need no tuning for some time, and then only as a result of a change in

workload pattern or perhaps volumes. If the system needs tuning soon after going "live," questions should be asked of the development and operations teams.

■ Providing *looking-ahead* input to capacity management or *capacity planning*.

Difference between Management and Monitoring

This topic might generate an erudite book on the subject, but I will settle for a simple picture to illustrate the difference (Figure 7.5). I think it illustrates the principle perfectly.

There is little point in investing in people and software to monitor things you have no intention of managing.

Desired PM Solution Capabilities (BMC)

A commissioned study conducted by Forrester Consulting on behalf of BMC Software (November 2014) listed 15 *must-haves* from U.S., UK, and German IT decision makers. I have listed the top six here:

1. Ability to rapidly perform root cause analysis (RCA) if a performance or availability issue occurs
2. Ability to automatically fix availability or performance issues
3. Ability to do Deep Dive analysis of infrastructure and application components
4. Ability to avoid or predict potential performance or availability issues before they impact the end user
5. Ability to integrate all monitoring data on a customizable dashboard to foster cooperation between IT support and development
6. Ability to monitor enterprise business applications

The source of this data can be found at the following link:

Digital Business Requires Application Performance Management
http://media.cms.bmc.com/documents/BMC-APM-TAP-FINAL.pdf

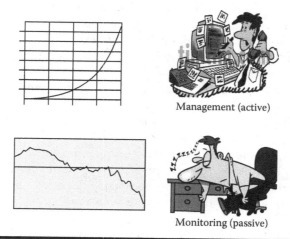

Management (active)

Monitoring (passive)

Figure 7.5 Monitoring vs. managing.

(You will probably have to register to view this report.)

The reference below has a very readable coverage of the elements of systems (resources) that need visibility and their usage quantifying for performance assessment and problem determination. It is by Brendan Gregg, cited elsewhere in this book.

The USE Method [utilization saturation and errors]
http://www.brendangregg.com/usemethod.html

These requirements may not match your own organization's 100%, but they are worth bearing in mind when evaluating products and techniques covered in this book.

Performance Management (PM)

What Is PM?

Performance management of IT systems is the monitoring, quantification, result interpretation, and action from data related to IT systems, namely (but not exclusively),

- CPUs or processors, including clusters
- Memory, including cache memory
- Storage I/O (mainly disk and solid-state drive [SSD])
- Network activity (response times and throughput)
- LAN activity
- Internet activity in its various forms
- Other devices, such as tapes, other storage devices, printers, and other devices not covered in this book, but nevertheless important in many environments

The action part of this activity involves

- An agreed upon and documented PM methodology along with roles and responsibilities.
- Knowledge of your workload (OLTP, batch, query, etc.). This includes awareness of normal loads, peak loads, and seasonal and other variations: month-end and year-end processing, sales promotions (load spikes), and other abnormal situations.
- Adequate monitoring tools, products, and skills to operate and interpret data.
- Concise reporting of performance for *consumption* at various levels in the organization (management, operations, systems, and users).
- Change management and connection to performance management.
- Predictive activity; "If this continues, we will be running our disks at 92% utilization in 3 months, and we know what that means."
- Capacity planning from growth trends and anticipated new business.
- Liaison with users or their representatives.

It is *not* simply

- The production of dozens of pretty graphs; visual or hard copy
- The papering of walls and stuffing reports with the same

- The interpretation of PM data without adequate knowledge
- Someone else's responsibility

Importance of Performance Management

Performance management, along with change management, represents a key factor in maintaining availability and complying with performance clauses in any service level agreements (SLAs). Performance management is covered briefly here as a "pointer" to texts that show the "how and why" of the discipline.

One issue with performance management is, do we monitor and optimize the performance of every service and application we have? The answer is probably no, unless you have resources and money to burn. That leaves the same decision to be made that applied to disaster and normal recovery: What are the most important services, and what performance characteristics do they require?

In addition, the monitoring aspect will need some consideration. Do we monitor, report, and analyze everything, or do we work on an *exception reporting basis*? If yes, then you will need an acceptable baseline and threshold for the things you don't report on, which might include

- Maximum CPU load
- Maximum disk utilization
- Maximum network traffic
- Maximum memory utilization

If one or more of these limits is breached, alerts and appropriate action should follow. This is not as simple as it sounds since an exceptional utilization of a resource does not really tell us who or what was responsible. It could be poor coding, bad database design, unexpected growth in numbers of users, and so on. This often requires monitors that are *application-aware*, so they can give some indication of what is causing the problems. These used to be called *knowledge modules*.

Performance management lives in a hierarchy of several management disciplines, as illustrated in Figure 7.6. This figure shows the interfacing of performance management and its data with not only systems management, but also operations management (short-term need for operational data) and user support and help desk, who need to know what is going on when complaints about performance are received. The disciplines are generally lumped under the acronym ITSM (IT service management). However, overall superiority in ITSM does not necessarily mean superiority in every subdiscipline, such as PM.

The reference below is the 2015 Gartner Magic Quadrant report covering IT service management tools vendors' ratings in the usual Gartner manner.

Magic Quadrant for IT Service Support Management Tools (August 25, 2015)
http://www.gartner.com/technology/reprints.do?id=1-2M9EOOU&ct=150901&st=sb

In my experience, unless you cater to this cross-discipline requirement, the results may be worse than if you didn't bother with PM.

Figure 7.7 shows schematically the range of application and other software that may contribute to resource utilization exceptions, which might allow a deeper insight into performance issues.

A lot of papers talk about application performance management (APM), which can be a little confusing, especially if it is buried in marketing hype. There are factors that affect the performance of an application in itself: lines of code, structure, and other aspects. The overall performance as

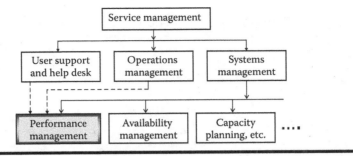

Figure 7.6   Performance in the context of service management.

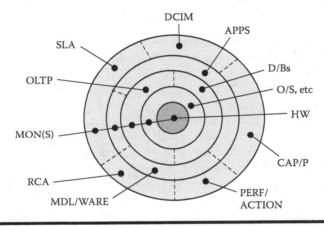

Figure 7.7   Key elements of the performance management "onion."

seen by the end user of that application depends on myriad other aspects, as illustrated in the onion structure in Figure 7.7.

In general, the system elements supporting an application (and hence its performance) are in series, and each element in this chain of resources has a part to play. The normal performance issues can usually be tracked to out-of-line situations of the major resources—CPU, disk, network, and so on—but the more intractable ones may require knowledge of what the other, less obvious resources are doing, for example, Domain Name Systems. For example, using ipconfig/flushdns on a PC every so often can often work wonders for sluggish performance.

Figure 7.8 illustrates a typical web or commercial workload configuration to outline the elements in the chain of processing activity, any of which can slow the system down. This is a long way from classical (legacy) architecture and demands more system and network visibility to be able to monitor, analyse, and act on performance information. There are also extra availability considerations since there are more elements in the service chain, but that is another story.

Service Flow Overview

Usually, the most important services are online, and it is at these services that monitoring, analyzing, reporting, and so forth, are aimed. What is of interest for critical online services, aside from availability, is the total response time as seen by the user.

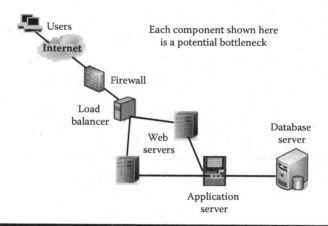

Figure 7.8   Performance factors: a complex configuration.

This is the sum of the times spent in the various components of the journey through the system from user back to user. These times are made up of the actual time to service the request for that resource plus the time waiting to be served by that resource. A schematic service flow is shown in Figure 7.9.

Monitors need to be available to measure the utilization of those service resources and the total response time in that resource. In the diagram, an "injector" and monitor system are shown. The injector system is a *user emulator* injecting or pinging transactions into the system to check for availability and performance by monitoring the return of the same. Suitable monitors are used to measure (or allow calculation of) traffic, response times, and utilizations.

For a transaction, N_i is the network time for input traffic, N_o is the network time for output traffic, and S is the time in the system, including disk and other input/output (I/O). Equation 7.4 shows the user's view of the transaction response time.

$$\text{Transaction Response Time at Screen} = N_i + S + N_o$$
$$= \text{Time Seen by User} \tag{7.4}$$

The "report" represents analysis of captured data, reporting, and notification of off-baseline numbers. This of course is a simple case that assumes screen painting time is zero and the system

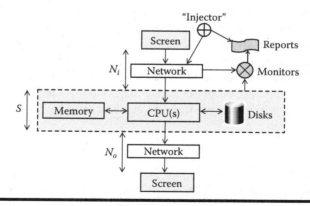

Figure 7.9   Performance management flow.

does not interact with other systems or agents (see the "System Performance Concepts" section later in this chapter).

References: There are some useful general sections in the following references that will help in setting up a performance management process with suitable products for any particular organization:

End to End Performance Management on IBMi
http://www.redbooks.ibm.com/redbooks/pdfs/sg247808.pdf

Capacity and Performance Management: Best Practices White Paper
http://www.cisco.com/c/en/us/support/docs/availability/high-availability/20769-performwp.html

More information specific to a vendor's own environment can be found by searching "[vendor name], performance management," for example, "Windows, performance management."

Stages of the Performance Life Cycle

The achievement of optimum performance in practice involves many factors and considerations aside from raw performance of the constituent parts of the hardware and software. These factors can be grouped together under the heading of "System Design." It is quite possible, and it has been observed, that a poorly designed application system running on one machine can perform worse than a well-designed application system running on a slower machine. Tuning is often useless in the former case, rather like trying to tune a tractor to race a motor car.

The need for performance management, as we have indicated, does not begin at commencement of productive use of the applications. It needs to be considered in the design, coding, configuration, and testing phases of the project. Design covers the application, database, network, and system aspects of the work to develop new applications. Experience of RDBMS problems indicates that poor application or database design accounts for the majority of reports of poor performance.

In such cases, tuning has little effect on the problem. The answer, then, is eternal vigilance of performance throughout the life cycle of applications. Figure 7.10 shows many of the areas where performance can be impacted at the various stages of the development life cycle. The same considerations also apply to the implementation of an application package, such as enterprise resource planning (ERP).

It is often said that you can overelaborate this performance management game, but the plain fact is that getting it wrong costs money in putting it right, instead of getting it right in the first place. Figure 7.10 shows the flow, but it also implies that the process is cyclical and keeps going around as long as the business or volumes change. There is no "Well, that's the job done, we can all go to sleep." There are always change and impending *gotchas* lurking.

Figure 7.11 illustrates schematically how the cost of correction of applications varies with time and the effort required to correct parts of the system, from the hardware architecture to operating systems tuning.

The details of the mechanics of setting up a performance management (and any other) project are covered in Chapter 17 under "Performance Management: The Project."

Performance Definitions and Terms

The shorter *Oxford English Dictionary* (OED) defines *performance* as "the accomplishment, carrying out, doing of any action or work." This is what computers do: they perform work on behalf of users. The definition, however, says nothing about how quickly the work is done, which is what

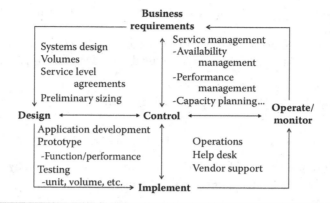

Figure 7.10   Performance life cycle.

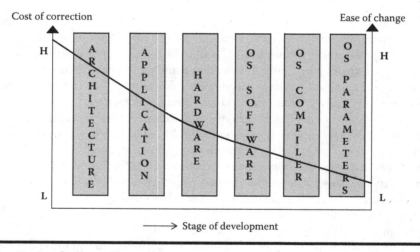

Figure 7.11   Cost and effort of correction.

most people mean when talking about computer performance. My definitions follow, and I will discuss the issue of speed in the next section.

Sizing is the measurement, calculation, or estimation of the resources needed to do certain tasks, for example, run payroll, and the configuration of the system needed to support them with a certain level of performance. There are a variety of sizing techniques, but very detailed ones are beyond the scope of this book. Not only that, but many of them don't work.

Benchmarks

There are formal definitions of benchmarks from a variety of sources, but tying the subject down to a single sentence can be counterproductive. In essence, a benchmark is a set of tasks designed to

- Compare the capacities or throughput capabilities of two or more systems
- Estimate real capacity or throughput capability requirements for a particular application or application set

Tuning

Tuning is the manipulation of certain objects to optimize the performance of a system or eliminate detected bottlenecks. Objects here might include operating system parameters, database design or modification, and the placement of data. Physical tuning might mean adding memory or disks, upgrading a CPU, or installing a faster network or LAN. Detailed tuning is not covered in this book, although the determination of physical bottlenecks is.

Tuning soon after implementation is often an admission of failure in the design and coding parts of the development cycle and is sometimes ineffective because of inherent design faults.

There are basically four things you can do about system performance in the production stage:

- Ignore it and hope for the best
- Measure it (performance monitoring)
- Predict it (sizing and capacity planning)
- Change or correct it (tuning)

To take action implies some performance threshold has been crossed and that such thresholds can be quantified in some way. This quantification of performance is the subject of the next section.

Simple Performance Model

A simple numerical model has been proposed (by A. Nonymous) that performance (P) can be assessed numerically by the indicator of performance equation:

$$\text{Performance Indicator } P = \frac{\text{Resource Available}}{\text{Resource Used/Required}} \tag{7.5}$$

If P is greater than 1, everything is fine, as we have resource on hand; if it is less than 1, we are short of resource and users of that resource may be forced to "queue" for access to that resource.

Telephone Example: The exercise to decide how many phones to provide is based on anticipated usage ("Logical Bottleneck Example 1"). It is, in effect, a sizing exercise just like those in IT with a compromise between cost incurred and the quality of service provided.

The subject of queues is very important in the performance area, and we will deal with them in some (not too much) detail shortly.

Performance Measures

Numeric performance measures, often called metrics, will depend on the workload in question and the requirements of the users. Vendors quote numbers to show the performance characteristics of their hardware; users normally employ different metrics, albeit often without knowing it.

Vendor Measures

Vendors, in general, quote performance characteristics from public benchmarks with the aim of demonstrating the power* of their system, either absolutely or by comparison with competitors. What they actually quote depends on the hardware they are selling, for example, CPUs, disks, or hubs.

■ Millions of instructions per second (MIPS), normally useful in commercial environments, although spreadsheets do make use of good floating-point capability
■ Millions of floating-point operations per second (MFLOPS) for floating-point performance, normally in scientific compute intensive applications (high-performance computing [HPC])
■ SPECint and SPECfp, measures of CPU performance
■ TPC-C, TPC-H, TPC-W, and TPC-R transactions per minute or second, used for commercial work and web commerce
■ Other SPEC benchmarks and web-oriented measures, such as SPECjbb
■ Graphics measures, such as shaded polygons per second and the like
■ Performance of network software, such as TCP/IP, NFS, and so on
■ Performance of network hardware, such as LANs, switches, and hubs, and so on

These vendor measures often consist of figures for standard benchmarks, perhaps with internal benchmark figures such as IBM's Commercial Processing Workload (CPW). Such numbers should form only a part of any system evaluation process along with the ability to deliver, support, services on offer, and so on. The criteria used by the Aberdeen Group, the Magic Quadrant, might be useful to employ.

User Measures

Although users are interested in the vendor measurements when evaluating vendor hardware, they are interested in different measurements when their applications are in full production, for example,

■ Response time for transactions and queries
■ Throughput of transactions (transactions per second)
■ Elapsed time and throughput for batch jobs
■ Times for backup and recovery activities for vital applications (disaster recovery)

For commercial transaction processing work, the combination of response time and throughput is of more interest than the individual elements. A typical user requirement might be stated in terms of desired throughput with certain response time constraints. The specification of user requirements of a system is often called a service level agreement (SLA), a topic covered in Chapter 8.

---

* They also often claim that their products are *modular, flexible, and easy to use,* but so is a garden hose.

Performance: Good and Bad

The subject of performance is probably unique in IT since it seems rarely to get much consideration or press coverage until it is bad. If people can identify "bad" performance, then there must be a notion of "good" performance. Let us settle here on the idea of good performance as getting adequate response or throughput to work submitted to a system, as either a transaction or a batch job. This, however, begs the question of what is adequate.

The normal answer is that it all depends on expectations and business, in its broadest sense, requirements. For instance, a telephone query desk using a computer to answer customer queries could reasonably expect a response in a few seconds. A system handling a real-time application, such as nuclear plant control, would consider 5 s an age and would expect a response of the order of fractions of a second. At the other end of the scale, a molecular modeler would be delighted if a new system turned around a large calculation in 10 h when in the past he had to wait several days. Thus, response time is relative to the workload.

At the end of the day, whatever the business, the best response time is one that doesn't have a negative impact on the business—like losing customers—and doesn't cost more than it contributes to the business. The happy scientist above apart, it seems logical that every application should have the fastest response time possible, say 0.1 s.

The simple curve in Figure 7.12 shows the truth of the saying "You get what you pay for." In reality, there has to be a compromise, and a system is (or should be) sized around an acceptable response time, and not the other way round. In addition, it has to be decided whether that response time applies to the average workload on the system or the peak, be that daily, weekly, or yearly. There will be businesses that offer special promotion deals that generate abnormally high online loads.

Abnormal Systems Loads

An occasional *peak* has occurred in the UK Lottery (and similar activities) where rollover prizes accumulate to very large amounts and generate hectic activity. When this activity occurs in the hours just before the draw, the system is often swamped and forced to close down. I am not sure what the solution to this problem is, but a queuing system, rather than a direct real-time processing of activity, might help. I am certain peak *whammies* like these occur in many countries.

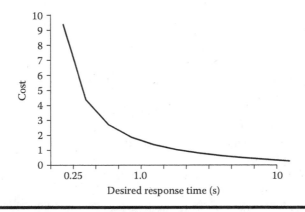

Figure 7.12 Cost of reducing transaction response time.

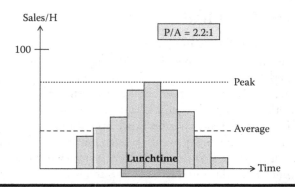

Figure 7.13 Sample workload vs. time.

Similar huge peaks of processor demand are caused by distributed denial-of-service (DDoS) malware, but these are handled in a different way than normal work. This is a security issue, but monitoring is a key part of detecting these attacks.

Suffice it to say here that another decision regarding peaks has to be made. That decision is whether to cater to the average peak over an hour, several minutes, or an even smaller period. The effect of catering to the peak compared to the average workload is shown in Figure 7.13.

The curve shows the number of sandwiches sold during 15 min periods over a working day, say, 8:00 a.m. to 6:00 p.m. It is evident that the peak selling activity is much greater than the average selling activity over the whole day. It is possible that within the peak 15 min there will be selling activity even greater than the peak shown in Figure 7.13. The shop owner will have to make the decision whether to provide enough resources (people, shelf space, etc.) for the peak 5 min of activity, the peak 15 min of activity, and so on. In effect, his decision is what level of service to provide or cater to any instantaneous peak, or settle for handling the 15 min average peak, for example.

This implies a reduced level of service at those peak times, but a lesser cost in terms of resources, including people, needed to cope with them.

Activity Peaks

Most computer systems experience "peaky" activity of this type (not necessarily the same curve), and the same "service level" decision has to be made regarding the provision of computer resources (CPU, disks, etc.). A common mistake made in sizing computer configurations is to calculate the average activity, say, two transactions per second, while neglecting the shape of the daily workload pattern. A second mistake is to cater to the peak of daily activity, but forget there may be even greater peaks at month end, year end, holidays, and so on. A classic peaky activity is shown in Figure 7.14, illustrating the activity in a computerized time and attendance recording system in a company with many employees.

The reason for emphasizing the importance of peak-to-average ratios is that even in systems with regular activity, it is rare not to have a peak 50% greater than the average, and in most commercial enterprises it is more like two or more. Errors of factors of 2 (100%) or more in sizing systems can be catastrophic if averages are taken as the baseline workload.

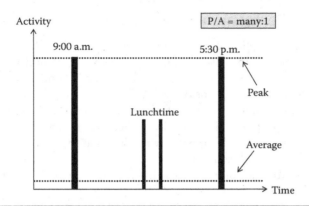

Figure 7.14 **Time and attendance peaky workload.**

Peakiness Lesson

I learned a valuable lesson some years ago when doing some performance work for a UK government legal department where peaks of high CPU utilization were causing concern. It looked like an upgrade was needed to their system. However, after I plotted the daytime CPU utilization for several days' activity, I noticed that the peaks were always in the midmorning and midafternoon periods, far higher than in other periods, and showed a large peak-to-average ratio. As Holmes would have said, "Most singular, Watson."

I asked what workload was carried out at those times and was told it was the main processing they carried out from letters delivered just prior to those periods. The solution was elementary: spread out that processing over a longer period, possibly by using fewer people to do the processing. I am against pretty performance plots that simply adorn walls, but they can sometimes give a lot of information if the alert eye is cast over a selection of them, preferably with some knowledge of the business activity.

In the electrical industry, the equivalent of an IT system or network of systems is a power network for the delivery of electricity. Many years ago, hand calculations were sufficient to plan a new network since each item (lines, transformers, etc.) was overconfigured to allow for contingency and growth. In more competitive days, electricity companies now use power systems analysis tools to design networks that have safety factors but are also cost-effective. The planning is done with graphical applications using well-known equations like Ohm's and Kirchhoff's laws, together with the more abstruse transport theory, sparse matrices, and numerical methods.

Such tools are not available to the IT industry except for some tools for modeling or simulating systems and subsystems, such as a disk or a network. These can help in many cases, but the data has to be estimated since the real data can only be measured on a live system with users, databases, and so on. There are also more unique elements in an IT system than there are in an electrical network, which renders pure simulation even more difficult. This leaves the pragmatic, or rule-of-thumb, approach as the optimum method for estimating, measuring, and controlling the performance of a system.

There are many elements in an IT system that affect performance, although some may be beyond the performance person's control. For example, an existing machine with its operating system and database is beyond his control to influence, although he may be able to do post-purchase work on performance.

What Degrades Performance?

It is often the case that an application performs adequately one day but does not the next. Why does this happen? The answer in most cases is that there are bottlenecks in the system, slowing down the servicing of, for example, a transaction. Everyone is familiar with bottlenecks in any road system, especially in London or Los Angeles.

Bottlenecks occur in computer systems at various points in the journey of work through it. In the context of our simple model (introduction to Section I), they occur when P is less than 1, where demand on a resource exceeds supply. The result is that the units of work the system is trying to process have to queue for resources.*

There are basically two kinds of bottleneck that can "throttle back" the flow of work through a system.

Physical Bottlenecks

Physical bottlenecks are tangible constraint on the flow of work through a system, which then results in a longer response time. Examples are networks with high latency or insufficient bandwidth to handle the load imposed, overutilized disks or servers, or outages of parallel items in a flow of work.

Logical Bottlenecks

In the absence of physical bottlenecks, there are often performance problems that sometimes baffle people. This can be due to logical bottlenecks in the system that can degrade performance even when sufficient physical resources are available. Let us look at some illustrative examples of this phenomenon.

Logical Bottleneck Example 1: An example of a logical bottleneck is that of the telephone booths outside a motorway (or freeway) service station. If there are 10 telephone booths and six potential users, performance is good since they all get to use a phone immediately ($p > 1$). Or do they?

Some telephone booths will only accept phone cards, others cash, and some both. In this example, there should in theory be no queues for the phone. However, if six of the booths are card only and only one person has a card, then the remaining five people will be competing for four phones and a queue of one will form. However, if there are 10 booths and 25 people trying to use them, many people will have to queue for the telephone service.

In theory, the solution is to provide a very large number of booths to cater to all eventualities. In practical IT, cost considerations need to be addressed in providing configurations that match SLA requirements.

Logical Bottleneck Example 2: Other logical bottlenecks can occur when system parameters intervene to throttle back the throughput of a system. There are some generic types, illustrated, using artificial names, below:
- Maxtasks = 50 (maximum number of tasks allowed)
- Maxprocs = 60 (maximum number of active processes allowed)
- Maxstor = 4000 (maximum storage allocated, e.g., in kilobytes)

---

* An Italian colleague of mine pointed out that queuing theory does not apply in Italy.

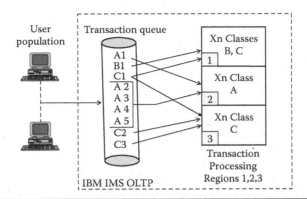

Figure 7.15   Sample service dispatching mechanism.

- Maxusers = 70 (maximum number of users allowed)
- Appmax = 20% (maximum CPU percentage this application can use)
- Maxbufs = 8 (maximum number of I/O buffers)

Logical Bottleneck Example 3: A real example of this kind of logical constraint is illustrated below. IBM's Information Management System (IMS) has a transaction dispatching mechanism that can be controlled by the use of certain parameters, set by operations personnel. Getting these wrong or, in some cases, failing to change them with changing circumstances can produce bottlenecks as the examples above would also do.

The transactions on the incoming queue are dispatched (executed) on the basis of their class as assigned by operations and the regions of the system assigned to process those classes, as shown above. A performance issue will arise if the incoming transactions are predominantly of a class for which few regions are assigned to process them.

If, for example, nearly all the incoming transactions are class A and there is only one processing region assigned to process them, it is likely there will be a queue of A transactions resulting in poor response time for that class. Other classes will be quite happy with their lot. This is an example where physical resource is not the issue, and the situation might be termed a selective performance issue, resulting in complaints from users of class A transactions, but not from users of the other classes (Figure 7.15).

The way around this is to understand the composition of the workload transactions and assign regions appropriately. If there is a variation in the arrival rate of different class transactions, it will need to be monitored and class or region adjustments made to handle the situation.

Let us now look at some of the components of a computer system that affect its performance.

System Performance Concepts

Three computer "timing" concepts should now be familiar to the reader:

- Time to run a job (commercial batch or scientific)
- Response time of a transaction (mean or percentile specification)
- Number transactions processed per unit time, usually a second (throughput)

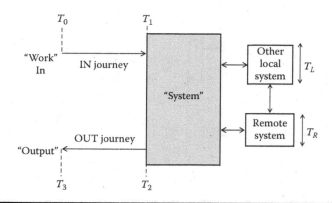

Figure 7.16 Journey through a general computer system.

The overall performance of, say, a transaction depends on its history in traversing whatever systems and resources it requires for its completion. Not all transactions will travel the same path since often a single transaction can performance one or more tasks, depending on the input parameters. It may work only on the primary system that first receives it, but might need access to other systems, which might be local or remote.

Thus, a transaction invocation may be of the form $XN1(a, b, c)$, where a, b, and c are parameters that tell the program dealing with $XN1$ how to proceed with its processing. The need to access other systems might come from using distributed systems or perhaps moving applications across to a new system, but not all the data resides on that system until some later date.

These concepts are shown schematically in Figure 7.16. This figure shows a transaction request or a job of work entering the system (In) and the transaction answer or the job results emerging (Out). The times T_0, T_1, and so on, mean different things, depending whether we are discussing batch jobs or transaction processing. We introduce here the notions of internal response times and external response times for system transactions, assuming that other local and remote systems are not involved:

- For the transaction processing case, $(T_2 - T_1)$ is the internal response time for the transaction or the time between the first character of the transaction data entering the system (server plus storage) and the last character leaving.
- The time $(T_3 - T_0)$ is the external response time, or that observed by the user entering the transaction. This is normally defined as the time between the last character entered on the input screen and the arrival of the first character of the output on the screen.
- The times $(T_1 - T_0)$ and $(T_3 - T_2)$ would typically represent communications line time in a simple case. For the batch job processing case, $(T_2 - T_1)$ is essentially the time taken to run the job, and $(T_3 - T_2)$ and $(T_1 - T_0)$ might be accounted for as job setup, scheduling, and input/output spooling.

The "system" might be a variety of things, but typically could be

- A traditional mainframe or minicomputer, that is, a single system or a client/server configuration comprising a user's workstation or PC and a server
- A heterogeneous network that, in the extreme case, might involve distributed databases and distributed transaction processing

- An Internet or intranet system, perhaps cooperating with an existing, non-Internet IT system
- A cloud system incorporating virtualization
- A mixture of these cases

In the more complex distributed case, the system time $(T_2 - T_1)$ will become

$$\text{Response Time} = (T_2 - T_1) + f(T_L, T_O)$$

where the function $f(..)$ is some time elements of the other systems, depending on what they are asked to do and whether only one or both are involved. The prediction of the response time or throughput of transactions in this environment by queuing theory is virtually impossible, by calculation very nearly so, and best done by ROTs or a pilot benchmark.

In any of the cases, there will be a number of elements through which the transaction or job must pass, and each will add a certain time to the *journey*. For a transaction, the journey time is called the *response time* for that transaction or *elapsed time* for a batch job. This is what the user sees, and this is the important factor in performance, as it relates directly to a service level agreement (SLA).

Another key performance number is the number of transactions completed per second (throughput rate), preferably with reasonable response times. However, an impressive throughput rate can be less attractive if the associated response times are long. For example, a system supporting five transactions per second with average response times of 5 s may be less desirable than one supporting four transactions per second with an average of 3 s.

But wait, surely a transaction rate of five per second must give a response time of 0.2 s and a rate of four per second, 0.25 s? To resolve this apparent dilemma, consider the following analogy, which should explain the dichotomy.*

Military Analogy of Throughput

There are some new recruits to the army who need to be supplied with various types of military clothing and equipment. These items are issued in a large hut that has several tables, each containing a specific item, and entrance and exit doors. The recruits enter the hut, pass in order among the tables, collecting items as they go, and depart through the exit door. It will probably take several minutes for each recruit to acquire a full set of items even though they will be moving quite quickly.

We might observe from an external position that the recruits are entering and leaving at a rate of about three per minute. This rate will vary depending on how queues build up at the various tables because of variations in the times to be served at each of them. This observation might lead the external observer to the conclusion that it takes 20 s to pick up a full complement of military items.

However, closer examination shows that the three people leaving the hut in any 1 min are not the same three that entered a minute previously. This leads to the conclusion that the recruits must spend some time traversing the hut.

---

* Division into two mutually exclusive, opposed, or contradictory groups.

In data processing terms, the hut is a *system* and the time to traverse the hut from entering to leaving the *response time*. To ensure an orderly flow into and out of the hut, there may be soldiers lining up the recruits as they enter, and releasing them from the queue every so often to regulate the flow of recruits around the tables. A similar operation may happen at the exit. This input queue, output queue method is often used in transaction processing systems, such as IBM's Information Management System (IMS) and many message queuing (MQ) systems.

A refinement of this recruit queuing technique is the selective release of recruits to go to certain tables that are not serving since they do not need items from previous tables that may be occupied. The soldier then acts as a "queue manager" based on criteria other than first in, first out. Again, IMS works in this way, and we will come across it later in the discussions on performance.

Percentile Responses

Returning to transaction processing again, it will be evident that response times for individual transactions, even of the same type, will vary. In attempting to compare the capacities of two or more transaction processing systems, we need some way of quoting these times meaningfully, rather than a long list of each response time. One way is to quote the average and some number representing the variation of response times around this number.

We will examine this number, called a percentile, in more detail in Appendix I on queuing theory.

Since all transactions, even of the same type and execution parameters, do not have the same response time, a useful form of measure for transaction response times is a graph of the numbers of transactions and their associated response times, the *response curve*. A schematic response curve is shown in Figure 7.17.

Although the graph shows a continuous curve, it really represents a smoothed-out histogram for measurements on a finite number of transactions and their response times. In Figure 7.17,

- n_1 is the number of transactions with response times between t_0 and t_1.
- n_2 is the number of transactions with response times between t_1 and t_2, and so on, for n_3, ..., n_i.

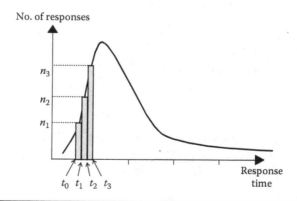

Figure 7.17   Sample response time curve.

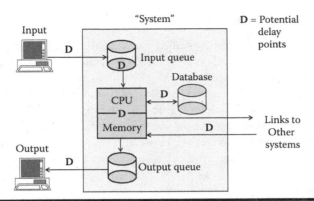

Figure 7.18 Elements of response time and delays.

For measurements on larger and larger numbers of transactions, the histogram would approach a smooth curve as the intervals, $(t_1 - t_0)$, $(t_2 - t_1)$, and so on, approach zero.

The response curve we have just discussed was illustrative only, and the types of curves arising in real situations are covered later. However, a practical aspect of response times and response curves should be noted here.

Experience has shown that users prefer a system that has an average response time made up of a narrow range of individual response times to one with a lower average composed of widely varying response times. For example, an average response time of 2.5 s derived from response times between 1.7 and 3.1 s is preferable to an average of 2.2 s made up of responses between 0.1 and 12.1 s.

The latter often results in irritation and loss of concentration by the user. This highlights the idea of a "distribution" of response times instead of a single number for every transaction entered. The latter case has a good average response but a wide distribution of component responses, whereas the former has a worse response time but a narrower spread.

Another *trick of the trade* is also relevant to this discussion. It is often the case that a new computer system has much spare capacity when initially installed, but fills up over a period as the planned user base increases. In the early days, the users will probably see a very good response time, which will deteriorate as more users come onto the system. Since their expectations will have been set by this early experience, they will become dissatisfied with the later level of service.

Imagine that the predicted response time when the system was fully loaded was a mean of 3 s, but in the early days users were getting responses between 0.5 and 1.0 s. If it is possible, steps should be taken at the start to add time to the responses so that they start off at, and hopefully remain, at the agreed and calculated times by reducing the delay as the user population increases.

Stability, as illustrated by the two examples above, is important in the design and use of interactive computer systems.

Looking back for a moment at the recruits traversing the equipment hut, we see that the time taken was the sum of the different times taken to be served at the various tables. A set of transactions make a similar journey through their equivalent of the hut, the system, taking time to traverse the various elements that make up the system.

Performance in Distributed Systems

The cases we have discussed so far have assumed a single CPU machine processing work (usually transactions) from a "dumb" terminal on a line or LAN. Today, however, there is a move toward client/server computing and distributed processing, both of which are illustrated in Figure 7.19.

Imagine a transaction being initiated on the client or host with part of it processed on the server or second host, rather like the schematic in Figure 7.19. The total response time seen by the user or client will be the sum of the time spent in the client system or host and that spent in the server or second host *plus* the time taken in interactions between them. This "interaction" time is not simply data movement time, but can include protocol, security, and other interchanges between the two or more systems.

The total response time (T_R) then will be

$$T_R = T_{R(System1)} + T_{R(System2)} + \text{Interaction/protocol delay}\,(s)$$

These examples are not parallel server cases, but single servers in a series so that single server rules apply to the calculations of $T_{R(System1)}$ and $T_{R(System2)}$ for each element in the chain. The "interaction delays" may be composed of communications protocols, distributed database protocols, and other elements, as well as the speed and reliability of the communications medium.

Aside: One reason for distributing systems is to separate "warring" workloads, for example, massive CPU consumers or I/O eaters. This is very often an issue on single servers where mixed workloads are run without the facility for prioritizing resource access. This is a factor to be considered in design for performance, as CPU hoggers can cause all kinds of problems if their characteristics are not fully understood. Runaway tasks have the same effect, but will continue to wreak havoc until killed.

Distributed Systems Examples

The best known example of distributed systems is probably the client/server model. Client/server systems can be implemented in a number of ways, depending on the user requirements. For remote UNIX file access, the Sun Network File System (NFS) is often used. In the case of Oracle client/server, SQL*Net or perhaps Oracle Gateways may be used to access data on another system.

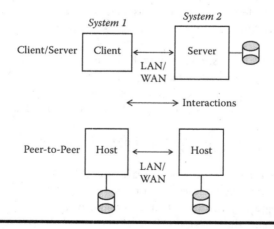

Figure 7.19   Generic distributed systems.

In other cases, some sort of peer-to-peer connection might be used to access data on a remote system. An example of this is program-to-program communication, such as IBM's Advanced Program-to-Program Communication (APPC).

Let us now examine the case where a mainframe application is accessed via a fixed function (dumb) terminal changed to operate as a client/server application.

Systems Network Architecture Mainframe Example

This is presented as an example of a *classical* IT system that prevailed in the 1970s and 1980s and performance was simpler to measure and predict than it is in today's more complex environments. Imagine that the user has retrieved some stock and cost figures for 12 items of inventory sold by the company. He or she wishes to change the stock figures of six of the items. The situation is illustrated in Figure 7.20.

When the screen is first received, the whole of the data and field markers are shipped down to the terminal buffer and displayed on the screen, say 1200 bytes. On changing six of the stock fields, the mainframe (usually via an OLTP system) issues a "read modified fields" command and only retrieves the changed fields, say 50 bytes.

Similarly, to write the changed stock figures back to the screen would require a "write modified fields" command to update the screen, perhaps highlighting the changes. Again, about 50 bytes plus a new field character will be transmitted. This makes efficient use of the links between user and system by minimizing the data traffic.

As a matter of interest, there are at least two ways of achieving this interaction:

1. Shipping the necessary transaction to the other system for it to handle and pass the results back to the initiator
2. Program-to-program communication where an application on system 1 interacts with a cooperating application on system 2

If the links between the terminal and mainframe are adequate, this sort of interaction can take place in fractions of a second. This is an example of the relatively simple classical or legacy world. This is *not* necessarily the case when the client/server mode of operation is adopted.

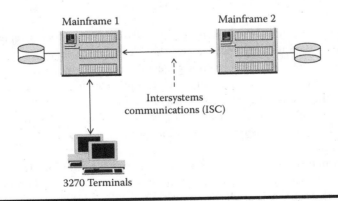

Mainframe 1   Mainframe 2

Intersystems
communications (ISC)

3270 Terminals

Figure 7.20   Systems Network Architecture mainframe distributed processing.

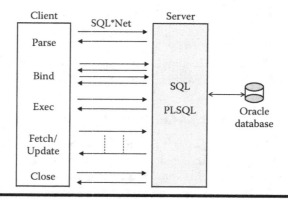

Figure 7.21   Client/server interaction example: Oracle.

Client/Server Example

Figure 7.21 shows the interactions between the client and server systems when the mainframe application is reproduced in this environment. The example uses Oracle terminology simply to illustrate the client/server mode of operation.

When a server receives a Structured Query Language (SQL) statement from the client, it performs the following tasks, generic to most RDBMSs:

1. Parse the statement
   - The syntax is checked.
   - The shared SQL area is searched to see if the statement already exists.
   - The data dictionary is searched for object resolution, security privileges, and the most effective search path.

   If the statement is not already stored in the shared SQL area, the server determines and stores the execution plan.
2. Bind
   - A bind is required if the statement does not have literal values.
3. Execute
   - The parse tree is applied to the data buffers.
   - Physical reads or logical reads and writes are performed.
4. Fetch or update
   - The appropriate row is retrieved and updated and the process repeated for six rows, where stock data is being updated and the client informed.

   There are ways of reducing the traffic generated by this "row at a time" update or retrieval method. The best way is to do an array fetch or update of several rows in one statement, the equivalent of chained reads of records from a disk. However, it means that the client code must have a dialogue with the user to receive and, where possible, validate the six changed rows of data. This may be time-consuming if the validation needs data stored on the server only.
5. Close the connection

   The performance of such a system compared to that of a dumb terminal with a central server depends very much on how the communications protocol and programming is implemented. If such a scheme is used, then monitoring and management, as well as initial design, are a must.

Internet Example

This is where it can get tricky in trying to establish what path a transaction takes through the Internet and other connections, such as the "tangle" of equipment involved in the Internet schematic in Figure 7.22.

Why Bother at All?

One of the biggest bugbears in performance issues is extreme variations in response times or job times, although the latter is less of a problem and more amenable to analysis. The ways of minimizing this kind of issue involve the following areas:

- Definition of service levels (SLAs)
- Design against these criteria with some contingency
- Performance monitoring
- Performance management
- Capacity planning and forecasting
- Use of key performance indicators (KPIs), particularly in resource utilizations
- Clear knowledge of volumes and changes of workload types and mix, which can affect response times

The latter point caused a minor war at one customer I was involved with when resource utilizations were rising regularly with no apparent reason until someone found that the business was adding users willy-nilly without informing IT. This emphasizes:

- The importance of a service level agreement (SLA) and its volatility.
- The use of clauses that can invalidate the terms of the SLA; in the example above, the users failed to inform the IT people of the increases in volumes.

The subject of SLAs is outlined in Chapter 8 and covered in more detail in Chapter 17 as part of the immersion process of learning.

Remember that without an SLA, it doesn't matter what you measure in performance terms; nobody in IT will care, the users will.

PERFORMANCE IN PRACTICE

The art and science of performance management has a reason to exist, and that is to satisfy the requirements of the users of the IT systems in the course of their business. It is not an academic exercise or an ego trip for IT gurus, and if this is borne in mind, then the systems and accompanying networks can be managed professionally.

It is easy to generate masses of performance and other data, especially if you are using commercial tools. However, if your SuperMonitor Mark III produces reams of data and graphs that are not translated into information and thus into usable knowledge, then such data is useless. If this operation is successful, then a plan of action can be developed to solve performance (and possibly other) issues. Having this data and not making optimum use of it is like having a large garage with a Porsche, a Rolls Royce, and a Ford Mustang in it, but being unable to drive.

The key message about all this is, if you can't measure it and interpret it, you can't manage it, and if you can't manage it, you are probably in trouble.

Chapter 8

Performance: Design, Sizing, and Management

The first thing to cover here is "Why are we doing all this?" and the answer is to satisfy a service level agreement (SLA) we have made with our clients or end users. There are arguments that say the benefits of application performance management (APM) are outweighed by the costs, which we address boldly up front.

Is the APM Cost Worth It?

There is also a possible return on investment (ROI) in managing performance:

The ROI of Application Performance Management
http://www.xo.com/resources/white-papers/the-roi-of-application-performance-management.pdf

This paper offers "examples and simple calculations [that] can provide a starting point in building a business case for an application performance management solution."

We will cover the topic of service level agreements first, before launching into the sea of performance data we will inevitably have to navigate successfully.

Service Level Agreements

Q: What have these got to do with performance?
A: Everything.

SLAs: The Dawn of Realism

If you want to buy a Ferrari or Maserati and walk into a car showroom dressed like Detective Columbo, the salesman will immediately think, "Can this guy afford one?" The same sort of question is often asked when the business user states his business service requirements to the IT people as "responses of 0.02 s (or less) and 100% availability (or greater) until judgment day (and beyond if required)." The IT department will dutifully go away and do their total cost of ownership (TCO) calculations for such a system or service and present it to business user management, to the nearest £10 million (ca. $15 million), and ongoing, operational, and depreciation costs, in rounded millions.

The businesspeople, having seen the estimate, will then retire crushed.* Over a coffee or a Jack Daniels and some financial reflection, they will modify their demands and settle for something the enterprise can afford, and then the serious business of planning, designing, delivering, and operating before the service delivery can begin. I know, because I saw a scenario similar to this played out at a well-known aerospace company in the United Kingdom where the users were setting impossible service level targets for IT. They too were crushed.

> Chargeback in real money is a useful way of ensuring realism in user demands.

When the dust settles, the parties involved will need to draw up an agreed on set of deliverables, requirements, constraints, and charges for a service and penalties on IT for nonfulfillment. There should also be penalties against the users if the workload differs markedly from that specified as the basis for the SLA, for example, adding 50% to the number of service users without informing IT.

> *Note*: This set is called a *service level agreement* or *SLA*. Notice the word *service* as opposed to *system*.

Idea of User Service

In the old legacy days, the computer center had little concept of serving the users and attending to their needs. They had a job to do, and that was managing the complex monster called the IBM mainframe—business users were just a blip on the horizon, a necessary evil who earned the money to pay their IT salaries. As the applications on offer moved out of the purely financial arena to areas like engineering, data warehouse, and online transactions, users were often charged for their use of the system, which finance used to claim as their own.

Gradually, these users started asking what they were getting for their money and began to demand quantifiable *levels of service*, such as hours of service availability, uptime, and response times.

Eventually, this led IT and users to the concept of *service management*, a conscious effort by IT to offer a quantifiable service and not just CPU power and disk storage when they happened to be available. This concept of a service evolved into an agreement between users and IT as to what it should and should not include, together with costs, either internal (often called *Mickey Mouse* or *funny*) money or real (*greenback*) money.

These management disciplines in IT are aimed at quantifying and improving the service offered to users in a variety of areas, including

---

* A wonderful expression for retreat, paraphrased here from the G.K. Chesterton Father Brown story called "The Queer Feet."

- Application and service availability and times of service
- Application and service costs (real or internal)
- System availability: Percent availability of the service platform within agreed service times
- Network availability: Ditto except that it should be available outside the service times for automatic file and data transmissions at any time
- More rapid recovery from failures, including disaster recovery (DR), quantified
- Adequate response times in terms of *means* or *percentiles*
- Extended service hours when needed, for example, quarter or year end
- Service level agreements (SLAs): Their structure and revision criteria
- Service level reporting (SLR): How are we doing against targets?
- Penalties for nonachievement of agreed on service levels
- Regular review and renegotiation of the SLAs between parties involved

Add to this list the two other vital "*ations*": *documentation* and *communication*. It helps to demonstrate due diligence when the fur starts to fly in difficult user IT situations and possibly provide the means of getting out of them amicably. It is quite possible that the service requirements for a *standard SLA* will be different from those for a *cloud SLA*, mainly in the reported metrics, but the users may not appreciate this distinction. The differences are covered later in the book under "SLAs and the Cloud" in Chapter 17.

Systems Design

Taking a step back for a moment, it may be instructive to look at the architectural aspects of a whole system or set of systems to see where performance management fits in. The list of architectures in Table 8.1 is ambitious and might take years to complete. A few things to note about architectures before we go any further include

- The architecture design methods of today are often overelaborate and practically opaque to most IT people.
- They should be simple* and not throwing terms like *abstraction* and *third normal forms* about like confetti,
- They should, wherever possible, be based on recognized standards.
- The subarchitectures are interlinked so that compromises will need to be made to avoid requirements clashes, for example, performance with availability or performance with security.[†]
- They need some form of management to monitor and maintain them where necessary, most usefully by reference to the IT Infrastructure Library (ITIL) standards and best practices.
- They should be capable of being manipulated to give different viewpoints of them to people in different functions within an organization.
- They should, in the main, be capable of being implemented in different ways, rather like an architect's drawing of a building that is open to being constructed by wood, brick, or other materials.

---

* The scientist Lord Rutherford always said we should keep things simple enough so that they can be explained to a barmaid.
[†] This can impose an overhead on performance depending on its implementation.

Table 8.1 List of IT Architectures Including Performance

Architecture	Definition
Information architecture	This architecture defines the business questions that IT is to address, including the major information repositories in the business, the information flow between them, and the access methodology. This is in essence a flow diagram that should be easily understood by businesspeople.
Storage architecture	This architecture defines the storage strategy for the business. It is also a subarchitecture to many of the other architectures, such as the availability, application, coexistence, and management architectures.
Application architecture	The application architecture defines the major applications, their interaction, and their delivery, e.g., client/server, thin client, web based, and *n*-tier.
Coexistence architecture	This architecture defines the integration of the major systems supporting the information architecture. It will include the definition of the interfaces between major systems, for example, provision of services for both homogeneous and heterogeneous environments. This type of architecture is mandatory for migrations from one system to another, for example, *modernizing* a legacy system where old must coexist with the new for a period.
Security architecture	This architecture defines the security requirements for the information architecture. This will probably be a requirement for multilevel security. For example, the demands of an Internet installation will typically be more stringent than those of an extranet. Anything in the public domain (as the Internet is) is prone to hacking and other malware intrusions; thus, its greatest advantage is its biggest exposure.
Availability architecture	This architecture defines how the availability criteria that are required for each major component of the information architecture will be met. It include subarchitectures such as backup and recovery strategy, archive strategy, and disaster recovery planning. It links with availability since software reliability is a key issue in overall availability of services.
Management architecture	This architecture defines the support strategy for the services that maintain the information architecture, including systems, storage, networks, and applications.
Development architecture	This architecture defines the development environment, test and quality assurance (QA) processes, and deployment strategy.
Production (or operations) architecture	This architecture defines the production schema for applications and day-to-day operations, such as backup and housekeeping.

Table 8.1 (Continued) List of IT Architectures Including Performance

Architecture	Definition
Data architecture	This architecture defines the characteristics of the data that flows through the information architecture. It would typically provide data volumes, storage technologies (relational database management system [RDBMS] and text files), availability and security requirements, volatility, and data importance.
Web or e-commerce architecture	This architecture defines the web or e-commerce infrastructure, the delivery targets and mechanisms, and how the security, performance, and availability requirements are addressed.
Performance architecture	This defines the characteristics of the resource components that support the business applications in the manner dictated by the SLAs. It is essentially a performance viewpoint of the application architecture with requirements and the chosen "feeds and speeds" to meet them.
Enterprise printing architecture	This describes the framework for supporting the printing needs of the organization or strategic business unit (SBU): factors such as security, priorities, color, remote printing, and synchronous and asynchronous printing.

Performance Architecture

A difficult concept to pin down or explain as *architecture* means different things to different people, particularly in an IT context. For our purposes, I would like to define an IT architecture as a set of standards and components, which can preferably be represented diagrammatically, that form the basis of systems aimed at maximizing performance of work running on it.

Such an architecture might comprise other architectures, for example, x86, relational database, I/O attachment architecture, and a network specification. It is impossible for me, as the author, to lay down an architecture for everyone to follow, but I can simply illustrate the principles of an architecture aimed at performance. The architecture documentation should explain its components and their relationship with the workload they are designed to optimize; this is the difficult bit. Costs and ROI will also be an issue when proposing an architecture.

> *Lesson*: A customer of mine once proposed a new data center to the board of his company without a cost–benefit analysis that he had been advised by a data center guru to prepare. He was dispatched by the board with a flea in his ear and told to prepare such a case. He promptly put the onus on me, representing IBM, to help him out, but we managed it in the end. The solution, incidentally, was centered on people productivity and some consolidation of system and human resources.

Sample Performance Architecture

Figure 8.1 shows a sample (not necessarily perfect) of a performance architecture where you will note that specific products are not named.

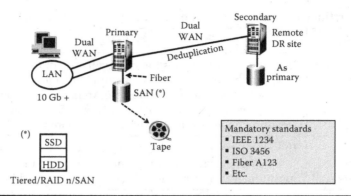

Figure 8.1   Sample performance architecture specification.

This architecture is vendor product neutral, although it does contain techniques and standards in its specification, and this is normal in my experience. I have seen diagrams purporting to be architectures when in fact they were more like wiring diagrams for a nuclear missile. If an architecture is to have any longevity, it should be

- As independent as possible of product specifics apart from some necessary ones, like minimum speeds, which may dictate a particular component of a solution
- Simple to understand (remember the Rutherford barmaid)
- Implementable by human beings
- Able to be dovetailed with other architectures in the organization
- Documented
- Reusable "as is" (i.e., the modular portions, if possible) or in diluted form in other architectures*

Performance Architecture White Papers

The two links below point to Dell and Intel papers that describe a Dell system architecture and a high-performance storage architecture. They illustrate the principle of developing architectures within an explanatory document and are fairly free of product implications. The papers not only have diagrams, but also explain why certain techniques are employed in the illustrated architectures and represent a good example of what I am trying to convey in differentiating between architectures and implementations.

Dell Fluid File System: A Dell Technology White Paper
http://i.dell.com/sites/doccontent/shared-content/data-sheets/en/Documents/DSFS_White_paper_r4-0.pdf

Architecting a High Performance Storage System [Intel]
http://docs.media.bitpipe.com/io_11x/io_117307/item_963935/architecting-lustre-storage-white-paper.pdf

---

* Sun Microsystems in the late 1990s was developing a reusable enterprise architecture library (REAL) along these lines, but I think it floundered due to high ambitions and inadequate skills (I had left). Proves the KISS method is best (keep it simple, stupid).

WoW: Unless they are proven to be absolutely necessary, I would steer clear of elaborate architecture models that are more aesthetic and elegant than useful in the real IT world. Take some useful practices or checklists from them by all means, but don't become addicted to *third normal forms*, *functional abstractions*, and other *architectural gymnastics* at the expense of pragmatic designs.

Life is too short and your organization's business won't wait.

System Sizing

System sizing is the activity of estimating resource requirements for performance and is often done via *testing* in simulated environments. There are a variety of test types for applications and other software:

- *Functional testing.* Does it do the job the users want it to do? Is it user friendly?
- *Performance testing.* Does it give adequate performance—as requested in a service level agreement (SLA)—and is the performance consistent?
- *Load testing.* At what point in the load does the system become unstable or give unacceptable response times or throughput volumes? This is often called *stress testing*.
- *Security testing.* Is the system open to unauthorized access by external or internal agents?

Our main interest is clearly in performance and load testing, but the choice of tool or technique may be influenced by the other testing requirements.

Sizing Background

In days gone by, estimation of resources needed to operate IT applications properly was important, not only for the performance, but also for the cost of providing those resources, particularly processor power, disk storage, and main memory. Processor power was not as granular as it is today, and the difference in cost between one model and the next model up was usually prohibitive.

Similarly, increments in storage and main memory could be very expensive, and a breed of IT staff worked hard to *shoehorn* (cram) as many applications and as much functionality into as little resource as possible. This IT breed is now extinct or redeployed elsewhere in IT departments. Some were possibly redeployed as rail commuter crammers on Japanese trains, a job to which they would be eminently suited.

Today, resources such as those discussed above are much more granular and orders of magnitude cheaper than in the old days, but they still need sizing for performance.

Peak-to-Average Concept

One of the most important concepts in sizing systems is that of peak-to-average ratios of workload. If, for example, one sizes a system that will run at 50% utilization (average) and the nature of the workload is such that there are peaks 1.5–2.0 times that load, the system is in trouble. Those peaks can occur as known peaks, month end, year end, spring sales, and so forth, or unexpected ones needing "catch-up" processing after some delay or outage of a service.

A typical peak-to-average is 1.75, which means that if you do not want your system to operate over 70% CPU utilization, then your average operational utilization should be no more than 40% (70% = 1.75 × 40%).

Remember that we do not wish to operate any resource at very high utilization because of its adverse effect on response time.*

Remember also that the peak acceptable utilization before serious queuing delays set in depends on the *service time* of the resource. A very slow link will probably *max out* at 30% utilization, whereas a very fast CPU will roll along quite happily at 75% (peak)—you would not want to run at this as an average if your peak-to-average was 1.75 or higher.

However, in the case of web servers that operate 24 h per day, the ratio maybe much higher, perhaps 3 or 4 to 1, depending on whether the site is global or specific to a country or contiguous area. A site accessed from across the world will probably have a load profile that is flatter than that which is accessed mainly from a single country since people tend to go to bed at night.

Sizing What?

In general, we would like to size and predict the requirements and usage of resources needed in IT to support the business. Traditionally, these resources were physical, namely,

- Processor power
- Memory, including cache and levels of cache
- Disk† I/O capacity and spread of I/O across devices
- Disk storage capacity
- Network capacity
- Capacity provided by other necessary resources, such as tapes for backup
- Printer and other peripherals
- Environment equipment (cooling, power, floor space, etc.)

The normal course of events in systems design, implementation, and operations are design it, size it, install it, monitor it, and predict it into the future, the *it* being the necessary resources listed above. With the advent of virtualization and the cloud, the water is muddied somewhat as we tend to talk about logical resources (virtual machines and software-defined resources), as well as physical ones.

It is probably appropriate at this stage to think about baseline parameters that form the basis of performance measurements, upgrades, and capacity planning. Examples are an action ceiling, say 40%, for average utilizations over a period (say 1/2 day) and of a peak utilization greater than a certain number, say 70%, and lasting more than a stated period, say 20 min.

When these baselines or ceilings are breached, action needs to be taken. In any case, the users will tell the IT department indirectly when their response times start to climb, but it is professional to notice it before the users pick up the phone to complain.

System sizing is the estimation of system resources required to support a given workload at service levels specified by a service level agreement (SLA) or informally agreed upon. The system resources calculated in such an exercise are usually designed to support a given workload at production inception and for some agreed period afterward. There should be no statements like "It

---

* An exception is batch work, where it is advantageous to run at very high utilizations as long as there are not response-sensitive applications running alongside.
† For *disk*, read direct access devices to cover flash and solid-state storage devices (SSDs).

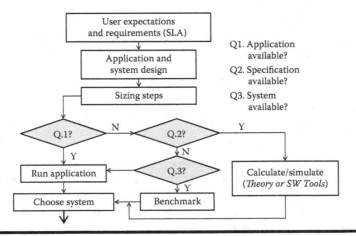

Figure 8.2   Preinstallation: design and sizing work.

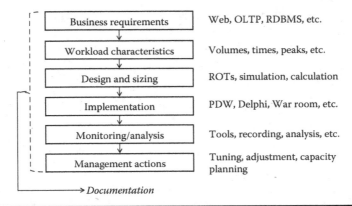

Figure 8.3   Performance design, sizing, and management flow.

will support the workload on day 1, but after that, who knows?" This is where capacity planning enters the arena.

System sizing, which includes the connecting networks, can be carried out in several ways or variations on one way. An overarching entity in performance is *workload*, that is, the things that the server and its attendant components need to process in the appropriate manner.

Figure 8.2 shows the ways sizing can be done, depending on what information and resources are available, and this slots into the overall flow of a project, as shown in Figure 8.3.

The metrics that define the workload* are

- Composition of the work: transactions types, batch types, query types, and so forth.
- The business importance of the work types for designing priority mechanisms where necessary.

---

* In this book, I will often use *work unit* (WU) as a generic term to describe whatever the characteristics of the workload thrown at the system. It can cover transactions, batch jobs, database queries, web page retrieval, log writing, and anything else that runs on the system, has a beginning and an end, and moves the system from one state to another permanently.

- The time profile of this work during the active periods of the day with a note of expected peak (if known) and peak time. This time is important in assessing the performance implications of the superimposition of other workloads on the system to see if they coincide and cause an unacceptable peak in demand.
- The volumes of the components of the workload and anticipated growth.

The life cycle flow of the performance design, sizing, and management architecture is important in at least two respects:

- It is formalized, documented, and understood by all concerned.
- Documentation (not necessarily *War and Peace* size) should be the watchword throughout the management cycle. This will form the basis of evidence to be used in brainstorming sessions (Delphi technique) and the war room (see Chapter 17 for this and other IT process management tools and techniques).

The complete process is shown in Figure 8.3.

Some of the main characteristics that are important to the resources comprising the system are listed in Table 8.2.

WoW: You will need estimates of growth rates for all these areas, and bear in mind the ability of chosen components to be upgraded with minimum disruption.

Outline

Classical Systems

The method adopted for this type of sizing is based on determining the number of business transactions or units of work done on the system in a given period. A business transaction translates into system transactions on a 1:n basis; that is, one business transaction might generate n system transactions. An illustrative example of this is the deletion of an applicant from the system.

From the user point of view, this is a single *business* transaction, but it may generate more than one *system* transaction, for example, checking the status of bills associated with the application, the actual deletion of the application, and any "housekeeping" needed to tidy up the system after deletion, for example, removing records relating to this application and perhaps archiving the application details.

Processor

Unless a new system is available for benchmarking to assess the resource requirements, it is necessary to relate the anticipated workload to workloads whose performance on the suppliers' machines is known or estimable. In the ideal world, the suppliers would furnish the organization with results for standard benchmarks, such as TPC-C and SPECthruput to compare machine capacities.

This method is not foolproof or even proven accurate, but it will often give a feel for the expected performance in the absence of any other data other than guesswork. As I have said, it has worked for me on simple systems sizing.

Table 8.2 System Sizing Resources and Components

Resource	Component	Sizing Factors
Whole system	• System applications	• Throughput • Transactions per second • Number of users supported • Service level agreement
Operating system	• Paging	• Thrashing • Overcommitment virtual:real
Processor	• CPU power • Memory • Transactions	• SPEC units • Megabytes or gigabytes • CPU/XN, I/Os/XN, memory/XN
Storage	• Disk	• Actuators to support I/O rate • Capacity or organization of data—RAID, etc. • Contingency
	• Controllers	• Database type (DBMS, etc.) • Hardware and software versions
Network (includes features like compression)	• Links	• Protocol (frame relay, ATM, etc.) • Capacity and acceptable loading (%)
	• Hardware	• Bandwidth and latency
	• Remote access	• Routers, etc., and capacity • Remote access bring your own device (BYOD) traffic • Errors and retransmissions • Dropped packets, etc.
Backup storage (local)	• Media/capacity • Write speed • Readback speed	• Recovery times
Backup storage (remote for DR)	• As above plus recovery requirements	• WAN bandwidth • WAN optimization features (effect on sizing)

Note: XN = transaction.

The flow of the generic sizing methodology is to break the workload into its smallest components, which are normally single system transactions, and use those as the sizing blocks of an application by relating them to known transactions in standard benchmarks. This might be called the workload decomposition and is illustrated in Figure 8.4.

Rough Sizing Method

The essence is to decompose what users know as a business transaction or query into system components called *system transactions*. For example, the business transaction to add an amount to a customer's account is one transaction to the user, but to the system it may consist of several transactions: get record, update balance field, record the activity in a log or ledger, and so on. It

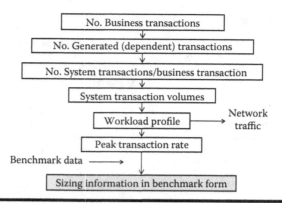

Figure 8.4 Flow of sizing mechanism: classical system.

may then be possible to size the business transaction in terms of resources used by comparing it with known and benchmarked transactions, such as TPC-C.

Thus, if you determine that your average system transaction is 1.5 times the resource consumption of a TPC-C transaction mix, and you know the average and peak rate of your system transactions, then it is possible to estimate the system size. If you determine that your load is 1.5 times TPC-C load and there are 50 transactions per second, then you need a system supporting 75 transactions per second, or 4500 TPC-C per minute. You have to understand roughly the structure of your system transactions and those of TPC-C (if that is your chosen sizing baseline).

The paper referenced below covers this sort of sizing in some detail if you can follow the logic in it.

Hardware Sizing Method for Information System in Korea
http://www.sersc.org/journals/IJMUE/vol1_no4_2006/IJMUE-2006-01-04-04.pdf

It is not a foolproof or rigorous method, but it is more professional than guesswork, and I have used it reasonably successfully in the past. There are other methods described in the sections in describing IBM tools for sizing of pSeries (UNIX) system resources:

IBM eServer pSeries Sizing and Capacity Planning
https://www.redbooks.ibm.com/redbooks/pdfs/sg247071.pdf

The accuracy of any sizing estimate is determined by the reliability of the volume and profile data supplied and the ability to assess the resource consumption of the transactions in terms of known workloads, such as TPC benchmarks or others that are trustworthy and show characteristics similar to those of the workload in question.

Disk Space Requirements: This is organization, system, and storage configuration (RAID, etc.) dependent and I have no ready formula. However, the guidelines are to include the following:

■ Basic data size, for example, 10 million records at 4800 bytes per record.
■ Data organization overhead; for example, normal, RAID 6, or mirroring will have totally different capacity and I/O capability needs.
■ A growth headroom of, say, 40%, but this depends on the growth volatility of the applications involved.
■ A contingency allowance, say, an extra 10% over and above any base calculations.

In terms of input/output (I/O) capability, this will involve understanding the characteristics of the storage medium and the peak-to-average I/O rates (IOPS) for each workload, bearing in mind you cannot run the disk at 100% utilization unless you want an infinite response time.*

The Adobe link below discusses hardware sizing for Adobe authors, but has a very useful set of lists for areas that need to be covered in sizing and outlines good generic advice that can help you perform almost any other sizing exercise.

Hardware Sizing Guidelines
https://docs.adobe.com/docs/en/cq/5-6-1/managing/hardware_sizing_guidelines.html

Network Sizing: This is amenable to calculation or simulation, and some of the tools pointed out in the next section can be of use in non-web environments.

Web-Based Applications

Web-based systems are hard to handle simply with calculations to which *clear-cut* classical systems are amenable because of the latter's relative simplicity and the probable existence of systems with similar characteristics.[†] Web systems do not handle simple transactions with known input sizes and an estimated output size; they are extremely variable in data characteristics, including size, number per web request, and link requests.

As with any complex system, the way to handle this effectively is by simulating user activity against a real or simulated website.[‡] This would normally take the form of a client/server configuration, with the client simulating the user accessing the server in ways that are expected by the organization or by its clients in the case of a public website. The desired response characteristics will be dictated by an internal service level agreement (SLA) or a pseudo-SLA based on known customer needs and preferences, including their *patience limits* with slow servers.

There are tools to aid this process, particularly in the web environment, but also in the non-web, for example, Systems Network Architecture (SNA) environment. In the simpler, non-web case, it is relatively simple to have a workstation accessing the server by generating real transactions and measuring their response time. This measurement might be done using simple timing code in the simulating workstation or via a commercial performance tool where appropriate (see next section).

Web Server Sizing: One Method

Sizing of web servers is the nearest thing to the eternal query "How long is a piece of string?" It all depends on whether the content is static or dynamic, the page size, the number of pages per request, the number of requests per unit time (e.g., a day), the peak number of requests in some smaller interval (e.g., an hour), the amount of memory, the use of caching, the similarity of requests to leverage the cache, the use of color, the use of image compression, and probably 50 or more other things.

What documentation there is concentrates on the network sizing, which is the easier bit of the sizing puzzle. The upshot of this is that whatever you do, you will probably get it wrong, so

---

* Believe it or not, some gurus preach this very fact, implying or even stating, "If your disk access time is 10 ms, you can get 100 I/Os per second (IOPS) from it."
† I have done such calculations for a website of known characteristics, but only for network loading, given the page sizes and volumes.
‡ Calculations and queuing theory would struggle in this area of sizing for multiple types of resource.

it might make sense to skip calculations and simulations and run a pilot with a testing tool and load testers such as NeoSense or NeoLoad* (see "Web Server Sizing: Another Method" section).

For the record, here are two links to server sizing exercises from Dell and Oracle:

Web Server Sizing
http://www.dell.com/content/topics/global.aspx/power/en/ps3q01_graham?c=us&l=en&cs=04

Oracle iPlanet Web Server 7.0.9 Performance Tuning, Sizing, and Scaling Guide
https://docs.oracle.com/cd/E19146-01/821-1834/abygs/index.html

Web Server Sizing: Another Method

NeoSense: NeoSense, from the Neotys stable, allows the user to navigate different paths through transactions to observe the performance and availability of a transaction or, in our terms, a work unit (UoW). Data about these journeys is recorded in some detail to allow the presentation of key performance indicators (KPIs) and more detailed drill-down data for them.

The setups for these paths and what KPIs and warnings are required are done by the IT department, which is guided in the business flow by end (business) users. In this way, the scenarios can mimic true business applications and exhibit the following characteristics:

- Support for the latest web and mobile application technologies (HTML 5, etc.; see the data sheet link below for an icon list of supported technologies and a diagram of the whole scenario)
- Realistic user paths through business activities
- Fast creation of test scenarios
- Full collaboration between IT development and operations and business users

NeoSense: 24×7 Synthetic Performance Monitoring for Web and Mobile Apps
http://www.neotys.com/product/overview-neosense.html

NeoSense: Synthetic Monitoring for Application Performance and Availability
http://www.neotys.com/documents/datasheets/neosense_ data_sheet_en.pdf

NeoLoad: NeoLoad, also from the Neotys stable, automates simple tasks to create use cases using an intuitive graphical user interface (GUI), which can be used to load test hybrid cloud environments, including those from leading cloud providers. It also facilitates load testing via mobile devices with support for different devices and WAN emulation as part of the test environment.

NeoLoad Technical Features [what it actually does]
http://www.neotys.com/product/neoload-features.html

Sizing a Web Server Farm with NeoLoad [a practical use of the product]
http://www.infoworld.com/article/2627564/application-testing/sizing-a-web-server-farm-with-neoload.html

Mobile Load & Performance Testing Solution [web and mobile testing]
http://www.neotys.com/documents/datasheets/mobile_ data_sheet_en.pdf

---

* These products are taken as examples of requirements for this task. It is not a recommendation and does not imply there are no other tools that can do a similar job.

Design Process [for using NeoLoad; there are other useful links within this link]
http://www.neotys.com/documents/doc/neoload/latest/en/html/#1518.htm

Web Server Sizing: Other Sources

Web Server Sizing
http://www.dell.com/content/topics/global.aspx/power/en/ps3q01_graham?c=us&l=en&cs=04

Sizing a Web Server Farm with NeoLoad
http://www.infoworld.com/article/2627564/application-testing/sizing-a-web-server-farm-with-neoload.html

Web Server Sizing: Testing and Simulation

There are a variety of applications out there that will simulate web traffic in various forms, some of them a repetition of the same query. What is needed to be a true simulation is a script of different web access patterns, for example,

- Load a page
- Click on a link
- Wait for the next page to display
- Wait and study the page
- Click on another link

Some load simulators simply are not *real world* enough in many cases, and any candidate product will need assessing to check if it fits your organization's bill. The base element of such a test or simulation environment is the ability to create your own access patterns via some sort of scripting language. It is also useful if the tool can build a representative test web server database to host these accesses and report back on the relevant metrics.

You should ascertain your organization's requirements in this area and do a search on suitable tools. As a guide, the following links are to information on load testing tools for creating and running automated load tests for web servers and services and in other environments.

LoadComplete 3 Documentation
http://support.smartbear.com/viewarticle/64794/

Features of Webserver Stress Tool
http://www.paessler.com/tools/webstress/features

Performance Test Tools (53 Found)
http://www.opensourcetesting.org/performance.php

User's Guide: Article Reprints: CSIM 18—The Simulation Engine
http://www.mesquite.com/documentation/articles/simengine.htm

Simulating OLTP Queries: How to Run Load Tests against SQL Server with HammerDB
http://www.brentozar.com/archive/2012/06/load-test-sqlserver/

IBM Workload Simulator for z/OS and OS/390
ftp://public.dhe.ibm.com/software/htp/pdtools/info/DatasheetWS.pdf

This is such a minefield if there are tight constraints on web response times, and if the websites are for businesses that live or die by users remaining on their website, a great deal of work has to be done at the organization level. I hope the links above will prove useful in most situations.

Network Simulation Tools

In any design of an IT resource there is normally a design and feasibility stage before implementation and operations. There are a number of tools to aid in sizing and other things, from calculations on the back of a cigarette packet to full-blown simulations. The more realistic ways of designing systems for performance can take several forms, three of which are

- Benchmark the system or a similar one
- Calculate performance using queuing theory and other math facilities
- Use a simulation tool to do the job

Which level is chosen depends on the need for accuracy in the results. Some of the tools available are outlined briefly below, and a reference to sources of further information given. *Their inclusion does not constitute a recommendation or imply they are the only suitable tools available.*

NetSim

NetSim is a popular network simulation tool used for network design, planning, and network research and development and comes in standard and academic versions. Various technologies such as wireless sensor networks, wireless LAN, Wi Max, TCP, IP, Ethernet, and Token Ring are covered in NetSim via its model libraries. The full list can be found in the Wikipedia entry for this product.

The basic method of operation is

- Create a network scenario with a GUI or Extensible Markup Language (XML).
- Click and drop applications, links, and devices into the scenario using the GUI.
- Set the relevant properties and parameters.
- Run the model.
- Examine output performance metrics at multiple levels—*network, subnetwork, link, queue, application*, and so forth.
- Analyze a variety of metrics, such as *throughput, delay, loss, packet error, link utilization*, and so on.

NetSim was developed by Tetcos, in association with the Indian Institute of Science, with the first release in June 2002. The current release is v 10.10. Search on term Netsim for the latest information and links.

NetSim: Simulation Platform for Network R & D [product brochure]
http://www.tetcos.com/downloads/brochure.pdf

NetSim Emulator
http://www.tetcos.com/downloads/NetSim_Emulator.pdf

The link above explains clearly the difference between a network simulator and a network emulator.

TETCOS Releases NetSim
http://tetcos.com/blog/category/netsim-product-release/
As of September 2015, NetSim has scalability and speed enhancements to simulate very large networks. These enhancements, available with NetSim v9 included

- Multicore processing with separate threads for different subprocesses within the simulation
- 64-bit simulation kernel with quicker event handling
- Acceleration algorithms for packet processing
- Data structure optimization for intense compute operations
- Memory overflow detection and integrity checks for packets and events

As of October 2015, you can view this introductory video on network emulation and how the NetSim emulator works:
https://www.youtube.com/watch?v=OwOwl0LuYbQ

Wireshark

Although strictly speaking it is a monitor and not a simulation tool, Wireshark interfaces with NetSim, which substantiates its claim to a certain extent. Wireshark is a free and open-source packet analyzer used for network analysis, troubleshooting, software and communications protocol development, and education. Although it performs network monitoring, it can interface with NetSim and thus claim to be part simulation tool.

Originally named Ethereal, the project was renamed Wireshark in May 2006. It is very similar to tcpdump, but has a graphical front end, plus some integrated sorting and filtering options. tcpdump is a common packet analyzer that runs under the command line. It allows the user to display TCP/IP and other packets being transmitted or received over a network to which the computer is attached.

Distributed under the BSD license, tcpdump is free software. tcpdump works on most UNIX-like operating systems—Linux, Solaris, BSD, OS X, HP-UX, Android, and AIX, among others.

Because protocols are growing and becoming more complex, new diagnostics methods, and therefore products, are essential. NetSim (see above) now enables the capture of packets from inside the simulator as it flows from one node to another using Wireshark, the industry standard network protocol analyzer. Users can create network scenarios across a wide range of protocols in NetSim, model application traffic, and then use Wireshark for postprocessing.

Wireshark
http://en.wikipedia.org/wiki/Wireshark

Wireshark Download
https://www.wireshark.org/download.html

ns-3

ns-3 was developed to provide an open, extensible network simulation platform, for networking research and education. It provides models of how packet data networks work and perform, and provides a simulation engine for users to conduct simulation experiments. Some of the reasons to use ns-3 include to perform studies that are more difficult or not possible to perform with real systems, to study system behavior in a highly controlled, reproducible environment, and to learn about how networks work.

The available model set in ns-3 focuses on modeling how Internet protocols and networks work, but ns-3 is not limited to Internet systems; several users are using ns-3 to model non-Internet-based systems.

Because ns-3 is a research and educational simulator, developed by and mainly for the research community, it will rely on the ongoing contributions of the community to develop new models, debug or maintain existing ones, and share results.

Its use in real-life IT might be questioned, but there is no harm in trying it out and perhaps learning something about simulating network protocols and properties.*

ns-3 Tutorial
https://www.nsnam.org/docs/release/3.21/tutorial/singlehtml/index.html

ns-3 Home Page
https://www.nsnam.org/

OPNET

OPNET is a network simulation tool, now acquired by Riverbed and renamed, which aids the design and simulation of many types of networks, as described in the links below.

Modeling Overview
http://suraj.lums.edu.pk/~te/simandmod/Opnet/01%20Modeling%20Overview.pdf

OPNET Simulator
http://users.salleurl.edu/~zaballos/opnet_interna/pdf/OPNET%20Simulator.pdf

Simulations and Tools for Telecommunications 521365S: OPNET—Network Simulator
http://www.telecomlab.oulu.fi/kurssit/521365A_tietoliikennetekniikan_simuloinnit_ja_tyokalut/
Opnet_esittely_07.pdf

Riverbed Modeler (OPNET)
http://www.riverbed.com/products/performance-management-control/network-performance-management/network-simulation.html#Overview

A Survey of Network Simulation Tools: Current Status and Future Developments
http://www.cse.wustl.edu/~jain/cse567-08/ftp/simtools/

GNS3

GNS3 is a graphical network simulator that allows networkers to design complex network topologies. They may run simulations or configure devices ranging from simple workstations to powerful Cisco routers.

The GNS3 website lists the following as some of the features provided by the simulator:

■ Design of high-quality and complex network topologies
■ Emulation of many Cisco router platforms and private Internet exchange (PIX) firewalls
■ Simulation of simple Ethernet, asynchronous transfer mode (ATM), and frame relay switches

---

* The ns-3.21 version came out in September 2014. ns-3.1 is dated June 2008.

- Connection of the simulated network to the real world
- Packet capture using Wireshark (see "Wireshark" above)

GNS3 Website [see "Technology" section via this home page]
http://www.gns3.com/

Using the GNS3 Network Simulator [other useful information here too]
http://blog.pluralsight.com/using-gns3-network-simulator

GNS3 Network Simulator Raises Its Game
http://www.networkcomputing.com/networking/gns3-network-simulator-raises-its-game/d/d-id/1319279
   You can download GNS3 from https://sourceforge.net/projects/gns-3/.

> ***Note***: If the organization's work is carried out totally on a vendor cloud service, it should still be possible to perform the same kind of measurements from the workstation client with a view to obtaining your own take on whether the service provided meets the SLA requirements demanded of that vendor. The same applies to a hybrid cloud, except that the cloud user has more control over its part of the cloud scenario.

Web Network Sizing

With the usual rules of running at queue-friendly utilizations and remembering the peak-to-average concept, web network sizing can be done as follows. The basic information you need here is

- The number of site visitors per day (or hour, or whatever time unit you choose)
- The number of pages accessed per visitor
- The average page size accessed, including images that form a large part of many web pages

This will yield information about the traffic generated by these numbers:

- Traffic in megabytes per day (or other time unit and remembering peak-to-average especially for websites)
- Bandwidth needed
- Download time per page

Web server traffic is determined by the simple relationship (based on quantity averages)

$$\textit{Traffic } T = V \times P_V \times P_S \text{ bytes} \tag{8.1}$$

where V is the number of visits per day, P_V the pages accessed per day, and P_S the page size in bytes, including *control metadata*—headers and so on. If you don't know this number of bytes, it might be calculated in bits by multiplying by 8, but that doesn't allow for the header or trailer metadata bits accompanying a block of transmitted data. It might be safe to multiply by 10 (12 to be safe if you are a pessimist) to allow for this, in true sizing *make doubly sure* fashion. Thus,

$$T = 10 \times V \times P_V \times P_S \text{ bits}$$

The scenario of 1,000 visits/day at 30 pages/visit and 40,000 bytes per page might be typical, yielding 1,000 × 30 × 40,000 bytes per day or 10 × 1,000 × 30 × 40,000 bits/day, which equals 12 × 10^9 bits/day spread over 86,400 s (1 day). However, this assumes a flat rate of accesses, which may not be the case, and peak-to-averages will definitely have to be considered.

You may find your communication speed fixed by the Internet service provider (ISP), so you may have to limit your workload to fit what bandwidth is available. Remember the potential loss of business through poor response times on websites, borne out by many studies and, more than likely, your own experience as a potential customer.

Monitoring Overview

Introduction

If you wish to acquire information on someone or something, you monitor it or read about it in hard copy or on the Internet.

System knowledge is there, but basically hidden from us unless we monitor and measure it.

There is a world of difference between performance *measurement* and performance *management*. The former is the passive recording of information in tabular and graphical form, whereas the latter implies active control and action taking where necessary. The necessity for taking action may depend on

■ The rules of the installation and any service level agreements (SLAs) in force
■ Physical limits to resource utilizations that are fixed by nature and queuing rules

Once the key resource measurements have been decided on, they can be monitored and reported on an exception basis, for example, flagging heavily loaded CPUs rather than reporting on them all, especially if you have scores or hundreds of them.

For all resources, a process of *monitoring* and projecting the increases in utilizations of key resources is called capacity planning or capacity management. This cannot be carried out without good performance management to supply data. The obvious reason for capacity planning is to anticipate overutilization of key resources so that measures can be taken to alleviate it. Such measures might include tuning or, where this is not feasible, the purchase of more resource, for example, memory.

Monitoring, in what my grandchildren call the *olden days*, was a relatively simple task of measuring what the physical resources comprising the system were doing and hopefully being able to take some action when things were going awry on the performance front.

Today, the panorama we see is littered with new concepts, architectures, and technologies, and taking stock of all the parameters in these environments is a little trickier than it was in the olden days.

We now have the basic environments of physical, virtual, and cloud resources to contend with, as illustrated in Figure 8.5.

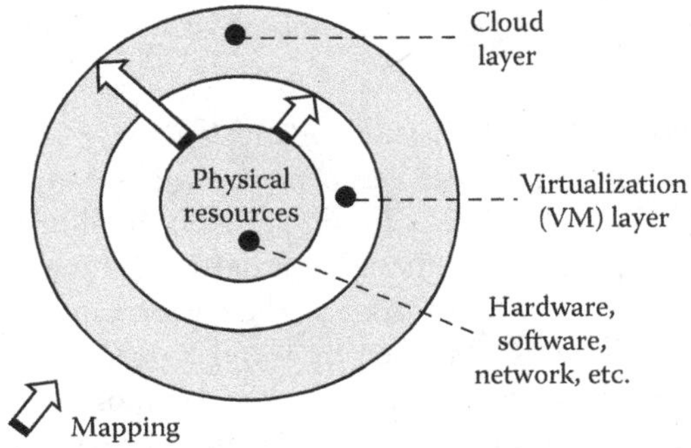

Figure 8.5 The monitoring environment today.

The Issue: In the absence of an automated mapping of physical resources to virtual machines and clouds, the measurement of physical resource characteristics alone makes it very difficult to ascertain what is happening to virtual machine (VM) or cloud services using those resources.

Generic Monitoring or Management

This seeks to answer the questions

- What performance entities do we measure and why?
- How do we measure these entities?
- How accurately do we need to measure each entity?
- What do we do with these measurements (the "so what" test)?
- What does the end user see from his or her vantage point (certainly not what central operations thinks he or she sees)?

These questions may sound trite to the performance *cognoscenti*, but they are important as we shall see. The first thing to do is to say what performance is and what good, average, and poor performance are. The first item is the subject of the first part of Chapter 1. The other items—good, average, and poor performance—are the very essence of service level agreements (SLAs). There are no standards for what is good, average, and poor since they are each *relative* to requirements of the business and its workload.

Synthetic Workload: Generic Requirements

In the "old days," workload metric gurus measured everything tangible—CPU utilization, memory utilization, I/O queuing, I/O times, and so forth, and were able to declare that everything was fine, or not, as the case might have been. In complex environments with interlinking software of various kinds, simple calculation or the application of queuing theory is not going to yield believable results for what is seen at the "sharp end," that is, the user's workstation.

There is a useful document (eBook) from Catchpoint, outlining their product, but also giving good insight into *synthetic monitoring.*

The Ultimate Guide to Improving Web Performance with Monitoring
http://pages.catchpoint.com/Ult-Guide-Web-Performance-ebook.html

Real user monitoring (RUM) is different from synthetic monitoring in that it more closely matches a user's perspective (it is claimed), though it is hard to see the difference when a synthetic driver or monitor is scripted with real-user work and the output captured at the user source.

However, one difference is that RUM often measures aspects of web performance from the user's browser or application, whereas synthetic drivers or monitors generally measure availability and response times. This mode will not necessarily be the user's view in today's environments, which are much more complex than they were in the old mainframe days. Units like pages accessed, pages transmitted, and average page size will be involved in Internet considerations.

Reasons for Synthetic Monitoring, Real User Monitoring & Measurements
https://www.neustar.biz/resources/whitepapers/why-real-user-monitoring-and-measurements

It is really a matter of tools understanding and catering to a multiplicity of software environments and services. Figure 8.6 illustrates a schematic monitor of an application system. In theory, one would like to pretend to be a user and experience what the user sees at various times in the operating cycle of a system, that is, the period over which it is meant to offer an available service.

One thing you should note: the view the user has of work and data *entering* his or her environment, together with its speed of access, is not the same as what the server operator sees *leaving* his or her system environment. Figure 8.6 illustrates the principle of this *pseudouser* or observer, plus the flow of two modes of "injection" into operational servers.* The observer injects pseudo- or real transactions into the system and measures the resulting response times and also the ongoing availability of the target systems. The real users work as usual.

There are local and remote observers to allow for a broken network, suggesting to the remote observer that the system or server component is down, when in reality it is not. This mode of operation is often called synthetic transactions, and the exercise the end-user experience, since in this environment, communication with a system can be via web browser emulation or scripts that

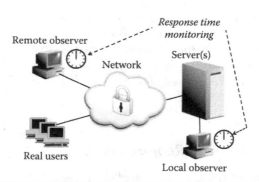

Figure 8.6 "Perfect" monitor: observer of system behavior.

---

* Compuware calls them "robot" workstations that execute synthetic, scripted transactions. These agents "simulate user activity so issues are discovered and fixed before they degrade your end-user experience" (Compuware dynaTrace).

generate transactions for the server in web or non-web mode. Results can be observed live (real time) or in post-operation processing, and might constitute part of the SLA report.

However, without proper monitoring, "all-seeing" tools and knowledge of what is happening end to end are limited to what various log files and intelligent network devices can tell the operations people. Compuware, for example, claims to sidestep these blind spots to monitor, among other things, activity on web clients and servers, Java/.NET servers, messaging and database systems, services, and transaction gateways.

What Entities Do We Measure?

The short answer is *everything you have in your system*, in its broadest sense. This means all elements that can influence the performance of *work* passing through them:

- The monitoring tools themselves—agent based or agentless.
- End-user access.
- Firewalls.
- Network components, including links.
- Bandwidth usage.
- Traffic flow.
- Packet sniffing.
- Routers.
- Availability (uptime). A system not working has a very long (bad) response time.
- Servers and front end, and application and database servers.
- Storage devices.

The last two items contain the applications and middleware, which are normally monitored by standard vendor packages. The detailed network aspects of routers, and so forth, will depend on the package chosen.

Many of these entities (elements) operate in serial mode, and so the performance of the whole system end to end can depend on the slowest entity if the system is delivering suboptimal performance.

However, response times of synthetic transactions will vary depending on the number of active users and their resource consumption—storage, network, CPU, and so forth. The *ping mechanism* has a very short path to travel on the server; the transaction has a longer journey through some middleware and application code.

The ping method (Figure 8.7) will give an indication of network net speed, whereas the actual transaction, less the prorated network time, will yield an approximate server time for that transaction. A ping is a 64-byte packet that travels to a server and is "batted" back, just like a tennis ball. It has several purposes, but is useful in checking the availability of a server—no return ball means the server is down or inaccessible.

Use of a Ping* Transaction

On the assumption that the ping occupies zero CPU resource, it can be used to estimate line times in an unconstrained environment; that is, the time taken for the ping to make its journey is

---

* A utility to determine whether a specific IP address is accessible. It works by sending a packet to the specified address and waiting for a reply. Ping is used primarily to troubleshoot Internet connections (Webopedia).

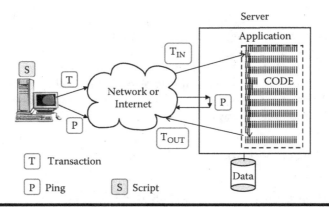

Figure 8.7   Synthetic user of a system: flow schematic.

measured. We can then calculate the time for a series of packets from a transaction, Xn, length n, since we know the time for a 64-byte packet, $Tping$:

$$T_{Xn} = \frac{T_{ping}}{64} \times n$$

The unconstrained factor means that the ping time has no wait component, whereas in real life a transaction will have a wait component. Thus, the transaction timing should be done in a test environment where no delays are encountered.

Performance Monitoring Methodology

Before diving into the internals of the various tools, it is instructive to think about what you are going to do with the potential plethora of numbers and percentages that will be generated, and you will need an organized way of handling them for problem analysis, tuning, root cause analysis, and performance prediction (short term, leading to capacity planning).

There are people who say you need the most comprehensive tools that produce exotic graphs and charts, and others who say you can do most of the job with the basic, free tools that normally come with an operating system. Based on personal experience, I side with the latter view—the KISS (keep it simple, stupid) method.

If you know what you are doing, then you can do great things with simple commands. If you don't understand the basics of performance and don't know what you are doing, then the best commercial tools in the world won't help you; remember the adage "A fool with a tool is still a fool." That said, there is a place for commercial tools, but they should be used on a "it fits our requirements" basis.

This presupposes you know your requirements and that you know enough to see if a product fulfills those requirements.*

---

* *Hint:* That's what this book is all about. My experience and that of others can help you avoid the issue of "those who do not learn from history are doomed to repeat its mistakes."

The reference below has very strong ideas about what to use and what not to use in UNIX (and presumably other OS) monitoring (underlined words I have corrected).

... are open source systems which you can try free and which usually <u>have</u> lower maintenance costs *than* proprietary systems. That does not mean that they can compete in all areas and, for example, agent-based monitoring and event correlation is still done much better in proprietary, closed source systems, but they are usually more adaptable and flexible which is an important advantage. Here is one apt quote:

"Command X is frankly not very good, ***but it's better than most of the alternatives in my opinion***. After all, you could spend buckets of cash on Product A or Product B and still be faced with the same amount of work to customize it into a useful state."

UNIX System Monitoring
http://www.softpanorama.org/Admin/system_monitoring.shtml

Solaris Troubleshooting and Performance Tuning
http://www.princeton.edu/~unix/Solaris/troubleshoot/

The link above is related to Sun Solaris, but is practically all applicable to general UNIX. It covers the following in some detail:

- CPU load
- Disk I/O
- Interprocess communication (IPC) parameters
- Kernel tuning
- Lock contention
- Memory and swap (PDF)
- Name service tuning
- Network File System (NFS) tuning
- Network debugging
- Process accounting
- Resource management
- Resource pools
- Scheduling

It also covers related commands, such as sar, iostat, and vmstat, in some detail.

Network Management Tools

Network Monitoring

Network monitoring is generally thought of as covering the following areas:

- Performance
- Availability
- Fault or diagnostic
- Configurations

- Security
- Account information

We are concerned mainly with the first entity, performance. The main tasks of network monitors are the collection and interpretation of data to provide meaningful information to operations and other functions. The uses of this information include

- Establishing a performance *baseline** for any future assessment and judgments on performance status.
- Alerts and warnings of performance or availability issues (fault or problem) management. You will need the baseline mentioned above to decide on trigger levels for alerts and warnings.
- Performance assessment and any tuning required. Service level agreements (SLAs) will dictate the bounds of what we need to measure.
- Augmenting network configuration management.
- Planning for the future in terms of capacity and capital expenditure (CAPEX) and any charging mechanisms in place.
  Edmund Wong, in the paper cited below, states what some of the key reporting entities are

Network Monitoring Fundamentals and Standards
http://www1.cse.wustl.edu/~jain/cis788-97/ftp/net_monitoring.pdf

- *Circuit availability*: The actual time that a user can dial up to a network and the network connection is available for the user.
- *Node availability*: The actual time that a user can use network nodes, multiplexers, and routers without having error.
- *Blocking factor*: The number of users who cannot access the network because of a busy signal in theory.
- *Response time*: The time to transmit a signal and receive a response for the signal.

These are the sorts of key performance indicators (KPIs) of interest in an SLA, the contract between the business users and IT.

This readable document goes on to cover some of the standard tools for monitoring, such as RMON and RMON2, which are extensions to the Simple Network Management Protocol (SNMP) developed from a request for comment (RFC).

In another document, the author, Chris Hoffman, claims,

> The most accurate way to monitor this would be on your router itself. All the devices on your network connect to the Internet through your router, so this is the single point where bandwidth usage and data transfers can be monitored and logged.

He then suggests a series of products and techniques to achieve this aim.

How to Monitor the Bandwidth and Data Usage of Individual Devices on Your Network
http://www.howtogeek.com/222740/how-to-the-monitor-the-bandwidth-and-data-usage-of-individual-devices-on-your-network/

---

* This word means an expectation for normal values of some resource in a system.

Network Factors

These are some of the key factors that an SLA would specify to the IT department.

The term *network* applies not only to the physical cable or fiber, but also to the hardware and software parts of the transmission setup, for example, routers and switches. The software aspects of these network elements include software or firmware currency and buffer sizes, which may need attention in solving performance or availability issues.

The main performance factors to assess when evaluating a network are throughput and response time plus any occurrence and duration of any failure of users to access the network. The detection of transmission errors and availability of routes through the network are, of course, also important. Also important is the logging of accumulated data for subsequent analysis for forecasting.

The Gartner Group has a methodology of assessing and evaluating various software products, resulting in their well-known Magic Quadrant display. When seeking input from vendors, they lay out areas they will consider, vendor product inclusion criteria, and other factors. Below I have summarized their *needs list* for network monitoring products:

A Gartner blog dated August 2014 states the criteria it would use in developing its familiar Magic Quadrant for tools in the area of network performance monitoring and diagnostics (NPDM). They are a solid foundation for assessing tools to suit your organization's needs in this area:

- The ability to monitor, diagnose, and generate alerts for network endpoints (servers, storage systems, or anything with an IP address) and network components—routers, switches, and so forth—and network links
- The ability to monitor, diagnose, and generate alerts for dynamic end-to-end network service delivery in the areas of end-user experience, business service delivery, and infrastructure component interactions
- Support for the analysis of real-time performance and behaviors, historical performance and behaviors, and predictive behaviors
- Leverage data from network devices, SNMP, and network packet analysis
- The ability to support the following capability and performance requirements: real-time monitoring of 10-gigabit Ethernet at full line rate via a single instance of the product and handling sampled flow records at 75,000 flows/s via a single product instance.

The relevant blog can be found at

Introducing the Criteria for the 2015 Network Performance Monitoring and Diagnostics (NPMD) Magic Quadrant
http://blogs.gartner.com/jonah-kowall/2014/08/15/introducing-the-criteria-for-the-2015-network-performance-monitoring-and-diagnostics-npmd-magic-quadrant/

I am a little surprised that this list by Jonah Kowall does not specifically mention *response times*.

Network Entities

These are some of the functions that network monitors and managers should have ideally:

- Packet capturing
- Capture of remote frames
- Viewing of bandwidth consumption by protocol
- Viewing of bandwidth consumption by user
- Modification and retransmitting of network traffic
- Differentiation between routers and network hosts
- Resolving of device names into media access control (MAC) addresses

There are also indicators of network viability that may be needed:

- Circuit availability—The time a network *connection** is available.
- Node availability—The time that a user can use network nodes, multiplexers, and routers without having an error.
- Blocking factor—The number of users who cannot access the network because it is busy.
- Response time—The time between *send* and *receive* of a signal or packet. This is not quite the same as the response time of a transaction or query, but it is an integral part of it.

These are part of what we call *network visibility*. At first, it may be assumed that network availability is not something a performance person should worry about, but they are inextricably linked. A very slow network is considered *down* by end users, and a network or part of it that is down represents a very *poorly performing* part of the service to the end users.

Network Performance Tools

Network *performance* monitoring solutions provide information on the makeup of traffic traversing critical network links with no need for probes. Using technologies like those outlined in this section, organizations can understand how applications are utilizing the network, and enable them to locate and manage bandwidth *hotspots*. They also yield valuable information about users, applications, peak usage periods, traffic patterns, and other key metrics.

In addition, none of these alternative tools offer every capability needed to diagnose problems, so several are required, each for a different purpose. Unfortunately, the requirements of any specific organization necessitate the assessment of which tools are suitable.

> Paraphrasing the motto of the British SAS elite squad once more, "Who reads, wins."

Internet2

This is a leading-edge research and innovation site, with a broader remit than the title suggests.

Internet2 Tools

The Internet2 site is interesting, containing much current and leading-edge information on aspects of the Internet. Its mission follows:

---

* There may be multiple connections in a single network.

Internet2 is an exceptional community of U.S. and international leaders in research, academia, industry and government who create and collaborate via innovative technologies. Together, we accelerate research discovery, advance national and global education, and improve the delivery of public services. Our community touches nearly every major innovation that defines our modern digital lives—and continues to define "what's next."

The site has a simple search window that gives access to many papers, from practical to research and *blue skies*.

Internet2 Home Page
http://www.internet2.edu/about-us/

These software tools, developed with the support of Internet2 members, aim to enhance the deployment and usefulness of high-performance networks:

Performance Tools [network]
http://www.internet2.edu/products-services/performance-analytics/performance-tools/

> *perfSONAR*: The pS-Performance Toolkit is a downloadable, preconfigured collection of network performance tools, including NDT, BWCTL, OWAMP, and perfSONAR tools and services that are outlined below.
> *Bandwidth Test Controller (BWCTL)*: BWCTL is a command-line client application and a scheduling and policy daemon that wraps Iperf (bandwidth measurement tool) and Thrulay (network measurement tool).
> *Network Diagnostic Tool (NDT)*: NDT is a user-friendly client/server program that provides network configuration and performance testing to a user's desktop or laptop computer.
> *One-Way Ping (OWAMP)*: OWAMP is a command-line client application and a policy daemon used to determine one-way latencies between hosts.

Extrahop

This product works at the *wire* level and is thus able to aggregate data from the lowest levels, which aggregates it to the top of the seven-layer model. Wire data is all the L2–L7 communications (seven-layer model) between all systems on the network, including full bidirectional transactional payloads. Transforming this raw wire data into meaningful business and IT insight is what the Extrahop analysis products do.

The functionality of Extrahop depends on its analysis of the communications traffic at the six layers it monitors. The two viewpoints of transit data are

- Upward aggregation and analysis (Extrahop viewpoint)
- Downward look at this data for response times and throughput (SLA viewpoint)

Somewhere between the meeting point of these views there is a need for tailored analysis for the upward movement of Extrahop data and information. This can be provided in some cases by Extrahop, but in other cases the user organization needs to perform the analysis via application programming interfaces (APIs) supplied by Extrahop. These provide access to data aggregated to level 7 in the Open System Interconnection (OSI) model and to the many metrics accumulated by Extrahop, a sort of do-it-yourself activity.

For example, Extrahop can provide timing information for a HTTP request or response, but it is the province of a tailored query to group several of these HTTP timings to comprise an access as requested by the application. Extrahop can aid the development of this work if the users provide identifiers for the application requests, for example, Oracle or a web query.

The following list* outlines the data captured at these levels and for what protocols:

- Web: *Supported protocols*: HTTP/HTTPS, AMF, and SSL
- VDI: *Supported protocols*: ICA, CGP, and PCoIP
- Middleware: *Supported protocols*: ActiveMQ, IBM MQ, CICS, and other HTTP-based protocols
- Database: *Extrahop-supported RDBMS*: IBM DB2, IBM Informix, Microsoft SQL Server, MongoDB, MySQL, Oracle, PostgreSQL, and Sybase
- Storage: *Supported protocols*: iSCSI, CIFS, and NFS
- Industry-supported protocols: *Supported protocols*: HL7, FIX, and SMPP
- Directory services and AAA: *Supported protocols*: LDAP, RADIUS, and Diameter
- Infrastructure services: *Supported protocols*: DNS, FTP, ICMP, LLDP, memcache, MSRPC, and SMTP
- Voice over IP (VoIP) and video: *Supported protocols*: SIP, RTP, RTCP, RTCP XR, and DSCP

Legend: If you do not know the meaning of the protocols listed above, the following links provide excellent sources of acronym meanings.

http://www.consp.com/it-information-technology-terminology-dictionary
http://techterms.com/category/acronyms

Extrahop also provides a framework for parsing any protocol not listed above that is based on TCP or UDP.

Figure 8.8 shows the points at which Extrahop (and other wire data analyzers) can gather data. You will appreciate that wire data, although very detailed, can be used for many monitoring and analysis purposes, for example, performance and, with the right analysis tool, security, by looking for unusual or out-of-normal patterns of data flow. This is a common security technique.

Products and Metrics

Extrahop produces metrics of the relevant kind for application, business, availability, security, performance, and capacity sets of data. We are interested here in *performance* metrics:

- Use of caching
- Use of compression
- Base HTML load time
- Network round-trip time
- Request transfer time
- Response transfer time

---

* List is skippable if you are not too network literate.

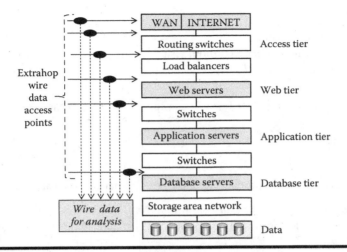

Figure 8.8 Network access points for wire data monitors.

- Server request processing time
- Total time taken

The basic resource metrics, such as utilizations, are available as usual for operational purposes.

Products supported include many network and related protocols (Citrix ICA, SMTP, FTP, LDAP, etc.) and several more application-oriented products, such as databases and queuing products:

- Oracle MongoDB
- Postgres
- MySQL
- ActiveMQ
- IBM MQ
- MS SQL
- Sybase
- Sybase IQ
- DB2
- Informix

The full list can be found at https://www.extrahop.com/platform/modules/ on the Extrahop website.

What Is Wire Data?
https://www.extrahop.com/our-approach/what-is-wire-data/
https://www.extrahop.com/our-approach/power-platform/

Extrahop Overview: How It Works
https://www.extrahop.com/platform/how-it-works/

Platform Value and Real-World Uses Cases
https://www.extrahop.com/platform/platform-value/

Extrahop Demonstration
https://www.extrahop.com/demo/
For more information or to contact Extrahop, visit
https://www.extrahop.com/contact/

See "Wire Data" in Appendix III for a brief explanation of wire data and the seven-layer OSI model.

ManageEngine
https://www.manageengine.com/products/applications_ manager/?application-monitoring

End User Experience Management & End User Monitoring
https://www.manageengine.com/products/applications_manager/end-user-monitoring.html

Cisco

Introduction to Cisco IOS NetFlow: A Technical Overview
http://www.cisco.com/c/en/us/products/collateral/ios-nx-os-software/ios-netflow/prod_white_paper0900aecd80406232.html

Sflow

http://www.sflow.org/

Overview Documents
http://www.sflow.org/about/presentation.php

Paessler

Monitoring Virtual Machines [network]
http://www.paessler.com/monitoring_virtual_machine
The reference above is quite comprehensive in network tools and covers

- Firewall monitoring
- Bandwidth monitoring
- Net flow monitoring
- Packet sniffing
- Router monitoring
- Usage monitoring
- Uptime monitoring
- Bandwidth manager
- Network monitoring
- VoIP network monitoring
- Server monitoring software

SevOne

Network Performance Management
https://www.sevone.com/search?keyword=network+management&=Search

Juniper Networks

Network Management
http://www.juniper.net/us/en/products-services/network-management/

Riverbed

Network Performance Management
http://www.riverbed.com/products/performance-management-control/network-performance-management/

Capterra Product Sources

Top Network Management Software [a huge list of products A–Z]
http://www.capterra.com/network-monitoring-software/

Fluke Networks eBook

Diagnosing the Cause of Poor Application Performance
http://freecomputerbooks.tradepub.com/?p=w_aaaa510&w =d&email=tcritchley07@gmail.com
&key=2qn1wWzsvrdHVZ1FSzmF&ts=55609&u=09202510902 41425855590&e=dGNyaXRj
aGxleTA3QGdtYWlsLmNvbQ==

A link of this size (unless you are reading online) is best found by searching using the vendor and article title or part thereof.

Other Sources

The links below are useful in outlining free network management products, but also, in some cases, for picking up snippets of general information about the topic.

The Top 20 Free Network Monitoring and Analysis Tools for Sys Admins
http://www.gfi.com/blog/the-top-20-free-network-monitoring-and-analysis-tools-for-sys-admins/

Top 5 Licensed Network Troubleshooting & Monitoring Tools
http://www.solarwinds.com/top5tools/network-monitoring/

Network Performance: Aberdeen Magic Quadrant

Gartner has produced a document outlining network performance monitoring and diagnostics, dated February 2015, which covers vendors in this monitoring space. The major vendors appearing in their Magic Quadrant for this include

- JDSU (Network Instruments)
- Riverbed
- Netscout Systems
- Fluke Networks
- Cisco
- CA Technologies
- SevOne

■ HP
■ Six other vendors

A complimentary copy of this report can be obtained from Riverbed (by registering) at http://www.riverbed.com/about/document-repository/Gartner-Magic-Quadrant-for-Network-Performance-Monitoring-and-Diagnostics.html.

Web Response Time Metrics

Web servers, like other servers and software packages, write a log for analysis or recovery purposes. The server activity is recorded in a web server log file, and every line of the web server log file contains the following items:

■ ISO standard time stamp, source of timing information
■ Virtual host name
■ Request method (GET or POST normally)
■ URL path
■ Query string
■ HTTP status code
■ Size of the requested entity itself
■ Size of the response message containing the entity and the HTTP response headers (these two items will help to estimate network latency)
■ *Possibly* the response time (see below)

For example, one can add a new parameter to the Apache log to ask the Apache web server to log the *time spent to serve the request*. This is done by adding *%T* to get the time taken to serve the request, in *seconds*. Unfortunately, the fact that this is represented in seconds will not be very useful, as the aim is to serve most of the requests in less than 1 s. Apache 2 introduced a new log value, *%D*, that logs the time spent to serve the request in *microseconds* instead of seconds.

The reported time contains not only CPU time spent by the different software components (web server, server-side scripting languages, databases, etc.), but also the wait times involved (disk I/O waits, database lock waits, and network latencies).

The time is measured on the web server and reflects the time spent to generate a single response. The server obviously doesn't know about dependencies between content items. The time needed on the client to fetch everything and render the page is definitely higher. In addition, it is important to note that for obvious reasons, the elapsed time measured on the server side always differs from the actual response time seen by the client.

There will be network time (latency) and possibly other interactions on the server to add on.

Customizing WebSphere Access Logs to Include the Response Time
http://veithen.github.io/2013/05/22/was-access-logs-response-time.html

Logging Apache Response Times
http://www.moeding.net/archives/33-Logging-Apache-response-times.html

Apache Logs: How Long Does It Take to Serve a Request?
http://www.ducea.com/2008/02/06/apache-logs-how-long-does-it-take-to-serve-a-request/

Other Uses of the Log: There are some other diagnostic uses for the server log:

- Recording response times from the *client device or browser* can give you an even more complete picture since it also captures page load time in the application or browser, as well as *network latency.*
- Chasing slow response times at the server or on the network.
- Memory issues and garbage collection, the latter being a harbinger of out-of-memory issues.
- Deadlocks and threading issues. These are pauses or halts when software is waiting for a resource locked for use by another piece of software.
- High resource usage, particularly of disk, processor, and network. High utilizations lead, as we have seen, to rocketing response times.
- Database issues and slow queries, possibly from a time-out or long query that breaks some time criterion.

Website Response Times
http://www.nngroup.com/articles/website-response-times/
   A paper, link shown below, discusses five other ways of finding web response times in addition to the methods outlined above.

Five Tools to Measure Website Response Times
http://www.websitemagazine.com/content/blogs/posts/pages/five-tools-to-measure-website-response-times.aspx
   Finally, there is a detailed master's thesis about web application monitoring, albeit pioneering, which you may find of interest:

High-Precision Web Application Monitoring [thesis]
http://www.few.vu.nl/~sna210/pubs/Master_thesis.pdf

WoW: As with all product and vendor lists, including mine, your organization is the final arbiter of which is best, based on your requirements.

Network Documentation

There are some free tools to help with automating some of the network documentation, which all the best IT departments do, don't they?

Network Documentation Tool Project: Overview [documentation tool]
https://osl.uoregon.edu/redmine/projects/netdot

IPplan: IP Address Management and Tracking [documentation tool]
http://iptrack.sourceforge.net/
   Networks are becoming so complex these days that it is foolish to neglect documenting them as well as possible.

Types of Performance Tool

There are two basic sets of tools available across the popular operating systems:

■ *Command line* or *native* tools, usually specific to an operating system
■ *Commercial* (or vendor-supplied) tools

The latter are mainly manipulation and presentation tools that feed off the native tools for basic information and perform various types of manipulation of this basic *data* to provide what we call *information*. Information is the entity that tells us something about the performance of our system or network and is, in essence, *cooked data* prepared for human "consumption." This analogy means the data must be digestible by a human being.

Native System Performance Tools

Windows Performance

Windows performance analysis used to be performed by Xperf, a command-line tool that is still supported, and Xperview, which is no longer supported.

Xperf Performance Analyzer is built on top of the Event Tracing for Windows (ETW) infrastructure. ETW enables Windows and applications to efficiently generate events, which can be enabled and disabled at any time without requiring system or process restarts. ETW collects requested kernel events and saves to an etl file.

It provides extensive details about the system: context switches, interrupts, deferred procedure calls, process and thread creation and destruction, disk I/Os, hard faults, processor P-state transitions, and registry operations.

A detailed discussion with examples and installation and operational tips for Xperf can be found at

Windows Performance Toolkit—Xperf
http://blogs.msdn.com/b/ntdebugging/archive/2008/04/03/windows-performance-toolkit-xperf.aspx

Xperf Command-Line Reference
https://msdn.microsoft.com/en-us/library/windows/hardware/hh162920.aspx

The later Windows Performance Toolkit (2013) consists of two independent tools:

■ Windows Performance Recorder (WPR)
■ Windows Performance Analyzer (WPA)

Windows Performance Toolkit Technical Reference
https://msdn.microsoft.com/en-us/library/windows/hardware/hh162945.aspx

UNIX Performance Commands

In this section, we will cover the main UNIX commands that deliver information about the different resources in a system that can have an impact on overall system performance. We will also briefly review VMS measurement commands, along with the functions offered by commercially available packages.

Many of the UNIX commands have found their way over to the Linux camp, and both sets have much in common. The overlap is possibly not 100%, so the UNIX commands are spelled out here as per the UNIX manual and other pages. There are a number of commands and techniques in UNIX systems that allow us to monitor what is going on at the physical level in a system.

The following are the main commands that can be employed to gather data.

- **sar**: UNIX utility that produces system activity reports of CPU, memory, and disk usage.
- **vmstat**: Command used to display statistics of virtual memory, kernel threads, disks, system processes, I/O blocks, interrupts, CPU activity, paging, and much more.
- **iostat**: Simple tool that will collect and show system input and output storage device statistics. This tool is often used to trace storage device performance issues, including devices, local disks, and remote disks such as NFS.
- **mpstat**: Reports processor statistics in tabular form.
- **netstat**: Command-line tool for monitoring incoming and outgoing network packet statistics, as well as interface statistics. It is a very useful tool for every system administrator to monitor network performance and troubleshoot network-related problems.
- **nfsstat**: Displays statistics kept about NFS client and server activity.
- **ps**: Reports a snapshot of the current processes operating in the system.
- **adb**: An interactive, general-purpose debugger. It can be used to examine files and provides a controlled environment for the execution of programs.

For the purposes of our discussion, we will limit our attention to important subsets of the first three. The others can be referenced in the standard texts on UNIX commands. You should note that not all commands are available on all versions of UNIX, and sometimes when they are, the details of implementation may be different. There are also some commands that are specific to a particular flavor of UNIX.

sar

sar is parameter driven and enables the collection of data in the following areas:

- Collective CPU usage
- Individual CPU statistics
- Memory used and available
- Swap space used and available
- Overall I/O activities on the system
- Individual device I/O activities
- Context switch statistics
- Run queue and load average data
- Network statistics
- Report sar data from a specific time

vmstat

vmstat is parameter driven and enables the collection of data in the following areas:

- Number of processing jobs waiting to run
- Details about memory usage, swapping, and allocated and unallocated memory

- Rate that memory is sent to or retrieved from the swap system
- Amount of input and output activity per second in terms of blocks read and blocks written
- Data that reflects the number of system operations per second, the number of system interrupts per second, and other related data
- Use of the system's CPU resources, including system time, idle time, user (application) time, and wait time

These are important numbers in assessing where problems lie, for example, excessive CPU wait time.

iostat

iostat is parameter driven and enables the collection of data in the following areas:

- *CPU utilization report*
  - CPU utilization that occurred while executing at the *user* level (application)
  - Percentage of CPU utilization that occurred while executing at the *user* level with nice priority
  - Percentage of CPU utilization that occurred while executing at the *system* level (kernel)
  - Percentage of time that the CPU or CPUs were idle, during which the system had an outstanding disk I/O request
  - Percentage of time that the CPU or CPUs were idle and the system did not have an outstanding disk I/O request
- *Device utilization report*
  - Device name.
  - Number of transfers per second that were issued to the device. A transfer is an I/O request to the device.
  - Amount of data read from the drive expressed in a number of blocks per second.
  - Amount of data written to the drive expressed in a number of blocks per second.
  - Total number of blocks read.
  - Total number of blocks written.
  - Percentage of CPU time during which I/O requests were issued to the device (bandwidth utilization for the device). Device saturation occurs when this value is close to 100% (as we well know).
  - Other data about input/output characteristics.

> *Note*: Several of the UNIX commands overlap in what they measure and report, so just be aware of the fact.

AIX Quicksheet [detailed UNIX [AIX] command reference]
http://www.tablespace.net/quicksheet/aix-quicksheet.pdf

LINUX Performance Commands

This section is for reference and skimming, and general readers might wish to pass over it and rejoin the book at "Management of Performance Data."

There are a number of native or command-line performance commands in Linux, some of them lifted from UNIX, either singly or in combinations. Some of them are listed below with a brief description of their functions. More details can be found at the links at the end of this section and below each tool listed. Some of these tools also operate in other OS environments, so take care before dismissing them.

Remember, in all evaluations of tools, "Who reads, wins." The tools are as follows:

- **dstat**: Replacement for vmstat, iostat, netstat, and ifstat. Eliminates some of their limitations, as well as adding extra features and resource counters.
  http://www.simplehelp.net/2008/11/13/how-to-use-dstat-to-monitor-your-linuxunix-server/
- **atop**: http://linux.die.net/man/1/atop
- **nmon**: Nigel's performance Monitor for Linux. Command-line utility that can display information about various system resources like CPU, memory, disk, and network. It was developed at IBM and later released as open source.
  http://www.tecmint.com/nmon-analyze-and-monitor-linux-system-performance/
- **slabtop**: The modern Linux kernel implements this caching memory allocator to hold the caches called the slabs. It gives information about cache and other kernel resources.
  http://linoxide.com/linux-command/kernel-slab-cache-information/#sthash.4BFtCneo.dpuf
  http://www.tutorialspoint.com/unix_commands/slabtop.htm
- **sar**: System activity reporting gives information about CPU and processes and other resource information.
  http://www.slashroot.in/examples-using-sar-command-system-monitoring-linux
- **saidar**: Simple tool for system information—uptime, CPU, memory plus disk, and network interfaces.
  http://linoxide.com/monitoring-2/linux-performance-monitoring-tools/
- **top**: Displays the top CPU processes' information and can be sorted by CPU, memory usage, and runtime.
  http://www.tecmint.com/12-top-command-examples-in-linux/
- **sysdig**: Tool aimed at administrators and troubleshooters that captures system calls and other operating system events that can be filtered via command parameters to provide specific information.
  http://bencane.com/2014/04/18/using-sysdig-to-troubleshoot-like-a-boss/
- **netstat**: Useful tool for checking network configuration statistics and activity. It is a collection of several tools lumped together to provide this information, which is filtered by *flags* (or parameters) to tailor the command.
  http://linux.about.com/od/commands/l/blcmdl8_netstat.htm
- **tcpdump**: Prints out a description of the contents of packets on a network interface that matches a Boolean *expression* to specify the desired output.
  http://www.tcpdump.org/manpages/tcpdump.1.html
  http://www.thegeekstuff.com/2010/08/tcpdump-command-examples/ [examples]
- **vmstat**: Reports information about processes, memory, paging, block IO, traps, and CPU activity.
  http://linuxcommand.org/man_pages/vmstat8.html
- **free**: Command that gives valuable information on available random access memory (RAM) in a Linux machine, for example, details like total available RAM, used RAM, shared RAM, RAM used for buffers, and RAM used of the caching content.

http://www.computerhope.com/unix/free.htm

- **htop**: Tool in Linux that allows you to monitor your system's vital resources and the processes (applications) that are running in near real time.
  http://www.nextstep4it.com/htop-interactive-process-viewer-linux/
- **ss**: Used to dump *socket* statistics. It displays information similar to netstat. It can display more TCP and state more information than other tools.
  http://www.binarytides.com/linux-ss-command/
- **lsof**: Command-line utility that is used to list the information about the files that are opened by various processes. Since in UNIX and Linux, everything is a file, pipe, socket, directory, device, and so forth, it tells much about what is going on in the system.
  http://www.thegeekstuff.com/2012/08/lsof-command-examples/ [examples]
  https://danielmiessler.com/study/lsof/ [primer]
- **iftop**: Shows a table of current bandwidth usage by hosts, giving the Linux bandwidth usage.
  http://community.spiceworks.com/how_to/show/1251-using-iftop-to-monitor-bandwidth-in-near-real-time
  http://en.wikipedia.org/wiki/Iftop
- **iperf**: Open-source tool that can be used to test network performance. Iperf is much more reliable in its test results than many other online network speed test providers.
  https://iperf.fr/
  http://www.slashroot.in/iperf-how-test-network-speedperformancebandwidth
- **thrulay**: A network tester.
  http://www.internet2.edu/presentations/jt2006feb/ 20060207-thrulay-shalunov.pdf
- **smem**: Tool that can give numerous reports on memory usage in Linux systems. It can report *proportional set size* (PSS), which is a more meaningful representation of the amount of memory used by libraries and applications in a virtual memory system.
  http://linuxaria.com/pills/linux-terminal-check-who- uses-all-your-memory-with-smem
  http://xmodulo.com/visualize-memory-usage-linux.html
- **icinga**: Open-source host, service, and network monitoring program. It monitors specified hosts and services, providing alerts for any developing issues, errors, or improvements.
  http://www.tecmint.com/install-icinga-in-centos-7/
- **nagios**: Has the capability to monitor applications, services, operating systems, network protocols, system metrics, and infrastructure components with a single tool (see "Cloud Monitoring and Performance" section).
- **procexp**: A graphical process explorer for Linux. Shows process information such as process tree, TCP/IP connections, and graphical performance figures for processes. It is a replica of procexp in Windows Sysinternals.
  http://www.howtogeek.com/school/sysinternals-pro/lesson2/
- **collectl**: Used to measure, monitor, and analyze system performance on Linux systems. It can gather information on many different types of system resources, such as CPU, disk, memory, network, sockets, TCP, inodes, infiniband, luster, NFS, and processes.
  http://collectl.sourceforge.net/
  http://www.tecmint.com/linux-performance-monitoring-with-collectl-tool/
- **MRTG**: Multi Router Traffic Grapher. A tool to monitor the traffic load on network links. MRTG generates HTML pages containing PNG (graphical) images that provide a LIVE visual representation of this traffic.
  https://wiki.archlinux.org/index.php/Multi_Router_Traffic_Grapher

- **monit**: Utility for monitoring services on a UNIX system—processes, programs, files, directories, and file systems.
  http://linux.die.net/man/1/monit
- **munin**: Group of programs to gather data from hosts, graph them, create HTML pages, and optionally warn contacts about any off-limit values.
  http://linux.die.net/man/8/munin
  http://munin-monitoring.org/wiki/faq

Linux Performance Tool References

Linux Performance [master paper link; the three below are diagrams within it]
http://www.brendangregg.com/linuxperf.html

Linux Performance Tuning Tools
http://www.brendangregg.com/Perf/linux_tuning_tools.png

Linux Observability: sar
http://www.brendangregg.com/Perf/linux_observability_sar.png

Linux Performance Benchmark Tools
http://www.brendangregg.com/Perf/linux_benchmarking_tools.png

The Linux links above contain *three informative diagrams* as to where commands fit in the scheme of the system and network, both hardware and software. A version is shown in Figure 8.9 with permission from Brendan Gregg to use the original as a template.

This Linux version can also serve as a model for other operating systems since it shows which elements of a total system can impact performance and hence should, if possible, be monitored. Typical OSs might be HP-UX, IBM AIX, Microsoft Windows, IBM's z/OS, and others, although it is unlikely that there will be a one-to-one correspondence in their tools to those in Linux.

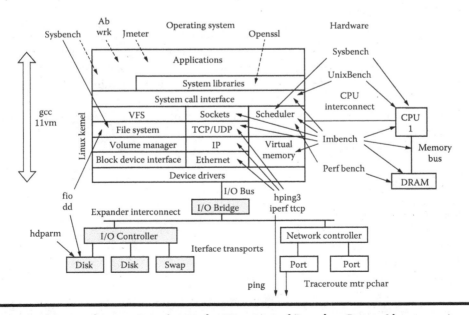

Figure 8.9   Linux performance tuning tools. (Courtesy of Brendan Gregg, Linux guru.)

The following IBM Redbook link is a useful adjunct to the Gregg references given above.

Linux Performance and Tuning Guidelines
https://sanet.me/blogs/ninanikol/linux_performance_and_tuning_guidelines.32171.html

Amazing! 25 Linux Performance Management Tools
http://linoxide.com/monitoring-2/linux-performance-monitoring-tools/
For Linux Black Belts only, it also covers

- Command-line tools
- Network-related performance tools
- System-related monitoring
- Log monitoring tools
- Infrastructure monitoring tools

80 Linux Monitoring Tools for SysAdmins
https://blog.serverdensity.com/80-linux-monitoring-tools-know/
On the similarities and differences between Linux and UNIX commands (which are covered next), Brendan Gregg, Linux guru, has the following to say:

> In general, UNIX tools can be more polished, as enterprise customers have paid to use them. They are also generally better documented, and marketed. Linux tools are often created by the community ad hoc, and have less documentation, and sometimes more rough edges. People comparing the two often think that UNIX has more tooling than Linux, but you need to dig deeper into Linux (and often browse the kernel source) to find out the truth—Linux can do a lot, and often more. (Private communication)

MVS and z/OS Performance Tools

The main monitoring tool for MVS and z/OS is Resource Measurement Facility (RMF), which covers the statistics for most resources involved in IBM mainframe computing. RMF is IBM's strategic product for z/OS performance measurement and management and is the base product to collect performance data for z/OS and Sysplex* environments to monitor systems performance behavior.

This information allows the configuring and tuning of systems, often to suit service level agreements (SLAs).

RMF consists of several components:

- Monitor I (base collection)
- Monitor II (snapshot monitoring)
- Monitor III (short-term data collection)
- Postprocessor
- Spreadsheet reporter
- Client/server enabling
- Sysplex data server

---

* High-availability mainframe clustering and resource-sharing system.

- Distributed data server for z/OS
- Distributed data server for AIX, Linux, and Windows systems (RMF XP)
- RMF performance monitoring

Monitor I and Monitor III provide long-term data collection for system workload and resource utilization, and cover all hardware and software components of a system—processor, I/O device, and storage activities and utilizations.

> A typical first pass at getting to the bottom of performance issues is to check utilizations of processor, memory, I/O channels, I/O devices, and paging rates. They will furnish clues as to where the issues lie.

The Redbook reference below is a detailed but clear coverage of RMF in the z/OS environment.

Effective zSeries Performance Monitoring Using Resource Measurement Facility
http://www.redbooks.ibm.com/redbooks/pdfs/sg246645.pdf
The reference below is a (very) detailed exposition of disk and tape I/O in z/OS systems, but much of it applies to most versions of MVS, the precursor to z/OS.

Analizing [sic]/*Monitoring Performance of z/OS I/O Operations: DASD and Tape Performance View*
https://share.confex.com/share/119/webprogram/Session 11491.html

OpenVMS Performance Tools

VMS, like some other operating systems, can give more information about the jobs and transactions running than UNIX can. UNIX treats every job, task, or transaction simply as a numbered process and is unable to tell whether a process belongs to an application, a relational database management system (RDBMS), and so forth. It is up to the IT user to correlate information on processes belonging to the software subsystem of interest to him or her.

VMS records system activity continuously for analysis and other purposes. The $MONITOR command allows various aspects of this system activity to be observed in real time, that is, as it happens. The system activity records can be examined in retrospect to check for peaks in activity of various kinds and for trends.

> While interpreting MONITOR statistics, keep in mind that the collection interval has no effect on the accuracy of MONITOR *rates*. It does, however, affect *levels*, because they represent sampled data. In other words, the smaller the collection interval, the more accurate MONITOR level statistics will be.

The above extract is taken from

OpenVMS Performance Management
http://h71000.www7.hp.com/doc/73final/documentation/pdf/ovms_73_perf_mang.pdf
This publication by Compaq, dated 2001, details the following sets of information from the MONITOR command:

- Memory MONITOR statistics
- I/O MONITOR statistics
- CPU MONITOR statistics

The publication overall is useful as a general introduction to performance management, as well as being a specific OpenVMS manual.

A more recent publication (by CA and dated 2008) is

CA Performance Management for OpenVMS r3.1
   http://www.ca.com/gb/~/media/Files/ProductBriefs/perf-mgmt-openvms-product-brief-us.pdf

$ Monitor Command

The general format of the MONITOR command is

$$ \$ \text{ MONITOR nnnn/INTERVAL} = \text{tt} $$

where nnnn is a parameter indicating what kind of system activity is to be examined and tt is the length, in seconds, of the sampling interval.

nnnn can take the following forms (there are several others too). See "OpenVMS Performance Management" reference above)"

> SYSTEM: For general system CPU, I/O, and memory usage
> MODE: Activity in the five different CPU modes: user, supervisor, exec, kernel, and interrupt
> PROCESS/x: Displays the processes with the highest page fault rate
> DISK: Displays I/O rate and I/O request queue for one or more disks
> IO: Displays I/O system statistics, including direct disk I/O, buffered (terminal) I/O, and various paging statistics
> FCP: Displays other file access statistics

The performance data from the MONITOR command can be stored on disk in either full or summary form, or displayed on an operator terminal.

$ MONITOR SYSTEM Command

This form of the MONITOR command initiates the monitoring of system statistics of various forms, including

- Time spent in various program modes (kernel, etc.)
- Process counts
- Idle time
- Page fault rate
- Direct I/O rate (physical)
- Buffered I/O rate (logical)

The MONITOR command can also record useful statistics about online transaction processing (OLTP) transactions under the control of DECtp services.

MONITOR DISK/Qualifier

See the previous references for details of this form of the MONITOR command to collect details of disk activity on a system—single or clustered.

Management of Performance Data

There are four basic ways of collecting and hence analyzing performance data:

■ For immediate consumption during, for example, short term or sudden loss of performance, often called real time. In the cases such as using wire data (see Appendix III), quite powerful analytics tools may be needed to provide real-time warnings and alerts.
■ Regular, time-based collection for later analysis and capacity planning.
■ Collections and real-time analysis for alert purposes.
■ Retrospective analysis of historical data for problem analysis.

These can be achieved by using native operating system tools or commercial performance tools for the various resources that comprise systems: processors, disks, and so on.

The essence of the whole process is not just to draw attractive, aesthetically pleasing graphs, but to do something with the data if only to say the IT equivalent of "All quiet on the Western front." The mantra should be "Collect, analyze, act and learn (and don't repeat)."

Collection of Data

Whatever operating system environment is being used, data normally needs to be divided into *interval data* and *average data* over various periods. For example, data may need to be sampled at 30 s intervals for graphical and other analysis, hourly averages, and peak-to-average ratios established and longer-term (shift, day, week) averages and other derivations of collected data to aid performance management.

For example, in the UNIX and Linux environments,

$$vmstat\,(parameters)\,30\ 1200$$

will collect data at 30 s intervals for 10 h (twelve hundred 30 s intervals), which might cover the online activity during prime shift. Again,

$$iostat - d30\ 1200$$

will collect physical volume data in a fashion similar to that of the vmstat command above.

Analysis of Data

Data output from the commands is often directed to the screen, but this is not necessary where long-term monitoring is taking place. Instead, it is possible to store the results in a file and analyze the file using grep, awk, or Lotus 1-2-3, for example. The UNIX commands offer powerful file and data manipulation facilities for such stored data, but can be difficult to use. Lotus 1-2-3 or equivalent spreadsheet packages can take the data and plot it in various ways for analysis.

Virtual Machine Performance

Also note that the virtualization arena is volatile, and vendors and products come and go. In addition, existing products may change names and vendors may be taken over by other vendors. The vendors and products in this section are the current players at the time of writing this book.

Performance management in virtual environments and clouds is different from traditional, physical server environments inasmuch as it is sometimes difficult to isolate your application from the herd, so to speak. It is like trying to spot your child in a mass of children on school sports day.

Cloud or Virtualization Gotcha

In the cloud (virtual) environment, it is possible that all physical indicators show that all is well—CPU, storage, and network utilizations OK—so we need not worry. However, it may be that your application is not getting the resource it needs, and this will probably show up in the application response time.

The continuation of the child analogy is that there might be enough food at the children's party for all the guests, but it could well be that some of them are hogging the food and others are going short, even though the calculated average amount of food per child (total food divided by number of children), is acceptable.

What this implies for IT is there must be a better way to verify that your workload is getting the resource it needs. The most obvious one is response time and throughput, which, in the case of your using a cloud service, is easier for you to measure than the physical resource characteristics of the systems.

In Figure 8.10, the dark textured boxes represent the workload of a company or part of a company, and our interest is how that is faring in the virtualized melee of this environment.

The *internal measures* that served us well in the physical environment are considered a little suspect in the virtualized world with its added complexity. Such measures are probably valid in looking at the overall resource performance in terms of utilizations, but they don't tell us how the individual applications are faring in this new regime.

A first-class paper on aspects of performance monitoring in a virtualized environment is

Performance Monitoring in Cloud [Infosys]
http://www.infosys.tuwien.ac.at/Staff/sd/papers/SOCA%202012%20Ph.%20Leitner%20 Application-Level%20Performance.pdf

I recommend you take a look at it, if convenient, before proceeding with the rest of this book.

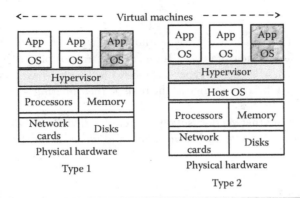

Figure 8.10 Virtualized environments: types 1 and 2.

Monitoring Virtual Environments

One key difference between the physical and the virtualized environments is that in the first case, there is a one-to-one relationship of operating system (OS) and the hardware. In the second case, there is an interposed virtual machine (VM) monitor or OS that acts as a go-between between the (guest) OS and the hardware, where the monitor simulates a hardware environment for each of its guest OSs (see Figure 8.10).

Scope of the Problem

To find out what is happening in this new environment, Srinivas Ramanathan (CEO and founder, eG Innovations) has written a paper:

Managing the Performance of Red Hat Virtual Structures
http://www.eginnovations.com/white-papers.htm [paper is a selection in this link]
   In this paper are suggested areas that require monitoring if the virtualized systems are to be understood, measured, and managed. These areas include*

- Monitoring the hypervisor and its resource consumption. The main hypervisors are listed in the next section of this book.
- Automatic discovery of virtual machines (VMs) and their status and resource allocation and consumption.
- Understanding why a VM is taking excessive resource or is abnormally slow. Can it be workload variation or perhaps a rogue application looping?
- Tracking and understanding the storage aspect of the virtualized environment.
- Having the ability to monitor every tier (or level) within this infrastructure.
- Having an alert methodology to raise alarms when baseline resource levels are exceeded.
- (Hopefully) being able to pinpoint and correct performance problems and ensuring they aren't repeated via root cause analysis (RCA).

---

* My interpretation added.

Hypervisors

There are a number of players in the VM monitor and hypervisor field and others in the VM monitoring field, if you see the difference. The major hypervisor players are Citrix (XenServer), VMware (vSphere/ESXi), Microsoft (Hyper-V), and KVM (Kernel-Based Virtual Machine; modified Linux). Others use Citrix Xensource as the basis of their offerings—Oracle VM and Virtual Iron.

There are a number of other vendors supplying peripheral virtual environment products, such as *security*, *backup*, *monitoring*, *reporting*, *automation*, and *file conversion* from one hypervisor environment to another.

Virtualization Management

The management areas singled out for attention by an article in *CIO* magazine are

■ Capacity management
■ Performance optimization
■ Storage management
■ Virtual enterprise management suites
■ Desktop virtualization planning and management

A good springboard for diving into virtualization management is the following papers from VMware and TechTarget:

How to Select a Virtualization Management Tool
http://www.vmware.com/files/pdf/vrealize/vmw-howt-virtualization-management-tool-wp.pdf

Top 10 Hypervisors: Choosing the Best Hypervisor Technology
http://searchservervirtualization.techtarget.com/tip/Top-10-hypervisors-Choosing-the-best-hypervisor-technology
The references below list another batch of virtualization hypervisors and management of virtualized environments.
The virtualization management vendor list comprises (but not exclusively) the following:

BMC: *Virtualization Management from BMC*
http://documents.bmc.com/products/documents/55/15/ 215515/215515.pdf

IBM: *IBM Cloud Manager with Openstack*
https://www.ibm.com/developerworks/servicemanagement/cvm/sce/resources.html

HP: *HP Software Virtualization Management Solutions*
http://h20229.www2.hp.com/partner/isv/resources/Virtualization.pdf

HP: *Virtualization Performance Viewer (vPV)*
http://www8.hp.com/us/en/software-solutions/vpv-server-virtualization-management/

Dell: *Optimize Infrastructure Performance and Capacity*
http://software.dell.com/solutions/virtualization-management/
A Dell paper on some characteristics of the virtual environment that can be monitored with some benefit can be found in

Top 10 Ways That Foglight for Virtualization, Free Edition Can Help You
https://software.dell.com/docs/top-10-ways-that-foglight-for- virtualization-free-edition-can-help-you-
whitepaper-13775.pdf

The Definitive Guide to Virtualization Management Software [eBook]
https://software.dell.com/docs/the-definitive-guide-to-virtualization-management-software-eb-
ook-15113.pdf

Clabby Analytics/IBM: *Virtualization and Cloud Management Using Capacity Planning*
https://www.ibm.com/developerworks/community/files/form/anonymous/api/library/75d26e43-
17d6-4754-8782-ff55209b2ee4/document/1af76034-20f5-4ad4-a4ec-7258662b2524/media/
Virtualization%20and%20Cloud%20Management%20Using%20Capacity%20Planning%20
-%20by%20Clabby%20Analytics.pdf

Virtualization Management: 5 Tools That Matter Most
http://www.cio.com/article/2415009/virtualization/virtualization-management--5-tools-that-
matter-most.html

Top 10 Virtualization Management Tools
http://searchservervirtualization.techtarget.com/tip/Top-10-virtualization-management-tools

Compuware: *Java Enterprise Performance: Chapter 7: Virtualization and Cloud Performance*
https://info.dynatrace.com/rs/compuware/images/JEP_7_Cloud_Virtualization_Performance.pdf

The exposition above is the best paper on the topic of virtualization performance I have come
across in my research. There are a total of seven chapters, four of which are as yet unpublished at the
time of writing this book (December 2015).

So, with all these managers, what can possibly go wrong? A lot of things if you don't know
what key *metrics* your organization needs, and it depends on how you interpret the output of tools
to make these *metrics* meaningful.

Virtualization Performance Metrics

The performance metrics that are of use in virtualized environments are sometimes the same as those
in traditional physical environments, but with some exceptions and several additions to cater to the
extra dimension of the virtual world. Probably the first practical commercial use of virtualization was
IBM's VM/370 (Virtual Machine/370), announced in 1972.

Initially, VM/370 treated all its guests equally, but application priorities dictated that some
were more equal than others,* and they should be treated accordingly. This led to classes of guest
and, in particular, a preferred virtual machine (PVM) where the major applications ran. This
highlights the main issue with VM metrics, and that is, who is getting what resource and is it
enough?

The link below, from TechTarget, discusses why physical monitors are not up to the task
of monitoring virtual worlds and goes on to outline the areas in those worlds that need special
attention.

Why Physical Performance Monitoring Tools Aren't Enough
http://searchservervirtualization.techtarget.com/tip/Why-physical-performance-monitoring-
tools-arent-enough

---

* From *Animal Farm* by George Orwell (Eric Blair).

Further, a hypervisor provides the mapping between a virtual machine's hardware and the host's physical hardware. Because a guest OS is not aware of the virtualization layer, it believes it has the host hardware all to itself. As a result, an OS cannot detect or measure underlying resource bottlenecks in the virtualization layer. So performance monitoring tools from the physical world can produce inaccurate results. (TechTarget article above)

Another useful link, from ManageEngine, provides a very thorough *review of metrics* to aid the management of virtual environments.

Virtual Machines
https://www.manageengine.com/it360/help/meitms/applications/help/monitors/virtual-machines.html

Some of the key metrics in the virtual world that ManageEngine includes are

- *Monitor information (hypervisor)*
  - Some virtual machine details
- *CPU and memory data*
  - CPU utilization of the VM (%)
  - CPU usage in megahertz
  - Memory utilization of the VM (%)
- *Disk and network data*
  - Disk I/O utilization of the VM (Kbps)
  - Network utilization of the VM (Kbps)
- *Memory data*
  - Active (recently used) memory
  - Overhead memory, allocated to the VM
  - Swapped memory
  - Shared memory
  - Ballooned memory
  - Granted memory
- *Datastore data*
  - Name, type of datastore
  - Capacity (GB)
  - Used GB
  - Free GB
  - Health—overall health of the datastore
- *Other disk I/O data*
  - Logical unit number
  - Disk read rate of logical unit number (LUN) (Kbps)
  - Disk write rate of LUN (Kbps)
  - Number of disk reads to this LUN during defined interval
  - Number of disk writes to this LUN during defined interval
  - Overall health of this LUN
- *Other network data*
  - Network interface card (NIC) IP and MAC address plus network name
  - NIC health
  - Data receive rate for this NIC (Kbps)

- Data transmit rate for this NIC (Kbps)
- Number of packets received
- Number of packets transmitted
■ *Configuration data*
  - Name (universal unique identifier [UUID]) of VM, OS name assigned to VM, and other information outlined in the cited document above

Whatever the source and nature of the metrics in the virtualized environments is, remember that utilization of a resource is a good indicator of performance information *quality*.

Remembering also that efficient utilizations depend on the service time of the resource in question,* Equation 8.2 gives an indicator of performance quality:

$$\frac{\text{Resource Consumed}}{\text{Resource Available}(\text{Capacity})} \tag{8.2}$$

Maturity of Virtualization Monitoring

Many of the papers on the subject are dubious about the quality of performance information gathered internally to the virtualized systems, particularly of that involving time and time intervals.

If you plan to swim in the cloud and virtualization world, you would be advised to look out for sharks.

VM Time

There is a remarkable paper about timekeeping in virtual machines that presents an almost Einsteinian view of the variability of time, depending on your viewpoint in the universe:

Timekeeping in VMware Virtual Machines
http://www.vmware.com/files/pdf/Timekeeping-In-Virtual Machines.pdf
Another paper, cited below, also explains some issues in the definition of time in the VM world.

Hyper-V: Clocks Lie … Which Performance Counters Can You Trust?
http://blogs.msdn.com/b/tvoellm/archive/2008/03/20/hyper-v-clocks-lie.aspx
Many similar articles suggest that anything observed by a virtual machine involving CPU cycles or time might generate inconsistent or inaccurate metrics and should be treated with respect (or even suspicion).

This variability of time in virtualized environments leads some authors to question just which internal measurements can be trusted, and some, like TeamQuest, opt for looking at external measures, measured or derived (see Appendix IV), to quantify performance in this arena.

VM Interference

A novel paper by Novakovic et al. discusses the topic of interference between VMs and its detection and measurement, claiming that interference can severely diminish the trust of customers in

---

* Faster service times support a higher operating utilization than slower ones before hitting the knee of the performance curve due to excessive queue lengths.

a cloud's ability to deliver predictable performance. The authors claim that the DeepDive tool or analyzer can detect performance degradation due to interference to within 5% (average) and 10% (worst case) and suggest a migration of the offending virtual machine.

Figure 10 in the document shows that the DeepDive placement manager properly predicts interference on the possible destination PMs and suggests a near-optimum placement for a VM.

DeepDive: Transparently Identifying and Managing Performance Interference in Virtualized Environments
http://www.cs.rutgers.edu/~ricardob/papers/usenix13.pdf

Cloud Monitoring and Performance

An SLA (and sub-SLAs) agreeing with a cloud provider can be either believed implicitly or checked by the customer (your organization). How might this be done to avoid being sold *snake oil?** This is not to say that cloud service vendors cheat, but interpretations of key performance indicators can vary organization to organization.

When in total control of one's IT, the monitoring responsibility and interpretation is that of the organization, but in IT (in part or in total), the visibility of what is happening is not so clear. Whichever guise your organization takes, there is merit in being able to monitor your cloud computing to make sure you meet internal service level agreements (SLAs) and the cloud providers meet theirs.

> *Note*: The outlines and references that follow are generic to fit any particular solution your organization requires knowledge of it and your SLA specifications. I do not have knowledge of either, but there should be enough information in this section for you to do some homework and decide.

Cloud Visibility

Network World tested and ranked four tools in the cloud monitoring arena. As before, skimmers and generalists can skip to "Cloud Monitoring Metrics":

1. Exoprise CloudReady
   SaaS Performance Monitoring
   http://www.exoprise.com/solutions/
   Ensuring High Service Levels for Apps in the Cloud—Best Practices
   http://www.exoprise.com/bpwp20140927/
2. AppNeta
   PathView: Network Health Monitoring over Any Network
   https://docs.appneta.com/pathview

---

* An expression used in Western movies and also by the late Ken Olsen when describing the value of UNIX.

3. Dynatrace
   Cloud Monitoring
   http://www.dynatrace.com/en/initiatives/cloud.html
   Performance Analysis of Cloud Applications [very good and detailed]
   http://www.dynatrace.com/en/javabook/performance-analysis-and-resolution-and-a-cloud.html
4. ThousandEyes
   ThousandEyes Website
   https://www.thousandeyes.com/
   Rethink Network Troubleshooting: Your Applications Are a Mix of Cloud and On-Premises
   https://www.thousandeyes.com/solutions/why-thousandeyes

The Network World winner, "with some caveats," was AppNeta, partly because of its breadth of vision and granularity of data it accumulated; the caveats related to cost and the attendant learning curve for the product.

Reference A (below) should be consulted for detailed results of the survey and tests, and reference B for a recent (September 2015) paper on cloud management tools.

A. Top Tools to Manage Cloud Apps
http://www.networkworld.com/article/2915837/cloud-computing/top-tools-to-manage-cloud-apps.html

B. 11 Powerful Cloud Management Tools
http://www.networkcomputing.com/cloud-infrastructure/11-powerful-cloud-management-tools/d/d-id/1322004

Cloud Monitoring Metrics

Metrics are things we measure, record, and analyze as an aid to managing the environment, in our case, the performance world. It is known that the metrics and tools used to monitor physical environments (classical or legacy computing) do not give the right information when run against virtualized and cloud environments. It is like the move from classical mechanics to quantum mechanics and relativity to explain the new environments.

The reason for monitoring the performance (and other metrics) of the cloud is mainly to satisfy service level agreement (SLA) demands. In many cloud situations, there are two *demanders*: (1) the internal user of the system, who will have an SLA with the organization's IT department, and (2) the organization itself, who will want to vet the cloud provider's performance against its SLA.

> In such environments, the service level agreement reporting will only be as reliable as the data that feeds it.

There are basically two sets of data providing metrics:

■ The data about the individual elements of the virtualized systems: utilizations, paging, I/O rate, and so on. These are visible only to the systems people at the cloud supplier or organization using the cloud. They mean little to the end user.

■ What the end user can see is the response time for transactions, queries, and similar functions and work throughput for batch and other, similar work.

The Itpro paper (reference C) cited below states that this dilemma needs solutions to "view external components and performance as if they were a part of their [own] internal network." In this context, the report suggests the use of synthetic transactions and cites "Observer Infrastructure" (see reference below the list) as a tool for observing their cloud performance.

The functionality of this tool includes

■ Active discovery and configuration
■ Up and down monitoring
■ Network mapping
■ Route monitoring
■ Event notification—alarms and alerts
■ Device inventory
■ Public and private cloud management
■ Storage enclosure and storage area network (SAN) details
■ Virtualization visibility
■ Application availability
■ Synthetic transactions
■ Configuration monitoring

Observer Platform
http://www.viavisolutions.com/en-us/products/product-families/observer-platform-gigastor?_ga=
1.245163141.1460598391.1458215900

C. 3 Key Cloud Monitoring Metrics
http://research.itpro.co.uk/content43815

Reference D is written by ManageEngine and lists the management challenges presented by movement of applications to the cloud, be it public, private, or hybrid. The solutions suggested, under the heading *"Capabilities Needed,"* are as follows:

■ Tools for measuring the impact of rules for assigning cloud resources for quality of end-user experience (QoS), taking advantage of the ability to assign resources to applications within the cloud.
■ The ability to compare cloud service delivery to performance of the internal environment, with the intention of getting the same performance in the cloud as that experienced in the organization's internal environment.
■ Using an independent tool for monitoring and validating performance of a heterogeneous set of applications in the cloud. This is to allow monitoring of applications for SLA compliance beyond the details supplied by the cloud vendors. There is no implication of skulduggery by the vendor, just that the information supplied by it may not fit the requirements of all organizations for assessing SLA fulfillment, which is essentially what this book is all about.
■ The ability to monitor cloud applications alongside internal IT systems, which is mainly a requirement in hybrid cloud situations. They maintain that a single tool is better for this purpose than two separate ones.

They then outline the business benefits of achieving these goals and describe how the ManageEngine Applications Manager fits into the role of achieving them.

D. Four Keys for Monitoring Cloud Services
https://www.manageengine.com/products/applications_manager/four-keys-for-monitoring-cloud-services.pdf

There are numerous other papers on cloud SLAs, and I have had to be selective in quoting those that give as full coverage to the topic as possible, along with the names of vendors who provide tools for cloud monitoring. The reference below (E) is a short paper but contains names of vendors that complement those already mentioned in this chapter. They are

- AlertSite
- CA
- LogicMonitor
- Monitis
- Novell
- Panopta
- RightScale
- Servoy
- Tap in Systems
- Webmetrics
- Zenoss
- Zeus

E. Accurately Monitoring Cloud SLAs
http://www.cloudbook.net/resources/stories/accurately-monitoring-cloud-slas

Other tools, not mentioned in the previous reference but having a lot of exposure, are Nagios and BMC's Cloud Lifecycle Management, details of which can be found at

Nagios
http://www.nagios.org/
http://library.nagios.com/
http://www.thegeekstuff.com/2008/06/how-to-monitor-remote-linux-host-using-nagios-30/

Cloud Lifecycle Management
http://www.bmc.com/it-solutions/cloud-lifecycle-management.html

> **WoW**: Your evaluation method should be to draw up what information you need to fulfill SLAs and match any tools to that list of requirements, and not vice versa. If you do it the latter way, you may end up with a solution to which there is no problem, a big bill, and irate end users.

Cloud Benchmarking*

Benchmarking cloud and other services can masquerade as *load testing*, which is essentially benchmarking until the system under test (SUT) creaks at the seams.

---

* The companies referenced in this section are not unique in this area. Others can be found by a simple search on "cloud benchmarking."

Brendan Gregg has written a book from which a sample chapter can be found on the web (see reference below). It is an interesting and thorough article, though to be fair, it concentrates more on the *benchmarking* aspects than the *enterprise* and *cloud* aspects, but it is useful nonetheless, coming from a guru.

Benchmarking Enterprise and Cloud Systems Performance
http://www.informit.com/articles/article.aspx?p=2144597

Google has thrown its hat in the ring with a cloud benchmark called *PerfKit Benchmarker*. The tool is open source, and Google says the tool will measure "the end to end time to provision resources in the cloud, in addition to reporting on the most standard metrics of peak performance," giving a way to easily benchmark across cloud platforms, while getting a transparent view of application throughput, latency, variance, and overhead. The documentation link below tells us

> PerfKit Benchmarker is an open effort to define a canonical set of benchmarks to measure and compare cloud offerings. It's designed to operate via vendor-provided command-line tools. The benchmarks are not tuned (i.e., the defaults) because this is what most users will use. This should help us drive to great defaults. Only in the rare cause where there is a common practice like setting the buffer pool size of a database do we change any settings.

Google Cloud Platform/PerfKit Benchmarker
https://github.com/GoogleCloudPlatform/PerfKit Benchmarker

There are offerings in this area from *ProfitBricks*, claiming to specialize in workload-based cloud computing performance benchmarks and synthetic cloud computing performance benchmarks.

PROFITBRICKS: The IaaS-Company
https://www.profitbricks.com/cloud-performance-testing/

The company below (Cloudspectator, a relatively new one) offers services in assessing cloud services for infrastructure as a service (IaaS) environments. They cover enterprise services and hosting providers, providing services and information on both performance and price per performance in these areas.

Cloud Performance Benchmark Services
http://cloudspectator.com/

Cloud Performance Variations

Xangati (www.xangati.com) provides solutions for tracking what it calls *performance storms* in cloud and virtualized infrastructures. Such a storm is due to resource contention in these environments and can come and go just like ordinary storms. It is the rough equivalent of response time *jitter* in communication systems.

These performance glitches, due to resource contention, can manifest themselves as

- Storage storms
- Memory storms
- CPU storms
- Network storms

Such phenomena are foreign to legacy (precloud) infrastructures, and their unpredictability requires visualization of these resources in real time, which means on a second-by-second basis. In other words, it is necessary to track key IT metrics continuously to detect and remedy these performance *gotchas*.

You may want to be aware of these offerings if you come across any three-pipe* performance problems and add them to your emergency kit.

Intelligent Tracking of Performance Storms in Complex Cloud Infrastructures
http://xangati.com/wp-content/uploads/2014/04/WP-Intelligent-Tracking-of-Performance-Storms-04012014.pdf
Xangati Products
http://xangati.com/products/

SLAs for the Cloud

This topic is covered, alongside normal SLAs, in Chapter 17, to which reference should be made. There are some detailed references given here to cloud service level agreement documents that may be useful in some cases.

Service Level Agreement in Cloud Computing
http://corescholar.libraries.wright.edu/cgi/viewcontent.cgi? article=1077&context=knoesis

An Overview of the Commercial Cloud Monitoring Tools: Research Dimensions, Design Issues and State-of-the-Art
http://arxiv.org/ftp/arxiv/papers/1312/1312.6170.pdf

External Performance Measures†

This is a key measure that users will latch onto as proof that their application is being looked after in the virtualized and cloud *scrum*, and that is the observed *response time* at their workstation or, in some cases, the throughput of some workload or other, such as batch jobs.

In the following discussion of this, I have to thank TeamQuest for their assistance in the task of illustrating the use of external measures in performance measurement and management in virtualized environments.

The first generic step in this response time journey is to collect the data, and this can be done with numerous different tools, depending on the environment. I am using TeamQuest products as examples (because of the fine granularity of data that it is able to collect, going down to 1 s data collection in cases where the operating system or hypervisor updates its counters at that fine granularity).

Data collection is performed by *TeamQuest CMIS* (Capacity Management Information System). This can be a bit of a misnomer since the data collected can be used for operational (day-to-day) purposes, as well as tactical and strategic resource planning (using *Analyzer*).

---

* A three-pipe problem is what Sherlock Holmes called very difficult and apparently intractable criminal problems, necessitating sitting up all night and consuming three pipes of tobacco.

† In this discussion, I have to thank TeamQuest for their assistance in the task of illustrating the use of external measures in performance measurement and management in virtualized environments. Use of this material does not constitute a recommendation or imply there are no other vendors offering facilities similar to those of TeamQuest.

The next step in the journey is to be able to visualize the data and do a drill-down analysis to determine the root cause of performance issues (i.e., root cause analysis [RCA]). We do this with TeamQuest Analyzer. Visualizing the data and being able to perform RCA is a manually intense task that is sometimes necessary. There is also an automated correlation discovery that is built into Analyzer. This function discovers other metrics that correlated over time to the metric of interest, thus greatly speeding up the RCA process.

Operational Metrics

The key *overall metric* here is *TeamQuest Performance Indicator* (TPI), a single number (scale of 1–100) that indicates how much queuing is occurring on the system. A score close to 100 indicates little to no queuing. A score of 50 indicates that jobs are spending equal amounts of time processing and waiting in the queue. A score lower than 50 indicates that there is more queuing going on than processing, and of course a score of 0 indicates complete thrashing with no work actually getting done.

There are more than 1500 metrics taken in each sample interval (1 s upward), from which the TPI is derived. A few of them are reproduced here (we don't have space for all 1500+):

- CPU percent used
- CPU queue length
- Disk space used
- Disk I/O throughput
- Disk I/O response time
- Memory percent used
- Page rate
- Swap rate
- Network I/O rate

These metrics are the raw indicators of good and poor performance at an operational level. What about response time? you may ask.

TeamQuest products do not capture response time directly. Rather, using Little's law (see Appendix I) and network queuing theory, the predictor product calculates infrastructure response time and throughput. All this in consolidated into the TPI, described above. Also included in the output of the predictor are *components of response*, so you know which resource (e.g., CPU) is responsible for the degradation in response time or throughput.

Capacity Planning

For these purposes, we need to do two other things: (1) predict when throughput and response time objectives will not be met (along with identifying the cause of such issues), and (2) conduct automated exception-based reporting so that we can monitor thousands of virtual instances with a limited staff and direct that staff to take a closer look at the true exceptions, rather than having to cull through tens of thousands of data points to find the issue.

To address the accurate prediction of throughput and response time issues, *TeamQuest Predictor* can be both used in a manual what-if scenario manner and fully automated to predict future issues based on analysis of historical behavior. The TeamQuest solution set is complemented with *Surveyor*, which is used to create exception-based reporting against any variety of data sources.

These data sources can be TeamQuest CMIS data or other performance data (such as Tivoli, HP, and BMC) or other, more business-focused sources, such as hardware costing data.

The CMIS, Analyzer, Predictor, and Surveyor can be found at the link below.

Products and Services
http://www.teamquest.com/products-services/overview/

Cloud KPIs

An article in Data Center Knowledge (October 2015) discusses the ability to monitor cloud infrastructure KPIs, noting that a private, public, or hybrid cloud may require its own set of tools for this purpose. The article is aimed at aiding the *selection* of cloud management tools.

- User count
- Resource management
- Alerts and alarms
- Failover capabilities
- Roles and privileges
- SLA considerations
- Testing and maintenance

How to Select the Right Cloud Management Tools
http://www.datacenterknowledge.com/archives/2015/10/02/how-to-select-the-right-cloud-management-tools/?utm_source=DailyNewsletter&utm_medium=email&utm_campaign=DailyNewsletter B&utm_content=10-03-2015

Cloud Vendors' Performance

A 2015 report on the performance of cloud services from two different suppliers is contained in the following link:

Performance Analysis: Benchmarking Public Clouds [Amazon and Internap Services; white paper, Data Center Knowledge; better accessed via a search of the terms above]
http://whitepapers.datacenterknowledge.com/?option=com_categoryreport&task=viewabstra ct&pathway=no&title=47024&frmurl=http%3a%2f%2fforms.madisonlogic.com%2fForm. aspx%3fpub%3d81%26pgr%3d68%26frm%3d293%26autodn%3d1%26src%3d744%26ctg %3d1%26 ast%3d47024%26crv%3d0%26cmp%3d15442%26yld%3d0%26clk%3d614976784 4692428932%26em%3d%2525%2525%2521contact_email%2525%2525%26embed%3d1

> *WoW*: With a URL of this size and complexity, it may be more productive to search the title and vendors involved. This applies to large URLs elsewhere in this book.

There are other reports on cloud service suppliers (by Gartner Magic Quadrant and Forrester on private cloud solutions), but their main emphasis is not on performance.

Commercial Performance Tools

System Performance Tools

There are tools needed for monitoring and managing nonvirtualized server environments (the classical world), and these have been around for some time in the main. Some of the tools have been adapted for the virtualized world, a necessary step since the worlds are very different.

BMC: *TrueSight Operations Management* [with links to various products]
http://www.bmc.com/it-solutions/truesight-operations-management.html

CA: *CA Performance Management*
http://www.ca.com/us/opscenter/ca-performance-management.aspx

SolarWinds: *Application Performance Management*
http://www.solarwinds.com/solutions/application-performance-management.aspx

Riverbed: *Application Performance Management*
http://www.riverbed.com/products/performance-management-control/application-performance-management/

IBM Tivoli: *Application Performance Management*
http://www-03.ibm.com/software/products/en/category/application-performance-management

Dell: *Foglight Application Performance Monitoring*
http://software.dell.com/products/foglight-application-performance-monitoring/

HP: *Application Performance Management (APM)*
http://www8.hp.com/us/en/software-solutions/application-performance-management/

Metron: *athene Capacity and Performance Management Software*
http://www.metron-athene.com/products/athene/index.html

There will be other tools that perform application and server performance management, but those above are the ones that spring to mind, and no superiority over other products is implied.

> *WoW*: I find some of the data sheets are written in impenetrable jargon, and finding out precisely what they do (as opposed to how they do it) can be difficult. If in doubt, ask them what *powerful, flexible, leading edge, modular, industry leading, standards based, intuitive,* and other buzzwords mean, since half of them could refer to a garden hose. Simply ask, "What does the product do?"

Application Performance Management

Application performance management (APM) is a set of disciplines, part of performance management, designed to provide accurate information on how business applications are performing. Many organizations rely on APM to give them sufficient information to see if their internally developed applications and third-party applications are performing well. The purpose of this exercise is both operational and, in the longer term, for capacity planning purposes.

The overarching reason is to match delivered performance with the service level agreements (SLAs) developed between IT and businesses. There are other reasons, not least of which are organization productivity and external customer acceptance of the online service, particularly websites.

> The cruel fact of the matter is that poor or erratic performance (response times and throughput) are bad for business. Zero performance when the system is down doesn't help the cause either. Availability is an essential component of performance.

There are several aspects of applications that need to be monitored since an application makes use of other software in its execution. The number of aspects needing consideration depends on the complexity of the supporting environment. Typically, one might need to be aware of the performance of

- Internet services.
- Response times (overall).
- Network traffic and latency.
- Transaction tracking (visibility) where applicable.
- The infrastructure—operating system, hypervisors.
- The database.
- Web server software.
- Other middleware.
- Enterprise resource planning (ERP) and other application systems. These sometimes have their own resource and reporting monitors.
- File servers, messaging systems, and so forth.
- Use of what are known as *Deep Dive diagnostics*, producing reams of data, for knotty problems.

Viewpoints: An important aspect of performance (and availability) monitoring is where the observer stands in the IT scenario. If a complaint says the performance of an application is dreadful, the network man might say, "Everything is fine," and the database man may agree, both saying, "What's the problem?"

These are what I call *viewpoints*, a popular concept in IT architecture design and all valid in their own way. Each participant has a different view of what is bad performance—network, database, web, system, or user personnel.

All these people, with the exception of the user, will be interested in

- Percent utilizations
- Wait times
- Disk space used
- Disk I/O throughput
- Disk I/O response time
- Memory percent used
- Page rate

These are meaningless to the user of the application who is interest in

- Response times (overall latency, percentiles, and variation)
- Throughput where applicable
- Availability

The trick here is to marry these viewpoints, which means translating the operational data into user and service level agreement (SLA) terms. All this is complicated when one moves from the relatively simple classical IT environment to the mixed web and application environments, rendered even more difficult to fathom by virtualization and clouds. This new world is outlined next.

Modern Applications and Architectures: Today, the IT world that needs management looks something like this:

- Some three-quarters of medium to enterprise-sized companies are developing and hosting custom applications.
- The majority of these use J2EE or other Java-based languages.
- Tiered web systems and applications are common.
- About half of these are using what is termed hybrid clouds, a mixture of public and private.
- Obviously, a common characteristic is virtualization with its attendant addition to complexity and visibility requirements.
- This world is made even more baffling with additions like live server migration and cloud-bursting (offloading excess work to an external cloud).
- Some organizations are in the middle of migrating from a monolithic (classical) environment to this new one.

This is where vendor monitoring and analysis tools come into their own, supplementing any native tools available with the base infrastructure software.

The reference below might take some of the bafflement out of making sense of what I have just outlined, starting with the sentence "Not sure which Application Performance Management vendor to choose?"

White Papers: APM Solutions by Real Users
http://apmdigest.com/white-papers
Slightly old (2007), this paper nevertheless outlines the needs and pitfalls in chasing APM solutions.

Application Performance Management: Best Practices Do Work
http://www.netforecast.com/wp-content/uploads/2007/05/ApplicationPerformanceManagement BestPractiesDoWork.pdf
An IBM paper, actually revolving around SmartCloud, is useful in understanding the modern IT environment, alluded to above. It is worth a perusal.

IBM SmartCloud Application Performance Management for Dynamic and Cloud Infrastructures
https://www-947.ibm.com/support/entry/portal/product/tivoli/ibm_smartcloud_application_ performance_management?productContext=2118294912
The outcome of all this is the urgent need for visibility of such environments in order to develop resource management and monitoring at the appropriate level of detail, hence the need to select the appropriate monitoring and management tools for your needs.

Gartner and APM

Gartner defines APM has having five facets to be covered to be the complete package:

1. End-user experience monitoring (EUM)
2. Application topology discovery and visualization
3. User-defined transaction profiling
4. Application component Deep Dive (fine-grained monitoring of resources consumed)
5. IT operations analytics (ITOA), the combination or usage of the following techniques:
   a. Complex operations event processing
   b. Statistical pattern discovery and recognition
   c. Unstructured text indexing, search, and inference
   d. Topological analysis
   e. Multidimensional database search and analysis

A complimentary copy of this report can be obtained via the link below.

Gartner's 2014 Magic Quadrant for APM
http://www.appdynamics.com/gartner-magic-quadrant-2014-application-performance-monitoring/
Their top three in APM (October 2014) were New Relic, AppDynamics, and Compuware, with CA Technologies some way behind. However, a new paper by Network World and Layland Consulting put the top four application performance management (APM) vendors as

- CA Technologies
- New Relic
- AppNeta
- Emulex Endace

The paper covers quite a bit of ground, with contributions from the above vendors. To be fair, to compare the results of the two studies and explain the differences would require a similar set of criteria for judging each vendor's product.

The 2015 Application and Network Performance Management Challenge
http://resources.idgenterprise.com/original/AST-0145464_2015_ANPM_Challenge_Document_FINAL.pdf
There is an excellent document on application performance monitoring by Don Jones in a Real-time Publishing document:

The Five Essential Elements of Application Performance Monitoring
http://www.realtimepublishers.com/book?id=168

Database Performance Management

RDBMS Monitors

In assessing database performance, the usual low-level metrics are often of use, but there are some that are specific to databases. A selection of these, at various levels, are shown below:

High-Level Metrics

- *Response time*: The maximum, median, and minimum response times for database queries by the selected node in milliseconds
- *Transactions per unit time*: The total number of database transactions per minute by the selected node
- *DB connection use*: The maximum, median, and minimum number of database connections in use by the selected node

Database Metrics

- *Database throughput*: The count (per minute) for each type of database operation (inserts, deletes, etc.) over time.
- *Database response*: The response time (in milliseconds) for each type of database operation.
- *DB connection use*: How many connections this instance has opened to the database. Select to display as a maximum, a minimum, or a mean.
- *Access diagnostics*: Database products usually have some sort of tools for assessing the efficiency of database access and organization and reporting on these as a tuning or retrospective design aid.
- *Deadlocks*: Should be zero with proper design of application and database.
- *Physical reads and writes*: This should tie in with the cache hit rate, which should be high and the read and write I/O optimum.

Operational Metrics

These may be used if any performance issues are not strictly database design issues, and it may be necessary to resort to these component-level tools to see if lack of resource is the issue.

- *CPU stats*: sar, vmstat, mpstat, iostat
- *Virtual memory stats*: sar, vmstat
- *Disk stats*: sar, iostat
- *Network stats*: netstat
- *Specific RDBMS stats (possibly)*: depends on what the RDBMS vendor offers

These metrics, as usual, will focus on utilizations and wait times.

Note, however, that low, acceptable utilizations on physical media used by the database do not mean that all is well with performance. It is quite possible that indexing and application design issues are causing excessive I/Os to do their jobs, but not at a high rate, so the response times might be very poor while the utilizations are looking fine.

General

There are a number of software packages for checking the health of relational databases, which is a way of solving performance problems in advance of their occurrence. The prevailing opinion is that an ideal health check should provide an overview of a database's stability across three major areas:

- Availability
- Performance
- Scalability

An article on SQL Server health checks is also a useful vehicle for learning the principles of such checks in heading off performance problems:

Database Properties Health Check (2011)
https://www.simple-talk.com/sql/database-administration/database-properties-health-check/
Another article, although majoring on IBM's DB2, is also useful as a generic guide to such checks:

An *"Ideal Database Health Check"—What Does That Really Mean?* (2007)
http://vdevraj.blogspot.co.uk/2007/04/ideal-database-health-check-what-does.html
In addition, there exist a number of articles and tools that cover the health of specific RDBMSs, such as Oracle, DB2, and SQL Server, which can be unearthed using the simple search "database health check," possibly adding the name of your database as well to narrow the search field.

Oracle

Oracle offers a number of ways to monitor and manage performance of both the Oracle database itself and Oracle applications.

Enterprise Manager 12c provides a complete application performance management (APM) solution for custom applications and Oracle applications (including E-Business Suite, Siebel, PeopleSoft, JD Edwards, and Fusion Applications). The APM solution is designed for both cloud and enterprise data center deployments, and is supported on Oracle and non-Oracle platforms.

Oracle Enterprise Manager
http://www.oracle.com/technetwork/oem/enterprise-manager/overview/index.html

Database Performance Management [Oracle 12c]
http://www.oracle.com/technetwork/oem/db-perf-mgmt- 496651.html

(Oracle) Application Performance Management
http://www.oracle.com/technetwork/oem/app-performance-mgmt/index.html

Oracle Performance Monitoring and Tuning Software
http://www.solarwinds.com/database-performance-analyzer-oracle.aspx

SolarWinds

The link below leads to a paper on the details of response time analysis (RTA, as they call it), looking at *wait points* in the Oracle database access elements of response time.

Response Time Analysis: A Pragmatic Approach for Tuning and Optimizing
Oracle Database Performance [SolarWinds/Confio]
http://launch.solarwinds.com/rs/solarwindsworldwide/images/Response_Time_Analysis_
Oracle_WP.pdf

The next reference is to a very useful paper by Confio (now part of SolarWinds) containing an objective discussion of metrics and techniques key to monitoring and assessing database performance. The software involved can be used for Oracle, DB2, Sybase, and SQL Server on physical or virtual machines.

Response Time Analysis
http://www.confio.com/media/353784/responsetimeanalysis_wp_confio_jan2013b.pdf

IBM DB2

IBM Data Server Manager is a new (March 2015) monitoring tool for managing performance and administering DB2 for Linux, UNIX, and Windows DB2 databases. The tutorial referenced below starts with a brief introduction of Data Server Manager and a high-level explanation of the quick up-and-running process.

It provides database administrators (DBAs) and other IT staff with the information they need to manage performance proactively and prevent problems before they impact the business. It is cloud ready, easy to deploy, and offers expert recommendations on courses of action in various situations.

Tutorial
http://www.ibm.com/developerworks/data/library/techarticle/dm-1503db2-data-server/dm-1503db2-data-server-pdf.pdf

IBM Data Server Manager
http://www-03.ibm.com/software/products/en/ibm-data-server-manager

DB2 Performance Management Offering
http://www-03.ibm.com/software/products/en/db2-performance-management-offering

MySQL

MySQL Enterprise Monitor continuously monitors MySQL queries and performance-related server metrics. Receive alerts on significant deviations from the baseline performance trends, and best practice advisors recommend changes to configuration and variable settings to improve performance.

Real-Time MySQL Performance Monitoring and Alerts
http://www.mysql.com/products/enterprise/monitor.html

Informix

A variety of statistics are available to monitor the performance of any of the Informix database servers, and a number of tools are available with which to measure and display these statistics. These are provided by both the UNIX operating system and IBM and Informix themselves. Knowing the appropriate tool to use for measuring each statistic is key to quickly building a complete picture of current system performance. This means either you have such skills or you need to learn them or hire people with them.

The above is paraphrased from what looks like an old Informix-related document (http://debian.fmi.uni-sofia.bg/~ tomecks/Inf/ch21.htm), but the sentiment is still true.

Informix is part of the IBM product line.

The document above is a chapter of *Informix Unleashed*, an online book from SAMS Publishing, seemingly undated, but it appears useful in many areas.

http://debian.fmi.uni-sofia.bg/~tomecks/Inf/fm.htm

There are a number of tools for this RDBMS from both IBM and third parties.

IBM Informix Database Monitoring
https://www.manageengine.com/products/applications_manager/help/monitors/informix-db-monitoring.html

IBM Informix 12.10 Performance Guide
http://www-01.ibm.com/support/knowledgecenter/SSGU8G_ 12.1.0/com.ibm.perf.doc/perf.htm

Sybase

Tools for Sybase management include

AseTune: Sybase ASE Performance Monitor
http://sourceforge.net/projects/asetune/

Foglight for Sybase
http://software.dell.com/products/foglight-for-sybase/

SYBASE Performance and Tuning: Monitoring and Analyzing
http://infocenter.sybase.com/help/topic/com.sybase.dc20022_ 1251/pdf/monitoring.pdf

SolarWinds Database Performance Analyzer (formerly Confio Ignite) for Sybase ASE is a database performance monitoring and analysis solution for DBAs, IT managers, and application developers. Database Performance Analyzer eliminates performance bottlenecks, improves application service, and reduces overall cost of Sybase ASE operations (thus spake SolarWinds).

SolarWinds Database Performance Manager for Sybase ASE
http://web.swcdn.net/creative/pdf/datasheets/SW_DPA_Sybase_DataSheet.pdf

NoSQL

NoSQL (not only Structured Query Language [SQL]) is a new database access method, propelled in part by the advent of large amounts of structured, semistructured, and unstructured data (big data). It has made little impact on the use of traditional RDBMSs for normal commercial workloads, but is finding its own niche. It provides a method of storage and retrieval of data, but not using the tabular form employed by traditional relational products.

NoSQL
http://en.wikipedia.org/wiki/NoSQL

NoSQL Explained
http://www.mongodb.com/nosql-explained

Why NoSQL
http://info.couchbase.com/rs/northscale/images/why NoSQL.whitePaper.FINAL.pdf

MongoDB

MongoDB is an implementation of NoSQL and is a document-oriented data management tool.

Agility, Scalability, Performance: Pick Three
https://www.mongodb.org/

Dell

Proactive Performance Management for Enterprise Databases
https://software.dell.com/whitepaper/proactive-performance-management-for-enterprise-databases821269/

Other Databases

There are still non-SQL databases in the field, some of them of vintage status. IBM's DL/I (Data Language 1) and VSAM (Virtual Storage Access Method) are still with us, as are other examples of indexed file structures:

- Star schema model
- Hierarchical model
- Network model
- Object[oriented model

Introduction to Computer Information Systems/Database
http://en.wikibooks.org/wiki/Introduction_to_Computer_Information_Systems/Database#Database_Models

Interpreting Wait Events to Boost System Performance [concerning databases]
http://www.dbspecialists.com/files/presentations/wait_events. html

In-Memory Databases

There are moves to enhance RDBMS performance by placing the database in main memory as opposed to traditional hard storage, such as disk or solid state. This is very useful for applications and queries that do a lot of data reading and writing for analysis purposes.

> A database that uses a system's main memory for data storage rather than the disk-based storage typically utilized by traditional databases. In-memory databases, or IMDBs, are frequently employed in high-volume environments where response time is critical, as access times and database requests are typically considerably faster when system memory is used as opposed to disk storage, particularly hard drive storage.
>
> In-memory databases are also sometimes referred to as main memory database systems, or MMDBs, and have become more popular in recent years for handling High-Performance Computing (HPC) and Big Data applications. The distinction between traditional databases and in-memory databases has been blurred recently with the advent of hybrid databases, which support both in-memory and disk-based storage in order to maximize performance as well as reliability. (Webopedia definition)

Order of magnitude performance enhancements are claimed for this use of databases. Obviously, very large databases (VLDBs) cannot reside totally in main memory, but rely on a caching-type mechanism with the high-usage data remaining in memory, rather like virtual storage does. The obvious downside to this is the potential data loss on a power failure since memory loses its data in such an event. This can be dealt with by logging and other recovery procedures—see the first reference listed below.

A very readable and impartial description of this mechanism can be found at the following link:

In-Memory Database Systems: Questions and Answers
http://www.mcobject.com/in_memory_database
This reference covers issues such as

- Isn't this just database caching?
- Comparison of performance enhancements
- Don't we lose data in a system crash?
- What types of application can benefit from this technique?
- How does it handle very large databases (terabytes in size)?
- Time taken to populate an in-memory database
- Sharing of an in-memory database by more than one system

Also, there is a Gartner survey on the topic that can be downloaded at

Gartner Market Guide for In-Memory DBMS
http://www1.memsql.com/gartner.html?gclid=CPT78Yj32sYCFUKWtAodhQIHSA
In addition, a *list* of databases capable of in-memory operation can be found in Wikipedia at

List of In-Memory Databases
http://en.wikipedia.org/wiki/List_of_in-memory_databases
This link shows the main RDBMSs having an in-memory option, and there are many other niche databases listed too. Oracle, for example, claims that in-memory operation boosts analytic work and online transaction processing (OLTP) significantly.

In-Memory Database Performance

This is the definitive "How long is a piece of string?" conundrum. There are numerous articles on the topic, but few verifiable figures as far as I can make out. What information there is indicates performance enhancement of factors of a few to nearly 100, but they all depend on the workload. For example, small transactions in an OLTP system using in-memory database show significant improvements. There are some illuminating papers on the topic:

TATP Benchmark [telecommunication application transaction processing]
http://en.wikipedia.org/wiki/TATP_Benchmark

In-Memory Databases: Do You Need the Speed?
http://www.informationweek.com/big-data/big-data-analytics/in-memory-databases-do-you-need-the-speed/d/d-id/1114076

Information Week: In-Memory Databases [edition]
http://dc.ubm-us.com/i/268861-informationweek-2014- 03-03

Aside: The IBM AS/400, announced in 1988, adopted 64-bit addressing (lifted from the abandoned Future Systems project) and was aimed at addressing vast quantities of data in a single address space, although the data might physically reside in memory and on tiered data storage. Accessing the data would then be similar to accessing data in a data field in storage.

The data would actually be in memory, but present the appearance of not being so. mcobject.com, authors of the first in-memory reference above, offer "eXtremeDB-64: McObject's 64-Bit Embedded Database," which reads precisely like the AS/400's 64-bit addressing architecture. *Plus ça change.*

Capacity Management and Planning

Introduction and Justification

If you look at the Internet or books for inspiration on this topic, you will probably come away completely *blitzed* with different ideas and methods for what is not rocket science at the end of the day. It depends mainly on knowledge of the current and projected business environments and their impact on the IT resources required to support them.

The Aberdeen paper referred to below maintains that organizations that employ capacity planning do a better job of managing and getting the most out of their virtual environments than those that do not. This, of course, is in addition to maintaining application performance at an SLA-acceptable level. The planners gain advantages over nonplanners in the vital areas of

- Disaster recovery
- Reduced downtime
- Lower service expense

The figures quoted in this paper are from an Aberdeen survey dated October 2014.

Optimize Your Virtual Environments with Capacity Planning [Aberdeen Group]
https://software.dell.com/docs/knowledge-brief-optimize-your-virtual-environments-with-capacity-planning-technical-brief-14915.pdf

What Is Capacity Management?

We defined *management* earlier as the following:

$$\text{Management} = \text{Design} + \text{Measurement} + \text{Analysis} + \text{Action}$$

Capacity management follows the same definition, with the meaning of the parameters as follows:

- *Design* is the design of the original system with an eye to tactical performance management and a view to using the data for capacity planning purposes. It is no use deciding suddenly that you need data for the capacity plan that you didn't start collecting from time zero.
- *Measurement* is what we and the industry normally call *monitoring*.
- *Design* plus *monitoring* is the basis of capacity plans.
- *Design* plus *monitoring* plus *analysis* is what I call *capacity planning*.
- *Analysis* and *action* apply to tactical performance work, but are ongoing for capacity planning purposes.

I hope this clarifies the differences (it does in my mind anyway) between management, planning, and monitoring. I think the order of hierarchical seniority is management, planning, and monitoring.

ITIL View

The IT Infrastructure Library defines three subprocesses of the capacity management process:

1. Business capacity management (knowledge of current and future business requirements)
2. Service capacity management (IT application services)
3. Resource capacity management (components)

I combine the elements of these areas in what follows. See the link below for further information of the ITIL approach.

ITIL Capacity Management
http://www.itlibrary.org/index.php?page=Capacity_Management

Capacity Planning Scope

The resource capacity task will of course cover the core system areas:

- Processors.
- Network (and components therein).
- Storage.
- Environment (cooling, space, power, etc.). Neglect these at your peril.
- Impact on disaster recovery resources (failover site must cope). Neglecting this aspect can be severe.

It might ostensibly include capacity attention in other areas, depending on how the business is supported:

- printing, for printing businesses and organizations with huge print volumes
- CD/DVD producers and manufacturers
- Other system-produced output

These latter areas won't be covered here.

Capacity planning is, generically, the ongoing projection of system resource requirements needed to support a growing or evolving workload. It is, in essence, the policing of the original system sizing and beyond. The workload pattern of a production system may vary from that used to produce the initial sizing estimate, and hence capacity planning is needed at the outset of production. Capacity planning relies very much on data and information from a number of sources:

- Performance measurements on production systems
- Transaction and job mixes and changes to these
- Application enhancements of jobs, transactions, reports, and so on
- Increased volumes of jobs, transactions, reports, and so on
- Additional applications using performance measurements from pilot and prototype systems
- New versions of operating systems, RDBMS, OLTP, and so on. These can have a dramatic effect on resource consumption, even for the same number of users or transaction rates, and may well need the rerunning of original load tests

As daily workloads grow, it is a wise precaution to check out the effect of this on overnight batch and housekeeping activity, in case the overnight "window" spills into the daytime activity of users and prevents application access by the users.

The simple extrapolation over time of current resource consumption is no substitute for real capacity planning. I have seen an example of a dramatic increase in resource consumption for a particular application that could not be explained by the IT support staff. It transpired that an extra 100 or so users had come online without informing the IT staff of the fact. This sort of behavior obviously breaks the spirit of any SLA in force at the time.

Methodology

The goal of capacity planning, in a nutshell, is to predict the peak utilization of system resources over time, and this will include

- Organic growth,* including growths in peaks as well as averages
- Business growth leading to higher IT workloads
- New applications and methods, such as analytics and use of big data

The key to not over- or underproviding extra resources is to decide what peak of activity to cater to: the average over an hour of peak activity, 10 min, 1 min? The cost of resourcing the last peak (1 min) might be so high as to overwhelm any business benefits in meeting it, so a compromise has to be made.

It should be clear that *averages* are less important than *peaks* that must be met, and the growth of the latter must be monitored, as well as means and averages.

---

* A company I worked with once put a case to the board for a bigger system based on workload growth. A senior board member queried how this could be so: since their actual business growth was close to zero, why was the business IT load increasing? We never figured this one out, but just be prepared for this eventuality.

Steps to Take

Assuming your system was installed with possible growth in mind, there are some generic steps you might want to take and supplement them with your own tailored needs.

1. Specify and quantify your business workload and its activity pattern—OLTP, query, backup, batch work, and so forth, by time of day or night.
2. Translate the activity into resources—CPU, I/Os, megabytes of storage, and so on.
3. Check what headroom you have in the current system against sensible baselines, for example, OLTP peak CPU is 44% and we can tolerate 70%, current batch work overnight runs from 11:00 p.m. to 6:00 a.m., but an extension of this will impact the OLTP systems, which commences at 7:00 a.m.
4. Assess possible growth in activity from:
   a. Organic business growth
   b. New applications or business, including business analysis on big data
   c. Possible migration of workload from other systems or, conversely, possible retirement of systems, both offloading resource that needs to be catered to on an existing system

   It is also a good idea to have an idea of the growth in resource requirements of system software upgrades and new versions, as they have a habit of growing, sometimes as much as 10% between versions.
5. Change management or control is a key aspect of this, but it is a key aspect in its own right in IT installations.
6. Staffing, including third parties and tools for capacity management.
7. Don't forget to try to measure capacity by workload, if possible, rather than just work on average or peak resource utilizations since the individual workloads will need separate *treatment*.

A capacity planning guide from the Centers for Disease Control and Prevention (CDC) can be found at

CDC: Capacity Planning Practices Guide
http://www2.cdc.gov/cdcup/library/practices_guides/cdc_up_capacity_planning_practices_guide.pdf

There is also an associated CDC checklist you may find useful at this link:

CDC: Capacity Planning Checklist
http://www2.cdc.gov/cdcup/library/checklists/CDC_UP_Capacity_Planning_checklist.pdf

There may be peaks in IT activity during company year-end processing, but a slowdown may be acceptable, as the results are not minute crucial. On the other hand, not being able to meet a rush of orders for Christmas goods may damage the business finances and company's credibility, and the requirements may have to be met. Company year-end processing may also produce one-off peaks of activity.

It may be possible to design around the peaky peaks by some means, for example, leveling out a short peak of activity by some form of queuing mechanism so that a 2 min peak can be smeared over 4 or 5 min to ease the load on resources. Another method is to smooth out the workload where possible; for example, if 10 people work on transactions generated by mail delivered, slow it down a little by using 6 people.

I have seen a workload like this where the peaks suggested a new set of resources were required, but it transpired that the peaks were only at times when mail was delivered and immediately acted upon, creating large peaks around midmorning and late afternoon.

The solution? Slow it down a bit. Problem solved (Figure 8.11).

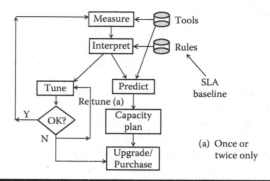

Figure 8.11 Outline of performance and capacity planning.

Modes of Operation

There are three modes of implementing capacity upgrades according to some literature, a fourth if you don't care:

- Muddling through and hoping for the best, tuning as best you can
- Leading method, where a just-in-time (JIT) upgrade of necessary resources is done
- Matching method, where smaller, incremental upgrades are performed on a shorter timescale to meet growing demand
- Lagging method, where the upgrades are performed, possibly incrementally, just as capacity runs out

These methods put one in mind of the types of people; there are those people who make things happen, those who watch things happens, and those who say, "What happened?" Figure 8.12 illustrates the three modes involving action and shows the lead, match, and lag techniques of capacity upgrades. These philosophies assume, of course, that the resources are upgradable without too much CAPEX or disruption.

Thirty years ago, an upgrade from a mainframe that ran out of steam meant moving to the next model up—usually a very expensive option. Today it can be less of an issue, but still needs bearing in mind in the early days, which is the *design* part of capacity management.

There are a number of useful papers to be found at the link below, some very useful, others somewhat wordy without saying too much, but overall worth a few hours of study:

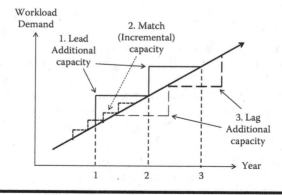

Figure 8.12 Capacity upgrade: three modus operandi.

Metron-Athene Capacity & Performance Papers
http://www.metron-athene.com/products/athene/index.html

Network Capacity Planning

If you know the nature, size, and frequency of the units of work traversing your network, it is relatively easy to do the calculations if you know your link speeds, the capacity of the hardware within the network, and so on. For public web traffic, this can be a headache since the volumes can vary enormously. For example, the UK Lottery once had weeks of money rolling over (accumulating) to the following weeks because nobody had a winning ticket.

They advertised that this particular week the jackpot stood at something like $75 million (about £50 million), and about 30 min before the lottery tickets sales were due to close, millions of people tried to enter online (from home or a shop).

The result was that the system fell down in a big heap since such volumes were never anticipated in such a short period. I do not know how the lottery system works, but my first thoughts were they should have implemented a queuing mechanism to handle the load, rather than trying to do it in real time. This could have been done in the time before the draw, which was some 2 h later, but with all entries received and time-stamped before the cutoff time of 7:30 p.m.—therefore valid, but processed in an orderly fashion.

Suggested Method

The job of the network links is to get the data to and from destination and source

- As fast as possible (good response time and adequate bandwidth)
- With as few errors and retransmissions as possible
- As consistently as possible (little jitter or wide variations)
- Fit for purpose and not costing the earth (throwing bandwidth at poor design)
- So it is capable of smooth upgrade in the future
- With high availability (important, but not to us presently)

The same considerations apply as to the server and storage loads, that is, a breakdown of the workload into activity and times of that activity—batch, remote backup, OLTP, file transfer, and so on. The things that affect link performance and need consideration are

- Traffic volumes and work unit priorities, for example, preference to be given to business OLTP and other vital work.
- Peaks of activity and coincident peaks that may cause problems over certain periods. These will be dictated by your own plan of what runs when and is a baseline profile of the design stage.
- Link bandwidth (for speed) and reliability (to reduce retransmissions).
- Baseline capacity and utilization of LANs and WANs, interfaces, and intermediate nodes in the network links. Tools are needed to measure these.
- Capacity of intermediate nodes, such as network interfaces (NICs), routers, and switches.
- Transmission protocols used (frame relay, MPSL, ATM, etc.; see Appendix V) and any broadcast traffic, which can often overwhelm other traffic. Network "sniffers" can be used to find out what traffic is transmitted by what method.

■ Any network speed enhancements used—*congestion control, WAN acceleration*, and so forth. It may be the case that these are kept in reserve and used only when the network is creaking and its life before upgrade is increased to some degree by these measures.

The basic message here is "know your network and its traffic," which means in monitoring terms *network visibility*. You should also know what applications use the links to assess volumes and also what is affected by slowdown or failure of the link.

There are two very good network planning documents I have come across (and there are many others) that are a good starting point for those who are not network planning *Black Belts*. The first document, from IBM, is a generic one with little or no marketing slant, and the second is from Cisco, who should know about this topic.

Network Performance and Capacity Planning: Techniques for an e-Business World [IBM]
http://www-07.ibm.com/services/pdf/nametka.pdf

This IBM document takes the reader through some charts and illustrates how to use the figures in them and what they mean in practice. One useful chart that might serve as a template for your thinking is Chart 3, which shows traffic volumes, error rates, and discards by different network technologies in the study (Ethernet, WAN, systems development life cycle [SDLC], Token Ring, and Integrated Services Digital Network [ISDN]).

Best Practices in Core Network Capacity Planning
http://www.cisco.com/c/en/us/solutions/collateral/service-provider/quantum/white_paper_c11-728551.pdf

This document uses the service level agreement (SLA) as the springboard for capacity planning activity. It defines three main steps in the capacity planning process:

1. Collecting the core traffic data and adding to it via a demand forecast
2. Determining overprovision factors (headroom for growth)
3. Running simulations to overforecasted demands over the network topology

It also introduces the IP Flow Information Export (IPFIX) developed by the Internet Engineering Task Force (IETF), which is a standard for the export of IP flow information from network routers, probes, and other network devices to enable collection of IP flow statistics. The paper also covers the retrieval and analysis of statistics.

Summary

In summary, it is important to get the user requirements and your design right; know your baseline resource numbers; monitor, collect, and analyze resource data; and use it for general operations, error analysis, and capacity planning. Remember,

■ If you can't see it, you can't measure it.
■ If you can't measure it, you can't manage it.
■ If you can't manage it, you are in trouble.

Here endeth the lesson.

BENCHMARKS AND BENCHMARKING

Apart from earning bragging rights for vendors, benchmarks are used first as comparison vehicles for hardware and software and second as estimators of the size and number of resources needed to support a specific workload mix.

As a comparison vehicle, benchmarks are used in at least three different guises:

1. To compare systems from different vendors, often for aiding purchasing decisions.
2. To compare the performance of systems of different architectures within a single vendor, for example, IBM looking at AS/400 and S/370 performance. This is often important for pricing purposes.
3. As a way of measuring increases or decreases in performance of new models and versions of hardware and software. The latter sometimes decreases in performance as function is added.

As a workload estimator, organizations sometimes assess resources needed for a new workload by looking at the performance characteristics of a system running a benchmark that approximates very roughly to their own workload type. These benchmarks can be

- Standard benchmarks such as Systems Performance Evaluation Corporation (SPEC) or Transaction Performance Council (TPC)
- A benchmark of the actual workload or simulated version of it using program loops and synthetic databases created by software
- A simulation using a "driver" to represent multiple users entering a mix of online transactions, for example

There are more than likely other uses, but I have found these the main (sensible) ones. The benefits of the relative cheapness of power and capacity today make the task of sizing less onerous than in the dark ages of IT, when a 10% error in processor sizing sent you up a model in the range and cost about $1 million more. I know this because I was there.

Chapter 9

Overview of Benchmarking

There used to be a handful of information sources regarding benchmarks and the associated results, some independent, others biased toward a vendor. With the advent of websites on the Internet, there are hundreds, if not thousands, of sources. Unless the searcher is *au fait* with all home pages, it is probably best to do a "search." That aside, the following sources should prove useful in that they contain useful information and act as doorways to other sources on the web:

http://www.spec.org
http://www.tpc.org

Notes on Benchmarking Metrics

The following riders should be understood when reading Section IV of this book:

- In many of the benchmarks discussed in this part of the book, we will use benchmark results to illustrate the problem of assessing the relative capacities of two or more systems with a single number. This is not to denigrate the benchmark but to highlight limitations of a single number reported in the exercise.
- Since the performance of systems delivered by vendors increases dramatically every few months, numbers used in this book should not be used as the basis for assessing computer performance in purchases since they will almost certainly be out of date by the time you read this book. All numbers and graphs in this book are illustrative only and meant to complement and expand upon the text. Some of the graphs have been liberally interpreted to show key points but should still be recognizable as representing the original. For the most up-to-date figures, you should contact the relevant benchmarking body or your vendor, but ensure you fully understand the benchmark in question and its metrics.
- Some of the benchmarks discussed are rarely, if ever, quoted nowadays. However, they have some historical interest and lessons for future IT historians and performance people. I'm not sure they are covered elsewhere in this depth.

■ There are probably two classes of benchmark. One is the class where different systems are compared in detail in various aspects of performance. These have strict rules and conditions—they are to be reproducible, consistent, and so forth. The other class is a benchmark to give a feel for the size of system one might be looking at for handling a particular set of jobs. In the latter case, I wouldn't get too hung up on points of benchmark *law* since in the long run you will probably run some of your own work on that systems anyway.

What Is a Benchmark?

Artis and Domanski (a long time ago) defined a benchmark thus:

> A benchmark is a carefully designed and structured experiment that is designed to evaluate the characteristics of a system or subsystem to perform a specific task or tasks.

Although not explicitly stated in the definition, they go on to say that a benchmark can be used to evaluate alternative systems doing certain work. If you are using a benchmark to *measure* performance, then the system or subsystem workload must be very close to the planned production workload. This sort of exercise is usually installation specific and invariably entails considerable effort and skill.

Today, most general benchmarks are produced and agreed on by consortia of vendors* and, in the main, cannot be used to measure performance. For example, the statement "The X2000 has a SPECfp rating of 92.2" has no meaning in terms of real workloads. It might, however, have more meaning when used to *compare* the performance of two or more systems. It still falls short of measuring the capacity of a system to do normal computing tasks where more than just a certain element of CPU speed is involved.

> What, you may ask, is the difference between *performance* and *capacity*?

Performance, as we saw earlier, has connotations of speed, *but* speed does not necessarily equate to *power* (in physics, power is the capacity to do useful work). Take the example of a sports car and a Cadillac. The two-seater sports car generates greater revs per minute and has a higher top speed than the Cadillac, but it has a smaller brake horsepower (bhp). So what? Well, if the job in hand is to carry three people from New York to Boston, the sports car, although traveling much faster, will take three journeys to deliver the passengers, assuming the driver occupies seat number 1. The Cadillac will need only one and will complete the work before the sports car despite being a slower vehicle.

Consider another analogy:

Q: Is a 10 V transformer less powerful than a 20 V transformer?

A: It depends on the current delivered. The power (or capacity to do useful work, as opposed to generating heat) in such devices is the product of the voltage and current:

$$\text{Power}\,(P) = \text{Current}\,(I) \times \text{Voltage}\,(V)$$

---

* For an excellent and readable exposition of rules and regulations for rigorous benchmarks plus extensions to cater for clouds and real-time work, see the 14-page document "Benchmarking computers and computer networks," http://www.ict-fire.eu/uploads/media/Whitepaperonbenchmarking_V2.pdf.

A 10 V transformer delivering 2 A of current is more "powerful" than a 20 V transformer delivering 0.7 A.

For the purposes of this section of the book, we will treat a benchmark as a set of jobs, tasks, or transactions to compare the "capacity" of systems doing various types of work. This, in essence, agrees with the definition of Dongarra, Martin, and Worlton: "running a set of well-known programs on a machine to compare its performance with that of others."

This capacity, depending on your application viewpoint, can take the form of

- Fixed-point or integer instructions per second (MIPS)
- Floating-point operations per second (FLOPS—usually expressed as KFLOPS or MFLOPS)
- Throughput of transactions or batch jobs per unit time
- Response time for a transaction or time to run a job
- Scripts executed per unit time for workloads such as time sharing, program development, and office workloads
- X-terminal and other client device operations
- Graphics functions
- Some mixtures of these
- Others, including real customer workloads, the only true benchmark

They are, in the main, not created to simulate a particular type of user workload but to assess all-round performance in various areas of computing. They do not necessarily show what throughput might be obtained by any particular customer with his specific workload, unless, of course, the benchmark *is* his workload.

> **Note:** There are rarely any *absolute* benchmarks around—only *comparison* benchmarks. A benchmark used by only one system is like having the first telephone. Also, comparing two systems via a floating-point benchmark when your planned workload is mainly fixed-point work and non-math functionality is quite silly.

Benchmark Metrics

In the discussion above, we referred to MIPS, MFLOPS, and so on, as parameters giving numeric values to performance. In any benchmark, it is important to state exactly what the test is measuring, under what conditions, and how the results are to be presented and what *interpretation* can be placed on them. These performance reporting "rules" are often called *benchmark metrics*, which are necessary to allow a fair comparison of benchmark results for different machines.

It is the anomalies in older benchmarks discussed in this chapter that have given rise to carefully defined benchmarks with stated metrics to measure or compare system performance for various types of workload. It is important to understand not only the figures produced by any given benchmark and where they apply, but also their inherent (not just run-time) limitations.

Why Run Benchmarks?

From what has gone before, the reader may think that running benchmarks is a goal in itself. This is not the case. The reason for running benchmarks is to obtain and use information about IT workloads that cannot be obtained by other means. The use to which the benchmark results are put will vary. Benchmarks are used

- By vendors to show the superiority of their hardware and software products.
- By vendors to compare the performance of their own systems, either models in the same range or systems of different architectures. An example might be comparing a VAX/VMS system with a VAX/UNIX system of the same or different processor model.
- By users (or their agent) to compare the capacities of different systems performing work that is roughly representative of their planned workload.
- By users (or their agent) to measure the capacity of one or more systems performing work that is closely representative of their planned workload (sizing).
- By writers of articles, books, and promotional literature.

If the user can run his own workload with adequate metrics and measurement tools, then artificial benchmarks are not necessary. If this is not possible, then the careful selection of a benchmark will probably be necessary if they are to be used for realistic sizing purposes.

Choosing a Benchmark

W. Nicholls lists four general requirements of a "good" benchmark:

- It must be meaningful and test things that are relevant to the user.
- It should be accurate with a stated accuracy measure published with the actual results. It is important to understand the difference between *accuracy* and *precision*. The TPC-A results are very often quoted to two decimal places, for example, 120.96 tpsA (transactions per second TPC-A). This is a very precise figure, but it is foolish to take much notice of figures after the 1 and 2 of the number. The accuracy for planning purposes is simply not there and should be treated as guidelines.
- The test should be repeatable, with any variance in the results also reported. If the results of repeat tests show significant variation, the benchmark is probably being operated in unstable environments or is an inadequate tool (see next point).
- The benchmark should be able to differentiate between systems that are really different and give similar results for similar systems. For example, if a benchmark gives widely different results for two systems known to be comparable via a variety of other observations, then the benchmark must be questioned.

In choosing a benchmark to do machine comparisons, it is often useful to specify the characteristics of the planned production workload and use the "performance triangle" shown in Figure 9.1 to see where the workload lies. The triangle points are floating point, integer, and (disk) input/output (I/O). By assessing the proportion of these types of load in the planned application, it is possible to select the appropriate benchmark to do the comparison with. Note that not all possible benchmarks are contained in the figure as drawn, but the selection principle is established, I hope.

Summary

If you are using standard benchmarks to *size* a system, make sure you choose one that is of a nature similar to that of your proposed or anticipated workload and assess its accuracy to set realistic expectations.

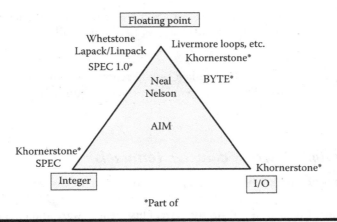

Figure 9.1   Benchmark triangle.

If you are using standard benchmarks to *compare* the capacity of two or more systems, make sure you choose workloads that are the same on each system and representative of the workload for which the customer is planning. However, even some of the apparently all-round benchmarks (*decathlon* benchmarks) can be misleading for this purpose.

Running Benchmarks

Introduction

Figure 9.2 shows a typical benchmark (schematic) environment showing the main elements involved. The names and detailed configurations may change, but the functional parts of it will remain.

The word *scripts* in the figure is nominal and might refer to anything that drives the server during the test—people, scripts, applications, and so forth—in other circumstances.

Running a simple benchmark properly is a big job. Running a complex benchmark properly is a major undertaking in design, execution, and analysis, not to mention control. A benchmark is

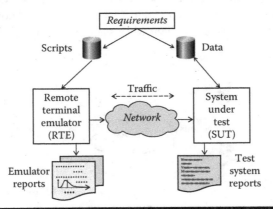

Figure 9.2   Typical benchmark environment.

a project and, as such, requires a sponsor, objectives, a personnel plan, and defined deliverables—many benchmarks do not and are hence failures or, at best, indeterminate.

> The complexity of a benchmark undertaken should reflect the importance of the accuracy and relevance of the results. They are generally expensive to run properly and shouldn't be undertaken for fun.

Simulating Multiple Users: Character Terminals

To run a full-scale benchmark representing a production environment would require

- The application, OLTP and DBMS software, plus the hardware and operating system
- A full population of real users working in typical production mode

The former is feasible, but the latter, in most cases, is difficult or impossible. To cater to such cases, there are tools known as *remote terminal emulators* (RTEs) that simulate the activity of many users entering different transaction mixes.

In Figure 9.3, the RTE represents a screen and keyboard operated by the user, whose activities are represented by "scripts."

The RTE runs on a *driver system* that drives the *system under test* (SUT). Functions of the RTE might typically include

- Keystroke capture facility to capture the pattern of keying from a real user
- Script production from the keystroke capture facility
- Workload definition facility, including user think times
- Run-time facilities that produce user actions from the scripts
- Evaluation tools to produce graphs, tables, and so on

In the case of external drivers, the SUT must do extra work to handle the characters coming from and going to the terminal or driver. To the SUT, there is little difference between real users and a well-designed driver. One reason for having "real" terminal I/O is that inefficient adapters, through which the terminals are supported, can impose a bigger demand on the system CPU than one that can carry out many of the terminal I/O tasks itself. This inefficiency will not be apparent in the multitasking case and will often only come to light when the system is installed and in operational use.

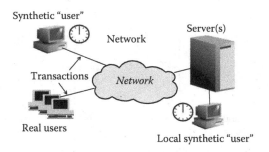

Figure 9.3   Transaction system test environment: real and synthetic system users.

There is a world of difference between character-mode access to server systems and client/server access, and benchmarking the two types of architecture requires different benchmarking environments. Examples of character-based systems are

- IBM 3270 block-mode (buffered) terminals accessing an IBM mainframe across an SNA network
- Digital Vtxxx character-mode terminals accessing a VAX across a WAN or LAN

These are really history now, but the concept of a remote or local *driver* to simulate real-user activity still holds in benchmarking.

Benchmarking "Do's"

A benchmark needs a business as well as an IT sponsor to cover all aspects of the exercise. The former sponsor should be a senior manager who will benefit from a successful outcome. Such a sponsor is vital in the resolution of nontechnical issues in a benchmark, such as funding.

The reasons for the benchmark should be clear to all involved, documented, and spell out what is to be measured and why, for example,

- Application function and performance
- Hardware performance
- Response times
- Throughput
- Upper bounds of various resources
- Interpretation of results

Any exclusions and assumptions should also be documented. The benchmark should have a clear timescale with several checkpoints where progress, or otherwise, can be assessed against the plan. Benchmarking personnel, users, and sponsors should then agree on what has been documented so that no one is in any doubt about the *what, why, when, where,* and *who* of the exercise.

The benchmarking plan should be drawn up, agreed on, and documented and not be made up as the benchmark proceeds. A benchmark is a project and should be treated as such, laying out responsibilities, resources, timescales, and deliverables.

The transaction types (or batch jobs) that form the basis of the benchmark should be selected and analyzed for measurement purposes. If there is more than one type of job or transaction involved, then representative mixes will need to be agreed on with the appropriate users. The chosen work should consist of stable code and not test modules since there is always the temptation to modify failing ones in the course of the benchmark (goalpost moving).

Test scripts need to be drawn up to represent the workload mixes, volumes, and execution pattern of the business processes they represent. Most benchmarks will require special hardware and software configurations, application and database software, and other supporting software to

- Run the application
- Simulate a user population and hence "drive" the benchmark
- Monitor performance statistics and store the results
- Analyze and report statistics, averages, peaks, and so on
- Allow for reruns (regression testing) to check for results consistency

It should be agreed on at the outset whether any competing vendors involved run the benchmark once (first past the post) or whether retrospective system (not the application?) modifications and tuning are allowed, perhaps once or twice (best of three).

As well as measuring response times, throughput, and so on, it is often worthwhile to measure resource consumption and component utilizations, for example, disk I/Os per second and disk utilizations. These can be used in extrapolating workloads composed of the work under test. Components of interest in such cases could include

- Workstations and adapters (e.g., graphics)
- LANs and WANs
- CPU, memory, and disk
- System interfaces (e.g., Advanced Program-to-Program Communication [APPC], file transfer, and Network File System [NFS])
- Database characteristics (e.g., I/Os per call and memory per user)

It may be necessary to report results in a variety of contexts, for example, minimum, maximum, and average

- Number of users
- Amount of data
- Number of transactions per unit time
- Batch streams, if applicable

At the end of the day, there has to be some expectation about the results, perhaps a service level agreement (SLA) or response time requirement; otherwise, the results are simply a set of numbers without a home.

Structured Approach to Performance Testing

Lessons learned in days gone by using character terminals and reputedly ponderous mainframes still hold today if you are doing *real-life benchmarks* and not relying on standard benchmarks.

Preliminary considerations include the following:

- Consider performance requirements at the design stage as well as later.
- Build an isolated test environment so that tests can be run without mutual interference between testers and normal users.
- Use stable applications and databases; otherwise, problems will compound, especially in repeat test cases.
- Involve the *sponsor*, business users, IT support, and operations at all stages.
- Take care with client/server testing—it is not the same as dumb screen or CPU testing. There are more combinations of people, hardware, and software to consider.
- Make estimates of testing time and numbers of people involved.
- Use *production volumes* for data and transactions if possible.
- Consider network aspects carefully; they play a great part in performance.
- Ensure the right skills are available at the right time.

One feasible and sensible approach to testing of this sort is outlined in the following list:

- Confirm business and IT groups for tests.
- Understand the system to be tested.
- Agree on the detailed approach.
- Specify or acquire the hardware and software required.
- Acquire or learn the performance tools required.
- Agree on parts of the system to be tested.
- Agree on volumes and SLAs to which the benchmark applies.
- Use stable application, middleware, and database software, preferably that to be used in the live environment.
- Capture performance scripts.
- Edit scripts and test.
- Run performance tests.
- Analyze results and publish to relevant personnel.
- Agree on and prioritize areas to be "enhanced" to meet SLAs.
- Document everything.

There are many papers on performance testing, found by a search of "performance testing, best practices," many of them with a marketing angle. The references below are quite generic and are complemented by material and other references to more specific testing in Chapter 8 of this book.

Introduction (to Performance Testing) [Microsoft]
https://msdn.microsoft.com/en-us/library/bb924376.aspx

Meaningful Website Testing: Understanding Performance [O'Reilly/Limelight]
http://www.oreilly.com/pub/e/3106

Types of Benchmark

Multitasking

In this book, *multitasking* is used to define a set of tasks running in a system without external terminal I/O. This mode of operation is usually initiated by a program within the system itself.

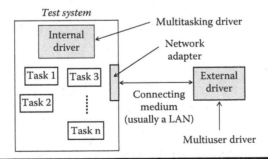

Figure 9.4 Multitasking and multiuser benchmark types.

A multitasking operation might be a single simulated user initiating many tasks or multiple simulated users doing multiple tasks. If the number of tasks in both cases is the same, then the system resources consumed should be the same. The basic difference is that the schedule might do a little more work in the multiuser case (Figure 9.4).

Multiuser

The term *multiuser* is used in the case of tasks being initiated externally, via either real users at terminals or another system (e.g., a workstation) acting as a "driver," as we saw in "Why Run Benchmarks?"

The multitasking benchmark will produce higher transactions per second than the multiuser one because of extra work to be done by the latter. This is borne out by TPC-B benchmarks compared with TPC-A benchmarks for the same system, about 1.25:1.

There are today numerous benchmarks covering the scientific, Internet, and commercial areas (including product-related benchmarks), and these are dealt with in Chapter 10.

Summary

Multitasking implies no external driver or terminals. Multiuser implies an external driver or terminals with any overheads associated with that mode of operation. Of course, the multiuser case can be, and usually is, multitasking as well.

We have not covered web-based benchmarking and testing here since this is covered in Chapter 8 under "Web-Based Applications." Unless you know precisely what you are doing, steer clear of benchmarking cloud applications and leave them to cloud gurus.

In essence, benchmarks with drivers on the same system as the test applications will give better results that those involving LAN or WAN connections.

Chapter 10

Commercial and Scientific Benchmarks

Integer and Fixed-Point Benchmarks

There is little emphasis on pure integer and floating-point-oriented benchmarks except perhaps within a manufacturer who wishes to compare systems of different types of generations of the same architecture. This is a perfectly valid use of these *kernels* or tight routines to test the speed of computation, usually without I/O. There is a move to test speed and throughput using benchmarks with the actual software that the organization intends to use in practice.

Commercial Benchmarks

Sometimes a project needs to assess the performance characteristics of a system using the actual software that will be used in production, especially if large volumes and complex usage of the application are envisaged. One such benchmark is that involving the SAP enterprise resource planning (ERP) application and database.

SAP Standard Application Benchmarks

SAP Standard Application Benchmarks help customers and partners find the appropriate hardware configuration for their commercial applications. Working in concert, SAP and its hardware partners developed the SAP Standard Application Benchmarks to test the hardware and database performance of SAP applications and components.

> The benchmarking procedure is standardized and well defined. It is monitored by the SAP benchmark council made up of representatives of SAP and technology partners involved in benchmarking. Originally introduced to strengthen quality assurance, the SAP Standard Application Benchmarks can also be used to test and verify scalability, concurrency, power efficiency, and multi-user behavior of system software components, RDBMS, and business applications.

While the majority of benchmarks are run online, the SAP APO, SAP BW, HR (Payroll), PS, Retail, and ISU/CCS Benchmarks are run in the background, and the TRBK Benchmark has both an online section and a batch section. (http://global.sap.com/campaigns/benchmark/appbm_overview.epx)

SAP Standard Application Benchmarks test the hardware and database performance of SAP applications and components. Access the two-tier and three-tier results for the Sales and Distribution (SD) benchmark. There is also a benchmark for testing power usage, rather like the Systems Performance Evaluation Corporation (SPEC) equivalent.

Measurements in SAPS: The SAP Application Performance Standard (SAPS) is a hardware-independent unit of measurement that describes the performance of a system configuration in the SAP environment. It is derived from the Sales and Distribution (SD) benchmark, where 100 SAPS is defined as 2000 fully business-processed order line items per hour.

In technical terms, this throughput is achieved by processing 6000 dialog steps (screen changes), 2000 postings per hour in the SD benchmark, or 2400 SAP transactions.

In the SD benchmark, fully business processed means the full business process of an order line item: creating the order, creating a delivery note for the order, displaying the order, changing the delivery, posting a goods issue, listing orders, and creating an invoice.

SAP Standard Application Benchmarks: Glossary
http://global.sap.com/campaigns/benchmark/bob_glossary.epx#SAPS

If you have a sizing in SAPS, it is then recommended that you use the SAP Quick Sizer to find a configuration from the two-tier or three-tier SAP benchmark results for the benchmarked configurations of these denominations.

Three-Tier Results
http://global.sap.com/solutions/benchmark/sd3tier.epx

Two-Tier Results
http://global.sap.com/solutions/benchmark/sd2tier.epx

SAP Quick Sizer
http://global.sap.com/solutions/benchmark/pdf/Quick_Sizer_Factsheet.pdf

Oracle Applications Benchmark

The Oracle Applications Standard Benchmark is a comparable standard workload that demonstrates the performance and scalability of Oracle Applications and provides metrics for the comparison of Oracle Applications performance on different system configurations.

The benchmark has the two standard forms of work, namely, online and batch. The online component exercises the common User Interface flows, which are most frequently used by Oracle Applications customers, and the batch flow consists of the Order Management and Payroll Processes. The benchmark metrics are

■ User count and average response time for the online part
■ Throughput for the batch part

Details of the benchmark *audit procedure* and composition of the *Oracle Applications* Standard Benchmark Council can be found in the references below.

There are other Oracle-related benchmarks, and associated documentation which is also listed below:

Oracle E-Business Suite Standard Benchmarks
http://www.oracle.com/us/solutions/benchmark/apps-benchmark/results-166922.html

Oracle PeopleSoft Benchmark Performance Reports
http://www.oracle.com/us/solutions/benchmark/apps-benchmark/peoplesoft-167486.html

Oracle Siebel Benchmark White Papers
http://www.oracle.com/us/solutions/benchmark/white-papers/siebel-167484.html

Oracle E-Business Suite White Papers
http://www.oracle.com/us/solutions/benchmark/white-papers/white-papers-e-business-177385.html

Oracle R12 E-Business Standard Benchmark Overview
http://www.oracle.com/us/solutions/benchmark/apps-benchmark/ebs-standard-benchmark-overview-192676.html

Oracle Applications Benchmark
http://www.oracle.com/us/solutions/benchmark/apps-benchmark/index-166919.html

Relational Database Benchmarks

Sysbench

Sysbench is a cross–operating system (OS) multithreaded benchmark designed to test OS features that are important in running a database system under intensive load.

> The idea of this benchmark suite is to quickly get an impression about system performance without setting up complex database benchmarks or even without installing a database at all. (From the reference below)

The benchmark is designed to test the ability of the OS in handling

- File I/O performance
- Database server performance
- Scheduler performance
- Memory allocation and transfer speed
- POSIX threads' implementation performance

It runs by running threads in parallel, executing database calls (which can be batch operations as well as online transaction processing [OLTP] mode).

The benchmark is often used with the MySQL database running in a Linux environment where the database is set up by specifying the number of tables in the database, as well the number of rows per table.* A simple search of "sysbench" will produce a lot of useful articles on the benchmark.

---

* I first came across this type of database creation and test environment by using IBM's DBPROTOTYPE program in the 1970s. It was designed to be used in the IMS/DL/I (Data Language 1) environment rather than DB2, which had not been invented yet.

SysBench Manual
http://imysql.com/wp-content/uploads/2014/10/sysbench-manual.pdf

AS3AP

The AS3AP (often written AS³AP) benchmark is an American National Standards Institute (ANSI) Structured Query Language (SQL) relational database benchmark. This benchmark provides the following features:

- Tests database processing power
- Has built-in scalability and portability that tests a broad range of database systems
- Minimizes effort in implementing and running benchmark tests
- Provides a uniform metric and straightforward interpretation of benchmark results

An early relational database management system (RDBMS) benchmark was the Wisconsin benchmark (WISC), which served its purpose for a while but was considered limited in scope and lightweight. Further developments of the Wisconsin benchmark led to the first release of the AS3AP benchmark. The original AS3AP consisted of two sections:

- Single-user tests, including
  - Utilities for loading and structuring the database
  - Queries designed to test access methods and basic query optimization—selections, simple joins, projections, aggregates, one-tuple updates, and bulk updates
- Multiuser tests modeling different types of database workloads:
  - Online transaction processing (OLTP) workloads
  - Information retrieval (IR) workloads
  - Mixed workloads, including a balance of short transactions, report queries, and long transactions

Systems tested with the AS3AP benchmark must support common data types and provide a complete relational interface with basic integrity, consistency, and recovery mechanisms (*ACID properties*). The AS3AP tests systems ranging from a single-user microcomputer database management system (DBMS) to a high-performance parallel or distributed database system.

Measuring Relational Database Server Transaction Speeds Using the AS3AP Benchmark [thesis]
https://cdr.lib.unc.edu/indexablecontent/uuid:35e8c391-0f56-49ea-a7d6-82c969b2b2b0

AS3AP: An ANSI SQL Standard Scalable and Portable Benchmark for Relational Database Systems
http://research.microsoft.com/en-us/um/people/gray/benchmarkhandbook/chapter5.pdf
There is an interesting, if somewhat dated, article on RDBMS benchmarks at

A Study on Industry and Synthetic Standard Benchmarks in Relational and Object Databases
http://nccur.lib.nccu.edu.tw/bitstream/140.119/40031/1

Scientific Benchmarks

Standard scientific benchmarks are normally about pure speed in solving mathematical representations of physical and chemical properties of various things. Most of these came from laboratories of other science agencies in the course of their work, more often than not solving large numbers of equations, where the words *matrix inversion*, *Monte Carlo methods*, and *nonlinear equations* abound.

Other benchmarks, in the broadest sense of the word, often involve commercial application software such as molecular modeling, electrical design, and nuclear reactions, but these are not standard benchmarks in any sense.

Linpack

The Linpack benchmark was introduced by Jack Dongarra, Jim Bunch, Cleve Moler, and Gilbert Stewart, and was intended for use on supercomputers in the 1970s and early 1980s. A detailed description, as well as a list of performance results on a wide variety of machines, is available in postscript form from netlib. There it is possible to download the latest version of the Linpack report.

The Linpack benchmark is used to solve a dense system of linear equations in matrix format. The TOP500 *league table* uses the version of the benchmark that allows the user to scale the size of the problem and optimize the software in order to achieve the best performance for a given machine. This performance does not reflect the *overall performance* of a given system, as no single number ever can.

It does, however, reflect the *performance of a dedicated system for solving a dense system of linear equations*. Since the problem is very regular, the performance achieved is quite high, and the performance numbers give a good correction of peak performance. One Linpack metric is Toward Peak Performance (TPP) for large matrices.

In an attempt to obtain uniformity across all computers in performance reporting, the algorithm used in solving the system of equations in the benchmark procedure must conform to certain math manipulations. In particular, the operation (benchmark) count for the algorithm must be $2/3n^3 + O(n^2)$ double-precision floating-point operations. This excludes the use of fast matrix multiply algorithms or algorithms that compute a solution in a precision lower than full precision (64-bit floating-point arithmetic) and refine the solution using an iterative approach.

A *parallel* implementation of the Linpack benchmark and instructions on how to run it can be found at

High Performance Linpack
http://www.netlib.org/benchmark/hpl/

There is also a Java implementation of Linpack:

Linpack Benchmark: Java Version
http://www.netlib.org/benchmark/linpackjava/

> More information on the structure of Linpack can be found in Appendix II under "Floating-Point Benchmarks."

Lapack

Since 1993, Jack Dongarra, distinguished professor of computer science at the University of Tennessee, has led the ranking of the world's top 500 supercomputers. The much celebrated biannual TOP500 list (computer hit parade) is compiled using Dongarra's benchmark system, called

Linpack. It is the most widely recognized and discussed metric for ranking high-performance computing systems. But Dongarra has said that Linpack hasn't kept pace with supercomputing needs and must be updated. "Linpack rankings of computer systems are no longer so strongly correlated to real application performance," Dongarra has said. Lapack is a follow-on from Linpack, but it does not have the longevity or pedigree of Linpack.

> Lapack is written in FORTRAN 90 and provides routines for solving systems of simultaneous linear equations, least-squares solutions of linear systems of equations, eigenvalue problems, and singular value problems. The associated matrix factorizations are also provided, as are related computations. In all areas, similar functionality is provided for real and complex matrices, in both single and double precision.

The original goal of the Lapack project was to make the widely used EISPACK and Linpack libraries* run efficiently on shared-memory vector and parallel processors. On these machines, Linpack and EISPACK are inefficient because their memory-access patterns don't understand the multilayered memory hierarchies of these machines, thereby spending too much time moving data unnecessarily instead of doing useful floating-point operations. Lapack addresses this problem by reorganizing the algorithms to use block matrix operations, such as matrix multiplication, in the innermost loops.

These block operations can be optimized for each architecture to account for the memory hierarchy, and so provide a transportable way to achieve high efficiency on diverse modern machines. We use the term *transportable* instead of *portable* because, for fastest possible performance, Lapack requires that highly optimized block matrix operations be already implemented on each machine.

Lapack Benchmark
http://www.netlib.org/lapack/

NAMD V2.7b1

NAMD is a parallel molecular dynamics code designed for high-performance simulation of large biomolecular systems. NAMD was designed to run efficiently on such parallel machines for simulating large molecules. Based on Charm++ parallel objects, NAMD is a simulation engine implementing the molecular dynamics algorithm as applied to biomolecular systems with higher optimization and efficiency.

NAMD was developed by the Theoretical and Computational Biophysics Group in the Beckman Institute for Advanced Science and Technology at the University of Illinois at Urbana-Champaign.

Details
http://www.ks.uiuc.edu/Research/namd/
There are other molecular modeling programs, among them General Atomic and Molecular Electronic Structure System (GAMESS).† In this arena, words like *docking substrates* and *Hartree–Fock* fill the documentation (and me with fear).

---

* These libraries are preprepared standard subroutines to be used by such benchmarks.
† There is also (I believe) a UK molecular modeling program called GAMESS.

ANSYS V11

ANSYS is a finite-element analysis simulation software package that provides solutions for conceptual design through final-stage testing and performance validation from design concept to final-stage testing and performance validation. The ANSYS product suite is used in structural, thermal, mechanical, acoustics, computational fluid dynamics (CFD), electrical, and electromagnetic analyses.

Ansys Benchmark
http://www.ansys.com/Support/Platform+Support

HPCG

Jack Dongarra (Linpack) and Michael A. Heroux suggested a new HPC benchmark to overcome the drawbacks of High Performance Linpack (HPL). They suggest a new high-performance conjugate gradient (HPCG) benchmark. HPCG is composed of computations and data access patterns more commonly found in HPC applications. The benchmark and the limitations of Linpack are discussed in the reference below.

Toward a New Metric for Ranking High Performance Computing Systems
http://www.netlib.org/utk/people/JackDongarra/PAPERS/HPCG-Benchmark-utk.pdf
    Dr. Dongarra seems to enjoy dispatching his own children.

HPCC Benchmark

The High Performance Computing Challenge (HPCC) benchmark is a relatively new benchmark designed to supplement the High Performance Linpack (HPL) benchmark used to measure the TOP500 scientific computing machines in terms of megaflops. Linpack has for many years been the *benchmark* role model for high-performance computing performance evaluations. The HPCC is aimed at testing multiple resource attributes that can contribute substantially to the performance of real-world HPC systems and applications.

The initiative is cosponsored by the DARPA High Productivity Computing Systems program, the U.S. Department of Energy, and the National Science Foundation and features on its committee the ubiquitous Jack Dongarra of the University of Tennessee and Oak Ridge National Laboratory (ORBL).

The HPCC benchmark consists of seven tests designed to exercise programs in a variety of areas and also seeks to provide information to allow optimization of performance in the computer resources used in HPC. These are mainly registers, cache, main memory, and disk drives (or other equivalent media). These are

1. *HPL*, the High Performance Linpack, the objective of which is to solve a system of linear equations. The restrictions on running it are no complexity-reducing matrix multiply and it must use 64-bit precision throughout.
2. *DGEMM*, a double-precision general matrix–matrix multiply designed to test compute matrix functionality with the same restrictions as for HPL above.
3. *STREAM* is a test that measures sustainable memory bandwidth in gigabytes per second and the corresponding computation rate for four simple vector kernels. It has to use only 64-bit precision.

4. *b_eff* measures the effective bandwidth and latency of the interconnect by exchanging messages in ping-pong, natural, and random ring patterns; eight for latency and 2 million for bandwidth for simultaneous communications. The messaging routines must conform to the Message Passing Interface (MPI) standard.* Remember that MPI is used for communication between processors in a multiple-processor environment, such as parallel processors.

5. *PTRANS*, parallel transpose, is to update a matrix with the sum of its transpose and another matrix using 64-bit precision arithmetic.

6. *FFT*, fast Fourier transform computation.

7. *Random access*, calculates a series of integer updates to random locations in memory by performing computations on a table, which should occupy half the memory available. Restrictions apply (see second reference below).

Message Passing Interface (MPI) Tutorial
http://polaris.cs.uiuc.edu/~padua/cs320/mpi/tutorial.pdf

HPC Challenge Presentation
http://polaris.cs.uiuc.edu/~padua/cs320/mpi/tutorial.pdf

HPP Challenge Benchmark Website
http://icl.cs.utk.edu/hpcc/

---

* Message Passing Interface Standard 3.0, http://www.mpi-forum.org/docs/mpi-3.0/mpi30-report.pdf. It is 852 pages long and not recommended as breakfast or bedtime reading.

Chapter 11

SPEC Benchmarks

SPEC Glossary [definitive definitions]
https://www.spec.org/spec/glossary

Origins of SPEC

The System Performance Evaluation Cooperative, now named the Standard Performance Evaluation Corporation (SPEC), was founded in 1988 by a small number of workstation vendors who realized that the marketplace was in desperate need of realistic, standardized performance tests. The key realization was that an ounce of honest data was worth more than a pound of marketing hype.

SPEC has grown to become one of the more successful performance standardization bodies with more than 60 member companies. SPEC publishes several hundred different performance results each quarter spanning a variety of system performance disciplines. (http://www.spec.org/spec/)

SPEC Subgroups

SPEC evolved into an umbrella organization encompassing four diverse groups: the Graphics and Workstation Performance Group (GWPG), the High Performance Group (HPG), the Open Systems Group (OSG), and the newest, the Research Group (RG). More details are on their website.

1. The Open Systems Group (OSG). The OSG is the original SPEC committee. This group focuses on benchmarks for desktop systems, high-end workstations and servers running open systems environments.
2. The High Performance Group (HPG). The HPG is a forum for establishing, maintaining and endorsing a suite of benchmarks that represent high-performance computing applications for standardized, cross-platform performance evaluation.

3. The Graphics and Workstation Performance Group (GWPG). SPEC/GWPG is the umbrella organization for project groups that develop consistent and repeatable graphics and workstation performance benchmarks and reporting procedures.
4. The SPEC Research Group (RG). The RG is a new group within SPEC created to promote innovative research on benchmarking methodologies and tools facilitating the development of benchmark suites and performance analysis frameworks for established and newly emerging technologies.

SPEC benchmarks are widely used to evaluate the performance of computer systems; the test results are published on the SPEC website. Results are sometimes informally and generically referred to as *SPECmarks* or just *SPEC*.

Current SPEC Benchmarks

There are too many SPEC benchmarks to cover in this book, and they can be examined on the SPEC website. I do, however, cover a few that fill the gap left by older benchmarks, which majored on millions of instructions per second (MIPS), Dhrystones and Whetstones, and a few of the older, superseded SPEC benchmarks.
For full details of all the SPEC benchmarks, see
http://www.spec.org/benchmarks.html

SPEC's Benchmarks

CPU

- SPEC CPU2006
- SPEC CPUv6
- SPEC CPU2000 [retired]
- SPEC CPU95 [retired]
- SPEC CPU92 [retired]

Graphics and Workstation Performance

- SPECviewperf 12
- SPECviewperf 11
- SPECwpc
- SPECap for 3ds Max 2015
- SPECap for May 2012
- SPECap for PTC Creo 2.0
- SPECap for Siemens NX 8.5
- SPECapc for SolidWorks 2013
- Previous versions of SPECapc and SPECviewperf benchmarks

Handheld

SPEC has formed a committee chartered for the development of, and support for, a compute intensive benchmark suite for handheld devices.

High-Performance Computing, OpenMP, MPI, OpenACC, OpenCL

- SPEC ACCEL
- SPEC MPI2007
- SPEC OMP2012
- SPEC OMP2001 [retired]
- SPEC HPC2002 [retired]
- SPEC HPC96 [retired]

Java Client/Server

- SPECjAppServer2004 [retired]
- SPECjAppServer2002 [retired]
- SPECjAppServer2001 [retired]
- SPECjbb2013
- SPECjbb2005 [retired]
- SPECjbb2000 [retired]
- SPECjEnterprise2010
- SPECjms2007
- SPECjvm2008
- SPEC JVM98 [retired]

Mail Servers

- SPECmail2009 [retired]
- SPECmail2008 [retired]
- SPECmail2001 [retired]

Solution File Server

- SPEC SFS2014 (chargeable)
- SPECsfs2008
- SPEC SFS97_R1 (3.0) [retired]
- SPEC SFS97 (2.0) [retired]
- SPEC SFS93 (LADDIS) [retired]

Power

- SPECpower_ssj2008
- Server Efficiency Rating Tool (SERT)
    Other SPEC benchmarks incorporating power measurement
    - SPEC ACCEL
    - SPEC OMP2012
    - SPECvirt_sc2013
    - SPECvirt_sc2010 [retired]
    - SPECweb2009 [retired]

SIP

SPECsip_infrastructure2011

■ **SOA**

SPEC has formed a new subcommittee to develop standard methods of measuring performance for typical middleware, database, and hardware deployments of applications based on the service-oriented architecture (SOA).

Virtualization

■ SPECvirt_sc2013
■ SPECvirt_sc2010 [retired]

Web Servers

■ SPECweb2009 [retired]
■ SPECweb2005 [retired]
■ SPECweb96 [retired]
■ SPECweb99 [retired]
■ SPECweb99_SSL [retired]

SPEC Tools

■ Server Efficiency Rating Tool (SERT): Intended to measure server energy efficiency, initially as part of the second generation of the U.S. Environmental Protection Agency (EPA) ENERGY STAR for Computer Servers program.
■ Chauffeur Worklet Development Kit (WDK): Chauffeur was designed to simplify the development of workloads for measuring both performance and energy efficiency.
■ PTDaemon: The SPEC PTDaemon software is used to control power analyzers in benchmarks that contain a power measurement component.

SPEC CPU2006*

SPEC CPU2006 contains two suites that focus on two different types of compute intensive performance:

■ The *CINT2006* suite measures compute intensive integer performance.
■ The *CFP2006* suite measures compute intensive floating-point performance.

The SPECint 2006 (CINT) benchmark contains 12 different benchmark tests, and the SPECfp 2006 (CFP) benchmark contains 19 different benchmark tests.

---

* At the time of writing, the current version of the CPU 2006 benchmark suite is V1.2, released in September 2011. Most benchmark names in the documentation are marked as Copyright.

Table 11.1 Sample Results Table for SPEC CPU2006 (CINT2006)

Benchmark	Hardware Vendor	System	No. Cores	No. Chips	No. Cores per Chip	Result	Date
CINT2006	Acme	HK1	12	2	6	35.8	December 2012
CINT2006	Acme	HK2	12	2	6	41.5	December 2012
CINT2006	ICM	PS2	12	2	6	37.5	July 2011
CINT2006	ICM	PS4	8	2	4	28.8	September 2008
CINT2006	Echo	E12	8	2	4	31.4	December 2008
CINT2006	Echo	E14	16	2	8	59	February 2013

System names in this table are artificial.

SPEC 2006 has two base metrics within the benchmark:

- The "speed" of the CPU in terms of time to complete a task, for example, the SPECint 2006 benchmark
- The throughput capacity in terms of tasks completed per unit time, for example, the SPECint_rate 2006 benchmark

To run the benchmarks and publish them publically, there are some run and reporting rules that need to be followed. These rules may be changed from time to time and can be found at http://www.spec.org/cpu2006/Docs/runrules.html.
Results for, for example, OSG benchmarks can be found at

SPECint2006 Results: Results
https://www.spec.org/cgi-bin/osgresults
A set of results for some imaginary vendors and machines are shown in Table 11.1, although the figures to the right of the "System" column are genuine.

SPEC CPU2006 is designed to emphasize the performance of the *CPU*, the *memory* subsystem, and the associated *compilers*.

Specjbb

Specjbb is a SPEC benchmark aimed at measuring server-side Java performance, and there have been several versions issued: SPECjbb2000, SPECjbb2005 (retired in October 2013), and SPECjbb2013.
The *SPECjbb2013* benchmark has been developed from the ground up to measure performance based on the latest Java application features. It is relevant to all audiences who are interested in Java server performance, including Java virtual machine (JVM) vendors, hardware developers, Java application developers, researchers, and members of the academic community.

New Features in SPECjbb2013

- A usage model based on a worldwide supermarket company with an IT infrastructure that handles a mix of point-of-sale requests, online purchases, and data mining operations.
- Both a pure throughput metric and a metric that measures critical throughput under service level agreements (SLAs) specifying response times ranging from 10 to 500 ms.
- Support for multiple run configurations, enabling users to analyze and overcome bottlenecks at multiple layers of the system stack, including hardware, OS, JVM, and application layers.
- Exercising new Java 7 features and other important performance elements, including the latest data formats (XML), communication using compression, and messaging with security.
- Support for virtualization and cloud environments
  SPECjbb documentation can be found at
  http://www.spec.org/jbb2013/.

The SPEC benchmarks are essentially aimed at raw performance in various environments and now include power and other entities previously absent.

The Transaction Performance Council (TPC) benchmarks, covered in Chapter 12, aim at the commercial online environment.

Chapter 12

The TPC and Other Benchmarks

TPC Organization

The Transaction Processing Performance Council, formed in 1988, is an independent organization devoted to the specification and standardization of publicly available measures of computer performance. It initially comprised workstation vendors but soon expanded to the larger vendors. Its membership today is comprised of computer manufacturers and software providers and includes Oracle, IBM, and HP.

The reason for the formation was the unsatisfactory nature of existing commercial benchmarks, notably TP1 and debit/credit. The formation of the Transaction Processing Council (TPC) was driven by Omri Serlin, a stern critic of "sloppy" benchmarks.

In November 1989, the TPC membership approved the specification of TPC Benchmark A, summarized below. In August 1990, the council approved the specification of TPC Benchmark B: a benchmark that could be loosely described as a batch version of TPC Benchmark A. Benchmark B is designed to stress only high-contention data accesses and transaction integrity. It bears little resemblance to a full system environment and has many similarities to the older TP1 benchmark.

Benchmark results were eventually accompanied by a *full disclosure report* (FDR) by means of which the validity of the results could be established. FDRs were, and still are, quite large documents and not intended for holiday reading.

TPC Benchmark C (TPC-C) was approved by the TPC in July 1992. It was designed to be more representative of medium transaction processing applications in a complex environment. TPC-A was, in contrast, a simple benchmark and not really representative of real online transaction processing (OLTP) workloads.

For example, a certain IBM RISC System/6000 weighed in with a tpsA of 101 per second, whereas its TPC-C rating was 6.6 per second (396 per minute), a ratio of 15:1. Similarly, an HP 700 series machine had an A/C ratio of 17:1. These ratios clearly reflect the differences in complexity and resource consumption between TPC-A and TPC-C, and the latter was more satisfactory to many vendors and customers in representing "real" workloads.

The TPC went on to define other benchmarks, which we will address in this chapter and Appendix I. The rest, as they say, is history.

TPC-C Benchmark

The TPC-C suite was designed to measure the performance of systems running OLTP workloads and to be reasonably "heavy" in terms of resources demanded from the system under test (SUT). It might be asked why this benchmark was not used to test IBM mainframes. One reason is that such mainframes carry a massive instruction overhead when dealing with interrupts, for example, from transactions running over TCP/IP instead of the usual IBM SNA network. It differs from earlier benchmarks in that it specifies certain constraints and time limits so the measurements approximate to real life and not just a test of how many transactions get be crammed into a fixed time.

This would render any comparisons with UNIX and similar machines based around the TCP/IP protocol invalid and unfair.

TPC-C Workload

The TPC Benchmark C (TPC-C) reflects a manufacturing environment and consists of five transaction types. Like TPC-A, it has *descriptions* and *constraints* plus *response time rules*. TPC-C represents the administration of an order for items that are stored in warehouses to fulfill orders from customers. In brief, this complex benchmark comprises five transaction types:

1. The *new order* transaction is the entry of a new order through a single database transaction.
2. The *payment* transaction updates the customer's balance and reflects the payment on the district and warehouse statistics.
3. The *order status* transaction queries the status of the customer's last order.
4. The *delivery* transaction involves the processing of a batch of 10 orders, to be executed in "deferred mode," that is, not interactively.
5. The *stock level* transaction determines the number of recently ordered items that have a stock level below a specified threshold.

A summary of the constraint specifications for TPC-C is given in Table 12.1.

Note that for single-server systems with random arrivals and random service times, the 90th percentile response (T_{90}) is related to the mean response time (T_{Mean}) in the case of exponential distributions by Equation 12.1:

$$T_{90} = T_{Mean} \times \ln(10) = 2.3T_{Mean} \tag{12.1}$$

Table 12.1 TPC-C Transaction Characteristics and Constraints

Transaction Type	Minimum % of Transaction Mix	Minimum Keying Time (s)	90th Percentile Response Time (s)	Minimum Mean of Think Time Distribution (s)
New order	n/a	18	5	12
Payment	43	3	5	12
Order status	4	2	5	10
Delivery[a]	4	2	5	5
Stock level	4	2	20	5

[a] Delivery has two components—interactive and batch. The batch portion has a 90% limit of 80 s.

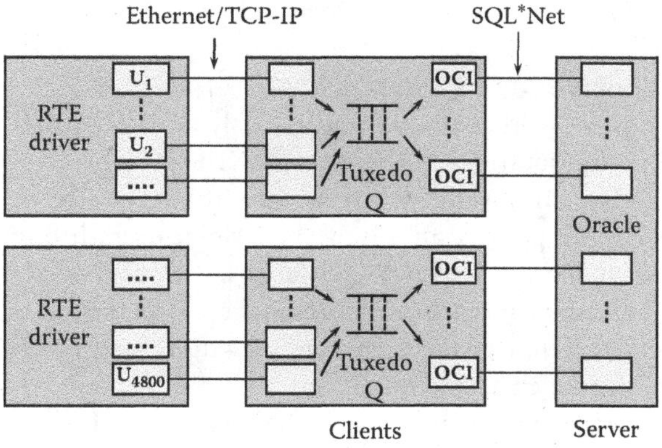

Figure 12.1 Typical TPC-C benchmark configuration with 4800 users (Oracle).

where ln is the logarithm to the base e, that is, natural logarithms. See Appendix I for the general formula for percentiles featuring an exponential distribution.

Incidentally, most benchmarks in this area do not specify a database type, and in theory, one could use something simple and quick to get maximum speed, but it is expected that a relational database management system (RDBMS) be used in most cases.

Typical TPC-C Setup

The setup shown in Figure 12.1 illustrates a TPC-C benchmark configuration based on Oracle. Most benchmarks do not mandate an RDBMS, but using one is the accepted practice, as we have already seen. The diagram could apply to DB2, Sybase, Informix, and so on, by replacing SQL*Net with the relevant vendor's equivalent software. Similarly, an online transaction processing (OLTP) monitor is used.

In this case it is Tuxedo, the veteran UNIX OLTP, although IBM CICS has been employed in some instances. OCI is the Oracle Call Interface to facilitate access to Oracle instances.

The references below relate to Oracle 12c as well as earlier versions.

Oracle Call Interface
http://www.oracle.com/technetwork/database/features/oci/index-090945.html

Setting Up an Oracle Tuxedo Application
https://docs.oracle.com/cd/E35855_01/tuxedo/docs12c/pdf/ads.pdf

TPC-D Benchmark

TPC-D was developed to represent a broad range of decision support (DS) applications that required complex, long-running queries against large complex data structures. This was deemed necessary when data warehouses and data marts were becoming popular as business tools for data analysis and TPC-C was not really representative of this kind of work. The characteristics of such work are heavy data access and no real expected response time, especially if the information sought is for planning purposes.

The basic structure of the benchmark was 17 complex queries and 2 update functions:*

■ Update functions insert or delete.
■ Modeled after an *ad hoc* workload on a continuously available database.
■ Designed with business questions built first, followed by SQL.
■ No think time: A constant flow of SQL requests within each stream.
■ Primary metrics: Two for performance (power for single user, throughput for multiuser) and one for price–performance.
■ Volume: May be published at one of eight distinct scale factors.
■ Secondary metrics: (1) Reported load time and (2) a disk storage ratio (total disk space in the system divided by the scale factor).
■ ACID tests: Concurrent update and query capability required.
■ Version 1 was completed in April 1995 with a view to a version 2.

SIGMOD '97 Industrial Session 5
http://www.tpc.org/information/sessions/sigmod/sld025.htm

TPC-D was declared obsolete as of June 4, 1999.

TPC-H Benchmark

The TPC Benchmark H (TPC-H) was a decision support benchmark. It consists of a suite of business-oriented *ad hoc* queries and concurrent data modifications. The queries and the data populating the database have been chosen to have broad industry-wide relevance. This benchmark illustrates decision support systems that examine large volumes of data, execute queries with a high degree of complexity, and give answers to critical business questions. Response time, unlike transaction-based benchmarks, is not a major metric, although throughput *power* is.

The performance metric reported by TPC-H is called the TPC-H Composite Query-per-Hour Performance Metric (QphH@Size), and it reflects multiple aspects of the capability of the system to process queries. These aspects include the selected database size against which the queries are executed, the query processing power when queries are submitted by a single stream, and the query throughput when queries are submitted by multiple concurrent users. The TPC-H price–performance metric is expressed as $/QphH@Size.

TPC-H results are still being reported and can be found (November 2014) at

TPC-H: Ten Most Recently Published Results
http://www.tpc.org/tpch/results/tpch_last_ten_results.asp

TPC-R Benchmark

TPC-R was a business reporting, decision support benchmark that, along with TPC-H, replaced TPC-D. This was a decision support benchmark similar to TPC-H, but which allows additional

---

* http://research.microsoft.com/en-us/um/people/gray/benchmarkhandbook/chapter3.pdf (referenced elsewhere in this book).

optimizations based on advance knowledge of the queries. It consists of a suite of business-oriented queries and concurrent data modifications.

The performance metric reported by TPC-R is called the TPC-R Composite Query-per-Hour Performance Metric (QphR@Size), and it reflects multiple aspects of the capability of the system to process queries. These aspects include the selected database size against which the queries are executed, the query processing power when queries are submitted by a single stream, and the query throughput when queries are submitted by multiple concurrent users.

The TPC-R price–performance metric is expressed as $/QphR@Size. It was rendered obsolete as of January 1, 2005.

Virtualization Environment Benchmarks

The virtualization world of benchmarks is different from the traditional physical world of IT, not least in new terminology. The first section of this discussion outlines some of this jargon and associated products that have no equivalents in the physical world. Mention is made of the VMmark benchmark, which is covered a little later.

Virtualization Performance Terminology

Ballooning: Memory ballooning is a feature of most virtualization platforms to make more efficient use of physical memory for virtual servers. In essence, it is *stretching* or *ballooning* of the regular physical memory to a larger amount. This allows a server with 32 GB of memory to host, say, 64 GB worth of virtual machines, the actual size depending on the workload composition.

If a guest virtual machine (VM) is running short of storage, it can request extra storage from the hypervisor on a temporary basis via a *balloon driver*. The balloon driver can inflate up to a maximum of 65%. For instance, for a VM with 1000 MB memory, the balloon can inflate to 650 MB.

Understanding VMware Ballooning
http://www.vfrank.org/2013/09/18/understanding-vmware-ballooning/

DVD Store: A simulation of a DVD store where customers browse and buy DVDs after logging in and searching. It is used as stand-alone or in conjunction with the VMware VMmark benchmark.

The DVD Store Version 2 (DS2) is a complete, online e-commerce test application, with a back-end database component, a web application layer, and driver programs. The goal in designing the database component as well as the mid-tier application was to utilize many advanced database features (transactions, stored procedures, triggers, and referential integrity) while keeping the database easy to install and understand. The DS2 workload may be used to test databases or as a stress tool for any purpose.

DVD Store
http://en.community.dell.com/techcenter/extras/w/wiki/dvd-store

Dell DVD Store Video
http://en.community.dell.com/techcenter/extras/w/wiki/dvd-store

Relocation: Another term for *migration*. Migration refers to the process of moving a virtualized guest image from one virtualization server to another. This other server could be on the same server or a different server, including servers in other locations. This is an integral part of the VMmark benchmark.

Dynamic Resource Management in Virtualized Environments through Virtual Server Relocation
http://www.thinkmind.org/download.php?articleid= soft_v3_n34_2010_2

Tile: The unit of work known as a tile is best defined as a collection of VMs running a diverse set of workloads, such as those specified in VMmark, encapsulated in a diverse set of VMs. In the context of VMmark, a data center's consolidation capacity, which measures scalability and individual application performance, is thus measured as the number of tiles that the data center platform can handle while at the same time supporting the required administrative operations.

VMware VMmark Virtualization Benchmark
http://www.storagereview.com/vmware_vmmark_virtualization_benchmark

vMotion: Storage vMotion is a component of VMware vSphere that allows the live migration (relocation; see above) of a running virtual machine's file system from one storage system to another, with no downtime for the VM or service disruption for end users. This migration occurs while maintaining data integrity.

TPC-VMS Benchmark

Benchmarks in the virtualization field are a fairly recent addition to the furious physical benchmarking taking place despite the rapid uptake of cloud and hence virtualized computing. Virtualization and benchmarks remind me of what I think was a Mark Twain quotation about the weather: "Everyone is talking about it, but nobody is doing anything about it." This could in the past be leveled at virtualization benchmarks until recently.

> The TPC Virtual Measurement Single System Specification (TPC-VMS) leverages the TPC-C, TPC-E, TPC-H and TPC-DS Benchmarks by adding the methodology and requirements for running and reporting performance metrics for virtualized databases. The intent of TPC-VMS is to represent a Virtualization Environment where three database workloads are consolidated onto one server. Test sponsors choose one of the four benchmark workloads (TPC-C, TPC-E, TPC-H, or TPC-DS) and runs one instance of that benchmark workload in each of the 3 virtual machines (VMs) on the system under test. The 3 virtualized databases must have the same attributes, e.g. the same number of TPC-C warehouses, the same number of TPC-E Load Units, or the same TPC-DS or TPC-H scale factors. The TPC-VMS Primary Performance Metric is the minimum value of the three TPC Benchmark Primary metrics for the TPC Benchmarks run in the Virtualization Environment. (TPC website)

The TPC website makes reference to the paper below, which I have attempted to summarize here.

Virtualization Performance Insights from TPC-VMS
http://www.tpc.org/tpcvms/tpc-vms-2013-1.0.pdf

The TPC Virtual Measurement Single System Specification (TPC-VMS) mandates three identical TPC benchmarks to be run in separate virtual machines (VMs):

- Three TPC-C VMs
- Three TPC-E VMs
- Three TPC-H VMs or three TPC-DS VMs

The TPC-VMS *performance metric* is the minimum value of the three performance metrics for the three TPC benchmarks run on the TPC-VMS system under test (VSUT). The TPC-VMS performance metric is reported by prefixing a "VMS" to the TPC benchmark performance metric, for example, VMStpmC, VMStpsE, VMSQphDS@ScaleFactor, or VMSQphH@ScaleFactor (see tpc.org for details of these metrics).

The VSUT includes a consolidated database server that supports the virtualization environment where the three VMs are run. To prevent a test sponsor from minimizing the number of VMs, the consolidated database server must support a large number of VMs. In this way, all I/O must be virtualized by either the hypervisor or the I/O controllers managing the I/O devices, without which a test sponsor could simply partition the I/O by assigning an I/O device exclusively to each VM.

The authors point out that there are existing virtualization benchmarks such as SPECvirt_sc2010 and VMmark, but they focus on smaller workloads and claim TPC-VMS was designed to address this issue. SPECvirt_sc2013 and VMmark V2 probably go some way to neutralizing this claim.

The authors summarize TPC-VMS thus:

The TPC-VMS benchmark leverages the TPC-C, TPC-E, TPC-H, and TPC-DS benchmarks to provide a measure of database performance in a virtualized environment.

SPECvirt_sc2013 Benchmark

The Systems Performance Evaluation Corporation's (SPEC) first virtualization benchmark, SPECvirt_sc2010, was well received and considered appropriate until, like many benchmarks, it was overtaken by the events and technology it was designed to model and predict. Organizations are virtualizing much heavier workloads than they did in the *suck it and see* era of virtualization.

Its successor, SPECvirt_sc2013, is the new benchmark and is meant to measure the end-to-end performance of all system components, including the hardware, virtualization platform, virtualized guest operating systems, and application software. Its design caters for both hardware and operating system virtualization. It was developed by the SPEC virtualization subcommittee, whose members and contributors include HP, IBM, Intel, Oracle, Red Hat, Microsoft, and VMware.

Kunal Singh Sodhi, an IBM content manager, attributes the changes leading to the new benchmarks as

- Each VM requires more resources than the 2010 version.
- Many VMs have much more variability in their resource usages (*burstiness*).
- The previously *idle* VM (in sc2010) is now a *batch* VM.

The official description of this benchmark (see link below it) is

The benchmark utilizes several SPEC workloads representing applications that are common targets of virtualization and server consolidation. We modified each of these standard workloads to match a typical server consolidation scenario of CPU resource requirements, memory, disk I/O, and network utilization for each workload. These workloads are modified versions of SPECweb2005, SPECjAppServer 2004, SPECmail 2008, and SPEC INT 2006 benchmarks. The client-side SPEC virt_sc 2013 harness controls the workloads. Scaling is achieved by running additional sets of virtual machines, called "tiles", until overall throughput reaches a peak. All VMs must continue to meet required quality of service (QoS) criteria.

Note: Many of the terms above are registered trademarks of the SPEC organization.

SPECvirt_sc2013
http://www.spec.org/virt_sc2013/

SPECvirt_2013sc Run and Reporting Rules
https://www.spec.org/virt_sc2013/docs/SPECvirt_Run Rules.html
The results of any vendor benchmark using SPECvirt_sc2013 follow the format below:
Performance section

■ Performance summary
■ Performance details
■ Validation errors

Configuration section

■ Physical configuration
■ Virtual configuration

Notes section

■ Physical system notes
■ Virtualization software notes
■ Hosted VM notes

SPECvirt_sc2013 Metrics

The metrics reported for SPECvirt_sc2013 are

■ SPECvirt_sc2013 number of VMs: The benchmark presents an overall workload that achieves the maximum performance of the platform when running a set of four application workloads against one or more sets of virtual machines called *tiles*. The power metric format is <no.> @ <no.> of VMs.

Scaling the workload on the system under test (SUT) consists of running an increasing number of tiles. Peak performance is the point at which the addition of extra tiles causes performance to drop.

■ SPECvirt_sc2013_PPW (server and storage performance per watt)
■ SPECvirt_sc2013_ServerPPW (server performance per watt)

Sample Results: To see typical performance summary tables for IBM and HP executions of SPECvirt_sc2013, visit

SPECvirt_sc2013 Result: IBM Flex System x240, Red Hat: Enterprise Linux 6.4 (KVM)
http://www.spec.org/virt_sc2013/results/res2013q3/virt_sc2013-20130730-00003-perf.html

New HP ProLiant DL360 Gen9 Server Achieves World Records on SPECvirt_sc2013 Benchmark
http://h20195.www2.hp.com/V2/GetDocument.aspx? docname=4AA5-6825ENW&cc=us&lc=en

An interesting paper looks at virtual machine metrics over and above those of SPECvirt and includes a discussion of multicore system benchmark metrics. It introduces the metrics *total normalized throughput* (TNT) and *average normalized reduced throughput* (ANRT), which aim to quantify the loss in per-VM performance (overhead) due to consolidation of workloads. TNT is a quantification of the total aggregate system performance that is derived from the normalized throughput NTP.

Performance Metrics for Consolidated Servers
http://users.elis.ugent.be/~leeckhou/papers/hpcvirt10.pdf

Costs: SPECvirt_sc2013 is available for download on the SPEC website for $3000 for commercial licensees and $1500 for academic and eligible nonprofit organizations.

vConsolidate Benchmark

The SPECvirt benchmarks effectively rendered another benchmark, *vConsolidate*, redundant. This benchmark was developed by Intel and involved benchmarking multiple VMs running together with different workloads.

VMmark Benchmark

The 1970s and 1980s saw a move toward what was considered *the future* by moving work from mainframes to smaller machines (*distributed computing*), not always in a data center, but often in other locations. Latterly, there was an opposite migration to bigger systems (*consolidation*) in the name of economies of scale and ease of maintenance. This consolidation could take two basic forms:

■ Consolidation of similar architecture systems (*homogeneous* consolidation), for example, a plethora of HP systems moving to an HP Superdome in that era.
■ Consolidation of *heterogeneous* systems—different architectures and operating systems. This would require some form of migration or conversion exercise to consolidate into a single-architecture environment.

The consolidation trend took a dramatic turn when virtualization matured and allowed the combining of disparate systems onto a larger system, but retaining their original form and operating system environment. Thus was the cloud born.

The traditional environments, whether distributed or consolidated, had their benchmarks that formed the ammunition for the *benchmark wars* of the 1970s and 1980s. As the cloud environment matured with a growing number of adherents and suppliers, it became evident that the standard physical benchmarks did not cater adequately to the new environment.

It was also clear that the current monitoring tools did not fit into this new world comfortably either. Thus were born new benchmarks and new monitoring and analysis tools.

Original VMmark

This consolidation benchmark was constructed on a set of relevant data center workloads, not synthetic code, as in some older benchmarks. A survey of data center applications led to the inclusion of the following workloads as the basis of VMmark:

- Mail server (Microsoft Exchange 2003)
- Java server (modified SPECjbb2005)
- Standby server (extremely lightly loaded or idle)
- Web server (SPECweb2005 under Linux)
- Database server (Swingbench [OLTP], Oracle 10g, or Red Hat Linux)
- File server (dbench under Red Hat Linux)

For reasons of reality, existing benchmarks were used wherever possible. This reduces implementation effort and provides a well-understood foundation upon which to build. However, the run rules of the various benchmarks occasionally conflict with the design goals of VMmark, requiring some modifications to the benchmarks to make them suitable for multi-VM benchmarking.

There are sections in the reference link below discussing each of these workloads and any necessary modifications to make them *virtualization-friendly*.

Table 12.2 shows the VMmark workload metrics.

VMmark: A Scalable Benchmark for Virtualized Systems
http://www.vmware.com/pdf/vmmark_intro.pdf

VMmark V2.x*

The proven benchmark "VMmark V1" was mothballed in October 2010 and was succeeded by "VMmark V2," which requires a cluster of at least two servers and covers data center functions, like cloning and deployment of virtual machines (VMs), load balancing, and the moving of VMs with vMotion and Storage vMotion. In late 2012, VMmark V2.5 was extended to include optional *power scores* to determine the energy efficiency of servers or servers and associated storage (power per kilowatt).

Three proven benchmarks were integrated in VMmark V2 that cover the following application scenarios (Table 12.3):

- Mail server
- Web 2.0
- E-commerce

---

* VMmark 2.5 was current at the end of 2012, and 2.5.2 at the end of 2014.

Table 12.2   VMmark Benchmark: Workload Metrics

Workload	Metric
1. Mail server	Actions per minute
2. Java server	New orders per second
3. Standby server	None
4. Web server	Accesses per second
5. Database server	Commits per second
6. File server	Megabytes per second

Table 12.3   VMmark 2.5 Applications Trio and VM Configuration

Application Scenario	Load Tool	No. of VMs
Mail server	LoadGen	1
Web 2.0	Olio client	2
E-commerce	DVD Store 2 client	4
Standby server	idleVMtest	1

Each of the three application scenarios is assigned to a total of seven dedicated virtual machines. Then add to these an eighth VM called the standby server. These eight VMs are said to form a "tile." There can then be several tiles running at the same time for the purposes of the benchmark.

The benchmark is run with multiple tiles and the results tabulated and registered; the section below illustrates the process and objectives of the benchmark using predefined *tiles* or configurations to make valid comparisons between systems. VMmark measures the performance and scalability of real applications running in a virtualized environment.

A typical VMmark benchmark run is structured as follows:

■ Virtual Microsoft Exchange Server 2007 and 1000 heavy profile users
■ Two Olio VMs (web and database) simulating a Web 2.0 application
■ Four DVD Store Version 2 (DS2) VMs: Three DS2 web servers and one DS2 database, simulating an e-commerce application
■ One virtual Windows Server 2003 that serves as a standby system

As well as running these applications, VMmark performs the following tasks during the test:

■ VM cloning and deployment
■ Dynamic VM relocation using vMotion
■ Dynamic storage relocation using Storage vMotion
■ Automated VM load balancing

Dell Paper
http://www.dell.com/downloads/global/solutions/poweredge_vmmark_final.pdf

VMmark Results

These are a little complex to reproduce here, but they can be found at the link below under the heading "High-Precision Scoring Methodology":

http://www.vmware.com/products/vmmark/features.html

One thing to note about the differences between results from V1 and V2 is that the latter has a power index rating in it, in addition to performance ratios of the various throughputs of the VMs in a tile and quality of service (QoS) rating.

The additional references below give more details about the benchmark and the running and reporting of results.

VMmark 2.5: Virtualization Platform Benchmark
http://www.vmmark.com/

Run and Reporting Rules for VMmark® Version 2.x
http://www.vmware.com/files/pdf/vmmark/VMmark_Rules_2.5_20121119.pdf

Benchmark Overview VMmark V2 [Fujitsu white paper]
http://globalsp.ts.fujitsu.com/dmsp/Publications/public/wp-benchmark-overview-vmmark-v2-ww-en.pdf

TPC Benchmarks That Didn't Make It*

A few TPC benchmarks did not make it to the final lap for various reasons, mainly because full agreement on them could not be achieved and would add considerable extra expense to vendors' already expensive benchmarking efforts. Running rigorous benchmarks with a full disclosure report to produce is a money-eating process, especially across multiple machine sizes and architectures.

> Benchmarking expense for vendors is prominent, so the fewer (but representative) benchmarks there are, the better they like it. They wouldn't like you to invent new ones, thank you.

TPC-S

The TPC-Server benchmark was planned to be a server version of TPC-C, which was normally a client/server benchmark. The benchmark did not gain popular support and was thought to introduce confusion between TPC-C and TPC-S, to say nothing of the extra expense of running them both. However, TPC-S rose phoenix-like from the ashes to become the TPC-W benchmark.

---

* See "History and Overview of the TPC" by Kim Shanley (February 1998).

TPC-E

The TPC-E (Enterprise) benchmark began development shortly after TPC-C was approved and was aimed at stressing large enterprise systems more rigorously than TPC-C. It was to demand faster response times and high I/O bandwidth with concurrent batch processing. This work pattern is very similar to what IBM mainframes had been doing for years and played to its strengths. Again, the benchmark failed to get the necessary majority and was abandoned as a full benchmark, but many of its elements were preserved for use in later versions of TPC-C and TPC-D.

Another reason for its demise was that vendors saw it would cost even more than TPC-C to run and would only apply to a few vendors at the upper end of the computing world systems, the so-called big burners.

TPC-CS

Work was carried out on a client/server benchmark, TPC-CS, which was to utilize much of the TPC-C workload in its specification. This new benchmark was worked on but never voted on since, as Kim Shanley stated, "by mid-1996 ... the World Wide Web was changing the computing paradigm" and a web benchmark group was formed by people who had worked on TPC-CS.

TPC: State of the Art*

There are a few benchmarks that we have not covered above, but they are documented on the TPC website listed below. In summary, they are

    TPC benchmarks
        TPC-C (older OLTP)
        TPC-DS (new decision support)
        TPC-E (new OLTP)
        TPC-H (son of TPC-D)
        TPC-VMS (virtualized environment)
        TPCx-HS (big data environment)
        TPC-Pricing (common pricing)
        TPC-Energy (energy metrics)
    Obsolete TP benchmarks
        TPC-A (son of debit/credit)
        TPC-B (son of TPC-A)
        TPC-D (old decision support)
        TPC-R (son of TPC-D)
        TPC-W (web e-commerce)
        TPC-App (web application server)

TPC Benchmarks
http://www.tpc.org/information/benchmarks.asp

---

* December 2014.

Classic Benchmark Reference

There is classic text from 1993, edited by the late Jim Gray, which attempted to put benchmarks on a classified footing at a time when they looked like they were running amok. Although some of the benchmarks covered in the book either are superseded by later versions or disappeared altogether, there are sections on benchmarks and benchmarking in general that are still useful. The chapters can be accessed online, and the following references will take the reader down *benchmark memory lane.*

TPC-C
http://research.microsoft.com/en-us/um/people/gray/benchmarkhandbook/chapter12.pdf

TPC-D
http://research.microsoft.com/en-us/um/people/gray/benchmarkhandbook/chapter3.pdf

Early SPEC [to 1992]
http://research.microsoft.com/en-us/um/people/gray/benchmarkhandbook/chapter9.pdf

Neal Nelson [draft]
http://research.microsoft.com/en-us/um/people/gray/benchmarkhandbook/chapter10.pdf

Jim Gray* *(Ed.): The Benchmark Handbook for Database and Transaction Systems (2nd Edition),* *Morgan Kaufmann 1993*
http://research.microsoft.com/en-us/um/people/gray/benchmarkhandbook/toc.htm

Storage Benchmarks

Some years ago, storage benchmarks didn't have high visibility and were often the hobby of *techies*, as storage was just a bunch of disks (JBODs). Today, storage has a much higher profile and is much more complicated to cater to the demands put on it by new types of data—big data, video data, audio data, sensor data, and so on. Each has different requirements in the areas of capacity, access times, availability, and recovery, which have fostered the development of hard disks, solid-state storage, network-attached storage (NAS), storage area network (SAN), and redundant array of independent disks (RAID).

As alluded to before, and it bears repeating as part of the immersion process, there are several ways of estimating storage performance, as well as other IT resources:

- Calculation
- Simulation tools
- Rules of thumbs (ROTs)
- Standard benchmarks
- Special or tailor-made benchmarks

The latter may already be developed by others. It is not very difficult to create a synthetic benchmark program to mimic a planned program or a real, existing one if such a ruse is needed. Creating loops to simulate processor time used by it and generating an I/O profile based on real

---

* Jim was posted "missing at sea" some years ago and declared "dead" a few years later, although no body was ever found. A sad loss to IT.

data can be applied to a pilot configuration of any new storage subsystem for which the test is needed, and perhaps a new processor configuration.

The following description and Table 4.1 will illustrate this principle. Let's imagine we have an existing application that requires $p\%$ of a processor of type A using storage type X and generates n I/Os per second. The method a colleague and I used to test I/O capability of the new IBM Risc System/6000 was, in essence, as follows:

1. Generate a large (empty) database of the required size consisting of N records. We used C language for this, or at least my colleague did.
2. Start the measurement commands.
3. Generate simple code in a loop to generate a random record number between 1 and N.
4. Start timing and retrieve that (empty) record.
5. Tighten the loop to increase the frequency of I/O and retrieve more records.
6. Close and analyze.

At the end, you should have enough data to plot an I/O rate against the disk utilization to give you an I/O profile of a particular disk or disk configuration.

Standard Storage Benchmarks

SPC

The Storage Performance Council (SPC) offers storage benchmarks intended to show storage performance in different business environments. A current list of tests is

- SPC Benchmark 1 (SPC-1), SPC Benchmark 1/Energy Extension (SPC-1/E)
  Reference below the SPC-1 description
- SPC Benchmark 2 (SPC-2), SPC Benchmark 2/Energy Extension (SPC-2/E)
  Reference below the SPC-2 description
- SPC Benchmark 1C (SPC-1C), SPC Benchmark 1C/Energy Extension (SPC-1C/E)
  http://www.storageperformance.org/specs/#spc1c
- SPC Benchmark 2C (SPC-2C), SPC Benchmark 2C/Energy Extension (SPC-2C/E)
  http://www.storageperformance.org/specs/#spc2c
- SPC Benchmark 3BR (SPC-3BR)
  http://www.storageperformance.org/specs/#spc3br

We will cover SPC-1 and SPC-2 here as illustrative and provide references to the others.

SPC-1

SPC-1 is a business-oriented benchmark.

Business and Application Environment

SPC-1 is comprised of a set of I/O operations designed to demonstrate the performance of a storage subsystem while performing the typical functions of a business critical application. SPC-1 represents a segment of applications characterized by predominately random I/O operations and requiring both queries as well as update operations (for example: OLTP systems, database systems, or mail server applications). (http://www.storageperformance.org/specs/SPC-1_SPC-1E_v1.14.pdf)

The SPC-1 data includes a performance profile that relates response time to I/Os per second (IOPS) along with a price calculation per IOPS based on the supplied cost data.

The reported results look as follows (for a hypothetical storage device, the HK2000).

Summary of Results SPC-1 Reported Data	
Tested Storage Product (TSP)	Name: Hokey Cokey 2000
Metric	*Reported Result*
SPC-1 IOPS	151,250.50
SPC-1 price–performance	$0.52/SPC-1 IOPS
Total ASU capacity	1,420.578 GB
Data protection level	Protected 2 (mirroring)
Total price	$xxxxxx
Currency used	U.S. dollars

The format roughly follows that of the other performance benchmarks with *speed* and *bang per buck* as major elements in the report. The other is the form of *protection* that means, how safe is your configuration from failure? It should be obvious that a simple disk format will perform better than a RAID 6 configuration doing the same job, as the latter has parity calculation and other work to do.

SPC-2

SPC-2 is for business-critical applications.

Business and Application Environment

SPC-2 is comprised of a set of I/O operations designed to demonstrate the performance of a storage subsystem when running business critical applications that require the large-scale, sequential movement of data. SPC-2 represents a segment of applications characterized predominately by large I/O's, organized into one or more concurrent sequential patterns.

Frequently encountered examples of such applications include:

1. *Large file processing*: applications, in a wide range of fields, which require simple sequential processing of one or more large files. Specific examples include scientific computing and large-scale financial processing.
2. *Large database queries*: scans or joins of large relational tables, such as those performed for data mining or business intelligence.
3. *Video on demand*: individualized video entertainment provided to a community of subscribers, by drawing from a digital film library. (http://www.storageperformance.org/specs/SPC-2_SPC-2E_v1.5.pdf)

SPC-2 Reported Data

The SPC-2 tables are not easy to follow, so I will present here the items reported. A set of results tables can be found in the reference above. SPC-2 reported data consists of three groups of information:

The following SPC-2 primary metrics, which characterize the overall benchmark result

- SPC-2 MBPS
- SPC-2 price–performance
- Application storage unit (ASU) capacity

Supplemental data to the SPC-2 primary metrics

- Total price
- Data protection level
- Reported data for each SPC test: large file processing (LFP), large database query (LDQ), and video on demand delivery (VOD) test.

Again, the results feature *performance*, *protection*, and *bang per buck*.

SPECsfs Benchmarks

SPEC has produced a number of benchmarks, some of which relate to storage performance.

SPEC SFS2014 is the (chargeable) successor to *SPEC sfs2008*, which was used to measure the performance of a Network File System (NFS) or Common Internet File System (CIFS) server. It creates a mixed workload that simulates a typical server environment. The user could use the tool to measure the performance of an NFS or CIFS server and compare the results with other servers that have results published on the SPEC website. More details on SPEC sfs2008 can be found at the link below.

SPECsfs2008 User's Guide
http://www.spec.org/sfs2008/docs/usersguide.pdf

SPEC SFS2014

The SPEC SFS 2014 benchmark is used to measure the maximum sustainable throughput that a storage solution can deliver. The benchmark is protocol independent. It will run over any version of NFS or SMB/CIFS, clustered file systems, object oriented file systems, local file systems, or any other POSIX compatible file system. Because this tool runs at the application system call level, it is file system type agnostic. This provides strong portability across operating systems, and storage solutions. The SPEC SFS 2014 benchmark already runs on Linux, Windows Vista, Windows 7, Windows 8, Windows Server 2003, Windows Server 2008, Windows 2012, Mac OS X, BSD, Solaris, and AIX, and can be used to test any of the files-system types that these systems offer.

The SPEC SFS 2014 benchmark is throughput oriented. The workloads are a mixture of file meta-data and data oriented operations. The SPEC SFS 2014 benchmark is fully multi-client aware, and is a distributed application that coordinates and conducts the testing across all of the client nodes that are used to test a storage solution. (From the reference below)

Spec SFS2014 User Guide
https://www.spec.org/sfs2014/docs/usersguide.pdf

SPEC SFS2014 Results

VDA: Video data acquisition
VDI: Virtual desktop infrastructure

These workloads are discussed in the SNIA presentation:

SPEC SFS2014: An-Under-the-Hood Review
http://www.snia.org/sites/default/files/SpencerShepler_SPEC_Under-the-Hood_Review_Final.pdf

SPEC SFS2014 Database Results
https://www.spec.org/sfs2014/results/res2014q4/sfs2014-20141029-00001.html

SPEC SFS2014 Software Build Results
https://www.spec.org/sfs2014/results/sfs2014swbuild.html

SPEC SFS2014 vda Result
https://www.spec.org/sfs2014/results/res2014q4/sfs2014-20141029-00003.html

SPEC SFS2014 vdi Result
https://www.spec.org/sfs2014/results/res2014q4/sfs2014-20141029-00004.html

Other Storage References

Another storage performance reference, cited below, is not a survey of storage benchmarks but of various considerations in measuring performance in this environment, for example, complexity, storage peculiarities, reproducibility, defining your applications' characteristics, and choosing your test load. It is in the format of a presentation.

Table 12.4   SPEC SFS2014 Results Metrics

Workload	Business Metric	Workload Metric
Database	Databases	SPEC SFS2014_database
SWBUILD	Builds	SPEC SFS2014_swbuild
VDA	Streams	SPEC SFS2014_vda
VDI	Desktops	SPEC SFS2014_vdi

Storage Benchmarking Cookbook
https://www.terena.org/activities/tf-storage/ws3/IV_StorageBenchmarkingCookbook-StijnEeckhaut-final.pdf

The following DZone paper contains a plethora of links to various aspects of storage I/O and other performance aspects.

Server and Storage I/O Benchmarking and Performance Resources
http://java.dzone.com/articles/server-and-storage-io?mz= 110215-high-perf

Chapter 13

Network Performance Benchmarks

Network performance is just as important as processor and peripheral's performance but does not seem to have the depth of function accorded the latter resources.

Network Benchmarks

As with other resources, there are some benchmarks developed by various gurus that have disclaimers of every sort. Most of them, I'm sure, have their merits, and one way of finding out is to use more than one to seek a consensus. This section could almost be called network performance testing, as the activity is more of an experiment than a formal benchmark.

Netperf

A Hewlett-Packard engineer developed Netperf to help the UNIX network benchmarking community many years ago, and this benchmarking tool remains popular in UNIX and Linux environments today. It measures the effective bandwidth between two hosts.

http://www.netperf.org/netperf/

Netperf is designed around a basic client/server model. The bulk of this write-up is from the Netperf manual, link of which is found at the end of this section.

There are two executables: netperf and netserver. Generally, it will only be necessary to execute the netperf program, with the netserver program being invoked by the remote system or having been previously started as its own stand-alone daemon.

When netperf execute begins, it will establish a *control connection* to the remote system, and this connection will be used to pass test configuration information and results to and from the remote system. Regardless of the type of test to be run, the control connection will be a Transmission Control Protocol (TCP) connection using BSD sockets. The control connection can use either IPv4 or IPv6.

Once the control connection is up and the configuration information has been passed, a separate "data" connection will be opened for the measurement itself using the application programming interfaces (APIs) and protocols appropriate for the specified test. When the test is completed, the data connection will be discontinued and results from the netserver will be passed back via the control connection and combined with netperf's result for display to the user.

Netperf places no traffic on the control connection while a test is in progress. Certain TCP options, if set as your system's default, may put packets out on the control connection while a test is in progress, but generally speaking, this will have no effect on the results.

CPU Utilization

CPU utilization is an important, but all too infrequently reported, component of networking performance. Unfortunately, it can be one of the most difficult metrics to measure accurately in this environment. Netperf will do its best to report accurate CPU utilization figures, but some combinations of processor, OS, and configuration may make this difficult.

CPU utilization in netperf is reported as a value between 0% and 100% regardless of the number of CPUs involved. In addition to CPU utilization, netperf will report a metric called a *service demand*. The service demand is the normalization of CPU utilization and work performed. For a data transfer test, it is the microseconds of CPU time consumed to transfer 1 KB of data. For a request or response test, it is the microseconds of CPU time consumed processing a single transaction. For both CPU utilization and service demand, lower is better.

Netperf is coded to be able to use one of several, generally platform-specific CPU utilization measurement mechanisms. Single-letter codes will be included in the CPU portion of the test banner to indicate which mechanism was used on each of the local (netperf) and remote (netserver) systems.

Using Netperf to Measure Bulk Data Transfer

The most commonly measured aspect of networked system performance is that of bulk or unidirectional data transfer performance. Everyone wants to know how many bits or bytes per second they can push across the network. The classic netperf convention for a bulk data transfer test name is to tack a "_STREAM" suffix to the test name.

Issues in Bulk Transfer

There are any number of things that can affect the performance of a bulk transfer test. Certainly, absent compression, bulk transfer tests can be limited by the speed of the slowest link in the path from the source to the destination. If testing over a gigabit link, you will not see more than a gigabit. Such situations can be described as being *network limited* or *network interface card (NIC) limited*.

CPU utilization can also affect the results of a bulk transfer test. If the networking stack requires a certain number of instructions or CPU cycles per kilobyte of data transferred, and the CPU is limited in the number of instructions or cycles it can provide, then the transfer can be described as being *CPU bound*.

Distance and the speed of light can affect performance for a bulk transfer; often this can be mitigated by using larger transfer windows. One common limit to the performance of a transport using window-based flow control is

$$\text{Throughput} \leq \text{Window Size/Round-Trip Time}$$

As the sender can only have a window's worth of data outstanding on the network at any one time, the soonest the sender can receive a window update from the receiver is one round-trip time (RTT), or what we might normally call response time. TCP and Stream Control Transmission Protocol (SCTP) are examples of such protocols.

Packet losses, as one might guess, are bad for performance, and the packet losses result in retransmission time-outs for the protocols involved. By the time a retransmission time-out has happened, the flow or connection has sat idle for a considerable length of time. (Information from the Netperf manual.)

CPU Utilization in a Virtual Guest

The CPU utilization mechanisms used by netperf are "in line" in that they are run by the same netperf or netserver process as is running the test itself. This works just fine for "bare-iron" tests, but runs into a problem when using virtual machines.

The relationship between virtual guest and hypervisor can be thought of as being similar to that between a process and kernel in a bare-iron system. As such, many CPU utilization mechanisms used in the virtual guest are similar to "process-local" mechanisms in a bare-iron situation. However, just as with bare-iron and process-local mechanisms, much networking processing happens outside the context of the virtual guest. It takes place in the hypervisor, and is not visible to mechanisms running in the guests. For this reason, one should not really trust CPU utilization figures reported by netperf or netserver when running in a virtual guest.*

If one is looking to measure the added overhead of a virtualization mechanism, rather than rely on CPU utilization, one can rely instead on netperf _RR tests; path lengths and overheads can be a significant fraction of the latency, so increases in overhead will appear as decreases in transaction rate.

CPU Rate Calibration

Some of the CPU utilization measurement mechanisms of netperf work by comparing the rate at which some counter increments when the system is idle (wait state) with the rate at which that same counter increments when the system is running a netperf test. The ratio of those rates is used to arrive at a CPU utilization percentage: running/(running + idle).

This means that netperf must know the rate at which the counter increments when the system is presumed to be "idle." If it does not know the rate, netperf will measure it before starting a data transfer test. This calibration step takes 40 s for each of the local or remote systems, and if repeated for each netperf test, it would make taking repeated measurements rather slow.

Netperf Benchmark Manual
http://www.netperf.org/svn/netperf2/tags/netperf-2.7.0/doc/netperf.html

Five Free Network Performance Tools

The tools in the link below have useful screen shots to help in understanding each tool.

5 Free Tools to Test and Benchmark Your Network Speed
https://www.raymond.cc/blog/network-benchmark-test-your-network-speed/

---

* We know that virtualization-aware tools are needed for these environments.

1. *LAN speed test.* The lite version is basically the free version of the shareware LAN speed test and is a simple tool for measuring the speed on a LAN by copying a file to another computer that is located at the same local network. All you need to do is browse the location of another computer on the network where you have write access and click the Start Test button. You will then be prompted to set the file size of the dummy file to be transferred.

2. *LANBench* is also a free and portable utility that tests the network using TCP only. You need to run LANBench on both computers, one as server and the other as client, which will be the tester. The server part will only need to click on the Listen button, while at the client side it will require a bit of configuration, such as specifying the server's IP address from File > Configure. You can also define the test duration, packet size, connection, and transfer mode. During benchmark you can see the live transfer rate and also the average performance.

3. *NetIO-GUI* is a command-line application for benchmarking the network throughput, and there is a portable graphical user interface (GUI) version that works as a front end. It is necessary to run NetIO-GUI on both computers that you want to test, one as client mode and the other as server mode. The server will only require to click on the Start Server button, while for the client, you will need to enter the server's IP address and optionally selecting the protocol (TCP or Universal Datagram Protocol [UDP]) that needs testing. NetIO will then test the connectivity based on a few different specified packet sizes.

4. *NetStress* is a free and simple network benchmarking tool created as an internal tool by Nuts About Nets, but it is now being released generally. Like NetIO, NetStress also needs to run on both computers that you want to test, but the good thing about it is it can automatically find the receiver IP address. The Start button will start sending and measuring the TCP and UDP throughput.

   A unique feature found in NetStress is the ability to change the maximum transmission unit (MTU) (of a protocol) size.

   NetStress—Network Benchmarking Tool
   http://nutsaboutnets.com/netstress/

5. *AIDA32* is actually the first and free version of the popular hardware information and benchmarking tool known as EVEREST and now AIDA64. AIDA32 comes with a network benchmark plug-in that is no longer found in EVEREST or AIDA64. Just like most of the network benchmarking tools, it is necessary to run the network benchmark plug-in on both computers (client and server) in the test.

Also check out the following:

Network Benchmark Methodology: The link below points to a large document setting out the best practices and a lot of details about running network performance benchmarks.

Benchmarking Methodology for Network Interconnect Devices
https://tools.ietf.org/html/rfc2544

PassMark Advanced Network Test:

Almost all computers these days have a network connection of some description. Whether it be a modem connection to an ISP, or an Ethernet connection to a corporate intranet, sending and receiving data to and from other computers is an essential part of day-to-day operations. A myriad of applications use TCP/IP networking technology: Email, Web browsers and games to name a few popular applications. In most cases, there is one performance factor the user is most concerned with the speed or transfer rate.

The PassMark Advanced Network Test (which is part of PerformanceTest*) is designed to test the data transfer rate between two computers both of which must be running PerformanceTest. One of the computers must act as the server and will sit waiting for a connection. The other computer acts as a client. It connects to the server machine and sends data to it for the duration of the test.

The network benchmark test will work with any type of TCP/IP connection. Including Ethernet, dial up modems, ADSL, cable modems, local area networks (LAN), Wide area networks (WAN) and wireless networking (WiFi). The software has been optimized to use a minimum amount of CPU time, allowing even high-speed gigabit Ethernet connections to be benchmarked.

Users have the ability to change the following test parameters.

- The IP address of the machine acting as the server and the port number used for the test to help with firewall issues.
- The size of the data block used for each send request. It is also possible to select variable-sized blocks to measure performance deltas as block size increases or decreases.
- The duration of the test.
- The protocol, either TCP or UDP. The TCP protocol is when data integrity is important (Errors are corrected using data retransmission). UDP is used with applications that are tolerant to data loss such as video streaming.

The results of all completed tests may be graphed using our custom graphing components. (From the reference below)

Network Benchmark: Test Your Network Speed
http://www.passmark.com/products/pt_advnet.htm

Commercial and Other Tools

There are a number of vendor products in this area, and a few are outlined and referenced here. Not all are chargeable.

Paessler: This tool is primarily a network monitor, but according to Paessler, the PRTG Network Monitor can also do a network performance test for virtualized environments using special VMware sensors.
Network Performance Test
https://www.paessler.com/network_performance_test
Windows: There are a number of tools referenced in the link below; some of them were already covered above in the "Five Free Network Performance Tools" section.

---

* http://www.passmark.com/products/pt.htm.

Network Throughput Testing Tools

http://www.windowsnetworking.com/articles-tutorials/netgeneral/network-throughput-testing-tools.html

The link adds the following tools to our little inventory:

IxChariot is a commercial enterprise-level network assessment tool that can simulate real-world network environments and applications at the transport layer (layer 4), supporting testing via TCP, UDP, Real-Time Transport Protocol (RTP), IP Exchange (IPX), Sequenced Packet Exchange (SPX), IPv4, IPv6, IP Multicast, and voice over IP (VoIP). You can measure throughput, jitter, packet loss, end-to-end delay, mean opinion score (MOS), and Media Delivery Index (MDI). It's offered as a Windows-based console, but also provides endpoint software for many platforms, including Windows CE, Linux, Sun Solaris, and Novell Netware.

TamoSoft Throughput Test is a free Windows-based utility, one of many network tools TamoSoft offers. It can test TCP and UDP simultaneously in both directions, or TCP by itself, supporting either IPv4 or IPv6. Once started, it continuously sends data streams and reports the upstream and downstream throughput values in megabits per second, UDP packet loss percentage, and round-trip time. It gives a numeric readout and offers live chart views as well. You can also test with varying quality of service (QoS) settings too. For more details, see

TamoSoft Throughput Test

http://www.tamos.com/products/throughput-test/

Iperf is an open source, cross-platform, command line throughput testing tool. It runs on various platforms, including Linux, UNIX, and Windows. It's also accessible via a GUI with jperf. It can test using TCP and UDP data streams unidirectionally or bidirectionally and reports throughput, delay jitter, and datagram loss. It has various customizable testing parameters to tailor the tests.

Other Tools: Can be found at the following link:

Network Troubleshooting Tools

https://fasterdata.es.net/performance-testing/network-troubleshooting-tools/

NetSpec

NetSpec strives to implement more realistic network performance testing scenarios than the standard utilities by accounting for variable traffic flows. NetSpec is an academic research project that includes source code.

NetSpec provides a wider range of test types and scenarios than current methods (e.g., Test TCP [TTCP] or netperf), because accurately characterizing network behavior and performance requires more subtle testing than what is provided by a "full-blast" data stream from point A to point B.

NetSpec offers a scripting language that allows the user to define multiple traffic flows from or to multiple computers. This allows an automatic and reproducible test to be performed.

http://www.ittc.ku.edu/netspec/

Nettest

Nettest is a simple latency and bandwidth performance benchmark for point-to-point TCP connections on Solaris and Linux. NetTest 2.0 is a simple network connectivity tester designed for remote support environments. It's easy to deploy through active directory or email. It is also extremely easy to use so that in remote support situations, the end users unfamiliar with detailed scripts can help diagnose network issues by simply hitting a button. You would be well advised to read the documentation before hitting *any* buttons.

http://sourceforge.net/projects/dorkwarenettest/

TTCP

The Test TCP (TTCP) utility can be used to measure TCP throughput through an IP path. In order to use it, one starts the receiver on one side of the path, and then starts the transmitter on the other side. The transmitting side sends a specified number of TCP packets to the receiving side. At the end of the test, the two sides display the number of bytes transmitted and the time elapsed for the packets to pass from one end to the other. These figures can then be used to calculate the actual throughput on the link. For general information on TTCP, refer to

http://www.cisco.com/c/en/us/support/docs/dial-access/asynchronous-connections/10340-ttcp.html

We could spend the rest of the week looking at further network performance monitoring and testing tools, but if that is what you want to do, simply do a search on "network performance testing."

Network Load Testing

Networks are now being hit with mixtures of data types—video, voice, and image, as well as the normal business data we are familiar with. Adding the traffic from an application is no longer a guesswork exercise since then it may impinge adversely on existing work. This is one very good reason for *load (or stress) testing* of networks. This is normally achieved by generating live network traffic, rather like a remote terminal emulator (RTE) used in processor benchmarking, and analyzing the results.

It is desirable to do such tests while varying the mix of data types to assess the impact of changes to the data transmission profile.

Load testing allows an organization to run realistic and *worst-case* testing scenarios in a controlled way, establishing how the application will perform under both normal and anticipated peak load conditions. Simulating the traffic on the production environment at high load allows understanding of how the current configuration will stand up to real-time user stress. This allows the system or devices to be modified, predeployment, and updated to appropriately meet the needs of end users.

Stress and load testing products focus on the network or application performance and may need to be integrated with other test tools, such as WAN emulators or application analyzers.

There are a number of commercial products aimed at this test area, and a few are outlined in the reference below:*

---

* There is no implication that products mentioned here are superior to others. They are simply illustrative of available load testing functionality.

Network Performance and Load testing
http://www.telnetnetworks.ca/en/technology-solutions/network-performance-testing.html

Wi Fi Benchmarking
The benchmarks covered so far are not Wi Fi (IEEE 802.11) oriented but here is one.

NetStress—Network Benchmarking Tool [Wi Fi networks]
http://nutsaboutnets.com/netstress/

Chapter 14

Virtualization Overview

What Is Virtualization?

Virtualization is the logical division of a physical machine into multiple *virtual machines* (VMs), sometimes called *guests*. The concept of virtual systems came mainly from ideas developed in the 1960s and made into a time-sharing software product called Control/Program Cambridge Monitor System (CP/CMS). CP/CMS became CP-40 and evolved into CP-67, which appeared in 1967. (It also owes something to MIT's Multics* [1969].)

The development of CP-67 culminated in the announcement of VM/370 on August 2, 1972, along with enhancements to the System/370 range of machines. A nuance that amused me at the announcement was that you could run VM/370 under VM/370 *ad infinitum*.

VM/370 was used as a time-sharing system and for program development, and CMS came to mean Conversational Monitor System. It was also the vehicle for running different operating systems on a single machine, for example, Disk Operating System (DOS) and OS, the main operating system for large machines and workloads.

Within cloud computing, virtual machines go under different names, although the base architectures are the same. IBM VMs are called logical partitions (LPARs), and x86-based machines are called virtual machines.

Virtual Machines Today

Full Virtualization

The structure of a virtualized environment as recognized today looks as shown in Figure 14.1, where "App" stands for applications. The "Host OS" is the one that normally controls the hardware platform, which now hosts the VMs. The operating systems (guest OSs) on the VMs are unaware that they have been "virtualized" and are completely isolated from the underlying hardware. They think they are accessing and controlling the hardware themselves, but their hardware requests are handled for them by the hypervisor. Figure 14.1 shows the structure of two types of hypervisor:

---

* The name *UNIX* (originally Unics) is itself a pun on *Multics*.

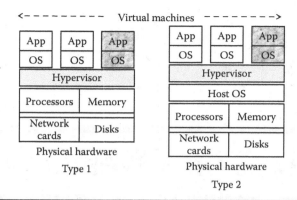

Figure 14.1   Two full virtualization environments.

Type 1: This configuration comprises a series of VMs, each containing an operating system and applications and a hypervisor "operating system" to control the allocation of resources—processors, memory, disk, and network interface cards (NICs)—across the VMs. This is commonly called a *bare-metal* or *native* hypervisor environment. Examples of bare-metal hypervisors are IBM z/VM for zSeries platforms; IBM PowerVM for Power 5, 6, and 7 platforms (what was Risc System/6000); VMWare ESX/ESX1 Server for Windows x86 platforms; and Microsoft Hyper-V.

Type 2: This configuration comprises a series of VMs, each containing an operating system and applications and a hypervisor operating system and the host or native operating system for the hardware platform to control the allocation of resources—processors, memory, disk, and NICs—across the VMs. These are commonly called *hosted hypervisors*. Examples of these include VMware Workstation, VMware Server, Oracle VM VirtualBox, and Kernel-Based Virtual Machine (KVM).

Paravirtualization

Paravirtualization (PV) is similar to full virtualization, but has a "thin" hypervisor and necessitates alterations to the guest operating systems to function.

It therefore has its pluses and minuses, as we will see. Paravirtualization is a technique introduced by Xen and is now adopted by other virtualization solution providers. Guests on a paravirtualized system require a modified OS kernel that must be ported to run with Xen. However, because the guest (OS) is aware of the hypervisor, it can run efficiently without any emulation.

Thus, paravirtualization offers better performance and scalability than full virtualization, although it has the downside of involving OS modification and all that entails, and some *ad hoc* flexibility is lost because of this need to modify the OS and, of course, test it before going operational.

Performance Aspects of Virtualization

The outline of PV is shown in Figure 14.2. Table 14.1 shows the efficiency, in terms of the resource "cost" virtualization of the paravirtualization mode against that of the full virtualization mode.

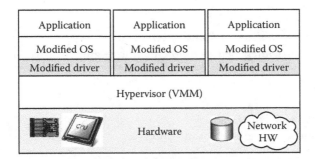

Figure 14.2   Paravirtualization schematic.

Table 14.1   Virtualization/Paravirtualization Overheads Compared

Mode	Guest Instances	Virtualization Overhead %	System Needs %	Total %
Full virtualization	5	10 (50 total)	10 (50 total)	100
Paravirtualization	8	2 (16 total)	10 (80 total)	96

Source: Taken from http://searchservervirtualization.techtarget.com/tip/Paravirtualization-explained.

Performance and modifications aside, the choice of virtualization type will ultimately depend on the requirements of the system the solution supports. See the reference below for more detailed aspects.

http://searchservervirtualization.techtarget.com/tip/Paravirtualization-explained

Monitoring Virtual Machines

Virtual machines have been around since the late 1960s and found their métier in software and system development. The move to production environments was delayed, sensibly, since management of such environments was hit and miss without tools. A virtual machine is a ghostly entity that can occupy different machines and storage sets and parts thereof. We can measure the physical characteristics of the hardware supporting this virtual environment, but where is a particular virtual machine?

Virtual machine performance monitoring entails monitoring virtualization and private cloud-specific performance problems in proactive fashion. Proactive means not just measuring numbers and plotting them, but interpreting them and actively managing the environment. Private cloud and virtualization have created new performance monitoring challenges with the need to monitor and manage shared pools of CPU, memory, network, and storage resources. Contention for these shared resources makes it increasingly difficult to determine the source of application and workload performance problems.

One good reason to get a grip on what is happening is for service level management and reporting on service level agreements (SLAs). Another is good capacity planning so that lack of knowledge of what is going on does not lead to overprovisioning of hardware and possibly software.

There is a good paper produced by Dell on this topic:

The Definitive Guide to Virtualization Management Software
https://software.dell.com/whitepaper/ebook-the-definitive-guide-to-virtualization-management-software872556/

SolarWinds has also produced a paper on this topic:

Virtual Machine Monitoring & Management
http://www.solarwinds.com/freetools/vm-monitor.aspx

> ***Note***: Both papers have a marketing slant, and there are other vendors providing software that is similar in function, so these mentions do not constitute a recommendation. For example, VMware and Zabbix also have products in this area.

Risks of Virtualization

A paper by the Cloud Security Alliance (CSA) considers the risks involved in moving to and using a virtualized environment. It summarizes the risks under 11 headings and then deals with the consequences of falling foul of these pitfalls:

1. VM sprawl, leading to lack of manageability.
2. Sensitive data within a VM, inviting compromise due to ease of transportation.
3. Security of offline and dormant VMs can introduce security vulnerabilities.
4. Security of preconfigured VMs and active VMs; exist as files that can lead to unauthorized access.
5. Lack of visibility and control over virtual networks; virtualized network traffic may not be visible to security protection entities.
6. Resource exhaustion where uncontrolled physical resource consumption may impact availability.*
7. Hypervisor security must be secure throughout its life cycle.
8. Unauthorized access to hypervisor: access controls must be adequate to protect against hacker and other attacks.
9. Account or service hijacking through the self-service portal: portal vulnerabilities can lead to privilege escalation attacks (good for the attacker).
10. Workloads of different trust levels located on the same server, ensuring sufficient segregation of workloads on a physical host.
11. Risk due to cloud service provider application programming interfaces (APIs), a hybrid cloud security risk.

This paper elaborates on these points:

Best Practices for Mitigating Risks in Virtualized Environments
https://downloads.cloudsecurityalliance.org/whitepapers/Best_Practices_for%20_Mitigating_Risks_Virtual_Environments_April2015_4-1-15_GLM5.pdf

---

* Remember that nonavailability = infinite response time = poor performance.

Cloud Overview

Origins of Cloud Environment

Clouds and virtualization go hand in hand in the provision of adaptable services to end users. This partnership is often classed as phase 3 of the development of computing services to end users. The first was the mainframe or mini–dumb terminal model, typified in the 1960s and 1970s by IBM, HP, and DEC machines with nonintelligent screens attached. The second phase, commencing in the 1980s, was the client/server era where intelligent *user stations*, normally PCs, shared functions with the central computer. The main shared functions were

- Presentation logic
- Application logic
- Database logic

Exactly how these were split (and each could be split down the middle) defined which client/ server model they represented. These models ranged from presentation logic on the client and the rest on the central computer (X Window) through about four models, depending on how you break it down, to everything on the client (workstation computing).

What Is Cloud Computing?

The National Institute of Standards and Technology's (NIST) definition of cloud computing is

> Cloud computing is a model for enabling ubiquitous, convenient, on-demand network access to a shared pool of configurable computing resources (e.g., networks, servers, storage, applications, and services) that can be rapidly provisioned and released with minimal management effort or service provider interaction. This cloud model is composed of five essential characteristics, three service models, and four deployment models. (NIST Special Publication 800-145)

Cloud Characteristics

- Cloud computing centralization of applications, servers, data, and storage resources.
- Selective virtualization of IT entities such as servers, storage, applications, desktops, and network components such as switches and routers.
- Reliance on the network as the connector between the client and the provider.
- Often used in a *pay as you go* mode, rather like purchasing electricity or using a cell (mobile) phone.
- Control and automation shifted to the *provider* for the *client* or *user*, for example, resource management, troubleshooting, change management, and other data center disciplines.
- The dynamic creation and modification of virtual resources to meet changing requirements, for example, the addition of a virtual machine or virtual disk. This is often called elasticity in a cloud context.
- Different manifestations of cloud computing depending on what functions the organization's IT wished to keep and which it offloaded to a cloud provider.

Cloud Characteristics (NIST 800-145)

On-demand self-service: A consumer can unilaterally provision computing capabilities, such as server time and network storage, as needed automatically without requiring human interaction with each service provider.

Broad network access: Capabilities are available over the network and accessed through standard mechanisms that promote use by heterogeneous thin or thick client platforms (e.g., mobile phones, tablets, laptops, and workstations).

Resource pooling: The provider's computing resources are pooled to serve multiple consumers using a multitenant model, with different physical and virtual resources dynamically assigned and reassigned according to consumer demand. There is a sense of location independence in that the customer generally has no control or knowledge over the exact location of the provided resources, but may be able to specify location at a higher level of abstraction (e.g., country, state, or data center). Examples of resources include storage, processing, memory, and network bandwidth.

Rapid elasticity: Capabilities can be elastically provisioned and released, in some cases automatically, to scale rapidly outward and inward commensurate with demand. To the consumer, the capabilities available for provisioning often appear to be unlimited and can be appropriated in any quantity at any time.

Measured service: Cloud systems automatically control and optimize resource use by leveraging a metering capability at some level of abstraction appropriate to the type of service (e.g., storage, processing, bandwidth, and active user accounts). Resource usage can be monitored, controlled, and reported, providing transparency for both the provider and consumer of the utilized service.

Cloud Service Models

There were four initial service models recognized and on offer in cloud computing:

- Infrastructure as a service (IaaS)
- Platform as a service (PaaS)
- Software as a service (SaaS)
- Information technology as a service (ITaaS): EMC

Since then, there have been other *<entity> as a service* entries into the cloud arena, such as disaster recovery as a service (DRaaS), high availability as a service (HAaaS) (see reference below), network as a service (NaaS), optimization as a service (OaaS), database as a service (DBaaS), and probably others by now as the "as a service" bug bites. I have seen one recently, laboratory as a service (LaaS); I have no idea what it offers.

DRaaS and HAaaS Discussion
http://virtualizationreview.com/Whitepapers/2014/03/VRTVISSOLUTION-5-Reasons-to-Consider/Asset.aspx

We will examine four major XaaS contenders here:

1. **IaaS**: This model provides users (or tenants) with shared computing capacity, such as processors, network, and storage, which are virtualized, and an operating system. They are not aware of the hypervisor function. All over "facilities" the users install for themselves are not shared.

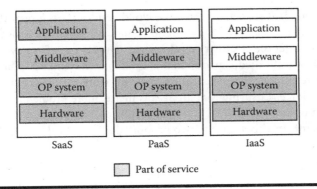

Figure 14.3   Three major cloud services models.

2. **PaaS**: In this service, a layer above IaaS, the user is provided with middleware components, databases, storage, connectivity, caching, monitoring, and routing, plus reliability features. These may vary with cloud supplier.
3. **SaaS**: Here users share things that are shared in IaaS and PaaS environments plus an application. The application may be shared, but data is isolated for the user's purposes. An application might be installed on multiple machines to provide scalability.
4. **DRaaS**: This disaster recovery service is offered by cloud vendors to clients. An example is the offering by Windstream, a video of which can be seen at https://www.youtube.com/watch?v=QT_tymQSDIg

Figure 14.3 shows where the XaaS elements (X = I, P, or S) fit in the virtualized cloud environment.

For a good source document on the main cloud service models, see

Cloud Computing
http://explainingcomputers.com/cloud.html

Cloud Deployment Models

These cloud models represent the residence and responsibility of the cloud deployment:

Community deployment: A community cloud is for the exclusive use of a community, defined as groups of people from different organizations that share a common interest or goal, for example, vertical markets, scientific institutions, or organizations working together on a joint project.

Private deployment: The private cloud is deployed for the exclusive use of the client organization. If the cloud is managed by the client, it is known as a *managed private cloud*. If this cloud environment is hosted and operated off the premises, it is called a *hosted private cloud*.

Private clouds offer the client the ability to use existing hardware investments, reduce security fears when sharing infrastructure with others, and eliminate any resource contention between different clients.

Public deployment: In this deployment, the cloud resides on the provider's premises but is "open to the public." Usage in this scenario is on a *pay as you go* basis and is often termed *utility computing* after the electricity model where you pay for what power you use. They give the impression of unlimited capacity that is available on demand.* The user or client need not know or care exactly what machine or where his work is run, as long as it fits in with any SLAs he has in force. Ensuring that an SLA is met is more problematic than it is when the · IT is wholly in-house.

Hybrid deployment: In this scenario, two or more distinct cloud infrastructures coexist, but they share technology that enables the porting of data and applications from one to the other.

Resource Management in Virtualized Environments

Cloud management means the software and technologies designed for operating and monitoring applications, data and services residing in the cloud. Cloud management tools help ensure a company's cloud computing-based resources are working optimally and properly interacting with users and other services. (Webopedia)

Resource management covers the management of the key resources in a cloud and their measurements (quantification). Major entities, which in the main relate to SLAs, and hence the business, are performance, availability, change, and problem or fault management. Who is responsible for what, when, and why depends on which of the deployment models above is in operation for a particular client of the cloud provider. Resource management is a key component of meeting SLAs in a cloud environment, and this is discussed next.

Physical versus Virtual Management

Managing a physical environment is simpler (but not so simple in absolute terms) than managing a virtual environment. In a physical environment, resources usually have a one-to-one relationship with the throughput or utilization of that resource and are easier to interpret. In virtual environments, although metrics similar to those in the physical world can be measured, they are not open to the same unique interpretation.

For example, a measurement of resource utilizations in the virtual world which shows everything is OK with that world, it does not mean that every VM and the applications on it are OK too. Studies have shown that there in enough food on this planet to feed everyone to a reasonable degree, but we know there is still an imbalance. Some people have too much food and others too little.

Differences like this can generate issues in charging, chargeback, and meeting SLA targets for organizations' work buried somewhere in the virtualized scrum. Some of these issues of monitoring and interpretation of metrics in the virtualized world are covered in Chapter 17. The references below are tastes of life in this virtual world.

---

* This puts me in mind of the old Amdahl CPU accelerator on its systems, which a customer could switch on to get temporary extra CPU horsepower and was charged for it later by Amdahl on a metered basis.

The reference below has the following quote:

> Virtualization and cloud vendors often play down the need for increased security management, but in reality the shared resources model could pose more risks and put you more under the microscope of regulators.

Managing a Virtual Server vs. Physical Server: What's the Difference?
http://searchcio.techtarget.com/tip/Virtual-server-management-vs-physical-servers-Whats-the-difference

Another paper discussing aspects of virtualizing physical environments has several very good diagrams showing, among other things, *before* and *after* images of environments.

Aspects of Virtualization [VMware]
https://pubs.vmware.com/vsphere-50/index.jsp?topic=   %2Fcom.vmware.vsphere.introduction.doc_50%2FGUID-7EE617A2-4A10-424F-BAE2-56CA6692A93F.html

One aspect of virtualization (and hence cloud computing) is security, which has been recognized since the outset. Fortunately, this is being addressed, but the sheer opaqueness of what is going on in virtualized environments is still a concern to *nonbelievers*.

SLAs and the Cloud

SLAs for cloud computing are probably more difficult to define since the operating environment is not controlled by the client organization, who must define the service expectations, and the cloud provider will need to map these onto the cloud environment. The SLAs will obviously vary depending on which service model (IaaS, PaaS, or Saas) is chosen by the organization.

The document footnote referenced in the title above discusses 10 areas of SLAs that a cloud client and cloud vendor need to consider and agree on:

1. Understand roles and responsibilities.
2. Evaluate business-level policies.
3. Understand service and deployment model differences.
4. Identify critical performance objectives.
5. Evaluate security and privacy requirements.
6. Identify service management requirements.
7. Prepare for service failure management.
8. Understand the disaster recovery plan.
9. Define an effective management process.
10. Understand the exit process (in case of nonachievement of SLA criteria, for example).

Before the client can discuss and agree on SLAs with the provider, he must discuss the requirements of the client's own end users, that is, the business users. This implies two "translations":

1. The translation of the user requirements into an SLA
2. The translation of this SLA into one or more SLAs by the provider between him and his providers, for example, a network carrier.

The cloud provider will then need an SLA, derived from the client/provider SLA, agreed on with the carrier. It might well be the case that there is more than one carrier, and hence possibly more than one provider to deliver SLAs. It could get complicated unless you sublet these *secondary* SLAs to the primary cloud provider (tertiary SLAs don't bear thinking about).

The subject of SLAs and the cloud may well sway the selection of which cloud provider to use, as the choices available are widening.

For a more detailed discussion of SLAs, both classical and cloud, see Chapter 17. There are some references presented there with the proviso they are used as an aid and not as instructions from on high.

Chapter 15

High Availability and Disaster Recovery

Relationship to Performance

What, you may ask, has performance got to do with high availability (HA) and its sister discipline, disaster recovery (DR)? Quite a lot. If the system fails and you cannot recover it, that is a serious performance problem. You may be worried if your planned 2 s response time averages out at 5 s, but think, what happens if the response time is measured in days if the system goes down or encounters a disaster?

To cut this discussion short, an installation has to consider the performance aspects of backing up and restoring data in its various forms so that recovery can be effected in minimum time according to the service level agreement (SLA) made with the business users. The users will be aware (or should be made aware) that outages can occur and will need to specify achievable recovery times in the SLAs.

We have been looking at performance aspects of the operational environment, but attention must be given to the nonoperational environment when the system fails. In essence, the installation needs to ensure that the backup and recovery mechanisms are fast enough to fulfill the SLA requirements for the recovery point objective (RPO) and recovery time objective (RTO). These will be discussed, along with their IT implications, after we have looked briefly at HA and DR.

What Is HA?

High availability is a status of an IT installation that is designed to minimize failures that would impact business operations and to recover as quickly as possible from those that do occur (as Murphy's law says they will). Availability as a metric is normally expressed as a percentage of time for which a system or service is available and functioning correctly against the elapsed time it is meant to be operating, not the wall clock time. A system that is not operating (down) is one with zero performance, and this is why availability and performance go hand in hand.

Thus, the availability of a system or service can be expressed as follows:

$$\text{Availability } A = \frac{\text{Time Operating as Designed}}{\text{Time Supposed to Be Operating}} \times 100\%$$

So, if in a period of 10,000 h of operation (not necessarily contiguous) the system is not functioning as required for 2 h, its availability would be 9,998/10,000, which is $A = 99.98\%$ (sometimes expressed as the decimal 0.9998).

What Is DR?

An IT disaster is a failure over and above a normal outage caused by a hardware or software failure or operator *finger trouble*. These are normally dealt with *in situ* and normal service resumed after a period of time. A disaster is an event that essentially renders the IT site useless, for whatever reason.

Disasters are a reality that every business needs to face, and according to a Forrester survey, they are not a rare event. Forces of nature, acts of terrorism, fires, theft, and even careless (or malicious) employee actions can cause downtime that impairs day-to-day business activity. While there is certainly nothing new about disaster, many businesses are reexamining their preparedness and response plans. Recovery from such situations is two orders of magnitude greater than recovery from normal outages.

Recovery involves issues beyond the scope of this book, but the one that does concern us in the context of performance is the storage and recovery of data. Businesses that do not recover or take a long time to do so often go out of business according to surveys.

Backup and Recovery Performance Requirements

There are at least two metrics that will drive the specification of backup and recovery procedures. These are defined below, and they are derived from a business continuity plan (BCP) for the various parts of a business. Normally, these plans are geared to meet the demands of different business aspects on the basis that one size does not fit all, a philosophy that can be time-consuming and costly.

The two basic entities in backup and recovery, apart from requirements, are method and speed—how you do the backup or recovery and how fast it can go.

RTO and RPO

Recovery Time Objective

The recovery time objective (RTO) is the maximum tolerable length of time that a computer, system, network, or application can be down after a failure or disaster occurs. This is the factor that dictates how often backups are made, which, together with transaction logs, can restore the system to its prefailure state within this time.

Recovery Point Objective

The recovery point objective (RPO) is the maximum acceptable amount of data loss measured in time. It is the age of the files or data in the backup storage required to resume normal operations if a computer system or network failure occurs.

RPO is measured in time and then dictates the backup requirements for disaster recovery procedures. For example, if the RPO is set to 90 min, then a backup of the system is required to be done every 90 min. Backing up every 3 h is useless in meeting this criterion.

Backup and Restore

Overview

The normal reasons for making backups or archiving are for future use. This might be for short-term recovery (high-availability recovery) or disaster recovery (backup) or litigation (archiving). Many years ago, backup procedures were relatively simple since they only involved just a bunch of disks (JBODs) and the backup mechanism was usually provided by the provider of the online transaction processing (OLTP) or database, for example, IMS Data Base/Data Communications (IMS DB/DC). The receiving medium for the backup was invariably tape, except perhaps in special circumstances.

Today (2016), the IT landscape has changed and we have to consider what to do in various circumstances with which data. Depending on the business situation, you may need to recover:

- The whole server and all databases (in case of disaster recovery)
- A whole disk or set of disks
- Specific databases
- Specific database tables
- Specific transactions' data

These requirements and their solutions may need to be mapped onto one or more of the following environments:

- Simple JBOD.
- Storage area network (SAN) and network attached storage (NAS) environments.
- Redundant array of independent disks (RAID) with various levels of RAID employed.
- Relational database management systems (RDBMS) systems.
- "Big data" situations.
- Object databases.
- Cloud and virtual machine environments.
- Erasure code storage methods (forward error correction, etc.). Some of these newer methods for error correction beyond that offered by RAID allow the distribution of pieces of data across a network. Whatever benefits this accrues will be counterbalanced by the need to back up this data in a consistent and recoverable manner in such a dispersed environment.

It has been suggested in various papers and seminars that the following steps should be considered to categorize backup requirements and make it a "horses for courses" method, which means not duplicating expensive solutions for all parts of the business:

- Group data by business value (i.e., by criticality).
- Identify backup goals plus RPOs and RTOs (for each group).
- Identify optimal backup infrastructure solution (tape, disk, geomirrors, etc.)

- Define a backup strategy based on this infrastructure—data targets, frequency, reporting, logs and retention plan including transport and locations
- Test it for functionality and performance. My view is that mathematical modeling on the complex environments of today will not work. The empirical "suck it and see" approach is really the only sensible one.
- Ongoing management, deploying (appropriate) combinations of backup, replication, continuous data protection, and failover (see next sections).

I have no generalized solution to offer in this area since it is complex and dictated by the existing IT environment and needs of a particular organization.

There are a number of ways (modes) of taking copies of or archiving data. Which one is chosen depends on how you plan to recover, to *what point* (RPO) and at *what speed* (RTO), to minimize the business impact of a major failure. Remember, we have outlined RTO and RPO above and that these times and points of recovery are the key aspects of recovery.

Let us look at some ways of making "copies" of data and associated metadata (indexes, pointers, data definitions, some logs, etc.) plus data and files associated with supporting software, such as OLTP, Domain Name System (DNS), and other "middleware."

Backup and Restore Environment

Backing up and restoring data can be achieved in two basic ways:

- **Locally**: This is easier to control and comfortable and is probably the best option in geographies where natural disasters are unlikely. This is the normal mode of operation for normal and high-availability recovery after a failure.
- **Remotely**: This involves more effort but is invaluable if your primary site suffers a catastrophic outage that destroys your local backups along with it.

Figure 15.1 illustrates these scenarios in a schematic way and is followed by a discussion on backup techniques.

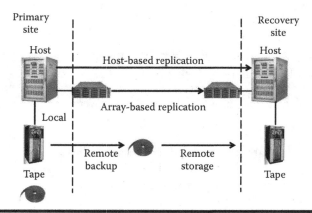

Figure 15.1   Data backup modes and methods: local and remote.

Backup Modes

Cold (offline): A copy made when all components (processes) of a system are stopped and the stable data, metadata, and other volatile data backed up without consideration of data changing while being backed up. Copies can be of everything on the system storage or by application or service. It is important for all backup types and modes to know exactly what data (volatile or other) is needed for each service or application.

For DR purposes, nonvolatile (fixed) data needs to be backed up and stored safely in the event of an invocation of DR when perhaps all primary disks and tapes are lost.

Warm (online): A warm online backup is made where users still have access to the system, but with reduced functionality to simplify the backup to preserve consistency between files and data and metafiles being backed up. An example of this reduction might be the suspension of database writes, where writes may be cached and permanently applied later.

Hot (online): An online hot backup is made with no restrictions on user access, but can present difficulties in synchronizing in-flight data and is often ignored.

Backup Types

Full backup: A full backup backs up all files in a storage area or service irrespective of archive bit settings, last change date, and so forth. This means that even dormant data is backed up each time this kind of backup is run. A study of time-sharing users (IBM TSO) once discovered that only 3% of the data involved was altered on any given day. The backups employed were full backups resulting in repeatedly backing up unchanged data. The solution? Incremental backups (see below).

Incremental backup: This backs up files that have been modified since the last full or incremental backup, which saves storage space. One downside of this is that should a restore be necessary, the restore must take place from the most recent full backup and then sequentially from each subsequent incremental backup. Unfortunately, files that have been deleted since the last full backup may also be restored in this operation.

Multilevel incremental backup: This type of backup is akin to an incremental backup except, on the nth backup, it backs up the files that have been modified since the last $(n - 1)$ level backup. The preceding full backup is considered the level 0 backup version.

Differential backup: A differential (or delta) backup backs up only the files that have been modified since the last *full backup*. As an example, if a full backup is made on Sunday, a differential backup on Monday would back up files modified since Sunday. However, a differential backup made on Thursday would back up all files modified since Sunday. It thus loses the incremental backup benefit of space saving, but usually gains restoration time.

Synthetic backup: This is a combination of a full backup and subsequent incremental or differential backups. To combine a full backup with subsequent incremental or differential backups to *masquerade* as a new full backup requires the host to have records of changes and deletions. However, this "new" backup increases the restore speed over that using backup plus incremental or differential.

Progressive backup: These are scenarios where a single backup is made and thereafter only incremental backups are made. This tends to be proprietary since its use requires system knowledge of inactive and deleted files that can be kept for a specified period and then removed.

Data Deduplication

Deduplication: Data deduplication is the replacement of multiple copies of data at various levels of granularity with references to a shared copy in order to save storage space and/or bandwidth. (Storage Networking Industry Association definition).

Data deduplication looks for redundancy of sequences of bytes across very large comparison windows. Sequences of data (over 8 KB long) are compared to the history of other such sequences. The first uniquely stored version of a sequence is referenced rather than stored again. This process is completely hidden from users and applications so the whole file is readable after it's written. (EMC Glossary)

Data deduplication can operate at the *file*, *block*, or *bit* level. In file-level deduplication, if two files are exactly alike, one copy of the file is stored and subsequent iterations receive pointers to the saved file. However, file deduplication is not highly efficient because the change of even a single bit results in a totally different copy of the entire file being stored.

However, care must be taken if using deduplication on account of its minimizing data volumes and ostensibly speeding up the backup process, as the following reference discusses (see the extract after the link).

Deduplication and Restore Performance
http://wikibon.org/wiki/v/Deduplication_and_restore_ performance

Action Item: When reviewing or considering deduplication solutions, you must review restore performance. Remember that with most solutions restore performance will decrease over time and so you must evaluate its impact with data retention. Just running one or two backups to a solution and testing restore performance is not an accurate indication of long-term restore performance.

Data Replication

Definition: Data replication is continuously maintaining a secondary copy of data— possibly at a remote site—from a primary volume for the purposes of providing high availability and redundancy. (Storage Networking Industry Association definition)

Replication is a mode of "backup" where changes to a primary data source are reflected elsewhere in "real time" for synchronous replication or in a delayed "store and forward" mode for asynchronous replication. It is a common method of backup in DR plans and architectures; which mode is used depends on the distance over which the replication needs to take place.

SYNCH usually operates for distances of more than 300 km, usually for services where data loss cannot be tolerated, and ASYNC from 50–300 km.

Replication Agents

With the advent of intelligent storage subsystems or arrays, a lot of function is taken off the host system and performed by the storage array, assuming it has an intelligent array to "converse" with. One sort of replication is the normal *host-based replication* where the system performs the replication in communication with another one. The second way, offloaded from the host, is *array-based replication*, where the action may be initiated by the host, but the transfer work is done by the arrays involved. The data is replicated array to array, possibly over a distance.

Reference: A good source of information on replication is our friend Wikipedia at

http://en.wikipedia.org/wiki/Replication_(computing)

where a detailed exposition of the many vendor replication products and techniques can also be found.

Restoring Data

This is a subject that depends on what data is being restored, how it was backed up, what its importance to the business is, and a host of other factors. The simplest case is a flat sequential file where it is dumped and restored in the same format. The next level is an indexed, relational, object, and so on, type of file. In these cases, there are options, including

- Image copy, a direct *photocopy* of the data, warts and all. Any poor indexing and other discrepancies will reappear in the restored database or file. An image copy can be of a database or file, or in some cases, the whole disk is copied as is, rather like a photocopy.
- Reload, where the database or indexed file is reconstructed as if being entered for the first time so that good indexing, space allocation, and so forth, can be implemented. This, however, is normally slower than the image dump and restore option on account of rebuilding the database and indexes.

Again, different considerations might be applied to the data from different sections of the business (strategic business units [SBUs]).

Backup and Restore Performance

We come here to the nuts and bolts of the performance aspects of recovery, both short term (high availability) and longer term (disaster recovery). This normally distills into discussions of hardware and software. Traditional backup and restore took place using tapes as the preferred medium, but today, disk is a major contender as the backup medium of choice.

The speed of the chosen devices or, more accurately, the effective speed or rate at which data can be handled is the deciding factor. As we have seen in our discussions on networks, effective transmission speeds are not necessarily the rated speed of the transporting medium since other factors play a part.

However, it is not always the fastest physical medium that is the best for these purposes. There are some neat tricks employed by some vendors to speed up the process of recovery. One of these is Veeam, and it is used here in the "Backup Products" section simply as an example of these techniques. Other vendors also have techniques for optimizing backup and restore.

Backup and Restore Media

The speed at which backup and restore of data occurs depends on the backup medium (tape, disk, etc.), the method of backup (volume dump, record dump, and image copy), and restore (image restore and recreation of data from base records), plus the compression algorithm. It can also depend on the organization of the file (flat, RAID X, etc.) and its fragmentation status. It will also depend somewhat on the backup window available each dump time, in which case it makes sense to cater to the worst case.

The required speed of restoration will be dictated by the organization's RTO and RPO, which will probably be different for different sorts of applications.

Virtual Environment Backup

In this arena, it is common to differentiate between *traditional* (classical) environments and *virtual* environments. Traditional methods and backup software can work, and indeed are apparently being used in virtual environments. However, there are drawbacks to this approach, one of which is that traditional methods do not understand the virtual world. The other is the overhead of backup and the potential impact on resources needed to keep multiple virtual machines operating at service level agreement (SLA) levels.

Thus, one has a choice of backup methods—traditional and VM-aware. The traditional methods have an overhead, as they back up everything they can see, whether it has changed since the last backup or not. VM-aware techniques can take a snapshot of the VM and put a copy of its virtual disk file on the backup medium.

There are a number of products that are VM-aware, both from VMware and third parties. According to VMware, *all major backup vendors fully support using consolidated backup to protect virtual machines.*

VCB

> VMware Consolidated Backup [VCB] provides a centralized backup facility for virtual machines that works in conjunction with many leading backup tools. The software enables third-party backup tools to protect virtual machines and their contents from a centralized backup server rather than running directly from VMware ESX™ hosts. (From the reference below)

The benefits of VCB are also outlined in this reference:

Understanding VMware Consolidated Backup
http://www.vmware.com/pdf/vi3_consolidated_backup.pdf

Backup Products

This is a selection of products; there are others that offer similar facilities for virtual machine backup. You should note that backup performance is not just a function of the speed of the physical media involved, as many of the products listed will show.

It often involves techniques such as snapshots to enhance the performance of the backup and restore, for example, in the Veeam products.

VMware Consolidated Backup
http://www.vmware.com/files/pdf/consolidated_backup_datasheet.pdf

VMware Consolidated Backup: Best Practices
http://www.vmware.com/files/pdf/vcb_best_practices.pdf

Microsoft Virtual Machine Manager (VMM)
https://technet.microsoft.com/en-us/library/Gg610610.aspx

Veeam Backup
http://www.veeam.com/vmware-esx-backup.html

Symantec NetBackup
http://www.symantec.com/netbackup/

IBM Tivoli Storage Manager
http://www-03.ibm.com/software/products/en/tivostormana/

Quest vRanger
http://software.dell.com/products/vranger/

Other vendors of VM backup solutions can be found in the Datamation paper:

Data Backup: Virtual vs. Conventional [see page 2]
http://www.datamation.com/data-center/backing-up-virtual-vs.-conventional-2.html

Other VM Backup Literature

Backing Up Your Virtual Environment
http://cdn.ttgtmedia.com/searchDataBackup/downloads/Vmwarech09060909.pdf

Virtual Machine Backup Guide
http://www.vmware.com/pdf/vi3_35/esx_3/r35u2/vi3_35_25_u2_vm_backup.pdf

Disaster Recovery and Backup
http://cdn.ttgtmedia.com/searchStorageChannel/downloads/DR_VMware_12.pdf

Backup and Restore: Speedup Methods

Aside from raw speed of hardware devices, there are techniques (including software) that can enhance the dump and restore performance of data in recovery situations (HA and DR). One of them, deduplication, has already been dealt with in this section, along with warnings about its incorrect usage.

Some of these techniques apply to network backup as well.

Compression and Decompression

Compression and decompression of data is often done for the purposes of transmission over a network, but it is equally valid as an exercise for magnetic media data devices.

A test carried out some time ago showed the results given in Table 15.1 (with link given below the table); even if are not 100% representative, they demonstrate the differences in speed and resource consumption of compression and decompression for a 332 MB file.

It illustrates (for this case) that if you can afford the extra CPU, then compression is a great help in backup and restore.

Table 15.1 Compression and Decompression Comparison

Backup		CPU Used	Time Taken (s)
	Uncompressed	5%	39.5
	Compressed	25%	21.6
Restore			
	Uncompressed	8%	71
	Compressed	14.5%	36

SQL Server 2008: Backup Compression CPU Cost
http://www.sqlskills.com/blogs/paul/sql-server-2008-backup-compression-cpu-cost/
The conclusions in this paper about the usefulness of compression and decompression are broadly supported in the following paper:

Reasons Why the Data Throughput Rate Can Be Slower than the theoretical maximum
http://www.symantec.com/business/support/index?page=content&id=TECH8326

WAN Optimization

One of the main considerations in locating a DR site is avoiding the *double whammy* of both sites being hit by the same outage cause—flood, earthquake, and so forth. This is normally solved by having the primary and backup sites geographically separate, but this brings with it possible issues of backup and replication across large distances.

The basic equation is that the slower and less frequent the backup from the primary to the DR site, the longer the RTO in a DR situation. This is often tackled by *WAN optimization* and *WAN acceleration* techniques and technology, which are usually combinations of other techniques and specific products.

WAN optimization is achieved by lowering the volume of data and the latency of the network by several techniques, sometimes called data reduction:

- Data deduplication to reduce the amount of data shipped.
- Data compression to reduce the size (not amount) of data transmitted by some ratio x:1, where x might be in double figures.
- Latency optimization via transmission protocol "tweaks," such as window size scaling and selective acknowledgments (TCP, UDP, CIFS, NFS, MAPI, HTTP, and HTTPS network protocols). This offers the chance to optimize mixed traffic, for example, production data and backup or replication data streams.
- Data center and local office caching of data with only changes shipped over the network when cached data is requested.
- Application acceleration for applications such as RDBMSs.

Figures of 30× data transfer speedups are quoted in various places, but I don't think they are the norm, just marketing hype in some cases. There are some methods that rely on *optimized deduplication* and raw speed to aid backup and recovery processes to meet stringent service level agreements (SLAs), and one is outlined in the next link:

GFI MAX Backup: Speed Is the Essence
http://cloud-computing.tmcnet.com/features/articles/365277-gfi-max-backup-speed-the-essence.htm

QoS: Networks are now carrying increasing amounts of audio and video data that threaten to clog the transmission "pipes." Important, time-sensitive data needs special treatment in such heavy traffic. This can be achieved by rationing bandwidth based on the importance of the data transmitted with less important work having less bandwidth allocated. Optimization technology should also monitor traffic and warn network administration of imminent gridlocks, as well as identifying current trouble spots.

Chapter 16

Other Topics

Performance Overheads

Not everything in life comes free of cost, guilt, or waistline, and some IT enhancements, such as virtualization, carry their own *costs*. Developments like virtualization, emulation, and similar techniques always carry a performance overhead, which, in days gone by, might be very costly in terms of speed and dollars.

Today, disk, network, and processor resources are much cheaper than those dark days where programmers might be put forward for a Nobel Prize for saving 100 instructions in a program. However, it is necessary to be aware of such resource overheads and their possible impact on systems performance.

Virtual Machine Overheads

Figure 16.1 shows a virtual machine (VM) configuration with a hypervisor and three virtual machines, VM_1, VM_2, and VM_3, each possibly with a different operating system—OS_1, OS_2, and OS_3. In schematic form, the time taken for a hypothetical job X to run on operating system 3 is T_N, N meaning native mode. The time taken for the job to run under the hypervisor is T_V, V meaning running in virtual machine mode.

The overhead caused by using a VM environment is $[(T_V - T_N)/T_N] \times 100\%$. My first brush with virtualization was shortly after IBM announced VM/370, a hypervisor under which other IBM operating systems, such as Disk Operating System (DOS) and Multiple Virtual Storage (MVS), could run as virtual machines. There was obviously going to be a performance overhead when running an application under a VM–operating system combination compared to when running it native under the operating system alone.

For a simple batch job, the system appeared to be only 60% the throughput per unit time under the VM than running native; that is, there was a 40% overhead or resource "tax" levied by the VM. This overhead was reduced in VM/370 development, and facilities were provided to favor one VM over another if the application needed it. The bias was known as preferred virtual machine (PVM).

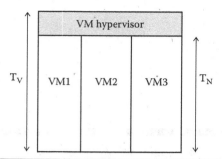

Figure 16.1 Job runtimes in native and VM modes.

VMs today still carry an overhead, but not too great, and with the cost per unit of processor power today, this overhead can be catered for quite easily financially—not the case in the dark days of expensive IT resources.

> *Note*: It is sometimes a salutary exercise to question some disciplines that were developed in resource-constrained days as a way of saving money. They may still be valid in many ways but need to be understood. They may be a solution to which there is no problem. An example is massively detailed planning for system size, although the parameters involved may still need to be assessed and included.

Network Overheads

Protocol overhead in computer networking refers to the information that must be sent with data being routed through the network toward a destination. The information is stored at the start of the packet and is called a header. Depending on the exact network protocol being used, there can be a wide variety of information in the header, but most importantly are the destination address and the originating address. Even if a protocol between two applications uses little or no protocol overhead, the information will be wrapped in a network protocol with overhead to be sent through routers to reach the correct destination. (http://www.wisegeek.com/what-is-protocol-overhead.htm)

These overheads are usually caused by extra traffic generated over and above the native payload (or actual data), with this extra traffic normally comprising metadata. This overhead is normally associated with headers and trailers to payload data; the trailer often consists of check data for error correction. The overhead depends on

- Network protocol employed
- Error correction algorithm(s)

In addition, there may be extra traffic due to retransmissions of *erroneous packets* detected upon receipt and recognized by the metadata, for example, error correction code (ECC). Table 16.1 shows a *generic* form of a transmission "chunk" or "packet," as they are often called, showing the data over and above the payload or real data that is destined for the application. In the different protocols, the metadata does not fit tidily into this schematic, but the principle is the same, namely, that there is extra traffic generated over and above the native application data.

Table 16.1   Generic Packet of Transmitted Data

Header Data	Data (Payload)	Cyclic Redundancy Check (Error Correction)

Note: The outline to Table 16.1 is not to scale.

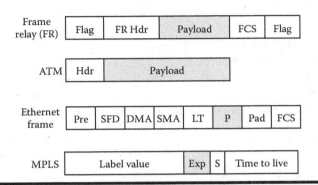

Figure 16.2   Structure of several network transmission protocols. FSC, frame sequence check.

As we stated above, the detailed format of the packet depends on the protocol in use, some of which are shown Figure 16.2, together with a brief definition and an outline of the fields in the transmission packets or frames. See the relevant references below for an explanation of the frame and cell components and lengths.

Frame Relay

Frame relay is a high-speed packet-switching protocol used in wide area networks (WANs). Providing a granular service of up to DS3 speed (45 Mbps), it has become popular for LAN-to-LAN connections across remote distances, and services are offered by most major carriers. Frame relay provides *permanent virtual circuits* (PVCs) and *switched virtual circuits* (SVCs). They are logical connections provisioned ahead of time (PVCs) or on demand (SVCs).

Frame Relay
http://www.packet-lab.com/main/images/stories/framerelay_intro/frame%20relay%20-%20 introduction%20and%20concepts%20slides.pdf

Frame Relay Glossary
http://www.cisco.com/c/en/us/support/docs/wan/frame-relay/47202-87.html#glossary

ATM

Asynchronous transfer mode (ATM) is a network technology based on transferring data in *cells* or *packets* of a fixed size. The cell used with ATM is relatively small compared to units used with older technologies. The small, constant cell size allows ATM equipment to transmit video, audio, and computer data over the same network, and ensure that no single type of data hogs the line.

Asynchronous Transfer Mode
http://technet.microsoft.com/en-us/library/bb962019.aspx

MPLS

The basic idea of multiprotocol label switching (MPLS) is labeling of data packets traversing a network in tandem with other protocols. In a traditional network, a router does some homework to decide the route the packet should take next. Using MPLS, as a packet enters a network, it is assigned a forwarding equivalence class (FEC) via a *label* (see Figure 16.2). The routers have a table of FEC types and how to handle them so the overhead of the router's *think time* is eliminated.

MPLS offers network management a great deal of flexibility to divert and route traffic around link failures, congestion, and bottlenecks.

MPLS can encapsulate packets of various network protocols. MPLS supports a range of access technologies, including T1/E1, ATM, frame relay, and digital subscriber line (DSL).

MPLS Reference Information: These are listed below in order of difficulty.

Introduction
http://www.networkworld.com/article/2297171/network-security/mpls-explained.html

MPLS Tutorial
http://www.cisco.com/web/about/ac123/ac147/archived_issues/ipj_4-3/mpls.html

12-Part Detailed Exposition [change the trailing 1 to 2, 3, 4, ..., 12 for each part]
http://blog.globalknowledge.com/technology/cisco/routing-switching/mpls-part-1/

Ethernet

Ethernet is a computer network architecture consisting of various specified local area network protocols, devices, and connection methods. It has a collision detect discipline to avoid message collisions due to simultaneous transmission.
http://computer.howstuffworks.com/ethernet8.htm

Routing in TCP/IP

Figure 16.3 shows where router function lies in the TCP/IP model layer.

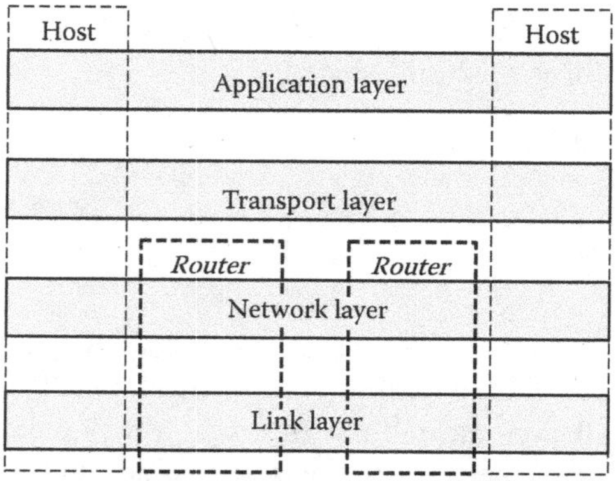

Figure 16.3 Position of host and router functions in TCP/IP layers.

Simple Transmission Math

There is a simple equation for quantifying this overhead for the generic case, but it can be applied to the specific protocols as well. Let us use the following parameters to develop this equation and then test it with some numbers to check its sensitivity. Although this treatment does not map one-to-one with all the protocols, it is basically a way of stating that the transmitted bytes consist of data or payload + control information, including error correction facilities.

$$EDR = \frac{P}{(h + P + e)} \times \frac{T}{(T + A)} \times \rho \times R \qquad (16.1)$$

where:

h is the length of the header data
P is the length of the payload data (data for the applications)
e is the length of the error correction data
T is the total number of packets (or frames) transmitted
A is the number of retries due to erroneous transmission of a packet or frame
R is the rated speed of transmission of the medium
ρ is the maximum utilization of the network to avoid excessive queuing
EDR is the *effective data rate*, that is, the rate of transmission of data useful to the application

Note that *EDR* is not the rated transmission speed of the network medium, which is the whole point of the equation.

It is easy to see that the effective rate of transmission and receipt of application data depends very much on these parameters.

- If P is much larger than h and e, then the first expression in the equation will be roughly 1.
- If A is much smaller than T, then the second expression in the equation will be roughly 1. The more reliable the network, the smaller the value of A.
- If the network is fast, the acceptable value of ρ (as a fraction) can be higher than that for a slow network. For a slow network, ρ might be 0.4, and for a much higher speed, ρ might be 0.7. In general, the faster the component, the higher the utilization that can be tolerated before response times are adversely affected.

> **Note**: This equation does not take account of lost packets, but that factor might be added to A to compensate if the loss rate is a known factor.

More Transmission Considerations

The math above is a simple way of looking at effective transmission rates for network data in general. See the "Latency: An Examination" section below.

Monitoring Overheads

The performance characteristics of systems is often determined by monitoring tools rather than operations staff using stopwatches. Although these tools are often minimal resource consumers, they do take up some horsepower in a system. In theory, they can never measure resources used by small applications or test modules precisely because they disturb the measurement by their very intrusion, a kind of IT Heisenberg uncertainty principle.

If the measurements are broad numbers, then normally the monitor overhead should not matter too much, but if a small resource is being measured with a requirement for some accuracy, then allowance will have to be made in some way.

Other Overheads

There are other areas that may impact what we call *native* performance, such as emulation of protocols, protocol wrapping and diverse modifications, and commercial add-on products, which will be specific to an organization and its requirements. Suffice it to say that such factors should be taken into account when predicting performance.

I distinctly remember an account that used a Systems Network Architecture (SNA) emulation product to merge into a DEC DNA network for some purpose or other. The performance was such that it could be measured by a calendar rather than a stopwatch.

Latency: An Examination

Overview

Latency is normally defined as the total time taken to perform a unit of work in IT, normally a transaction of some sort. This is often referred to as the response time. The latency of a unit of work is usually made up of subunits, such as processor work, disk I/Os, and transit times in a network, each of which has a latency related to it. While not disagreeing with the common concept of latency, I feel there are advantages in dividing the latency time into two components.

Let us break the time into the following two components: the *native* latency and the *extra* latency. The native latency is the time taken for the unit of work to execute in an unconstrained environment, that is, without queuing, retransmission, retries, and other items that might add to this time. This is fixed in the absence of upgrades or, in the case of a network, techniques such as data compression. Thus, for a disk access, this native time would be equal to seek time plus search time plus data transfer time or, for a network link, the data size (payload + control data) divided by the line speed.

The extra latency comes into play when the traffic of work units (transactions) becomes such that queuing occurs, as well as other time elements, such as data retransmission, disk retries, and so on. Queuing, for example, will add a *wait* (or queuing) *time* to the native latency, and this time will depend on the utilization (busyness) of the resource in question. For a single resource, this can be expressed as

$$T_{latency} = T_{native} + T_{extra}$$

Table 16.2   Native Latency for Various System Resources

Resource	Access Time (Native Latency)	Added to by Queuing? (Extra Latency)
CPU	0.3 ns	Y
L1 cache	0.9 ns	Y (misses)
L2 cache	2.8 ns	Y (misses)
Main memory	100 ns	Y
SSD	50–150 μs	Y
HDD seek	4 ms	Y
HDD rotational delay	10–12 ms	N
Line/link	Variable	Y

In online transaction processing (OLTP) parlance, these terms are, respectively, response time, service time, and wait time (see Appendix I on queuing). This can then be written as a response time (latency) breakdown equation:

$$T_{response} = T_{service} + T_{wait} = T_{service} + \frac{T_{service} \times \rho}{(1-\rho)} \qquad (16.2)$$

where ρ is the utilization of the resource. To show what typical native latencies are, look at the following Table 16.2.

Latency: More Detail

In order to expand on this simple notion of *native* and *extra* latency, let us take a network link as an example. As the network transit time becomes a bit slower, let us take a deeper look. In a simple network connection driven by a simple program sending blocks of data across a single link that is not shared with other work, the transfer rate will approach the rated speed of the network medium. This means in essence zero latency, as there are no performance *gotchas* involved.

In realistic networks, there are a number of hardware elements involved, as well as the source and target servers, namely, routers, switches, multiplexers, signal boosters, and so on. This involves the use of some form of signaling called *protocol*, which is a set of rules involved in communication between parties.

An example of human communication protocol is, when in front of the Queen of England, you do not speak unless you are spoken to. Another human protocol is teaching children to say please and thank you to adults at the appropriate time.

Hardware and software protocols needs to be well defined as the entities involved cannot make judgments as a human being could when the protocol seems to breaking down.

Some Transmission Physics

It is perhaps important to get a feel for the scale of things which affect network transmissions so that major entities are not missed or minor entities overemphasized. Data is carried along transmission media via electrical signals at speeds varying between 50% and 99% of the speed of light, symbol *c*.

Table 16.3   Speed of Light/Electrical Signals

Medium	Speed of Light/Electrical Signal
Vacuum	c (ca. 300,000 km/s)
Air	0.9997 c
Glass	0.66 c
Copper coax	0.7 c
Copper wire	0.75 c
Water	0.75 c

Signals are carried over networks composed of either copper or fiber-optic material or, in the case of wireless transmission, through the air. This was sometimes done in the past with dishes using microwave links between, for example, line-of-sight data centers. The characteristics of these media are shown in Table 16.3.

In fact, the speed of light in a medium depends on the refractive index of the material, that property that bends the light as it enters that medium. The speed of light in a medium of refractive index μ is

$$\frac{c}{\mu}$$

Thus, for normal glass, the refractive index is about 1.5, giving a speed of light of c/1.5 or about 0.66 c. Similarly, the speed of light in air is c/0.9997, which is very nearly c.

This applies to wireless transmission, and the speed of light in air depends on its density. If the air temperature rises, the density decreases and it becomes closer to a vacuum; hence, the speed of light will be a little higher.

In reality, these differences will be lost in the delays involved in other elements of the transmission setup for wireless transmission. There can also be losses even in wireless transmissions so that retransmissions may be needed. For a review of causes of loss, see

Experimental Anatomy of Packet Losses in Wireless Mesh Networks
http://spirit.cs.ucdavis.edu/pubs/conf/yu-secon-2009.pdf

ER: Efficient Retransmission Scheme for Wireless LANs
https://www.cs.utexas.edu/~erozner/papers/conext07.pdf

Losses are basically bit errors that can be caused by a number of things, including Rayleigh scattering (proportional to $[1/(wavelength)^4]$) and energy absorption by molecules of gas or optical fiber. I'll leave it there before I get out of my depth.

Latency: Some Math

The word *latency* is bandied about without a common understanding, as I see it. To my way of thinking, a delay is something expected but should not really happen in a well-designed, balanced system. It is like a traffic jam adding 30 min to your journey that normally takes 20 min. Hence, we have the fact that

Normal (native) time = 20, delay (extra) = 30, total time = 50 (latency)

Another way of looking at this is via equations, exemplified here using network scenarios:

$$Network\ Time = \frac{M}{B} (Simple\ point-to-point\ in\ the\ medium)$$ (16.3)

Equation 16.3 is the "best you'll ever get" result (native latency). Call this time *t*.
Equation 16.4 is the response or throughput time elements:

$$Network\ Time = \frac{M}{B} + Delay (Network\ with\ nodes)$$ (16.4)

where *M* is the message size (headers + data payload) and *B* the bandwidth of the transmitting medium. Call this delay time τ. This is the realistic equation that recognizes there are extra hardware *and* software involved in such transmissions.

However, in real life, there are probably extra delays added to the overall time given by Equation 16.4. These can be due to bit losses, congestion and general queuing, router buffer overflows, suboptimal packet sizes, and a few other things. We'll call this *DelayX*:

$$Network\ Time = \frac{M}{B} + Delay + Delay \cdot X$$

Call this third term (second delay term) τ_O, the overhead delay. The total network time *T* is therefore

$$T = t + \tau + \tau_O$$ (16.5)

To summarize this,

■ *t* is the *native* line or link time based on payload size and line bandwidth.
■ τ is the *extra* delay added by intermediate nodes (routers, switches, multiplexers, etc.) between sender and receiver.
■ τ_O is another *extra* delay time due to other causes—queuing, buffer overflow, processing packet headers, ECC, and longitudinal redundancy code (LRC), plus retransmissions because of bit dropping and so on.

The Logic

The total time taken is thus $T = (t + \tau + \tau_O)$.

If we take random actions to reduce *T* and manage to do that, which element was responsible: t, τ, τ_O? Since in the short term, *t* is fixed and data size probably so, the task to reduce the response or transit time of the network revolves around τ and τ_O. Not rocket science.

However, in a normal network there will be multiple links (*n*) and possible routes through it from requestor to receiver, and the equation changes from the one above to

$$T = \sum_{1}^{n} t_i + \sum_{1}^{n} \tau_i + \sum \text{all } \tau_O \qquad (16.6)$$

where t_i is the transit time of a link in the ith link of the data route and τ_i the latency (delay) in that link, caused by hardware, software, and protocol. Thus, it clearly makes sense to treat each element represented by the equation separately in analyzing where changes might be made to decrease the total time T transit time.

This is the reason I suggest splitting the time up into three (at least for a network) and calling the time over and above that which might be calculated, t, based on the characteristics of the medium and the added delays τ and τ_O, which I have called *extra latency*.

Importance of Differentiation

Apart from sticking to the meaning of latency in the English language, reasons for recognizing and maintaining the split include:

- The three entities are different in their nature.
- As such, separation assists when overall response time or throughput is excessive and corrective action needs to be taken. Each component of this time requires different actions.

Treatment, that is, minimization, of the excessive response time or throughput using the composite time is more difficult. The reason for splitting latency into native (fixed) and extra (variable) is to be able to concentrate on the latter to reduce overall latency.

Latency: Visual Detail

1. Figure 16.4 illustrates the components of latency, using a network as an example; this could be repeated for other resources in a system. It reinforces the idea of breaking down extra

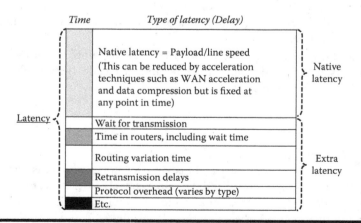

Figure 16.4 Latency schematic (total and extra) for a network.

latency so that it can be addressed in reducing overall latency. The native latency is fixed, in the absence of upgrades or acceleration techniques.

If these components of the extra latency can be measured or estimated in some way, then steps may be possible to reduce the delay elements.

2. Figure 16.5 shows a schematic network (not a working one) to illustrate where latency arises in data transmissions.

In the more realistic network shown, there is an interchange of messages between the elements of the network—servers, routers, firewalls, and switches—the servers via these elements. This interchange carries an overhead however fast the individual components. If bits of the transmitted data are lost, then retransmissions will take place between sender and whomever made the discovery of the error. Look at Figure 16.6 for a breakdown of *expected times (native)* and *latent (extra)* times.

Thus, we have a built-in overhead of time in addition to the actual time taken by the data to traverse the network medium. Thus, for example, a 1 Mbps link will have an effective speed of less than this nominal figure, the shortfall depending on the speed of the components, how busy they are, and the reliability of the transmission medium, which will dictate the retransmission rate and hence extra latency.

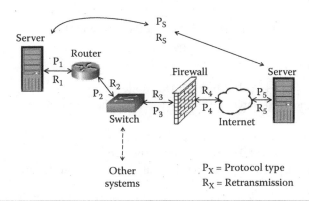

Figure 16.5 Latency: Protocol interchange schematic.

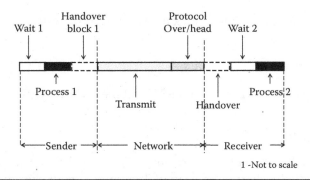

Figure 16.6 Transmission latency: Native and extra.

Note: This data rate I call (and always have) the effective data rate (EDR), which will be the rate *observed* when transmitting data.

Figure 16.6 shows the times involved in a single (no retransmission) transfer of some data from sending server to receiving server via a network, and an explanation of the elements of that transmission are as follows:

WAIT 1: The time that the process has to wait to send the first block of data to the receiving server. This wait time will depend on the utilization ρ of the system.

PROCESS 1: The time for the system to handle the data to be transmitted across the network to the receiving server.

HANDOVER: The transfer of the first block of data across the network interface card (NIC) to the network medium.

After that the subsequent transfers will overlap with the network transfers (hopefully).

TRANSMIT: The transfer of the data across the network and intervening network devices (routers, switches, signal boosters, etc.). This is the *expected time* as given by the simple equation

$$\frac{\text{Message Size} (= \text{Header} + \text{Payload and Trailer})}{\text{Bandwidth}} \quad (16.7)$$

PROTOCOL OVERHEAD: The overhead of node protocol exchanges within the network, essentially the network latency (τ) plus the overheads from other sources (τ_O), discussed above *ad nauseam*.

HANDOVER: The retrieval of the blocks from the network by the NIC and receiving server, the reverse of the HANDOVER at entry to the network.

WAIT 2: The time the actual transfer has to wait, depending on the utilization of the receiving server.

PROCESS 2: The retrieval of the transmitted data.

The total *latency* in the payload transmission is

$$\text{WAIT 1} + \text{PROTOCOL OVERHEAD} + \text{WAIT 2} \quad (16.8)$$

The *expected time* is

$$\text{PROCESS 1} + \text{HANDOVER BLOCK 1} + \text{TRANSMIT} + \text{HANDOVER} + \text{PROCESS 2} \quad (16.9)$$

Effective Data Rate

Effective data rate (EDR) is a common expression in IT, particularly when referring to peripheral devices such as tape. EDR is the measured rate of data transfer, as opposed to the raw speed of the transmitting medium, and the ratio of EDR to rated raw speed as a percentage is a good measure of minimal latency. A tape drive that can process tapes at L inches per second and has a bit density of D bits per inch should handle data at $L \times D$ bps, but it never does because of various things, including start, stop, pause, and interblock gaps.

Reference 3 below shows figures for the EDR of network transmissions as a percentage of bandwidth (raw speed), and illustrates that it varies from 21.43% for 64-byte packets to 95.66% for 1500-byte packets. This is because the header and other overheads are fixed and form a bigger percentage of the packet for small payloads than for larger ones (see table on p. 11 of reference 3).

> **Note**: The definition of *latency* from the *Shorter Oxford Dictionary* (1988) is reproduced below:
>
> > *Latent*: Hidden, concealed; present or existing but not manifest, exhibited, or developed.
> > *Latency*: The condition or quality of being latent.
>
> This is why I have called the added latency extra, meaning it isn't always there.

Reference 3 cites the definition of latency as

> network latency of packets is the delay from the time of the start of the packet transmission to the time of the end of packet reception at the receiver host.

The reference also points out that other definitions are the same, except they specify the end time to be the start of packet reception and not the end. In addition, the following delay (latency) areas are highlighted (and explained in some detail):

- Network interface card (NIC)
- Network processing (firewall, routers, and other nodes)
- Signal propagation delay (the time the signal takes to travel the physical medium)
- Inherent router and switch delay
- Queuing delay (wait time at any service point)

Measuring Latency

Latency is initially of academic interest if the end users' SLA is being fulfilled, especially with respect to response time and throughput. However, its measurement may well be needed if things start to go astray and an understanding of slow parts of a network forms part of its visibility.

Ping Method: The *ping* utility can serve as a quick and simple tool to measure latency—how long it takes one packet to get from start point to end point—and latency information is reported directly by ping itself:

10 packets transmitted, 10 received, 0% packet loss, time 1756 ms
Ping times are roughly proportional to distance traveled.

Measuring Latency with the Ping Utility
http://homepage.smc.edu/morgan_david/cs70/assignments/ping-latency.htm

However, see the following paper for a warning about its use in studying Internet latency:

The Story of the PING Program
http://ftp.arl.army.mil/~mike/ping.html

Monitors: Various application performance monitors (APMs) give latencies, normally in the form of a response time, for a total application *journey* (normally a transaction or query) and sometimes for individual elements of that journey—CPU, storage I/O, network, and possibly other elements.

Latency: Summary

I have agreed with common usage of the word *latency*, but added the rider that it should be dealt with in (at least) two parts—the short-term unchangeable latency (*native* latency) and the possible additional latency (*extra* latency). In general, you can do little about native latency without significant change, and so concentrating on the elements of the extra latency can bear fruit in terms of enhancing performance.

> **Note**: Trying to reduce an overall latency of 4 s to 2 s is impossible if the *native* latency is 2.5 s, so your efforts would be better concentrated on the 1.5 s *extra* latency, pending upgrades or acceleration techniques. You are unlikely to attend to this unless you understand the split of latency I have been talking about and plan to tackle each component.

Monitoring Tools: To take two examples, Paessler's PRTG Network Monitor measures latency in two ways:

- By use of ping (see warning above about ping)
- The quality of service (QoS) sensor, which determines packet delay, packet loss, duplicate packets, and jitter by sending Universal Datagram Protocol (UDP) packets between two computers in your network.

Network Latency: Improving Network Performance with PRTG's Network Latency Test
https://www.paessler.com/network_latency

ExtraHop (www.extrahop.com) monitor network traffic at the *wire level*, that is, at level L2 and onward up to L7 of the seven-layer model. This minutiae enables them to do what they call real-user monitoring (RUM), which includes latency and other response time delays. There is also a lot on analysis work that can be done and information gained from working at this level of data collection. See a more detailed ExtraHop discussion under "Network Performance Tools" in Chapter 8 plus a reference to wire data.

ExtraHop Drives Customer Engagement with End-to-End Real-User Monitoring
http://www.extrahop.com/post/press-releases/extrahop-offers-free-real-user-monitoring/

The link below is to a useful Cisco document about latency reduction and areas where latency is most prominent.

Design Best Practices for Latency Optimization
https://www.cisco.com/application/pdf/en/us/guest/netsol/ns407/c654/ccmigration_09186a008091d542.pdf

A valuable figure in the above reference (Figure 2) gives details of network latency *issues* and *possible solutions* in these areas, as well as monitoring suggestions for

- Application layer, application, OS, and so forth
- Transaction layer
- Network layer, security, encryption, and TCP/IP overhead
- Interface layer, buffering, and fragmentation

This paper is well worth a perusal.

Empirical Analysis: Minseok Kwon, in reference 4 at the end of this section, likens the distribution of latency times in various networks (including clouds) to roughly following a Rayleigh distribution with a narrow spread and a displacement along the *x*-axis.

For the record, a Rayleigh distribution is described by the following probability density function (pdf: see Appendix I). For the initiated, look at it; for the uninitiated, just ignore it.

$$\frac{x}{\sigma^2} e^{x^2/2\sigma^2} \quad x \geq 0 \tag{16.10}$$

where σ denotes the shape of the curve (basically how wide or narrow it is) and *x* moves the distribution along the *x*-axis. The same curve is used in software development stages to measure effort in them.

> In summary, *my* (breakdown) *definition* of latency is the difference between the theoretical time it would take to transmit a certain amount of data (say *t*) and the actual time taken (say *T*). The latency is therefore $(T - t)$ since $T > t$.
>
> In my thinking, the latency is not *t* but $(T - t)$, the overhead. You may call it what you wish as long as you understand what I am saying. See the "'Latency: Corroboration" section below.

Latency: Corroboration

A quote from *High Performance Browser Networking* by Ilya Grigorik supports what I am saying 100%; that is, you need to know *what makes up latency* to be able to reduce it. It can be read online free of charge at
http://chimera.labs.oreilly.com/books/1230000000545

> Latency is the time it takes for a message, or a packet, to travel from its point of origin to the point of destination. That is a simple and useful definition, but it often hides a lot of useful information—every system contains multiple sources, or components, contributing to the overall time it takes for a message to be delivered, and it is important to understand what these components are and what dictates their performance. (Quoted with permission from the author)

The Many Components of Latency
http://chimera.labs.oreilly.com/books/1230000000545/ch01.html#LATENCY_COMPONENTS

References

1. One of these papers puts forward the thesis that bigger router buffers do not necessarily mean better performance—quite interesting. They are both quite advanced, however.

   Part I: Buffer Sizes for Core Routers
   http://klamath.stanford.edu/~nickm/papers/Buffer Sizing.pdf.pdf

   Part II: Control Theory for Buffer Sizing
   http://www.wischik.com/damon/Work/Research/Part-II.pdf

2. There is an interesting paper from ZDnet on improving network performance and one from Wayne Rash, a latency guru:

   10 Ways to Improve Network Performance
   http://www.zdnet.com/article/10-ways-to-improve-network-performance/

   A Sensible Guide to Latency Management [Wayne Rash]
   http://business.comcast.com/docs/default-source/white-papers/cb_latency_whitepaper.pdf?sfvrsn=2
   This guide is a useful look at latency, with examples and describing cause, effect, and reducing it. It also delves into the components of latency that are important for understanding what and how to *fix* it.

3. There is another interesting detailed paper from cpacket (networks) on latency and network performance:

   Pragmatic Network Latency Engineering Fundamental Facts and Analysis
   http://cpacket.com/wp-content/files_mf/introductiontonetworklatencyengineering.pdf

4. *A Tutorial on Network Latency and Its Measurements*
   https://www.network-visibility.com/downloads/cPacket_Whitepaper_Introduction-to-network-latency-engineering.pdf

This document covers not only the technical aspects of latency, but also the consequences of high latency on transmissions such as voice over IP (VoIP), interactive video conferencing, and so on. It also quotes research that suggests that high latency in responses in financial trading can result in financial loss, which takes latency beyond a technical issue. One source talks about losses of millions of dollars for every extra millisecond of latency.

This puts a different perspective on what is acceptable latency in a network, especially when transmissions take place over large distances. Since the speed of light is fixed (at least in our environments) and signals travel at about two-thirds of that speed, distances are of crucial importance.

It is not just the distance and signal speed that cause latency, but the number of hops (e.g., as measured by *traceroute*) that the data goes through, meaning intervening nodes such as routers can add delays.

Future Developments

Network Speeds

There are noises about 100 Gbps networks that, alone, will add nothing to performance unless the supplier and receiver of data can handle it. If not, the receiver will be like a person trying to drink

Table 16.4   Network Bandwidth Needs

Application	Mbps per User
Video streaming	5.0
Telepresence	4.0
WebEx (with video)	1.5
Skype HD video	1.14
Data backup	1.0
Distance learning	1.0
Social networking	0.6
Audio streaming	0.6
Web browsing/streaming	0.4
BYOD usage	0.025

Source: ACG Research 2013.

from a fire hose. Not recommended. As with a wagon train in the old West, the speed of the train is that of the slowest member.

User requirements and usage will dictate what is needed from innovation, and aside from Nielsen's law, more detailed predictions can be gained from the survey below by ACG Research (2013), showing the estimates of business application bandwidth requirements per user (Table 16.4).

This is where the debates about *unified communications* enter the fray—the handling of multiple types of data in network transmission. A point coming out of the survey is the fact that video streaming and voice over IP require a continuous data flow to ensure quality of delivery.*

Everyone knows the irritation of trying to follow poor video delivery from whatever cause. This is not usually the case with normal data or email, where simply getting it from A to B intact is considered success.

ACG Research
http://acgcc.com/

Business Case Analysis
http://acgcc.com/home/business-case-analysis/

Ethernet Alliance "Speed" Road Map

The Ethernet Alliance published a road map in March 2015 that shows the previous developments in Ethernet transfer speeds and estimated future speeds with tentative dates. It indicates alongside these dates whether the speed is current, in development, or a possible future speed. The speeds shown on the *road* imply 1 Tbps sometime after 2020 and 6.4–10 Tbps much after 2020. I would

---

* For UK readers, patchy voice over IP transmission might sound like the late Norman Collier using his faulty microphone in a night club.

take the *delivery* dates with a pinch of salt, as I have never seen a series of dates in predictive documents met.

2015 Ethernet Roadmap
http://www.Ethernetalliance.org/wp-content/uploads/2015/ 03/Ethernet-Roadmap-2sides-Final-5Mar.pdf

> *Note*: The Ethernet Alliance is a global, nonprofit industry consortium of member organizations that are dedicated to the continued success and advancement of Ethernet technologies. Its members include system and component vendors, industry experts, and university and government professionals.

Photonic Chip

In May 2015, IBM announced the successful development of a chip that uses pulses of light to transmit data instead of electrical signals and could revolutionize the connections within parallel processors and between data centers.

The new CMOS chips use four distinct colors of light traveling within an optical fiber, each acting as an independent 25 Gbps optical channel, giving 100 Gbps total bandwidth over a duplex single-mode fiber. IBM says it has demonstrated pushing 100 Gbps over a range up to 2 km, but it is uncertain whether current manufacturing techniques can make these chips as a commercial proposition.

> *WoW*: These attractive speed enhancements should be considered in terms of the whole system's performance. It is pointless having superfast connections if nothing else in the delivery chain can keep up with them. This includes processors, storage, and other elements of connection mechanisms: network interface cards (NICs), photonic chips, routers, and so on. Any IT service delivery system is as fast as its slowest link in the chain.

Storage Speeds

It probably goes without saying that the cost per unit of storage will continue to decrease from the massive cost per kilobyte of the IBM RAMAC of 1956 to the relatively minuscule cost per unit of today's storage. The limiting factor in increasing areal storage density on magnetic surfaces is the physics of it—the magnetization of small areas so they can be detected as separate entities.

> This means that densities of perhaps tens of gigabits per square inch might be achievable.

Whatever happens to densities, there will have to be corresponding increases in delivery speed of data via faster channels, other technologies, such as flash and solid-state storage, and faster cache, all in some cooperating hierarchy or tier. The sheer volume of data today (big data) means that large storage *buckets* such as standard disks still have a place alongside faster, newer technologies to cope with it.

The issue with bigger and bigger disks is the recovery time when data is corrupted. Current redundant array of independent disks (RAID) storage can take up to days to reconstruct data after a failure, and new recovery techniques will have to complement any technology advance. In this case, erasure codes are mooted at a solution to the RAID drawbacks in recovery.

An idea, once mooted in IBM, was to have bits going *down* into the medium instead of being recoded linearly along the surface. I am not sure where this concept is today.

The death of *tapes*, like that of Mark Twain, has been greatly exaggerated, and tapes will probably have a part to play in storage hierarchies for some time to come. My feeling is that no great theoretical breakthrough will announce the solution to all this. It will evolve in its own way (empirically), depending on issues as they arise and are tackled and solved.*

Future Storage Trends and Technologies
http://siim.org/books/archiving/chapter-10-future-storage-trends-technologies

Processor Speed: Futures

There is a lot of speculation on how to get more performance out of systems, ranging from hardware advances to software techniques. Again, as with networks above, requirements will run side by side with technological developments to develop empirical solutions.

The paper referenced below foretells of possible speeds on computing millions of times faster than today:

> University of Utah engineers have taken a step forward in creating the next generation of computers and mobile devices capable of speeds millions of times faster than current machines. The engineers have developed an ultra compact beam splitter—the smallest on record—for dividing light waves into two separate channels of information. The device brings researchers closer to producing silicon photonic chips that compute and shuttle data with light instead of electrons. Electrical and computer engineering associate professor Rajesh Menon and colleagues describe their invention May 18, 2015, in the journal *Nature Photonics*.

Next-Gen Computing: Closing in on Speeds Millions of Times Faster than Current Machines
http://www.scientificcomputing.com/news/2015/05/next-gen-computing-closing-speeds-millions-times-faster-current-machines?et_cid=4580535&et_rid=784345100& location=top

In 2015, we were told about biodegradable *computer chips* made almost entirely of *wood*, which might be the future of circuitry.

Computer Chips Made of Wood Promise Greener Electronics
http://www.infoworld.com/article/2926806/components-processors/computer-chips-made-of-wood-promise-greener-electronics.html?phint=newt%3Dinfoworld_hardware_rpt&phint=i dg_eid%3D36d5d934825c41283fc0e9c68846524d#tk.IFWNLE_nlt_hdwr_2015-05-28

Memory Futures?

> A team of NIST scientists has devised and demonstrated a novel nano-scale memory technology for superconducting computing that could hasten the advent of an urgently awaited, low-energy alternative to power-hungry conventional data centers and supercomputers. (reference 1 below)

---

* This is known as the cloudy crystal ball syndrome.

The increasing problem with installations (made bigger by cloud services) is power consumption. These and other large data center facilities typically run 24 h a day and employ arrays of semiconductor-based servers that require substantial amounts of electricity. They also generate correspondingly substantial amounts of heat—which in turn requires yet more energy to remove from the systems.

A possible replacement technology is superconducting computing (SC), which offers the prospect of moving information without loss over zero-resistance channels. Instead of using semiconductor transistors to switch electronic signals, SC systems employ tiny components called Josephson junctions, an innovation surmised by Brian D. Josephson in 1962 that never found a home in the years immediately following. Experimental work proved that he was right, and Josephson was awarded the 1973 Nobel Prize in Physics for his work.

Josephson junctions operate near absolute zero (in the range 4 K to 10 K [−269°C to −263°C]), dissipate minuscule amounts of energy (less than 10^{-19} J per operation), and can be switched between states at hundreds of billions of times a second (frequencies of gigahertz), compared to a few gigahertz for semiconductor computers.

1. *Hybrid Memory Device for Superconducting Computing (January 23, 2015)*
   http://www.nist.gov/pml/electromagnetics/grp09/hybrid-memory-device-for-superconducting-computing.cfm
2. *What Are Josephson Junctions? How Do They Work?*
   http://www.scientificamerican.com/article/what-are-josephson-juncti/
3. *Josephson Effect* [these are detailed documents]
   http://en.wikipedia.org/wiki/Josephson_effect
   http://en.wikipedia.org/wiki/Pi_Josephson_junction

Other Useful Documents

1. The quotation below comes from an appropriate U.S. Academy of Sciences publication (2011):
   The Future of Computing Performance: Game Over or Next Level?
      International Standard Book Number 13: 978-0-309-15951-7
      International Standard Book Number 10: 0-309-15951-2
      Library of Congress Control Number: 2011923200

The following should have high priority:

- Algorithms that can exploit parallel processing;
- New computing "stacks" (applications, programming languages, compilers, run-time/virtual machines, operating systems, and architectures) that execute parallel rather than sequential programs and that effectively manage software parallelism, hardware parallelism, power, memory, and other resources;
- Portable programming models that allow expert and typical programmers to express parallelism easily and allow software to be efficiently reused on multiple generations of evolving hardware;
- Parallel-computing architectures driven by applications, including enhancements of chip multiprocessors, conventional data parallel architectures, application-specific architectures, and radically different architectures;

- Open interface standards for parallel programming systems that promote cooperation and innovation to accelerate the transition to practical parallel-computing systems; and
- Engineering and computer-science educational programs that incorporate an increased emphasis on parallelism and use a variety of methods and approaches to better prepare students for the types of computing resources that they will encounter in their careers.

The publication discusses limitations on technology, the role of software, and surprise, education in these areas of development.

It also includes an appendix on a history of computer performance and a reprint of Gordon E. Moore's seminal paper "Cramming More Components onto Integrated Circuits."

2. A paper from the Enterprise Strategy Group (ESG) outlines in readable detail the value of contemporary tape, the advances in reliability and lifetime, and the future of tape as a storage medium (using barium ferrite).

The Technical and Operational Values of Barium Ferrite Tape Media
http://www.bitpipe.com/fulfillment/1415829317_906

3. IBM and Fujifilm announced a dense storage tape prototype at the IBM Edge conference, which was held in May 2014 in Las Vegas.

Anticipating a storage crunch spurred by big data, IBM and Fujifilm are advancing the state of the art in magnetic tape with a prototype capable of storing 85.9 billion bits of data per square inch. In an industry standard, linear tape-open (LTO)-size cartridge tape like that could store up to 154 TB of uncompressed data. In May 2014, an LTO version 6 cartridge held 2.5 TB. A terabyte is a trillion bytes, or about 1000 GB.

The announcement seems to extend the life of tape as a backup medium into the foreseeable future on counts of capacity, cost, and energy efficiency.

IBM and Fujifilm Show Super Dense Storage Tape for Big Data Work
http://www.infoworld.com/d/storage/ibm-and-fujifilm-show-super-dense-storage-tape-big-data-work-242846?source=IFWNLE_nlt_storage_2014-05-21

4. There are pundits who dismiss tape as a future storage medium and plump for developments in disk and related storage. Here is one pro-disk article. It mentions helium-filled disk drives as a future option.

The Future of Storage: Disk-Based or Just Discombobulated?
http://www.theregister.co.uk/2014/01/21/discombobulations/?page=1

The real future of performance increases will lie to some extent with the advancing technologies outlined above, but sloppy use of resources and poor coding and program design can swallow up a lot of this bonus performance. Shortly after I joined IBM, large companies were running their business on 256K IBM 370/158s, the standard workhorse in those days. Today, the PC I have has 8 GB of main memory and 500 GB of disk storage and still groans at the seams sometimes.

I realize that there is extra function available today, and this is paid for in extra resource usage, but I do feel that sloppiness and profligacy with those resources have something to do with it. The motto that applies here would seem to be "use it or lose it" with respect to additional resources granted by technological advances, with the rider "respect it" too. Treat the resources as if they were your own money.

Endnote: If you are planning that far ahead, I think it is a matter of "you pay your money and you make your choice."

Chapter 17

Performance-Related Disciplines

Introduction

Why Discipline?

Performance gurus might argue that their vast experience dispenses with the need for discipline and documents as "I carry it all in my head." Therein lies the problem. In my book *High Availability IT Services*, I relate a story from a company that had two first-class database administrators (DBAs). A major outage occurred that was quickly recognized as a database issue. The obvious course of action was to call one of the DBAs. As luck would have it, one was on vacation and the other at a wedding half a continent away.

The author of the article confessed that the company had no sensible documentation or detailed problem determination procedures and no contract with outside agencies for assistance. They were in it up to their necks and took a long time to sort things out. If they had an availability clause in their service level agreement (SLA), it was blown into the middle of next week.

The measurement and management of performance does not only involve the use of monitoring tools and interpretation of resulting data; there are other factors that can impact performance. One of them is the SLA, which will almost certainly demand some form of performance guarantee and change management that has the potential to either improve performance or kill it stone dead.

SLAs are discussed in some detail next, but in the final count, it is the requirements of the organization that will dictate the content, not the references given. They will act as reminders of areas to be considered for inclusion, but not a prescriptive set of commands.

Content

Not every technique covered here is mandatory, but they may be useful in some situations where blind faith in one person's ability is not the answer to a pressing issue.

- Service level agreements (SLAs)
- Project definition workshops (PDWs)

- Change management
- War room
- Delphi technique

Service Level Agreements

SLA Introduction

In the days before IT, computing was done in the data processing department by gurus with little or no contact with the business users. The primary use of the systems was in accounting, and very often, the DP manager reported to the finance director. As more applications were put on the system, it often became necessary to give priority to certain applications at peak times, and this was done without reference to the users.

As chargeback became more prevalent, users began to ask what they were getting for their money and would make certain demands about the service they wanted to receive. This developed into the idea of agreements about levels of service, which became known as service level agreements (SLAs).

A service level agreement is a document drawn up between the organization's IT service providers and representatives of the business users. The agreement covers the levels of service needed by the users. Often, there will be SLAs for individual applications whose requirements differ from those of other applications; for example, order entry may demand a higher level of service than the HR application.

The link below takes you to an excellent reference to the many aspects of providing a service and should prove useful to anyone seriously involved in IT service provision.

Service Management Toolkit
http://its.ucsc.edu/itsm/index.html

We will now examine the reasons why SLAs are a good thing for IT accounts.

SLA Metrics

> **WoW**: The first thing to note here is that it is easy to get confused when reading about metrics, particularly in academic texts and presentations. In the main, they talk about metrics to assess performance of systems with a view to comparing systems, and there is lots of information about means and averages plus warnings about accuracy, reproducibility, and so on. This is fine, but when you are talking about quality of service (QoS) for IT business systems, the emphasis is different, as we shall see.

Performance Metrics Environment

All this sounds very complex, and it probably is, but perhaps Figure 17.1, which shows the whole environment, will make it clearer. There are a number of *players* in the performance game, as the diagram shows; many of them are part of a chain of resources through which units of work (transaction, email, etc.) must pass.

Metrics are normally numbers that *quantify* the quality of service (QoS) over and above words like *poor*, *average*, *good*, and *excellent*. There are basically five sets of system metrics and application that are usually of interest:

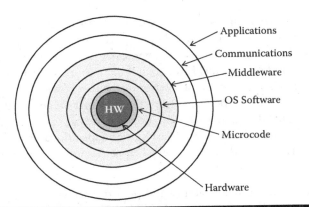

Figure 17.1 Performance monitoring metrics environment.

1. Internal metrics for operational people within an organization. These can be quite detailed and used for operational and capacity planning purposes.
2. Summary or *single-sheet* metrics for IT management to assess QoS delivered internally.
3. Metrics required by an SLA with internal users, often business users.
4. Metrics required by an organization from a cloud or other third-party SLA running IT on their behalf.
5. Application or middleware metrics that indicate performance in user terms.

Of course, they are not limited to performance management, but that is what we are mainly concerned with here. The metrics will also be organization dependent, but I will present a representative set for each category, A–E.

> *Note*: The metrics listed here do not imply there are no others—we simply do not cover them in this book. Measurements like *availability, recovery times, security* metrics, and others are all important in defining QoS.

A: Internal Metrics

Internal data collected by operating and middleware systems themselves and by software packages like IBM Tivoli, BMC, and SolarWinds,* when printed out, can sink a small battleship, so even for operational staff these need some sort of structure to give relevant *information* from the mass of *data*. The most important data is that which tells us of a serious situation or foretells of a possible one in the future.

Hardware engineers often run tests on equipment to detect *soft* errors, that is, those which are recovered from but may become *hard* (nonrecoverable) errors in the near future. Action is then taken to schedule maintenance or replacement of the ailing hardware.

A similar philosophy can be adopted for performance by initially reporting mainly on systems and subsystems (like storage area network [SANs] and just a bunch of disks [JBODs]) that exceed or are close to the baseline limits set for them. If an organization has 300 servers and 2000 disks, it makes no sense to lump them all in the same report with servers and disks that are close to the

---

* These are simply examples and not recommendations.

knee of the performance curve. This is called *exception reporting*, but it does not exclude *recording* everything ready for future analysis if required (disk space is cheap enough to do this).

An obvious fact is that if you don't record it, you can't report it, so recording can be done on a wide basis for systems and subsystems. If we are talking performance, there are parameters that are specific to devices and some that are of interest to the user. I will leave the latter to category C, but bear in mind they must be derivable from the information collected, or capable of being calculated, in data collected during normal operation of systems.

There are metrics that are for immediate consumption (operational) and some not for immediate consumption (trends and planning). I've called these A1 and A2, respectively, and tabulated them below:

A1: Factors that show operational stability and performance within baseline limits set at the design stage. These include those shown in Table 17.1.

A2: Factors that are meant to show trends, warn of impending doom, and provide information for capacity management and planning. These include those shown in Table 17.2:

Table 17.1 System Metrics: Operational

Resource	Metric	Comment
Processor	*Utilization* • Baseline • Average • Peak • Peak to average • I/O wait time • Idle time	These and other numbers will give IT a feel for how the system is performing. However, there should still be an awareness of what the end user sees as the final arbiter. I/O wait is indicative of resources serving the processor not keeping up. Idle time is just having nothing to do.
Channel/ connection	As above	It is useful to have a feel for the balance between the work rate of the processor and the disks to see if their connection mechanism is in balance.
Disk	*Utilization* • I/O rate • Response time characteristics • Soft errors • As above	
Storage capacity	*Capacity* • Baseline • Used	This has more than a physical dimension. Fragmentation of files and databases can cause performance issues, and attention should be paid at this level.
Network	• Bandwidth line/link utilization at various speeds • Throughput: frames etc./ second • Latency (delays) • Jitter • Error rates	Tools, such as wire data analyzers, will be needed for detailed network information.

Table 17.2 System Metrics: Trends and Planning

Resource	Metric	Comment
Processor	*Utilization* • Baseline • Growth over a period • "Panic" level	In essence, this yields information on real growth rate and can be used to predict when saturation might be reached, which means upgrades.
Network	*Used bandwidth* • Baseline capacity • Average used • Peak usage • Growth pattern • Link quality (retries)	http://en.wikipedia.org/wiki/Network_performance
Network processors	*Recorded performance characteristics; vary by vendor*	The routers, switches, and other devices on network links are sources of latency or delays and need to be monitored.
Disk usage	*Used capacity* • Baseline capacity	
	I/O rates • Baseline • Average • Peak	
Paging/memory	*Page rates/memory utilization*	Basically, looking for excessive rates (thrashing), which may indicate memory shortages. It is desirable to run V = R, that is, have enough real storage to avoid paging except for occasional situations.

B: Internal Management Metrics

This really depends on what management wants to see (in the performance context), but a base would be the following:

■ Report on exceptions, for example, high utilizations shown against baselines
■ Projections as to possible upgrade paths
■ Percentile response times against SLA specifications

C: Internal SLA Metrics

Internal here means within the organization involved.

■ Percentile response times by application
■ Available service hours (*not* availability percentage)
■ Other performance items specified in the SLAs

The following links show two sets of report portfolios that present pictorial views of various reports that cover categories C and D:

CA Unified Infrastructure Management Gallery
http://www.ca.com/us/lpg/ca-uim-gallery.aspx

Halcyon SLA Reporting Sheets
http://www.halcyonsoftware.com/suites/advanced-reporting-suite/Halcyon%20SLA%20
Statistics%20-%20Monthly%20Service%20Report.pdf

Halcyon Performance Reporting Sheets
http://www.halcyonsoftware.com/suites/advanced-reporting-suite/Halcyon%20Performance%
20Statistics.pdf

D: External SLA Metrics

External metrics are those provided by an outside agency that is running some or all of an organization's computing, normally a cloud facility. In such cases, the organization is not primarily interested in detailed internal metrics of the systems that run its business applications, but some overall numbers that allow it to assess the QoS it is receiving.

The references provided below are detailed and cover aspects of provided services other than performance, such as security, availability, data integrity, and roles and responsibilities. In this section, we are mainly interested in the performance aspects of the service, which can then be relayed in total or in summary to the business end users in normal SLA reporting style.

This, however, may present a problem in reconciling the information from the cloud service provider and that observed by the end users in the organization. The provider may report an availability of the service of X%, which he claims represents an outage of, say, 22 min. "Nonsense," say the users, "we were out for over an hour on two successive days." This is the old argument about whose viewpoint you believe, how it was measured, and it is vital that the organization and provider (and its subproviders) thrash this aspect out at the very beginning.

Some organizations may want to know how their applications are distributed across virtual machines (VMs) and when they change. This may be of interest in correlating incidents or events with changes to the VM configurations, which will happen, for example, when there is a physical outage at the service data center. In such cases, reconfiguration across other physical and VMs may be required.

In short, the organization should ask itself, "If this cloud service were an airplane, would I fly in it'?" This means doing your homework on your requirements versus service offered.

Service Level Agreements in the Cloud: Who Cares? [good introduction, but scope is wider than just performance]
http://www.wired.com/2011/12/service-level-agreements-in-the-cloud-who-cares/

Practical Guide to Cloud Service Level Agreements Version 1 [Cloud Standards Customer Council]
http://www.cloud-council.org/2012_Practical_Guide_to_Cloud_SLAs.pdf

Cloud Service Level Agreement Standardisation Guidelines [Digital Agenda for Europe]
https://ec.europa.eu/digital-agenda/en/news/cloud-service-level-agreement-standardisation-guidelines

General Metrics Reference: You can wallow in 100 different and often esoteric metrics in the paper by Nicholas Spanos, Computer Aid, Inc. Some are business oriented, others IT facing.

IT metrics listed are

- Infrastructure incidents (6 metrics)
- Infrastructure availability (2 metrics)
- Infrastructure utilization and performance (6 metrics)
- Application problems (7 metrics)
- Application availability (2 metrics)
- Application utilization and performance (2 metrics)
- Change management (16 metrics)

There are then the remaining metrics, which are related to staffing, finance, and value delivery, and there are submetrics within these categories. It can be a useful document to use as a *picking list* for your particular needs, bearing in mind it is not 100% comprehensive, but certainly more than one can carry in one's head.

100 IT Performance Metrics
http://www.compaid.com/caiinternet/ezine/Spanos-Metrics.pdf

E: Application Metrics

These numbers are the ones that will mean something to the *business end users* since most of the data discussed above is of no interest to them in that form. Some things need to be stressed up front about this area of metrics:

1. There are as many of them as there are application types.
2. The metrics are formulated in styles suited to the application type.
3. They are not, as a rule, generated by the operating systems.*
4. They are usually monitored by tools from the vendor or vendor agents.
5. They should produce end user–friendly information.
6. They will fight shy of resource utilizations, paging rates, and the like, but concentrate on business work units processed per unit time—emails, queries, and transactions per shift for a particular business application. I think you get the drift of this argument.

Most commercial off-the-shelf (COTS) application vendors provide some kind of application performance statistics that can often be tailored for SLA and management reporting.

Middleware and database products can be monitored as well as coded applications, say, payroll and together provide a view of how well or badly the computer system is handling them. If we take a look at some of the application and middleware types, it will become clear why the whole gamut of them is not covered in this book. They are, as they say, left as an exercise for the reader. Modern applications and support often cover

- Transaction processing (online transaction processing [OLTP])
- Database processing and relational and other flavors, such as Information Management System (IMS) or "big data"

---

* Although some OS do. For example, varieties of IBM Multiple Virtual Storage (MVS) understand Customer Information Control System (CICS) and its transactions and other IBM products and can provide data about their activities. In general, though, they do not know much about the applications running under their control.

- "Link" software such as Citrix, DNS, NFS, FTP, replication, and firewalls
- Virtual machines (VMs)
- Email
- Query tools
- Office applications (text, spreadsheets, graphics, etc.)

The main interest in all these is

- How fast do they do it (time to complete an action—response time)
- How many do they do in unit time (throughput)

The numbers for these will vary across the application types where a complex query giving a response in 5 min is considered lightning fast, whereas a transaction response time of 5 s is considered appalling. Previously, it may have been the case that the complex query would take a week, having to go to a department that carried all the necessary data to answer it.

Again, these numbers depend on your point of view and expectations.

Using Performance Metrics

Mission: Metrics are data. They must be turned into meaningful information and actions planned and executed to deal with out-of-line situations (which assumes you have a baselines to see if you are out of line).

How Do We Measure Them?

Measurements of performance metrics can be done in one of four ways:

- Don't bother or just make a guess: not recommended
- Use operating system internal tools: needs some internal skills
- Use a vendor software tool: easier, but can be expensive or overkill
- Use a combination of the last two items: reasonable option

Exactly how and what is measured is organization dependent and will be driven by any SLAs in force. The basic idea is to see how hard the IT resources are working and make sure they don't collapse under the strain.

What Do We Do with Them?

WoW: A customer I dealt with, ca. 1985, had a performance person in IT. His office wall was covered with multicolored charts of *anything* versus *everything* plotted on them. One day I plucked up courage and asked him what they all meant (the "so what" test). He confessed he wasn't really sure, although we both agreed they were very beautiful and covered the ugly wall of his office nicely. This is a true story—only the name of the man has been left out, as I can't afford to fight a libel case.

Since the beginning of (IT) time, men have sought to show exactly how systems were performing using data on a single sheet of paper. This has proved elusive and other means have been established to achieve the aim of seeing performance "at a glance." This involves setting *baselines* for what is good and bad in the performance arena.

The main driver for setting baselines is the service level agreement (SLA) and their expression in terms that meet the SLA requirements. To take a simple example, an SLA might ask for certain performance overall, but specify that reasonable performance must be delivered at certain peak times.

For a dedicated server environment, this may mean normally running the CPU at, say, 40% average utilization so that it can handle an increased load (say 75%) without excessive response times caused by high CPU utilizations.

A similar requirement may be enshrined in an SLA for a cloud service provider (and its sub-providers). In such cases, the actual detailed performance numbers may be of little interest to the organization—only the final outcome in terms of meeting the users' SLAs. The picture is clouded somewhat when you realize that there are web customers to be catered to, and in general, SLAs aren't normally agreed on between supplier and customer where the classical IT world meets the digital world.

Performance Visualization

Most results will provide insight into performance if presented in graphical format,* either internally or from the cloud service provider. In addition, alerts should be raised when certain performance exceptions occur, reporting on an exception basis instead of reporting on everything: "server 1 OK, server 2 OK, ... server 101 OK, ..." This is counterproductive; reporting "servers 3, 7, and 9 exceed baseline limits" gives far better insight into performance status and reduces root cause analysis (RCA) time.

It is probably far more informative to report results by application server, for example, *invoicing server* rather than *server 6 bd007*.

This does not mean that apparently unimportant data isn't collected or is discarded after a day or so. The mantra is *collect everything, use what you need*. This data may be of retrospective use in RCA of deeper problems, to understand them and prevent recurrence. The data is almost certain to be of some use in capacity planning, management in tracking organic growth, and possibly other retrospective needs.

Figures 17.2 and 17.3 show ways of presenting data in forms far more useful than tables and lists. One way of looking at the data at the physical resource level is shown in a radar chart (sometimes called a Kiviat chart).

The "panic" line (-------) is the limit of resource utilization before the system starts to creak and the utilization causes large increases in response time.

Figure 17.3 shows a real system where everything is not perfectly balanced as it is in Figure 17.2. We observe wait times for CPU, channels, and disk I/O, with scales on each axis to match the range of numbers expected for that entity.

Commercial performance packages have their own ways of displaying data that are often, to my simple mind, overelaborate and based on the simpler numbers you and I can get from system commands anyway. However, such packages have merit in the way they can manipulate data to order when you carry out investigations into performance and other issues.

(I'm afraid you will have to consult the relevant books to learn how to do these things.)

---

* Remember, a picture is worth a thousand words.

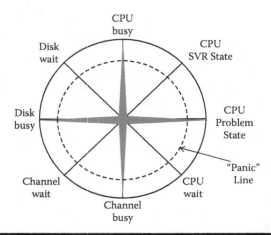

Figure 17.2   Balanced system: Kiviat or radar chart. SVR = server.

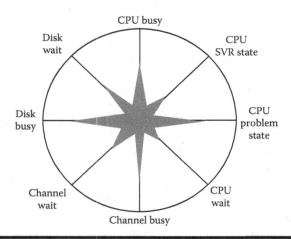

Figure 17.3   Real system: Kiviat or radar chart.

Cloud Scenario

Figure 17.4 shows the chronology of computing from the dedicated, organization-owned servers through the private cloud phase to the public and hybrid cloud phases. This undoubtedly has benefits, but plays havoc with the idea of an SLA, as there are many new fingers in the IT pie.

SLAs and the Cloud

The cloud SLA arena is a minefield of information, misinformation, and well-meaning checklists and standards. Remember that an SLA is exactly what you and your organization want it to be (Humpty Dumpty quote). There is a place, however, for the checklists and guidelines as an *aide-mémoire* in the development of SLAs, like the reminder "don't forget your clean handkerchief when you go out." This is valuable information (unless you don't have a nose).

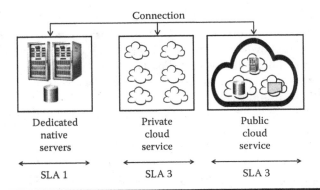

Figure 17.4 Cloud scenario spectrum.

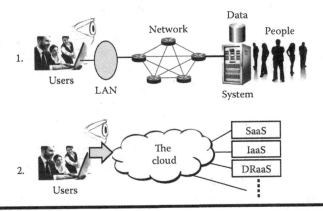

Figure 17.5 SLAs: classical vs. cloud viewpoint.

Despite this, I have included references to several sites that contain guidance and checklists on SLAs for cloud services, rather like an online catalog, for you to choose from to suit your personal cloud SLAs. I have tried here to sift and categorize the base differences and hope that this treatment and a perusal of the supporting references will suffice in helping your organization with SLAs in this new environment.

The main difference between a standard SLA with in-house IT and an SLA for a cloud service is that there are several different cloud services: infrastructure as a service (IaaS), desktop as a service (DaaS), software as a service (SaaS), disaster recovery as a service (DRaaS), and so on. Another difference is the accessibility of IT personnel to kick when things go wrong, and this is where a cloud service SLA needs to be watertight. Figure 17.5 illustrates the viewpoints of the end user when having an application service delivered by an internal IT facility and that delivered from the cloud.

A hybrid cloud is a cloud computing environment in which an organization provides and manages some IT resources in-house and has others provided externally.

Dedicated servers: The usual environment that is normally designed, implemented, and operated by the organization itself. Vanilla SLAs will apply, and this environment is business as usual.

Private cloud: The cloud environment that is normally operated by the organization itself, which maintains ultimate control. Such a cloud comprises a set of resources (hardware, networking, storage, etc.) owned and often operated by an organization for its own purposes. It can be created and managed by a third party, but it is still dedicated to that organization and often makes use of automated operations for predictability, and hence ability, to meet SLAs in such an environment.

Cloud SLAs will apply, which include *nested* SLAs with any outside suppliers of resources to the primary cloud service provider.

Public cloud: The cloud environment that is normally operated by the outside organization (third party) itself, which maintains ultimate control but is regulated by cloud SLAs from the organization using the cloud service. Such a cloud setup of resources (hardware, etc., as above) is owned and operated by the third party, who offers it as a service to other companies. This is normally done on a *pay for what you use* basis, rather like electricity from a utility company. A *hybrid cloud* is a mix of public and private clouds.

To get an indication of how one can check the cloud vendors, SLA can be found in the reference "A Practical Guide to Cloud SLAs" below.

One benefit of such an environment is the elasticity it offers in resource availability to organizations where the load is unpredictable or has unexpected high resource requirements at certain times. In the old dedicated server environment, this sort of workload would need a system big enough to handle the peaks, which might be rare but important to satisfy.

SLAs in these cases will need to be agreed on with the primary supplier, who may have to negotiate further SLAs with others who supply him with resources or services.

The public cloud is a shared environment, so security will feature largely in any SLAs, alongside performance, availability, and so on.

It is normal to connect these environments if they have any commonality, but what to feature where is an exercise in itself.

A Practical Guide to Cloud SLAs
http://www.cloud-council.org/2012_Practical_Guide_to_Cloud_SLAs.pdf

The guide referenced above is from the Cloud Standards Customer Council, which is "an end user advocacy group dedicated to accelerating cloud's successful adoption, and drilling down into the standards, security and interoperability issues surrounding the transition to the cloud" (from their website).

http://www.cloud-council.org/

On this site, under "Resource Hub" you will find a number of useful documents that may well fit your requirements and settle any queries you may have.

A guide to check out the quality of a cloud suppler and the offered environment can be found at

Guidance on Cloud Computing
http://www.nen.gov.uk/wp-content/uploads/2014/09/Guidance-on-cloud-computing.png

Aside on Viewpoints

Viewpoints is a useful concept to grasp in the IT world. It is a representation of something connected with IT that is tailored to the audience it addresses and excludes detail of no interest to that audience. In presenting an IT topic, for example, a development proposal, the proposer might need to construct several viewpoints for the various stakeholders involved.

Consider a proposal to develop a high-availability system for an organization to run a new key application. The *CEO* will be interested in the flow of the work and where the benefits lie, for example, faster production of invoices or better stock control. The *operations manager* will be interested in the configuration, volumes, feeds and speeds, monitoring and maintenance, and so on. The *software manager* will be concerned with the various layers of software, skill gaps to support it, and possibly development requirements. *Users* will want yet another view of the system and its functions, and so on.

This will probably necessitate different diagrams with different descriptions aimed at different people, that is, multiple viewpoints.

Figure 17.5 shows the viewpoints of their delivery system seen by the users, and this will color their thinking about what needs to be included in an SLA, be it a normal (classical) one or a cloud version. They will be familiar with the components of a normal system (even if they don't understand them) and can talk to internal staff about what they need.

Multilayer SLAs

In the cloud environment, they only see what has been sold to them as a cloud with certain services on tap. What happens then? The simple solution is to layer the SLA so that users talk to internal IT staff, who then interpret the requirements and translate them into a cloud-oriented SLA. If the business users talk to the cloud vendor, the result could be a disaster waiting to happen.

This is what I term the *three-layer model*. If the cloud vendor uses subcontractors, he must distill the SLA to specify their responsibilities. Figure 17.6 illustrates the dilemma of multiparty SLA agreements using a classic set of diagrams. It could become a multilayer issue if the cloud vendor uses subcontractors for certain services. The essence of it is to make sure all parties understand the SLA and are *all reading the same page of the book.*

1. What the user said he wanted
2. How IT understood it
3. How it was specified for the cloud vendor
4. How the cloud vendor understood it
5. How it was passed to subcontractors
6. How it was documented

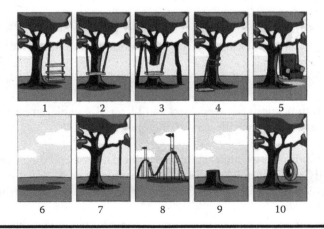

Figure 17.6 Three-layer cloud SLA model.

7. How it was implemented
8. How it was billed
9. How it was supported
10. What the users really wanted

SLA: Availability and Quality of Service

Depending on how an SLA is phrased, it is possible for its terms to be met but the quality of the service delivered not what was expected. For example, a service might comfortably meet its target for availability, but with poor or erratic response times, giving an uneven and substandard quality of service. Performance and response time variations might be caused by unexpected increases in the numbers of users' unforeseen peak loads, which were not reflected in the drawing up of the SLA then in force.

If these increases are deemed to be permanent, the existing SLA should either be *ignored* or *renegotiated* by both sides. I have seen "undeclared" extra users affect a system considerably.

Elements of SLAs

The following are things to consider and, where appropriate, include in an SLA. They are in no particular order and not necessarily complete:

■ Background and brief description of the application and its importance, that is, why it needs the requested level of service.
■ Parties to the agreement—IT and user.
■ Roles and responsibilities.
■ Current system workload and capacity.
■ Growth forecasts for the application.
■ Workload pattern forecasts, for example, changes in transaction mixes toward the heavier transactions.
■ Measurement methods for SLA reporting—hours of service, uptime, response times, and so forth. This can get quite involved with the 90th percentile and so on. If you are not sure about this topic, take advice.
■ *Response times* and deadlines, for example, for batch reports.
■ Business *security* requirements.
■ Recovery times and status of recovered data (recovery time objective [RTO], etc.).
■ Charging mechanism, for example, by transaction, CPU second, disk occupancy, lines printed, and so forth.
■ Service level metrics, that is, what is to be measured and why.
■ Service level reporting, for example, *availability* for IT and for users.
■ Ongoing communications between users and IT on SLA achievements and changes.
■ User compensation for nonachievement of targets by IT.
■ User and IT staff training.
■ User responsibilities, for example, not deleting the database and then demanding immediate recovery, notifying IT of unusual working, for example, weekends or evenings.
■ Any exclusions, for example, acts of God, floods, and so forth, unless these are covered by a disaster recovery plan.
■ Another exclusion might say, "Response times cannot be guaranteed during quarter, half-year, and year-end processing when these workloads are superimposed on the normal workload."

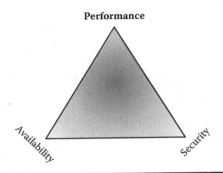

Figure 17.7 Service level agreement key metrics triangle.

■ The term of the agreement, for example, 9 months when the SLA will be either revised or renegotiated. SLAs have a "sell by date," especially in a volatile business environment.

There can be many elements of service in an SLA, but three are important in designing and maintaining high availability (obviously), performance (logical outages), and in modern times, security, illustrated in Figure 17.7 as an *aide-mémoire*. These, in my view, are the major showstoppers in IT, hence my first book *High Availability IT Services* (CRC Press).

https://www.crcpress.com/High-Availability-IT-Services/Critchley/9781482255904

The following are expansions of some SLA specifics:

1. *Hours of service* for the application access. This can range from 9:00 a.m. to 5:00 p.m. 5 days a week to 24 h a day, 365 days a year. The hours of service put constraints on certain activities, such as backup, scheduling maintenance, and the duration of housekeeping activities. It is necessary for the non–prime shift activities (usually overnight batch) to complete before the start of the prime shift user activity.
2. The *actual availability* of the system during those hours of service. If it is 100%, then availability equals hours of service divided by hours of service.
3. *Response times* for application transactions or elapsed time for batch and reporting applications. Interactive transactions usually have a response time requirement phrased something like "the application will, at peak times, deliver 90% of the transactions within 2 s." This is called a 90th percentile.
4. *Security requirements*. This implies setting up the system to block unauthorized access to the system, the application, and the associated data. It often means that attempts at unauthorized access should be logged and kept for audit and other reporting.
5. *Advance notification* to users of planned downtime, for example, hardware or software upgrades and new installations, and immediate notification of unplanned downtime.

Note: Poor *system performance* can often present a logical outage, especially in Internet applications, such as online finance. Studies have shown that a user's "patience span" in browsing websites is about 7 s, which, in terms of the general public, means he or she will not use the system if the response time is longer than this or is very erratic. The service is then effectively unavailable for its purpose.

Types of SLA

An SLA is usually related to a business function and its specific requirements for service. A single SLA does not normally cover a whole business since this might prove expensive and, in the case of minor functions, unnecessary. Examples of SLA types are shown below:

1. Production systems that are 24/7. Planned downtime notification is needed.
2. Systems that are normally available for extended working hours, say, 6:00 a.m. to 9:00 p.m. Planned downtime notification is needed.
3. Systems that are available during normal working hours but can be taken down after hours without official notice.
4. Systems that can be taken down during working hours with 1 or 2 h notice.
5. Systems that can be taken down with little or no notice.
6. Systems that can be taken down immediately if the resource they use is needed for the more important system. An example is a power outage where minimal power is available and is devoted to the most important systems.

Notifications here should form part of the *change management* procedures.

Potential Business Benefits of SLAs

Some of the potential benefits of an SLA can be classified under "business benefits" and "IT benefits."

- Stable production environment
- Consistent response times
- Resilience, especially for mission-critical work
- Improved quality of service
- Competitive edge

Potential IT Benefits

- Skills development
- Increased productivity
- Helps IT to be viewed as a benefit, not just an overhead

Reasons for SLAs*

1. Define performance levels required	58%
2. Measure service level provided	52%
3. Measure customer satisfaction	35%
4. Set and manage customer and user expectations	34%
5. Expand services	30%

---

* *Source:* Lucent Technologies (acquired by Alcatel in 2006).

Cloud Supplier SLAs

It may appear at first sight that an SLA is an SLA whichever supplier you choose. I am not sure. There are a number of suppliers in this area:

- Amazon C 2
- Google App Engine
- Microsoft Azure
- Slice Host
- Prgmr
- Linode
- Heroku
- GoGrid
- Rackspace

If you wish to transfer an existing cloud SLA from one supplier to another,* you should understand the characteristics of their services. For example, the web application languages used vary across supplier and include

- PHP
- .NET
- Java
- Python
- Ruby

It is also useful to understand what resource monitoring the supplier has, and what usage scenarios and metrics are on offer, so that the output can match your SLA reporting requirements. It's no good if the cloud vendor speaks Japanese and you only understand English.

Cloud SLA References

Getting Stared with Cloud Computing (DZone Refcardz)
http://refcardz.dzone.com/refcardz/getting-started-cloud

Standardisation Guidelines for Cloud Computing Service Level Agreements Developed by Industry
http://www.out-law.com/en/articles/2014/june/standardisation-guidelines-for-cloud-computing-service-level-agreements-developed-by-industry/

Practical Guide to Cloud Service Level Agreements Version 1.0
http://www.cloudstandardscustomercouncil.org/2012_Practical_Guide_to_Cloud_SLAs.pdf

Service Level Agreements in the Cloud: Who Cares?
http://www.wired.com/2011/12/service-level-agreements-in-the-cloud-who-cares/

Cloud Service Level Agreement Standardisation Guidelines
http://ec.europa.eu/digital-agenda/en/news/cloud-service-level-agreement-standardisation-guidelines

---

* Or even from a dedicated (noncloud, nonvirtual) environment, a much trickier proposition.

Managing Cloud Service Provisioning and SLA Enforcement via Holistic Monitoring Techniques [dissertation]
http://www.infosys.tuwien.ac.at/staff/vincent/pub/Emeakaroha_thesis.pdf

Performance Management: The Project*

In an IBM paper (other than the one referenced below), Joseph Gulla writes,

> Have you ever noticed there are two basic kinds of IT projects? The first is a project in name only. It has executive interest but not true support. It has a team, but its members have other jobs as well. The project has a goal but it might not be firm or it changes in an unmanaged way. Let's call them "self-styled projects."
>
> The second category is the formal project with funding, executive support, dedicated resources, deadlines and serious consequences for failure. These are the "real projects."

Start-Up and Design Phase

There is a diagram I used to use to illustrate the *cost of correcting errors* in software development and other projects. It was a curve that showed rapidly increasing costs involved in correcting problems as the project proceeded. The curve was used to demonstrate that *well begun is half done'* and getting the project out of a hole after much digging became a massive task.

That is why the start-up and design phase is singled out here for attention. Most of what follows can be used in other projects apart from high availability (HA). I have found that using the time notation *P-w*, where *P* is production day and *w* the number of weeks before *P* that a particular activity should start, is a useful header to documented project activity. It focuses the mind quite effectively. Thus, *P-12* is an activity due 12 weeks (3 months) before production date.

This is a documentation method I find very useful, particularly with fellow IT people who have an aversion to calendars and clocks.

Management Flow

Figure 17.8 shows the activity flow from concept, through design, and onto implementation and operation. It is roughly chronological and suggests tools and techniques that might be employed in this sequence of activities.

Design and Start-Up

As I said before, the use of these tools is not prescriptive or mandatory, but knowledge of the tools and techniques can generate synergy of thinking among participants of Delphi, project definition workshops (PDWs), and so forth. The process should start with the need, which is normally a business request for a new or modified service.

---

* See "Seven Reasons Why Projects Fail" by Joseph Gulla (ex-IBM, now Alazar Press), http://www.ibmsystems-mag.com/mainframe/tipstechniques/applicationdevelopment/project_pitfalls/.

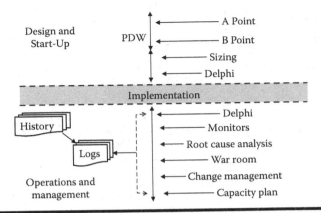

Figure 17.8   Design and operation: flow of activity.

The next step would normally be a PDW to give the project an initial shape and scope. This will require someone skilled as a facilitator to oversee this activity, though he or she need not be a project manager.

Operations and Management

The next phase after implementation of the service is the day-to-day running of the service, which is just as important as the design stage since it is here that SLAs are achieved or not. There are a number of areas involved here, and the basic ones are shown in Figure 17.9.

Note: Operation and management are not passive activities, but an active discipline that not only records, but also acts on service events.

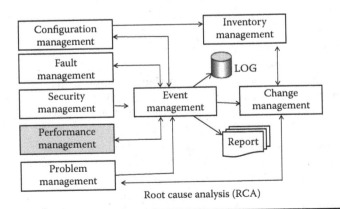

Figure 17.9   System management (SYSMAN) framework.

Management Framework

Project Definition Workshop

A short conversation from Lewis Carroll's *Alice in Wonderland* will outline the need for, and indicate the direction of, a project definition workshop (PDW):

> **Alice:** Would you tell me, please, which way I ought to go from here?
> **Cheshire Cat:** That depends a good deal on where you want to get to.
> **Alice:** I don't much care where …
> **Cheshire Cat:** Then it doesn't matter which way you go.
> **Alice:** … so long as I get *somewhere*.
> **Cheshire Cat:** Oh, you're sure to do that, if you only walk long enough.*

This conversation illustrates to a T my take on PDW, a simple principle that you can expand to implement in several ways. The bare bones of the process are as follows:

■ Define the A point, which is where you are now.
■ Define the B point, which is where you want to get to.
■ Develop and refine the activities needed for a transition from state A to state B.
■ Classify them under disciplines—operations, development, systems management, security, and so on.
■ Develop an action plan against these items and assign to people.
■ Document in a PID (see below) and get on with it.
■ Seek a peer review by someone not involved directly (devil's advocate).

The beauty of the PDW is that it works. I know, because I've been there.

Outline of the PDW

Today, a PDW is a common vehicle for setting up projects and was common fare at IBM in the 1970s and 1980s. It still exists today, but under a different name. A PDW is *not* a project management and control technique, but is a way of defining a project as unambiguously as possible. It does not replace project management tools and technologies and is usually independent of them, although such tools can be used in carrying out the actions and work items coming out of the PDW.

The purpose of the project definition workshop is to allow an organization to reach a common understanding of the business requirements and operational parameters for the delivery of an identified project, in this case a performance design and implementation. This information will allow the development of a solution to meet the users' requirements, and to manage the integration of the proposed project approach into the users' business with maximum chance of success and minimum disruption.

A project definition workshop can be used at several stages of the project. Outputs from the workshop enable the top-level deliverables, project acceptance, and sign-off criteria to be agreed on. The key skills and resources are identified and the project pricing expectations are set.

---

* I have lived in Cheshire (United Kingdom) all my life and very close to Lewis Carroll's original home at Daresbury. However, I still have no idea what a Cheshire cat is or how if differs from other cats.

Input: To aid the PDW process, a project brief should be prepared that describes the requirements and environment for the project, and will normally include

- Background—where it came from and who it is for and the sponsor
- Outline business case and drivers—cost and business impact of downtime
- Project definition, explaining what the project needs to achieve and including
  - Project goals
  - Project scope—setting boundaries to change and technology
  - Outline of project deliverables or desired outcomes
  - Critical success factors (CSFs), but not cost, as that is a constraint, not a CSF
  - Exclusions, constraints, assumptions, and interfaces
- Success and acceptance criteria (IT and user)
- Risks involved—these are to be addressed in the PDW
- Project organization (overall responsibilities only); detailed roles and responsibilities come out of the PDW actions

Output: The output of a PDW will be a draft *project initiation document* (PID), covering many of the same topics, but eventually in more detail and with more certainty.

PDW Method Overview

The normal way of running a PDW is via a facilitator, internal or external. That person will direct operations, but an overview will be presented here. It is assumed that the A point and B point are defined in some way or another, perhaps via a Delphi session.

It is then necessary for the team and facilitator to extract all the actions needed for the journey from A to B. A typical rough output of such a session is a series of activities across a number of charts or black- or whiteboards. It is then necessary to decide what area each activity comes under (operations, security, application development, database, OLTP, etc.), and a manager is assigned to that area. In Figure 17.10, they are the responsibilities of Jim, Fred, …, and Sue.

The progress in these areas should be subject to frequent meetings, within both the discipline and cross-discipline, and hence be subject to the organization's *change management* methodology. All this is driven by, and feeds into, the PID. The PID is the project start-up *blueprint*. You can see this graphically in Figure 17.10.

Project Initiation Document

The project initiation document (PID) is a core document for the project, and its format and content are pretty consistent across vendors, consultants, and the like. I have worked on several of these documents in a big UK bank, not all initiated by me, but maintained, updated, and used as input to various reviews. The documents were a very useful inheritance for me at contract start and for people who took over from me at contract end. We'll examine a typical structure and content headings and discuss its creation, maintenance, and use.

Of course, if your organization has its own mandatory document standards, it shouldn't be difficult to fit a PID around the appropriate ones.

There are two basic ways of developing a high-availability solution:

1. *Ab initio*, that is, from nothing through to a working solution
2. A *delta* increment across the whole of an existing configuration

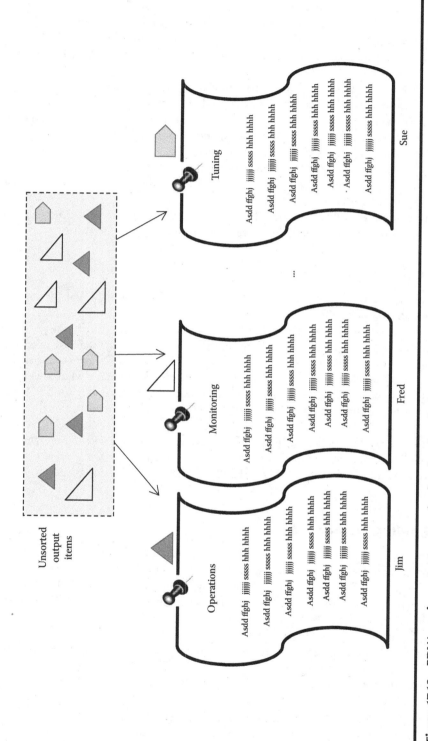

Figure 17.10 PDW: session output categorized and assigned.

The output of the PDW will obviously be different in both cases. In my view, the second scenario will be the messiest to handle, partly because nearly everything done will be a change. A third possible route is specific *delta* work on a few components of an existing system that are proving the most vulnerable to outages. The route chosen will depend on users' requirements, costs, and available skills.

PID Structure and Purpose

Purpose: The PID is the document that will answer the questions why, what, when, and who, which covers management information and approval, what it entails, progress via milestones, and who is doing what to ensure that progress. Whatever project management method is used, it can fit in with a PID, even if it mandates its own documentation. PIDs are recognized by PRINCE2 (projects in a controlled environment), and so cooperation is not a big issue. A major thing to remember is that the PID should be a living document nurtured by progress and any changes rendered necessary by circumstances.

Input: The working flip charts and notes generated at the PDW, plus the events and documentation leading up to the PDW, including previous attempts or experience from similar projects.

Structure: PRINCE documentation suggests the following table of contents for a PID, but *it is not carved in stone*. I have seen variations used to cater for an organization's own needs,* often using its own documentation standards:

- Purpose of the document—what is this project all about? Relate to business.
- Background to the need for it.
- Project definition—I would hammer the "A point to B point" and viewpoints way of looking at things.
- Method of approach, probably devised and communicated by the facilitator.
- Business case, including losses if we don't do it.
- Project organization.
- Communications plan.
- Project quality plan.
- Initial project plan.
- Project controls.
- Initial risk and issues log—these pages will get "red hot," I can assure you. The document should chart actions and progress against these issues and risks.
- Financial management—this could be a totally different document. This log needs frequent review and follow-up.
- Contingency plans.
- Project filing structure, that is, where can I find things out regarding this project?

PID Notes:

1. The beginning of the document can contain the usual features of your organization—who has copies, contact names, revisions and dates, and so forth.
2. A PID need not be a single monolithic document, but an outline and holding document that points to other, separately maintained documents.

---

* See Appendix III for an expansion of these topics à la PRINCE2 and my comments and additions.

3. The document will obviously state what is in the project plan, but equally important, it is an understanding of what is *not* in the plan, in other words, exclusions. This has been found necessary to avoid situations where certain things have been assumed as implicit in the plan when they have not been requested or designed explicitly.

4. The reader will be aware by now of my discomfort at following prescriptive activities blindly. The key here is to use common sense, decide on who the document is written for, and ask yourself if everyone involved disappeared, would the PID be enough for a new team to take up the reins and drive on?

There are several sample PIDs to be found on the Internet. Searching on "PID, sample document" will yield a number of PIDs from various sources.

Multistage PDW

Where a project is large or requires phasing, it is convenient to have several A points and B points, where the B point of phase 1 is the A point of phase 2, and so on. Each one then requires a mini-PDW, handled exactly the same as before, while ensuring continuity from one phase to succeeding phases. It may be advisable to have a multistage PID unless you wish to produce a single PID, resembling *War and Peace* in size and scope.

Delphi Techniques and Intensive Planning

These topics cover activities where raw brain power, prejudices, and pet ideas are subjugated to the pursuit of solutions to defined objectives by a superior being called a facilitator.

In performance planning and implementation, it is not acceptable to take the opinions of *n* people, add them together, and divide by *n* to get a mean solution. It should be more like a decision made by an informed jury so that the end result is sound and you don't find the wrong man guilty.

Delphi Technique*

One process used to "facilitate" the meeting is called the *Delphi technique*. Its name comes from the all-knowing Oracle at Delphi, and the actual method was developed during the Cold War to forecast the impact of technology on warfare.

This technique was further refined and developed by the RAND Corporation for the U.S. Department of Defense in the 1950s. Although originally intended for use as a psychological weapon during the Cold War, it has since been adapted for use in business and other areas of endeavor. Before going into the technique itself, I have a little tale about the surprising outcome of a Delphi-like session involving an IBM facilitator and senior executives from a large chemical company.

The facilitator asked them to work alone and produce a list of the six most pressing issues in the business, and then present them briefly to the rest of the executives.

The outcome was an eye opener. They disagreed totally on what the major issues were and expressed surprise at some of the issues raised by their peers in their own sector of the business.

---

* For the knowledge geek, http://is.njit.edu/pubs/delphibook/delphibook.pdf is a 618-page document on Delphi and, for all I know, the Freudian and Jungian implications of the method.

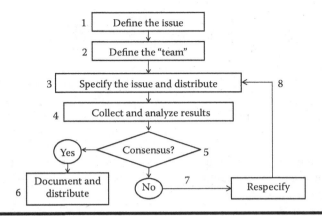

Figure 17.11 Delphi technique flowchart.

"I didn't know that stock levels were a serious issue," said the finance director. "I could have helped you there."

The same scenario was repeated among them for other important issues, each new to someone on the team. Even though their expectation was one of immediate consensus on what the issues were, they found the exercise very useful in bringing these thoughts to the surface. That is one of the beneficial effects of Delphi.

Although the executives were unaware of the technique, they were actually partaking in a diluted, short-term version of it.

Note: In general, the Delphi method is useful in answering one specific, single-dimension question. There is less support in the field for its use to determine complex forecasts involving multiple factors. Such complex model building is more appropriate for other, more esoteric models, perhaps with Delphi results serving as inputs. This makes it useful for single IT issues in the right circumstances, and with today's communication methods and networks, the traditional snail-mail and days or weeks time frames can be short-circuited.

This is what I have called the turbo-Delphi technique, an exercise tailored to fit the necessary decision timescale for an IT issue. Look at the simplified flowchart of the technique in Figure 17.11, with the steps explained below.

Delphi: The Steps

The essence of the technique is as follows (refer to the diagram):

1. A *facilitator* is chosen, probably for the whole project or subproject. It should be someone familiar with the project and having some leadership and analysis skills. If this is part of a major project, it should already have a *sponsor.*

   He or she should initiate any documentation on the project.

2. A *panel of experts* is chosen. This is more than likely the IT team involved in the availability working together with a business contact. An *expert* can be defined as "an individual with relevant knowledge and experience of a particular topic."

3. Define the *problem* that needs to be understood and input given on.

4. Set out the *questions* that require input from the experts. The answers should be correlated for commonality of views. A second set of questions based on the input should then be

issued. In a "turbo" version of Delphi, the whole thing might be done in conference mode around a table with "think" breaks to gain independent input from the team. Collect the results.

5. *Analyze* the input and findings and put an *action* plan together for the issue in question. If the facilitator finds broad agreement, the "solution" is documented and distributed. If not, the variations of opinion are documented and distributed, and a second round of opinions is sought and the analysis repeated.

6. When some form of consensus is reached, initiate the project.

There are other design and evaluation methods, one of which is discussed below. They sometimes overlap, and it is up to the account which elements of which method it uses. The common-sense method should be applied here.

Change Management

Change or Configuration Management

It is fairly well known that change and operational *volatility* can have an adverse effect on performance (and other things) or, at least, predispose systems to performance problems.

Change management and configuration management are very close together in terms of what they seek to achieve. Change management seeks to make changes to resources in a system in a controlled and consistent manner, while understanding the impact on other parts of the system.

Change Management and Control: Best Practice

The basic elements of this key discipline are (Figure 17.12)

■ Identify a change management team (virtual, containing relevant skills) plus a change controller.

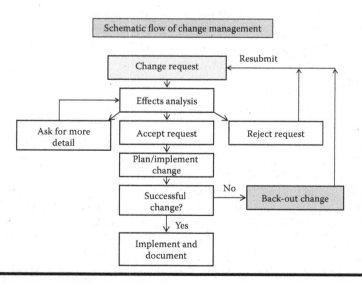

Figure 17.12   Change control flow: schematic.

- Devise documentation and meetings plans (what, where, and when).
- Request for a change (initiation) from the business, IT, user, or problem resolution.
- Change impact analysis—will a change to system software X related to application A have an adverse effect on application B?*
- Authorization for the change from an appropriate authority.
- Publish the impending change to IT staff concerned and any users who might be affected. You don't need to tell everyone about every minor change, though.
- Scheduling and tracking the changes as a mini-project.
- Change installation, coordination, and verification.
- Back-out procedures for the change where the change causes other problems. This ability is vital to an installation making changes.
- If the change does not have the desired results, then a root cause analysis should be carried out to avoid repetition in the future.
- Review the change, document, and publish the results.
- Areas where change management is required include
  - Operating environment patch management.
  - Application patch or upgrade management.
  - Concurrent upgrade of hardware or software.
  - Installation of new hardware or software.
  - Changing system or application parameters, for example, tuning the operating system or reorganizing an application database.
  - Other changes that might impact business services' availability or correct functioning. A service that doesn't deliver what it is supposed to deliver can be considered *unavailable* without necessarily involving outages of hardware or software. These I call *logical outages*.
- As ever, update and maintain the change documentation. You never know when you might need it for internal, legal, or job preservation reasons.

The box *back-out change* is a vital step in the change management process. If this cannot be done, or is very slow to complete, the service will remain in limbo until the *status quo* is restored.

> **WoW**: Back-out is necessary for a failed change since performance will be adversely affected; that is, there won't be any.

Change Operations

This is the job of the change team—using the established, agreed on, and understood procedure for IT changes.

They must assess impact on IT outside the actual change being made and on the end users:

- The request for a change to be made is generated.
- A change impact analysis is performed, especially clashes with other changes.
- The change is authorized by IT and management of the requestor.

---

* I've seen it happen when the A-to-B connection wasn't raised in a customer: the result was a big problem.

- The change is scheduled and tracked.
- The change is performed and verified.
- The change is backed out if unsuccessful.
- The requestors are informed, who provide change feedback.
- The change is reviewed and documented.

Patch Management

A major factor in the volatility of service performance is the application of patches to the various layers of software, including the operating system. This is a change management issue, and as it assumes greater importance, the more patches that will need to be applied. There are at least three philosophies pertaining to patch management:

- Put them all on ASAP.
- Only put on the patches that our system needs.
- Don't bother with any of them: not recommended.

The decision of which route to take may be different for different types of patch. Hot fixes are usually offered to fix a specific problem that your organization may or may not have. Others are a series of patches (roll-ups) and service packs.

There are several papers on the topic that might be useful in deciding the patch philosophy your organization should adopt in the HA environment. The second reference (from Cisco) contains other references, including the National Institute of Standards and Technology (NIST) documentation on patch management. Two general references are listed below:

http://docs.media.bitpipe.com/io_11x/io_113690/item_831844/patch-management-ebook%5B2%5D.pdf

http://blogs.cisco.com/security/patch-management-overview-challenges-and-recommendations/

NIST Special Publication 800-40, Revision 3, Guide to Enterprise Patch Management Technologies
http://nvlpubs.nist.gov/nistpubs/SpecialPublications/NIST.SP.800-40r3.pdf

Six Steps for Security Patch Management Best Practices
http://searchsecurity.techtarget.com/Six-steps-for-security-patch-management-best-practices

This is not such a big task as it may appear here. Myself and the customer did it without expensive software tools—just common sense and the commitment of management to the process.* Looking at the myriad statistics about what factors contribute to poor performance, whichever set you study, the *human factor* looms large.

The output of change management can be of vital importance in root cause analysis (RCA) inasmuch as it may give a clue to the possible cause from the sequence of events preceding the performance issue.

---

* If you don't have a senior management sponsor for this type of activity or any other extensive IT projects, you will almost certainly hit intractable problems. A sponsor is needed to support the project and remove nontechnical hurdles, such as "we need reinforcements or money."

WoW: A word from Sherlock Holmes on problem solving (apart from smoking multiple pipes): "When you have eliminated the impossible, whatever remains, however improbable, must be the truth" (*Sign of Four*).

War Room

Quote: "There are people who make things happen, people who watch things happen and people who say 'what happened?'" Which category are you?

I came across the war room concept in my early days in IBM. The *war room* was a room dedicated to problem and issue management in its broadest sense, mainly for extensive problems. It contained charts, listings, and so forth, concerning the current issues being handled. It also contained operations manuals, the history of resolved issues, and related Component Failure Impact Analysis (CFIA) and RCA documents in case they might throw light on current problems being experienced.

War Room Location

Today, if all necessary data is online and accessible, the war room can be a virtual room, convened wherever needed, as long as the necessary information is available. In true high-availability fashion, it may be wise to have two rooms, similarly equipped and with key information duplicated, depending on the size of the organization. One might indeed be a movable vehicle if there is a possibility of the original room being unavailable because of a disaster affecting the location. This could possibly be called "peripatetic" operation after the walking Greek philosopher.

A gathering of the *war cabinet* would be called by a designated *problem manager*, attendees being decided on when the rough area of concern is ascertained—hardware, software, network, and so on. IBM had a system called RETAIN, which was a worldwide system of symptoms and solutions.

An engineer in Tokyo experiencing a problem could dial into this system and, with appropriate keywords, initiate a search for problems matching his own. Where there was a "hit" on the particular symptoms, there might be one or more solutions posted that could solve or help to solve his current problem. Typical attendees would be the application owner, operations manager or deputy, and so on.

Once the *size and shape* of the problem are determined, the issue is assigned to an *owner*, who pursues the issue using any resources he or she needs to get to the bottom of it. This owner needs temporary empowerment to pursue his or her mission from the service sponsor.

Documentation

Documentation, quality and pictorial systems visibility, is essential to the success of the war room and should contain information pertaining to any SLAs in force relating to the issues in progress. They are enterprise specific but should contain at least

- Location and backup location
- Scope of the war room activity (which services are covered)
- Communication channels for all stakeholders: very important
- Facilitator name and contact details plus stand-in
- Service representatives and contact details plus stand-in
- Business impact analyses (BIAs) and SLAs for the services covered
- Roles and responsibilities of participants by service (not necessarily specific names)
- The process that should be followed for a major issue or DR invocation
- Access to previous problems, preferably on a dedicated "server," for example, a simple search facility* on a PC (with a standby of course)
- Visual equipment for viewing all aspects of the issue in hand, even to the extent of walls full of handwritten flip charts
- Anything else you feel would help the situation

War room staff groups are sometimes called *failure review boards*.

The war room is for all intents and purposes a command and control center (CCC) for IT problems. One major benefit of the technique is it minimizes the "headless chicken syndrome," which involves everyone running around shouting, "What shall we do? What shall we do?"

---

* A customer of mine used a simple PC search tool to access previous or similar problem situations along with suggested lines of progressing and possible solutions. It worked beautifully and eliminated the need for and expense of commercial tools.

APPENDICES V

The appendices are here as backup material to the main body of this book. I have tried not to make the mistake of putting detail, above and beyond the call of understanding the topic in question at the desired level, in the body text. An example is the breakout of slightly more advanced (but necessary) queuing theory from the discussion in Chapter 7 and its placement in Appendix I. I became tired when reading books that drowned me in queuing theory before I could swim a few strokes in the subject. Most of it is purely academic anyway.

Similarly, I have included as an appendix a detailed discussion of some old benchmarks that may soon disappear from the literature on the subject to act as a record of things past.

Appendix I: Basic Queuing Theory

Introduction

Basic queuing theory stems to a large degree from the work of Erlang (ca. 1909) on telephony systems, using theory to predict and change the service perception of users of the systems. Queues and wait times are the factors that cause dissatisfaction in customers, which is bad for business.

It is therefore important to a business that the flow of work, queries, and other *units of work* or *work units* (WUs) pass through a system at an optimum rate, and queuing theory can help in this task. Some of the many factors of interest in queuing theory are listed below, not all of which are obvious to the customer but can have an effect on things he or she can witness, such as long wait times for service at a counter or supermarket checkout. Long, visible queues are bad for business.

A queue in a transaction processing system is not a visible problem unless it causes an unacceptable rise in response times. The upshot of this is that out of all the various quantities that can be derived via queuing theory, only some are of direct importance to any particular business or activity.

One thing to note about queuing is that, in general, there is a randomness about the traffic of work units arriving at a server for execution. These go under the name of stochastic processes. The other thing to note is that almost all quantities coming out of queuing calculations or simulations are averages (or means), and hence have a variation about this average or mean.

The queuing situations encountered can be classified thus:

- Constant arrivals, constant service times
- Random arrivals, constant service times
- Constant arrivals, random service times
- Random arrivals, random service times

The subject is made more difficult than simple math because the random arrivals and service profiles are described by math distributions that may or may not approximate to your own situations. In addition to this factor, there are others, such as queue limits—finite or infinite, multiple servers and multiple queues, and networks of queues.

Queuing Entities of Interest

- Type of system and environment
- Queuing discipline
- Population to be served
- Dispatching discipline within the servers
- Server service times
- Server idle time
- Number of servers
- Work unit (UoW)* arrival rate (λ)
- Service rate per server (μ)
- Service rate distribution (probability distribution function [pdf])
- WU arrival rate distribution (pdf)
- Average server utilization (ρ %), a measure of its busyness
- Peak server utilization (ρ_{MAX} %) before degradation occurs in either response time or throughput
- Peak-to-average utilization ratio (x:1), important in sizing exercises
- Average number of UoWs in the queue, for example, transactions
- Average number of UoWs in the system
- Average time a UoW spends in the queue (T_W) (waiting time)
- Average time a UoW spends in the server (T_S) (service time)
- Average total time for service (T_R), response time, which equals $T_S + T_W$
- Probability that all servers are idle
- Probability that an arriving UoW waits
- Average rate of balking UoWs
- Maximum UoWs in the queue
- Average queue length
- Maximum queue length (capacity)
- Kendall's notation
- Little's theorem
- Transaction throughput rate
- Transaction response time and percentiles
- Batch work throughput
- Batch work job time
- Bottlenecks in workflow

Which entities are of interest depends on the organization involved. In transaction processing, the queue length isn't a concern for the end user, only the resulting response time. However, for a supermarket planning checkouts and other facilities, a large, visible queue of customers creates a bad impression of the service offered and may affect whether they stay or even ever come again.

---

* These are called work units (UoWs) in some documentation, but I have always used UoW in these contexts—they are one and the same entity—and it maintains continuity in the book.

Service and Wait Times

In real life, total service times depend on the time spent waiting to be served (*wait time*) plus the time actually taken to be served (*service time*). These will depend on other factors, such as how busy the server is. In transactional systems, this time is often called the response time to a request. For example, if I enter a shop to buy a newspaper, the time I spend waiting to be served and the time taken to get and pay for the newspaper is called response time of the *purchase of a newspaper* transaction.

If the shop is empty and the newsagent is doing nothing else, there is no wait time and the system is said to be unconstrained; that is, there are no bottlenecks to impede service. Where there are bottlenecks resulting in wait times, the service is constrained. Thus, the equation for service time and wait time is

$$\text{Constrained service time} = \text{Unconstrained service time plus wait times} \qquad \text{(A1.1)}$$

This is the whole topic of latency, response time, wait times, and the rest in a nutshell.

Response Time: Unconstrained System

In an unconstrained system where utilizations are low (zero in theory), the response time is the sum of the elements of the response times, in this case, the sum of the service times of all the elements in the work unit's journey.

The response time of a transaction is basically the time it takes to service the workload generated by it. There is an added complication sometimes in that other systems are involved and updates to them must be coordinated before the original transaction can be said to have completed.

This is called two-phase commit and can be found in Appendix III.

Response Time: Constrained System

In real life, unless there has been some spectacular overconfiguration, a system will have constraints of some kind due to the utilization of its constituent parts, as shown in Figure A1.1. What it shows is the additional time added to the unconstrained response time by delays or waits at each of the service points in the work unit's journey—network in, network out, disk, and server.

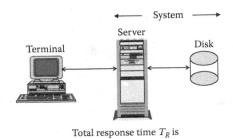

Total response time T_R is

Line time (in) + CPU time + disk I/O time + line time (out)

◄—— Time in system ——►

Figure A1.1 Response time: unconstrained system.

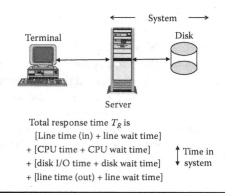

Total response time T_R is
  [Line time (in) + line wait time]
  + [CPU time + CPU wait time]   ↑ Time in
  + [disk I/O time + disk wait time] ↓ system
  + [line time (out) + line wait time]

Figure A1.2 Response time: constrained system.

The queuing theory side arises from the quantification of these factors comprising the response time in terms of means (averages) since they will vary over time as queues ebb and flow in size. It is sometimes the case with certain systems that the queues may vary in length from what is later perceived to be an average, but they may settle down after a *bedding-in* (or stabilization) period to a more closely spaced set of queue lengths.

Figures A1.1 and A1.2 are illustrative only to introduce the idea of things that cause delays or, in server, storage, and network terminology, latency.

Factors We Will Consider

We will now develop the relationship between service time, wait time, and total response time, as well as looking at the concept of response time *percentiles*. This is a review of the coverage in Chapter 7 under the heading "System Performance Concepts."

We saw earlier that response times are made up of the time to be served plus the time spent waiting to be served. Percentiles are a measure of what percentage of the user population receive response times within a certain range, as opposed to some number representing average response times.

Percentile Review: Thus, the *90th percentile* response is the response that covers 90% of responses, and the *mean response* time is that for which 50% are greater and 50% are less. Other percentiles split the response across the response curve according to the percentage chosen. For certain arrival distributions, the 90th percentile response is 2.3 times the mean response.

A percentile response time specification is often used in a service level agreement (SLA) instead of a simple average or mean response time (Figure A1.3).

Simple Queuing Theory

Introduction

Queue Characteristics

Queuing is part of life and occurs in many aspects of life—shops, supermarkets, traffic roundabouts, computer systems, cash machines, and many others. These queues share many characteristics but

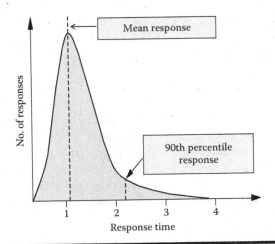

Figure A1.3 Response time percentiles.

vary in some. For instance, a queue of online transaction processing (OLTP) transactions doesn't have a mind of its own and so cannot show human characteristics like cursing and leaving the queue (*reneging*) or even refusing to join it (*balking*). In queuing theory, allowances have to be made for such defections, but less so in IT situations, fortunately for us.

We will now cover the essentials of queuing and queuing theory with a view to gaining a practical understanding of where it applies in computer systems. A key thing to note is that many parameters in queuing are variable in nature or in time. This means that we are nearly always dealing in means, averages, and probabilities, as opposed to fixed quantities throughout. Some of these variables are dealt with in the following sections.

As we have seen in the queuing introduction in Chapter 8, there is a series of activities and participants in the population, arrival, queuing, and processing of work units (UoWs) in an IT system.

Why Bother about Queues?

First, nobody likes to be in one, secondly, it can be bad for business, and third, it can cause congestion in undesirable circumstances, like a traffic situation. Businesses (and websites) that suffer excessive balking and reneging do not stay around too long. Given that consideration of queues is important, different businesses will focus on different aspects—average and maximum waiting times, average number in a queue, call center holding times, and so on. Why bother with all this work and math?

In the end, it boils down to two aspects:

■ Service to the customer
■ Cost–benefit (dollars or pounds) = staying in business

Population

Population is a term applied to the number of potential UoWs (sometimes referred to as customers in queuing terminology) forming the system. This can be *finite* or (in theory) *infinite*, and then the mathematical treatment will vary. *Infinite* normally means large in the sense that it is much larger than any queue that might form and is then amenable to simpler math treatment. In the finite case, a sizable queue might deplete the population such that the mathematical treatment needs to diverge from the infinite population scenario.

Arrival Patterns

The arrival pattern is the manner in which UoWs arrive to be served in some way. In the simple case where UoWs arrive at regular intervals, say one every 5 min,* and always take just 3 min to be served, there will be no queue and everyone is happy. This is not the normal case, however, since humans are nearly always involved, even in IT, where UoW submissions will have a pattern.

Queuing theory normally works on a random exponential arrival rate, described as a Poisson distribution. Here the interarrival time is variable with an average value, which is normally denoted λ.

Service Time Patterns

It should be obvious, given the number of different queuing scenarios, that service times for a UoW will not always be fixed, even in a single scenario like a small shop. In the queue there may be one person who simply wants a newspaper, but another who may ask for a basketful of goods.

Incidentally, in the case of a supermarket, the queuing is at the checkout and not the receipt of goods phase of the operations. If the shop has a serving assistant and a separate checkout, there will be two queues involved in servicing the WU.

Here the service time might be variable, described by a distribution, with an average value, which is normally denoted μ.

Number of Servers

One obvious way of reducing waiting times in queues is to have more than one server. Basically, the number of servers is decided by what level of service is being offered or can be afforded. In private banks or very exclusive restaurants, there are normally enough staff serving customers that none of the latter need ever wait. In bars at football matches, waiting in a queue for a beer at the interval is the norm.

Number of Queues

In some cases, there may be a need to use multiple queues, usually with multiple servers. A typical scenario might be a supermarket where some checkouts are assigned to handle customers with baskets of less than 10 items or checkouts for credit cards only. In such cases, there will have to be multiple queues, clearly marked, to avoid people joining the wrong one and reneging with choice language.

In cases where any server can serve any UoW (customer), the single queue, multiple server configuration works best. For example, in a post office, a multiple queue, multiple server situation always find a person in one queue involved in a huge transaction, causing others in the queue to renege and join another queue. We've all seen this happen.

---

* This is nearly always referred to as the interarrival time.

Service/Queue Discipline

When the UoWs are in the queue awaiting service, in which order are they served?

Like a shop or bar, you would expect the first come, first served protocol to be observed, wouldn't you?

This is not necessarily the case for various reasons. In the United Kingdom, if you enter a strange pub, it is likely that you will be served after the regular customers have been dealt with, but these are exceptions.

There are a number of service disciplines or patterns designed to make the service more efficient, but this can depend on the type of server, at least in IT. The normal order is first in, first out (FIFO), where the queue of UoWs is served in strict order of arrival, but not always.

Let us examine just two examples of non-FIFO service patterns:

Packet shaping. In communications, it is sometimes necessary to give certain classes of traffic precedence over other forms. This is done by assigning priorities to classes of traffic and favoring the important ones. For example, key financial transactions will be given precedence over the transmission of historical data for planning purposes.

Transaction classes. In IBM's Information Management System (IMS), transactions are processed by programs in regions, each of which has a class assigned: A, B, C, and so forth. Incoming transactions also have a class designated, which dictates which regions can process them. The manner in which these classes and regions are assigned dictates the service pattern of the incoming transactions. Figure A1.4 illustrates this mode of service selection.

There are other service patterns in existence that are designed to suit various service requirements, for example, last in, first out (LIFO).

Queue–Service Configurations

There are a number of combinations of queue and server configurations, some better suited to certain situations than others.

Figure A1.5 shows the scenario of a system dealing with and servicing UoWs in a selection of queue–server combinations:

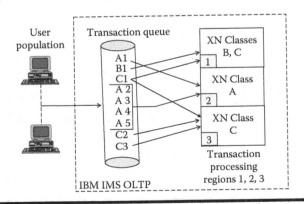

Figure A1.4   IMS transaction service discipline example.

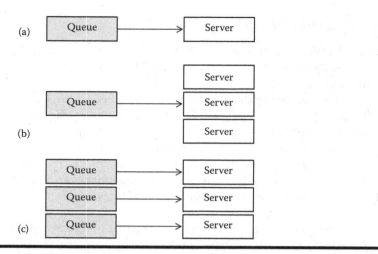

Figure A1.5   Queue–server configurations.

- **A**: Single queue, single server (simple OLTP system)
- **B**: Single queue, multiple server (post office; reneging not feasible)
- **C**: Multiple queue, multiple server (servers designed for different queues, e.g., supermarket payment methods; reneging practically impossible)

Queuing Review

The queuing–service mechanism can be shown alphabetically using what is known as the *Kendall–Lee* notation, mentioned briefly earlier. This is summarized in Figure A1.6, and some of the less esoteric terms are explained afterwards.

Many expositions of the Kendall–Lee notation (or convention) use different letters to denote the six parameters involved: A/ B/ C/ ..., T/X/C/K/P/Z, and so on. In Figure A1.6, I have used numbers 1–6 to signify these parameters, with a brief explanation underneath each one.

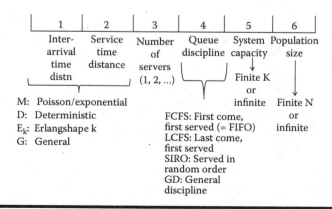

Figure A1.6   Kendall–Lee service notation and convention.

Although this seems complicated, most models we deal with in IT can have items 4/5/6 as G/infinite queue/infinite population and omitted, assumed. As examples, the two notations that follow illustrate the principle:

■ M/M/2 is an exponential arrival pattern, a similar service time distribution, and two servers in parallel.
■ M/E2/4/FCFS/10/infinite might represent a surgery with 4 doctors dealing with patients on a first come, <u>two</u>-phase Erlang service time, first served basis (FCFS) in a clinic of maximum capacity 10 patients from the huge population outside.

However, if a serious emergency case arose, the FCFS might change to LCFS (last come, first served) or some other medically decided priority.

Note: Parameters 4–6 can be omitted if the source and queue are infinite and the queue discipline is FIFO/FCFS.

Poisson and Erlang Distributions

These cover the interarrival and service time distributions and are shown in Figure A1.7. What do they look like mathematically? The equations for these shapes are given below. As noted elsewhere, these distributions apply to arrivals at a queue–sever combination, and it is not a certainty that the shape of the distribution at the server exit and entrance to the following server will be the same.

I discuss this at the end of this Appendix under "Limitations of Theoretical Approaches."

Poisson Distribution

Equation A1.2 shows the Poisson distribution:

$$P(n) = \frac{e^{-\lambda}\lambda^n}{n!} \tag{A1.2}$$

for $n = 0, 1, 2, \ldots$.

Distributions that do not fit the Poisson pattern are sometimes based on the Erlang distribution given below.

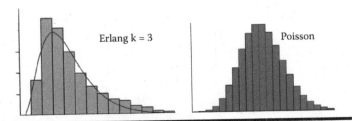

Figure A1.7 Erlang and Poisson distributions.

Erlang k Distribution

The Erlang distribution was developed by A.K. Erlang in the early 1900s to examine the number of telephone calls that might be made at the same time to the operators of the switching stations. This work on telephone traffic has been expanded to consider waiting times in queuing systems in general, in particular IT. Equation A1.3 shows the Erlang distribution.

$$F(t) = \mu \frac{(\mu t)^{k-1}}{(k-1)!} e^{\mu t} \tag{A1.3}$$

The Erlang distribution with shape parameter *k equal to 1* simplifies to the exponential distribution. It is a special case of the gamma distribution and is the distribution of a sum of *k* independent exponential variables with mean μ in Equation A1.3.

Figure A1.7 illustrates these distributions as a function of time.

There are other distributions in vogue, such as hyperexponential and hypoexponential, but these two are the most frequently used. We shouldn't get too hung about which distribution relates to which work profile since you will almost certainly be using software tools to handle queuing issues.

Simple Server Math

The following equations are illustrative of properties of queues, and a few more rigorous math equations are given later in this appendix under "Other Queuing Formulas."

Single Server: See Figure A1.8.
Two Servers: See Figure A1.9.

Arrival Patterns

Scenario 1: Fixed IAT, Fixed Service Time

The first queuing scenario we will deal with is that where transactions arrive at regular intervals. We will call this case fixed interarrival time (IAT). The time is broken into six units across the foil, and we will examine three cases as a function of time:

1. Where the service time, denoted by two-ended arrows, is less than the time between arrivals. Arrivals might be people, transactions, or whatever.

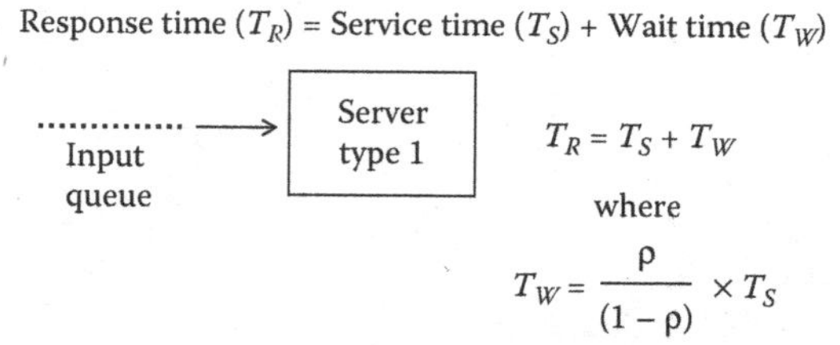

Response time (T_R) = Service time (T_S) + Wait time (T_W)

Input queue → Server type 1

$$T_R = T_S + T_W$$

where

$$T_W = \frac{\rho}{(1 - \rho)} \times T_S$$

Figure A1.8   Wait and response times: single server.

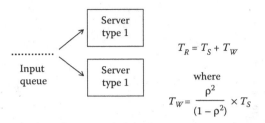

Response time (T_R) = Service time (T_S) + Wait time (T_W)

$$T_R = T_S + T_W$$

where

$$T_W = \frac{\rho^2}{(1 - \rho^2)} \times T_S$$

Figure A1.9   Response and wait times: two servers.

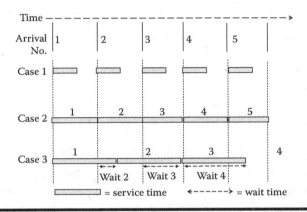

Figure A1.10   Three cases of fixed IAT and fixed service time.

2. Where the service time is equal to the time between arrivals (IAT).

3. Where the service time is greater than the IAT.

We will develop the analogy using the example of a post office with customers requesting service. Again, refer Figure A1.10.

Normally, the arrival distribution is not fixed like case 3, and we get a variation of queuing lengths (but it never returns to an average of zero) and times.

Case 1: At time 1, a customer arrives but is served before time 2, when the next one arrives. He too has been served before the next customer arrives. This can go on indefinitely (or until the post office closes) without anyone having to wait to be served.

Case 2: The first customer has *just* been served when the second arrives, so again no queues develop. In this case, the time to be served is greater than the time between arrivals so that before the first customer has been served, the second arrives. He has to wait for time Wait2 before being served. While customer 2 is being served, a third arrives and has to wait for time Wait3. Succeeding customers always have to wait.

Case 3: In these scenarios of fixed IAT and fixed service time, case 3 will result in an ever-lengthening queue, each customer waiting longer than his predecessor to be served. We should point out that this is not the case in normal IT situations, but illustrates the concepts and effects of queuing very well.

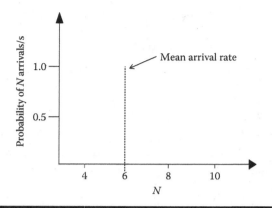

Figure A1.11   Arrival pattern: fixed IAT and fixed service time.

The fixed arrival rate leads to the simple graph shown in Figure A1.11.

The probability on N arrivals in any second versus N is a single line at six arrivals since there is no rate other than 6.

Scenario 2: Random Arrivals, Random Service Time

Take the post office as an analogy with an average interarrival time of 2 min, but no longer fixed.

If we assume that the first service time of the clerk is 1.5 min, then take the first case where two arrivals are 2 min apart. Obviously, the second person does not need to queue because the first person will have been served. Now consider the second person taking 2.5 min to be served and a third person arriving 1 min after the second. The third person will have to wait to be served.

Looking Figure A1.12, you will see that the need to queue will vary depending on various factors. Although the IAT equals the service time on average, you might not expect there to be a queue. Because we are averaging periods where there is no queue (IAT less than service time) with periods when there is a queue (IAT less than service time), there is on average going to be a queue. Another way of looking at this is to see that once there has been a queue, there can never

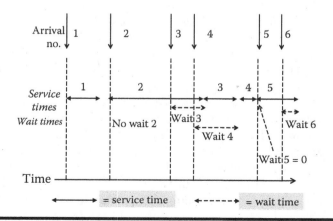

Figure A1.12   Arrival pattern: random IAT and random service time.

be a negative queue to average out to zero queue length. We will give the simple formulas you need in a few foils' time.

The curve at the bottom of the foil shows the probability of *N* arrivals in any minute against *N*. The random arrivals and service times often follow a Poisson distribution in their variation. In analyzing IT situations where queuing is involved, there are a number of other "probability" curves one might plot, such as

1. Probability of there being *n* in the queue at any time
2. Probability of queue length being greater than *m* at any time

Note: Do not use these curves in dealing with real life situations—they are meant to illustrate queuing *principles* only.

There is a spread of arrival rates in the case of random arrival pattern spread about some mean arrival rate, shown in Figure A1.13 at horizontal number 6. There will be rates less than, and some greater than, the six per interval (second, minute, etc.).

Note: Believe it or not, you have a measure of control over the arrival pattern in your organization. Arrival distributions can be defeated and their math defused. Let me give an example of this.

Years ago I was doing some performance work at a legal organization in the United Kingdom where they were having intermittent response time problems. I looked at the graph of CPU load against time on a typical day and noticed two pronounced peaks; one midmorning and the other midafternoon. The rest of the day was relatively quiet.

I thought about this and asked what their work pattern for the day was and was told they did all their data entry and processing in two slots when the mail arrived. Bingo! I suggested they slow down these processing periods by perhaps having less people doing the jobs or staggering the workload. Problem solved, no upgrade needed, much chagrin from their hardware supplier (I was working for a software company at the time).

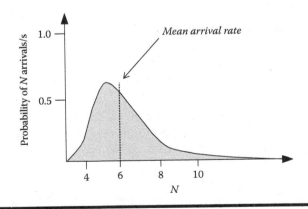

Figure A1.13   Arrival distribution: random IAT and service time.

Random IAT and Service Time Factors

The following list shows some of the factors and key parameters in queuing theory. Taking a transaction processing system (OLTP) as an example, it can be shown that the following equations hold:

- Probability that system is idle = $(1 - \rho)$
- Probability that transaction has to wait (queue) = ρ
- Probability of n transactions in the system (in queue plus being served) = $(1 - \rho)\rho^n$
- Expected number of transactions in system (in queue plus being served) = $\rho/(1 - \rho)$
- Average time transaction is in system = $T_S/(1 - \rho)$
- Expected number of transactions in the queue = $\rho^2/(1 - \rho)$
- Average time transactions in the queue = $T_S \times \rho/(1 - \rho)$

where ρ is the resources utilization, T_S is the service time of the resource.

Queuing Theory: Parameters

To simplify the approach to queuing theory from which we can get numeric information, we will consider the base case of

- Infinite population with random arrival rate
- Single queue of infinite length, that is, no overflows
- Single server with variable service time

The *resource utilization* ρ of a server executing a request (work unit WU) is often defined as shown in Equation A1.4:

$$\frac{\text{Time to Service a Request}}{\text{Elapsed Time}} \tag{A1.4}$$

An example of this is a CPU executing three jobs or tasks in 1 s, where each job or task needs 200 ms of CPU processing time. The utilization of that particular CPU during that 1 s period would be

$$600\text{ms}/1000\text{ms} = 60\%$$

It is interesting to note here that in reality, a CPU cannot actually be 60% busy—it is either 100% busy or 0% busy (operating or not operating); not many people know or realize this. However, over a long period in terms of the CPU cycle time, there can be an average figure for busy CPU:

$$\text{Average Busy \%} = \frac{\text{No. Periods at 100\% Busy}}{\text{No. Periods at 100\% Busy} + \text{No. Periods 0\% Busy}} \tag{A1.5}$$

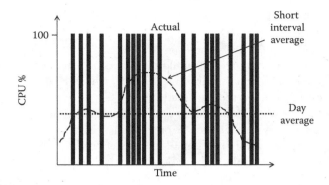

Figure A1.14 CPU utilization: Actual vs. recorded averages.

This is illustrated in Figure A1.14 as if you measured what the CPU was doing every fraction of a nanosecond. You would get only two answers: it is working (100% busy or utilization) or idle (0% utilization), as illustrated the figure.

Queuing theory points to certain times that need to be measured or calculated, and simple theory yields the following wait and response time equations for a single server:

$$1.\ \text{Wait Time } T_W = \frac{T_S \times \rho}{(1-\rho)} \tag{A1.6}$$

$$2.\ \text{Response Time } T_R = T_S + T_W \tag{A1.7}$$

where T_W is the waiting time, T_S is the service time, and ρ is the utilization of the server. T_R is the total response time or time taken to queue and then be served. If there are several types of servers needed to complete the service, then the total response time is the sum of the total response times for each element. If we consider a single computer system, then the response time seen by the end user will be

$$T = T_R\left(\text{Link or LAN}\right) + T_R\left(\text{CPU}\right) + T_R\left(\text{Disk}\right)$$

or expressed another way,

$$T = \sum\left(T_S + \frac{(T_S \times \rho)}{(1-\rho)}\right) \tag{A1.8}$$

for all three elements—line/LAN, CPU, and disk—but see the "Remember" note below.

It is evident that the total response time (T_R) depends not only on the service time (T_S), but also on the utilization (ρ) of that server. For more complex, distributed systems, the calculations become a little more difficult.

However, for single-server systems, the question arises, "At what utilization should we plan to run the system? 10%, 70%, or 100%?" The answer is that optimum utilization depends on the type of server and the type of workload.

Remember two things:

1. The CPU + Disk time equations should be understood in terms of the words under "Response Time Interpretation" in Appendix VII, where the difference between CPU time and time in the CPU are explained.
2. The summation of all response times and wait times assumes a totally serial system where each UoW goes through each resource sequentially, whereas in fact some operations may overlap. This will yield a small total system transit time. Examples of overlap are full-duplex network links and rotational position sensing (RPS) in disk accesses.

A Word on Utilizations

Since the wait (or queue) time is given by the equation

$$T_W = \frac{(T_S \times \rho)}{(1 - \rho)} \tag{A1.9}$$

unless someone has been seriously overbuying, it is likely that ρ will lie between 0.2 and 0.7 on average, a scalability factor of 3.5. T_S, however, can vary greatly across the server elements in an IT system, as shown in Table A1.1.

The scalability of T_S (service time) can be 100 or more, but the utilization factor does not move pro rata

1. For interactive or transaction loads. This utilization can be 100% for batch work, whereas we are interested in throughput and not response time.
2. Because of the randomness of the Ethernet collision detection protocol. Token Ring is deterministic and can be run at higher utilizations (say 80%) than Ethernet without the same detrimental effect on performance.

Table A1.1   Optimum Utilization vs. Service Time

Resource	Service Time	Peak Utilization Norm
Processor	Micro- or nanoseconds	70%–85%
Channel/bus	Microseconds	40%–60%
Disk (hard disk drive [HDD])	Milliseconds	40%–50%
Ethernet	Milliseconds	40%[a]
Network link	10s of milliseconds	40%–50%

[a] Due to *collision detect protocol* with back-off and retry. Token Ring arbitration, a sort of referee or umpire, allows ca. 70% without degradation.

For sequential data access and batch work, it is usually possible to run most elements of the system at high utilization rates. However, for transaction-based systems with significant random disk accesses, there are guidelines indicating which utilization percentages are best for good response.

It is possible to show that the optimum utilization for any server varies with the service time so that, for example, servers that exhibit short service times can work reasonably well at utilizations higher than those for slower servers. In this context, server can be taken as a real server, a disk subsystem, or a network link—the same principle applies.

> Exceeding these guidelines may cause the wait time and total service (response) time to deteriorate rapidly and eventually result in unacceptable delays.

We will consider a simple example of the change in response time with increases in the utilization of the server elements (disks, lines, and CPU) in a system.

The maximum figures quoted above are for workloads that do not have extremes of activity, such as normal office work, which often peaks midmorning and midafternoon, with a peak-to-average intensity of about 1.5 or 2.0 to 1. For workloads with more extreme variations, the maximum should be the guideline, since the average may be meaningless.

As an example, consider the case of a time card system where workers in a factory register their arrivals and exits in four 10 min periods: in the morning, before and after lunch, and in the evening. The average load means little as the activity, though intensive, is sparse in terms of time.

For illustrative figures, see the "Abnormal Systems Loads" section in Chapter 7.

Queuing Theory: Useful* Output

In the analysis of practical queuing situations, the types of information we might be interested in is typically concerned with measures of system performance and might include for a supermarket *counter* or *checkout*

1. How long do customers expect to *wait in the queue* before they are served, and how long will they have to *wait* before the service is complete (mean waiting time and service time)?
2. Waiting time *percentile*, that is, what percentage of customers wait longer than a time T_w? Alternatively, what is the wait time for which 90% of customers wait less (*90th percentile*)?
3. What is the *probability* of customers having to *wait* longer than a given time interval before they are served?
4. What is the distribution of waiting customers, that is, what is the probability or percentage of there being 0, 1, 2, 3 ..., customers in a queue?
5. How many might *balk* (walk away) at seeing a long queue?
6. How many might *renege* and leave a queue before being served?
7. What is the *average length* of the queue (number of customers)—counter or checkout?
8. What is the *throughput*, that is, number of customers served per unit time?
9. What is the probability that the queue will *exceed* a certain length? This might be of interest in providing a queuing area large enough so that it doesn't impede other shoppers.

---

* This excludes useless pretty graphs and mind-blowing screen shots so beloved of marketing performance tool publications.

10. What is the expected *utilization* of the server and the expected time period during which he or she will be fully occupied. This is a human factor, but it is still important when talking about IT resources and their costs.

So What 1? If we can assign costs to factors such as customer waiting time and server idle time, then we can investigate how to design a system at minimum *total cost* and customer *dissatisfaction*. We might not care how long a disk I/O request might have to wait, but the end user does.

So What 2? An old IBM colleague makes his living out of performing these sorts of calculations for various organizations, such as call centers, website providers, supermarkets, and similar organizations who need to plan for these factors in their space, financial, and customer satisfaction considerations.

Note: Not every situation demands the answers to all these questions, but they can be asked and normally calculated using queuing theory (for simple cases) or rules of thumb (ROTs). See *Limitations of Theoretical Approaches* below for a short discussion of where I feel that overuse of theory can give erroneous results and expectations.

Practical Examples of Queuing

Line Loading

It is simple to calculate the line traffic load that will produce a 30% utilization figure. Both synchronous and asynchronous communications methods have an overhead, so that the full bandwidth of a line or LAN is never used fully to carry data. The overhead for synchronous communications is less than that for asynchronous communications.

For the purposes of sizing calculations, using the rule of thumb that there are 12 bits to each character is usually adequate for both modes of transmission.

Imagine a terminal attached to a computer system entering transactions over a 9600 bps telephone line. The user at the terminal enters a transaction every minute with input consisting of 200 characters and the output 1000, a total of 1200 per transaction. Assuming that there are roughly 10 bits for each character (to allow for headers, etc.), the time to transmit the characters will be 12000/9600 or 1.25 s. This is without the transaction execution or queue time (latency) added.

Make the further assumption that there are other users sharing the same line, either via a multiplexer or a control unit hosting multiple terminals. The guideline to keep the line utilization to 30% means that the line should only be busy 3 s in every 10, or 18 s in every 60. A single user occupies the line for 1.25 s every 60; thus, the maximum number of users on the line is 18/1.25 or 14 users.

CPU Loading

It is also easy, given the CPU time consumed by a transaction, to calculate what transaction rate will produce a 70% load on the CPU. Look at Table A1.2, outlining the resource characteristics of some transactions that might be used in system sizing.

Table A1.2 CPU Loading via Transaction Characteristics

Transaction	Resource	Usage Frequency
XN-1	100 ms CPU	54%
	16 I/Os	
	80K working storage	
XN-2	200 ms CPU	26%
	28 I/Os	
	140K working storage	
XN-3	420 ms CPU	20%
	54 I/Os	
	250K working storage	
Etc.	Etc.	Etc.

Note: The numbers in the table may not represent real life or your organization's work, as they are illustrative of the method, which is the crux of the matter, to be shown next.

Assuming we wanted to work our CPU at a maximum of 70% (or thereabouts), it can be seen that seven of XN-1 per second will run the CPU at 70% (7 × 100 ms/1000 ms). This will yield a requirement for 7 × 80K working storage = 560K and 77 × 16 I/Os per second (IOPS) = 112 IOPS.

Transaction Mix: To see what transaction load or mix would require the agreed 70% of CPU, we proceed as follows:

Math: In any 1 s, XN-1 will take 0.54 × 100 ms = 54 ms; XN-2, 0.26 × 200 = 52 ms; XN-3, 0.2 × 420 ms = 84 ms; and so on to XN-*n*, to make up all transactions. So in any 1 s, our three transactions, assuming they are the total load for the purpose of this calculation, will occupy 54 + 52 + 84 = 190 ms. So we can support 700/190 = 3.7 transactions of our transaction mix per second with the CPU running at 70% utilization (we have 700 ms to play with out of 1000 ms, giving us the 70% utilization). This is essentially the weighted mean of the transactions' consumption of CPU resource.

Similarly, the working storage and I/Os can be prorated to generate the required storage and I/O rate needing support.

In the *general case of n transactions*, XN-1, XN-2, ..., XN-*n*, each needing CPU milliseconds of C_1, C_2, ..., C_n and representing P_1, P_2, ..., P_n percent of the transaction profile, the sustainable transaction rate N at 70% CPU utilization is

$$N = \frac{700}{\sum_{1}^{n}\left(C_i \times \left(P_i/100\right)\right)} \; XNs \text{ per second} \qquad (A1.10)$$

A similar exercise can be done with this equation substituting working storage and IOPS for CPU milliseconds describing the transactions.

See the following section for the case of disk estimation.

Disk Loading

In the use of the equation above for a disk, the calculation proceeds as follows:

> We wish to have the disk utilized to 40%,* and we have a disk that will support N IOPS at 40% utilization (= 0.4 × 1000/access time [ms]); then the number of such disks required to support the mix is [(Total IOPS for mix)/N].

In the case of the transactions above, the I/Os required are given by the sum

$$N(0.54 \times 16 + 0.26 \times 28 + 0.2 \times 54) = 3.7(8.64 + 7.28 + 10.8) = 99 \text{ IOPS}$$

Thus, the disk or solid-state drive (SSD) configuration must provide ca. 100 IOPS at 40% utilization, and that it must be capable of (but never run at) 100% means it must support $100/40 \times 100 = 250$ IOPS.

For applications that are heavily oriented toward sequential disk I/O, the sequential rates will provide you with the maximum (100%) utilization at which sequential accesses can be processed. Disk utilizations can be converted into I/O rates. Most commercial applications will tend to exhibit a more random nature.

The listed rates are again at 100% utilization. The random utilizations are fairly linear in nature, so by multiplying these rates by 0.40, you can come up with a good estimate of 40% utilization. Note that the CPU utilization for disk access must be added to the CPU utilization for a particular application when calculating the overall CPU utilization.

Note that a 40% utilization on a fast disk will convert into a higher I/O rate (IOPS) than a 40% utilization on a slow disk, as shown in Figure A1.15.

Curves like these are fairly easy to generate using data from a simple read, write, or timing program (see "Do It Yourself Method" section in Chapter 4).

A Word on Resource Utilizations

Why do recommended utilizations vary so much across physical resources. Shouldn't they all be the same?

No, they maximum utilization before unacceptable queuing occurs, which varies from resource to resource.

- If service time, T_S, is small, then a larger utilization (ρ) can be tolerated.
- The increase in Q length, and hence wait time (T_W), is proportional to T_S for a given increase in traffic.

---

* Change this if you wish, but remember that excessive queuing will increase the response time.

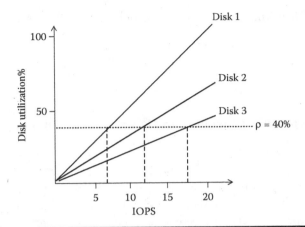

Figure A1.15   I/O and utilization characteristics of disks.

This means, in essence, that faster servers can tolerate higher utilizations than slower servers before wait times, and hence response times (latency) become an issue.

Little's Theorem*

This is sometimes known as *Little's result, law, lemma, or formula.*

> The long-term average number of customers in a stable system, L, is equal to the long-term average effective arrival rate, λ, multiplied by the average time a customer spends in the system, W; or expressed algebraically: $L = \lambda W$. (Wikipedia).

Or spelling out these quantities and expressing them in Little's words.

L is the average number of items in the queuing system
W is the average waiting time in the system for an item
λ is the average number of items arriving per unit time (arrival rate)

This disarmingly simple equation holds whatever the arrival process distribution, the service distribution, the service order, or seemingly anything else. One use often pointed out is that by knowing two of the parameters (perhaps by measurement), the other can be deduced. Other corollaries of Little's theorem or law are

Queue Length: The number of customers per UoW waiting for service, L_q, is

$$L_q = \lambda W_q$$

where W_q is the time spent in the queue and λ is the arrival rate.

---

* By John Little, not to be confused with Little John, employee of R. Hood, of Sherwood Forest.

Typical Wait Time: The average time a customer per UoW has to wait before receiving service is

$$W = W_q + \frac{1}{\mu}$$

where μ is the service rate minus customers per UoW served per unit time.

Example of the Theorem

A coffee shop owner calculates that 17 customers arrive at his shop every hour (λ) and the typical, (average) number of customers in the shop is 5 (L_q). He wants to know how long the customers spend in his shop. Little's theorem tells us that

$$5 = 17 \times W_q$$

Thus, wait time (average time in coffee shop) = 7/17 = about 25 min (ca. 0.4 h which is our time calculation unit).

Other Uses

As for other uses, there is an article coauthored by Little that outlines many uses of the law. See under heading "Usefulness of Little's Law in Practice" at the link below:

http://web.mit.edu/sgraves/www/papers/Little's%20Law-Published.pdf

There are any number of articles and presentations covering Little's law, but a good one that also covers the proof and applications of the law can be found in the presentation by Raj Jain:

Introduction to Queueing [sic] *Theory*
http://www.cse.wustl.edu/~jain/cse567-08/ftp/k_30iqt.pdf
Queueing Networks [J. Virtamo]
https://www.netlab.tkk.fi/opetus/s383143/kalvot/E_qnets.pdf

Jackson's Theorem

Jackson's network is an example of a *queuing network* in which a unit of work* (UoW) may pass through several servers (called *nodes* or *Jackson nodes* in this parlance), which may be serial or in parallel, with work passing through several servers via a series of queues at each. This is shown schematically in Figure A1.16.

A typical queuing network might be a single server issuing I/O requests to a series of disks in *partitioned mode* (see below, and Jain early in his presentation at the following link):

Queueing Networks [Raj Jain]
http://www.cse.wustl.edu/~jain/cse567-08/ftp/k_32qn.pdf

The servers in this figure have a queue, each of which the UoWs have to join to gain service. Jackson networks have the following characteristics:

---

* Some authors call these units *applications*.

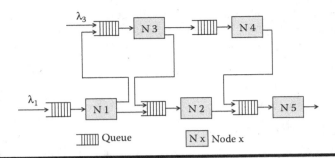

Figure A1.16 Queuing network: Jackson network.

- All outside arrivals to each node queue must follow a Poisson process (or distribution.)
- All service times are exponential.
- All queues are of infinite capacity.
- When a UoW leaves one node, the probability it will go to another node is independent of its past history and of the location of any other UoW.
- The whole system is in a steady state.

The Jackson network can then be thought of as a collection of M/M/1 queues with these known parameters. It is also an *open queuing network* as the UoWs come in, pass through the system, and disappear. A *closed system* is one where the UoWs go round the nodes in a closed loop and is known as a Gordon–Newell network. If work entering a node splits up after passing through, the process is known as *traffic partitioning*. Two streams of traffic merging into one node are known as *traffic merging*.

In the case of partitioned traffic, there is a simple equation showing that after the split, the total traffic intensity is as it was before partitioning. This is analogous to the conservation of energy and, for physicists, Kirchhoff's law, which says the currents entering and leaving a "node" in a circuit are the same, that is, conserved.

Both Jackson and Gordon–Newell networks have theorems associated with them that, in essence, develop the math needed to predict how such systems would operate.

Queueing Networks [covers Jackson and Gordon–Newell]
http://omikron.eit.lth.se/ETSN01/ETSN012015/lectures/queueing_networks.pdf
Open and Closed Networks (Jackson's Theorem for Open and Closed Networks)
http://www.iitg.ac.in/skbose/qbook/Slide_Set_14.PDF

Burke's Theorem

Burke's theorem (sometimes the Burke's output theorem) is a theorem (stated and demonstrated by Paul J. Burke while working at Bell Telephone Laboratories) asserting that for the M/M/1 queue, M/M/c queue, or M/M/∞ queue in the steady state with a Poisson arrivals process with rate parameter λ:

1. The departure process is a Poisson process with rate parameter λ.
2. At time t the number of customers in the queue is independent of the departure process prior to time t.

Assertion 1 flies in the face of my assertion in "Limitations of Theoretical Approaches" below, which says the output distribution of a server may not be the same as the input distribution. However, Burke's theorem applies to Poisson processes, and I may be right for other cases.

Open and Closed Networks [Sanjay Bose]
http://www.iitg.ac.in/skbose/qbook/Slide_Set_14.PDF

Queue Service Priority

In a *nonpreemptive model*, the service to a customer or unit of work (UoW) cannot be interrupted, this model being denoted in the fourth parameter in the Kendall (–Lee) notation as NPRP.

In a preemptive model, lower-priority work can be ejected from service whenever a higher-priority customer arrives, and once all higher-priority work has been serviced, the ejected work reenters the system for service; this is at the point of interruption in a preemptive resume model. In a *preemptive repeat* model, the service begins from scratch again.

The preemptive queuing model is denoted in the fourth parameter in the Kendall (–Lee) notation as PRP.

Response Time Percentiles

The Xth percentile of the value V of a variable means that X% of the relevant population is below the value V. The formula for percentiles in queuing theory usually relates to response time (latency) and depends on the arrival distribution of the queuing system. The formula for the Xth percentile of response time T_R for an *exponential* distribution is given by

$$X(T_R) = T_R \times \ln\left(\frac{100}{100 - X}\right) \qquad (A1.11)$$

where ln is the logarithm to base e. This gives, for example, the value of the 90th percentile of 2.3 T_R. Table A1.3 shows some value characteristics for three distribution types.

As a corollary (add-on fact), the formula for *wait time*, T_W, percentiles (exponential distribution) is

$$X(T_W) = \frac{T_W}{\rho} \times \ln\left[\frac{100\rho}{(100 - X)}\right] \qquad (A1.12)$$

Table A1.3 Response Time of the 90th Percentile for Two Distributions

Distribution Type	C Value[a]	Percent Less Than Average	90th Percentile
Hypoexponential	0.5	57	2.0 × Average
Exponential	1.0	63	2.3 × Average
Hyperexponential	2.0	69	2.8 × Average

[a] All we need to know about C is that it is a *squared coefficient of variance* (SCV), which basically indicates the *spread* of response times for that distribution, rather akin to a root mean square deviation (RMSD).

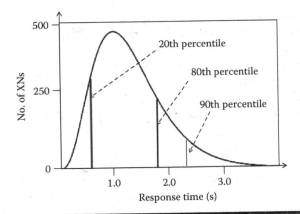

Figure A1.17   Response time percentile examples.

Percentiles are the usual way of specifying response times in a service level agreement (SLA), rather than a specific time with a plus and minus leeway or an average response time. Figure A1.17 shows three percentiles on a typical response time curve.

Other Queuing Formulas

General Queuing Math

This section represents a potpourri (selection) of items you may come across in articles on performance that involve queuing theory or techniques. Remember also that these metrics are not all relevant to the same people; for example, users and management will be interested in the last four items, and operational people mainly in the preceding metrics.

Queuing Parameters and Notation

In some formulas you may come across, the following parameters may occur when the arrival and service rates are in a steady state:*

λ = mean arrival rate (expected number of arrivals per unit time)
μ = mean service rate for a busy server
$1/\lambda$ = expected interarrival time (IAT)
$1/\mu$ = expected service time
$\rho = \lambda/\mu$
    = utilization factor for the service facility
    = expected fraction is in use of time the system's service capacity (μ)
    = is being utilized by arriving customers (λ)
c = number of servers

---

* In systems theory, a system in a steady state has numerous properties that are unchanging in time. This means that for those properties p of the system, the rate of change with respect to time is zero.

P_n = probability that there are *n* customers per UoW in the system
L = mean number of customers per UoW in the system
L_q = mean number of customers per UoW in the queue
L_s = mean number of customers per UoW being served
W = mean wait in the system
K = capacity of the queue (limited or infinite)
T_S = mean *service* time in developing simple queuing formulas
T_W = *wait* time
T_R = *response* time = $T_S + T_W$

Variances: There are a number of coefficients of variation for service and interarrival time (IAT) plus a figure for the variance of service time (response) of that server.

WoW: Much of the math in queuing will involve these parameters, as demonstrated in the articles at the two links below. One important difference in the significance of these quantities for us is whether they have a real meaning in IT. Some—number in queue, waiting time, and so forth—have important significance to supermarket planners hoping to minimize queue lengths.

They do not have much significance in IT unless they adversely affect the response time or throughput.

Simple Queuing Formulas

Single Server: These are some of the simpler queuing formulas that you may encounter. More detailed material can be found in the references at the end of this section. UoW (unit of work) is shorthand representing customer, transaction, query, job, and so forth.

1. The following formulas apply to a single server, Poisson arrivals, exponentially distributed interarrival times (IATs) and service times, infinite queues and population capacity, and FCFS dispatching.
   a. Probability of 0 (zero) in system: $(1 - \rho)$
   b. Probability of exactly *n* UoWs in the system: $P_n = \rho^2(1 - \rho)$
   c. Mean number of UoWs in *system*:

$$L_s = \frac{\lambda}{\mu - \lambda}$$

   d. Mean number of UoWs in the *queue*:

$$L_q = \frac{\rho\lambda}{\mu - \lambda}$$

e. Mean time of UoW in *system*:

$$W_s = \frac{1}{\mu - \lambda}$$

f. Mean time of UoW in *queue*:

$$W_q = \frac{\rho}{\mu - \lambda}$$

2. The next formulas apply to a single server, Poisson arrivals, exponentially distributed interarrival times (IATs) and service times, infinite queues, and population.
   a. Probability of 0 (zero) in system:
      Prob (0) Complex equation (see Baker reference below)
   b. Probability of exactly *n* UoWs in the *system*:

$$P_n = Prob(0)\left[\frac{(\rho M)^n}{n!}\right] \ if \ n \le M$$

$$P_n = Prob(0)\left[\frac{\rho^n M^M}{M!}\right] \ if \ n \le M$$

   c. Mean number of UoWs in *system*:

$$L_s = L_q + \frac{\lambda}{\mu}$$

   d. Mean number of UoWs in the *queue*:

$$L_q = Prob(0)\left[\frac{M^M \rho^{M+1}}{M!(1-\rho)^2}\right]$$

   e. Mean time of UoW in *system*:

$$W_s = \frac{L}{\lambda}$$

   f. Mean time of UoW in *queue*:

$$W_q = \frac{L_q}{\lambda}$$

Multiple Servers (N): These are some of the queuing formulas that you may encounter in dealing with multiple servers.

We know that $T_R = T_S + T_W$ (Response = Service + Wait times). The following are *wait times* for various numbers of servers $N = 1, 2, 4$, and n.

$$N = 1 \qquad T_W = T_S \times \frac{\rho}{(\rho - 1)}$$

$$N = 2 \qquad T_W = T_S \times \frac{\rho^2}{\left(1 - \rho^2\right)}$$

$$N = 4 \qquad T_W = \frac{T_S \times 8\rho^4}{\left(3 + 6\rho + 3\rho^2 - 4\rho^3 - 8\rho^4\right)}$$

Formula Links

Introduction to Queueing Theory [Raj Jain]
http://www.cse.wustl.edu/~jain/cse567-08/ftp/k_30iqt.pdf

Queuing Analysis [William Stallings]
http://cse.csusb.edu/ykarant/courses/f2006/csci530/QueuingAnalysis.pdf

Traffic Behavior and Queuing in a QoS Environment
http://web.mit.edu/dimitrib/www/OPNET_Full_Presentation.ppt
The above link contains some good general queuing theory and very good diagrams illustrating various principles.
A very detailed but readable account of the math of transaction processing systems can be found at

Performance Analysis of Transaction Processing Systems
http://www.amazon.com/Performance-Analysis-Transaction-Processing-Professional/dp/0136570089

Pollaczek–Kinchin(e) Formula for M/G/1

An M/G/1 queue is a queue model where arrivals are Markovian (described by a Poisson process), service times have a general distribution, and there is a single server. This formula is often called the P-K formula or theorem for obvious reasons, and even the full spelling of the names varies paper by paper. Put in comprehensible terms, it looks as follows:

$$\text{UoW in Total System} = \rho + \frac{\rho^2}{2(1-\rho)}\left[1 + (\lambda\sigma)^2\right] \qquad \text{(A1.13)}$$

James Martin uses the reciprocal of the mean service time instead of λ in the formula.

This represents the UoWs (customers, transactions, queries, or other piece of work) in the system as a whole, both queuing and being served.

λ = arrival rate
μ = service rate of server
ρ = server utilization $=\lambda/\mu$
σ2 = variance of service time

Two references are useful in trying to follow this formula or theorem:

Networking Theory & Fundamentals [detailed]
http://www.seas.upenn.edu/~tcom501/Lectures/Lecture10.pdf

The P-K Formula [from a manufacturing fabrication site!]
http://www.fabtime.com/p-k.shtml

Operational Analysis Math

Some performance monitors don't monitor certain metrics directly but need to deduce them by manipulating what data they do measure to give the metrics that operations people and users would like.

This sort of operational method is used by *TeamQuest* in their analysis of raw data to produce the metrics and their Teamquest Performance Indicator (TPI) dealt with earlier. For details of this process, see Appendix IV under "Operational Math Analysis Details."

Queuing Formulas: References

1. The queuing theory cookbook reference below summarizes succinctly the various metrics for different server configurations.
   Queuing Theory Cookbook [Samuel L. Baker]
   http://hspm.sph.sc.edu/Courses/J716/pdf/716-8%20Queuing%20Theory%20Cookbook.pdf
   Since the IT world moved from the classical mainframe–communications–disk world to the complex environment of today, some beloved queuing metrics begin to lose their value as performance indicators.
2. The paper at the link below is a short but useful discussion of disk queue lengths versus disk latency as metrics when looking for performance bottlenecks (in database systems, but the logic remains the same elsewhere). I feel it is useful to challenge certain queuing theory conclusions against the modern environment of clusters, storage area network (SAN), network attached storage (NAS), cache (memory and head of string [HOS]), and so on. I veer toward a pragmatic and hands-on approach.
   Disk Queue Length vs. Disk Latency Times: Which *Is* Best for Measuring Database Performance?
   http://www.r71.nl/index.php?option=com_content&view=article&catid=7:technical-docs&id=185:disk-queue-length-vs-disk-latency-times-which-is-best-for-measuring-database-performance&Itemid=50

The documents in the two links below (3. and 4.) concentrate mainly on queuing formulas for various server configurations and arrival and service time distributions.

3. *Queuing Theory Cookbook*
   http://hspm.sph.sc.edu/Courses/J716/pdf/716-8%20Queuing%20Theory%20Cookbook.pdf

4. *Queuing Formulas*
   http://web.mst.edu/~gosavia/queuing_formulas.pdf

5. A *Black Belt* reference for queuing formula across the Kendall–Lee notation range is *Basic Queueing* [sic] *Theory*
   http://irh.inf.unideb.hu/user/jsztrik/education/16/SOR_Main_Angol.pdf

Limitations of Theoretical Approaches

The theory of queuing as we have seen it here assumes particular types of distributions for the arrivals at a server in order to calculate the parameters of interest in service performance analysis. Get the distribution wrong, and you have the calculation based on this fact, that is, fairly useless. In addition, it is sometimes possible to alter the input distribution if you have control over the input, for example, how many people can enter data over what period.

In other cases, for example, a public website, this regulator mechanism is not readily available. This is my view and experience of online work and the applicability of standard arrival queuing theory to it.

- Normal data entry and business as usual (BAU) online OLTP work. This is dictated by the number of people involved and the availability of the work to be processed. My feeling is that this will be constant or constant in phases, like a bar chart with zero activity gaps between the bars, rather than a continuous distribution.
- Web-based work with a large enough population that users will be the closest to standard queuing arrival distributions, mainly because of this and its randomness.
- Standard queries and *ad hoc* queries might be random, but probably with a relatively small population of users.

Whatever the arrival pattern, when the first server has processed work with an arrival profile $f(t)$, the outgoing profile proceeding to the next server will not necessarily be the same $f(t)$. An example of this is a server processing transactions and passing requests on to a disk, and then passing resultant output to a user or other system via communications, and so on, through the system.

I have called this phenomenon *dispersion*, for want of a better term. I have never seen this discussed anywhere in the vast literature on queuing theory, although I have seen it hinted at in *traffic queuing analysis*. This sort of analysis finds its way into theoretical traffic (motorcar) analysis. For example, the approach pattern of traffic at a roundabout is not the same as the exit pattern at any exit point from that roundabout, even if there was only one exit, that is, straight ahead (Figure A1.18).

How this can be treated rigorously is anyone's guess, and so arrival distributions must be assumed for each server—first server in the chain and succeeding ones. I feel the lesson to be learned is not to try to model several resources in the chain as one exercise.

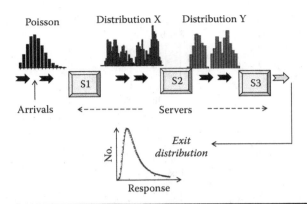

Figure A1.18   Queuing: dispersion of incoming distribution.

The reference link below has a table that tries to show the applicability of various theoretical and simulation approaches to IT issues, and it implies that there are several holes in the wholly theoretical approach.

Traffic Behavior and Queuing in a QoS Environment
http://web.mit.edu/dimitrib/www/OPNET_Full_Presentation.ppt

Sample Scenario

This scenario features an organization with 200 users accessing the system for transaction-based work and Internet work. Let us just examine the transaction work as an example to see where input distributions and service time distributions lead us.

First, the pattern of access will be dictated by the working day and the availability of data and queries, and so forth, for system access to be required. This pattern may or may not conform to any distribution and, in my experience, will be either a steady stream or very little activity, depending on what needs to be done. My feeling is that such an environment will generate a bar chart sort of distribution rather than a neat mathematical function as outlined above.

Second, look at the journey to and from the system by a transaction (XN). A typical input might be 100 or so characters and an output of many hundreds; data entry may be hundreds in and fewer out to the submitter. If all the messages are the same length, there would be a constant service time according to theory. I do not believe this would be true for transactions (XNs) as the arriving "customer."

A XN is driven by program invocation, the input telling it how to proceed and then the XN executes. The service time for the *input* is likely to be fixed (fixed length), but the service time for the ensuing XN might not be. For example, a payroll transaction (XN-1) may be executed with the flag "No tax due" on the input, but a second may have "Tax due," meaning extra processing (and extra I/O and network traffic too, probably) to handle the tax part of its work.

The input length may be fixed, but the service time will not be constant in this case. In fact, depending on how many paths and related actions there are in the XN, the service time could vary quite markedly and almost certainly will not follow a mathematical distribution.

There may also be a mix of transactions, XN-*a*, XN-*b*, ..., XN-*n*, each with its own variations in path length, and hence service time to confuse the issue further.

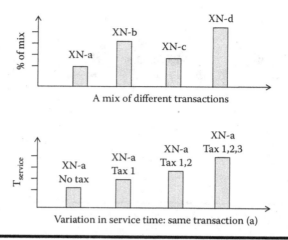

Figure A1.19   Variation in transaction service time or mix.

I could be miles off target in my assertions here, but am willing to be convinced by reasoned argument of the error of my ways. This is illustrated schematically in Figure A1.19.

There will be, in general, a pattern of work by people entering these transactions that is often flat during the whole working day or, in some circumstance, a series of flat peaks throughout the working day.

Summary

My view as expressed above is formed by the difference between formal mathematics and the actual behavior of IT equipment. My concern is not to take the theory too far, as it is mainly based on the following principles:

- The arrivals fit a distribution pattern—Poisson, exponential, and so forth—which may not be true.
- The service time also follows a mathematical pattern, which may not be true.
- A fixed dispatching mechanism is used—first come, first served (FCFS), and so forth.
- The queue length can be unlimited.
- The incoming population can be infinite or not.
- Even simple transactions and web requests travel through several resources where queues may form and the arrival patterns may change from one resource to the next. For example, if data arrives at a network for transmission with arrival pattern $f(t)$, there is no guarantee it will arrive at the next resource after transmission with the same pattern.

The combination of these choices can be analogous to taking about six or so different medications each day without anyone really knowing how they combine in effect (and believe me, they don't). The variances from the stated assumption may (or may not) assume great significance in the final outcome of the calculations if their effect is amplified by the differences.

All this is not to decry tools and simulations, but their limitations should be recognized. Website work may well follow queuing theory to some extent, but transaction and query work may not, resembling the distributions in the figure above rather than Poisson and the rest. The potential variation in service time for a single transaction muddies the water still further.

My own way would be to seek some consensus, where feasible, from

- Similar situations and configurations ("our system looks just like that one, whose behavior is understood")
- Rules of thumb (ROTs), guidelines developed from experience and consensus
- Simple calculations (in the appropriate circumstances)
- Modeling and simulations (as above)
- Performance testing tools
- Standard benchmarks of the appropriate type, that is, resembling the workload you are trying to size and understand
- Personalized benchmarks that match your requirements closely

Consensus means looking at different approaches (opinions in real life) and seeing where maximum agreement lies.

Support for my thesis comes from Bob Wescott in his performance book:*

Most computer performance books are fairly useless for solving your problems. Why? Because:

- Some have hundreds of pages of very difficult math that most people can't do and most problems don't require
- Many focus on a specific version of some product, but you don't have that version.
- There is no performance book for a key part of our transaction path.
- There are so many different technologies in your transaction path; to read all the necessary books would take longer than the average corporate lifetime.

I agree with Bob, and his words are a reflection of my own feeling that abstruse queuing theory is often a solution to which there is no problem or suffers from over-mathing.

---

* Bob Wescott, *Every Computer Performance Book*, http://www.amazon.com/Every-Computer-Performance-Book-Computers/dp/1482657759/.

Appendix II: Historical Benchmarks

Benchmark: A standard or point of reference against which things may be compared or assessed. In IT terms, this can usually be written as "a problem designed to evaluate the performance of a computer system, either directly or as a comparison with another system or systems."

In IT terms, historical means "over 10 years old," and knowledge of some benchmarks, historical and prehistoric, needs to be preserved, I feel. It may puzzle the reader as to why older benchmarks should be included in this book, but there are several good reasons, apart from my personal preference. First, they are *instructive** in learning about the pitfalls of performance comparisons and absolute measurements. Secondly, it is often necessary to compare the performance of systems that are of different generations in benchmarking terms.

For example, a customer wishes to replace his old AS/400 with a UNIX system but only has Transaction Performance Council (TPC)-A figures for the former and TPC-C figures for the latter. How does he compare them in terms of the extra performance he will get from the new UNIX system? Finally, there is a place for chronicling IT topics, and benchmarks are no exception for, as has been said, history has a habit of repeating itself.

They are also rather interesting, some of them in their own convoluted way, others in how they reflected contemporary thinking about what constituted a good test of performance.

> *WoW*: The whole field of benchmarking also generated the derogatory old chestnut about the speed of competitive systems: *"You don't need a stop watch to time the jobs on their systems; you need a calendar."*

Integer Benchmarks[†]

Dhrystone Benchmark

The Dhrystone benchmark is a test of C-compiler maturity, processor performance, and, to some degree, processor architecture. It is a computer-bound program of about 100 statements in 12 procedures that utilizes no operating system calls and thus can, in theory, be run without an operating

---

* To quote Sherlock Holmes.

[†] Often called *fixed point* benchmarks.

system. The benchmark originally appeared in "Communications of the ACM," October 1984, volume 27, Number 10, in an article by Reinhold P. Weicker: "Dhrystone: A synthetic systems programming benchmark."

The benchmark does not use floating-point data types and, like the Whetstone (see later discussion), it is based on a statistically derived mix of instructions found in "average" programs. There were at least two versions of the benchmark. The latest version, V2, was available as one "C" version split onto three parts.

The two source code parts are to be compiled separately so that optimizing compilers are prevented from moving code out of the measurement loop. Limitations of the benchmark include the fact that the two versions can give different results for the same workstation, typically 10%–15% different. However, that is not always the case, as shown in Table A2.1.

Version 2 (2.1) was created to have a common version of Dhrystone for Ada, C, and Pascal, thereby avoiding confusion when comparing results. Another reason was to maintain the statistical distribution of statement execution while allowing the use of optimizing compilers. In version 1, some optimizing compilers suppressed the generation of "dead code," which did not vary, for example, code-to-print results. Version 2 has the printing of all main computed variables outside the measurement loop to prevent compilers discarding it. Also, code has been added in selected places to prevent the compiler moving the execution sequence outside the measurement loop.

One basic ground rule for 2.1 is that modules should be compiled separately, rather than using a single, merged program and then linking them together. Dhrystone is a "synthetic" benchmark that does no particular job; it can be sensitive to run-time parameters and it is operating systems and compiler dependent. It is possible to get results nearly 50% different for the same machine by using different operating systems (and hence compilers) for the benchmark.

For example, Table A2.2 shows figures for the same IBM PS/2 model 70 from the *UNIX Review*, May 1988.

Dhrystone can generally run in the high-speed cache of a workstation, and so it really measures the speed of the cache and not the whole memory and central processing unit (CPU). In addition, there is no "central control" body to oversee the benchmark and verify the results.

Despite these limitations, it is sometimes quoted as a measure of integer performance. Results are quoted in thousands of Dhrystones per second, where high is good. The floating-point cousin of Dhrystone is the Whetstone benchmark, named after the place in the United Kingdom where it was conceived.

Table A2.1   Variation in Dhrystone Ratings

Machine	Dhrystone 1.1	Dhrystone 2.1
Sun 3/80	4.9	4.7
Sun 4/50 IPX	43.5	14.4

Table A2.2   Dhrystone Variation by Operating System

AIX-PS/2	ISC-PS/2	SCO Xenix-PS/2
12,679	10,745	8,650

Derivation of MIPs Rating from Dhrystones

Often, workstations quote a "MIPs" figure along with a Dhrystone rating. This "MIPs" number is not the same as the one discussed previously; it is the figure derived from the fact that the VAX 11/780 is rated at 1757 Dhrystones and is often rated as "a 1 MIP" machine by DEC and users.

This we can call a "VAX MIP," and this is the rating called "MIPs" quoted in workstation performance. It is not the same as the IBM relative processor performance (RPP) number, although it is possible to relate the two to some extent. Thus, Equation A2.1, showing VAX MIPs from Dhrystone results, holds:

$$(\text{VAX}) \text{ MIPs} = \text{Dhrystones} (\text{Version 1.1}) / 1757 \qquad (A2.1)$$

We will examine MIPs again in the discussion of the SPEC integer benchmark and compare them as a measure of integer performance. To obtain "2.1" version VAX MIPs, divide the Dhrystone 2.1 rating by 1650.

MIPs from Dhrystones: Effects of Memory Cache

Cache, or high-speed memory, was introduced into mainframes many years ago to remove the imbalance between what the CPU demanded in terms of data and instructions and what the main memory could deliver. Cache memory was relatively expensive and typical sizes used were 8K to about 64K.

Today, instruction and data caches are common even in workstations and other machines, with cache sizes typically ranging from 32K up to 256K. Although cache memory is cheaper than it was, it is still expensive to populate the whole of memory with it. With cache sizes of this order, many programs can live and execute entirely in cache and never use main memory. If two machines are compared for performance on such cache resident programs, only a comparison of cache speed is being made. If, however, the jobs being run are big enough to need main as well as cache memory, then when the instruction needed is not in the cache, access to main memory will be necessary.

The percentage of occasions where such requests can be satisfied from the cache only is called the *cache hit rate*. This hit rate depends very much on the "cache handling algorithm" implemented in the machine. It is possible for a bigger, faster cache to be less effective than a smaller, slower one. The effect of cache speed becomes evident when the program being run on the system is contained entirely in the cache, which means that the CPU has a 100% "hit rate" within the cache when executing instructions.

When the program is too large for the cache and is spread across both cache and main memory, then the speed of execution will drop, as the cache often needs to take instructions needed by the CPU from main memory.

Figure A2.1 illustrates schematically what happens to the observed performance of a machine as the cache hit rate is reduced. It is feasible for one machine to appear faster than another when running "cache resident" programs (which are very small!) but to be slower than the other when running large programs across cache and main memory. This means that the drop-off in performance illustrated above is more rapid for the fast cache machine than the slower one.

What we are saying here is that a MIPs rating is not a reliable measure of machine performance, except possibly for machines with identical architectures. Reinhold Weicker observed

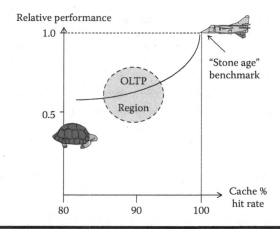

Figure A2.1   Effect of cache hit rate on performance.

more discrepancies when he ran the Dhrystone program on a VAX 11/780. Using Berkeley 4.2 Pascal, the benchmark yielded 483 instructions and executed in 700 μs, giving a native rating of 0.69 MIPs. When he used DEC VMS Pascal, 226 instructions were executed (on the same machine) in 543 μs, giving 0.42 MIPs.

In other words, the lower MIP "machine" ran the job faster than the higher MIP "machine." Weicker's paper* is an interesting look at several aspects of "popular benchmarks" and the paper below summarizes these and other aspects of the benchmark:

Dhrystone Benchmark: History, Analysis, Scores and Recommendations
http://www.johnloomis.org/NiosII/dhrystone/ECLDhrystone WhitePaper.pdf

Gibson Mix

This was one of the first efforts to structure performance measurements and reduce reliance on pure MIPS, with its notorious dependence on *which* instructions are being executed. It was a mix of instructions that Jack C. Gibson of IBM developed in 1959 after studying traces of program instructions running on IBM 650 and 704 computers. The measurement is never quoted today but, for historical reasons, the instruction mix is reproduced here.

Instruction	Percentage of Mix
1. Load and store	31.2%
2. Fixed point add and subtract	6.1%
3. Compares	3.8%
4. Branches	16.6%
5. Floating point add and subtract	6.9%

---

* The benchmark originally appeared in *Communications of the ACM*, October 1984, volume 27, Number 10, in an article by Reinhold P. Weicker: Dhrystone: A synthetic systems programming benchmark.

6. Floating point add and multiply	3.8%
7. Floating point add and divide	1.5%
8. Fixed point multiply	0.6%
9. Fixed point divide	0.2%
10. Shifting	4.4%
11. Logical AND, OR	5.3%
12. Indexing	18.0%

The Gibson mix is now consigned to history, but what better place to record it than in a book on systems performance and benchmarks. Incidentally, there was a similar genre of benchmark called the (UK) *Post Office Benchmark*, again now consigned to the IT history books and the memories of IT veterans who fought in the *Benchmark Wars*.

DEC VUPs

VUPs stands for VAX units of performance, with the VAX 11/780 = 1.0 running a certain version of the VAX VMS operating system. The term was used in at least two senses during the 1980s. A VUP rating was derived by the simple Equation A2.24, showing the derivation of VUPs rating:

$$\text{VUPs Rating} = \frac{\text{Time Taken by Test System running same Job}}{\text{Time Taken by VAX 11 / 780 for that Job}} \tag{A2.2}$$

A stricter interpretation of the term was the geometric mean of the ratios of the execution times of 99 specific CPU-intensive benchmarks, including 71 FORTRAN benchmarks, 4 COBOL benchmarks, and 24 Lisp benchmarks. For example, using the strict interpretation, the VAX 6000 Model 410 achieved 6.64 VUPs.

Tables of DEC systems with VUPs rating were produced, and many of the systems also had a SPEC rating; thus, other manufacturers with SPEC ratings for their machine could make "guesstimates" of their power relative to DEC systems.

How many VUPs is that Alpha in the window? [Interesting and nostalgic for old timers]
http://h18002.www1.hp.com/alphaserver/performance/vups_297.html

Floating-Point Benchmarks*

Whetstone Benchmark

The Whetstone benchmark was originally published in *Computer Journal* Volume 19, No. 1, (February 1976) in the article "A synthetic benchmark" by H. J. Curnow and B. A. Wichman, who were then at the National Physical Laboratory in Whetstone, England.

---

* Some of these benchmarks are designed to test *parallelism* in scientific applications.

Benchmark Structure

The benchmark was initially written in Algol60 and was also offered in FORTRAN and PL/1 versions. The benchmark is based on a statistical distribution of Algol statements, which is not confirmed for any languages other than Algol, FORTRAN, and PL/1. The program is written such that a single pass through the benchmark executes 100,000 "Whetstone instructions."

The benchmark is currently, and has been for many years, run only in FORTRAN, with an iteration multiplier of 10 yielding the execution of 1,000,000 WHETSTONES. Thus, the resulting Whetstone rating is derived by dividing 1,000,000 by the execution time in seconds (i.e., if the benchmark executes in 0.8 s the machine is rated at 1.25M WHETSTONES, or 1250K WHETSTONES (1250 KWIPS), as shown in Equation A2.3 (Whetstone benchmark rating):

$$\text{Whetstone Rating} = 1{,}000{,}000/\text{Time of execution} \qquad (A2.3)$$

The Whetstone benchmark can be performed in both *single* and *double* precision floating-point formats, with the results being tabulated in Whetstone instructions per second. The higher this number, the better the floating-point performance of a computer system. It tests a combination of computer floating-point processing power and compiler maturity. The benchmark consists of a main program with three subroutines accounting for 47% of the time spent in the benchmark code. Library functions account for the other 53%.

The floating-point functions included in the Whetstone benchmark are
Convergent series:

- Trigonometric functions, such as sin, cos, and atan.
- Transcendental functions, such as exp, sqrt, and log; for example,

$$X = \sqrt{e^{(\ln(x)/t1)}}$$

The benchmark does, however, have some limitations:

- It is a *synthetic* benchmark that calculates no specific result; it is simply an amalgam of scientific functions.
- There is no check on the correctness of the results of computations.
- It is compiler dependent and, since the structure of the program is well known, it is possible to "tweak" compilers to increase performance.
- It can generally run in the high-speed cache of a workstation and so really measures the speed of the cache rather than the whole memory and central processing unit (CPU). R.P. Weicker estimates that 100% hit rates can be obtained with quite small caches, especially if the code is reordered in some way.
- Figures may be quoted for *single* (32-bit) or *double* (64-bit) precision. Some workstations have single-precision figures up to several times their double-precision figures (see Table A2.3).
- There is no "central control" body to oversee the benchmark, except for the Pascal version in the Pascal Evaluation Suite from the British Standards Institution (BSI).

Despite these limitations, it was quoted as a measure of floating-point performance.

Both the Whetstone and Dhrystone benchmarks are increasingly seen as less useful than the SPEC 1.0 benchmark and succeeding versions, which are described later.

Table A2.3   Linpack Double- and Single-Precision Performance

Machine	Single Precision	Double Precision	Ratio DP/SP
Sun SS10/41	16.2	7.3	2.22
H-P 710	24.3	10.8	2.25
H-P 730	32.1	25.8	1.24
Apollo 10010	2.5	2.3	1.09

Linpack Benchmark

Linpack, issued in 1979, is a program library package written in FORTRAN by Dr. Jack J. Dongarra, formerly of the Argonne National Laboratory and now at the University of Tennessee.

The Linpack benchmark is an example of a real work benchmark that uses a linear programming problem to test machine performance. Linpack solves dense systems of linear equations with a high percentage of floating-point operations. A "dense" system is one where few of the elements of the vector or matrix arrays are zero, that is, nonsparse (the solution of problems using sparse matrices is very different from this method).

Linpack solves a set of equations of the form* and is shown in Appendix IV under *Matrix Equations*. The Linpack equations are devised in different sizes.

Approximately $2/3(n^3) + 2n^2$ floating-point operations are needed to solve this system of equations. Normally, n is 100 in Linpack benchmarks, and the benchmark is then said to be "100 × 100" giving c. 700,000 instructions. Sometimes 300 × 300 is used (as in matrix300 in the SPEC 1.0 benchmark); or 1000 × 1000 (which aims to measure "peak" performance in millions of floating operations per second [MFLOPS]), called *towards peak performance* (TPP).

The programming problem is standardized so that results from a variety of machines can be meaningfully compared. The innermost computational loops of the Linpack benchmark are isolated into subroutines called the "basic linear algebra subroutines," or BLAS for short. Since most of the floating-point work is carried out by the BLAS, the overall performance of the workstation as measured by Linpack will be highly dependent on the implementation of BLAS.

The three basic implementations of BLAS are

Coded BLAS: These are coded in machine language for the machine in question, although these versions are no longer collected by Jack Dongarra.

Rolled BLAS: These are coded in FORTRAN for machines with *vector* capability.

Unrolled BLAS: These are coded in FORTRAN for *scalar* machines.

For use with *supercomputers*, there are versions called Extended BLAS or Level2 BLAS, but they need not concern a discussion on workstation performance (at least not yet!).

Some factors to note about Linpack are that

- It has reasonable "central" control and ownership.
- It can be compiler and cache dependent (particularly the BLAS). Over 75% of the benchmark time is spent in subroutine *saxpy*, which is less than 256 bytes long.

---

* The simple math of these equations is quite well explained in the link http://www.akiti.ca/SimEqR12Solver.html.

■ It can be quoted in single- or double-precision forms and the two should not be mixed when comparing systems, as indicated in Table A2.3.

It can be quoted as 100 × 100, 300 × 300, or 1000 × 1000 (TPP), and these should not be mixed when comparing systems. TPP in general gives a much higher MFLOP rating than 100 × 100. It is generally accepted as a good measure of the floating-point performance of a workstation and other systems in the absence of real customer applications.

The results of the Linpack benchmark are reported in units of MFLOPS or KFLOPS (thousands of floating operations per second). The larger this number, the better the floating-point performance. The Argonne National Laboratory report, which is updated about every 5–6 months, contains data on about 100 machines from Crays to IBM PCs and includes several of the more popular workstations.

There are several types of Linpack runs listed; in particular, figures for single precision and double precision may show some machines to be much worse at the latter than the former, in some cases by a factor of up to two.

Jack Dongarra issued the following disclaimer in the Linpack Performance reports:

"The timing information presented here should in no way be used to judge the overall performance of a computer system. The results reflect only one problem area—solving dense systems of equations using the Linpack programs in a FORTRAN environment."

Java Linpack Benchmark

This is a Java version of the numerically intensive Linpack benchmark, and while the results are often confusing, they often show the state of Java rather than the speed of the underlying processors it runs on.

Versions of Linpack are also available in C and FORTRAN.

Lapack Benchmark

Lapack is a library of FORTRAN 90 subroutines for solving the most commonly occurring problems in numerical linear algebra. It has been designed to be efficient on a wide range of modern high-performance computers. The name Lapack is an acronym for "linear algebra package."

Lapack's SGESV and DGESV functions solve, in *single* and *double precision*, respectively:*

$$A * X = B$$

where A is an M-by-N matrix and X and B are N-by-NRHS matrices.

The original goal of the Lapack project was to make the widely used EISPACK and Linpack libraries run efficiently on shared-memory vector and parallel processors. On these machines, Linpack and EISPACK (a software library for numerical computation of eigenvalues [valid solutions] and eigenvectors of matrices, written in FORTRAN) are inefficient because their memory-access patterns disregard the multilayered memory hierarchies of the machines, thereby spending *too much time moving data* instead of doing useful floating-point operations.

---

* Skip the math if you wish. In layman's terms, Lapack does *hard scientific sums* on various machines.

Lapack addresses this problem by reorganizing the algorithms to use block matrix operations, such as matrix multiplication, in the innermost loops. These block operations can be optimized for each architecture to account for the memory hierarchy and so provide a transportable way to achieve high efficiency on diverse modern cached machines.

Lapack is a freely available software package. It is available from netlib via anonymous ftp and the Internet at
http://www.netlib.org/lapack.

Lawrence Livermore Loops

This is a collection of kernels from the Lawrence Livermore National Laboratory including the 24 *Livermore FORTRAN Kernels* (LFK), which are samples of floating-point computations taken from many diverse scientific applications; and the Livermore loops (LL). They were designed to measure the efficiency of code generated by compilers for CDC (Control Data Corporation) machines. The primary purpose of these "tests" is to evaluate the performance of computers with *vector* and/or *parallel processing* capabilities.

The current benchmark consists of 24 LFKs, which represent types of computational work found on large-scale scientific processors. The kernels contain a wide range of FORTRAN coding practices and floating-point operations. A MFLOPS rating is obtained by assigning weights to the different types of floating-point measurements.

The benchmark consists of 24 *do loops*, some of which can be vectorized, and some of which cannot.

The benchmark was published in 1986 in *Livermore FORTRAN kernels: A computer test of numerical performance range*. The Livermore loops were originally written in *FORTRAN*, but have since been ported to many programming languages, including C. These kernels are listed in this link:

http://www.netlib.org/benchmark/livermore

The benchmark is also called Livermore FORTRAN kernels or LFK.

'*This LFK test may be used as a standard performance test, as a test of compiler accuracy (checksums), or as a hardware endurance test*' (Frank McMahon, author).

The major use of Livermore Loops can be summarized as;

■ A test of FORTRAN compiler development and maturity in terms of code optimization
■ A test of compiler accuracy
■ A test of the speed of different types of floating-point operations in the hardware of a processor
■ A test of the intrinsic speed of floating-point operations when the loops are recoded in machine language

The only useful measurement from the LFKs applicable to servers is the MFLOP rating, which in general will not be the same as the Linpack MFLOP rating because of the way in which it is derived. The MFLOP ratings can be reported for both scalar and vector performance.

PERFECT Club Benchmark

See the section *Benchmarks to End All Benchmarks* in this Appendix.

SPEComp2001 Suite

SPEComp is fashioned after the SPEC CPU2000 benchmarks, unlike the SPEC CPU2000 suite, which is split into integer and floating-point applications.

SPEComp2001 is partitioned into a medium and a large data set. The medium data set is for moderate-size shared-memory multiprocessor (SMP) systems of about 10 CPUs. The large data set is oriented to systems with 30 CPUs or more. The medium data sets have a maximum memory requirement of 1.6 GB for a single CPU, and the large data sets require up to 6 GB. Runtimes tend to be a bit long for people used to running SPEC CPU benchmarks.

SPEComp targets mid-size parallel servers. It includes a number of science and engineering and data processing applications, shown below as type/*language*.

1. Chemistry/biology/ *C*
2. Fluid dynamics/physics/ *FORTRAN*
3. Air pollution
4. FORTRAN image recognition/neural networks/ *C*
5. Face recognition/ *FORTRAN*
6. Crash simulation/ *FORTRAN*
7. Genetic algorithm/ *FORTRAN*
8. Fluid dynamics/ *FORTRAN*
9. Earthquake modeling/ *C*
10. Multigrid solver/ *FORTRAN*
11. Shallow water modeling/ *FORTRAN*
12. Quantum chromodynamics/ *FORTRAN*

SLALOM Benchmark

See *Benchmarks to End All Benchmarks* in this Appendix and this link:
http://hint.byu.edu/documentation/Gus/SLALOM/First Scalable.html

CERN* Benchmarks

The CERN *Benchmarks Suite,* appearing in my original benchmark notes, no longer appears on its website but can be found in *Old CERN Benchmarks* in this Appendix.

Performance Benchmarks
http://information-technology.web.cern.ch/book/cern-clo
There is also a section on the website about managing VMs, which might be useful in cloud environments:
http://clouddocs.web.cern.ch/clouddocs/
CERN has developed other benchmarks related to its work and these can be found on its website: http://home.web.cern.ch/

---

* The name CERN is derived from the acronym for the French "Conseil Européen pour la Recherche Nucléaire," or European Council for Nuclear Research.

Los Alamos Benchmarks

A collection of benchmarks extracted from applications at the Los Alamos National Laboratory by the Computer and Research Applications Group (Monte Carlo, particle-in-cell, matrix calculations, vector calculations, kernels, etc.).

NAS Parallel Benchmarks (NPB)

A collection of eight benchmark problems from NASA Ames Research Center designed to study the performance of highly parallel supercomputers. The eight benchmark problems are specified in a *pencil-and-paper* fashion, leaving benchmark staff free to select the language constructs and implementation techniques best suited for a particular system. Results are normalized against a Cray Y-MP and Cray C90.

The original eight benchmarks specified in NPB 1 mimic the computation and data movement in computational fluid dynamics (CFD) applications:

- Five kernels
  - IS: Integer Sort, random memory access
  - EP: Embarrassingly Parallel
  - CG: Conjugate Gradient, irregular memory access and communication
  - MG: Multi-Grid on a sequence of meshes, long- and short-distance communication, memory intensive
  - FT: discrete 3D fast Fourier Transform, all-to-all communication
- Three pseudo applications
  - BT: Block Tri-diagonal solver
  - SP: Scalar Penta-diagonal solver
  - LU: Lower-Upper Gauss-Seidel solver

The benchmark is developing, and versions NPB 2 and 3 (various versions) exist.

PARKbench Benchmark

Parallel kernels and benchmarks (PARKbench) is a parallel benchmark created by a group at Oak Ridge National Laboratory. Its initial focus is on the new generation of scalable distributed-memory message-passing architectures. The initial benchmark release concentrates on FORTRAN 77 message-passing codes using PVM (parallel virtual machine). Future versions will adopt MPI (message passing interface) and HPF (high-performance FORTRAN) over PVM.

SPEC Benchmarks

The SPEC Organization

The Standard Performance Evaluation Corporation (SPEC) (initially a cooperative), is an organization dedicated to producing benchmarks that are reasonably scientific, unbiased, meaningful, and relevant. It was formed in September 1988 with vendors as sponsors and released its first set of benchmarks, the *SPEC Benchmark Suite for* UNIX Systems version 1.0 (SPEC 1.0), in October 1989. There followed a series of revisions and updates, based on deficiencies found in each current version, which were sometimes suggested by vendors who were at the losing end of some of the tests! Other benchmarks and metrics were developed to take account of IT developments, for example, the web.

- SPEC92
- SPEC95
- SPEC2000
- SPEC2006

SPEC has broadened its portfolio of performance benchmarks and metrics, and today (December 2014) its benchmarks are as follows:

- CPU
- Graphics/workstations
- ACCEL/MPI/OMP
- Java client/server
- Mail servers
- Solution file server
- Power
- SIP
- SOA
- Virtualization
- Web servers

To keep up to date on SPEC, see the SPEC home page: https://www.spec.org/

SPEC 1.0 Benchmark

SPEC announced the availability of Release 1.0 of the SPEC benchmark suite in October 1989. Release 1.0, which consists of 10 engineering and scientific benchmarks, is endorsed by 12 of the leading computer-system vendors (including IBM) as a common means of measuring computing systems performance, particularly UNIX workstations and multiuser systems.

Benchmark Structure

SPEC 1.0 compares the performance of systems running single copies of the benchmark programs. In real life, there are likely to be many jobs running simultaneously on a uni- or multiprocessor system. SPEC has accordingly developed a new metric called the SPECthruput. Multiple copies of each of the 10 SPEC 1.0 benchmarks are run, and the new metric is calculated as will be shown.

Release 1.0 was a complex set of benchmarks that measure CPU-intensive (integer and floating-point) computations associated with engineering and scientific applications. In total, release 1.0 consisted of over 150,000 lines of C and FORTRAN code, and a high-end technical workstation or minicomputer would require up to 2–3 h to execute the complete series of benchmarks. Table A2.4 shows the SPEC 1.0 series of benchmarks.

The size and complexity of the SPEC benchmark suite, drawn from real application sources, make it a meaningful test of engineering and scientific performance and eliminates the "cache" resident aspects of some other benchmarks discussed previously.

Table A2.4 SPEC 1.0 Benchmarks

Program	Type of Benchmark	Language	Measure
gcc	Engineering (GNU compiler)	C	Integer
espresso	Engineering (PLA simulator)	C	Integer
spice 2g6	Engineering (ECASD Analog circuit simulator)	FORTRAN	FP
doduc	Scientific (Reactor physics)	FORTRAN	FP
nasa	Scientific (Synthetic - 7 kernels)	FORTRAN	FP
li	Engineering (LISP)	C	Integer
eqntott	Engineering (Boolean)	C	Integer
matrix300	Scientific (Monte Carlo)	FORTRAN	FP
fpppp	Scientific (Quantum chemistry)	FORTRAN	FP
tomcatv	Scientific (Fluid dynamics)	FORTRAN	FP

Future suites were stated to measure other important aspects of system performance, such as disk, graphics, and communications, although little has been seen of these at the time of writing. This benchmark will replace existing older common measures of system performance, namely

- Whetstones (floating point)
- Dhrystones (integer)
- MIPS

SPEC Metrics

The parameters used in the SPEC 1.0 benchmark are

SPEC Reference Machine: VAX 11/780

SPEC Reference Time: The elapsed time in seconds that it takes the reference machine to run a SPEC job

SPECratio: The ratio of the time taken by the reference machine to run a SPEC job divided by the time taken by the system under test to run the same job (definition of SPECratio number):

$$\text{SPECratio} = \frac{\text{Time taken by VAX 11/780}}{\text{Time taken by Test System}} \qquad (A2.4)$$

SPECmark: The geometric mean of the 10 SPECratios, denoted SR_1, SR_2, ... in Equation 2.5 showing the definition of SPECmark:

$$\sqrt[10]{SR_1 \times SR_2 \times SR_3 \times ....SR_{10}} \qquad (A2.5)$$

SPECthruput:

■ Start K*N copies of SPEC benchmark i (i = 1 to 10), N = number of CPUs on system, K=Number of jobs per processor (K = 2)
■ Measure the elapsed time (E(i)) to complete
■ Compute the throughput ratio as follows:

$$TR(i) = \frac{R(i)}{E(i)}$$

where R(i) is the throughput reference time (of the VAX 11/780).

■ Calculate the geometric mean of the 10 throughput ratios TR(i) using Equation A2.6, showing the definition of SPECthruput:

$$SPECthruput = \sqrt[10]{TR_1 \times TR_2 \times \dots TR_{10}} \qquad (A2.6)$$

This leads to the final metric, called the aggregate throughput:

$$Aggregate\ Thruput = Number\ of\ CPUs\ (N) \times SPECthruput$$

SPEC Integer and Floating-Point Breakdown

Sometimes the individual integer and floating-point SPECratios and SPECmarks were quoted for SPEC 1.0. The SPECmarks are calculated by taking the 6th root of the product of the 6 floating point measurements and the 4th root for the integer measurements.

SPEC is essentially a composite benchmark, and it is common practice to use the individual components *SPECfp*, the floating-point measure derived from the six floating-point programs in the same way SPECmark is derived; and *SPECint*, the integer element derived from the other four programs. If you are comparing machines for general scientific work with a large floating-point content, then quote the SPECfp figures (and/or Linpack) rather than the full SPECmark.

The most recent SPEC benchmarks emphasize the floating point and integer part of the benchmark as a matter of course.

SPEC SDE Benchmark

This benchmark, the Systems Development Environment (SDE), was devised as a test of efficiency in UNIX program development. It in no way represents the capacity of particular systems running the developed applications, as some vendors have implied. It is a close relative of the Australian (Monash University) MUSBUS benchmark.

MIPS and SPEC 1.0

It is often overlooked that there should be a close correlation between MIPS as derived from Dhrystones and the integer part of SPEC 1.0. In fact, they should yield the same number. Why is this the case? Simply because they both purport to be measures of integer CPU performance and are both derived using the VAX 11/780 as the basis for the measurement. The fact that they do not give the same number means that one of them is not reliable as a measure. MIPs are *still* quoted today as performance indicators quite erroneously. It is common to see a vendor of symmetric multiprocessors (SMPs) quoting X MIPs for the uniprocessor and 8X MIPs for the eight-processor version of their hardware. This gives the unwary purchaser the impression that the eight-processor machine can handle eight times the throughput of the single-processor machine. In fact, it is rare for an eight-processor SMP machine to handle more than about five times the commercial work-load of a one-processor machine.

SPEC 92 Benchmark (Retired)

There were some drawbacks to the initial SPEC metrics. A particular floating-point job was found to be sensitive to using a preprocessor and gained several factors in SPECratio, giving an artificially inflated overall SPECmark.

The matrix300 benchmark program, similar in nature to Linpack, was particularly helped by blocking up code in the system cache. Compilers can be helped, via a preprocessor, to achieve this aim. H-P and IBM were able to considerably increase the SPECmark and SPECfp ratings of their larger machines by the use of such preprocessors. Examine the figures in Table A2.5, which shows the matrix300 results before the use of a preprocessor and after. Two "after" cases are shown where the preprocessor was enhanced before running the benchmark again.

As a result of this and other less dramatic inconsistencies, SPEC decided to revise the SPEC 1.0 benchmark programs, although the metrics were preserved. SPEC 1.1/1.2 now uses a different job mix comprising 14 floating-point and 6 integers, and the separate integer and floating-point results (CINT92, CFP92) are shown, along with the individual SPECratios. The job list for SPEC92 is shown in Table A2.6.

SPEC 95 Benchmark (Retired)

This SPEC version differentiated between integer and floating-point performance with two variations of SPEC 95:

- SPECint 95, an *integer* benchmark, written in C and often written as CINT95
- SPECfp 95, a *floating-point* benchmark, also in C and often written as CFP95

Table A2.5   HP and IBM marix300 Rating Progression

Vendor	Initial Performance	Preprocessor (1)	Preprocessor (2)
HP	36.1	273.3	407.7
IBM	78.3	103.8	729.8

Note: Large numbers are better.

Table A2.6   SPEC92 Benchmarks: Integer and Floating Point

SPEC CINT92	008.espresso	*Circuit Theory*
	022.li	LIST Interpreter
	023.eqntott	Logic Design
	026.compress	Data Compression
	072.sc	UNIX Spreadsheet
	085.gcc	GNU C Compiler
SPEC CFP92	013.spice2g6	Circuit Design
	015.doduc	Monte Carlo Simulation
	034.mdljpd2	Quantum Chemistry (1)
	039.wave5	Maxwell's Equations
	047.tomcatv	Coordinate Translation
	048.ora	Optics Ray Tracing
	052.alvinn	Robotics: Neural Nets
	056.ear	Human Ear Modelling
	077.mdljsp2	Single Precision (as (1))
	078.swm256	Shallow Water Model
	089.su2cor	Quantum Physics
	090.hydro2d	Astrophysics
	093.nasa7	NASA Maths Kernels
	094.fpppp	Quantum Chemistry

The benchmark also considers two performance metrics—speed and throughput—and these are further divided into normal (conservative) compilation and aggressive (optimized) compilation. These are clarified in Table A2.7.

As with SPEC92, this benchmark consists of individual jobs that exercise the target system in various ways. These can be found in either of the two papers cited below.

A Brief Introduction to the SPEC CPU 95 Benchmarks
http://www-inst.cs.berkeley.edu/~cs266/sp10/readings/reilly96.pdf

SPEC Version Description (by same author as above)
https://www.spec.org/cpu95/news/cpu95descr.html

Table A2.7 SPEC95 Benchmark: Different Metrics Involved

Compilation	Speed	Throughput
Conservative (Normal)	SPECint95_base95 SPECfp95_base95	SPECint_rate_base95 SPECfp_rate_base95
Aggressive (Optimized)	SPECint95 SPECfp95	SPECint_rate95 SPECfp_rate95

SPEC CPU2000 Benchmark (Retired)

This, like SPEC95, is a split benchmark with:

- CINT2000: the integer benchmarks.
- CFP2000: the floating-point benchmarks.

Benchmarks are provided in two suites —an integer suite, known as CINT2000, and a floating-point suite, known as CFP2000. Like the SPEC95 benchmark, there are speed and throughput metrics, which are detailed on the links

SPEC CPU2000 Run and Reporting Rules
https://www.spec.org/cpu2000/docs/runrules.html

SPEC CPU2000 V1.3
https://www.spec.org/cpu2000/

SPECseis96 Benchmark

There is a mass of information about the SPEC benchmarks at the following link:
https://www.spec.org/hpc96/docs/RelatedPublications/seis-qa.html' and then a 6pt space
The SPEC Benchmarks [Describing the SPEC benchmarks, giving their history, a description of how they are measured and how the scores are calculated, and other useful information across the SPEC range of benchmarks.
http://mrob.com/pub/comp/benchmarks/spec.html

Real-Time Benchmarks

Rhealstone Real-Time Benchmark*

UNIX systems are not in general suitable for real-time control systems, in which rapid switching between tasks after an external interrupt is a vital requirement. Normal UNIX systems do not have *kernel preempt* facilities, whereby the kernel can switch from one task to another when a higher-priority task is waiting.

The Rhealstone real-time benchmark (vintage 1989) is a synthetic test for measuring the real-time performance of multitasking systems.

Digital (see footnote) reported on the following components of the Rhealstone benchmark:

1. Task-switch time: The time between two active tasks of equal priority. The typical results for the task-switch time are shown in Figure A2.2.

---

* See "Digital Alphastation Family Performance Brief DEC OSF/1" EC-N3890-10, November 3, 1994.

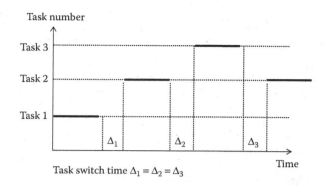

Figure A2.2   The Rhealstone benchmark schematic.

2. Preemption time: The time for a high-priority task to preempt a running task of lower priority
3. Interrupt time: The average delay between the CPU's receipt of an interrupt and the execution of the first instruction in an interrupt service routine
4. Intertask message latency: The delay within the kernel when a data message of nonzero length is sent from one task to another.

There are a variety of other graphical representations that accompany Rhealstone results. See http://www.drdobbs.com/cpp/implementing-the-rhealstone- real-time-be/184408332

Rhealstones are intended to provide a standard of comparison between real-time computers across the industry. Hence, their specification is

a. Independent of the features found in any CPU
b. Independent of any computer bus architecture
c. Independent of the features or primitives of any operating system or kernel

Rhealstone Measurements

The six Rhealstone components yield a set of time values (in the range of tens of microseconds to milliseconds, for most PCs). Although the individual benchmark measurements are of significance by themselves, it is useful to combine them into a single real-time figure of merit so that overall comparisons between real-time computers can be made.

Today, it is sometimes associated with real-time Linux systems as some of the "executives" it was previously associated with are no longer with us.

Implementing the Rhealstone Real-Time Benchmark

http://collaboration.cmc.ec.gc.ca/science/rpn/biblio/ddj/Website/articles/DDJ/1990/9004/9004d/9004d.htm

Composite Benchmarks

Introduction

The benchmarks discussed previously have, in the main, been "pure" benchmarks measuring specific capabilities of the CPU. Several other benchmarks have been developed to test the all-round ability of computer systems to do mixtures of work, including fixed point, floating point, and input/output (I/O). Some of these benchmarks form the substance of this chapter.

Descriptions and tables of output for some of the older benchmarks (and even older hardware) covered in this book can be found in

A Benchmark Tutorial (1989)
http://www-inst.eecs.berkeley.edu/~cs266/sp10/readings/price89.pdf

UNIXBench

UNIXBench started life in 1983 at Monash University (home of MUSBUS, which begat KENBUS and SDET and dates to 1983) as a simple synthetic benchmarking application.

It was then taken and expanded by *BYTE* magazine, some of whose varieties of it are outlined below.

The stated purpose of UNIXBench was to provide a basic indicator of the performance of a UNIX-like system via multiple tests, which are used to test various aspects of the system's performance. These test results are then compared to the scores from a baseline system to produce an index value, which is generally easier to handle than the raw scores. The entire set of index values is then combined to make an overall index for the system.

Some very simple graphics tests are included to measure the 2D and 3D graphics performance of the system.

byte-UNIXbench
http://code.google.com/p/byte-unixbench/

BYTE Magazine Benchmarks

There are several varieties of the BYTE UNIX benchmark. The one referred to as "old" in this book is the benchmark used prior to 1988, and many "BYTE" benchmark results in documents refer to the "old" BYTE benchmark specification. Another version was introduced in 1988, but this too has been superseded. The latest BYTE benchmark, called the Native Mode or BYTEMARK, is the latest version. The two older benchmarks are described in this Appendix.

> **Note:** The BYTE UNIX benchmarks should not be confused with the BYTE DOS benchmarks. Although similar in concept, they can give different results for the same machine. The *new*(!) DOS benchmarks are described in the August 1990 edition of *BYTE* magazine.

Pre-1988 BYTE Benchmark

The old BYTE benchmark consisted of seven programs and one shell command script. It was designed for the comparison of performance of both hardware and software on UNIX-based systems. The programs and script exercise typical UNIX system and compiler functions.

The BYTE benchmark includes

■ **The Pipe Program:** This creates a UNIX pipe and transfers 0.5mb of data. Operating system and disk overhead are measured since the pipe makes use of the kernel as well as disk I/O.

- **The Sieve Program**: The Sieve of Erastothenes determines and displays the prime numbers within a fixed numeric range. Looping, testing, and incrementing are heavily used. The program is a test of C-compiler efficiency and processor throughput.
- **The System Call Program**: The get-process identification system call is repeatedly issued by the program. Since the "getpid" call has little processing associated with it, the program essentially measures the system overhead to trap to the UNIX kernel and return to the user.
- **The Function Call Program**: The program is designed to complete a processing task in one of two ways: directly or via a user function call. Both versions of the program are compiled and executed. The difference in elapsed times of the two program versions is used to approximate the overhead associated with execution of a user function call.
- **The Loop Program**: The program repetitively increments a long integer. The instruction path length for the compiled program is relatively short. The program may be used to measure processor speed in a processor-bound environment.
- **The Disk Write Program**: The program opens a file and sequentially writes 256 512-byte records to disk. The program primarily measures disk speed since little processing is performed.
- **The Disk Read Program**: This program complements the disk write program. It reads 256 records from disk in random fashion and then the file is removed. The program measures random disk access performance as it may represent typical UNIX usage.
- **The Shell Script**: The shell script consists of a series of standard UNIX commands. The command functions include sort, octal listing, pattern matching, disk copy, character count, and file erase. I/O redirection is included. In its simplest form, the shell script is used to determine the elapsed time to complete a series of UNIX commands. The shell script can also be used to evaluate the performance of multiple concurrent tasks that might be found in a multiuser environment. Typically about six identical background tasks using the shell script might be started and the time taken to complete them recorded.

Figure A2.3 shows the consolidated results of the Pre-1988 BYTE benchmark.

1988 BYTE Benchmark

The new BYTE benchmark was "announced" in 1988 by *BYTE* magazine and is described in the March 1990 edition of *BYTE*. It is an evolving benchmark as the article implies. The benchmark covers eight areas divided into low-level and high-level benchmarks as follows:

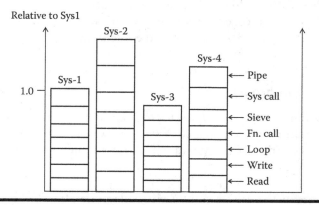

Figure A2.3   BYTE benchmark consolidated results.

Low-level

- Arithmetic
- System calls
- Memory operations
- Disk operations
- Dhrystone

High-level

- Database operations
- Random read, write, and add operations on a database file. It uses a server with one, two, four, or eight clients requesting database access.
- System loading
- Shell scripts generating one, two, four, or eight processes.
- Miscellaneous
- A C compile/link, the Tower of Hanoi (recursive operations), and the calculation of SQRT(2) to 99 places.

The magazine article expressed the intent to add the Whetstone benchmark to the suite as well as other high-level tests in the future.

Note: These BYTE measurements are presented in terms of the Everex 386/33 representing unit performance in each element of the benchmark. The old benchmark used actual times. The DOS benchmark uses the IBM PC/AT as the "unit" of measurement.

BYTEmark or Native Mode Benchmark

The BYTEmark benchmark test suite, dating from about 1995, is used to determine how the processor, its caches, and coprocessors influence overall system performance. Its measurements can indicate problems with the processor subsystem, and (since the processor is a major influence on overall system performance) give us an idea of how well a given system will perform. The BYTEmark test suite is especially valuable since it lets us directly compare computers with different processors and operating systems. The code used in BYTEmark tests simulates some of the real-world operations used by popular office and technical applications. Tests include numeric and string sort, bitfield working, Fourier and assignment manipulations, Huffman, IDEA, LU decomposition, and neural net test of the performance of CPU and memory (see below for an explanation of these entities).

Benchmark Structure

Release 2 of this benchmark was known as NBench and consisted of

- Numeric sort: Sorts an array of long integers
- String sort: Sorts an array of strings of arbitrary length
- Bitfield: Executes a variety of bit manipulation functions
- Emulated floating-point: A small software floating-point package

- Fourier coefficients: A numerical analysis routine for calculating series approximations of waveforms
- Assignment algorithm: A well-known task allocation algorithm
- Huffman compression: A well-known text and graphics compression algorithm
- IDEA encryption: A relatively new block cipher algorithm
- Neural net: A small but functional back-propagation network simulator
- LU decomposition: A robust algorithm for solving linear equations

The originator of this, *BYTE* magazine, ceased trading several years ago.

Khornerstone Benchmark

This benchmark was created by Workstation Laboratories (the United States). It consists of a balanced mix of

- Floating-point tests
- Integer (fixed-point) tests
- Disk I/O tests

and uses 21 separate programs coded in C and FORTRAN. They are run separately and then together, and the "Khornerstone" rating obtained is derived thus:

- 20% of the value is based on *disk* performance.
- 27% of the value is based on *integer* performance.
- 23% of the value is based on *floating-point* performance.
- 30% of the value is based on the *total time* taken to execute the entire set of tests.

The mix is meant to represent a typical single-user workload on a PC or workstation, and the results are expressed in units of thousands of Khornerstones per second. Large numbers indicate better performance.

Some features of the Khornerstone benchmark are

- It is a composite benchmark.
- It is single user.
- It is operating system dependent.
- It can be cache dependent.
- It is widely accepted (but long in the tooth).

This is sometimes referred to as the "Tested Mettle" benchmark after the name of a report that outlines the performance of various workstations, which includes Whetstones, Dhrystones, and Linpack as well as Khornerstone ratings.

MUSBUS Benchmark

MUSBUS (Monash University Suite for Benchmarking UNIX Systems) is a set of programs developed by Ken McDonell to control workload-based performance measurement.

The programs emulate a user typing commands with resulting terminal output. MUSBUS allows a benchmarker to control relevant variables like the number of users while handling extraneous details. MUSBUS is not a single program, and it gives no single figure of merit with which to compare systems.

MUSBUS
https://www.nas.nasa.gov/assets/pdf/techreports/1991/rnd-91-010.pdf

AIM Benchmarks

The AIM benchmarks are C programs used by AIM Technology to compare the performance of UNIX systems. There are several AIM benchmark suites:

- AIM Application Benchmark Suite II
- AIM Multi-User Benchmark Suite III
- AIM Workstation Benchmark Suite VI
- AIM Multi-User Benchmark Suite VII
- AIM X Windows Benchmark Suite X
- AIM Milestone Benchmark

Multiple versions of the benchmarks exist. AIM Technology, which was based in California, has performance reports based on the above benchmarks. The *AIM Performance Report* (used until June 1990) uses the older versions of Suite II and Suite III.

The *AIM Performance Report II* Uses newer versions of Suite II and Suite III, plus the new Milestone benchmark. AIM Technology also has other performance-related software offerings:

- AIM NETWORK File Manager for Sun NFS
- AIM Disk Tuner, Job Scheduler, Job Accounting

AIM II Benchmark

The AIM II Suite was introduced in 1984 to test the performance of different parts of a UNIX system simulating a single user. This means that a single program performs the whole suite sequentially. Using a program to analyze a "Results" database, it is possible to

- Assess the performance of a single system under various user conditions
- Measure the performance of multiple UNIX systems using a variety of application mixes
- Compare the performance of up to 20 systems at a time

AIM II uses 38 functional tests, which consist of different types of operation (disk I/O, pipes, etc.) usually in combinations.

AIM II Functional Tests

These tests are the basic building blocks of AIM II. For the older AIM Performance Report, the functional tests are used in combination to evaluate performance for

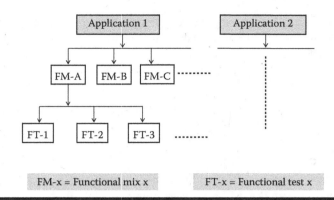

Figure A2.4   AIM II tests and mixes.

- Application mixes
- Functional mixes (FMs)

as seen in Figure A2.4.

Users can select and weight application mixes (for a charge) and run tests representing their own workload, for example:

- 20% word processing
- 10% spreadsheet
- 70% accounting

This might be done to compare several systems running the same (weighted) application mix. In addition, a user can compare different (weighted) application mixes on a single system. Details of the AIM II tests and mixes are shown the bullet list here.

AIM II Function Test Details

- Disk I/O
- Arithmetic operations
- Array references
- Fork
- Pipes
- RAM tests
- TTY (teletype) tests
- System calls
- Function calls

Interpreting AIM II Benchmark Data

There are two main versions of the AIM II benchmark. Version 1.1 presents

- The raw data from the *functional tests* and comparisons with other systems under test.
- The data from the *functional mixes* and comparisons with other systems under test.
- The raw data from the *application tests* and comparisons with other systems under test.

Version 2.1 dispenses with the last two items in the list above and graphs only the raw numbers for a system in the new AIM Performance Report II.

Multitasking Benchmarks

In this book, "multitasking" means a single user executing multiple tasks simultaneously. "Multiuser" means multiple users executing a single or multiple tasks generated by *external terminal I/O*, either via real terminals and users or a terminal emulator. In either case, the system then has to handle character I/O, which impacts the benchmark performance of a system.

AIM III Benchmark Suite

Note: For information on the AIM performance reports to which Suite III contributes, see the section on AIM Benchmarks above.

There were two versions of AIM Suite III 1.4 and 3.0. Version 1.4 was used for the old AIM Performance Report, and version 3.0 was used in the newer AIM Performance Report II.

AIM Suite III versions 1.4 and 3.0 contain all of the same tests, although the tests themselves have changed slightly. The disk tests do more reading and writing to disk, and others have been improved so that optimizers will not affect their operation. For Version 1.4, some of the tests were eliminated by optimization at compile time and therefore were compiled without optimization. For Version 3, all tests are optimized.

The following description applies to both versions.

AIM Suite III is a multitasking system-level benchmark. No external interactive users are simulated in the default mix that is used for the performance reports. The benchmark exercises functions from both the engineering/scientific and the commercial environments. It is very CPU intensive and emulates a large user load but does no terminal I/O (an internal driver and benchmark).

AIM Suite III is made up of 31 tests. The tests are C programs that stress specific functions of a system. Tasks are created to load a system. The greater the number of users simulated, the greater the number of tasks that are started. Each task runs all of the tests in a random order. The exact tests differ from version 1.4 to 3.0.

The tests stress the following components:

System calls: Calls to the UNIX system (kernel) to do a kernel function.
Disk I/O: Files are written, read, and copied using 10 KB block size.
Pipes: Pipes pass information between two segments of a program.
Arithmetic: They test addition, multiplication, and division for short (16 bit) and long integers (32 bits), and single (32 bit or "float") and double (64-bit) precision floating-point modes.
Function calls: The functions are called with zero, one, two, and three parameters.
Examine RAM: Tests, memory reads, writes, and copies are done in short, long, and character modes.
Directory search: Searches for 40 file names that exist and 40 file names that do not exist.

As a way of tailoring the benchmark, the user can select and weight functional tests to suit their own needs. However, AIM Suite III defaults to the following:

- 20% RAM
- 10% float
- 10% pipe
- 20% logic
- 20% disk
- 20% math

This is called the AIM standard mix and is used for the performance reports.

Interpreting AIM III Version 1.4 Benchmark Data

Two metrics are used in the original AIM Performance Reports for relative system performance positioning.

Performance rating: The percentage of power that the system under test has compared to the Standard AIM System (SAS), a DEC VAX 11/780 running Ultrix. It is a measure of "raw processing power" relative to the SAS.

User load rating: This is a measure of system throughput, excluding terminal overhead. It is the maximum number of simulated users that can be supported before response time becomes unacceptable. The response time cutoff is 1.2 jobs/minute/user. One *user load,* or one *simulated user*, is one process that executes all 31 of the tests, one at a time. One *job* is one of the 31 tests.

The "performance rating" is similar to the "AIMs" rating on the new APR II, but they are not directly comparable. Also note that this user load rating is not directly comparable to the "maximum user load" for APR II. The new reports uses a response time cutoff of 1 job/minute/user instead of 1.2, and the new Suite III Version 3.0 is slightly heavier (i.e., harder to run, as version 3.0 is more demanding for a given user load).

The Standard AIM System (VAX 11/780) has a User Load Rating of 12 and a performance index of 100, the baselines for performance assessments.

Interpreting AIM III Version 3.0 Benchmark Data

Three of the metrics presented on the first page of the AIM Performance Report II are for relative system performance positioning and come from AIM III Version 3. A chart is also included showing system throughput for varying user load levels. The following descriptions are from the APR II.

AIMs: The AIM Performance Rating reflects the overall performance of the system measured in AIM Multiuser Performance Units. A DEC VAX 11/780 (SAS) typically rates 1 AIM.

User loads: Maximum user load indicates the multitasking user load where the system's performance could become unacceptable, that is, less than one job/minute/user load. The user loads for the SAS is 9. One "user load," or one "simulated user," is one process that executes all 31 of the tests, one at a time. One "job" is one test, so each user load runs 31 jobs at each level of testing.

Jobs/minute: Maximum throughput, the point at which the system is able to process the most jobs per minute.

System throughput graph: The total amount of work the system processes per minute at various user loads. Graphed as jobs/minute, it shows how many jobs (or tests) a system can complete per minute as a function of the number of simulated users.

The AIMs rating is similar to the "performance rating" from the original APR, but they are different and not directly comparable. This is due to differences in Suite III versions.

Note that this maximum user load rating is not directly comparable to the "user load rating" for the original APR. The new reports uses a response time cutoff of 1 job/minute/user instead of 1.2, and the new Suite III Version 3.0 is slightly heavier (i.e., the old user load rating for the SAS is 12; the new user load rating for the SAS is 9).

The user load rating may not be appropriate for determining the number of users a given system can support. The two metrics do not necessarily reflect identical relative performance ratios between two given systems because the formulas and data used to arrive at these metrics are different.

Generally, AIM III results should not be used to represent a given customer's real application unless it can be shown that the customer's application and these tests exercise similar functions in approximately the same proportion. The AIM III Suite can also exercise the following resources:

TTY (tele-typewriter): simulates the actions of online users.

- Tape read/write
- Line printer

Virtual memory use: Allocates as much virtual storage as a system will give it (20 MB maximum!) and changes memory locations such that little locality of reference is possible and paging results.

Database calls: These resources can be exercised singly or in combination. Additionally, users can add any test written in C. There are, however, some points to note about AIM III:

- It is a multiuser, multitasking benchmark with possible *simulated* terminal I/O but no *real* terminal I/O.
- AIM III release 1.4 may not take full advantage of compiler optimization techniques. This limitation is removed in version 3.0 of AIM III.

It has the following advantages:

- It is portable to most UNIX implementations.
- It has a large database of results for several vendors' systems.
- It is regulated by AIM Technology.

AIM Benchmark Suite VII

This appears to be the only benchmark in the AIM stable that has documentation on the Internet.
http://sourceforge.net/projects/aimbench/

Neal Nelson Benchmark

The Neal Nelson benchmark is a product of Neal Nelson Associates and is aimed at measuring performance in a variety of commercial environments. It is, like the AIM benchmark, a multitasking rather than a multiuser set of tests. Neal Nelson offers a variety of performance tests and services, the main one being the Business Benchmark. Other services and tests available are

- Business Benchmark Reports
- Business Benchmark Source Code
- Benchmark Services
- A Remote Terminal Emulator (RTE) and Software
- Multi-User Benchmark with RTE for UNIX World
- An RPG Benchmark

The Business Benchmark is available in C, Basic, FORTRAN, and other languages.

The Business Benchmark

The Business Benchmark consists of 18 separate test programs ranging from very specific tests (e.g., 64-bit arithmetic) to composite tasks. These tests can be grouped to exercise a system doing work similar to tasks such as

- Word processing
- Spreadsheet
- Database management
- Engineering and scientific
- Programming and application development

The Neal Nelson Business Benchmark

- Runs 1 to 100 copies of the 18 test jobs, stressing the system with an increasing load
- Runs on UNIX systems only
- Has disk I/O buffers artificially fixed at 6 Mb
- Is multitasking, not multiuser
- Has no terminal I/O either *real* or *simulated*

The Neal Nelson benchmarks measure times for the various tasks in seconds, and so low values mean higher performance.

Neal Nelson Business Benchmark Reports

Each of the 18 tests of the Business Benchmark is reported separately. The report of each test consists of a response time graph and a bar chart showing the percentage difference in response time for two systems being compared.

The reports could be purchased directly from Neal Nelson & Associates. For publication, Neal Nelson combined the results from their numerous tests into four general categories:

- Integer performance
- Floating-point performance
- Disk performance
- Disk cache performance

The results are then charted for various machines. The benchmark is rarely seen today but, like others, is sometimes used to compare the performance of old systems with new where another benchmark is shared by those systems.

Today: Neal Nelson Benchmark Laboratory has developed benchmarks in a number of other areas, including new benchmarks—one for power efficiency and another to measure throughput for Sybase, Oracle, MySQL, and PostgreSQL. Documentation on what appears to be an embryo Neal Nelson relational database management system (RDBMS) benchmark can be found as part of the classic 1993 *Benchmarking Handbook* at

Neal Nelson (Draft)
http://research.microsoft.com/en-us/um/people/gray/benchmarkhandbook/chapter10.pdf
The latest web-site information I can find is:

Neal Nelson Benchmark Laboratory
http://www.worlds-fastest.com/

Conclusion: The latest online references I can find to Neal Nelson in its various disguises are dated 2008, and the website www.nna.com appears to grind to a halt at 2006.

ECperf (Java)

ECperf was designed for benchmarking J2EE application servers. It consists of a specification and a benchmarking kit that is designed specifically to test and measure the performance and scalability of J2EE application servers.

This Java Enterprise Edition (EE) benchmark from Sun (as was) was designed for measuring the performance of Enterprise Java Beans (EJB) containers. It is designed to measure internal functions such as memory management, connection pooling, and caching, rather than the graphical interface or database I/O. The ECperf workload focuses on manufacturing, supply-chain management, and order/inventory processing.

Results are measured in benchmark business operations per minute (BBops/min), which is the combination of the total number of customer transactions and manufacturing work orders processed in one minute.

PC Magazine Glossary
http://www.pcmag.com/encyclopedia/

ECperf Benchmark Specification
https://jcp.org/aboutJava/communityprocess/final/jsr004/index.html

ECperf Presentation
http://home.agh.edu.pl/~ajanik/links/J2EEPerformance.pdf

Currency: Seems to run out of steam in 2002. It is possibly replaced by SPECjbb of various denominations, e.g., SPECjbb2000 or, possibly SPECjAppServer2002.

See
http://user.it.uu.se/~martink/d/java-processor-study.pdf
http://www.spec.org/osg/faq/

Transaction Processing Benchmarks

Preamble

It may be useful to recall the difference between *internal throughput rate* (ITR) and *external throughput rate* (ETR). They are defined as follows:

$$ITR = \frac{Transactions/second}{Processor\ Busy\ Time}$$

$$ETR = \frac{Transactions/second}{Elapsed\ Time} \tag{A2.7}$$

ITR effectively measures the transactions per CPU second in an unconstrained environment, that is, enough memory, disk, and so on to drive the CPU to high utilizations.

ETR effectively measures the transaction throughput rate of the whole system as observed by the end user. It is not necessarily a measure of processor performance. The ITR measurement described above will provide this measure for a single system or, in the case of two or more systems, a comparison. IBM uses these concepts along with another relating to the performance of mainframes or large systems in general. This is the *large systems performance reference* (LSPR) developed in the 1970s.

The development of the LSPR was to have a more realistic measure of large systems performance, in all its aspects, other than the discredited MIPs. It measures the ITR (as defined above) via different LSPR benchmarks for CICS/DB2, IMS, TSO, and multiple-batch workloads. When the work completed (transactions or job steps) is measured, it is divided by the total elapsed time taken (wall clock time), giving the ETR (as defined above).

The ETR is divided by the average processor utilization (ρ) to give the LSPR ITR to normalize the results (Equation A2.8). This gets around the situation wherein a workload takes a longer elapsed time because (for some reason or other) the processor utilization is different in the different runs of LSPR.

$$ITR = \frac{ETR}{\rho} \qquad \text{(A2.8)}$$

Thus, dividing the ETR by the utilization normalizes the throughput to that which would be obtained if each test was run at 100% utilization and $\rho = 1$ (in theory) in Equation A2.8).

Debit/Credit Benchmark

This section is included for completeness. It should be noted that the TPC benchmarks essentially superseded the debit/credit and the TP1 benchmarks, which can give inconsistent results depending on the way the benchmarks are run.

In the summer of 1984, Jim Gray of Tandem Computers wrote an early version of what eventually became the celebrated "Anon et al." paper. This early version was distributed by Gray to a number of interested Tandem employees, as well as to 19 other professional acquaintances in industry and academia for comments and suggestions. "Anon et al." was graciously used by Gray to suggest that the paper was authored by this entire group*.

The paper recommended the adoption of three standard performance tests for OLTP systems: one on-line transaction processing test, dubbed debit/credit; and two batch tests, a sort and a scan. The rationale for these three tests was

> that they would adequately characterize the key aspects of a system intended for commercial on-line transaction processing work. For the on-line test, the paper proposed a highly stylized emulation of a teller support system in a large, multi-branch bank. (Omri Serlin)

The original debit/credit benchmark was created by the Bank of America for evaluating vendor bids for teller applications. Since then, numerous vendors have implemented it in different ways.

It is a benchmark measuring ETR. Two of the implementations of the benchmark are

■ *ET1*: This usually implies an *external* driver
■ *TP1*: This usually implies an *internal* driver and a relational database and is a batch (no terminal I/O) process.

The debit/credit benchmark has the following characteristics:

■ Single, simple file; update intensive application
■ Four files: account, teller, branch, and history
■ Transaction flow:
  – *Begin transaction*
  – *Read message from terminal (100 bytes)*
  – *Update account file*

---

* http://research.microsoft.com/en-us/um/people/gray/Benchmark Handbook/chapter2.pdf.

- *Write to history file*
- *Update teller file*
- *Update branch file*
- *Write message to terminal (200 bytes)*
- *Commit transaction (Xn)*

For each Xn/sec measured, it uses

- 100,000 account records
- 100 teller records
- 10 branch records
- 2,590,000 history records

Throughput measurement is that 95% of all Xns must have better than 1 sec *internal* response time irrespective of CPU utilization. The response time metric for the debit/credit benchmark warrants further consideration.

Consider the case of two competing systems, A and B. System A achieves a rating of 25 transactions per second while B achieves 20. System A is evidently a more powerful system than System B. Because of the very simple nature of the benchmark, it may not exercise many of the facilities of the system being tested. Figure A2.5 shows this in diagram form.

System A has the best result but is running at 80% utilization to achieve it, whereas System B, although apparently slower, is cruising at 55% utilization. This is another (early) example of the benchmark dilemma.

If you reread the topic LSPR above, you will see the logic behind its normalization of results.

Debit/Credit Details

- Debit/credit defines a total of 20 fields. The emphasis is on very simple screen definition with minimal terminal interaction. This is a typical requirement for banking ATM–type applications. Debit/credit sends and receives a relatively short data stream to the terminal—about 200 characters.
- Debit/credit has only one transaction type. Based on its CPU, disk, and terminal I/O activity, it falls somewhere between a RAMP-C "simple" and "average" transaction type.

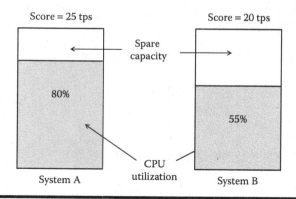

Figure A2.5 The debit/credit dilemma.

- Debit/credit executes approximately 25 COBOL statements per transaction when implemented in VSE/COBOL/CICS/VSAM.
- Debit/credit uses 100 s for *keying + think time* (see *Interactive Response Time Law* in Appendix V). This may be typical for an ATM network in a banking environment, but it is probably not typical for many commercial environments.
- Debit/credit specifies that transaction logging is required as part of the benchmark process.
- Debit/credit measures response time as "internal" response time, or the time interval between the point where the system receives the last character of input from the communications adapter until the system sends the first character of output to the communications adapter. This measured response time may not be representative of what the end-user experiences, since network transmission time is not taken into account.
- Debit/credit measures throughput as the number of transactions per second at the point.
- In other words, debit/credit measures throughput at a constant predefined response time, with variable system utilization.

A one-second response time criterion may be appropriate for a banking ATM application simulated by debit/credit, but it may not be representative for more complex commercial applications. There is no requirement to state at what system utilization the response goal was met, so it is difficult to estimate the true capacity of the system. For example, two systems can report similar throughput at a 1-s response time, yet one system could have a significantly lower system utilization than the other and therefore have more CPU capacity for doing extra work, perhaps by having more disks.

Debit/credit requires the use of an X.25 connection to a network for terminal attachment, although most vendors use their native terminal attachment protocol. The use of internal response time eliminates the communications related response time.

Debit/Credit Benchmark Summary

Application type

- Banking ATM

Disk I/O operations

- Data files accessed : 4
- Number of disk I/Os: 7

Terminal I/O description

- Number of fields: 20
- Characters input: 100
- Characters output: 200

Application description

- Transaction types: 1
- Transaction mix: 100%
- Average number of COBOL statements executed/transaction: 25

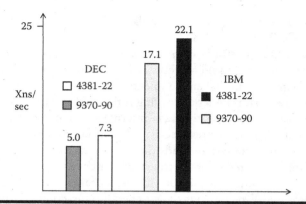

Figure A2.6 Another debit/credit dilemma.

- Key time + think time: 100 s
- Record level locking: Yes
- Transaction logging: Yes
- Network: X.25

Measurement metrics:

- Response time: internal
- Throughput: 95% < 1 s

The debit/credit benchmark is inherently unreliable as Figure A2.6, taken from the DEC/IBM midrange benchmark wars in 1988, illustrates graphically. The performance numbers differ by more than a factor of three, the price/performance numbers (not shown) by a factor of four. A similar chart could be drawn for IBM and DEC benchmarks on the DEC 8810, 6210, and MicroVAX 3600, but the point is made.

Giving credence to such discrepancies is like taking notice of aircraft test reports where one says the range is 2000 miles, another 6000 miles. The question then is, would you join the maiden flight across the Atlantic from London to New York on this aircraft?

There are other benchmarking tricks played by hardware and software vendors, which we will draw a veil over for the moment. The older TPC benchmarks, discussed in the subsequent sections, sought to bring some semblance of order to the unruly world of benchmarking and vendors in perennial commercial combat for supremacy.

TPC-A/TPC-B Benchmarks

TPC-A is a publicly available benchmark whose specification is more rigorous than the debit/credit benchmark it was designed to replace.

The debit/credit benchmark originated with the Bank of America in 1973 and was designed to compare systems suitable for their IT workload. It is therefore not applicable to other applications and workloads. TPC-A is a simple, single transaction program doing simple file updates in a bank teller environment with integrity and recovery characteristics.

These characteristics are defined by what are known as the *ACID Tests*, standing for

- *Atomicity*: The changes made to the system by a transaction must be accomplished entirely or not at all. If a transaction cannot complete, any changes made must be rolled back or undone.
- *Consistency*: The transaction must change the state of the system from one valid state to another valid state. The results of a transaction must be reproducible and predictable.
- *Isolation*: Changes made to shared resources by a transaction do not become visible outside the transaction until the changes are committed. This means, for example, that if a transaction has updated two out of four related records it intends to change, another transaction cannot access any of them until they have been committed.
- *Durability*: The changes made and committed by a transaction will survive subsequent system or media failure. This is normally achieved by logging changes to indexes and data and registering commit points within or at the termination of a transaction program.

The tested system must guarantee the ability to ensure database consistency after recovery from

- Permanent irrecoverable failure of database, tables, logs, and so on.
- System crash or hang requiring re-boot/re-IPL to recover
- Failure of all or part of memory (loss of contents)

These ACID properties are built into the TPC benchmark specifications to eliminate some of the loopholes in the debit/credit and TP1 benchmarks, which often yielded widely different results for machines of comparable power, as we saw in the RAMP-C and debit/credit discussions.

TPC-A, like any nonspecific benchmark, should only be used to compare the capacity of systems running simple transaction processing applications. In particular, the results in transactions per second achieved in a TPC-A benchmark will almost certainly not be achieved by normal business-transaction processing systems, unless the business just runs TPC-A. Similar riders apply to the TPC-B benchmark discussed later.

Overview of TPC-A

The TPC benchmark A (TPC-A) exercises the system resources needed to perform tasks associated with online transaction processing (OLTP) with database update activity. This OLTP environment is characterized by

- Multiple online terminal sessions
- Significant disk I/O
- Moderate system and application execution time
- Transaction integrity

The TPC-A workload is designed to represent a bank teller system, similar to debit/credit but with certain constraints and different metrics:

- Transactions/second (tps)
- Subject to a response time constraint
- The associated cost per transaction/second

The benchmark can be run on a local area network or a wide area network (tpsA-Local, tpsA-Wide). The TPC-A Standard contains rules, definitions, and descriptions for

- Transaction and terminal profiles
- Transaction system properties
- Logical database design
- Scaling rules
- Distribution, partitioning, and message generation
- Response time
- Duration of test
- System under test (SUT), driver, and communications definition
- Pricing of system
- Full disclosure of results
- Audit

The simulation of terminals is done by a *remote terminal emulator* (RTE), which is outside the SUT and is usually remote.

There are still some areas of OLTP not defined by TPC-A, but the benchmark is closer to *real-life* transaction processing than debit/credit and some other benchmarks (see the OLTP benchmark comparisons after the description of TPC-C).

TPC-A Details

There are several key areas of the benchmark as defined by the TPC. One thing that often escaped notice was that the file system used was the bench markers' choice. Although it was possible to choose a simple, performance-oriented file system, it was generally expected that a RDBMS would be used, as that was the likely choice in the real application.

Application Description

The TPC-A program performs three updates to indexed files, one addition to a flat file, one read of a workstation display, one write to a workstation display, and one commitment control function. Each workstation executes a transaction an average of once every 10 s. The program logic is as follows:

- Read 100 characters from display, including account, branch, and teller IDs, plus the amount, in dollars, of the transaction.
- Read and update account file
- Read and update teller file
- Read and update branch file
- Write history file record
- Commit transaction
- Write 200 characters to display
- Loop to top of sequence

There are a number of files, outlined next, that are used in TPC-A and accessed by the single TPC-A program.

History File

The history file is a flat file with 50-byte records. The required fields in this file are

- Account ID
- Branch ID
- Teller ID
- Date and time
- Delta
- Filler information to 50 bytes

Account File

The account file is an indexed file keyed on a unique account ID. It must have a capacity that is equal to

$$100,000 \text{ records} \times \text{tpsA}$$

For example, a test on a system supporting 120 tpsA must have an account file of 1200 Megabytes (120 × 100,000 × 100). Each record is 100 bytes long and has the following required field definitions:

- Account ID
- Branch ID
- Balance
- Filler information to 100 bytes

Teller File

The teller file is an indexed file keyed on a unique teller ID. It must have a capacity that is equal to

$$10 \text{ records} \times \text{tpsA}$$

Each workstation is assumed to be a teller and will access exactly one teller record. These records are 100 bytes long and have the following required field definitions:

- Teller ID
- Branch ID
- Balance
- Filler information to 100 bytes

Branch File

The branch file is an indexed file keyed on a unique branch ID. It must have a capacity that is equal to

$$1 \text{ records} \times \text{tpsA}$$

A branch is assumed to have 10 tellers, so 10 workstations access and update a single branch record. Each record is 100 bytes long and has the following required field definitions:

- Branch ID
- Balance
- Filler information to 100 bytes

The TPC-A specification imposes further requirements on the bench marker, which, like other things, must be reported on.

Other TPC-A Requirements

- The test system must be configured with sufficient disk space to hold 90 days of history records in order to force a realistic configuration for pricing. This works out at 2,592,000 records per tpsA.
- The system must be configured with sufficient journal space on disk to run continuously for 8 h at the claimed transaction rate (tpsA). The relationships between numbers of records and the measured tpsA are called *scaling rules*.
- Wait times between transactions from each workstation (teller) must vary across a *truncated negative exponential distribution*, essentially a random distribution with an upper limit. The times must be sufficiently large so that the average cycle time

$$\text{response time} + \text{think time} + \text{keystroke time}$$

is greater than 10 s. This effectively prevents testers making savings on terminal costs by pretending that a few terminals (tellers) can enter unrealistic numbers of transactions each second. At least 10 terminals must be simulated per tpsA generated.

Incidentally, testers were not allowed to simulate more terminals in the benchmark than the system under test can physically support in the real world.

TPC-A Metrics

There are several key metrics for TPC-A:

- Transactions per second (tpsA), where 90% of the transactions started and completed in steady state during the measurement interval must have a response time of less than 2 s. The response time is defined as *the time before the 1st byte of the transaction leaves the RTE until the time after the last byte of the response arrives at the RTE.*
- The reported tpsA rating must be measured and not interpolated or extrapolated.

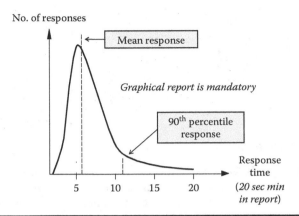

Figure A2.7 Typical response time distribution: TPC-A.

- The TPC-A benchmark requires a graphical report displaying the frequency distribution of response times from 0 to 20 s at least.
- The response time axis must have at least 20 1-s intervals. In addition, the maximum and mean values of response time must be reported.
- A price/performance ratio (K¢/tpsA), which shows the associated cost per transaction per second. The "price" is defined as the 5-year cost of ownership of the benchmarked system and includes
  - System and peripheral hardware, including terminals
  - All the software necessary to run the benchmark
  - Costs of five years of maintenance and/or warranty on the hardware and software used to obtain the tpsA rating

Figure A2.7 shows the typical response time distribution for TPC-A.

Full Disclosure of Results

The TPC insisted that all claims of TPC-A performance are accompanied by a report on how those results were obtained and the test sponsor's *proof of compliance* with the TPC-A benchmark specifications.

TPC-B Benchmark

The TPC-B benchmark was defined by the TPC as a follow-on to the TP1 benchmark. It is identical to the TPC-A benchmark in workload profile with the following notable exceptions:

- The transaction profile does not contain "terminal I/O"
- Internal response time (sometimes called *residence time*) is used in place of the external response time
- No think time or keying time ("cycle time") is required
- Terminals need not be simulated or priced
- It is basically a test of database performance and the maximum load the system can sustain

Incidentally, in the 1980s, I estimated the ratio of TPC-B results to TPC-A using figures for IBM and HP systems and got the ratio figure TPC-B/TPC-A = 1.4:1.

> *Note*: It is important to remember that the characteristics and *metrics* of TPC-B are very different from TPC-A, although the *basic transaction program* is the same.

IBM Internal Benchmarks

RAMP-C[*]: RAMP-C is an IBM synthetic benchmark, essentially measuring internal through-put rate (ITR), mainly midrange systems. It was designed to be a more realistic representation of OLTP than the lightweight TPC-A and TPC-B benchmarks.[†] RAMP-C has the following characteristics:

- Full screen terminal I/O
- Disk I/O (indexed not relational)
- Processor and main storage

It has four transaction types in its repertoire:

- Simple
- Average
- Complex
- Very complex

The RAMP-C benchmark work load allows uniform commercial performance comparisons between systems of differing architectures. The RAMP-C application is divided into four types of transactions or "classes." Each class consists of many separately compiled programs designed to execute a single transaction each time one is requested.

Each RAMP-C work station executes only one program. The programs are set up interactively so that a request is a simple return from the work station to the system.

Table A2.8 shows the characteristics of the four RAMP-C classes.

Table A2.8 IBM RAMP-C Transaction Mixes

Transaction	Class 1	Class 2	Class 3	Class 4
Transaction mix %	35	25	30	10

---

[*] Requirements Approach to Measuring Performance: in COBOL.

[†] Incidentally, I found by comparing results for old HP and IBM systems that the ratio of TPC-B/TPC-A was about 1.3 for the same machine. So, if system X had a rating of 130 TPC-B, its TPC-A rating would be about 100. I used this and other rule-of-thumb (RoT) numbers for other benchmarks, TPC-C and RAMP-C, as a basis for rough system sizing.

In Class 1 and Class 2 programs, control remains within the main program at all times; no calls are made to subprograms. The Class 3 and Class 4 programs call subprograms during execution. These calls are included to represent program-to-program transition within the system.

The subprograms are randomly selected every fifth transaction from within the main program. For each subprogram call, one transaction is performed, after which control is returned to the calling program. Subprograms perform the same work as the associated main program.

There are five subprograms shared by Class 3 programs and five subprograms shared by Class 4 programs. New copies of the subprograms (five each for Class 3 and Class 4) are generated for every 100 work stations. This means that a different set of subprograms are used by the Class 3 and Class 4 programs running on the first 100 workstations than those used by the Class 3 and Class 4 programs running on the second 100 workstations.

However, it is important to remember that even though each set of subprograms is named differently and uses different files, the actual code in each new set is the same as the code in the previous set.

For execution purposes, a RAMP-C work load is defined as a combination of classes, or a *mixture*. For this mixture, the number of transactions from each class comprises a certain percentage of the total number of transactions. To help maintain this mixture, each workstation is assigned a constant key and think time, depending on which class of program is being run on that workstation.

Files Access: The Standard DP database is used for all measurements. The size of the files created is dependent on the disk capacity of the system being tested, though not all files are accessed during each measurement. For example, in the five workstation case (Standard DP mixture), the main programs access only eight files. As the workload is increased to 10 workstations, the number of files accessed by the main programs increases to 12. The number of files accessed by each copy of the subprograms remains at 24 for all measurements.

Measurements were made using automated test equipment to ensure realistic keystroke rates and think times in all environments. The automated environment utilized in these measurements produces a *heads-down, no-breaks* operator environment, eliminating fatigue and interruptions. Human operators may not be able to sustain the throughput achieved in these measurements except for brief periods of time.

The RTE driver in RAMP-C provides the following data:

- Throughput in a given time period
- Actual average key-think time
- Average response time
- 90th percentile response time

From this data, two values are derived;

- Total system throughput at 70% CPU utilization (RAMP-C transactions per hour)
- Average response time over all workstations and all transactions at that throughput.

RAMP-C results are expressed in thousands of transactions/hour. Running the system up to 70% utilization means supplying whatever other resources are needed to achieve this (memory, disk, etc.); in other words, a balanced system. This means the RAMP-C tests are assessing the system capacity for processing transactions at a normally accepted limit for CPU utilization.

CPW (commercial processing workload): For iSeries, previously AS/400. IBM, along with some other vendors, developed some internal benchmarks to compare the performance of systems with different architectures or, in some cases, compare versions of the same hardware system. This was done on the premise that external public benchmarks might not suit the architecture or software configuration of their systems and thus may not represent what a customer might observe in real life.

- These vendors did comply with and run standard benchmarks but still maintained some internal ones for internal comparisons across architectures and levels of hardware. An early IBM internal benchmark was RAMP-C which was used across several systems. As transactions became more complex, RAMP-C was not considered up to the job of simulating such OLTP environments and a replacement was sought.
- The TPC-C benchmark emerged from the Transaction Processing Council and IBM eventually married some of the desirable features of it and the OLTP rules-orientation of RAMP-C to produce a new internal benchmark. This was the commercial processing workload or CPW to be used on AS/4000 and latterly iSeries systems for system comparisons and capacity planning.
- The CPW application simulates the database server of an OLTP system, receiving transactions form an outside source and processed by an application server against the CPW database. Like TPC-C it handles a variety (five) differing transaction-generated workloads in an admixture interaction with between three and eight of the nine databases simulated by CPW.

The benchmark also implements a level of commitment control (via the ACID properties) with a log enabling incomplete transactions to be backed out in some way.

CIW (compute intensive workload): Unlike CPW values, CIW values are not derived from specific measurements of a single workload. They are modeled projections that are based on the characteristics of internal workloads such as Domino workloads and application server environments, such as can be found with SAP or JD Edwards applications.

If there is a CPU-intensive application environment, consideration should be given to using the relative CIW rating rather than CPW rating among iSeries processors to size the server for acceptable performance.

MCU (mail and calendaring users)" This is an authorized mixed workload benchmark from the Lotus Corporation. It is used in the System i context as a more CPU intensive than CPW workload for performance rating of System i models.

IBM References: The first link below is a very readable introduction to CPW from *Ideas International*, covering not only the benchmark but the reasons behind it. The second one contains a lot of performance information about IBM iSeries, including more detailed information on CPW and its usage.

Ideas International Evaluation of IBM's Commercial Processing Workload (CPW) for Rating Relative Performance of IBM eServer iSeries Systems
ft//ftp.software.ibm.com/systems/i/perfmgmt/iicpw.pdf

System i Performance Capabilities Reference
http://www03.ibm.com/systems/resources/systems_i_solutions_perfmgmt_pdf_pcrmjan08.pdf

TPC-A and Debit/Credit Comparison

Although the basic structures of TPC-A, TPC-B, and debit/credit are similar, the results obtained from them should not be compared because of underlying differences.

Debit/credit is not as well defined as TPC-A by definition, since the latter was meant to replace Debit/credit and tighten it up.

Since there are no database consistency checks or forced commitment control in debit/credit, it is possible to take short cuts and to do things in any order since there are no checks on what has been done or the final state of the database or anything been done to avoid real I/O or striping the data across many disks when I/O is done in order to increase performance.

In a way, it is like a contest to play a Beethoven piano concerto as fast as possible. One contestant might play all the notes in the concerto, but not necessarily in the right order, while the other obeys the real score.

Some loopholes in the debit/credit benchmark were identified in an article by Omri Serlin of the TPC and published in *UNIX World* Vol. 6 No.1 January 1989 in an article entitled "Searching for meaningful OLTP benchmarks." The response time metrics are different.

- TPC-A requires 90% of all *external* responses to be less than 2 s, while Debit/Credit requires that 95% of all *internal* responses to be less than 1 s. TPC-A also requires a graphical response curve, like the one we discussed in Chapter 7, Figure 7.17, up to at least 20 s response time.
- TPC-A uses 10 workstations, each averaging a transaction every 10 s, to alter a single record in the smallest data file.
- Debit/credit uses 100 workstations, each averaging a transaction every 100 s to alter 10 records in the smallest data file.
- There are many more "active" sessions in a debit/credit run, but the TPC-A sessions are "more active," often involving record contention.
- TPC-A requires that the price of the system includes peripherals, terminals, and controllers. Debit/credit only requires the central system to be priced. Thus, an implementation that had external processors handling workstation I/O would not have to be reported with debit/credit, but would with TPC-A.

Of the differences between TPC-A and debit/credit, the most important is the last one. A vendor with inefficient terminal I/O can offload that I/O to a processor that is not included in the claimed price under debit/credit. This will effectively boost the work that was done on the system.

TPC-A and TPC-B Comparison

TPC-B can be executed in batch, which means that

- The priced configuration is much less expensive than TPC-A because terminals and controllers need not be costed.
- The performance, tpsB, is typically higher than tpsA for the same machine, especially if it has inefficient terminal I/O. As a rule of thumb, the greater the difference between tpsA and tpsB on the same machine, the worse the terminal I/O handling.
- TPC-B does not require as much disk space to be configured as TPC-A, with obvious effects on the system cost.

■ TPC-B requires many fewer jobs to be active to achieve the same number of transactions per second, since user "think time" is not included in the specification. For systems that require a large amount of memory for each job, the resources required for TPC-B are much lower than for TPC-A.

As with the debit/credit benchmark, a vendor with inefficient terminal I/O can claim a much higher performance rating by eliminating the key terminal I/O component of a commercial environment from the measurement.

TPC-A and RAMP-C Comparison

IBM still uses the RAMP-C benchmark, and so a comparison with TPC-A is appropriate here. The major characteristics of the two benchmarks can be found in Table A2.9, but other things are also of note.

1. RAMP-C and TPC-A represent different application environments and possibly operating system and terminal handling environments; for example:
   a. AS/400 running OS/400 with block-mode terminals
   b. RS/6000 running AIX with character-mode terminals

This leads to some performance anomalies. An AS/400 processor achieves about twice the number of transactions per second for TPC-A than it does for RAMP-C, but an RS/6000 achieves nearly four times the number of TPC-A transactions per second than it does RAMP-C transactions per second. One major reason for this is that the character-mode operation of the RS/6000 (and other UNIX systems) imposes a CPU overhead that is very small on a block-mode system with dedicated I/O processors, namely, the AS/400.

Comparing systems' performance using RAMP-C, therefore, unfairly depresses the power of UNIX systems compared to that of the AS/400.

This can be seen in Table A2.9.

2. Other factors differentiating the two benchmarks are
   a. RAMP-C is much more terminal intensive than TPC-A, causing large CPU overhead on systems using character-mode terminals.
   b. RAMP-C uses many more data files than TPC-A. TPC-A uses four files for any number of simulated users, whereas RAMP-C uses four files for every five users simulated.
   c. TPC-A requires more OLTP functionality than RAMP-C.

Table A2.10 shows how these benchmarks compare.

Table A2.9   RAMP-C and TPC-A Comparison

System (OS)	RAMP-C (Xns/sec)	TPC-A (Xns/sec)
AS/400 D60 (OS/400)	15.5	32.0
RS/6000 550 (AIX [UNIX])	8.6	32.0

Table A2.10   Commercial OLTP Benchmark Characteristics

Item	TPC-A	TPC-B	TPC-C	RAMP-C	Debit/Credit
Xn Type	Single	Single	Mix of 5	Mix of 4	Single
Application Description	Interactive flat file or relational	Batch subset of TPC-A	Interactive relational	Interactive flat file	Simple (TP1) RDBMS (ET1)
Complexity	Simple	Simple	Complex	Medium	Simple
Xn logging	Yes	Yes	Yes	No	Yes
ACID tests	Yes	Yes	Yes	No	No
Path/Xn	66	55	900	105	25
Data files	4	4	9	5	4??
#logical I/Os	7	7	9	5	4??
Contention?	High	High	High	Very low	Very low
# files	Fixed	Fixed	Fixed	Variable	Fixed
# recs/file	Variable	Variable	Variable	Fixed	Variable
# input fields	5	0	48	60	??
# chars	Variable	Variable	Variable	Fixed	
Think time	Exponential	None	Exponential	Constant	
Response time (RT)	External	Internal	External	External	Internal(*)
RT metric	90% < 2s.	90% < 2s.	90% < 5s.	70% utiln.	95% < 1s.
# terminals	10/Xn	0	10/ warehouse	16/Xn	No. of tellers
Price/perf	K$/tpsA	K$/tpsB	K$tpmC	None	None
Audit?	Yes	Yes	Yes	No	No

(*) Except for ET1 version of Debit/Credit.

Old Benchmarking Summary

This section outlines the areas of applicability of the major nongraphics benchmarks and the characteristics of the main commercial OLTP benchmarks. The reason for this is partly as a historical record, since details on these benchmarks seems to be fading fast, and partly as part of the immersion process in performance.* Table A2.11 presents a summary of major vintage commercial benchmarks.

---

* In this table, a blank implies a N(o).

Table A2.11   Summary of Major Vintage Commercial Benchmarks

Benchmark	Integer	FP	Disk I/O	Multiuser	Multitasking
Dhrystone	Y				
Whetstone		Y			
Linpack		Y			
Livermore Loops		Y			
SPEC 1.0	Y	Y			
SPECint 92	Y				
SPECfp 92		Y			
CINT95	Y				
CFP95		Y			
Khornerstones	Y	Y	Y		
BYTE	Y	Y	Y	Y	
TPC-A	Y		Y	Y	Y
TPC-B	Y		Y	Y	
TPC-C	Y		Y	Y	Y
TPC-D	Y		Y	Y	Y
Debit/Credit	Y		Y	Y(TP1)	Y(ET1)
Neal Nelson	Y		Y	Y	
RAMP-C	Y		Y	Y	Y
AIM II	Y	Y	Y		
AIM III	Y	Y	Y	Y	

See the link (if it still exists when you read this) for a gamut of results for many of these older benchmarks:

http://www.roylongbottom.org.uk/oldones.htm#anchor BenchDOS

SPEC 1.0 Benchmark

The Systems Performance Evaluation Cooperative (SPEC) announced the availability of Release 1.0 of the SPEC benchmark suite in October 1989.* Release 1.0, which consists of 10 engineering and scientific benchmarks, is endorsed by 12 of the leading computer-system vendors (including IBM) as a common means of measuring computing systems performance, particularly UNIX workstations and multiuser systems.

---

* It celebrated its 25th birthday in 2014.

Release 1.0 was a complex set of benchmarks that measure CPU-intensive (integer and floating-point) computation associated with engineering and scientific applications. In total, Release 1.0 consisted of over 150,000 lines of C and FORTRAN code, and a high-end technical workstation or minicomputer would require up to 2–3 h to execute the complete series of benchmarks.

The size and complexity of the SPEC benchmark suite, drawn from real application sources, make it a meaningful test of engineering and scientific performance and eliminates the "cache" resident aspects of some other benchmarks discussed previously.

Future suites were stated to measure other important aspects of system performance, such as disk, graphics, and communications, although little has been seen of these at the time of writing. Table A2.12 shows SPEC 1.0 benchmark programs.

This benchmark was to replace existing older common measures of system performance namely:

- Whetstones (floating point)
- Dhrystones (integer)
- MIPS

SPEC Metrics

The parameters used in the SPEC 1.0 benchmark are

SPEC reference machine: VAX 11/780

SPEC reference time: The elapsed time in seconds that it takes the reference machine to run a SPEC job.

SPECratio: The ratio of the time taken by the system under test to run a SPEC job divided by the time taken by the reference machine to run the same job.

Table A2.12   SPEC 1.0 Benchmark Programs

Program	Type of Benchmark	Language	Measure
gcc	Engineering (GNU compiler)	C	Integer
espresso	Engineering (PLA simulator)	C	Integer
spice 2g6	Engineering (ECASD Analog circuit simulator)	FORTRAN	FP
doduc	Scientific (Reactor physics)	FORTRAN	FP
nasa	Scientific (Synthetic 7 kernels)	FORTRAN	FP
li	Engineering (LISP)	C	Integer
eqntott	Engineering (Boolean)	C	Integer
matrix300	Scientific (Monte Carlo)	FORTRAN	FP
fpppp	Scientific (Quantum chemistry)	FORTRAN	FP
tomcatv	Scientific (Fluid dynamics)	FORTRAN	FP

$$\text{SPECratio} = \frac{\text{Time Taken by Test System}}{\text{Time Taken by VAX 11/780}}.$$

SPECmark: The geometric mean of the 10 SPECratios, denoted SR_1, SR_2, ... in the next equation.

$$\text{SPECmark} = \sqrt[10]{\left(SR_1 \times SR_2 \times SR_3 \times .... SR_{10}\right)}$$

SPEC 1.0 compares the performance of systems running single copies of the benchmark programs. In real life, there are likely to be many jobs running simultaneously on a uni- or multiprocessor system. SPEC has accordingly developed a new metric called the SPECthruput.

Multiple copies of each of the 10 SPEC 1.0 benchmarks are run and the new metric is calculated as follows:

- Start K*N copies of SPEC benchmark i (i = 1 to 10), N = number of CPUs on the system, K = number of jobs per processor (K = 2).
- Measure the elapsed time (E(i)) to complete.
- Compute the SPEC throughput ratio as follows:

$$TR(i) = \frac{R(i)}{E(i)} \tag{A2.9}$$

where R(i) is the throughput reference time (VAX 11/780).

- Calculate the geometric mean of the 10 throughput ratios TR(i) (SPECthruput specification):

$$\text{SPECthruput} = 10\sqrt[2]{\left(TR_1 \times TR_2 \times ....TR_{10}\right)} \tag{A2.10}$$

This leads to the final metric called the *aggregate throughput*:

$$\text{Aggregate Thruput} = \text{Number of CPUs}\ (N) \times \text{SPECthruput}$$

SPEC Integer and Floating-Point Breakdown

Sometimes the individual *integer* and *floating-point* SPECratios and SPECmarks were sometimes quoted for SPEC 1.0. The SPECmarks are calculated by taking the 6th root of the product of the 6 floating point measurements and the 4th root for the integer measurements.

SPEC is essentially a composite benchmark, and it is common practice to use the individual components SPECfp, the floating-point measure derived from the six floating-point programs in the same way SPECmark is derived; and SPECint, the integer element derived from the other four programs.

If you are comparing machines for general scientific work with a large floating-point content, then quote the SPECfp figures (and/or Linpack) rather than the full SPECmark. The most recent SPEC benchmarks emphasize the floating point and integer part of the benchmark as a matter of course.

SPEC SDE benchmark

This benchmark, the Systems Development Environment (SDE), was devised as a test of efficiency in UNIX program development. It in no way represents the capacity of particular systems running the developed applications, as some vendors have implied.

It is a close relative of the Australian MUSBUS benchmark.

MUSBUS

MUSBUS (Monash University Suite for Benchmarking UNIX Systems) is a set of programs developed by Ken McDonell to control workload-based performance measurement. The programs emulate a user typing commands with resulting terminal output. MUSBUS allows a benchmarker to control relevant variables like the number of users while handling extraneous details. MUSBUS is not a single program, and it gives no single figure of merit.

The MUSBUS program performed six basic functions:

1. Checks single-copy, workload execution
2. Meters output volume and rate
3. Prepares simulated user directories
4. Waits one minute
5. Runs a test based on desired test conditions
6. Cleans up

MUSBUS was the forerunner of SPEC SDE benchmarks SDET and KENBUS. What they all attempted to do was to see how UNIX workloads (mainly scripts) would scale onto larger machines using a plot of script throughput versus number of concurrent scripts to produce a unitless scaling factor against a reference machine, often the VAX 11/70. A typical schematic of such a graph is shown in Figure A2.8.

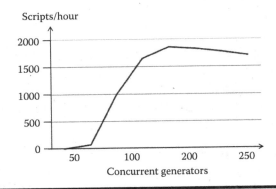

Figure A2.8   SDET typical output.

SPEC Benchmark Suites. A Summary
http://www-inst.eecs.berkeley.edu/~cs266/sp10/readings/balan92a.pdf

Perspectives on the SPEC SDET Benchmark
http://www.spec.org/sdm91/sdet/SDETPerspectives.html

> **Note**: This type of *tail-off and decrease* in throughput is often typical of adding a resource to increase throughput, for example, extra processors in a cluster and forecast by various scaling laws. It is a case of the last straw breaking the camel's back.

MIPS and SPEC 1.0

It is often overlooked that there should be a close correlation between MIPS as derived from Dhrystones and the integer part of SPEC 1.0. In fact, they should yield the same number. Why is this the case? Simply because they both purport to be measures of integer CPU performance and are both derived using the VAX 11/780 as the basis for the measurement. The fact that they do not give the same number means that one of them is not reliable as a measure. MIPs are *still* quoted today as performance indicators, quite erroneously, in the view of most people.

It is common to see a vendor of SMPs quoting X MIPs for the uniprocessor and 8X MIPs for the eight-processor version of their hardware. This gives the unwary purchaser the impression that the eight-processor machine can handle eight times the throughput of the single-processor machine. In fact, it is rare for an eight-processor SMP machine to handle more than about five times the commercial workload of a one-processor machine (see the laws of Amdahl, Gustafson, and Gunther in the section "Performance Scaling Laws" in Chapter 2.

SPEC 92 Benchmark

There were some drawbacks to the initial SPEC metrics. A particular floating-point job was found to be sensitive to using a preprocessor and gained in SPECratio several factors, giving an artificially inflated overall SPECmark.

SPEC Skulduggery?

The *matrix300* benchmark program, similar in nature to Linpack, was particularly helped by blocking up code in the system cache. Compilers can be helped, via a preprocessor, to achieve this aim. H-P and IBM were able to increase the SPECmark and SPECfp ratings of their larger machines considerably by the use of such preprocessors. Examine the figures in Table A2.5, which shows the matrix300 results before the use of a preprocessor and after. Two "after" cases are shown where the preprocessor was enhanced before running the benchmark again.

Other underhand benchmark tricks include:

- Benchmark-specific hardware
- Benchmark-specific compilers
- Benchmark-specific compiler flags
- Source-code modification

These issues are part of the reason for standard benchmarks now requiring *full disclosure reports* containing full details about published benchmark results and their execution environments.

Aside: Kuck and Associates, Inc. wrote, among other things, a compiler preprocessor called KAP, which attempts to do source-code optimization. It is used by all the vendors on the old SPEC89 benchmark because it considerably improved the performance on the matrix300 code. It is also used to do source code parallelization and so on. KAP is not an acronym for Kuck and Associates Preprocessor.

As a result of this and other, less dramatic, inconsistencies, SPEC decided to revise the SPEC 1.0 benchmark programs, although the metrics were preserved. SPEC 1.1/1.2 now uses a different job mix, 14 floating-point and 6 integers, and the separate integer and floating-point results (CINT92, CFP92) are shown, along with the individual SPECratios. The job list for SPEC92 is shown in Table A2.13.

Table A2.13   SPEC92 Composition and Modules

SPEC CINT92	*008.espresso*	*Circuit Theory*
	022.li	LIST Interpreter
	023.eqntott	Logic Design
	026.compress	Data Compression
	072.sc	UNIX Spreadsheet
	085.gcc	GNU C Compiler
SPEC CFP92	013.spice2g6	Circuit Design
	015.doduc	Monte Carlo Simulation
	034.mdljpd2	Quantum Chemistry
	039.wave5	Maxwell's Equations
	047.tomcatv	Coordinate Translation
	048.ora	Optics Ray Tracing
	052.alvinn	Robotics: Neural Nets
	056.ear	Human Ear Modelling
	077.mdljsp2	Single Precision 034.mdljpp2
	078.swm256	Shallow Water Model
	089.su2cor	Quantum Physics
	090.hydro2d	Astrophysics
	093.nasa7	NASA Maths Kernels
	094.fpppp	Quantum Chemistry

There followed other SPEC benchmarks, adding to and refining older versions. These included SPEC95, SPEC2000, and SPECseis96.

Old CERN Benchmarks

The nuclear research facility is not prominent in the public benchmark field, but it still covers on its website some benchmarks used there, which incidentally include bonnie++, our friend the disk I/O benchmark. The CERN benchmark suite, now no longer evident from its website, were as follows:

The CERN (European Particle Physics Laboratory) User Support Group collected a set of typical programs used for event simulation and reconstruction by the "users" of the CERN facilities. These programs were refined, ported to FORTRAN 77 (for portability reasons), and called the CERN benchmark suite. The suite comprised four scalar production tests:

- Two event generators (CRN3, CRN4)
- Two event processors (CRN5, CRN12)

Other programs were added to complement the production suite:

- CRN4C, for testing compilation times
- CRN7, CRN11, for vectorization
- CRN6, for character manipulation

The metric employed by the CERN Suite was CPU time, measured as the geometric mean of the four production tests, normalized to the VAX 8600. The resulting numbers were called "CERN Units."

$$\text{Mean} = \sqrt[4]{\left(T_1 \times T_2 \times T_3 \times T_4\right)/T_{8600}}$$

On the CERN website, a reference is made to others in a more modern vein, for example, virtual machines.

Benchmarks to End All Benchmarks

There was a spate of benchmark production in the 1980s to represent the *true nature* of performance characteristics. Some of these benchmarks are still in use for personal and organizational use but are rarely used by vendors except to promote their wares and demonstrate superiority*. Many of these benchmarks were aimed at the HPC market. John Gustafson, at AMD sometime in 2013, was prominent in this area. However, at the time of writing, he seems to have disappeared!

---

* Didn't Shakespeare say somewhere "The devil can quote scripture for his purpose"?

Perfect Benchmark

The PERFECT (performance evaluation by cost-effective transformations) benchmark was developed at the University of Illinois Center for Supercomputing with contributions from numerous academic, research, and vendor organizations. The underlying assumption of PERFECT is that no single benchmark test based on kernels or algorithms can adequately describe actual performance with real applications. With the advent of MPP, which accelerates some types of application processing dramatically while having little effect on other types, the need for specific application comparisons has increased.

Perfect Structure

PERFECT consists of 13 benchmark tests, each of which is a real FORTRAN application. Categories include fluid flow, chemical/physical analysis, engineering design, and signal processing. Results are given in run-time and MFLOPS for each test, and a harmonic mean is derived from all tests. Testing began in 1990 for a variety of systems. An interesting aspect of the PERFECT results is that performance can vary widely from test to test for the same machine.

A Cray Y-MP/832, for example, performs one of the fluid flow tests at 448.2 MFLOPS and one of the engineering design tests at only 5.7 MFLOPS. It should be noted, however, that all systems tend to exhibit the same pattern of high and low results, facilitating comparison of systems but comparing apples with apples.

The PERFECT benchmark should be of value to prospective buyers who wish to know how well a system can be expected to perform at their own type of application. For others who would rather have a single number to compare, the harmonic mean value provides a general performance metric.

SLALOM Benchmark

The scalable, language-independent Ames Laboratory one-minute measurement (SLALOM) was developed by John Gustafson et al. to solve some of the inherent limitations of other benchmarks. Rather than measuring the time it takes to solve a problem of fixed size, the SLALOM measures the size of problem a computer can solve in exactly one minute. This produces a highly scalable benchmark suitable for a wide range of computers, now and in the future, and allows a fair comparison between, say, an Apple Macintosh and a Cray supercomputer.

SLALOM was designed to resist the obsolescence of fixed-length programs and enable a huge spectrum of systems to be measured against a common metric. The order 100 Linpack in its current form, for example, requires only 1/200 s for a high-end Cray system and uses only 1/400 of its available memory space, hardly taxing the system or indicating the full limits of its application performance. Interestingly, the Linpack has been updated three times since its inception to provide more of a challenge for newer high-end systems.

The SLALOM, which is based on a radiosity calculation (the generation of realistic images with diffuse surfaces), measures the number of diffuse surfaces (called patches) a system can calculate from RGB (red, green, blue) color data in one minute. The smallest SLALOM run possible is one with only six patches, one for each surface of the cube. The developers rate this at 8812 FLOPS or 8.812 KFLOPS. It is then possible to get a KFLOP/MFLOP rating from the benchmark using this fact.

Table A2.14   SLALOM Component Programs

Task	Seconds	Operations	MFLOPS	% of Time
Reader	0.001	258	0.025800	0.0
Region	0.001	1148	1.148000	0.0
SetUp1	10.520	20532123	1.951723	17.8
SetUp2	23.130	39372520	1.702227	39.1
SetUp3	0.130	236856	1.821969	0.2
Solver	24.890	135282624	5.435220	42.1
Storer	0.480	25440	0.053000	0.8
TOTAL	59.160	195425529	3.303339	100.0

It is not solvable through known algorithms and is thus resistant to artificial optimization, and it measures set-up and I/O time (which Linpack does not) as well as computational time. The final performance measurement is provided in both number of patches and MFLOPS. The SLALOM is appropriate for measuring TERAFLOPS (1 million MEGAFLOPS) machines which are becoming available, and it is claimed that it accurately measures performance across vector processors, MPPs, workstations, and even low-end systems such as PCs.

SLALOM is claimed to fit any architecture, any word size, and any programming language (C, FORTRAN, and Pascal source code versions are currently available). Recorded benchmarks are published from a single source and are verified where possible. SLALOM testing began in 1990, and the illustrative results for a single machine[*] would look as shown in Table A2.14.

The claims made for the original SLALOM benchmark can be summarized as follows:

■ It was scalable, allowing comparisons of a large range of machines. This illustrated in a 1990 table of results wherein a Cray Y-MP/8 weighed in at 2130 MFLOPS, whereas an Apple Mac IIcx 68030 delivered 0.00239 MFLOPS.
■ It did not have a preferred computer language.
■ It was maintained by a vendor-independent organisation (Ames Laboratory, Department of Energy, Iowa).
■ It solved a real problem in its entirety and not just the computation portion.
■ It could be run on scalar, vector, and parallel machines of many kinds.
■ It identified the benchmarker, avoiding anonymous submissions.
■ It ranked performance by the size of the problem solved.
■ It stated precision in terms of the accuracy of the answer and not hardware word size.
■ It presented the machine as a single number and not a range.
■ It encouraged tuning, a double-edged sword with the opportunity to compare apples with oranges.

A summary comparison of many machines was represented as shown in Table A2.15.[†]

---

[*] In this case, a Silicon Graphics 4D/380S.
[†] Real systems are not represented in this table, since performance results age rapidly.

Table A2.15   SLALOM Results Presentation Format

Machine	Procs	Patches	Operations	Seconds	MFLOPS	Date
M/c 1	8	5120	126 G	59.03	2130	9/22/90
M/c 2	4	4096	65.2 G	54.81	1190	9/22/90
M/c 3	2	3200	31.6 G	56.7	556	9/17/90

HINT Benchmark

Hierarchical Integration (HINT) originated from John Gustafson and Quinn Snell at the Ames, Iowa, Laboratory (former authors of the SLALOM benchmark, outlined below) and is built on the SLALOM benchmark. The measure of performance is given in terms of quality improvement per second (QUIPS). HINT tries to remove the need for measures such as MFLOPS/sec., MIPS, or Mbytes/sec. HINT reveals memory band width and memory regimes, and it scales with memory size and increasing numbers of processors, allowing it to compare computing from PCs to the largest supercomputers.

This sounds like an interesting new approach since QUIPS will reveal, for example, the fact that many RISC workstations depend heavily on data residing in primary or secondary cache, and that their performance will drop drastically on large applications that do not cache well.

There is now a new web page called System Optimization Information, which contains the latest benchmark comparison lists and the locations of actual benchmarking programs.

A HINT of Things to Come
http://www.johngustafson.net/images/HINTofThingsTo Come.pdf

Graphics Benchmarks

Unless you are a graphics professional or guru, do not worry too much about the terms in the following sections; just get a feel for the nature of the test involved in graphics versus other entities in the IT world.

X-Terminal Benchmarks

X-Station performance is difficult to define and measure for the reasons given before. In spite of this, there are several emerging benchmarks designed for this purpose.

XBench Benchmark

The XBench benchmark was devised and released in 1988 by Claus Gittinger of Siemens, Munich. It was designed to test the graphical capabilities of X-Servers using a variety of tests.

The XBench Tests

Solid lines: This draws horizontal, vertical, and diagonal lines of different lengths.
Dashed lines: The *dline* benchmark draws dashed lines.

Wide lines: The *wline* benchmark draws wide lines of width five.

Rectangles: The *rects* benchmark draws a series of rectangles of different sides.

Filled rectangles: The *fillrects* benchmark draws solid filled rectangles.

Tiled rectangles: The *tiledrects* benchmark draws tiled rectangles (32 × 32 tile).

Stippled rectangles: The *stippledrects* benchmark draws stippled rectangles.

Inverting rectangles: The *invrects* benchmark inverts rectangles on the screen.

Arcs: The *arc* benchmark draws arcs of varying angle between 5 and 360 degrees.

Filled arcs: The *filledarc* benchmark draws filled arcs varying angles between 5 and 360 degrees.

Filled polygons: The *filledpoly* benchmark draws a filled polygon with five points.

BitBlts: A number of *BitBlt* tests are available within XBench:

- Screen-to-screen copy
- Scrolling
- Pixmap-to-screen copy using XCopyArea
- Bitmap-to-screen copy using XCopyPlane (more often used on color systems).

For monochrome systems, pixmap-to-screen copy and bitmap-to-screen copy are the same operation.

Drawing characters: The *imagestring* benchmark draws a string using a commonly available font.

Complex test: All the previous tests are low-level graphics function tests. To assess the working performance of a system requires a combination of tests. The *complex test* creates a window, creates a GC, clears an area, draws some text, scrolls the window, and finally destroys the window.

Results

The relative performance of the servers under test is compared to the performance of a monochrome Sun 3/50 running untuned X11 code.

X11perf

This is a suite of public domain programs for X-server performance tuning. It measures a wide range of operations and displays the results. x11perf measures window manager performance as well as traditional graphics performance. x11perf includes benchmarks for

- The time it takes to create and map windows, for example, at startup
- The time it takes to map an existing set of windows on the screen, for example, when you deiconify an application
- Rearranging windows, for example, moving windows around to find the one you want
- Graphics performance such as copyplane and scrolling

The x11perf benchmarks do not seek to produce a single number (HeXStones) to represent X windows performance. It rather seeks to analyse the strengths and weaknesses of a server in various areas of operation. For repeatable results, x11perf is run using a local connection on a freshly started server. Each test is run five times to check for consistency of results.

X-bench/X-stones

X-bench is similar to x11perf and is aimed at the server. It attempts to give a "feel" for the X-server performance by outputting a number of graphics commands and measures the time taken to put them on the screen. It is a useful tool for comparing different server implementations and for measuring server tuning effects.

Each test is run three times and the best rating, rather than the average, is taken to minimize the effect of daemons or other background processes. The benchmark includes the following operations:

- Lines (horizontal, vertical, dashed, and wide)
- Rectangles (filled, unfilled)
- Arcs
- Bit-blts
- Character output

X-stones are generic X-server display performance benchmarks based on X-bench data. X-stone performance numbers were achieved by running the X-bench suite of tests distributed by the xconsortium. These 40 tests are used as a mechanism to determine the relative and absolute performance of X-servers from various vendors.

X-bench times a series of X graphics output primitives with an emphasis on the server's ability to display and move graphic and bit patterns. It uses the performance of a monochrome Sun Microsystems 3/50 running an X11R3 MIT sample server as its reference point.

The ratings are scaled to give the Sun an X-stone rating of 10000. Ratings of other machines are normalized against this number. Therefore, a machine with better performance than the Sun (10000 X-stones) will be rated at more X-stones, while a machine with worse performance will be rated at less X-stones.

X-stones are the harmonic weighted means of the X-bench data. X-bench functions are weighted and grouped to get component stone ratings (e.g., linestones, textstones) or an overall rating. As always, the best indicator of performance is to use the terminal in customer specific applications. X-stones can be misleading because they are heavily impacted by factors not related to the actual X-station performance such as:

- Host performance
- Network performance
- Standard X-bench weighting tables (they may not be applicable to actual work to be done on the box)
- Number of bits per pixel the X-station supports
- UNIX timing functions

Furthermore, X-stones only measure output, and they do not consider mouse/keyboard response. The X-stones benchmark is a weighted composite figure which is/was intended as an overall benchmark but, as the benchmark author pointed out, it is only meaningful if the composition happens to match the application in question. No account is taken of networking.

Gem

Gemstones (or *Xwinstones*) are a set of graphics benchmarks for X windows and are shipped with the X11.4 distribution tape. They allow the user to specify a range of benchmark tests, possibly thousands. Gemstones provides standard scripts that exercise the benchmark options in specific combinations. They are a useful tool for users to identify the specific strengths and weaknesses of their X11 implementation. The tests do not test the performance of window-management functions nor do they measure CPU loads.

This old benchmark shouldn't be confused with GEM, the graphics execution manager, a relatively recent entrant.

There are some specific graphics benchmarks within the SPEC suites (q.v.) but others do exist and some are covered in this section.

OPC

The nonprofit *OpenGL Performance Characterization* (OPC) project is providing unambiguous methods for comparing the performance of OpenGL implementations across vendor platforms, operating systems, and windowing environments. Operating systems covered by the OPC group include, but are not limited to, OS/2, UNIX, Windows NT, and Windows 95. Windowing environments include, but are not limited to, Presentation Manager, Windows, and X. The intention of the OPC group is to characterize graphics performance for computer-systems running applications, not overall graphics performance.

Currently, there are eight OPC viewsets (test sets):

- Discreet's 3ds Max contains 14 different tests.
- Dassault Systemes's CATIA, which has 11 different tests, is a visualization application.
- CEI's EnSight, which replaces Data Explorer, has 9 different tests.
- Alias's Maya V5, which has 9 tests, is an animation application.
- Lightscape Technology's Lightscape Visualization System, which has 5 tests, is a radiosity visualization application.
- PTC's Pro/ENGINEER features 7 tests.
- Dassault Systeme's SolidWorks features 9 tests.
- UGS's Unigraphics V17, which has 8 tests, test shaded, shaded with transparency, and wireframe rendering.

All viewsets represent relatively high-end applications. These types of applications typically render large data sets, and they almost always include lighting, smooth shading, blending, line antialiasing, z-buffering, and some texture mapping. Remember, doing this sort of work in software would be painfully slow and this is where the hardware-accelerated functions resulted in the fast graphics we have today. It is inconceivable to have played complex games on the older graphics architectures.

Other, fuller benchmarks involving OPC and OpenGL are

1. SPECViewperf 8 Benchmark
2. SPECapc Benchmark
3. SPECglperf: Retired

These benchmarks are covered in the link below.

OpenGL Performance Benchmarks
https://www.opengl.org benchmarks//resources/

Other Benchmarks

The 1970s and 1980s were awash with benchmarks and program stress tests of all kinds, and these eventually settled down to SPEC and TPC models, except where the particular circumstances, such as HPC, demanded other tests. These might be used where circumstances do not fit the TPC or SPEC landscapes, and they are perfectly valid as long as they are designed to help the end user and not the vendors of particular hardware and software.

The list below presents (for history) many of these benchmarks, and short descriptions can be found at the URLs at the bottom (and elsewhere with an appropriate search):

- 007 (ODBMS)
- AGE Test Suite
- AIM Technology Benchmark
- BAPCo
- bc
- Bench ++
- bonnie, bonnie++
- cassandra_stress
- cluster_boot
- ycsb
- mesh_network
- copy_throughput
- aerospike
- object_storage_service
- memtier_benchmark
- mongodb
- fio
- coremark
- hadopp_terasort
- BYTE UNIX Benchmark
- Benchmark Suite
- CPU2
- DBMS Labs Benchmark
- Debit-Credit benchmark
- DEISA (HPC)
- Dhrystone
- Digital Review
- Euroben
- Fhourstones
- Flops
- fsanalyze
- gbench
- Gabriel

- Geek Benchmark
- Gibson mix
- GPCmark
- Hanoi
- Hartstone
- Heapsort
- HINT
- iobench
- ioblazer
- iocall
- iCOMP (INtel)
- iometer
- iostone
- iozone
- ipbench
- Kenbus1
- Khornerstone
- Laddis (NFS)
- lhynestone
- Linpack/C Linpack
- Livermore Loops
- LLCbench
- Los Alamos benchmarks
- Matrix multiply
- mendez
- McCalpin Kernels
- mhawstone
- MIT Volume Stress Test
- musbus
- NAS Kernels
- NCR benchmark
- Neil Nelson Business Benchmark
- netperf
- nettest
- NFSstone
- nhfsstone
- Nullstone
- Object Operations Benchmark
- PARKbench
- Parsec
- PC Bench/WinBench/NetBench
- PERFECT
- Performance Testing Alliance
- Picture Level Benchmarks
- plum benchmarks
- RAMP-C

- Rendermark
- Rhealstone
- RhosettaStone
- Rodinia
- SEI ADA benchmark
- Sieve of Eratosthenes
- sim
- SLALOM
- smith
- SPECmark (original)
- SPEC (various)
- Splash2
- SSBA
- Stanford Small Programs Benchmark
- Set
- STREAM
- SYSmark
- System Development Throughput
- Tak
- TATP
- tbench
- TFFTDP
- TPC (various)
- TPox
- ttcp
- University of Wisconsin benchmarks
- U.S. Steel
- VGX benchmark
- VMmark (virtualization)
- Whetstone
- Workstation Laboratories benchmark
- WPI benchmark suite
- x11perf
- xbench
- Xlib Protocol Test Suite
- xstone
- ZQH benchmark
- Others developed by organizations for their use.

Memory Lane: The next reference covers some of these old benchmarks in great detail and provides the code for many of them, for example, Whetstone, where different language versions are presented. It also covers some not in this list of venerable old time benchmarks.

PC Benchmark Collection Older Files
http://www.roylongbottom.org.uk/oldones.htm

Industry Standard Benchmarks: Summary

These are listed by Wikipedia as being classed as *industry standard* benchmarks inasmuch as they can be *audited* and *verified*, which normally means the production of a benchmark report laid out according to a specification dictated by the benchmark body:

- Business Applications Performance Corporation (BAPCo)
  www.bapco.com
  http://www.pcmag.com/encyclopedia/term/38418/bapco
- Standard Performance Evaluation Corporation (SPEC)
  www.spec.org
- Transaction Processing Performance Council (TPC)
  www.tpc.org
- Embedded Microprocessor Benchmark (EEMBC)
- Coremark (embedded computing standard benchmark)
  www.eembc.org

For a nostalgic stroll down benchmark memory lane, see the references below.

1. Look under "Vendor-Supplied Benchmarks" for an overview and access to detail of some of the benchmarks listed above.
   http://www.netlib.org/benchweb/
2. *Benchmarks*
   http://cs.fit.edu/~jpmcgee/classes/CSE5800/BENCH MARKS.ppt
3. *comp.Benchmarks FAQ*
   http://pages.cs.wisc.edu/~thomas/comp.benchmarks.FAQ.html
4. *Description of 56 Benchmarks*
   http://www.unf.edu/public/cda4102/ychua/bench/bench.descriptions.faq

---

Moral: There are doubtless dozens of other unsung benchmarks, but when it comes to the crunch, the actual company's workload is the only true test vehicle for performance assessment.

As Shakespeare said "The Devil can quote scripture for his purpose," and the trickster can quote benchmarks for his or her nefarious purposes.

Appendix III: Terminology

This section contains definitions of the key terms used throughout this book in discussing the performance of computer systems.

> *Note*: Some terms are unique to certain types of operating systems, others cross-operating system. Some are only applicable to High Performance Computing (HPC).

2PC: see **two-phase commit**.

7 layer model: see **seven-layer model**.

ACID properties: In nonsimple software interactions, particularly those involving middleware, there can be synchronization issues in data updates. One way of ensuring consistency is via the properties in the acronym ACID: *atomicity, consistency, isolation*, and *durability*. These are the mainstays of online transaction processing (OLTP) and databases, particularly in a distributed environment.

> **atomicity**: All changes to data are performed as if they are a single operation. That is, *all* the changes are performed, or *none* of them are. For example, in an application that transfers funds from one account to another, the atomicity property ensures that, if a debit is made successfully from one account, the corresponding credit is made to the other account. Doing one without the other is not allowed.

> **consistency**: Data is in a consistent state when a transaction starts and when it ends. For example, in an application that transfers funds from one account to another, the consistency property ensures that the total value of funds in both the accounts is the same at the start and end of each transaction.

> **isolation**: The intermediate state of a transaction is invisible to other transactions. As a result, transactions that run concurrently appear to be serialized. This property is sometimes called "independence."

add/drop multiplexor: see **transmission multiplexor**.

AIO: see **asynchronous I/O**.

Amdahl's law: A rule first formalized by Gene Amdahl in 1967. It states that if F is the fraction of a calculation that is serial and $(1 - F)$ the fraction that can be parallelized, then the speedup that can be achieved using P processors is

$$1/\left(F + (1-F)/P\right)$$

which has a limiting value of $1/F$ for an infinite number of processors. This no matter how many processors are employed; if a calculation has a 10% serial component, the maximum speedup obtainable is 10.

APM (application performance measurement): The monitoring and management of performance and availability of software applications. It also includes an element of the detection, diagnosis, and fixing of performance issues, mainly to fulfill the obligation to the service level agreement (SLA).

array processor: Any computer designed primarily to perform data parallel calculations on arrays or matrices.

asymmetric multiprocessing: A multiprocessor system is asymmetric when processors are not equally able to perform all tasks. For example, only the base processor is able to control input/output (I/O). Most machines acknowledged to be symmetric may still have some asymmetric features present such as only being able to boot using the base processor.

ATA (advanced technology attachment) (for disk connections): This is a type of disk drive that integrates the drive controller directly on the drive itself. Computers can use ATA hard drives without a specific controller to support the drive. The motherboard must still support an ATA connection, but a separate card (such as a small computer system interface (SCSI) card for a SCSI hard drive) is not needed. Some different types of ATA standards include ATA-1, ATA-2 (a.k.a. Fast ATA), ATA-3, Ultra ATA (33 MBps maximum transfer rate), ATA/66 (66 MBps), and ATA/100 (100 MBps). The term is interchangeable with integrated drive electronics (IDE).

asynchronous I/O: Provides nonblocking I/O access through a raw device interface.

ATM (asynchronous transfer mode): A network technology for both local and wide area networks that supports real-time voice and video as well as data. The topology uses switches that establish a logical circuit from end to end, which guarantees quality of service (QoS). However, unlike telephone switches that dedicate end-to-end circuits, unused bandwidth in ATM's logical circuits can be used elsewhere when needed. For example, idle bandwidth in a videoconference circuit can be used to transfer data.

balanced scorecard: (*ITIL Continual Service Improvement definition*). A management tool developed by Drs Robert Kaplan (Harvard Business School) and David Norton. A balanced scorecard enables a strategy to be broken down into key performance indicators. Performance against the key performance indicators (KPIs) is used to demonstrate how well the strategy is being achieved. A balanced scorecard has four major areas, each of which has a small number of KPIs. The same four areas are considered at different levels of detail throughout the organization.

balking: The refusal of a "work unit" to enter a service queue, most applicable to human queues.

bandwidth: The maximum I/O throughput of a system. A "system" might be a data or memory channel, a network, or a disk subsystem.

base processor: The first central processing unit (CPU) in a multiprocessor system. The system normally boots using this CPU. Also called the default processor, it cannot be deactivated.

bdflush: The system name for the buffer flushing daemon.

benchmark: Software run on a computer system to measure its performance under specific operating conditions. The word is also used to describe the act of running a benchmark or speed test.

benchmarking: The comparison between vendor performance and designated benchmark organizations or indexes. An index is a publicly available indicator for a factor that is associated with a pricing element.

internal benchmarking: The continuous process of measuring a company's products, services, and practices to determine whether the best possible job is being performed with the resources at hand. This can include comparing similar functions of different operating units in an organization or comparing the operations of a specific division from one year to the next.

external benchmarking: The continuous process of measuring a company's products, services and practices and comparing them with those of another company. This can include comparisons with industry peers, functional leaders, or best-in-class performers. [Gartner]

BGP (border gateway protocol): An Internet protocol defined by RFC 1163. It is a Transmission Control Protocol (TCP)-IP routing protocol that routers employ in order to exchange appropriate levels of information. When BGP peer routers first establish contact, they exchange full routing tables; subsequent contacts involve the transmission of changes only, a type of "send modified" protocol that reduces traffic.

BISDN (broadband integrated services digital network): This is a packet-switching technique that uses packets of fixed length, resulting in lower processing and higher speeds.

block device interface: Provides access to block-structured peripheral devices (such as hard disks) that allow data to be read and written in fixed-sized blocks.

blocking I/O: Forces a process to wait for the I/O operation to complete. Also known as synchronous I/O.

bottleneck: Occurs when demand for a particular resource is beyond the capacity of that resource and this adversely affects other resources. For example, a system has a disk bottleneck if it is unable to use all of its CPU power because processes are blocked waiting for disk access.

bss: Another name for data which was not initialized when a program was compiled. The name is an acronym for *block started by symbol*.

buffer: A temporary data storage area used to allow for the different capabilities (speed, addressing limits, or transfer size) of two communicating computer subsystems.

buffer cache: Stores the most recently accessed blocks on block devices. This avoids having to reread the blocks from the physical device.

buffer flushing daemon: Writes the contents of delayed-write buffers from the buffer cache to disk.

cache memory: High-speed, low-access time memory placed between a CPU and main memory in order to enhance performance. See also *level-one (L1) cache*, *level-two (L2) cache*, and *level-three (L3) cache* in this glossary.

cache consistency: The problem of ensuring that the values associated with a particular variable in the caches of several processors are never visibly different.

cache hit: A cache access that successfully finds the requested data. *Cache miss* is the opposite which then requires access to a lower cache level to find the data.

caching, server side: The process of storage data on a fast medium between a server and disk storage. The cost case depends on the cost of the fast medium per unit, the cache effectiveness (% fast hits), and caching algorithms, among other things. See *Server-side Caching*, the White Paper commissioned by StarWind Software, written and distributed by Langton Blue Ltd. (https://www.starwindsoftware.com/server-side-caching)

chaining: The ability to take the results of one vector operation and use them directly as input operands to a second vector instruction without the need to store to memory or register the results of the first vector operation, which can significantly speed up a HPC calculation.

channel I/O: A generic term that refers to a high-performance input/output (I/O) architecture that is implemented in various forms on a number of computer architectures, especially on mainframe computers. On IBM mainframes, the channels were byte, block multiplexor (MPX) channels, or selector channels. Byte MPXs were employed for slow peripheral devices such as printers and card readers and interleaved I/O at byte level so that one device did not monopolize the channel.

Selector channels were used for burst-mode devices like tapes and were usually dedicated to them. Block MPXs were a later creation that allowed burst-mode devices to interleave blocks (rather than bytes) of data to give fair shares access to the channel.

checkpointing: A point in time recording of the state of a computer system, or a component thereof, for later recovery to that point. Recovery to a later point is normally done by restoring the system/component to the checkpoint and then running a log of subsequent activity against it to bring it up to date. Examples of system components are Oracle RDBMS and IBM CICS OLTP.

child process: A new process created when a parent process calls the fork(s) system call. This is not a mainframe but originated in UNIX.

clean: The state of a memory page that has not had its contents altered.

client/server model: A method of implementing application programs and operating-system services that divides them into one or more client programs whose requests for service are satisfied by one or more server programs. The client/server model is suitable for implementing applications in a networked computer environment.

Examples of commercial and scientific applications of the client/server model are

■ page serving to diskless clients
■ file serving using network file system (NFS)
■ domain name service (DNS)
■ many relational database management systems (RDBMSs)
■ some scientific applications where a graphics front-end workstation creates a model and then submits jobs to a powerful back-end HPC system and subsequently receives output. An example of this might be molecular modeling.

CICS (Customer Information Control System): This is a TP monitor from IBM that was originally developed to provide transaction processing for public utilities (hence the inclusion of "customer") using IBM mainframes. It controls the interaction between applications and users and lets programmers develop screen displays without detailed knowledge of the terminals used—BMS or Basic Mapping Support. It provides terminal routing, password security, transaction logging for error recovery and activity journals for performance analysis. CICS has also been made available on nonmainframe platforms including the RS/6000, AS/400, and OS/2-based PCs, and a version that ran on HP equipment was produced.

clock interrupt: See *clock tick.*

clock tick: An interrupt received at regular intervals from the programmable interrupt timer. This interrupt is used to invoke kernel activities that must be performed on a regular basis.

cluster, HPC: Normally, the most obvious way to apply multiple compute cycles to a complex scientific problem is to use specialized supercomputing hardware—a solution with a very high cost of entry and technical complexity. However, software and hardware advances have made it possible to use existing IT skills and create an HPC environment using commodity servers with high-speed interconnections. These systems can deliver massive computing power at a significantly lower cost of entry and ownership than a supercomputer. This form of HPC is called a commodity HPC cluster. Power is not the only reason for using HPC commodity clustering—availability becomes important as longer jobs are being run, some taking weeks, and failures without a checkpoint mechanism waste a lot of time.

computer performance: The amount of useful work accomplished by a computer system compared to the time and resources used.

Depending on the context, good computer performance may involve one or more of the following:

- Short response time for a given piece of work
- High throughput (rate of processing work). This can include transactions, program compilations, HPC or commercial jobs, and other work
- Low utilization of computing resource(s)
- High availability of the computing system or application

contention: Occurs when several CPUs or processes need to access the same resource at the same time. The term applies to storage devices in the main, but it can apply to memory and other entities.

context: The set of CPU register values and other data, including the u-area, that describe the state of a process.

context switch: Occurs when the scheduler replaces one process executing on a CPU with another.

coprocessor: An additional processor attached to a main processor to accelerate arithmetic, I/O, or graphics operations.

copy-on-write page: A memory page that is shared by several processes until one tries to write to it. When this happens, the process is given its own private copy of the page.

core: A core is an individual processor—the part of a computer that actually executes programs. CPUs used to have a single core, and the terms were interchangeable. In recent years, several cores, or processors, have been manufactured on a single CPU chip, which may be referred to as a multiprocessor. It is important to note, however, that the relationship between the cores may vary radically: AMD's Opteron, Intel's Itanium, and IBM's Cell have very distinct configurations.

COW page: See *copy-on-write page*.

CPU: Abbreviation of central processing unit. One or more CPUs give a computer the ability to execute software such as operating systems and application programs. Modern systems may use several auxiliary processors to reduce the load on the CPUs.

CPU bound: A system in which there is insufficient CPU power to keep the number of runnable processes on the run queue low. This results in poor interactive response by applications.

daemon: A process that performs a service on behalf of the kernel. Since daemons spend most of their time sleeping, they usually do not consume much CPU power. The terminology does not really apply to mainframe architectures.

data striping (RAID): Data striping is a way of splitting data into sections and storing them across multiple hard disks. Striping is used to increase the efficiency of reading and writing in the disk array. This is because the hard disks work in parallel motion, making the file access faster than when using only one hard disk. Native striping is known as RAID 0. Data striping is used in combination with other techniques to deliver other forms of RAID.

database journaling: Database servers are one major category of server systems, and database software has provided storage redundancy through transaction journaling for many years. This redundancy defends against simple medium failure or can even be the basis of a remote-site disaster recovery plan.

deadly embrace: A system or application hang that occurs when two elements in a process are each waiting for the other to respond. For example, in a network, if one user is working on file A and needs file B to continue, but another user is working on file B and needs file A to continue, each one waits for the other. Both are temporarily locked out. The software must be able to deal with this based on some policy for delays. In terms of response times, this is "not a good thing."

DEC (Digital Equipment Corporation): An early mainframe pioneer and IBM's nemesis. It was absorbed by PC manufacturer Compaq, which was itself eventually swallowed up by Hewlett-Packard, which still markets and supports some of the DEC products.

deduplication: This is a method of copying data from one place to another while avoiding the transfer of duplicate blocks or records. This reduces the storage needed for copies or even source data and minimizes the bandwidth needed to carry the transferred data across a network. These and other reductions will also reduce costs. Once a deduplicated "file" has been transferred, only changes to the primary need to be transferred subsequently to keep the secondary "file" up to date.

delayed-write buffer: A system buffer the contents of which must be written to disk before it can be reassigned.

device driver: Performs I/O with a peripheral device on behalf of the operating system kernel. Most device drivers must be linked into the kernel before they can be used.

dirty: The state of a memory page that has had its contents altered.

distributed interrupts: Interrupts from devices that can be serviced by any CPU in a multi-processor system.

DMA (direct memory access): Allows devices on a bus to access memory without requiring intervention by the CPU.

DRAM (dynamic RAM): This uses a transistor and capacitor pair that needs frequent power refreshing to retain its charge. Because reading a DRAM discharges its contents, a power refresh is required after each read. Apart from reading, just to maintain the charge that holds its content in place, DRAM must be refreshed after a specified number of cycles. DRAM is the least expensive kind of RAM.

http://whatis.techtarget.com/reference/Fast-Guide-to-RAM

emulation: When hardware or software, or a combination of both, duplicates the functionality of a computer system in a different, second system. The behavior of the second system will closely resemble the original functionality of the first system. See also *virtualization*.

Erlang: The Erlang is a dimensionless unit that is used in telephony as a measure of offered load or carried load on service-providing elements such as telephone circuits or telephone switching equipment (Wikipedia).

event: This is a generic term signifying that something has happened in a system. It might be an interrupt, a data exception, a transaction completion, and so on. In the X Window System, an event is the notification that the X-server sends an X-client to tell it about changes such as keystrokes, mouse movement, or the moving or resizing of windows.

executing: Describes machine instructions belonging to a program or the kernel being interpreted by a CPU.

first mile: Bandwidth capacity of a website's connection to the Internet; the first leg of its journey.

FLOPs (floating-point operations per second): Used in HPC as a basis for specifying the speed of computation of a computer. In modern times, the FLOP is too small a unit, and multiples of FLOPs are used (kilo-, mega-, giga-, tera-, peta-, etc.) to measure and compare HPC results.

fragmentation: The propensity of the component disk blocks of a file or memory segments of a kernel data structure to become separated from each other. The greater the fragmentation, the more work has to be performed to retrieve the data. This can often be done deliberately to gain access benefits for OLTP. For example, IBM's Relative Byte (RBA) addressing for DL/I databases or RDBMS hash-key storage of records. These have a space overhead just like normal fragmentation because their distribution is dictated by the key-generating algorithm.

garbage collection: The process of compacting data structures to retrieve unused memory. It is also applied to the deletion of temporary entities when a process or program comes to an end, for example, temporary files or scratch pad areas for storing intermediate results in an OLTP system transaction.

hardware scalability: The number of physical processors (N) is incremented in the hardware configuration while keeping the user load per processor fixed. In this case, the number of users executing per processor (e.g., 100 users per processor) is assumed to remain the same for every added processor. For example, on a 32-processor platform, you would apply a load of N = 3200 users to the test platform.

HDLC (high-level data link control protocol): Based on the earlier IBM SDLC protocol,* HDLC was implemented in a great number of variants as a simple and robust Link Layer (layer 2 of the 7 layer model) protocol. The most popular current variant is probably Cisco HDLC (cHDLC). HDLC formed the foundation for PPP (point-to-point) protocol (q.v.). Frame Relay and X.25 also make use of HDLC.

hop: Each short, individual trip that packets make many times over, from router to router, on their way to their destinations.

HPC (high-performance computing): A term normally applied to intensive scientific computation wherein many numeric operations need to be carried out as fast as possible. Given sufficient speed, it is possible to use more sophisticated models to simulate the real world. An example of this is weather forecasting, in which a number of simultaneous equations describing the atmosphere can be increased to produce a more accurate forecast. Another is the simulation of cosmic events to explain and predict the behavior of the universe.

A glossary of High Performance Computing (HPC) can be found at:
http://www.nics.tennessee.edu/hpc-glossary

hypervisor: A hypervisor, also called a virtual machine manager, is a program that allows multiple operating systems to share a single hardware host. Each operating system appears to have the host's processor, memory, and other resources all to itself. However, the hypervisor is actually controlling the host processor and resources, allocating what is needed to each operating system in turn and making sure that the guest operating systems (called virtual machines) cannot disrupt each other.

Early examples of hypervisors are IBM's VM/370 (Virtual Machine/370) and Amdahl's MDF (Multiple Domain Facility), both of which are Type 1 hypervisors.

Type 1 hypervisor: Also known as a native or bare-metal hypervisor, a Type 1 hypervisor runs directly on the host computer's hardware.

Type 2 hypervisor: Also known as a hosted hypervisor, a Type 2 hypervisor runs under an operating system environment (OSE).

Hypervisors introduce a performance overhead on virtual machines when compared to native mode operation.

---

* IBM introduced SDLC as an systems network architecture (SNA) since it would not wait for the HDLC protocol to be finalized.

idle: The operating system is idle if no processes are ready to run or are sleeping while waiting for block I/O to complete. Normally, a processor is not completely idle as it nearly always scan queues for work and items for "posting" as complete and so on. This "workload" is often called a zero utilization effect.

idle waiting for I/O: The operating system is idle waiting for I/O if processes that would otherwise be runnable are sleeping while waiting for I/O to a block device to complete.

in-core: Describes something that is internal to the operating system kernel.

in-core inode: An entry in the kernel table describing the status of a file system inode that is being accessed by processes.

inode (index node): An inode is a data structure that represents a file within a traditional UNIX filesystem. It consists of a file's metadata and the numbers of the blocks that can be used to access the file's data.

instruction cycle: The time period during which one instruction is fetched from memory and executed when a computer is given an instruction in machine language.

interrupt: A notification from a hardware device about an event that is external to the CPU. Interrupts may be generated for events such as the completion of a transfer of data to or from disk, an impending error, or a key being pressed.

interrupt bound: A system that is unable to handle all the interrupts that are arriving. Operating systems have an interrupt structure and routines for handling the various levels which, in general, reflect the importance of each type of interrupt.

interrupt latency: The time that the kernel takes to handle an interrupt.

interrupt overrun: Occurs when too many interrupts arrive while the kernel is trying to handle a previous interrupt.

I/O: Abbreviation of input/output, that is, the transfer of data to and from peripheral devices such as hard disks, tape drives, the keyboard, and the screen.

I/O bound: A system in which the peripheral devices cannot transfer data as fast as requested. This may only be temporary but if it is a common occurrence, then palliative action needs to be taken. In the 1980s, I witnessed a company buy a bigger processor to solve a performance issue when the real problem was that the system was I/O constrained. This emphasizes the importance of performance management.

IOPS (input/output operations per second): A measure of performance of input and output devices. It is normally used in discussing HDD (disk) performance.

IPS (instructions per second): A measure of the performance of a processor in the execution of instructions in its instruction set.

This obviously depends on the mix of instructions, which normally need different cycles per instruction to execute.

ITOA (IT operations analytics): A term often associated with the collection and analysis of wire data (q.v.), which is the art and craft of streaming the mass of IT operations data into a single source for analysis and decision making.

jitter: In voice over IP (VoIP), jitter is the variation in the time between packets arriving, caused by network congestion, timing drift, or route changes. A jitter buffer (q.v.) can be used to handle jitter.

jitter buffer: A jitter buffer is a shared data area wherein voice packets can be collected, stored, and sent to the voice processor in evenly spaced intervals. Variations in packet arrival time, called jitter (q.v.), can occur because of network congestion, timing drift, or route changes. The jitter buffer, which is located at the receiving end of the voice connection, intentionally delays the arriving packets so that the end-user experiences a clear connection with very little sound distortion.

job: One or more processes grouped together but issued as a single command. For example, a job can be a shell script containing several commands or a series of commands issued on the command line connected by a pipeline. In older or proprietary systems, there was a language for controlling job dispatching and execution—Job Control Language (JCL—IBM) and Declarative Control Language (DCL—DEC).

kernel: The name for the operating system's central set of intrinsic services. These services provide the interface between user processes and the system's hardware, allowing access to virtual memory, I/O from and to peripheral devices, and sharing resources between the user processes running on the system.

kernel mode: See *system/supervisor mode*.

kernel parameter: A constant defined in the file */etc/conf/cf.d/mtune* that controls the configuration of the kernel.

kmdaemon: A kernel daemon that allocates pools on behalf of interrupt-level code and tries to give memory back to the system.

last mile: This is a common term that typically means the link between an end user and the telephone company central office—local, long distance, or Internet. It does not mean a mile but simply the last leg of the journey. The term has entered the language referring to the problems of communications making it that last mile. The last mile often runs over old, limited bandwidth copper wire that has been in the ground for years and the quality of whose cable is not optimal. It is the sibling of *first mile*.

level-one (L1) cache: Cache memory that is implemented on the CPU itself.

level-two (L2) cache: Cache memory that is implemented externally to the CPU.

level-three (L3) cache: Cache memory that is shared by processors and complements any on-chip cache.

load average: The utilization of the CPU measured as the average number of processes on the run queue over a certain period of time.

LOC (lines of code): Often used as a unit for various software measurements, for example, faults/LOC. Sometimes KLOC (1000s of LOCs) is used for larger programs.

logging: A generic term for information relating to hardware and/or software that can be used subsequently for statistics, problem determination, and so on. The log can also be used "in flight," for example, to recover a failed database.

lossless (compression): A compression technique that decompresses data back to its original form without any loss. The decompressed file and the original are identical. All compression methods used to compress text, databases, and other business data are lossless. For example, the ZIP archiving technology (PKZIP, WinZip, etc.) is the most widely used lossless method.

The term *lossless* is sometimes applied to data transmission since, in the bad old days, transmission media often dropped bits and was thus *lossy*. Today, the media have improved, and checksums are applied to detect and correct errors in transmission.

LRC (longitudinal redundancy check): A data communications error-trapping technique in which a character is accumulated at both the sending and receiving stations during the transmission and is compared for an equal condition, which indicates a good transmission of the previous block. It is a checking method that generates a parity bit from a specified string of bits on a longitudinal track. In a row-and-column format, such as on magnetic tape, LRC is often used with VRC, which creates a parity bit for each character.

marry driver: A pseudo-device driver that allows a regular file within a filesystem to be accessed as a block device, and, hence, as a swap area.

mean: This is a method of averaging numbers. For a discrete set of numbers, for example, a list of times taken to repair several occurrences of the same fault, the *arithmetic* mean is the sum of the repair times (T) divided by the number of such times, that is

$$\frac{\sum T_R}{\text{Number of Repairs}}$$

The other "mean" value is the *geometric* mean, which is the product of the set of numbers to the power of (1/N) where N is the number of numbers, that is

$$\text{Geometric Mean}\big(N \text{ numbers}\big) = (a1 \times a2 \times a3 \ldots \times aN)^{\frac{1}{N}} = \left(\prod_1^N a_i\right)^{\frac{1}{N}}$$

measurements of data:

- a bit = one binary digit (1 or 0) * "bit" is derived from the contraction bit (binary digit) → 8 bits = one byte
- K = kilobyte (1024 bytes)
- Kb = kilobit
- MB = megabyte
- Mb = megabit
- MB/s = megabytes per second
- Mb/s = megabits per second
- bps = bits per second

median: The *median* of a set of numbers is the number in the middle. For example, in the set of numbers 4, 6, 25, the median is 6. However the numbers must be in order for the median to be in the middle. If there is an even number of numbers, then the median is the average of the last two middle numbers.

For a distribution (as opposed to the discrete numbers), the median is the midpoint on the curve that divides it into even areas.

memory bound: A system that is short of physical memory, and in which pages of physical memory, but not their contents, must be shared by different processes. This is achieved by paging out, and swapping in cases of extreme shortage of physical memory.

memory leak: An application program has a memory leak if its size is constantly growing in virtual memory. This may happen if the program is continually requesting more memory without reusing memory allocated to data structures that are no longer in use. A program with a memory leak can eventually make the whole system memory bound, at which time it may start paging out or swapping.

metadata: The data that an inode stores concerning file attributes and directory entries.

monitor: Software that monitors the progress of activities within a computer system, particularly resources providing a service. This can be architected as a stand-alone system monitoring another system(s) or a stand-alone system cooperating with software (agent) on the monitored system. In theory, a system can monitor itself, but if the monitor is measuring availability, then it goes down with the system.

MPI (Message Passing Interface): A standard developed by the Message Passing Interface Forum (MPIF). It specifies a portable interface for writing message-passing programs and aims at practicality, efficiency, and flexibility at the same time. MPIF, with the participation of more than 40 organizations, started working on the standard in 1992. The first draft (Version 1.0), which was published in 1994, was strongly influenced by the work at the IBM T. J. Watson Research Center. MPIF has further enhanced the first version to develop a second version (MPI-2) in 1997. MPI 3.0 was released on September 21, 2012. For details about MPI and MPIF, visit http://www.mpi-forum.org/.

MPLS (Multiprotocol Label Switching): A protocol for speeding up and shaping network traffic flow. A candidate to replace frame relay and ATM protocols.

multiprocessor system: A computer system with more than one CPU.

multithreaded program: A program is multithreaded if it can be accessed simultaneously by different CPUs. Multithreaded device drivers can run on any CPU in a multiprocessor system. The kernel is multithreaded to allow equal access by all CPUs to its tables and the scheduler. Only one copy of the kernel resides in memory.

namei cache: A kernel data structure that stores the most commonly accessed translations of filesystem pathname components to *inode* number. The namei cache improves I/O performance by reducing the need to retrieve such information from disk.

NAND: NAND Flash architecture is one of two flash technologies (the other being NOR) used in memory cards such as the CompactFlash cards. It is also used in USB Flash drives, MP3 players, and provides the image storage for digital cameras. NAND is best suited to flash devices requiring high-capacity data storage. NAND flash devices offer storage space up to 512-MB and offer faster erase, write, and read capabilities over NOR architecture.

NAND flash architecture was introduced by Toshiba in 1989'. [Webopedia]

network adapter: See *NIC*.

network analyzer: See *traffic analyzer*.

NIC (network interface card): Also called a *network adapter*, this is a plug-in card that enables a computer to transmit and receive data on a local network. Today, the term refers to an Ethernet adapter, although in the past, Token Ring, LocalTalk, and FDDI networks were used. A network adapter/NIC may also refer to a Wi-Fi adapter. Ethernet circuitry is built onto the motherboard of every new desktop and laptop computer, and plug-in cards (NICs) are generally only used in servers and high-end workstations.

network topology: Describes the physical and logical relationship of nodes in a network, the schematic arrangement of the links and nodes, or some hybrid combination thereof. Topology is important for understanding the routes that data can take in a network.

nice value: A weighting factor in the range 0–39 that influences how great a share of CPU time a process will receive. A high value means that a process will run on the CPU less often.

nonblocking I/O: Allows a process to continue executing without waiting for an I/O operation to complete. Also known as asynchronous I/O.

OC-192: Optical Carrier Level 192. SONET channel of 9.953 thousand million bits per second (Gbps).

OC-48: Optical Carrier Level 48. SONET channel of 2.488 thousand million bits per second (Gbps).

OLTP (online transaction processing): An interactive way of working, normally via a workstation or terminal, and involving a remote server and database. It is in essence short pieces of work that have a beginning and an end, and whereby the state of a database is altered permanently. It is also used for queries where no permanent state change occurs (read-only).

Typically, OLTP systems are used for order entry, financial transactions, billing, and retail sales. Such systems have a large number of users who conduct short pieces of work (transactions). Database queries are usually simple, require subsecond response times, and return relatively few records.

Sometimes transactions are linked and need information passing between them when they execute. This is often achieved by using a "scratch pad area" where one transaction stores transient data for re-use later by itself or a related transaction.

Recovery from sudden failures in such systems is of paramount importance (see *Acid Properties*).

OpenGL: OpenGL is the premier environment for developing portable, interactive 2D and 3D graphics applications. Since its introduction in 1992, OpenGL has become the industry's most widely used and supported 2D and 3D graphics application programming interface (API), bringing thousands of applications to a wide variety of computer platforms. OpenGL fosters innovation and speeds application development by incorporating a broad set of rendering, texture mapping, special effects, and other powerful visualization functions. It also allows development across all popular desktop and workstation platforms, ensuring wide application deployment.

GL and the subsequent Open GL are examples of *de facto* standards upstaging *de jure* standards. Here, the *de jure* standard was PHIGS. Another example is TCP/IP versus OSI.

operating system: The software that manages access to a computer system's hardware resources.

OSPF (open shortest path first): A link-state routing algorithm that is used to calculate routes based on the number of routers, transmissions speed, delays, and route costs.

overhead: The load that an operating system incurs while sharing resources between user processes and performing its internal accounting.

packet: Generic term for a bundle of data, usually in binary form, organized in a specific way for transmission. The specific native protocol of the data network (for example, X.25, Frame Relay, ATM) may term the packet as a *packet*, *block*, *frame*, or *cell*. A packet consists of the data to be transmitted and certain control information, such as headers and trailing data, error correction code (ECC) or longitudinal redundancy code (LRC).

page: A fixed-size (4KB) block of memory.

page fault: A hardware event that occurs when a process tries to access an address in virtual memory that does not have a location in physical memory associated with it. In response, the system tries to load the appropriate data into a newly assigned physical page.

page stealing daemon: The daemon responsible for releasing pages of memory for use by other processes. Also known as *vhand*.

paging in: Reading pages of program text and preinitialized data from the file systems, or stack and data pages from swap.

paging out: Releasing pages of physical memory for use by making temporary copies of the contents of dirty pages to swap space. Clean pages of program text and preinitialized data are not copied to swap space because they can be paged in from the file systems.

parent process: A process that executes a **fork**(S) system call to create a new child process. The child process usually executes an **exec**(S) system call to invoke a new program in its place.

percentile: A value on a scale of 100 that indicates the percent of a distribution that is equal to or below it. For example, a service level agreement (SLA) may ask for a 90 (th) percentile response time of 3.5 seconds, meaning that 90% of response time must fall at or below 3.5 s. The rest will be above that figure.

performance management (PM): An activity intended to optimize performance and efficiency, and to plan for growth. PM is an ongoing process consisting of

- Setting the performance objectives and creating the baseline via service level agreements (SLAs)
- Collecting the performance and related data
- Analyzing the collected data to yield pertinent information
- Presenting this information at various levels, from management's single-page health checks to larger reports for operations and other people
- Changing the system resource parameters (*tuning*), bearing in mind you cannot tune a tractor to take part in a Formula 1 race
- Analyzing the performance trends, leading to capacity planning

Performance monitoring is part of this multipart process.

performance rating: see **benchmark**.

PHIGS (programmer's hierarchical interactive graphics system): This is an application programming interface (API) standard for rendering 3D computer graphics, considered to be the 3D graphics standard for the 1980s through the early 1990s. Subsequently, a combination of features and power led to the rise of OpenGL, which became the most popular professional 3D API of the mid to late 1990s.

PHIGS originally lacked the capability to render illuminated scenes, and was superseded by *PHIGS+*. PHIGS+ works in essentially the same manner but added methods for lighting and filling surfaces within a 3D scene. OpenGL (SGI) was generally considered to be much more "powerful" for 3D programming. PHIGS fell into disuse, another example of a *de facto* standard outlasting a *de jure* standard.

physical memory: Storage normally implemented using RAM chips.

PPP (point-to-point protocol): Essentially incorporating HDLC (q.v.), but with significantly expanded capabilities, PPP is used in various forms over a wide variety of serial connections. It is specified and extended in Internet Engineering Task Force (IETF) Request for Comments (RFC) 1661, RFC 1662*, and many others.

preemption: This occurs when a process that was running on a CPU is replaced by a higher-priority process.

priority: A value that the scheduler calculates to determine which process(es) should next run on the CPUs. A process's priority is calculated from its nice value and its recent CPU usage.

process: A single instance of a program in execution. This can be a login shell or an operating system command, but not a built-in shell command. If a command is built into the shell, a separate process is not created on its invocation; the built-in command is issued within the context of the shell process.

process table: A data structure inside the kernel that stores information about all the processes that are present on a system. Some OSs can generate CPU load by scanning through such lists looking for work, even if there isn't any to do.

---

* You should only refer to these (a) if it is part of your job (b) if you cannot get to sleep.

protocol: A set of rules and procedures used to establish and maintain communication between hardware or software subsystems.

protocol stack: Allows two high-level systems to communicate by passing messages through a low-level physical interface.

pseudo-device driver: A device driver that allows software to behave as though it is a physical device. Examples are ram disks and pseudo-ttys (tele typewriters, an ancient communication terminal).

pseudo-tty: A pseudo-terminal is a device driver that allows one process to communicate with another as though it were a physical terminal. Pseudo-ttys are used to interface to programs that expect to receive nonblocking input and to send terminal control characters.

queue: An ordered list of entities requiring a service of some sort.

queue balking: Some customers decide not to join the queue due to their observation related to the long length of queue, insufficient waiting space, or improper care while customers are in the queue. This is balking, and thus it pertains to the discouragement of the customer from joining an improper or inconvenient queue.

queue reneging: Reneging pertains to impatient customers. After being in queue for some time, some customers become impatient and may leave the queue. This phenomenon is called reneging of queue. This concept and the previous one (queue balking) are of interest to organizations who deal with real customers on the basis that unhappy customers may not return.

queuing methods (network): There are a variety of traffic queuing (engineering) methods that are used to regulate network traffic. Mostly dealing with queuing, they ensure that transmitted data are received in a timely manner. The following are some of the more the common methods:

- First come/first served or first in/first out (FIFO). Items are serviced in the order they are received.
- Last in/first out (LIFO). As above in reverse.
- Priority queuing: Items are placed in prioritized queues and served by queue in priority order; when one queue empties, the next in priority is serviced.
- Fair queuing: Each item is assigned a type (flow) and placed into the queue for that type. All queues are serviced round-robin: a packet from one queue, a packet from the next, and so on.

There are a number of other "selection" methods for handling queues; see

http://www.pcmag.com/encyclopedia/term/53063/traffic-engineering-methods

queuing methods (other resources): These vary depending on whether they are hardware or software entities. FIFO is the favorite, but priorities for dispatching items of work often depend on software and parameters decided by the business requirements. Queuing methods are often called *dispatching algorithms*.

race condition: The condition that occurs when several processes or CPUs are trying to write to the same memory or disk locations at the same time. The data that is eventually stored depends on the order that the writes occur. A synchronization mechanism must be used to enforce the desired order in which the writes are to take place.

RAID array: Abbreviation of redundant array of inexpensive disks. Used to implement high-performance and/or high-integrity disk storage.

ramdisk: A portion of physical memory configured to look like a physical disk but capable of fast access times. Data written to a ramdisk is lost when the operating system is shut down. Ramdisks are, therefore, only suitable for implementing temporary file systems.

raw device interface: Provides access to block-structured peripheral devices that bypasses the block device interface and allows variable-sized transfers of data. The raw interface also allows control of a peripheral using the **ioctl**(S) system call. This allows, for example, for low-level operations such as formatting a disk or rewinding a tape.

RCA: see *root cause analysis*

region: A region groups a process's pages by their function. A process has at least three regions for its data, stack, and text.

response time: In data processing, the response time perceived by the end user is the interval between

(a) the instant at which an operator at a terminal enters a request for a response from a computer
(b) the instant at which the first character of the response is received at a terminal

resource: An IT entity that can be divided into software and hardware resources. Software resources may be specific to applications, or they may be kernel data structures such as the process table, open file, and in-core inode tables, buffer and certain caches, multiphysical buffers, and character lists. Hardware resources are a computer's physical subsystems. The three main subsystems are CPU, memory, and I/O. The memory subsystem can be divided into two resources: physical memory (or main memory and caches) and swap space (or secondary memory). The I/O subsystem comprises one or more resources of similar or different types—hard and floppy disk drives, tape drives, CD-ROMs, graphics displays, network devices and *unit record* devices (printers, optical character readers [OCRs], card readers, etc.).

ready-to-run process: A process that has all the system resources that it needs in order to be able to run on a CPU.

reneging: The exiting from a queue by a "work unit" (customer, transaction etc.) before being served.

response time: The time taken between issuing a command and receiving some feedback from the system. This is not to be confused with turnaround time, which is a measure of how long a particular task takes from invocation to completion.

root cause analysis (RCA): (*ITIL Service Operation definition*). An activity that identifies the root cause of an incident or problem. Root cause analysis typically concentrates on IT infrastructure failures.

router: A network device that forwards data packets from one network to another. Based on the address of the destination network in the incoming packet and an internal *routing table* (q.v.), the router determines which port (line) to send out the packet. Routers require packets formatted in a routable protocol, the global standard being TCP/IP.

routing protocol: An algorithm used by routers to determine the appropriate path onto which data should be forwarded. The routing protocol also specifies how routers report changes and share information with the other routers in the network that they are in contact with.

A routing protocol allows the network to dynamically adjust to changing conditions; otherwise all routing decisions have to be predetermined and remain static. How clever a router is depends on its software.

routing table: A database in a router that contains the current network topology in a form that facilitates onward data transfers.

run queue: The list of ready-to-run processes maintained by the kernel.

runaway process: A process/program that is running in "useless" mode and consuming resources, especially processor cycles. These can continue *ad infinitum* unless identified and "killed."

runbook: A runbook is an electronic or physical document that lists detailed procedures for handling every expected situation that an IT system may experience. Based on changes in system operations, incoming requests, and other factors, system administrators determine which procedures to run and when to run them. In short, it is what "old timers" used to call an Ops Manual.

scaling: A computer system's ability to increase its processing capacity as processors are added. If the processing capacity increases in direct proportion to the number of CPUs, a system is said to exhibit linear scaling. These are tackled by Amdahl's, Gustafson's and Gunther's Laws, dealt with in this book.

In practice, a system's ability to scale is limited by contention between the CPUs for resources and depends on the mix of applications being run. It also depends on it having sufficient peripherals to feed an increase in processor power.

scheduler: The part of the kernel that chooses which process(es) to run on the CPUs.

service level agreement (SLA): (*ITIL Continual Service Improvement, ITIL Service Design definition*). An agreement between an IT service provider and a customer. A service-level agreement describes the IT service, documents service level targets, and specifies the responsibilities of the IT service provider and the customer. A single agreement may cover multiple IT services or multiple customers.

seven-layer model: The layers of the OSI communications model.

Physical (Layer 1): This layer conveys the bit stream—electrical impulse, light or radio signal—through the network at the electrical and mechanical level (wires, fiber). It provides the hardware means of sending and receiving data on a carrier, including defining cables, cards, and physical aspects. Layer 1 physical examples include Ethernet, FDDI, B8ZS, V.35, V.24, RJ45.

Data Link (Layer 2): In layer 2, data packets are encoded and decoded into bits. It furnishes transmission protocol knowledge and management and handles errors in the physical layer, flow control, and frame synchronization. The data link layer is divided into two sublayers: The media access control (MAC) layer and the logical link control (LLC) layer. The MAC sublayer controls how a computer on the network gains access to the data and permission to transmit it. The LLC layer controls frame synchronization, flow control, and error checking (ECC, etc.) Layer 2 Data Link examples include PPP, FDDI, ATM, IEEE 802.5/ 802.2, IEEE 802.3/802.2, HDLC, Frame Relay.

Network (Layer 3): The layer providing switching and routing technologies, creating logical paths, known as virtual circuits, for transmitting data from node to node. Routing and forwarding are functions of this layer, as well as addressing, internetworking, error handling, congestion control, and packet sequencing. Layer 3 Network examples include AppleTalk DDP, IP, and IPX.

Transport (Layer 4): This layer provides transparent transfer of data between end systems, or hosts, and is responsible for end-to-end error recovery and flow control. It ensures complete data transfer. Layer 4 Transport examples include SPX, TCP, and UDP.

Session (Layer 5): This layer establishes, manages, and terminates *connections* between applications. The session layer sets up, coordinates, and terminates conversations, exchanges, and dialogues between the applications at each end. It deals with session and connection coordination. Layer 5 Session examples include NFS, NetBios names, RPC, SQL.

Presentation (Layer 6): This layer provides independence from differences in data representation (e.g., encryption) by translating from application to network format and vice versa. The presentation layer works to transform data into the form that the application layer can accept. This layer formats and encrypts data to be sent across a network, providing freedom from compatibility problems. It is sometimes called the syntax layer.

Layer 6 Presentation examples include encryption, ASCII, EBCDIC, TIFF, GIF, PICT, JPEG, MPEG, MIDI.

Application (Layer 7): This layer supports application and end-user processes. Communication partners are identified, quality of service is identified, user authentication and privacy are considered, and any constraints on data syntax are identified. Everything at this layer is application-specific. This layer provides application services for file transfers, email, and other network software services. Telnet and FTP are applications that exist entirely in the application level. Tiered application architectures are part of this layer. Layer 7 Application examples include WWW browsers, NFS, SNMP, Telnet, HTTP, and FTP.

single-threaded program: A program is single threaded if it can only run on one CPU at a time. Single-threaded device drivers can only run on the base processor in a multiprocessor system.

sleeping on I/O: See *waiting for I/O*. This is logged in various ways, depending on the operating system in use.

software scalability: Here, the number of users or load generators (N) is incremented on a fixed hardware configuration. In this case, the number of users acts as the independent variable while the processor configuration remains fixed over the range of user-load measurements. This is the most common situation found in load testing environments where tools like HP's *LoadRunner* or Apache *JMeter* are used.

spin lock: A method of synchronizing processes on a multiprocessor system. A process waiting for a resource that is currently in use (locked) by a process running on a different CPU repeatedly executes a short section of kernel code (spins) until the lock is released.

SRAM (static RAM): This is more expensive and requires four times the amount of space for a given amount of data compared to dynamic RAM (DRAM q.v.) but unlike dynamic RAM, it does not need to be power-refreshed and is therefore faster to access (more recent advances in dynamic RAM have improved access time). Static RAM is often used for the level-1 and level-2 caches that the microprocessor looks in first before looking in dynamic RAM. SRAM often runs at the frequency of the host processor, which is very fast.

stack: A list of temporary data used by a program to handle function calls.

strd: The system name for the STREAMS daemon.

stream head: The level of the STREAMS I/O interface with which a user process communicates.

STREAMS daemon: The daemon used by the STREAMS I/O subsystem to manage STREAMS memory.

STREAMS I/O: A mechanism for implementing a layered interface between applications running in user space and a device driver. Most often used to implement network protocol stacks.

swap area: A piece of swap space implemented as a disk division or as a block device married to a regular file in a filesystem.

swap space: A collection of swap areas used to temporarily store the contents of stack and data memory pages while they are used by other processes.

swapper daemon: Part of the kernel that reclaims physical pages of memory for use by copying whole regions of processes to swap space.

swapping: The action taken by the swapper daemon when the system is extremely short of physical memory needed for use by processes. Swapping can place a heavy load on the CPU and disk I/O subsystems.

symmetric multiprocessing: A multiprocessor system is symmetric when any processor can perform any function. This ensures an even load distribution because no processor depends on another. Each process is executed by a single processor.

system mode: The state of a CPU when the kernel needs to ensure that it has privileged access to its data and physical devices. Also known as kernel mode.

T1: A speed designation of high-speed communication between systems over telephone lines at speeds of up to 1.544M.

T3: A speed designation of higher-speed communication between systems over telephone lines at speeds of up to 44.736M; it contains 28 T1 channels.

teraflops (TFLOPS): This is used to measure the performance of a computer's floating-point unit (FPU). One teraflops equals 1,000 gigaflops, or 1,000,000,000,000 FLOPS. The term "teraflops" may be singular or plural because FLOPS is short for "floating-point operations per second." Teraflops is often used to measure scientific computing performance, since most scientific calculations use floating-point operations.

text: Executable machine instructions (code) that a CPU can interpret and act on.

threads: A process can perform multiple computations, that is, program flows, concurrently within a program. In scientific applications (HPC), threads typically process their own subset of data, or a subset of loop iterations.

throughput: The amount of work (measured in number of jobs completed, disk requests handled, and so on) that a system processes in a specified time.

time: A fundamental property of the universe that ensures everything doesn't happen at once. It is also useful as the horizontal axis, symbol t or T, in many of the graphs in this and other books. It has no substitute and is not a renewable or repairable resource. It is also the stuff of which life is made so try not to waste it. Time on a computer is measured by a clock, and various time intervals—for example, an instruction execution time—are measured in clock cycles. Clocks with dates can falter, for example at Y2K.

The next blip will occur in January 2038, when the UNIX and similar clocks overflow.

time slice: The maximum amount of time for which a process can run without being preempted (interrupted). It is a simple way of assigning CPU cycles on a fair basis in some applications or time-sharing systems.

traffic: Control information (metadata) and data transmitted over a network. Traffic is a very general term and typically refers to overall network usage at a given moment. However, it can refer to specific transactions, messages, records, or users in any kind of data or telephone network. It can be used more generally to describe work accessing a storage system.

traffic analyzer: A hardware device or software in a desktop or laptop computer that captures packets transmitted in a network for routine inspection and problem detection. Also called a "sniffer," "packet sniffer," "packet analyzer," "traffic analyser" and "protocol analyzer," the network analyzer plugs into a port on a network hub or switch and decodes one or more protocols into a human-readable format for the network administrator. It can also store packets on disk for further analysis later on.

It is especially useful in detecting "broadcast" traffic where network devices are sending out "are you there" signals. These devices are also useful in analyzing LAN traffic.

traffic shaping: Traffic shaping is the practice of regulating network data transfer to assure a certain level of performance, quality of service (QoS), or return on investment. It is sometimes known as "packet shaping." The practice involves delaying the flow of packets that have been designated as less important or less desired than those of prioritized traffic streams. This is one way of ensuring that services that are critical or have stringent SLAs receive the necessary resources at the expense of other less important services or applications.

Although the term is often used synonymously with *traffic engineering*, traffic shaping deals with managing the network moment to moment, whereas traffic engineering refers to the overall strategies employed in a network. Typically deployed at the edge of the network, traffic shaping may be used to limit "burst-mode" traffic in general or to limit undesired traffic such as spam or peer-to-peer downloads.

This concept is of particular interest in the development of SLAs where competition for bandwidth and favoritism may be high to ensure business-process requirements are met.

Regulating the flow of packets into a network is known as *bandwidth throttling*. Regulation of the flow of packets out of a network is known as *rate limiting*.

transmission multiplexor: A device installed at an intermediate point on a transmission line that enables new signals to come in and existing signals to go out. In a typical example, most signals pass through the device, but some would be "dropped" by splitting them from the line. Signals originating at that point can be "added" into the line and directed to another destination.

Add/drop multiplexing can be done with optical or electronic signals. The device may deal only with wavelengths, or it may convert between wavelengths and electronic TDM signals. Sometimes called an *add/drop multiplexor*.

transaction intent logging: One of the functions of the **htepi_daemon**; writing the intention to change filesystem metadata to a log file on disk.

Two-phase commit (2PC): Another property of software that ensures consistency of results is two-phase commit, where database updates and transaction completions in related units of work are completed and abide by the ACID properties (atomicity, consistency, isolation, and durability.) q.v.

This type of discipline is key to consistent data and transaction integrity and has an implication for availability when one partner in the 2PC exchange fails and the whole task is not completed.

u-area: Abbreviation of user area and also known as a u-block. A data structure possessed by every process, the u-area contains private data about the process that only the kernel may access.

UIC (unreferenced interval count): An IBM MVS term that is a measure of how "old" a page in memory is and if it may be eligible for paging out to make room for more active pages.

user mode: The state of a CPU when it is executing the code of a user program that accesses its own data space in memory.

vddaemon: A kernel daemon that monitors and can reconfigure the operation of a virtual disk array.

vhand: The system name for the page stealing daemon.

virtual disk: A disk composed of pieces of several physical disks.

virtual memory: A method of expanding the amount of available memory by combining physical memory (RAM) with cheaper and slower storage such as a swap area on a hard disk.

VLN (very large number): A common field defined in HPC calculations to define the limit of large numbers derived in a program so that it fits the machine's architecture. Thus, if the calculation would yield a number too large for the architecture, it will be set by the programmer to be equal to VLN.

VPN (virtual private network): A VPN uses a public telecommunications infrastructure to provide secure access. This is a virtual network dedicated to providing a customer with more security within a cloud environment. Each VPN runs its own operating system, bandwidth, and disk space, and can be individually booted. The VPN is not necessarily a single line but a guaranteed path through a network dedicated to the user.

VSN (very small number): A common field defined in HPC calculations to define the limit of small numbers given by calculations. In the worst case, a very small number may end up as a zero to be divided into another number and is set by the programmer to be equal to VSN.

waiting for I/O: A process goes to sleep if it has to wait for an I/O operation to complete.

WAN acceleration: A wide area network (WAN) accelerator is an appliance that optimizes bandwidth to improve the end user's experience on a WAN. The appliance, which can be a physical hardware component, software program, or an appliance running in a virtualized environment, speeds up the time it takes for information to flow back and forth across the WAN by using compression and data deduplication techniques to reduce the amount of data that needs to be transmitted. Basically, an accelerator works by caching duplicate files or parts of files so they can be referenced instead of having to be sent across the WAN again. It is an adjunct to, and partially overlaps, WAN Optimization (q.v.).

WAN optimization: WAN optimization is a collection of techniques for increasing data transfer efficiencies across WANs. In 2008, the WAN optimization market was estimated to be $1 billion, and it was estimated to be about $4.4 billion by 2014 according to the Gartner Group.

There is a rather large eBook (250+ pages) that can be found at the following link:

How to Accelerate Your Internet: A practical guide to Bandwidth Management and Optimisation using Open Source Software

http://www.ws.afnog.org/afnog2014/extra/bwmo/bwmo-ebook.pdf

wire data:

> Wire data is the observed behavior and communication between networked elements which is an important source of information used by IT operations staff to troubleshoot performance issues, create activity baselines, detect anomalous activity, investigate security incidents, and discover IT assets and their dependencies. According to Gartner, wire data is one of five types of data that will need to be handled by emerging IT Operations Analytics platforms. Gartner defines wire data as "the data contained in the headers and payloads of packets and their associated flow data as traffic moves from one node to another across a distributed IT system." [Wikipedia]
>
> Wire data is all L2-L7 communications between all systems. This source of data has traditionally included including deep packet inspection and header sampling but recent advancements allow for far deeper, real-time wire data analysis. [ExtraHop]

With wire data, it is possible to assess what every component and server is doing in the *application delivery chain*. It is also possible with such data to spot emerging performance variances in behavior and predict potential larger variations. In addition, real-time views of application data can be inferred from L7 data, that is, application data and not just network traffic volumes. [*Information from ExtraHop*]

Some proponents of wire data collection and analysis claim that normal network performance and application performance monitors (NPM and APM) cannot keep pace with the volatility of present day IT and that wire data offers a more *elastic* solution since it encompasses most levels in the hierarchy.

Wire Data
http://en.wikipedia.org/wiki/Wire_data

10 Ways Wire Data Can help You Conquer IT Complexity
http://resources.idgenterprise.com/original/AST-0109886_10_Ways_Wire_Data_Can_Help_You_Conquer_IT_Complexity_Complete_11.15.13.pdf
[search "10 ways, wire data" and you should hit it.]

X-client: An applications program that communicates with an X-server to request that it display information on a screen or to receive input events from the keyboard or a pointing device such as a mouse. The client may be running on the same computer as the server (local), or it may be connected via a network (remote).

X-server: The software that controls the screen, keyboard, and pointing device under the X Window System.

X-terminal: A display device that is able to run X-server software. All of an X-terminal's clients must run on remote machines.

X Window System: A windowing system based on the client/server model.

Appendix IV: Some Performance Math

General Math

Sums and Products

Summation: The symbol Σ (Greek upper case *sigma*) denotes a summation of items. The example below should make the function clear.

$$a_1 + a_2 + a_3 + \ldots a_n = \sum_{i=1}^{n} a_i$$

Product: The symbol Π (Greek upper case *pi*) denotes a product of items. The example below should make the function clear.

$$a_1 \times a_2 \times a_3 \times \ldots a_n = \prod_{j=1}^{n} a_i$$

Mean Values of Quantities

The use of means or averages of some sort are common in IT since very few measurable parameters always have a fixed value. There are *mean response times, mean reliabilities, average utilizations,* and so on, often depending on mathematical distributions for their derivation and calculation.

Arithmetic Mean (Average)

This is the most common type of average. If we have n numbers, $a_1, a_2, a_3, \ldots, a_n$, then the arithmetic mean (AM) of these numbers is their sum divided by n.

$$AM = \frac{1}{n} \sum_{1}^{n} a_i = \frac{\left(a_1 + a_2 + a_3 \ldots \ldots a_n\right)}{n} \tag{A4.1}$$

Geometric Mean

The geometric mean (GM) of a series of n numbers, $a_1, a_2, a_3, \ldots, a_n$, is obtained by multiplying the numbers together and taking the nth root.

$$GM = \sqrt[n]{\prod_1^n a_i} = \sqrt[n]{a_1 \times a_2 \times a_3 \times \ldots a_n} \tag{A4.2}$$

Natural Logarithm

The logarithm of a number is normally the power of the base 10 that gives that number. So, on a base of 10, the logarithm of 3.1622 is 0.5000, that is, the square root, which is expressed as $10^{0.5000}$, so that we can say that

$$3.1622 = \log_{10} = 0.500$$

In the math of distributions, integration, and differentiation, there arises the concept of a natural logarithm the base of which happens to be approximately e = 2.71828. When a logarithm is generated in math, it is normally expressed to the base e. On this scale, the logarithm of a number is that number which, when used as a power of e, will yield that number. For example, the logarithm to base e of 1.6487 is 0.5000 since $e^{0.5000}$ is the same as $2.71828^{0.5000}$, which is written $\log_e (1.6487) = 0.5000$.

Sometimes a logarithm to base e is written as ln (x), which means the same as $\log_e$ (x). If the base e is assumed in any particular discussion, it may also be written as simply log(x).

Percentile

A percentile is a metric used in statistics indicating the value below which a given percentage of observations in a group of observations fall. For example, the 20th percentile is the value (or score) below which 20% of the observations may be found. Percentiles are frequently used in stating response time metrics, perhaps in a service level agreement (SLA).

In a graph or bar chart representation of the number of responses versus response time (small range), a line separates the area under the graph into 20% for the lower part and 80% for the other (upper) part. Thus, a statement saying the 90th percentile must be 3 s for the accounts application means that a vertical line drawn so that it breaks the response curve into a 90% and a 10% areas will cross the horizontal at the 3.0 s mark.

Weighted Mean

The weighted mean is an average that recognizes that a simple average of a number of entities does not allow for the fact that each entity may not be as prevalent or numerous as others, and so its influence on the mean is exaggerated.

To get a *fair* mean, it is necessary to *weight* the prevalent entities to give them more influence on the average.

As an example, consider a requirement to estimate the weight on a lorry when carrying a number of different items, so that it complies with transport regulations. Let's imagine there are n items, each of weight W_1, W_2, ...W_n. It might seem logical to say that the average weight of items, W_{AV}, is therefore a simple mean of quantities:

$$W_{AV} = \frac{(W_1 + W_2 + ...W_n)}{n} = \sum_1^n W_i \qquad (A4.3)$$

and that the load on the lorry of any n items will be n × W_{AV}. This may be a simplification since n items might consist of different numbers of each item so that, for example, if the load has a preponderance of the heaviest items, the weight will be far higher than that calculated above.

It is therefore necessary in such circumstances to bias any average toward the items according to their frequency of occurrence. This is what is called a *weighted mean*. So instead of Equation A4.3, we now have the relationship

$$W_{AV} = \frac{\sum_1^n W_i \times N_i}{\sum N_i} \qquad (A4.4)$$

where N_i is the number of item i in the average load. This is similar to the exercise of timing a software program by multiplying the number of instructions in it by the average instruction time of the CPU clock cycles needed to execute this *average instruction*.

We have already seen an example of this in Chapter 2 under "Processor Performance," showing this property for numbers of cycles per instruction.

Matrix Equations

These are blocks of numbers usually associated with multiple linear equations, for example in the Linpack benchmark, which solves sets of equations.

Linpack is essentially a tool for solving a large set of simultaneous equations with a number of unknowns in a number of equations. The example below is a three by three (3 × 3) set of equations to be solved:

$$a_{11}x_1 + a_{12}x_2 + a_{13}x_3 = b_1$$
$$a_{21}x_1 + a_{22}x_2 + a_{23}x_3 = b_2$$
$$a_{31}x_1 + a_{32}x_2 + a_{33}x_3 = b_3$$

where the a and b values are known *constants*. Knowing these constants, the task is then to solve for the values of x that satisfy this system. The notation a_{mn} means the value of a in row m, column n.

This system can be rearranged into matrix form:

$$[A](x) = (b)$$

a shorthand representation where [A] is a *square matrix* and (x) and (b) are *column vectors* and are written in the form:

$$[A] = \begin{pmatrix} a_{11} & a_{12} & a_{13} \\ a_{21} & a_{22} & a_{23} \\ a_{31} & a_{32} & a_{33} \end{pmatrix}$$

$$(x) = \begin{pmatrix} x_1 \\ x_2 \\ x_3 \end{pmatrix}$$

$$(b) = \begin{pmatrix} b_1 \\ b_2 \\ b_3 \end{pmatrix}$$

Linpack (and similar HPC calculations) are of this form but usually of greater matrix dimensions, such as 100×100 or 500×500. The solution of these equations by numerical methods is what provides the test for HPC systems in solving Linpack and Lapack. Incidentally, similar types of equations need to be solved in weather forecasting, and the availability of meteorological data and the ability to solve larger versions of these equations is what allows short-term weather forecasts to be more accurate. See the section "HPC and Weather" in Appendix VI.

Operational Math Analysis Details

Operational laws are simple equations, which may be used as an abstract representation or model of the average behavior of almost any system. The laws are very general and make almost no assumptions about the behavior of the random variables (*) characterizing the system.

[Jane Hilston, University of Edinburgh]

(*) the various queuing distributions

The Operational Laws were identified originally by J. P. Buzen in 1976 and later extended by Denning and Buzen in 1978. They are classified as follows (see Jain reference below this discussion):

- Little's law
- Forced flow law
- Utilization law
- General response time law
- Interactive response time law
- Bottleneck analysis

This concept takes me back many years before Buzen, when I taught elementary physics to mainly professional tradespeople at a night class. Many times they were stuck on a problem and would sit looking at it. My advice to them was *write down all you know and also what you don't know and then try to find relationships between them*. If, for example, you were perplexed by an Ohm's Law question, you might write down V (voltage) = 12, R (resistance) = 3, I (current) = ?? Eureka! There is an equation V = IR, so I can now deduce I! Simple, effective, and it works.

We employ the first five laws in our analysis of data that will be used to derive common performance metrics. The laws apply to what is known as *balanced job flow*, meaning that the number of arrivals is equal to the number of completions during the period of observation. Each arrival translates to a job, unit of work (UoW), or a customer, in general terms.

In some cases, however, a transaction may decompose into several transactions by calls to them from the primary transaction (arrival). For example, a payroll transaction may call a tax transaction or not, as the case may be.

Overview of Operational Laws

Little's Law

The mean number in the system or device* = arrival rate × mean time in the system/device:

$$N = XW$$

for a balanced workflow situation. Given that a system can be composed of subsystems, a new parameter can be defined: the *visit count*. This the number of requests for a particular resource, for example, a disk, and obviously, the sum of all these visit counts (V_i) is the ratio of requests to that resource to that of requests to the whole (parent) system:

$$V_i = \frac{C_i}{C}$$

Forced Flow Law

This relates the system throughput to the individual device throughput, throughput meaning jobs/UoW leaving the system per unit time. The law states that the ith resource's throughput is the throughput of the system x the visit count of that resource:

$$X_i = XV_i$$

Utilization Law

The utilization of a resource can be defined in various ways:

$$\text{Utilization} = \frac{\text{Processing required for a UoW}}{\text{Processing capacity of the resource}} = \frac{\text{Busy Time}}{\text{Total Time}}$$

---

* In our world, these devices could be processors, disks, or network links. A system can be thought of as consisting of a number of subsystems like these. Each can be treated as a system for operational laws and hence analysis.

A UoW visiting the ith resource requires, say, S_i amount of processing or service time. The amount of service that a system UoW requires from the ith resource is known as the service demand, D_i, which is

$$D_i = S_i V_i$$

The utilization law is

$$U_i = X_i S_i = XD_i$$

General Response Time Law

Some overall system quantities can be derived using the known quantities of subsystems if the former are not known. Little's law for the ith resource tells us

$$N_i = X_i W_i$$

The forced flow law tells us that $X_I = XV_i$ and so

$$\frac{N_i}{X} = V_i W_i$$

The total number of jobs in the system is the sum of the m jobs/UoW at the subsystems or resources, that is

$$N = \sum_{i=1}^{m} N_i$$

Jain's paper referenced below derives the fact that the response time R (=W/C) is

$$R = \sum_{i=1}^{m} R_i V_i$$

which is known as the general response time law, which (according to Jain) applies even if the job flow is not balanced.

Interactive Response Time Law

This factor takes account of the fact that in most cases, UoW input and output is done and read by humans. After receiving a response from the input, the user reads the response, thinks, and then probably enters another UoW (perhaps a transaction). This *think time* can be a limiting factor in throughput because of the number of people involved in this input.

This means that the real response time of the system as a whole, as seen from the user terminal, is not simply the system response time R (processor + network + disk I/O, etc.). It includes a mean think time, say Z, as well. Thus, the total turnaround time of a request is (R + Z) for each user, and each user then generates T/(R + Z) requests in our usual time T. If there are N users, the throughput X is total requests/total time, which is

$$X = \frac{N\dfrac{T}{(R+Z)}}{T} = \frac{N}{(R+Z)}$$

and, with some arithmetic we have

$$R = \frac{N}{X} - Z$$

This is the interactive response time law.

Bottleneck Analysis

An explanation of this can be found in the Jain or Hillston references below. *Operational analysis* is essentially the derivation of common performance metrics from other, related information. An example of such analysis is shown here, where use is made of measurements in calculating metrics that are not measured directly. The following list shows some of these measured quantities and the table following the derivation of the metrics we now know and love:

- **T*** is the length of the observation interval. This can vary from, say, 1 s to several minutes depending on the accuracy needed—with utilization peaks within a few seconds or averaged over a few minutes.
- **A** is the number of arrivals (UoWs) during time **T**.
- **B** is the time the server was busy during the interval **T** (**B ≤ T**).
- **C** is the number of completions (system departures) during time T. These completions might be transactions or queries, for example.
- **W** is the total time in the system for all requests (UoWs) during time **T**.

Assuming the measurement tool in question can deliver these quantities, then Table A4.1 can be constructed.

Derivation of Performance Metrics

The general performance information will consist of some direct metric measurements and some derived values. Operational analysis is based on five operational laws,[†] outlined next.

1. *Operational Laws* (Raj Jain presentation]
   http://www.cse.wustl.edu/~jain/cse567-08/ftp/k_33ol.pdf

---

* These notations are commonly used in this topic. I have translated them where applicable to the usual queuing theory notations.
† Much of this information was prompted by Teamquest and details from the references quoted, for example reference 2.

Table A4.1   Formulas for Service Metrics

Measured quantity	Formula for metric
Arrival rate	$a = A/T$ (λ)
Throughput	$X = C/T$
Utilization	$U = B/T$ (ρ)
Service time	$S = B/C$ (T_S)
Response time	$R = W/C$ (T_R)
No. of customers (UoWs)	$N = W/T$

2. *Fundamental Laws* [document]
   http://homes.cs.washington.edu/~lazowska/qsp/Images/ Chap_03.pdf
3. *Performance Modelling: Operational Laws* [Jane Hillston presentation]
   http://www.inf.ed.ac.uk/teaching/courses/pm/PM- lecture2.pdf

RAID Reliability

The eternal seesaw between performance and reliability in RAID configurations is not covered in this book, but there is a detailed treatment by M. and A. Shooman (father and son) if it is of importance to you as a performance guru (as by now you surely are). The math for the reliability of some RAID levels is contained in the references given below:

Reliability Models for Highly Fault-tolerant Storage Systems
https://www.researchgate.net/publication/257882767_Reliability_Models_for_Highly_Fault-tolerant_Storage_
  Systems

Andrew M. Shooman and Martin L. Shooman.
Reliability and Storage Capacity of Repairable RAID Systems
   Proceedings of the Computer Measurement Group (CMG) Annual Conference, November 2013.

Cache Memory Performance

Cache memory is a basic need generated by the fact that high processor speed can only be utilized if it can access data and instruction in memory quickly enough. Normal memory speed has not kept pace with that of processors—the latter ca. 50% per annum, memory less than 10% per annum. Based on the observed reuse of data and instructions, extra, fast memory was developed as a front end to standard main memory to feed the processor at higher speed.

The logic was that quite often, the data required might still be resident in a fast cache memory, and because the processor need not go back to main memory for it, the smaller size of the cache might be less of a problem. The speedup relies on there being an acceptable *hit rate* in cache so that minimum journeys to main memory are required.

Multilevel Cache Equation Math

The math associated with multilevel cache aims to calculate the access times involved when data is requested from main memory. It may reside in one or more levels of cache, and so the access time will be that of finding it and accessing it.

If it is found in level 1 cache (L1), then fine; if not, then we need to search in L2 and L3 and finally main memory if those searches fail to locate the data. Figure A4.1 shows the math of access times for multilevel cache.

The key parameters in this calculation are

- T_1, the access time for L1 data retrieval
- T_2, the access time for L2 data retrieval
- T_3, the access time for L3 data retrieval
- T_m, the access time for data retrieval from main memory
- h_1, the hit rate for L1
- h_2, the hit rate for L2
- h_3, the hit rate for L3
- h_m, the hit rate for main memory

The math below is essentially an exercise in the product of probabilities of access success though successive levels of cache/main storage, rather like the calculation of the reliability of a series of components (i.e., Lusser's law).

Access Time Equations

- Average access time for single-cache system (L1) plus main memory:

$$= h_1 \times T_1 + (1 - h_1) T_m$$

- Average access time for two-cache system (L1, L2) plus main memory:

$$= h_1 \times T_1 + (1 - h_1) \left[T_2 + (1 - h_2) T_m \right]$$

- Average access time for three-cache system (L1, L2, L3) plus main memory:

$$= h_1 \times T_1 + (1 - h_1) \left[T_2 + (1 - h_2) \left(T_3 + (1 - h_3) T_m \right) \right] \qquad \text{(A4.5)}$$

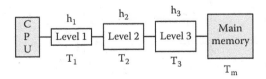

H_x = Hit rate of level **x** cache (**x** = 1, 2, 3)
T_x = Access time of level **x** cache/main memory

Figure A4.1   Math of access times for multilevel cache.

Some papers assume that h_1 is 1 so the first term in each case is T_1, that is, all the required data is accessed via cache L1 and no further searching is required as other factors in the equation become zero. In the absence of this eventuality, and when the data is no longer found by searching down the cache levels 1, 2, and 3, then access to main memory will be needed. It should be noted that there is no h_m (main memory hit rate) in the third equation as $h_m = 1$. In reality, sometimes access to hard disk/SSD will be necessary.*

In the following list, Reference 2 suggests the following as five categories of activity for optimizing cache performance:

1. *Reducing the hit time*: Small and simple first-level caches and way prediction. Both techniques also generally decrease power consumption.
2. *Increasing cache bandwidth*: Pipelined caches, multibanked caches, and nonblocking caches. These techniques have varying impacts on power consumption.
3. *Reducing the miss penalty*: Critical work-first and merging-write buffers. These optimizations have little impact on power.
4. *Reducing the miss rate*: Compiler optimizations. Obviously any improvement at compile time improves power consumption.
5. *Reducing the miss penalty or miss rate via parallelism*: Hardware prefetching and compiler prefetching. These optimizations generally increase power consumption, primarily due to prefetched data that are unused.

Figure A4.2 shows cache access times for various h2 values.

More detailed discussions of cache and the parameters that contribute to its performance can be found in the following papers:

Memory Design References

1. *Memory Hierarchy Design: Part 1. Basics of memory hierarchies*
   http://www.edn.com/design/systems-design/4397051/Memory-Hierarchy-Design-part-1

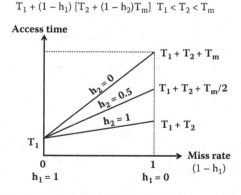

$$T_1 + (1 - h_1)\,[T_2 + (1 - h_2)T_m]\quad T_1 < T_2 < T_m$$

Figure A4.2 Cache access times for various h_2 values.

---

* I am indebted to Dr. Muhammad Ali Ismail for assistance with this section and permission to quote from his paper.

2. *Memory Hierarchy Design: Part 2. Ten advanced optimizations of cache performance*
   http://www.edn.com/design/systems-design/4397532/Memory-Hierarchy-Design---Part-2--Ten-advanced-optimizations-of-cache-performance-
3. *Memory Hierarchy Design: Part 3. Memory technology and optimizations*
   http://www.edn.com/design/systems-design/4398164/Memory-Hierarchy-Design---Part-3--Memory-technology-and-optimizations
4. *Memory Hierarchy Design: Part 4. Virtual memory and virtual machines*
   http://www.edn.com/design/systems-design/4398677/Memory-Hierarchy-Design---Part-4--Virtual-memory-and-virtual-machines
5. *Memory Hierarchy Design: Part 5. Crosscutting issues and the memory design of the ARM Cortex-A8*
   http://www.edn.com/design/systems-design/4399193/Memory-Hierarchy-Design---Part-5--Crosscutting-issues-and-the-memory-design-of-the-ARM-Cortex- A8-
6. *An Overview of Cache Optimization Techniques and Cache-Aware Numerical Algorithms*
   http://www.csd.uoc.gr/~hy460/pdf/AMH/10.pdf
7. *A Re-Usable Level 2 Cache Architecture*
   http://www.design-reuse.com/articles/20750/re-usable-level-2-cache-architecture.html
   (The reference above is detailed but readable and contains some of the necessary math in dealing with cache configurations.)
8. *On the Mathematics of Caching* [Thesis, advanced, 145 pages]
   http://web.eecs.umich.edu/~brehob/TW/cache.pdf

Also, see the reference under "cache, server side" in the glossary, Appendix III of this book.

Cache and Queuing

There is a rather unusual paper about cache that contains a section on the theory of queuing for analyzing hierarchical cache accesses.

> Any cache hierarchy may be analysed using queuing theory by considering every cache as a server and data request either by a CPU or the lower level of cache as a client. A complete cache hierarchy may be considered as an open queuing network where multiple servers (caches) are attached in a specific pattern. A request from a client is served by a specific server (cache). If the server (cache) fulfils the request then the client leaves the queue otherwise the request is sent to next server (upper level cache). Probability of a request being fulfilled or not at any server (cache) is the same as the hit or miss ratio. Similarly the mean response time of the server is same as that of average cache access time. Using queuing network, performance parameters like mean response time (average cache access time), marginal probabilities, utilization, throughput, mean number of jobs, mean queue length, and mean waiting time may be calculated for any individual server (cache) and for the complete network (cache hierarchy).

Author: Muhammad Ali Ismail, who kindly reviewed my material on cache math.
   Title: *Performance Behavior Analysis of the Present 3-Level Cache System for Multi-Core Systems using Queuing Modeling.*

Queuing model for 3-level cache system
http://psrcentre.org/images/extraimages/312034.pdf

Summary

In summary, the use of cache is to facilitate fast reuse of data stored in it rather than going to main memory which, in relative terms, is far slower. The effectiveness of cache does not solely depend on its size but also on the storage and retrieval algorithms for them. Well-designed caches can perform better than average caches of twice the size, as I have seen.

Cache memory is usually arranged in layers with hot data spread across these layers called Level 1, Level 2, and so on. In this section, we have dealt with cache at three levels: L1, L2, and L3. Currently, L4 cache is usually reserved for special purposes in some chips. Cache usage involves searching for data in L1 and moving down through L2 and lower until it is found. Failing that, the search goes to main memory. Each failed search is known as a *miss* and a successful one a *hit*.

The effectiveness of a cache configuration can be judged by the *hit* and *miss* rates, defined as [No. of hits]/[No. of accesses] and [No. of misses]/[No. of accesses], respectively. The speed of cache access is typically 10:20 times faster than that of main memory but costs much more per Mbyte than main memory.

Appendix V: Distributed Systems Topics

Introduction

Note: The purpose of this chapter is to outline ways in which disparate systems can cooperate in various ways—file transfer, program-to-program interaction, heterogeneous database access, and so on. This sort of interfacing will introduce resource overheads that can affect the performance of applications and other software being used.

Always remember that in choosing to use distributed processing, there are usability, manageability, security, and performance issues to consider as well as functionality ones. The words *pilot system* spring to mind in this context. In addition, a pilot can tell you whether a mix of products can work together in harmony—I know from personal experience on a PC that some products can fight each other even if they are performing different functions.

The reason for including a section on this topic is that network protocol and topology choices have a profound effect on the performance of that network and the application which rely on it.

The management and prediction of performance on a single system can be difficult enough; doing the same thing across two or more systems is extremely difficult, since there is normally a network between the participating systems. Nevertheless, it is important to understand the potential performance impact of functions such as distributed data, distributed processing, program-to-program communications, and so on.

This appendix outlines the architectures and mechanisms employed in various types of distributed computing and offers some areas which need to be addressed in a performance context. One purpose of it is to make the reader aware of protocols which may be encountered in network connections and also to understand that emulation of enveloping protocols can introduce performance overheads.

Distributed Computing Overview

This topic has evolved over the years, from being the only way to proceed, back to the mainframe, and then seeing a partial return to some form of distributed working. This reminds me of the big bang theory, according to which the universe began as an infinitesimally small point in space and exploded to cover the universe with distributed matter, eventually returning to the collapsed state and repeating the exercise over aeons of time.*

Topology vs. Protocol

Network *topology* is the arrangement of components of a computer network, that is, how it looks. The *physical topology* is the actual layout of the wires, cables, and functional units in the network; the *logical topology* is how the data flows.

For example, if there are two alternative routes for data, this might be shown as one line in a logical topology diagram.

Network *protocols* are the rules and conventions for communication between network devices. Protocols for computer networking all generally use packet-switching techniques to send and receive messages in the form of *packets*. Protocols in networking are closely akin to protocols used in addressing other people; for example, in England, you do not speak to the Queen unless she speaks to you.

An analogy for both these concepts is a road map (topology) showing the layout of roads and an indication of speed limits, no-entry roads, one-way streets, and so on (driving protocol).

These protocols are often arranged as functional *stacks*, each layer performing a particular job in liaison with the other layers. For example, there is a Transmission Control Protocol (TCP/IP) stack, an IBM systems network architecture (SNA) stack, and an open systems interconnection (OSI) stack, with the most common number of layers being seven. Some protocols combine what are separate stacks in others into one, for example TCP/IP, as illustrated below.

Seven-Layer Network Model

Layered network models were developed in the 1970s by competing vendors as a show of having an architecture-based product line rather than a confused mass of products and *ad hoc* standards. Among those introduced in the 1970s were DEC's distributed network architecture (DNA) and IBM's systems network architecture (SNA).

The architecture mantle was taken up by standards bodies, and the result was the seven-layer OSI model. This was regarded as a *de jure* model for the future but was usurped by the TCP/IP protocol as a *de facto* standard in communications.

However, most network protocols describe their functions in terms of these layers as a set of common terms of reference.

The layered seven-tier model is outlined in Figure A5.1, showing three implementations: OSI, SNA, and TCP/IP.

---

* Another view is that the expansion will cease and the universe will become a dead, dark "world" of dense matter—hopefully not too soon.

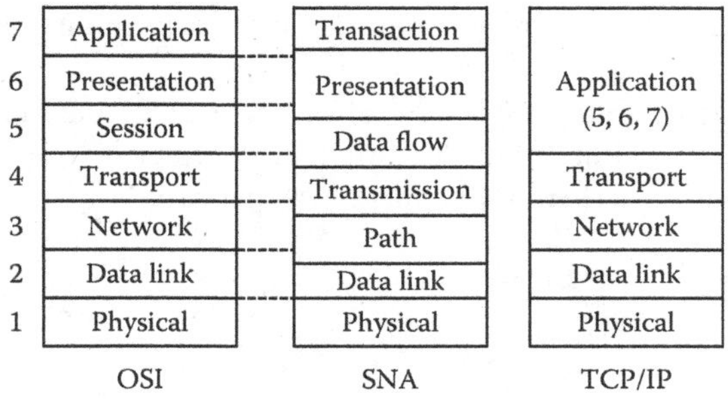

	OSI		SNA		TCP/IP
7	Application		Transaction		
6	Presentation		Presentation		Application (5, 6, 7)
5	Session		Data flow		
4	Transport		Transmission		Transport
3	Network		Path		Network
2	Data link		Data link		Data link
1	Physical		Physical		Physical

Figure A5.1 Seven-layer model and implementations.

OSI Layers

The basic functions of the OSI layers are as follows:

7. *Application layer*: Type of communication: email, file transfer, client/server
6. *Presentation layer*: Data conversion, encryption, ASDVII to EBCDIC, and so on
5. *Session layer*: Starts and stops sessions, maintains synchronicity
4. *Transport layer*: Ensures correct delivery of whole message or file
3. *Network layer*: Routes the data to different places based on the supplied network address
2. *Data link layer*: Transmits packets from node to node based on station address
1. *Physical layer*: Cabling and electrical signaling

TCP/IP Layers

The basic functions of the TCP/IP layers are as follows*:

Layers 7, 6, 5: NFS, NIS+, Domain Name System (DNS), Simple Network Management Protocol (SNMP), and others
Layer 4: TCP, UDP
Layer 3: IP (Internet protocol), ARP (address resolution protocol), ICMP (Internet control message protocol)
Layer 2: PPP, IEEE 802.2
Layer 1: Ethernet, Token Ring, RS-232, and others

Communications Methods

In distributed work activity, the network connecting systems have an important part to play if adequate performance, compatible with service level agreements (SLAs), is to be achieved. As well as the physical speed characteristics of the network components, there is the question of which protocol is best for the workload in question. For example, Transmission Control Protocol (TCP) transmission of data is slower than Universal Datagram Protocol (UDP) transmission, since TCP

---

* These TCP/IP terms are explained further in Appendix III, "Terminology."

is more *caring* about the validity of the transmitted data, asking for more delivery reassurance than UDP.

What follows is a brief canter through some of the transmission methods available and, where possible, the performance implications of their use. The coverage here is meant to serve as a background to network terminology that may be met in the performance arena and is not meant to be a tutorial.

Frame Relay (FR)

FR is a communications protocol designed for speed of transmission, which dispenses with the network layer of the OSI model and performs the routing and multiplexing functions itself. It does, however, require error-free or very low error transmission media as it is not a *caring* protocol.

These days, this sort of medium is more common than the days when transmission-error detection and correction was needed.

Overview

Data is sent in packets known as *frames*, which are shown schematically in Table A5.1.

FR is a virtual circuit connection; that is, it does not confine itself to a single physical connection but when established is a permanent one, or a private virtual circuit (PVA), for the duration of the work. Table A5.2 shows the basic characteristics of FR.

There are a number of articles on the Internet including the two below.

See: http://www.packet-lab.com/main/images/stories/framerelay_intro/frame%20relay%20 -%20introduction%20and%20concepts%20slides.pdf and

http://www.dcbnet.com/notes/framerly.html

Table A5.1 Structure of Frame Relay Packet

ADDRESS	CONTROL	DATA	CYCLIC REDUNDANCY CHECK (Error correction)

Table A5.2 Frame Relay Characteristics

Network Characteristic	Frame Relay
Propagation delay	Low
Error Correction	None; done by equipment at the end of the PVC link
Good at interactive work?	Yes
Protocol type	HDLC (Higher data Link Control), similar to IBM's SDLC
Good for LAN file transfer?	Yes
Voice?	Yes, with developing standards
Easy to implement?	Yes

Table A5.3   ATM Cell Structure

HEADER (5)	PAYLOAD (48)

Asynchronous Transfer Mode (ATM)

Many organizations are forced to operate multiple networks to support voice, data, and video, resulting in a degree of inefficiency and escalating communications costs. By combining the features from both technologies, ATM enables a single network protocol to be used in most cases.

The unit of transmission in an ATM network is the *cell*. Each individual ATM cell consists of a 5-byte cell header and 48 bytes of information encapsulated within its payload. The ATM network uses the header to support the virtual path and the virtual channel routing and to perform a quick error check for corrupted cells. This is in addition to the error checking done by the overall transmission stack.

The header contains six fields, each of different bit length, to control the flow and integrity of the cells' transmission. ATM operates independently of the type of transmission being generated at the upper layers *and* of the type and speed of the physical-layer medium below it. This allows the ATM technology to transport all kinds of transmissions (e.g., data, voice, video, etc.) in a single integrated data stream over any transmission medium, ranging from existing T1/E1 lines to SONET OC-3 at speeds of 155 Mbps, and beyond.

See:

http://technet.microsoft.com/en-us/library/bb962019.aspx# ID0EBG

https://www.scribd.com/doc/38184775/Chapter-08 (Power Point presentation)

Network Routing Reference

The reference below is a readable introduction to some network routing and network protocol stacks (but not all).

Networking and Network Routing: An Introduction [27 pages]
http://www.networkrouting.net/docs/mr-chapter_1.pdf

Multiprotocol Label Switching (MPLS)

Traffic on networks is often directed according to its *itinerary*, that is, how it should travel from source to destination. Routing information is usually carried in a packet header and interpreted as it travels (see previous section).

The basic idea behind MPLS is that of the labeling of packets. In a traditional routed IP network, each router makes an independent forwarding decision for each packet based solely on the packet's network-layer header. As a result, every time a packet arrives at a router, the router has to decide where to send the packet next.

With MPLS, the first time the packet enters a network, it's assigned to a specific class called a *forwarding equivalence class* (FEC), indicated by appending a short bit sequence (the label) to the packet (see Figure A5.2). Each router in the network has a table indicating how to handle packets of a specific FEC type, so once the packet has entered the network, routers don't need to perform header analysis. Instead, subsequent routers use the label as an index into a table that provides them with a new FEC for that packet.

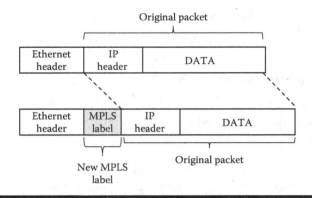

Figure A5.2 MPLS label on an IP packet.

This gives the MPLS network the ability to handle packets with particular characteristics (such as coming from particular ports or carrying traffic of particular application types) in a consistent fashion. Packets carrying real-time traffic, such as voice or video, can easily be mapped to low-latency routes across the network (if that is what is desired), something that can be difficult with conventional routing. The key outcome is that the labels provide a way to attach additional information to each packet—information above and beyond what the routers previously employed.

MPLS doesn't fit neatly into the seven-layer model but bypasses some elements of the model. MPLS can be used to create forwarding tables for ATM or frame relay switches (using the existing asynchronous transfer mode [ATM] or data link connection identifier [DLCI] header) or for plain old IP routers by appending MPLS tags to IP packets. For reference, see

MPLS for Dummies
https://www.nanog.org/meetings/nanog49/presentations/Sunday/mpls-nanog49.pdf

MPLS Explained
http://www.networkworld.com/article/2297171/network-security/mpls-explained.html

Multiprotocol Label Switching (MPLS)
http://searchenterprisewan.techtarget.com/definition/Multiprotocol-Label-Switching

MPLS and virtual private network (VPN)
http://infrastructureadventures.com/2011/02/20/network-virtualization-beyond-vlans-–-part-7-mpls-l3-vpns/

Remote Procedure Calls (RPC)

Remote procedure call (RPC) is a protocol that one program can use to request a service from another program located in another computer in a network, without having to understand network details. (A procedure call is also sometimes known as a remote function call or a subroutine call.) RPC uses the client/server model. The requesting program is a client, and the service-providing program is the server. Like a regular or local procedure call, an RPC is a synchronous operation requiring the requesting program to be suspended until the results of the remote procedure are returned.

There are several RPC models and implementations. A popular model and implementation is the Open Software Foundation's Distributed Computing Environment (DCE). The Institute of

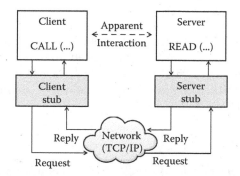

Figure A5.3   Sun remote procedure call overview.

Electrical and Electronics Engineers defines RPC in its *ISO Remote Procedure Call Specification*, ISO/IEC CD 11578 N6561, ISO/IEC, November 1991 (see below). RPC is the rough equivalent of the APPC CPI-C of IBM's Systems Network Architecture (SNA).

Microsoft has a form of DCE which has extensions to the DEC RPC and is normally known as MS DCE.

Sun RPC

The Sun RPC is a call to a function or service on a server remote from the caller, that is, a client in this case. The call is similar to calling a local function and, in essence, the caller is not aware that the request is being shipped across a network to be serviced. Other forms of RPC operate in a similar way and, schematically, look the same. The differences are in the detail. Figure A5.3 illustrates the Sun RPC.

Obviously, a service using RPCs across a network and not simply using functions resident on the same system will attract performance overheads. which may need to be taken into account in offering a service to users.

> **Note**: Sun's RPC forms the basis of many UNIX services, especially Network File System (NFS). However, RPC is extremely dangerous when left exposed to the Internet, which leads to the frequent compromise of servers based on Sun Solaris and Linux. RPC should never be exposed to the Internet.

http://www.iss.net/security_center/advice/Services/Sun RPC/default.htm

Distributed Computing Environment (DCE)

The DCE is a software system developed in the early 1990s and announced in 1993 by a consortium that included Apollo Computer (which later became part of Hewlett-Packard), IBM, Digital Equipment Corporation, and others. The DCE supplies a framework and toolkit for developing client/server applications. The framework includes an RPC mechanism known as DCE/RPC, a naming (directory) service, a time service, an authentication service, and a distributed file system (DFS) known as DCE/DFS.

HP/Apollo RPC

The DCE system was, to a large degree, based on independent developments made by each of the partners. For example, DCE/RPC (see below) was derived from the Network Computing System (NCS) created at Apollo Computer and subsequently enhanced when Apollo became part of Hewlett-Packard. There are different versions of this, and they are spelled out in detail in any standards that employ the RPC.

OSF DCE RPC

The acronym OSF DCE stands for Open Software Foundation Distributed Computing Environment and it includes an RPC based on the older HP/Apollo version.

The DCE comprises this RPC mechanism and subsidiary systems to aid distributed computing environments. Programs that use RPC perform some preliminary setup work. After that setup, predetermined programming language function calls get sent to a server somewhere else on the network. That server performs the function and then returns the results to the client.

OSF DCE RPC is just one of many methods used to organize a distributed system and one of a handful of RPCs. People often choose RPC to take advantage of programmers' current skills. When writing a distributed system, a programmer can structure the source code of the distributed system very much like a nondistributed version of the same system but where network communications hide behind what look like familiar function calls.

The framework of RPC exists mainly to ease difficulties programmers might otherwise have with distributed systems. See the following reference:

10 Reasons why OSF DCE sucks: A programmer's viewpoint
http://www.stratigery.com/anti_dce.html
> For asynchronous RPC details, see *A Survey of Asynchronous Remote Procedure Calls*
> http://www.ics.uci.edu/~cs230/reading/p92-ananda.pdf

Advanced Program-to-Program Communication (APPC)

APPC is the name IBM gave to the set of operations that transaction programs can use to talk to each other. The operations are simple enough to be used by programs written in COBOL or FORTRAN. It is part of IBM's systems network architecture (SNA)—which is what it says, an architecture—and then products are developed gradually using it as a basis.

It uses common programming interface—communications (CPI-C), which allows different IBM systems to use a common interface to APPC. Thus APPC software enables high-speed communication to take place between programs residing on different computers, and between workstations and midrange and mainframe computer servers. APPC is an open standard that is supported on most platforms and, in theory, non-IBM platforms can partake in APPC operations.

However, APPC is to a large extent limited to the IBM operating systems such z/OS (formerly MVS, then OS/390), z/VM (formerly VM/CMS), IBM i (formerly OS/400), OS/2, AIX, and z/VSE (formerly DOS/VSE). Microsoft also included SNA support in Microsoft's Host Integration Server. Major IBM software products have included support for APPC, including CICS, DB2, and WebSphere MQ.

Unlike TCP/IP, in which both communication partners always possess a clear role (one is always the server and others always the client), the communication partners in APPC are equal; that is, everyone can be both servers and clients equally.

With the wide success of TCP/IP, APPC has declined, although many IBM systems have translators (such as the iSeries ANYNET) to allow sending APPC-formatted traffic using Ethernet for the physical connection.

WoW: However, beware of protocols in sheep's clothing as emulated/enveloped communications protocols have a habit of being very slow and cumbersome.

Messaging Systems

An **enterprise messaging system** (EMS) is a set of published enterprise-wide standards that allows organizations to send semantically precise messages between computer systems. EMS systems promote loosely coupled architectures that allow changes in the formats of messages to have minimum impact on message subscribers. EMS systems are facilitated by the use of structured messages (such as using XML (Extensible Markup Language) or JSON (JavaScript Object Notation)), and appropriate protocols, such as DDS (Digital Data Storage), MSMQ (Microsoft Message Queuing), AMQP (Advanced Message Queuing Protocol) or SOAP (Simple Object Access Protocol) with web services. [Wikipedia]

Messaging
http://whatis.techtarget.com/definition/messaging

Distributed Relational Database Architecture (DRDA)*

DRDA is an architecture rather than a product specification for distributed relational databases. It defines the rules, but not an actual programming interface, for accessing the distributed data, but it does not provide the actual application programming interfaces (APIs) to perform the access. It was initially designed by a work group within IBM in the period 1988 to 1994, first used for DB2 and latterly adopted by The Open Group. The latter's definition follows:

DRDA is an open, published architecture that enables communication between applications and database systems on disparate platforms, whether those applications and database systems are provided by the same or different vendors and whether the platforms are the same or different hardware/software architectures. DRDA is a combination of other architectures and the environmental rules and process model for using them. The architectures that actually comprise DRDA are Distributed Data Management (DDM) and Formatted Data Object Content Architecture (FD: OCA).

The Distributed Data Management (DDM) architecture provides the overall command and reply structure used by the distributed database. Fewer than 20 commands are required to implement all of the distributed database functions for communication between the Application Requester (client) and the Application Server. [The Open Group]

---

* See The Open Group publication: http://pubs.opengroup.org/onlinepubs/9699959699/toc.pdf and Craig Mullins paper *DRDA* http://www.craigsmullins.com/drda.htm

The performance aspects of using this protocol are contained in various parts of The Open Group specification in the footnote.

Database Gateways

Database gateways are products that allow a system running one type of database to access data contained in a database of a different kind. This is sometimes known as database integration but on a logical rather than physical basis. Database gateways enable, for example, Oracle database integration with databases such as IBM DB2, Microsoft SQL Server, and Excel; transaction managers like IBM CICS; and message queuing systems like IBM WebSphere MQ.

For example, the Oracle Open Gateways (previously called SQL*Connect) is a typical gateway product that can be used to access data from non-Oracle databases (such as DB2, Sybase, Informix, etc.), and even nonrelational data sources like Adabas and conventional file systems like IBM's virtual storage access method (VSAM). Oracle also enables integration with ODBC-compliant data stores such as MySQL, Foxpro, Access, dBase, and nonrelational targets like Excel.

Gateways were a popular vote marketing tool in the 1980s and early 1990s, but the main proponent today appears to be Oracle wanting to connect to databases it hasn't yet managed to win over to Oracle RDBMS.

See these papers for an outline of gateways:

Database Gateway Use in Heterogeneous Environments (1997)
http://www.hp.com/products1/evolution/e3000/download/59660855.pdf

Oracle Database Gateway
http://www.oracle.com/technetwork/database/gateways/gateways-twp-131579.pdf

Online Transaction Processing (OLTP)

Teleprocessing, commonly known as OLTP, has been around since the "stone age" measured on IT timescales. The development phases I saw in IBM might be considered typical of the development of this online version of batch processing in other vendors.

Some TP Systems

The 1970s saw this type of rationalization across vendors, and some popular OLTP systems were in use:

- IBM CICS, a spin-off from an OLTP system developed for public utilities, using VSAM, DL/I, and eventually DB2 as its database partner.
- IMS/DC, the OLTP part of the information management system (IMS). The database partner was IMS DB, initially DL/I (Data Language /One), a hierarchical database and eventually the relational DB2.
- DECtp family, including ACMS OLTP which ran on most of its range of servers. It initially used Rdb (a relational product eventually acquired by Oracle) and other database facilities. The DEC products were acquired by Compaq and then by Hewlett-Packard, where several still remain.

- Encina (Enterprise Computing In a New Age*), the "great white hope" of Open Systems computing
- Tuxedo (Transactions for UNIX Extended for Distributed Operations†), a venerable OLTP war horse from the UNIX stable, still used today and the basis for TPC benchmarks in many instances.
- Other systems on servers that were available in the 1960s and 1970s: esoteric ones like Pick and MUMPS, whose adherents would die rather than convert to other systems.

A nostalgic journey awaits those of you who wish to pursue these products by searching for them on Wikipedia and elsewhere. The major OLTP systems today (often called TP Monitors) are:

- IBM CICS (customer information control system)
- IBM IMS (information management system)
- Transarc Encina (owned by IBM)
- TopEnd (BEA Systems)
- Oracle Tuxedo
- Microsoft Transaction Server

There are numerous books and articles on these products plus sections on application design and the performance and tuning of the supporting OLTP Monitor.

The maturing of these systems and the need for nonpartisan processing across heterogeneous platforms presented its own problems which, in part, the open-systems movement sought to address. Again, since this is not a treatise on OLTP; we will concentrate of availability and recoverability aspects here.

A typical OLTP and database system is illustrated in Figure A5.4, a real-life example of which might be CICS/DL/I or CICS/DB2.

Let's take an example. Imagine that for some reason, the Los Angeles emergency services consist of the LA Police Department and the London Fire Brigade, and a major incident occurred. The

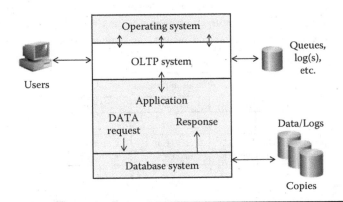

Figure A5.4   Schematic of OLTP with a database.

---

* Not many people know that.
† Not many people know this either.

chances that these entities would work together seamlessly are remote, unless they have a common *modus operandi* and commonly understood communications, code words, and so on.

The same problem awaited cross-system OLTP and associated database technologies. To wrap up this preamble, we'll take a short look at the collaborative modus operandi of OLTP and DBs.

X/Open Distributed Transaction Processing Model (DTP)

XA and XA+ Concepts*

The XA standard is an X/Open specification for distributed transaction processing (DTP) across heterogeneous data sources (e.g., Oracle Database and DB2) that was published in 1991. It describes the interface between the transaction coordinator and the data sources that participate in the distributed transaction. Within XA the transaction coordinator is termed the Transaction Manager and the participating data sources are termed the ***Resource Managers***. Transaction Managers and Resource managers that follow this specification are said to be XA compliant.

Some products such as the Oracle database and Oracle WebLogic Server can act as either Transaction Managers or Resource Managers or both within the same XA transaction. Examples of an XA Transaction Manager are: Tuxedo, Oracle WebLogic Server, the Oracle database and IBM WebSphere Application Server. Examples of an XA Resource Manager are: Oracle Database, IBM DB2, SQL Server, IBM MQ-Series and Java Message Service (JMS).

The XA+ specification was meant to be an enhanced specification that would enable distributed transactions to be coordinated across multiple heterogeneous Transaction Managers (e.g., Tuxedo and IBM Encina) as well as dictating how Transaction Managers should communicate with multiple RM instances (e.g., Real Application Cluster).

[Oracle documentation *XA and Oracle controlled Distributed Transactions*] http://www.oracle.com/technetwork/products/clustering/overview/distributed-transactions-and-xa-163941.pdf

The three "managers" in Figure A5.5 are called "resource managers" in the official documentation. Basically, the model shows an application program making calls to the RDBMS, the OLTP, and the communications system software. However, the issue is that each "resource manager" may

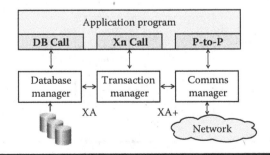

Figure A5.5 Distributed transaction processing (DTP) model.

---

* Transaction (<u>X</u>n) <u>A</u>PI and Transaction API plus (XA+). Even less people know this.

come from a different "stable" (speak a different language) and cannot communicate with the others to generate synergy across the board.

This is where the standards for the calls and the resource manager interfaces comes into play: standards for calls and the XA and XA+ interface specifications. It would be virtually impossible to handle transactions and two-phase commit without them.

Chapter Summary

This chapter has covered a diverse (some will say bewildering) set of communications protocols and products, including transaction processing (OLTP). The intention of this was not pure education, as there are good articles and books on these subjects, but to raise awareness of the network world and the communications flavors you may encounter. If you need to communicate with other systems using these protocols, you need to be aware of them and, importantly, that there may be performance considerations in such relationships and software that uses them.

WoW: Just because you connect your system A to a system B via an X Mb link, it is not necessarily true that you will talk at this speed. Think "pilot," "research," and "other peoples' experience," especially those who have meddled with emulation modes.

Appendix VI: High-Performance Computing

Introduction to HPC

High-performance computing (or computation, HPC) does not necessarily mean superfast transaction processing or the lightning execution of batch work. It is normally applied to scientific work more often than not involving iterations of similar code and equations. The work carried out is normally that which the computer can handle in a time amenable to progressing some study or other. The term *supercomputer* usually means those HPC systems at the top of the performance league at any point in time.

There are huge HPC problems that have eluded analysis because of the time it would take to solve them, and the solvers were keen to still be alive by the time the results were delivered. The most common users of HPC systems are scientific researchers, engineers, and academic institutions. Some government agencies, particularly the military, also rely on HPC for complex applications. In fact, many years ago the Western world was forbidden to export high-performance computers, as they were then to Eastern Bloc countries. High performance meant *able to calculate ICBM (intercontinental ballistic missiles) trajectories in real time*! This was not a desirable thing during the years of the Cold War.

Such computers are often constructed from commodity components (chips) to develop systems of hundreds or thousands of such components, which employ the software techniques of parallel computing (or processing) to utilize these components. Previously, such work was carried out on *vector processors*, which were more complex machines manufactured by Cray and others such as Stardent, Maspar, Meiko, Convex, Kendall Square Research, CDC, and others. Many died in the battle; others died and rose Lazarus-like to fight again or were absorbed by other manufacturers.

A *vector processor*, or *array processor*, comprised a central processing unit (CPU) that implements an instruction set containing instructions that operate on one-dimensional arrays of data called *vectors* (a scalar processor has instructions that operate on single data items). Vector processors can greatly improve performance on certain workloads, notably HPC numerical simulation and similar tasks, although they were quite expensive to produce and purchase.

Vector machines appeared in the early 1970s and dominated supercomputer design through the 1970s into the 1990s, notably the various Cray platforms (Cray 1, Cray 2, Cray XMP, Cray YMP), all designed by Seymour Cray. The relatively low cost of conventional microprocessor designs (commodity chips) and the emergence of sophisticated parallel processing techniques led to the vector supercomputer's decline in the later 1990s.

In around 1976, the Cray 1, weighing about 5000 pounds, cost US$8 M and its performance was 160 Megaflops. Today, 50 Gigaflops is available on commodity chips for about US$1000, coming in at 12 pounds weight.

HPC Overview

Parallel Processing

Serial computing, where one task leads to the next, is not up to the task of providing massive compute power for scientific and other HPC work. The progress in chip speeds is inadequate to deliver the power needed for this type of work.

Modern HPC computers are parallel computers, which comprise multiple processors, and attempts must be made to utilize them effectively. In order to exploit these multiple processors, measures have to be taken to distribute the computational tasks to these multiple processors via a process called parallelization. This technique runs nondependent tasks in parallel instead of sequentially, and with massive parallelism, large performance gains are possible.

In the simplest sense, *parallel computing* is the simultaneous use of multiple compute resources to solve a computational problem:

- A problem is broken into discrete parts that can be solved concurrently.
- Each part is further broken down to a series of instructions.
- Instructions from each part execute simultaneously on different processors.
- An overall control/coordination mechanism is employed, including communication between participating nodes.

The *computational resources* can be several processors (or nodes in HPC or cluster parlance) or multiple cores on a chip. These multiple nodes can be either in a single system or a network of nodes.

This assumes the computational problem is capable of being broken into discrete pieces of work that can be solved simultaneously, can execute multiple program instructions at any moment in time, and can be solved in less time with multiple compute resources than with a single compute resource.

There are different classifications of parallel processors and one, in use since 1966, is called *Flynn's Taxonomy*. This introduces the familiar:

1. *SISD*: Single instruction stream, single data stream
2. *SIMD*: Single instruction stream, multiple data stream
3. *MISD*: Multiple instruction stream, single data stream
4. *MIMD*: Multiple instruction stream, multiple data stream

For details of these, see the Lawrence Livermore reference below.

Processing Methods

In parallel processors and similar, nodes must be able to communicate with each other to share the processor load, which is often memory and current data or intermediate results of calculations. To do this and take advantage of fast processors, this communication cannot be slow; otherwise, it will negate the speed factor.

The main parallel programming communication paradigms are OpenMP and MPI:

- **OpenMP** (Open Multiprocessing) is an application programming interface (API) that supports shared-memory programming in C/C++ and FORTRAN. It consists of a set of compiler directives (parameters), library routines, and other variables that influence and control the program's run-time behavior. OpenMP programs run within a single instance of operating system and consist of multiple *threads*, which are lightweight processes sharing a common address space.
- **MPI** (message passing interface) is a language-independent communications protocol used to program computer clusters. Most MPI implementations consist of a specific set of routines (API) callable from FORTRAN, C, or C++. MPI programs consist of processes communicating with each other through the explicit exchange of messages through a fast interconnect mechanism. These processes are typically distributed across multiple nodes of a cluster, but it is feasible to run multiple processes within a single multiprocessor node.

MPI and OpenMP can be combined such that each MPI process consists of multiple threads; this approach is called *hybrid parallelization*.

The reference below is an excellent introduction to parallel processing and has very informative graphics illustrating the principles.

Introduction to Parallel Computing [Lawrence Livermore National Laboratory]
https://computing.llnl.gov/tutorials/parallel_comp/

A Short Introduction to High Performance Computing
https://doc.itc.rwth-aachen.de/display/CCP/A+Short+Introduction+in+High+Performance+Computing

HPC Performance Measurements

These are expressed mainly in terms of floating-point operations per unit time, usually per second—FLOPs. This is rather a small unit for today's HPC systems, and so units have progressed from FLOPs to kilo-, mega-, giga-, tera-, peta-, and even higher FLOP ratings.

However, simply measuring this metric using a FORTAN program is not really adequate since there are various other resources involved in HPC computing, for example, main memory and cache; and sometimes disk input/output (I/O) if massive swathes of intermediate results need to be saved for later calculations in the same job.

Such HPC calculations can now be run under various operating systems such as Windows, UNIX, Linux, and z/OS as well as specialist hypervisors for niche applications.

HPC Usage

Users of HPC are usually easy to qualify as those with *big sums* to do (as one IBM customer called HPC). The usage and numbers of the Top500 in 2014 (pre-November SC14) are shown in Table A6.1.

Table A6.1   Supercomputer Usage by "Industry"

Segment	Number	% of Top500
Academia	86	17
Industry	269	54
Classified	4	1
Government	18	4
Research	114	23
Vendor	8	2
Others	1	c. 0

Table A6.2   Number of Top500 HPC Systems by Country

Country (*)	Number	% of Top500
USA	253	50.6
China	65	13.0
Japan	30	6.0
United Kingdom	29	5.9
France	23	4.6
Germany	19	3.8
India	11	2.2

* The countries in the table with the top 10 most powerful systems are in bold letters. Listing HPC systems and their power here would be counterproductive as they will have changed out of recognition by the time this book is published.

Top500*

The Top500 is an annual list of the top 500 performing HPC systems based on HPL (high-performance Linpack), and in 2014, these top performers were spread across 27 countries. The top seven are shown in Table A6.2.

However, in June 2015, Top500 published a look back at a dozen or so of the high flyers in HPC:

http://www.scientificcomputing.com/articles/2015/07/look-back-top-1-systems-top500-list

HPC Clusters: Applications†

One category of applications where cluster computing is rapidly becoming the architecture of choice is Grand Challenge Applications (GCA). Grand Challenge Applications

---

* This is not a chart of pop music.
† http://www.cloudbus.org/papers/ic_cluster.pdf [with some corrections to the English].

(GCAs) are defined as fundamental problems in science and engineering with broad economic and scientific impact whose solution can be advanced by applying High-Performance Computing and Communications (HPCC) technologies. The high scale of complexity in GCAs demands enormous amounts of resource, such as processing time, memory and communication bandwidth. A common characteristic of GCAs is that they involve simulations that are computationally intensive. Examples of GCAs are applied fluid dynamics, environmental modeling, ecosystem simulation, biomedical imaging, biomechanics, molecular biology, molecular design, cognition, and computational sciences.

Obviously, *availability* is a key issue in very long-running simulations in applications like those outlined above.

HPC and Weather

At the time of writing, there has been a flurry of activity in the weather business, which is acquiring supercomputers for forecasting and other related activities. The US Weather Service, the UK meteorological body, and the German equivalent (to name three) are planning to spend hundreds of millions of dollars between them to improve the granularity of forecasting, both temporally and spatially.

For example, the US body aims to reduce the forecasting area from 27 km to 13 km while increasing the number of days they can forecast weather conditions with confidence. The German equivalent (the Deutscher Wetterdienst or DWD) plans to use 2 Cray XC30 systems in its work; these systems offer huge increases in storage capacity and bandwidth over current systems*.

Other disciplines are also looking at HPC to increase the granularity of their work where repetitive calculation is involved, and the goal is *more equations or "big sums" in less time* where time is of the essence, as it is in weather forecasting. It is pointless having a very good forecast for tomorrow's weather if it takes three days to produce.

There are a number of other industry stories about the use of HPC in the link below.

http://www.datacenterknowledge.com/archives/category/sectors/hpc/

HPC Futures

Over 2,600 attendees will gather in Frankfurt, Germany, from July 12 to 16, 2015[†] to celebrate the 30th anniversary of the ISC (International Supercomputing Conference) High Performance. They will discuss their organizational needs and the industry's challenges, as well as learn about the latest research, products, and solutions. The conference will be supported by a comprehensive exhibition, hosting over 160 vendors and international research organizations covering all areas of HPC.

---

* You may be interested in the Mark Twain view: "Everybody's talking about the weather, nobody's doing anything about it."
† After the writing of this book.

The agenda, I feel, indicates what the future may hold for HPC:

- Future design concepts of HPC systems
- Highly scalable operating systems (including run-time systems)
- From big data to smart data
- Life sciences: The next challenge for HPC
- HPC cloud services in the financial sector
- Highlights from Europe's Horizon 2020 ICT
- HPC trends in the chip market
- HPC in the public health sector
- Chip and node interconnects
- Human brain research worldwide
- Top 10 Exascale research topics
- Memory systems for HPC and big data
- Quantum computing
- HPC in Latin America

Benefits of HPC?

Are there any? I suppose it is a matter of opinion. My feeling is that medicine, meteorology, and other sciences do and will benefit in many ways from being able to perform bigger studies involving large equations and millions of iterations to aid understanding of our bodies and the environment, including outer space. The costs of supercomputing is easy to quantify, the benefits of using them less so.

Now a paper published in April 2015 claims that supercomputers give universities a competitive edge in scientific research, and they have some hard data showing that this is true. A team from Clemson University (South Carolina, the United States) found that universities with locally available supercomputers were more efficient in producing research in critical fields than universities that lacked supercomputers. The report below outlines this overview in more detail, including an assessment of which sciences benefit most fromHPC.

Data-enabled Science: Top500 Supercomputers Provide Universities with Competitive Edge
http://www.scientificcomputing.com/news/2015/04/data-enabled-science-top500-supercomputers-provide-universities-competitive-edge?et_cid=4507562&et_rid= 784345100&location=top

HPC Clusters

HPC has similar requirements to commercial computing, especially in the areas of availability and performance. High availability is necessary to avoid the rerunning of jobs that fail before completion, especially long jobs. The need for performance, however, is much greater than that of commercial work in the main, and clustering often morphs into a grid of hundreds or thousands of processors working in parallel to give the performance sought by HPC users and their "customers," the dependent sciences.

Scientific advances are fueling demand for more *number-crunching* power to handle increasingly complex and iterative jobs, such as weather forecasting at a greater granularity, molecular

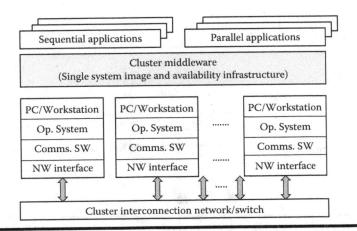

Figure A6.1   An HPC parallel cluster.

modeling, and complex biological problems such as neural networks and others outlined in the section "HPC Clusters: Applications."

The relatively slow increase in the power of chips that drove commercial clustering demands their aggregation into large configurations to supply the necessary power, given the ability of the programming to make use of these hundreds or thousands of chips or processors. Thus HPC clusters, and latterly grids, were born and are flourishing. Figure A6.1 shows an HPC parallel cluster.

Oscar HPC Cluster

Open Source Cluster Application Resources (OSCAR) is an initiative to develop high-performance scientific computing (HPC) without paying "mega bucks" for the privilege. Its philosophy is similar to that of RAID, using arrays of less expensive servers to perform the scientific calculations. OSCAR allows users to install a Beowulf-type high-performance computing cluster. Beowulf clusters are scalable performance clusters based on commodity hardware, on a private system network, with an open-source software (Linux) infrastructure. The OSCAR project aims to support as many different Linux distributions as possible. Some Linux distributions mentioned on the OSCAR website are OpenSUSE, Red Hat Enterprise Linux, and Ubuntu.

High availability (HA) computing has long been playing a critical role in industry mission-critical applications. On the other hand, HPC has equally been a significant enabler to the research and development (R&D) community for their scientific discoveries. The combination of HA and HPC will clearly lead to even more benefits to both industry, academic, and research fields of endeavor.

HA-OSCAR (High Availability Open Source Cluster Application Resources) is an open-source project that aims to provide a combined power of *high availability* and a *performance computing* solution. The goal is to enhance a Beowulf system (an earlier HPC cluster system) for mission-critical grade applications.

To achieve high availability, component redundancy is adopted in HA-OSCAR cluster to eliminate this single point of failure. HA-OSCAR incorporates a self-healing mechanism, failure detection and recovery, automatic failover and fail-back.

Figure A6.2 illustrates the concept of clusters of essentially commodity, cost-effective systems for scientific computing.

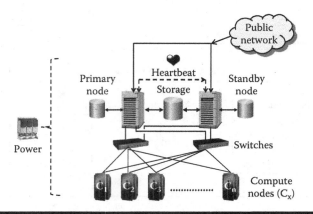

Figure A6.2   Basic HA-OSCAR HPC configuration.

More detail on OSCAR and more general papers on HPC clustering are available via the links below.

HA-OSCAR: High Availability Open Source Cluster Application Resources [Presentation]
http://www.csm.ornl.gov/oscar04/proceedings/leangsuksun_ha-oscar_slides.pdf

HA-OSCAR: Five Steps to a High-Availability Linux Cluster [Paper]
http://www.linuxdevcenter.com/pub/a/linux/2005/02/03/haoscar.html

High Performance Linux Clustering, Part 1: Clustering fundamentals
http://www.ibm.com/developerworks/library/l-cluster1/index.html

High Performance Computing
http://en.community.dell.com/techcenter/high-performance-computing/w/wiki/hpc-cluster-networks

Grid Computing

Grid computing is often likened to "pay as you go" to emulate a utility charging mechanism where one only pays for what one consumes in terms of electricity, gas, and so on. It has taken on a wider meaning in the sense that often it can use the power of many distributed systems or workstations in a "grid" to support a workload.

For example, workstations and desktop systems have been found to have average central processing unit (CPU) utilizations of 5% or less, offering scope for using the "spare" capacity in some way, provided the hardware and, more importantly, the software technology is available.

Not all workloads are suited to this grid "sharing" mode of operation, however. Those that are should be able to continue working if one of the nodes in the grid configuration is unavailable and be capable of parallelism.

Figure A6.3 shows the nominal CPU capacity of the grid systems (black fill rectangle) and the portion used, leaving spare capacity to be "soaked up" by the waiting distributed grid workload.

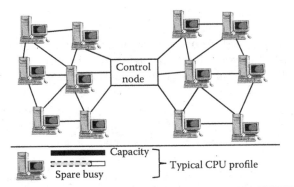

Capacity
Spare busy
Typical CPU profile

Figure A6.3   Grid computing schematic configuration.

Studies on workstations suggest that their CPU utilization is often quite low, and there is nearly always spare capacity to be had from them.

The main point regarding *availability* is that such a computing system needs software resilience as well as hardware resilience, which requires parallel execution of code and, where necessary, dual copies of code kept in the same "state."

Grid-computing and parallel-computing configurations often run very long scientific jobs, sometimes days or weeks long, and failures in the system during such jobs are very undesirable. Imagine running a 2-week job, failing at 1.95 weeks, and having to start again.

This would be necessary unless some complex checkpoint/restart is built into the program so that there are availability considerations in such jobs and configurations. These are outlined next.

Grid Availability

To ensure the availability of the workload in the absence of every participating node having HA characteristics, certain parts of the grid environment need to have HA properties, for example

- Workload management and the ability to run parallel copies of applications in case of failure in one of the nodes
- Grid directory (what resources are where and what can they do)
- Security services (such a distributed system is ripe for abuse)
- Data storage with redundancy, RAID
- Grid software clustering
- Load-balanced network
- High-availability routing protocols
- Redundant firewalls
- Parallel processing
- Backup and recovery
- Alerts and monitoring to signal a failure

As we have noted in the section "Grid Computing," not every workload is suited to this grid "sharing" mode of operation. Those that are should be able to continue working if one of the nodes in the grid configuration is unavailable and be capable of parallelism.

HPC: Uses

A common view of a HPC devotee is of a geek with wild hair, doing millions of calculations in designing weapons to rule the world. Nothing could be farther from the truth, as the IBM paper referenced at the end of this section demonstrates. It outlines the uses of HPC in research, manufacturing, life sciences, financial services, and banking using IBM solutions.

These are spreading into the analysis of *big data* for commercial and other intelligence information. The usage varies from expanding knowledge of science to competitive business advantage by big data analysis:

- *Hartree Centre*: a UK government science facility with locations at Daresbury, near Manchester, the United Kingdom, (home of Lewis Carroll of *Alice in Wonderland* fame) and two other sites. It does not only scientific work but also business applications that are amendable to HPC solutions.
- *University of East Anglia* (United Kingdom):: Research facilities and support.
- *Swift Engineering*: Maintaining global leadership in design and manufacturing, especially that needing aerodynamic analyses.
- *Red Bull Racing*: Basic HPC-supported innovation "to make cars go faster." The HPC system is used mainly for aerodynamic simulation and computational fluid dynamics (CFD).
- *A*CRC*: A*STAR Computational Resource Centre (Singapore), provides HPC resources to the entire A*STAR research community. Currently, A*CRC supports the HPC needs of a user community over 700 strong and manages several high-end computers.
- *Wellcome Trust Sanger Institute*: Genomic research. The trust was a key player in the Human Genome project, running half a million sequence matching jobs per day.
- *International Financial Services Company*: A major European insurance firm, it uses HPC in actuarial modeling in the life-insurance sector.
- *Major Wall Street Firm*: An investment bank which uses HPC in risk analysis, specifically counterpart credit risk and credit value adjustment (CVA).

This dispels the geek myth and introduces red braces and suits to the world of HPC.

Unleashing the power of high-performance technical computing
https://dsimg.ubm-us.net/envelope/158353/294142/1395161322_DCM03003USEN.pdf

HPC References

A Seven Part Discourse on HPC and the Future; by the "Daddy" of HPC, Jack Dongarra

A Beginners Guide to High-Performance Computing
http://www.shodor.org/media/content/petascale/materials/UPModules/beginnersGuideHPC/moduleDocument_pdf.pdf

High Performance Computing for Dummies
http://hpc.fs.uni-lj.si/sites/default/files/HPC_for_dummies.pdf

Introduction to HPC
https://secure.hosting.vt.edu/www.arc.vt.edu/wp-content/uploads/2015/04/Intro_HPC.pdf

Future Performance*

If the above findings on the value of supercomputing are true, then the future of HPC is important to those sciences that benefit most from progress. What follows are ideas as to where the subject is going over the next few years; only time and anyone who can remember the article above will tell.

> Future growth in computing performance will have to come from software parallelism that can exploit hardware parallelism. Programs will need to be expressed by dividing work into multiple computations that execute on separate processors and that communicate infrequently or, better yet, not at all.
>
> This chapter first explains how current software reaped the benefits of Moore's law and how much of the resulting software is not well suited to parallelism. It then explores the challenges of programming parallel systems. The committee explores examples of software and programming parallelism successes and possibilities for leveraging these successes, as well as examples of limitations of parallelism and challenges to programming parallel systems. The sudden shift from single-core to multiple-core processor chips requires a dramatic change in programming, but software developers are also challenged by the continuously widening gap between memory system and processor performance.
>
> That gap is often referred to as the "memory wall," but it reflects a continuous rather than discrete shift in the balance between the costs of computational and memory operations and adds to the difficulty of obtaining high performance. To optimize for locality, software must be written to minimize both communication between processors and data transfers between processors and memory.

The reference below was written by what looks like a soccer team (11) of distinguished people, including the ubiquitous David Patterson.

The Landscape of Parallel Computing Research: A View from Berkeley
http://www.eecs.berkeley.edu/Pubs/TechRpts/2006/EECS-2006-183.pdf

The advent of *quantum computing* is heralded by an article in *Scientific Computing*, dated March 2015:

Quantum Device Detects and Corrects Own Errors
http://www.scientificcomputing.com/news/2015/03/quantum-device-detects-and-corrects-own-errors?et_cid= 4449533&et_rid=784345100&location=top

Petaflops and Beyond

In April 2015, the US Department of Energy announced a $200 million investment to deliver a next-generation supercomputer, known as Aurora, to the Argonne Leadership Computing Facility. When commissioned in 2018, this supercomputer will be open to all scientific users—drawing America's top researchers to Argonne. The system will deliver 180 petaflops when fully commissioned. Uses are expected to include

---

* The Future of Computing Performance: Game Over or Next Level?
  ISBN 978-0-309-15951-7 (National Research Council)

- **Materials science**: Designing new classes of materials that will lead to more powerful, efficient, and durable batteries and solar panels
- **Biological science**: Gaining the ability to understand the capabilities and vulnerabilities of organisms that can result in improved biofuels and more effective disease control
- **Transportation efficiency**: Collaborating with industry to improve transportation systems with enhanced aerodynamics features, as well as enable production of better, more highly efficient, and quieter engines
- **Renewable energy**: Engineering wind turbine design and placement to greatly improve efficiency and reduce noise

There is no doubt that this progress will continue in areas far outside those that HPC was initially devoted to.

HPC Programming

Scientific programming in what my children and grandchildren call "the olden days" was carried out using binary code, assembler, Algol (A), C, and other languages (language B never quite made it). Some brave souls tried Common Business-Oriented Language (COBOL) if that was all they knew or reverted to the abacus for scientific work.

Just as COBOL became the language of commerce, Formula Translation (FORTRAN) became the language of science, and eventually the hardware became differentiated in a similar fashion. with parallel and vector processors advancing scientific programming in terms of performance.

FORTRAN is the main language for scientific computing, large and small. It was developed in the 1950s and, according to the article referenced below, it is going to be around for some time.

FORTRAN: 7 Reasons Why It's Not Dead
http://www.informationweek.com/software/enterprise-applications/fortran-7-reasons-why-its-not-dead/d/d-id/1321174?_mc=NL_IWK_EDT_IWK_daily_20150706&cid=NL_IWK_EDT_IWK_daily_20150706&elq=77370a7af10c417291e649411a763579&elqCampaignId=15362

The J3* FORTRAN Standards Committee is working on the next standard, tentatively titled FORTRAN 15, and should have met in London, August 2015.

http://www.j3-fortran.org/

J3 developed the FORTRAN 66, FORTRAN 77, FORTRAN 90, FORTRAN 95, FORTRAN 2003, and FORTRAN 2008 standards. FORTRAN 2008 is an upwardly compatible extension of FORTRAN 2003, adding, among other things, more expression of parallel computation, improved facilities for data organization (via enhancements to modules), and an enlarged intrinsic library (with more mathematical and bit-manipulating procedures).

Java is often touted as a scientific language and has its adherents. The paper below and its abstract illustrate the possibilities of Java. The abstract claims that "Java may be a natural language for portable parallel programming ... prospects for future Java-based parallel programming environments are also discussed."

---

* J3 is the US FORTRAN standards committee, known formally as PL22.3, a technical subcommittee of the International Committee for Information Technology Standards (INCITS), formerly known as the National Committee for Information Technology Standards (NCITS).

Java as a Language for Scientific Parallel Programming
http://www.researchgate.net/publication/2352295_Java_as_a_Language_for_Scientific_Parallel_
Programming
There is a presentation covering the use of Java as a scientific language at

Java for Scientific Computing
http://www.hpjava.org/theses/shko/thesis_paper/node12.html
and there are a number of other articles to be found with a search such as "java as a scientific language."

Appendix VII: Summary and Overview of the Book

What Have We Covered?

This book has covered a lot of ground, some from my own knowledge and experience but a lot from researching other people's work and seeking a consensus on any topic before including it in this book. I have learned a massive amount just by trying to write this book, writing what I had discovered but using the rule "if you don't understand it, don't cover it." I've nearly achieved that!

The coverage has been, I hope, thorough and useful and can satisfy any needs for deeper study by quoting references to topics in context. I believe in the immersion technique of learning, according to which repetition is a good way of picking up information as opposed to a single, intense run through a subject. I hope Appendix III ("Terminology") helps in this objective too.

Some of the URL links are large and, unfortunately, cannot be clicked on in a hardcopy version of the book. However, it is usually possible to find the paper/document by searching on the title or part title, which I have had to do when I have lost the URL but still have the hardcopy of a paper.

Response Time Interpretation

The traditional equation for response time is the sum of the time for network transit ($T_{network}$) + time for Xn in the server (T_{server}) + disk I/O time (T_{disk}).

This assumes all the elements in the equation are measured and reported.

As shown in Figure A7.1, the disk time is accounted for in the server time as t_{D1} and t_{D1}, the central processing unit (CPU) wait time pending input/output (I/O).

This is the wait time in the server for disk I/Os to complete, so adding the disk time again is incorrect and is double-counting. The answer is, referring to the figure:

- If server time interpretation is **CPU time** (Server Time = CPU Time):

$$T_R = \left[t_{S1} + t_{S2} + t_{S3} \right] + T_{network} + T_{disk} \left(t_{D1} + t_{D2} \right) \tag{A7.1}$$

- If server time interpretation is **elapsed time** (Server Time = Start − End Time):

$$T_R = T_{network} + T_{server} \tag{A7.2}$$

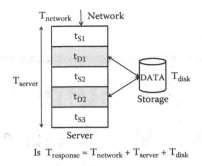

Is $T_{response} = T_{network} + T_{server} + T_{disk}$

Figure A7.1   E-to-E response time interpretation.

Since the disk time is accounted for as the wait times (t_{D1} and t_{D2}) in the elapsed server time T_{server}, this means we don't have to worry about finding what disk I/O times are.

The whole thing hangs on how a particular monitor measures and reports server time, whether as CPU time or unit of work (UoW, normally a transaction or query) elapsed time. Not rocket science but can cause confusion.

The Performance Universe

The discussion of individual elements or components of elements sometimes obscures the whole performance picture, and Figure A7.2 tries to show the whole picture.

The diagram represents the following:

■ A schematic of an end-to-end interaction of a user with a system and its subsystems (disk, etc.). The web approach is, in general, more complicated than a classical transaction (online transaction processing system [OLTP]) system and would be simplified. The principles remain the same, however.

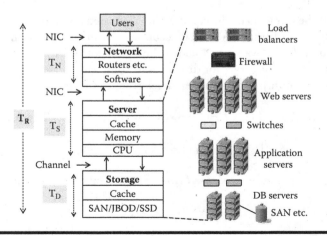

Figure A7.2   The scope of the performance universe.

■ There are times listed in the figure: T_N, T_S, T_D for the times that the UoW is present in each subsystem, x = N, S, D.

$$T_X = T_{service} + T_{wait} = \text{Latency for the component X}$$

■ Each component of the system has subcomponents that also have service times and wait times, not to mention an input distribution of some sort. An example of a subcomponent is a router in a network link:

$$T_X = \sum_{i=1}^{n} T_X^i = \sum_{i=1}^{n} T_{service}^i + \sum_{i=1}^{n} T_{wait}^i$$

where i is the ith component of n in the subsystem, for example, in this case, the network N. There are similar equations for the S(erver) and D(isk = storage) subsystems but see the section in this appendix "Response Time Interpretation" when using storage subsystem times for calculation purposes.

Limits of Theoretical Approaches to Performance

As I have iterated many times in this book, I am moving away from blind faith in theoretical modeling on modern-day IT systems because of their complexity and unpredictability. They were useful in what I have called the *classical era* of computing, when a terminal was attached by a communication line to a server with JBODs (just a bunch of disks) as the storage medium. A converged solution was more likely then than it is now.

Some of the ways of sizing systems and determining other parameters have been covered but are reproduced here as part of the immersion process.

■ *Guesswork*, which is not recommended unless you have knowledge of systems and applications closely resembling your own.
■ *Calculations* using queuing theory and other similar math. These can work fine for a single server (generic), but following though a system with the same math may not be wise, as the initial input distribution will almost certainly not apply to the next (generic) server in the service chain. This limitation is one reason I have not "gone to town" on esoteric queuing theory in this book. The other reason is that I don't know enough theory to do this!
■ *Simulation* methods and software that mimics the situation being modeled, for example, by generating transactions and measuring response times or incrementing use of some resource and repeating a simulation each time.
■ *Rules of thumb* (ROTs), which are guidelines based on experience and are found to be of use in similar circumstances.
■ *Standard benchmarks*, assuming your workload(s) can be related to these benchmarks. I have done this, relating the Transaction Performance Council (TPC)-C benchmark transactions to the customer's estimate of the resource requirements of his transactions.

■ ***Personalized benchmarks*** on the real application, for example, in a pilot scheme. The application might be a commercial off-the-shelf (COTS) one, in which case the vendor can assist. If it is an as yet unwritten in-house application, it can be simulated by coding the basic I/O and simulating the transaction code by timed coding loops.

I am leaning toward the lower items in this list for most system quantification situations, except for the simplest problems. If you try more than one method, and then you reach a consensus in the conclusion, that's fine.

What Have We Not Covered?

In the book, I have sought to illustrate performance principles by discussing some vendor software products. These are mentioned for just that reason; they are not recommendations for those products, nor does their inclusion imply they are unique in their coverage.

> ***Note***: I have left the detailed analysis of products in the various performance areas to Gartner and its Magic Quadrants and to other organizations performing similar analysis work.

What Do We Need to Know About?

There are some key basic items in the world of sizing and performance that we need to know about and do:

■ The workload characteristics
■ User requirements, decomposed into
  – Types of work *units* (OLTP, query, batch, HPC, web, big data)
  – Volumes of these units
  – Peak volumes
  – Baseline requirements for response times, throughput and availability, normally though service level agreements (SLAs)
  – The forward projection of these requirements, based on organic growth and additional applications (capacity management)
  – The workloads' time variation (by day, week, month, year end, etc.)
■ The selection and sizing of system components
■ Visibility of the operational environment (monitoring)
■ Ongoing operations activity (business as usual [BAU], tuning, root cause analysis [RCA] of performance issues, etc.)
■ Recognize that management of a resource, for example, *performance management*, has several stages as given by the relationship

$$\text{Management} = \text{Design} + \text{Measurement} + \text{Analysis} + \text{Action}$$

■ Document the whole lot. If you do not, it will almost certainly come back to bite you at unexpected times, and you will be partially clueless as to what to do

- Do as the Boy Scouts do and *be prepared*
- Remember the IBM exhortation *THINK*, sometimes laterally or out-of-the-box

An illustration of *lateral thinking* can be found in a story, possibly apocryphal, which tells of NASA spending $2 m on developing a pen that would write in weightless space environments. The parallel Soviet research recommended the use of a pencil.

We have covered a few metrics in this book, mainly when discussing examples of systems-monitoring products. The list of operations metrics below and the references therein should complete the picture of what may be relevant to your organization and perhaps aid in the selection of monitoring tools.

Note: Peak activity is key to raising alarms/alerts when they exceed your specified baselines. If your average activity blows these limits, sack the performance designer.

Operational Metrics Review

For most of these metrics, which vary, *average* and *peak* utilizations should be available for short-term operational and capacity planning purposes. These metrics apply to nonvirtualized and virtualized environments. Cloud environments have some extra things that need recording:

- Physical CPU utilization
- Virtual CPU utilization
- CPU queue length
- Disk space used: total, free, used
- Disk I/O throughput
- I/O per second for a storage controller
- Disk I/O response time/latency
- Physical memory utilization
- Virtual memory utilization
- Memory swapping: in/out
- Network I/O rate: in/out
- Network utilization
- Network interface utilization
- Network node metrics (routers, etc.) where appropriate and possible
- Transmission errors
- Availability and downtime metrics (not dealt with in this book)
- Batch work metrics (ditto)

There are other metrics when dealing with cloud environments, and these are discussed and listed very clearly in the documents referenced below.

The first reference contains links to other very useful cloud-monitoring documents:

Performance and Capacity Themes for Cloud Computing
http://www.infosys.com/engineering-services/features-opinions/Documents/cloud-performance-monitoring.pdf

Cloud Computing Service Metrics Description [Special Publication 500-307]
http://www.nist.gov/itl/cloud/upload/RATAX-CloudServiceMetricsDescription-DRAFT-20141111.pdf

If you need to formalize your use of performance metrics for a cloud environment, take a look at this document:

Craft a cloud performance metrics policy [IBM developerWorks]
http://www.ibm.com/developerworks/cloud/library/cl-cloudperformmetrics/cl-cloudperformmetrics-pdf.pdf

Another reference of a cloud *administration* nature can be found at

Design of a Performance Measurement Framework for Cloud Computing
http://www.scirp.org/journal/PaperInformation.aspx?Paper ID=17476

> *WoW*: We have covered a number of products in this book, many aimed at problem diagnosis and others covering performance monitoring and boosting. It is unlikely that an IT portfolio is likely to have all these products in it, but an awareness of them can help out in apparently insoluble situations. *"He who reads, wins."*

Performance Gotchas* Summary

The achievement of high performance means the elimination or reduction of things that impede that goal. This may sound trite, but it leads to the conclusion that you need to understand how units of work (OLTP transactions, queries, etc.) flow through the system that serves them. Once this is clear, it is possible to see what areas can cause bottlenecks (holdups) and to devise ways of minimizing them.

This is often referred to as *latency reduction*. Depending on how you define latency, some parts can be reduced, while others can't, unless you upgrade the resource involved. The list below, expanded on within the link following it, indicates the wide range of culprits who might be responsible for performance problems[†].

As an example, the following is a list of the computer components most likely to impact *network performance*.

File transfer: A file transfer may pass through the following components before it ever leaves the system: hard disk drive (HDD), system disk cache, transfer application, network stack, virtual private network (VPN) software, software firewalls and filters, network drivers, and the hardware network adapter.

Operating system: The operating system manages the resources and settings for all the other system components—hardware and software.

CPU usage: The CPU(s) must be shared by all of the software running on a system.

---

* *Gotchas*: Unexpected happenings and constraints stumbled over in the design, implementation, and operation of hardware systems and associated software. They are related to, and expressed by, Murphy's law, but their mathematics are beyond the scope of this book. Term *possibly* invented by IBM.

[†] A problem is something that prevents you reaching an objective (or target). If you don't have an objective, you cannot have a problem: Q.E.D.

Hard drive usage: Most data transfer begins and ends with a hard drive. Solid-state devices (SSDs) overcome many HDD performance issues but are not silver bullets.

Firewalls and Filters: Many operating systems now include software that performs network functions traditionally done in outside hardware. This includes firewalls.

VPN software: VPN software is similar to a firewall or filter in that it stops each data packet and processes it at some resource cost.

Memory (random access memory [RAM]): Inadequate system memory will cause the system to access the hard drive/SSD more often, leading to poor performance when reading or writing to external media.

Network interface card (NIC): The hardware component that moves data from the operating system to the physical media, which depends on correct drivers and settings to operate efficiently.

System clock: Many system functions depend heavily on the ability to accurately measure the timing of data transmission and arrival plus other functionality. It relies on the operating system to provide this timing information.

Virtual machines: Virtualized server environments involve multiple guest systems, all competing for limited access to CPU, memory, and hard drive. These different redundant systems can interact in unexpected ways.

Network devices: Switches, routers, and other interposing nodes in a network have the potential to slow things down, for example, suboptimal buffer sizes.

There are many areas of networks and networking which can give problems:

■ bandwidth requirements
■ compression and other errors on poor quality connections
■ RAID performance across networks
■ data loss, other latency, retransmissions
■ hardware – routers, NICs and similar – performance and availability
■ network emulator performance
■ UDP and tuning (for example, large file transmission)
■ NAS tuning
■ DNS problems
■ various parameter mismatches in connections
■ environmental issues
■ and so on

See the following references for more network *gotchas* and some solutions.

Network Performance
https://en.wikipedia.org/wiki/Network_performance

Ten top problems network techs encounter
http://www.newark.com/pdfs/techarticles/fluke/3450201_6511_ENG_A_W.PDF

The subject of performance is emotive and, as Humpty Dumpty said, "It means whatever I want it to mean, no more, no less"; that is, it is open to personal interpretation. The key thing is to have performance *objectives*; then you have something to aim at. These objectives are usually dictated by a service level agreement (SLA) agreed between users and IT.

You can approach performance management in one of three ways:

- Don't worry about it and hope for the best; the job market is flooded with people who have tried this. This approach is called *performance design by divine providence.*
- Rely totally on prescriptive documents and hope everything works. I know you would be worried if a surgeon operating on you had to consult a checklist every time he did anything during the operation; it wouldn't inspire confidence, would it?
- Know your subject, think your solution through, and, where appropriate, use checklists and other peoples' experiences as an aid. This leads to *performance design by anticipation.*

Performance Design by Anticipation

In this book, we have learned about performance parameters and ways of improving or messing up the performance of a system or systems. Messing up is the province of *gotchas* and poor design, for example, lousy indexing in a relational database management system (RDBMS). Anticipatory design means in essence that the designer should take the following approaches:

1. Design using the user requirements and select appropriate standard physical resources to meet them without sliding up the throughput-versus-utilization curve too soon. What I mean here is keep your powder dry for situations where demand exceeds initial forecasts, whether from poor forecasting or *gotchas*.*
2. I'm suggesting you perhaps might wish to keep wide area network (WAN) acceleration techniques, adding extra cache memory and other performance "goodies" for that rainy day, assuming that such boosters can be installed with minimum disruption.
3. If you don't take this route and play all your performance cards up front, then gaining extra power in times of need will probably involve disruption in terms of changing and adding physical resources.

Finally …

The purpose of this book is to help you achieve the first and, where appropriate, the second aims outlined above, hopefully in an educated and enjoyable manner. Think outside your personal box, encompassing the areas of functionality, usability, manageability, performance, and security, not to mention costs and cost of ownership. Your project, however, will require the following skills and tactics:

- Be prepared (Boy Scout motto).
- DYB (do your best—Boy Scout exhortation).
- Assume nothing.
- A fool with a tool is still a fool—don't throw technology at projects.
- Explore options and think out of the box (laterally).
- Be a team player.
- Remember (1) a lack of planning on your part does not constitute an emergency on someone else's part.

---

* This topic and a trick are covered in the section "Buffers and Performance" in Chapter 3.

- Remember (2) there are those people who make things happen, those who watch things happen, and those who say "what happened?"
- Listen as well as talk in the ratio 2:1 (no. of ears vs. one mouth).
- Challenge conventional IT thinking where it doesn't satisfy your requirements.
- Read voraciously—you'll never know it all.
- THINK (old IBM exhortation).
- If all else fails, read the instructions!

An excellent set of general reading articles on various queuing models can be found on Mike Tanner's MITAN website:
http://www.mitan.co.uk/

Mike has vast experience in the operational math of queuing, particularly as applied to commercial work in supermarkets and telephone call centers. As well as being a consultant, he has produced some analysis software for some of these commercial areas. His site is well worth a visit for an hour or two.

Read, learn, and go forth to provide high-performance IT services for your users, and may the force be with you.

Index